WORKS ISSUED BY
THE HAKLUYT SOCIETY

———

THE ENGLISH NEW ENGLAND VOYAGES

SECOND SERIES
NO. 161

THE ENGLISH
NEW ENGLAND
VOYAGES
1602–1608

Edited by

DAVID B. QUINN and ALISON M. QUINN

THE HAKLUYT SOCIETY
LONDON
1983

ISBN 0 904180 14 X

Printed in Great Britain at the
University Press, Cambridge

Published by the Hakluyt Society
c/o The Map Library,
British Library Reference Division
London WC1B 3DG

To the memory of
Wendell S. Hadlock
and Lawrence M. C. Smith

PREFACE

The English voyages to what was, from 1616, known as New England form a continuous sequence of discovery voyages from 1602 to 1606, and proceed from that to exploration and settlement in 1607–1608. They were distinct from one another and their paths did not, until 1606, cross to any great extent. The voyages of 1602–1605 were easy-going summery affairs, which nevertheless open our eyes to the first sight by Englishmen of shores which were to become significant for settlement from 1620 onwards. It is ironic that we should know relatively so much about them and so little about the final discovery voyage of 1606 as well as the settlement and exploration which followed in the last two years of the series. To Englishmen at the time these ventures were new and original. They overlapped only once with the more systematic exploration of the same coasts which Samuel de Champlain was making during the years 1604–1607. No attempt has been made here to integrate the two series of voyages but a determined effort has been made to see what indeed the English saw, recorded, and accumulated about the areas they discovered. This was quite a substantial amount and tracing it has occupied the editors intermittently, and mainly in summer time too, over the past generation. The John Carter Brown Library has been our base on most occasions and Lawrence C. Wroth, Thomas R. Adams, Jr., and Jeannette Black our mentors. In the earliest visits which the male partner made he depended much on Walter and Jane Whitehill and more on Warner F. Gookin at Edgartown. On later visits he owed more to Wendell S. and Susan Hadlock at Rockland (and we both continued our visits until 1978) and to S. E. Morison at East Harbor. When both of us spent some time together at Providence we were able to visit most of the sites the English visited, some changed utterly and many still, it would appear, very little altered. In later times we had hospitable help from Woods Hole Oceanographic Center and from the Gray Herbarium at Harvard as well as from the great libraries of Harvard University. On other occasions William F. Royall and Francis Jennings went out of their way to enable us to get to places we would otherwise not have visited. The Dukes County Historical Society under various Directors has been a constant source of help; Maine Historical Society at Portland, the Whaling Museum at New Bedford, Bronson Museum at Attleboro and the Rhode Island Historical Society assisted also. A host of ethnographers and anthropologists at the Peabody Museum in Harvard, the Peabody Museum at Andover, Gordon M. Day before and after his migration to the Museum of Man, Ottawa, and latterly members of the Smithsonian Institution far away in Washington (where our base was the Folger Library) have given specialist advice and help. Of these we wish to mention especially Wilcomb E. Washburn, William C. Sturtevant, Ives Goddard, and Mrs Waldo Wedel, but we owe much to many others as well. Dean S. Snow brought invaluable help on the Eastern Abenaki. Andrew J. Wahll came along at a late stage with new views on the 1607 colony site. Our American debts have been very great indeed, and we cannot hope to acknowledge them all. Lawrence and Eleanor Smith gave us encouragement and support at Philadelphia and Wolfs Neck to enable us to see Maine and to go on with our work in England. In England we worked especially closely with Helen Wallis and Paul Hulton both at a time when there was one British Museum and when there was a British Library, Reference Division, as well. The Public Record Office and Lambeth Palace Library in London and the Bodleian Library at Oxford gave us invaluable assistance, as did the 5th Marquess of Salisbury and his archivist Clare Talbot at Hatfield. Sir Henry Hanham and his sister at Dene House, Wimborne, in vain did all they could to locate the lost Hanham journal. We visited many county and city record offices in the search for materials and it will be clear that at Bristol we had the benefit of the great knowledge of Elizabeth Ralph and particular assistance too at both Plymouth and Exeter Libraries, as well as at the Lancashire County Record Office, Preston. We were doing many other things too while making our rounds, but we kept accumulating materials on these voyages so that what is given here is a rather arbitrary selection from a much larger mass. Whether we made the right choices remains to be seen. The experience of trying to see the new country through the eyes of its discoverers has been a happy one and we shall miss their company by bringing it to an end.

During the time we have been at work a vast amount of local history has been done in New England and we cannot claim to have kept track of all of it. So far as the exposition of the rather primitive but pioneering scientific material gathered by the discoverers is concerned we, again, cannot claim to have kept pace with all modern approaches, either in the life sciences or in anthropology and ethnography. For Hakluyt

Society readers we may have provided a little too much discussion and for specialists too little. This is a risk we had to take. We would hope, however, that men like Gabriel Archer, John Brereton, Martin Pring, George Waymouth and James Rosier, even the virtually undocumented Thomas Hanham and the anonymous author of the 1607 journal, Robert Davies as we have taken him to be, will emerge as individuals who have left us something of a personal insight into what they saw and how they saw it which will in turn throw some light on what early seventeenth century English explorers were like. We think they come out of it very well, even if Rosier exaggerated and most of Hanham's work is lost. The work they did had to be done again by John Smith and put together in a firmer, crisper synthetic view in his *Description* of 1616, but the freshness of discovery, so far as their contemporary editors allowed it to survive their pruning, does come through and will, we hope, communicate itself to a new generation of readers. We owe much to H. O. Thayer, Henry S. Burrage (whose daughter told us, at a delightful party at Wiscasset, how the memorial to Waymouth was raised on Allen Island in 1905), and Warner F. Gookin (working under physical difficulties from which he died before he had quite finished his work on Gosnold – it was completed and published by Philip L. Barbour). We cannot find too many words to thank Philip Barbour for working so long and successfully on the Rosier vocabulary which we are able to print as an appendix. We also owe very much to the patience of the officials of the Hakluyt Society, Peter Skelton, Eila Campbell and above all Terence Armstrong, who were promised this volume several times, but held out in the hope that it would come in the end.

We should point out that very many of the texts, un-annotated, are printed in the five-volume *New American world*, edited by D. B. Quinn, with the assistance of Alison M. Quinn and Susan Hillier (New York, Arno Press and Hector Bye Inc. 1979; London, Macmillan, 1979), mainly in volume III. We have taken the opportunity to add a few new documents in this volume and to abbreviate or quote from documents there we did not wish to print in full, while a number of additional documents in that collection are not reprinted since their interest for the Hakluyt society was more purely historical than geographical. The two collections, however, go together, and there are numerous cross-references to what we have, ungraciously, abbreviated to *NAW*.

Liverpool   *DAVID B. QUINN*
December 1980   *ALISON M. QUINN*

CONTENTS

CONTENTS

LIST OF ILLUSTRATIONS AND MAPS

page

PERMISSIONS

The editors and the Hakluyt Society are grateful to the following for granting permission to reproduce material and illustrations in their possession – The Director General, British Library, Reference Division (including figures 7, 15, 17, 18, 19); the Keeper of the Public Record Office (including figure 26); The Director, Archivo General de Simancas (including figures 25, 35); The Librarian, Bodleian Library, Oxford; The Librarian, Lambeth Palace Library (including figures 20, 21, 22); The County and City Archivists of Bristol, Devon (Exeter and Plymouth), and Lancashire; The Librarian, Ipswich Public Library; The Librarian, Stonyhurst College, Lancashire; The Marquess of Salisbury, Hatfield House; The Librarian of Congress; The Archivist of the United States (including figure 33); The Chief, Department of Anthropology, Smithsonian Institution, Washington, D.C.; The State Archivist, State Library (Archives Division), Augusta, Maine (including figure 32); The Librarian, John Carter Brown Library, Brown University (including figure 1); The Librarian, Harvard University Library; The Librarian of The New York Public Library, Astor, Lenox and Tilden Foundations (including figure 36 in the I. N. Phelps Stokes Collection); The Librarian, Alderman Library, University of Virginia, Charlottesville; The Director, Massachusetts Historical Society, Boston; The Librarian, American Antiquarian Society, Worcester, Massachusetts (including figure 29 from the Graphic Arts Division); The County Clerk, Dukes County, Edgartown, Massachusetts; The Director, Dukes County Historical Society, Edgartown, Massachusetts. Sketchmaps are the work of Philip and Brigid Wainwright and Sandra Collinge to whom much is owed.

LIST OF ABBREVIATIONS

B.L. British Library, Reference Division (formerly British Museum Library).

Cal. Cecil MSS. Historical Manuscipts Commission, *Calendar of the manuscripts of the Marquess of Salisbury at Hatfield House (Cecil MSS)*.

Driver and Massey, 'Comparative studies.' Harold E. Driver and William C. Massey, 'Comparative studies of North American Indians', American Philosophical Society, *Transactions*, XLVII, pt. 2 (Philadelphia, 1957).

Flannery, *Analysis.* Regina Flannery, *An analysis of coastal Algonquian culture.* Washington, D.C. Catholic University of America, Anthropological series no. 7. 1939.

Gleason and Cronquist, *Manual.* Henry A. Gleason and Arthur Cronquist, *Manual of vascular plants of northeastern United States and Canada.* Princeton, 1963. (Botanical identifications not given a reference will also be found in this volume.)

Handbook. William C. Sturtevant, gen. ed., *Handbook of North American Indians.* Vol. XV. *Northeast*, edited by Bruce E. Trigger. Washington, D.C., Smithsonian Institution, 1978. (In form 'Snow in *Handbook*', etc.)

NAW. New American World: a documentary history of North America to 1612. Edited by D. B. Quinn, A. M. Quinn and S. Hillier, 5 vols. New York and London, 1979.

P.R.O. Public Record Office, London.

Purchas, *Pilgrimes.* Samuel Purchas. *Hakluytus posthumus, or Purchas his Pilgrimes.* 4 vols. 1625. 20 vols. Glasgow, 1905–7.

Quinn, *Gilbert.* D. B. Quinn, ed., *The voyages and colonising enterprises of Sir Humphrey Gilbert.* 2 vols. Hakluyt Society, 1940.

Quinn, *Roanoke voyages.* D. B. Quinn, ed. *The Roanoke voyages, 1584–1590.* 2 vols. Hakluyt Society, 1955.

Quinn and Skelton, *Principall navigations (1589).* Richard Hakluyt, *The principall navigations (1589),* with an introduction by D. B. Quinn and R. A. Skelton. 2 vols. Hakluyt Society, Extra Series, 1965.

Taylor, *Hakluyts.* E. G. R. Taylor, ed. *The original writings and corres-*

pondence of the two Richard Hakluyts. 2 vols. The Hakluyt Society, 1935.

Venn. J. and J. A. Venn, *Alumni cantabrigienses.* 4 vols. Cambridge, 1922–1927.

DATING

English Style or Old Style, based on the Julian Calendar, is used for the days and months. It is ten days behind the Gregorian Calendar or New Style. Calendar year dating (i.e. from 1 January), which is also that of New Style, is used for the years, instead of the legal dating (beginning the year on 25 March). Where necessary double dating has been used.

INTRODUCTION

PRELIMINARY OBSERVATIONS

The exploration of North Virginia, 1602–8, the later New England (even if it was not known as such until 1616) came into being for English ears and eyes in these years, 1602–8, and in the longer run this was to be an important event. As a small chapter in maritime achievement it was not without significance that twenty-five direct crossings, one way or the other, were made in these years without the loss of a single ship, a notable record marred only by the taking of the *Richard* by the Spaniards in 1606 when she attempted the long, indirect route by way of the Caribbean. Moreover, navigators like Martin Pring, George Waymouth and Robert Davies showed that the combination of practical and theoretical knowledge which the Elizabethan pioneers like Hakluyt, Ralegh and Harriot had sought, now existed in the early seventeenth century. But alongside expertise in navigation and pilotage the routine of sending so many fishing voyages to Newfoundland on fishing fare had accumulated a body of knowledge of seamanship in the North Atlantic which, like the parallel expertise in carrying through privateering voyages further south, could be built on successfully. The voyages of 1602–8 may only have laid foundations for fishing, fur trading and colonisation between the latitudes 40 to 45 degrees North, but they proved to be foundations which stood later expeditions in good stead.

As an episode in exploration history the English New England voyages of these years must be considered alongside those of Samuel de Champlain, made over a similar coastline but extended to the head of the Bay of Fundy, during the years 1604–7. Each body of material had its own merits. Champlain's was systematically set out and contributed more directly to cartography, while its results became fully available with the publication of *Les voyages* in 1613: we could not do without this body of information in attempting to understand the character of northeastern North America in these years. Moreover, Lescarbot gave us an extensive survey of Indian life in the Bay of Fundy for 1606–7 in his *Histoire* in 1609. The English voyages were more episodic and discontinuous, but each provided more intensive evidence than Champlain had given for the particular parts of coast or river valley with which they were concerned. There is freshness and originality in many of their observations which are often naive but more often illuminating. The concentration on flora and fauna is more specific and the emphasis on language is not found in the published French accounts. There was, however, much less systematic publication of results, though for the voyages of 1602 and 1605 publication did follow within a few months of the return of the expeditions. There was no publication of the 1603 and 1606–8 voyages until a bare outline appeared in Purchas' *Pilgrimage* in 1614, their incorporation briefly in John Smith's *Description* in 1616, and the detailed publication in 1625 of important material by Purchas in his *Pilgrimes* who, however, rejected and so destroyed some of the most important records he had in his hands. Small items trickled out in 1622 and as late as 1658 in publications with which Sir Ferdinando Gorges was associated. From 1607 on, until after the Pilgrims had settled in Plymouth, much interest in North Virginia, the later New England, was swamped, and perhaps justifiably so, by material on South Virginia, *the* Virginia, on the Chesapeake. The materials for these years have to be put together from sources which are much less satisfactory or complete. This is not to say that they have been neglected in the past, since much devoted and effective work has been done on them, or to claim that it has been possible to add very significantly to the documentation already available. But they are worth collecting, analysing and annotating anew, so that their contribution to exploration history as a whole can become visible in both its assets and limitations, or at least in so far as can be seen down to this time, since later editors and interpreters are bound to look differently at other aspects and, who knows, there may after all be further documents to be discovered which can alter the perspective of one or a whole series of these voyages.

The New England voyages represent one small part only of the out-thrust beyond Europe which English state and society proved capable of making in the first decade of the seventeenth century, and which was to accelerate thereafter. This was not due to any great accession of economic strength but rather a diversion of resources, a small part of her total resources, from the export trade in cloth to other avenues of overseas commerce. Economic historians have measured England's capacity for export trade almost solely in terms of the cloth trade, the traditional trade in unfinished woollen cloths and the addition to them as they declined of the New Draperies for which many novel markets were to be found. For them, the early years of the seventeenth century were years of temporary prosperity and expansion followed by decades of crisis and decline. But this was not the whole or even entirely a true picture: the great trade in fish from Newfoundland, much of it direct to European markets, scarcely appeared in the English commercial records. The very large trade in men, women and children which grew out of the exploratory voyages of the late sixteenth and especially of those of the early seventeenth centuries – including those covered in this volume – is again virtually ignored in these records. The indirect results of exploration – shipbuilding, victualling, the payment of wages to seamen, the transport of capital as well as human beings overseas – is again largely hidden. Exploration and the development of new trades – and no doubt those of the Levant Company and the East India Company were the largest – played a major part, not always evident in customs accounts, in expanding capital investment and profits and in relieving distress and softening population pressures at home.

Over the whole period from 1600 to 1640 New England was to play a disproportionate part in English expansion. Some of this is due to the long-term effects of what were the superficially unsuccessful, or at least unproductive, voyages of these early years 1602–8, by indicating that New England was a place in which Englishmen could live and carry on a life much like that which they had lived in England but at a higher level of prosperity, and freed from ecclesiastical, economic and administrative restraints which were being found increasingly burdensome. This was put in more specific and seductive terms in Smith's 1616 *Description*, whose stroke of genius was his renaming of the area, long known as Norumbega, and then North Virginia, as New England. It is worth stressing that all the voyages related here, with the probable exception of Martin Pring's in 1603, had the objective of finding places where Englishmen might trade and settle, to be followed by English women and children, who could live there in a community. The lists of commodities, the ease of growing old and new food plants and of rearing livestock often exaggerated what was possible, as they did in the case of the Roanoke voyages of 1584–90, but they were not, except for optimism over the potential fertility of much of the Maine coast, misconceived, and many were in the end to be shown to be justified when settlement took place. Almost all voyagers went out in hope of mineral wealth, either precious metals

3

or useful minerals; if not gold or silver, at least alum, copper, lead, tin or iron, and in the long run they were almost all to be disappointed. The prospects for a fishery as rich as that of Newfoundland were often stressed, and they were genuine. The settlers when they came became vigorous fishermen in many cases, if only to supply their own needs in protein, though also to export. But, as in the case of Newfoundland, the major discovery which Waymouth was to stress in Rosier's tract in 1605, was that summer voyages from England to the Gulf of Maine, using an island such as Monhegan, or onshore rocky bays where fish could be dried, were more immediately profitable than settlements. The short-term result of the 1602–8 voyages was not settlement but the establishment of a seasonal fishery in the Gulf of Maine. The fur trade offered a genuine opportunity in these years and further north it was making considerable fortunes for the French, but southern New England, even the shores and rivers of the central Maine coast, was not the best place for it. Champlain had examined port after port and river after river and had concluded they were not profitable, not even in the end the more favoured shores of the Bay of Fundy. And this was the reason that the English were able to make their voyages without interference from the French, though Waymouth very nearly came into contact with Champlain in 1605. Fur-trading could be developed in New England and was to be a considerable resource later, but it could best be carried on after, not before, settlements of a permanent nature had been established, in complete distinction from the St Lawrence valley where the trade needed very few men and was maintained for a generation by a mere handful of resident Frenchmen. This was because most of the furs were available in the interior and not near the coasts of New England. But furs (with the hope of mineral gains) were what the voyagers of 1602–8 hoped would make their fortunes.

Each expedition before 1607 was a small one and its objectives were limited. Gosnold in 1602 hoped to find the happy and beautiful bay with its many islands where Verrazzano found rest and Indian friendship in 1524, though Narragansett Bay was to prove strangely elusive. There he expected to set up a small English trading post, selling English cloth and trinkets (with knives the most valuable object the Europeans had to offer to Indian peoples) in return for furs, medicinal roots and plants, dyes and such like – and of course minerals if they could be found. He was to settle for a small island fort on a lake in the Elizabeth Islands; but he had not enough stores to leave his men there, or indeed a sufficient number of them to guard such a trading post effectively, and so he had to abandon it unused, after much effort by those who constructed it, and it was never afterwards occupied. Even though it has been suggested that Pring's expedition was primarily one to extract sassafras roots and explore the chances of trade with the Indians, the possibility of future colonisation was kept in mind, since specimens of English vegetables and grain were test-grown for the short period of the ship's stay and were considered very promising. The Waymouth expedition, apart from its search for fishing grounds, was the first to search for extensive areas where settlement on a substantial area of land by Catholic gentlemen had been envisaged since the plans of Sir Humphrey Gilbert in 1582–3. The concentration on the St George River valley and the exaggeration of its considerable summer charms, amongst which great fertility was not one, and the extent of open ground not being very great, would have caused grave difficulty if it had been taken as a blueprint by Lord Arundell of Wardour to create a colony very much like that planned and effected by the Lords Baltimore in Maryland in 1632–4. It was perhaps not an unmixed blessing that it fell through and the Catholic gentlemen, though they played with the idea for a time, did not attempt any New England settlement on this basis.

The major effort of these years was that of the Plymouth division of the Virginia Company, created in 1606 to populate both North and South Virginia, the latter being left to the Londoners, the former to the West Country interests, urban and rural. The Indians taken captive by Waymouth in 1605 were the first members of the Eastern Abenaki people to be brought to England. As their economic base was a hunting, not an agricultural one, they could, as they learned English or taught Algonquian to their captors, tell much about the character and topography of their country, the land of Mawooshen, the territory dominated by the influential sagamore Bashabes, which extended from Saco Bay to just north of Penobscot Bay. They were wholly unfitted to provide information on the agricultural prospects of the area, and so undue reliance on them clearly handicapped the enterprise.

The two ships sent out in 1606, the first, the *Richard* under Henry Challons in early August and the relieving vessel two months later, about the beginning of October under Thomas Hanham, with Martin Pring as master, aimed at creating a base settlement to which a large party of settlers would come the following year. Starting so late, it may be thought that they intended in the first place to occupy, with the Indians' permission, the village of Pemaquid (which they said was their destination) during the absence of the village band for the winter hunting season, preparatory to building a post on the St George River as Rosier had recommended after his return from Waymouth's expedition. But Challons and his ship were captured by the Spaniards in Florida Strait in November and so were unable to do anything. Hanham and Pring, sent to reinforce them, probably had a few additional settlers on board. Their main task was to set Challons up for the winter. They were able to establish Nahanada as sagamore of the Pemaquid band but when they explored the St George River and other main entries into the interior they decided that the Kennebec River offered much better opportunities for defence, agriculture (though they were incorrect in this) and for the penetration of the interior to develop the fur trade and the minerals thought to be found there. Consequently, the main expedition which left Plymouth under Captain George Popham, with Raleigh Gilbert as his second in command, was to establish 100 (or 120) settlers on a strong post near the mouth of the Kennebec, as the advance guard of a more numerous colony. The leisurely progress of the expedition, the concentration on building a strong fort in case of French intervention and the limitation of exploration, though some valuable sorties were made, meant that no adequate preparations were made for wintering. The colony's administration did not realise that furs, except in small quantities, could only be traded in spring and early summer, having been brought back by the men from the winter hunting and prepared by the women after their return. The specimens of smilax and other miscellaneous plants brought back by the *Mary and John* and by the *Gifte of God* in February were considered of relatively minor value, and the derisory price obtained for masts in the Azores, when sold on their return voyage by the crew of the *Gifte of God*, convinced the adventurers in the enterprise that little good could come of it. A series of deaths, of George Popham at the fort in February 1608, and of two supporters, the vital one Sir John Popham in June 1607 and a significant one Sir John Gilbert in July 1608, weakened the drive behind the venture. Sir Ferdinando Gorges, Fort Major of Plymouth, took up the task of supplying the 45 or so settlers left in the Kennebec fort, since about half the settlers had come home in the two ships. Three vessels in all went out in 1608 and to begin with put heart into the colonists who eventually acquired a quantity of furs, but when the *Gifte* was ready to come back, apparently in September, the colonists would not face another winter, and insisted on deserting the fort and returning. The settlement was unlucky in suffering one of the earliest and most severe winters of a cold decade, but it was ill-conceived from the beginning and could have survived only as a small fur-trading post. There was, it was clear, no continuing inflow of capital, such as kept the Jamestown colony alive in spite of many tribulations, to be found in the West Country. Captain Robert Davis (or Davies) did consider that if the settlement moved south to the Casco Bay area it would have had better prospects and it is probable that this was so, but incentives and planned organisation, together with sufficient capital, were lacking. Except for summer fishing voyages, with a few of the ships doing some fur trading, there was little done in the years following 1608. The North Virginia venture had, it seemed, failed. Though the leading journals are lost, the surviving records provide some useful light on the Kennebec River valley and the coast between Richmond Island, just south of Casco Bay and the Georges Islands. Strategically (since the French had withdrawn) and economically little or nothing had been gained while a good deal of invested capital had been lost.

The venture was primarily one for the southwestern outports, Plymouth, Bristol and Exeter, and for such local gentry support as they could muster. The southwestern outports had done and were doing well out of the Newfoundland fishery but a good deal of the financing of this seems to have come from London and not all the profit remained locally. Capital accumulated from privateering ventures during the Spanish war tended, it might appear, to have been invested in land rather than in shipping or in high risk ventures such as the North Virginia voyages. Co-operation between the ports was difficult to maintain. The Plymouth corporation was determined to retain the headquarters at Plymouth, though the Popham, Hanham and Gorges families had links with Bristol as well as Plymouth, but only a little Bristol money went into these ventures. Very soon Bristol was to turn to plans for colonising Newfoundland instead. Guy's colony at Cupids in 1611 may be seen as the Bristolmen's alternative to a further New England venture. Exeter simply refused at first to have anything to do with the project, though the dean, Matthew Sutcliffe, was a strong supporter and a little money may have come in from individuals later. In the countryside, Lord Justice Popham, while he lived, had much influence. He was responsible for involving both the Seymour and Hanham families in the enterprise: we know little of other Somerset and Dorset investing gentry. So far as Devon was concerned it is probable that the Gilbert family played the major part. Sir John Gilbert,

Sir Humphrey's eldest son, was wealthy and his younger brother was second in command to George Popham and, ultimately, his successor. But, by and large, the outports were still declining in relation to London and had not the capital, or perhaps the will, to risk much on overseas voyaging which did not return the easily realised wealth that privateering had provided. The chances of a successful colony being established by the merchant-gentry group we must see as very small. On the other hand they had excellent seamen and ships and so could do very well the preliminary exploration work which was the main feature of these early seventeenth century voyages, followed by the creation of a fishery in New England waters.

The observers who have left us records were keen and relatively open-minded recorders of such Indian life as they saw. They have left us invaluable details of artifacts which help us to build up the ethnographic picture at an early stage in the contact period. They also conveyed many features of Indian society, though they did this in a fragmentary form and without any attempt to draw an articulated picture of Indian relationships and culture patterns. The early voyagers, 1602–5, saw the Indians only at a very limited phase of their annual cycle, the shore gathering season of the summer months. Almost all the individual observations made by Archer, Brereton (though his are limited), Pring (or his narrator), and above all Rosier are acute and objective, though the latter was helped by the Indians taken prisoner by Waymouth and, had he waited to publish until after he had examined them more closely, might have given us much more. Once settlement was attempted in 1607 the narrative, apparently by Robert Davies, is clearheaded enough but much more limited in his interests for 1607; our real loss is in the disappearance of the journals of Thomas Hanham for 1606 whose ethnographic notes were evidently especially interesting, and that of Raleigh Gilbert who had the longest continuous contact with the Eastern Abenaki bands in 1607–8, since these covered the autumn, winter and spring cycles between them. The English did not in general show as much sympathy with the Indians as the French, though perhaps Champlain's capacity for establishing a close and friendly rapport with such Indians as he met everywhere from southern New England to Lake Huron was exceptionally his own. The outstanding example of obtuseness by the English is their failure to appreciate the formal greeting and gift-exchange patterns of relationships between non-warring Indian groups and between them and visiting Europeans. This created misunderstandings and limited co-operation. But trade was not a new experience on these shores. Clearly there was much more coastal trade along the northeastern seaboard in the sixteenth century than was formerly realised, and it is evident that the Micmac took a considerable part in this right down the coast to Cape Cod Bay using, by the time the English arrived, stolen French or Spanish Basque shallops to carry on much of their commerce (while they also carried south war parties from time to time with which to attack the Eastern Abenaki or their southern neighbours). But Europeans had, on contact with a Pockanoket sachem or an Eastern Abenaki sagamore, to learn to listen to meaningless greeting harangues and were expected to reply to them, irrespective of whether there was a linguistic bridge or not. They were also expected to receive gifts and not raise questions about their value and return gifts in their place which might not (in English eyes) involve value for value. Only when such ceremonies had been satisfactorily performed would the Indians bring themselves to trade goods for goods. The English of the period with which we are concerned do not seem to have learnt this before at least 1608 and there are a number of cases where they sacrificed Indian co-operation by starting hard trade bargaining, refusing Indian ceremonial presents, before the right time had come for purely commercial relations. They missed the chance of doing more trade than they might have done since, when rebuffed, as they considered, by the reaction of the English, the Indians expressed little or no enthusiasm for trade *per se*. Their Abenaki tutors, Nahanada and Skidwarres, probably eventually taught the English at Fort St George something of the right way to trade during what appears to have been an effective trading season on the Kennebec River in the summer of 1608, but of that we have no surviving details. At the same time, considering that we now have less than half of the journal material known to be extant in 1625 it is remarkable how much of the information on early culture traits and contacts in a compendium such as the *Handbook of North American Indians*, xv (1978), comes from what has survived and is contained in this book.

The descriptions of the shoreline cannot have been very informative to those who first read them and they still offer us many difficulties in interpretation. But the map which George Waymouth made in detail of his expeditions (p. 299) was not published and has not survived. The so-called Velasco map of 1610 (fig. 35) probably did incorporate materials from sketches made on the 1602 voyage. It almost certainly has in it much on the Maine shoreline which comes from charting by the Hanham—Pring expedition of 1606. But compared with the manuscript map by Champlain of 1607, now in the Library of Congress, what we can trace of the cartographical contributions of the voyages is relatively small. John Smith said in his 1616 *Description* that he had a number of earlier maps and charts but found them greatly mistaken. This may be true but it may also be an exaggeration, to boost by comparison his own fine map of New England which he included with the *Description*. But if generalisations about shorelines and even the charts of particular harbours, which Champlain so generously provided in 1613, are lacking, the verbal descriptions which abound do bring the New England shore and river scenery to life. No one can visit Martha's Vineyard and the Elizabeth Islands, for example, without being grateful for the 1602 descriptions, or the St George River without appreciating Rosier, even if he exaggerated both its size and its charms. The material on the Kennebec, though scattered and incomplete, also conveys something of the character of that impressive river.

Climate was one of the misleading factors dealt with in the 1602—5 narratives. Between June and September, apart from occasional storms, the New England coast usually combines sunshine at a not intolerable level with fresh breezes and with clear skies — even though they cloud over and bring rain and cool spells rather more often in Maine. It is clear that the visitors conveyed the impression of a warmer and more pleasant England to their readers and raised hopes which were not to be satisfied when year-round settlement took place. What the summer visitors could not know was that New England, on the eastern side of a great continental landmass, has naturally a continental climate, the hot summer mitigated by sea breezes and currents, and cold winters, often with snow lying for months on end and with temperatures well below those of normal English weather. What was exceptional, however, was that much of the decade 1600—10 was a 'little ice age' over much of the northern hemisphere. Champlain met exceptional cold in 1604—5 at Ste Croix; Popham encountered it on the Kennebec in 1607—8 (and it may well have helped to kill him), but the Thames was frozen over in 1608 also. The hardships of the winter of 1607—8 helped to kill enthusiasm for settlement in the central and northern Maine coasts for a long time to come. The experiences of the settlers on the Kennebec tended to get translated farther south, since southern New England was also dubiously regarded by those in the know (since nothing had been published at the time) and certainly it was only Smith's assurance that if Maine was too cool, yet Massachusetts was not so, that gradually revived interest in the settlement prospects of the area as a whole.

What we can see now is that the lists of plants and animals and the descriptions of natural products, together with the limited growth-experiments that were made, did help, with what was said about the Indians, to give some idea of the ecology of the coastal regions. Archer, Brereton, Pring's narrator, Rosier and even Robert Davies were good observers and had a feeling for the landscape, its flora and fauna as well as its people, which made up something of a picture though one, of course, with very great gaps in it, due both to the short-term summer visits and to the eclectic choice of places to describe in detail. But close study does bring out the thoroughness with which descriptive and enumerative work was done, and helps to keep alive features of pre-contact New England which, if not always dead by any means, are often covered, altered, made less easy to comprehend as North American society exploits so thoroughly these most attractive shores. What the visitors did not understand is that many of the features which attracted them were the work of generations of aboriginal life. The Native Americans, as Indians are now tending to call themselves, had kept the shores cleared for their gathering and fishing; they had cleared great areas for their agriculture southwards from the Saco River, and the movement of their village agriculture, highly efficient in its own terms, from one site to another had made inroads on the unbroken forest which the later settlers were to meet as they moved inland. Even where there was thick forest but the land itself was reasonably level, Indian burning of underbrush to facilitate their hunting had opened up the woodlands so that they could offer easier routes to exploitation than if they had been left undisturbed in their climax state. It was in some considerable part a man-made landscape the visitors saw and of which they had no inkling at this time. It is also one of the ironies of later settlement from 1620 onwards that if European-carried diseases had not killed off the majority of the Indians of Massachusetts and adjoining areas the new settlers would have had to insinuate or fight their way into a fairly densely populated territory, which in the event lay open to them through the genocidal effects of such epidemics. But all this was, in 1608, still well into the future.

The topographic and linguistic records collected (since in this case the two cannot be effectively separated), so far as they survive, are important. James Rosier claimed, by the time he published his pamphlet, to have collected some 500 Eastern Abenaki words, but of these Purchas preserved only a limited number which, however, form the earliest vocabulary of this branch of the Algonquian language group. It is clear that Thomas Hanham too collected words, but only two have survived. The most remarkable achievement was the compilation of the description of Mawooshen, the territory of the Eastern Abenaki and part of its hinterland occupied by the Western Abenaki, compiled from material supplied by the Indians brought to England by Waymouth and discussed in connection with them below. It is the earliest document of this sort to have appeared from any of the early English voyages, apart from a certain limited amount of parallel information for the Roanoke Island neighbourhood supplied by the two Indians brought back in 1584 by Arthur Barlowe. It is almost certain that Thomas Harriot had a great deal of this type of documentation on that branch of the Algonquian linguistic group in his unpublished collections which were in Sion College from his death in 1621 until the Great Fire when they were destroyed. But it appears that subsequent to the Mawooshen document's compilation and use, attempts were made to keep it up to date and to extend it to other parts of New England, and a summary record of this appears in the instructions which were apparently prepared for Nicholas Hobson's voyage of 1614.

In the broad spectrum of English overseas activities in the first thirty years of the seventeenth century the New England voyages and such records as they left behind them have only a small place, but they were seminal in guiding attention to this area. Their contribution could come to be appreciated as New England emerged through publications by John Smith and others and by the Pilgrim settlement and its immediate small successors as indeed being a place where Englishmen might find land and seacoast, rivers and products to grow which were compatible with their way of life in country or town in England and into which they could import, without radical change though with many conscious reforms, English agriculture, craftsmanship and types of civil and religious organisation. In the synthetic picture of English colonial development which is emerging for the early seventeenth century assessment of the significance or non-significance of these voyages must be reached. This cannot be done until all the surviving evidence about these episodes has been set out and evaluated line by line and, almost, word for word. Only then can their 'placing' in the broader analytical context be attempted. Even so, it is hard to see how, with such a limited part of the mosaic of events which they represent alone surviving, that major generalisations can be derived from them which can materially affect the total assessment of the achievements of a particular generation in such a field as this. Their primary interest remains that of the record of the activities of a number of groups of outsiders, Englishmen in this case, in contact with a novel American environment and how they reacted in words and action to it. This interaction can be observed and commented on, where broader generalisations may, at this stage at least, give rise only to the encapsulation of the events in high-sounding but rather empty sociological terms. None the less, understanding of native American life in the immediate pre-conquest and early contact period is becoming wider and deeper as the attention of ethnologists has been drawn more systematically to the correlation of archaeological remains, early contact documents and later data acquired from Indian survivors so that understanding of the context of the early contact period has advanced substantially.

NATURAL HISTORY

A survey of the range and quality of the natural history observations made on the New England coast during the three voyages of 1602–5 invites comparison with those made, a generation earlier, by Thomas Harriot and John White on the Carolina Sounds. It would be too much to expect the summer visitors of 1602–5 to penetrate the ecology of an area as significantly as Harriot and White who not only were able to follow a year round cycle but had much more expertise, so far as can be ascertained, than any member of the ships' companies of Gosnold, Pring and Waymouth. As far as these narratives give any hint of who made the observations there was no one, with the possible exception of James Rosier, who matched Harriot in ability nor did they have an artist with them like John White. Nevertheless a mixed ship's company of captain, master, gentlemen, cape merchant and mariners could, out of a common pool of experience at sea on fishing or trading voyages to other parts of the world combined with the knowledge common to all who had lived in the English countryside, name trees, plants, fish, birds and animals that were the same, or approximately so, as those with which they were familiar. Since many of the fish and birds of the New England area are identical with or closely related to European species recognition was not difficult. Trees and plants, too, could usually be named from their similarity to European species. Mammals, as will be indicated, offered special problems even to list.

The information was collected by a simple process of enumeration and presented, for the most part, in lists of flora and fauna at the end of the narratives. These lists reflect this common knowledge with some confessions of ignorance and some complete novelties which simply had to be described. The underlying purpose of listing was economic, that is a search for commodities for trade but it was also a survey of natural resources which would assist in the survival of a settlement should one be made in the future. In addition each expedition was expected to plant selected European grains and vegetables to test soil fertility for the production of crops that would augment the natural products, again with a view to trade and self-sufficiency in food. In so short a time as the expeditions stayed in New England such tests could only be elementary.

The Gosnold and Waymouth voyages follow the same time pattern, both arriving on the shores of New England in the middle of May and remaining there for about four weeks. Both these voyages combined the economic and settlement reasons for collecting information. The Pring expedition arrived a month later and was a trading voyage only. Between them they cover the spring time and summer, a time of rapid change as growth, flowering and fruiting completed the cycle in a climate hot enough to promote the changes in the time they were there, even if some of the fruits were not wholly ripe. In May they would still be able to see something of the northerly migration of the birds and the swarming of the fish up the rivers to spawn. The lists of both Brereton and Rosier make mention of the 'large flocks of birds to vs vnknown' some of which were breeding in the Elizabeth Islands and off the Maine coast. In all three accounts the fish make an accurate and impressive list and fish as an abundant source of food is emphasized.

How many animals they saw is far from certain. They indicate, with the exception of Pring, that the information on them derived from the skins that the Indians traded, but deer they admit they saw. They mention seeing the tracks of animals but if they spent their nights mostly on shipboard they would be unlikely to glimpse the animals who came out at night in the scrubland between the forest and the shore. Yet the presence of live bears and wolves must surely have been known to the voyagers with Gosnold and Pring since they were in the Massachusetts area where the first settlement at Plymouth was made in 1620. The two earliest surveys of this area which were subsequently printed were made by Thomas Morton in 1622 and by William Wood between 1629 and 1633. Their remarks on bears and wolves make it plain that in spring and summer they were active, visible and noisy. Morton[1] in *New English Canaan*, published in 1637, says 'The beare is a tyrant at a lobster, and at low water will downe to the Rocks, and groape after them with great diligence.' Of the wolf[2] he says, 'On all these [deer] the Wolfes doe pray continually, the best meanes they have to escape the wolfes is by swimming to Islands, or necks of land, whereby they escape.' Wood[3] in *New Englands prospect*, published in 1634, makes the comment, 'For Beares they be common, being a great blacke kind of Beare, which be most feirce in Strawberry time, at which time they have young ones: at this time likewise they will goe upright like a man, and clime trees, and swimme to the Islands.' He also says[4] that the deer 'desire to be neare the Sea, so that they may swimme to the Islands when they are chased by the Woolves', and[5] 'in Autumne and the beginning of the Spring, these ravenous rangers doe most frequent our English habitations, following the Deare which come down at that time to these parts'; again,[6] 'Late at night, and early in the morning, they set up their howlings, and call their companies together at night to hunt, at morning to sleepe.' Such liveliness might not have been thought, in 1602–5, to be good propaganda for settlement.

The lists of the trees are comprehensive and show the same range of familiarity as is shown with fish, birds and plants. Timber was extensively used and had been a commodity much sought after in trade with Europe and the Baltic. There is mention, of course, of trees they did not recognise but those which could be used in shipbuilding or were known to be a profitable cargo are specified. The lists of plants are at the same time ordinary and curious. Some like the rose, the eglantine and the honeysuckle lend reassuring familiarity to the scene. So do the fruits they could name with the added advantage of their being a source of food. Some have specific medicinal properties, although all plants or parts of them were recommended by the herbalists and apothecaries for alleviating a host of ailments. The *Iris florentina* is especially interesting as it, like citrus fruits and olives, was a commodity which need not be imported from Europe if it grew in America where the English had control.

From these lists and the more generalised observations in the narratives something of the physical and climatic conditions of New England is conveyed and there emerges a picture of an environment

---

[1] Thomas Morton, *New English Canaan* (1637), p. 80.   [2] Ibid. p. 76.
[3] William Wood, *New Englands prospect* (1634), p. 19.   [4] Ibid. p. 21.
[5] Ibid. p. 23.   [6] Ibid. p. 24.

familiar to Englishmen to which they could adapt as colonists and in which they could make a prosperous living.

Little information is given on the identity of those members of the expeditions who named or commented on the fauna and flora. Only three names are directly connected with such activity. In the Archer narrative Master Robert Meriton appears as qualified to identify sassafras but no explanation is given for this expertise. He could have been on earlier voyages farther south that had collected cargoes of sassafras or he could have been an apothecary's apprentice a number of whom went on voyages to bring back specimens or plants. Gerard[1] mentions his servant William Marshall who was sent on a voyage to the Levant as surgeon on the *Hercules*. In the Pring narrative Robert Salterne collects and brings home to Bristol an unknown bush with the fruit like a pear-plum, and as he had also been on the Gosnold voyage he could have collected plants on that occasion too. With Pring was the gentleman, Thomas Bridges who was separated from the party engaged in digging up sassafras, possibly wandering too far from his fellows while searching for plants. That, however, is speculation. James Rosier, with Waymouth in 1605, is the only one who is shown to be actively engaged in compiling a list even if the primary purpose is listing Indian words. It is reasonable to assume that he could identify the fish and plants by their English names though he could well have had the assistance of the surgeon who is mentioned as being one of the company but who is not named.

No comparable study of the voyages and settlement of 1606–8 can be made. Thomas Hanham[2] may well have added to Rosier's natural history lists but we do not have his journal. Dr Turner[3] may have been able to report on the natural resources of the country of Mawooshen when he returned from Fort St George. The single journal we have is primarily one of sea and river exploration with the emphasis on action rather than natural history observations, though on one occasion the author makes the somewhat surprising claim that he could distinguish four distinct kinds of whortleberries on one island.[4] But with the journals of all the rest lost little more can be said.

---

[1] John Gerard, *Herball* (1597), pp. 1304, 1330.   [2] Pp. 76, 352 below.
[3] P. 334 below.   [4] P. 430 below.

The fauna and flora of the 1602 expedition

We can collate the list of fauna and flora following Brereton's printed narrative of 1602 with the narrative material supplied by him and by Gabriel Archer to make something of a synthesis. In the list of birds only the hernshaw (heron), crane and geese are mentioned by name in both narratives. The longer-ranging sea and coastal birds, mentioned by Archer, petrels, coots, hagbuts (shearwaters), murres, gannets, gulls and cormorants are recorded as the observers approach their first landfall after crossing the Atlantic and indeed are used as an indication that they were approaching land. All these birds would be familiar to experienced sailors. In addition Archer mentions birds as large as cliff pigeons which are probably represented by doves in the list. Penguins (Greak Auk) are seen as they approach land and later, farther south, are caught and eaten. The birds mentioned by Brereton alone are the bittern, mallard and teal, which would be commonly recognised in England. The eagle, osprey, hawk, crow, raven, seapie (oystercatcher) and redwinged blackbird are not specified in either narrative and again, with the exception of the redwinged blackbird, they are birds which could be identified by almost anyone in the company. They could have been seen at any time during the stay on the New England coast but their presence could also have been deduced from the feathers on the Indian arrows or head-dresses. This would apply particularly to the larger birds of prey, as can be seen from Pring's narrative which is the only one which mentions the vulture, not as having been seen but as a possible source for the arrow fletchings. Both Brereton and Archer mention more than once that some of these birds were breeding on the islands or cliffs, notably the herons, cranes and geese, and that the company supplemented their diet with young birds. One other bird is mentioned only by Archer, the shoveller, which is breeding on the cliffs of Capoag, the first Martha's Vineyard, along with the cranes, herons and geese. Whether Master Robert Meriton identified the redwinged blackbird as well as the sassafras we are left to guess but if he had been on voyages farther south he would have been familiar with both.

The cod, the mackerel and the herring are the three fish mentioned in both narratives, which is wholly appropriate, as they dominate all subsequent accounts of the fishing catch off the coast of southern Massachusetts and Cape Cod. To the herring must be added the alewife whose running and spawning at Plymouth John Pory describes vividly in his letter to the earl of Southampton.[1] Of the crustaceans and shell-fish both Archer and Brereton mention the lobster, crab and mussel but Brereton alone notes the whelk, cockle, scallop and oyster. The tortoise or turtle is mentioned twice by Archer, once as being eaten by the Indians and again as something to eke out their own diet when left on the island at the time Gosnold made his last exploring venture. It is Brereton, however, who notes that the tortoises were in the lake where the fort was built. Whales are referred to only by Brereton from the evidence of ribs on the shore of Capoag but both narratives record seals from the skins traded or worn by the Indians. They do not report that they were seen. One remaining fish that is on the list, and in Archer's narrative, is the dogfish, and in quantity, since a surfeit of the bellies made one of the company regret his indulgence. This leaves four names on the list, the bream, thornback, hake and rockfish, which are not specified in either narrative but were doubtless noted by someone, and may have been more plentiful in the waters to the north where they first caught fish.

Of the animals listed only the deer is mentioned by both Brereton and Archer as being seen on Martha's Vineyard as well as being a skin worn and traded by the Indians. While Archer writes of the rich furs that the Indians brought for trade it is Brereton who names them, adding marten to those named in the list. Live animals are introduced, by Brereton, only by their anonymous tracks. The dogs in the list would appear to be Indian dogs but here they are said to be like foxes and not like wolves, as in Rosier's list, thus avoiding any mention of the wolf. The bear does appear in the list and as it is not specified in either narrative as a skin the Indians traded, this may be an admission that they had been seen. The snake is permitted to intrude into this delectable country and appears at the end of the list as a further observation on Indian diet and clothing. Although the length and girth are given the impression is that they were dead snakes caught by the Indians.

The trees specified in both narratives are the sassafras, cedar, oak, walnut, beech and cherry, all growing either on Capoag, Martha's Vineyard or the Elizabeth Islands. They are important trees, useful for shipbuilding, trade in timber and for medicinal qualities. Brereton lists the hazelnut and Archer the witch-hazel which are both present and it may be that the hazelnut in the list is intended to cover both. Archer alone mentions the cypress, noted shortly after the first landfall, and

[1] Sidney V. James, ed. *Three Visitors to Early Plymouth* (1963), pp. 7–8.

Brereton alone picks up the elm and the holly on Cuttyhunk. The birch, ash and hawthorn are specified by Archer but do not appear on the list. The ash and the hawthorn are located in Cuttyhunk but the birch is recorded along with the cypress farther north. Brereton, however, on Cuttyhunk says that there are fruit trees he cannot name but with strange barks, one 'of an orange colour, in feeling soft and smooth like Veluet'. This, even if not a fruit tree, may have been a canoe birch. The cotton tree of the list does not appear in either narrative. It is possible that a verbal description to someone in England of one of these strange trees suggested the balsam poplar, but it is equally possible that it was added to the list as a tree they hoped would be found by another expedition. 'Fruit trees to vs vnknowen', added at the end of the list seems to indicate that there were a number of trees in flower but even when they left the fruits were not sufficiently formed to suggest familiar types of fruit trees, or conversely the ripening fruit showed clearly that they were something they had not seen before.

Almost all the plants in the list are noted also by both Brereton and Archer and they are, without exception, useful. They bear berries which they know can be eaten, as well as grapes for making wine. Groundnuts and peas are there for a staple food and tobacco can be had for pleasure, medicine and a substitute for food in times of shortage. Tobacco they do not see growing but they both make it clear that the Indians have it and will trade it. They do not suggest they might grow it themselves and here they may have been guided by those who knew from other voyages that it grew better farther south. Two plants on the list not mentioned by both are flax and sorrel. Sorrel is mentioned by Archer alone as growing on Cuttyhunk along with alexanders, tansy, eglantine and honeysuckle but the last four are not on the list. As alexanders were also eaten these would be included in the general reference to salad herbs which follows sorrel. The sorrels could have been several varieties of dock rather than the Wood Sorrel, the alexanders Angelica, Scotch Lovage or some other umbelliferous plant, the tansy one of the Yarrow family. The tansy was used for flavouring. What other herbs they noted we do not know. Later permanent settlers in southern Massachusetts confirm and extend the list of indigenous herbs. John Mason, in his *Discourse*,[1] says that the 'common wild herbs of the Countrie are Angelica, Violets, Mints, Scabius, Yarrow, Ferne, Salsaparilla, with divers other sorts whereof I am ignorant'. William Wood[2] lists among

---

[1] John Mason, *A briefe discourse of the New-found-land* (1625), sig. A4r.
[2] William Wood, *New Englands prospect* (1634), pp. 13–14.

the plants of New England such herbs as marjoram, purselane, sorrel, pennyroyal and yarrow. Some of these may not have been growing on Cuttyhunk but it is clear that when they were forced to eke out their food by eating salads they used only those plants with which they were familiar.

There are varieties of flax which are native to North America and if they saw and recognised flax growing wild it would most probably have been *Linum striatum* which is found on Cape Cod and the islands of southeastern Massachusetts. Archer does refer to hemp as being used by the Indians for making strings, but they may or may not have been using the wild flax. The practice in England where hemp and flax were separate crops was to use the fibres of the hemp, *Cannabis sativa*, for making cables and ropes and those of the flax for cloth. Here, too, the coarser fibres were probably those of Indian Hemp, *Cannabis indica*. John Smith[1] refers to the use by the Indians of 'A kinde...of Flax, wherewith they make nets.' The strings the Indians had may also have influenced Brereton when he describes the soil on Cuttyhunk as being 'of the colour of our hempelands in England; and being thus apt for these and like graines'. The eglantine and honeysuckle mentioned by Archer are not, as sweetbriar and some woodbind, native plants of North America, although they have been introduced. What they would have seen were the wild rose, *Rosa virginiana* and variants and the native azalea. Eglantine may have been used loosely as a name for a wild rose or deliberately, since the eglantine was a rose with medicinal value. Gerard[2] describes the briar balls that grow on the sweetbriar and goes on to cite Pliny '...that the little spungie Brier ball stamped with hony and ashes, doth cause haires to grow which are fallen away through the disease called *Alopecia*, or the Foxes euill, or in plaine tearmes, the French pockes'. Here might be something as effective as sassafras was thought to be. The honeysuckle known in England also had its medicinal uses but the shrubby plant called by Gerard[3] the 'Savoy honisuckle' which was native to Europe was not known to have such virtues.

We are left now with the *Iris florentina* which in this list occupies a place that is unique. It is not mentioned in the narratives specifically nor is there any oblique reference that would bring any kind of iris to mind. Orris root, as the root of *Iris florentina* was called, seems to have been widely used in the sixteenth century in the cloth trade as

[1] John Smith, *Works*, p. 216.   [2] Gerard, *Herball*, pp. 1087–9.
[3] Ibid. pp. 111–13.

well as in the apothecary business, and as it is not native to England nor, apparently, a plant that could be cultivated on a commercial scale, it had to be imported from the continent. We can then place the orris root among other imports like citrus fruits, olives, vines and the mulberry tree (for silk worms) which the English were anxious to find in North America or else be able to cultivate in a climate more favourable than in England. This suitable environment they would naturally expect southern Massachusetts to be as it lies in a similar latitude to Spain. *Iris florentina* is not, however, native to North America and the irises they could have seen, the Blue Flag and Slender Blue Flag do not have aromatic roots. They might have found the wild Sarsaparilla, *Aralia nudicaulis*, and the smilaxes with their aromatic roots, and possibly the Sweet Flag, *Acorus calamus*, also with an aromatic root, which is a native of Asia, was introduced into Europe by 1557 and regarded as naturalized by 1660.[1] In North America the Sweet Flag was regarded as being native only in the west, but Frank C. MacKeever describing the flora of Nantucket says that 'The Acorus of North America was believed to have been introduced from Europe but it is now proved to be fertile, diploid, and indigenous. Its correct name is *Acorus americana* (Raf.) Raf.'[2] If specimens of *Acorus* were brought to England they would have been recognised for what they were since Gerard had both *Iris florentina* and *Acorus calamus* growing in his garden,[3] as doubtless had other apothecary and private gardens. *Acorus* was used at a later time by snuff manufacturers and to scent hair and tooth powders, in the same way as orris.[4] There is, therefore, very little justification for calling anything they found in this area *Iris florentina*. Was this name included in the list because they still hoped to find it or because they hoped to be able to cultivate it? It is possible they brought some plants with them to America to 'make a triall of' under the watchful eyes of the party who were expected to stay there. It may, also, have been straight propaganda, an attempt to interest the Mercers and Drapers and encourage them to invest in future expeditions.

[1] Clapham, Tutin and Warburg, *Flora of the British Isles* (1962), pp. 1050–1.
[2] Frank C. MacKeever, *Plants of Nantucket* (1968), p. 6.
[3] *A Catalogue of Plants*, ed. B. D. Jackson (1876), pp. 23, 38.
[4] M. Grieve, *A Modern Herbal* (1959), p. 279.

The Pring voyage considered in relation to the Brereton and Archer narratives

The Pring voyage of 1603, following on the Gosnold voyage of 1602, supplements the natural history observations of the New England coast and Cape Cod. It arrived on the coast in the early summer, later than the Gosnold voyage, and by leaving in early August was able to observe almost to the end of the ripening season. In its range it took a closer view of the Maine coast, three weeks rather than three days, but did not go as far south. In some ways the record of the fauna and flora it contains reflects this pattern.

Pring adds to the Brereton list of trees the spruce, pine, fir and maple of the northern forests while omitting the cypress, elm and cotton tree. With Archer's additions the records tally closely if not exactly. Some emphasis is laid on the commercial uses for the trees, the witch hazel for making soap ashes and the holly for bird lime, not mentioned elsewhere. The list of plants growing wild agrees with that of Brereton but does not include groundnuts or any herbs, nor *Iris florentina* which is not altogether surprising. What is new is the description of the Indian gardens with crops of tobacco, pumpkins, cucumbers (as they thought) and, as they also surmise, maize so reassuringly like the gardens of the Algonquians which they knew from Harriot's description. It was important to establish that tobacco grew in New England. They could identify some of the bushes as being cherry from the fruit and note that the Beach Plum, with its white fruit, was almost ripe.

Here, too, we have a puzzling entry in the 'peare plum' a specimen of which Salterne so carefully packed in earth to bring back to Bristol. It is not at all easy to identify this precisely. The pear-plum, cultivated in Europe, was a variety of plum shaped like a pear, which gives us its colour and shape but not its size. That the pear plum was a smallish fruit might be inferred from Thomas Morton's description of Massachusetts in the early 1620s:[1] 'Plum trees, of this kind there are many; some beare fruit as bigg as our ordinary bullis; others there be, that doe beare fruite much bigger than peare plummes.' As identifications both the Prickly Pear, *Opuntia* Mill. and one of the many species of thorn, *Crataegus*, have been suggested. Gleason and Cronquist[2] say that the Prickly Pear grows on rocks, sand-dunes or sand prairies from east Massachusetts to south Ontario but this plant was already known

[1] Morton, *New English Canaan* p. 65.
[2] Gleason and Cronquist, *Manual* (1963), p. 483.

in England and described by Gerard[1] as the Indian Fig Tree, *Ficus Indica*. If Salterne had never seen or heard of it before surely he would have considered the plant just as remarkable as the fruit, certainly worthy of comment. If it was a thorn with a large berry of this shape and colour and with a calyx like a 'knop' he would have recognised so familiar an English bush or tree.

What was, it seems, abundant in the area where Pring had his encampment and was unfamiliar to the English was the Service Berry or Shad Bush, *Amelanchier canadensis*, with a berry the colour of a plum but more the contour of a pear and possibly with what he could call a 'knop'. Thoreau,[2] speaking of the sandy wastes between Truro and the Pamet River where once the sassafras grew says, 'the fruit of the shad-bush or *Amelanchier*, which the inhabitants call Josh-pears...is very abundant on the hills'. Fernald and Kinsey[3] give Sugar-Pear and Indian-Pear as colloquial names for the Service Berry and remark, 'Few wild fruits of such excellent quality are less known to the modern American although by the Indians and the early European explorers of the continent the berries were among the most esteemed of our native fruits.' The suggested identification here of the 'peare plum' is the Service Berry.

It is in Pring's narrative that we get the direct statement that animals were seen. The first group of names, fox, deer, stags, bears, wolves, lusernes (lynx) and dogs are associated with the exploration of the coast southwards from possibly Penobscot Bay. As they examined several inlets they would be close enough to the shore to see them at the watering places and possibly on short shore excursions. The second group is associated with their stay in the encampment on Cape Cod. The names are the same as in the first group with the addition of porcupine and a rumour of 'Tygres'. If this is the mountain lion it would not, of course, be seen on the coast. Snakes, six feet long, are introduced again as Indian girdles. Beavers and otters are not observed but appear in the context of the lucrative French fur trade farther north. Again, with a shore base, they were in a better position to observe the animal population than the 1602 expedition who probably spent the nights on board ship. As Pring's narrative was not printed until 1625 the variety of fauna with which settlers would share the environment was already well known from reports by the temporary settlers of

[1] Gerard, *Herball*, p. 1330.
[2] Henry D. Thoreau, *Cape Cod* (1865), p. 105.
[3] Fernald and Kinsey, *Edible Plants* (1943), pp. 230–1; see also below p. 225.

Sagadahoc, by the permanent settlers of Plymouth and from the publications of John Smith. It would not have been realistic to talk only of skins.

The list of birds in the narrative is brief compared with Brereton and Archer. The only sea bird is the gull. The eagle and vulture mentioned by Pring are a deduction from observing the feathered arrows. Although the kite is mentioned in this same context it does not appear on the list. While it is unwise to be dogmatic about what birds frequented New England in the early seventeenth century, today the kite would be a rare visitor. A general reference is made to the presence of many other birds. Coming on the scene in the summer months, reference to birds breeding is not to be expected nor, indeed, to birds such as geese most of which would have migrated northwards.

Again the list of fish is not as long as that given by Brereton and Archer but mullet and turbot are added. The cod, mackerel and herring on which they must have lived when collecting the sassafras are there and so are the more choice crustaceae like the lobster and crab, along with a novelty, the crayfish. Mussels are noted for their pearls. Seals are also mentioned not for their skins but for the oil that can be processed from the carcass as a reminder, perhaps, of the double trade value which they presented.

The aggregate of names for the fauna and flora is much smaller than we have from the Archer and Brereton narratives and list but this may well have been due to the editing of Pring's account of his expedition. What we get from Pring are additions and the 'peare plum'. To repeat in detail everything that had been noted in 1602 may have been thought to be unncessary.

James Rosier on the coast of Maine

While most of the plants, trees, animals, birds and fish which appear on Rosier's lists, that is the list of fauna and flora together with the list of Indian names, could have been identified by quite a number of the ship's company it seems clear that Rosier, possibly with the help of the surgeon, was responsible for collecting this information. As both the narrative and the first list printed by Purchas correspond closely with Rosier's *Relation* they are discussed together except where there are a few interesting divergences. The fauna and flora in the Indian word list[1] will be considered separately.

[1] Purchas, *Pilgrimes*, IV (1625), 1667, XVIII (1906), 358–9.

There is passing mention of cod and whales off Cape Cod but for the second landfall at Monhegan, where they anchor and go ashore, there is a short list of useful trees, fir, oak, birch and beech, some fruits, peas and the rose, and fish to eat, the cod and the haddock. Here they note that birds are breeding on the shore and the rocks and it is clear that apart from the taller trees the useful vegetation is growing on the shoreline. It is when they finally anchor in the Georges Islands, at Allen Island, that the systematic collection of names is made. Again it is noted that the plants are growing on the shore line and in clear spots where the tree cover is not heavy. The third set of observations was made when they explored the St George River and made one land excursion, the only occasion when herbs are noted. There are many more names given in the narrative for trees, fruit bushes, plants and fish than there are for birds and animals. The presence of animals is deduced from skins the Indians trade or are wearing and from tracks on the ground which seem to mean very little to them. They do not mention sea birds in the narrative and on land only the crane, goslings and large egg shells, bigger than a goose's egg, which would be those of the Great Auk. The final list contains, however, more names in all categories especially for birds, fish and animals, while for trees and plants the correspondence is much closer.

To the list of trees collected from earlier voyages are added the yew and the aspen, but the walnut is not mentioned. Rosier also notes that there are many fruit trees he cannot name and identifies only the cherry, a not very specific identification. Among the plants we have a rose but it is not eglantine. He has groundnuts but they are not mentioned in the narrative, and there is angelica which must have been similar to Archer's alexanders. He also notes a sweet smelling herb like marjoram to which Purchas adds camomile but does not attempt to be more specific.

In the list of fish Rosier adds to those mentioned in the narrative, herring, cunner, whiting and sole and to the crustaceae and shellfish, crab, cockle, whelk and oyster. Salmon which is in the narrative is not on the list, likewise Aloza or shad, while the tortoise appears only in the list. There are twelve names of birds in the list as against two only in the narrative – crane and gosling – while the large (auk) eggs appear as penguin. Purchas,[1] however, inserts into the first list the words Kite, Soga which could be *kitsuog*, a Narragansett name for a cormorant. At the bottom of the list in the *Relation* and in Purchas there is the legend

[1] Ibid. IV (1625), 1667, XVIII (1906), 357–8.

'Many birds of sundrie colors. Many vnknown fowles in flocks.' This is a handsome confession of ignorance and we are left to speculate on how the list was compiled. All the birds here are on Brereton's list with the exception of swan and 'shark' which could be a misprint for shrike (species in both England and America) or else shag which again is a cormorant. This earlier list may have acted as the model on the presumption that birds which frequented southern New England were likely also to be found farther north.[1]

As has already been indicated most of the animals mentioned in the list were seen only as skins but they would have seen Indian dogs and possibly heard the wolf pack and seen porcupine quills as decoration. The great wild cat could only have been the usual rumour. There is one interesting difference between the list in the *Relation* and that in Purchas. The former has 'raine-deer, stagges, fallow-deer' and the latter has 'deer, red and fallow' and at the bottom of the list 'deer with hornes and broad ears'. In the narrative Rosier has misleadingly gathered from the captive Indians that 'they make butter and cheese of the milke they haue of the Rain-Deere and Fallo-Deere, which they haue tame as we haue Cowes'. Somewhere among these kinds of deer we should have a reference to the moose but the deer with 'hornes and broad ears' is thought to be an elk.

The two statements made by Rosier on the collecting of Indian words appear only in the *Relation* whereas the list of words appears only in Purchas. Rosier informs the reader in the preface that he collected about five hundred items of vocabulary and later in the narrative that he started this collection on the shore of Allen Island in a meeting with the Abenaki devoted solely to this purpose. There were other occasions during the time the *Archangell* was anchored off Allen Island when Rosier could have added to the list, when engaged in trade and also when there were visits, voluntary and later enforced, by Indians to the ship. We must assume, if Rosier's statement in his preface is correct, that most of the five hundred words were collected from the five captives on the return voyage across the Atlantic. Of the eighty-five words printed by Purchas forty-one denote fauna and flora and the others are names of things to be seen round about them at Allen Island — parts of the body, a ship, the wind, the sea, rain and sand, and the trade items, knives and hatchets, to give some examples. This might suggest that the words printed by Purchas were Rosier's first list, collected before leaving the area.

There are ten names for sea creatures, cod, rockfish, cunner, plaice,

[1] See p. 306.

with lobster, cockle, mussel and crab, along the porpoise and tortoise. There is a name *Manedo* for a fish with horns. The word for whale, *Powdawe*, does not appear on the list but is given in the description of hunting the whale in the narrative. There is only one word for a bird and this is *Cagagoose*, the crow, which is vividly descriptive but suspect Indian. The crow may have been the only bird in sight, of the 'vnknown fowles in flocks', to which they could attach an English name. There are thirteen names for animals, three with no English equivalent, and one name for an insect, the garnepo fly. The animals named are bear, beaver, otter, rat, polecat, cat, hog and dog, along with two deer, *Coribo* the fallow deer, and *Moosurr* the red deer, which is undoubtedly the moose. There are only three trees, the fir, oak and birch, but to these we can add two fruit trees, the plum and the cherry. The plants are peas, tobacco, strawberry, gooseberry, currant, raspberry and rose with two other words, *Casterush* a weed, and *Nebeere* a leaf.

A scrutiny of all the natural history observations made during these visits from 1602 to 1605 and covering a large part of the coast of New England impresses with their accuracy if not their comprehensiveness. Considering that these were short visits and that observations of the fauna and flora were only part of their objectives and that they were slanted towards usefulness for trade and settlement, we can conclude that the work was done well. For the Massachusetts area a check can be made from *New English Canaan* and *New Englands prospect*, since in this early stage of settlement in Massachusetts the introduction of European plants would not have significantly changed the indigenous flora. The lists of fauna and flora in these reports are, naturally, much longer but what our voyagers list as being present, however they arrived at the names, were in fact to be found there at this time.

THE RECORDS OF THE VOYAGES, 1602–1608

When we look at the materials which we have for the English expeditions of the period we find record of ten separate voyages by one or two ships which were said to be setting out for, and actually made, a voyage to the area for which they were intended (or sufficiently close to it); while we find we have reasonably precise accounts of the voyages of 1602, 1603, 1605 and 1607 on which were performed a great part of the exploring, trading and settling attempted during these years. We have record of one expedition which, so far as we can tell, never got to sea, that of Sir John Zouche in August 1607, and of another, that of the *Triall*, which was taken over for piratical purposes and never got beyond European waters. We have full records of the one voyage which went seriously wrong, that of the *Richard*, Henry Challons captain, which was intercepted by the Spaniards late in 1606. We have very incomplete and unsatisfactory references to what was evidently a vitally important preparation voyage in late 1606, under Thomas Hanham and Martin Pring, the loss of whose records is a serious handicap to the understanding of the preparations for the 1607 colony and in particular of its decision to settle on the Kennebec rather than on the St George River farther north or on Saco Bay farther south. We have an appreciable amount of evidence on the founding voyage of 1607 which created the Sagadahoc colony, Fort St George on the Kennebec River, and on its activities between August and December 1607, though those for the months from October to December are fragmentary. We have very little evidence at all about the voyage of the two supply ships in May or thereabouts in 1608 and of another with a larger complement in July 1608, and consequently little solid information on the colony between January and September or October 1608 when it was abandoned and the personnel returned to England. So far as ancillary material is concerned we have only a small amount of information about what happened after the 1602 voyage, but nothing on what occurred before it started. We have no information on the Bristol reaction to Pring's voyage in 1603, or on the delay in sending out further expeditions (unless there was one of which we know nothing) in 1604. In 1605 we have only tantalising glimpses of what led to Waymouth's voyage of that year, and we have a complex of somewhat confusing information, not full enough to be precise, about some important aspects of what happened between October 1605 and April 1606. With 1606 we have the creation of the Virginia Company and if many things are obscure about this we can pin responsibility for the separate establishment of the Plymouth division of that company, which was to exploit North Virginia, on the shoulders of Sir John Popham. We have a reasonable number of documents on the ways and means sought to finance the proposed North Virginia colony but not enough to estimate the total investment available to the promoters – clearly early misfortunes cut away support which might have kept the colony, established in 1607, in existence for a longer period. The narrative of the *Mary and John*, in both of the forms in which we have it, is adequate for a reasonably clear account of the settlement down to 8 October 1607. We have also some reactions of promoters to her

28

return in December. There is some correspondence and legal proceedings which throw light on the return of the *Gifte of God* between December 1607 and February 1608, with accounts of what went on in the colony between October and December 1607. For the events of 1608 we are greatly handicapped since all the continuous narratives have disappeared along with journals of the two supply vessels sent in early summer and of the major supply voyage sent later in 1608 which ended by bringing the settlers home, thus abandoning the colony and bringing to an end the first phase of English enterprise. Our one additional asset is an account of part of Maine, based on Amerindian sources.

If we compare the documentation with the materials on the voyages to South Virginia and the foundation of Jamestown under the first charter which have been collected by Philip Barbour, we can see that we have there, for the shorter period, much less in the way of voyage narratives, very little after the first indeed, but enormously more on the exploration of the Chesapeake Bay and its attendant rivers, and more too on the problems of settlements (though we could do with still more), while the material on Amerindian life and culture is much more far-reaching. Thanks to John Smith and William Strachey we have a much more continuous narrative for the years 1607–9, than we have for the shorter life of the northern colony 1607–8. There was no such chronicler for the northern voyages as a whole while individual journals have disappeared. Thus the North Virginia voyage record is much more episodic, much more confined to specific and separate phases of exploration and to very limited information on the beginnings of settlement. But because we have a series of bird's-eye views of the voyages of 1602, 1603, 1605 and 1607 we have enough to establish something of a coherent series and to maintain a varied pattern of interest, even if we lack so much on the Hanham–Pring voyage and have lost journals such as that of Raleigh Gilbert which would have proved of inestimable value for the first English New England colonising episode and enabled us to compare it effectively with those at Ste Croix in 1604–5, Port Royal, 1605–7 and Jamestown, 1607–9. But we are not completely bereft of all materials on the periods where our sources are inadequate and the totality is substantial enough to enable us to see a pattern of development from beginning to an end which, however, was not a final terminus but an interlude before further spasmodic and ultimately systematic development took place in the New England area.

Apart from the Brereton pamphlet (or perhaps not wholly apart) and the Rosier tract of 1605, Hakluyt, and after him Purchas, are significant contributors to the documentation of the voyages, though our verdict on Purchas must inevitably be a very mixed one. After Hakluyt allowed Purchas in 1613 to use many of the manuscripts he had collected for a third edition of *The principal navigations*, his *Pilgrimage* in its second (1614) and subsequent editions contained reference to a number of crucial documents relating to the voyages and the colonial experiences of 1606–8, all of which he apparently obtained from Hakluyt (pp. 347–52 below). They included journals by Thomas Hanham, James Davies, John Elliott, Christopher Fortescue, and letters from George Popham to Sir John Gilbert and Edward Seymour. When he came to complete the *Pilgrimes* he admitted that he had prepared for the press the journals of Hanham, Raleigh Gilbert (not certainly obtained from Hakluyt's papers which had in the meantime, after Hakluyt's death, come into his possession), James Davies, John Elliott and others. He thought they would be too much for his readers (or more realistically perhaps for his publisher, as he was by this time far advanced in his fourth volume), and he omitted them, as well as narratives of later Virginia voyages by Edward Harlow in 1611 and by Nicholas Hobson in 1614. His failure to print the Hanham and Gilbert journals is particularly painful in that they provided essential links in the narrative chain which is now broken, probably for ever. He did reprint Brereton on the 1602 voyage (but attributed his journal by mistake to Rosier), and he had had from Hakluyt the original manuscript of James Rosier's journal of 1605 of which he gave extended extracts sufficient, however, as a collation shows, to reveal something of what was edited out in 1605, besides his partial vocabulary of the Eastern Abenaki tongue.

He preserved Hakluyt's copy of John Stoneman's journal of the fate of the *Richard* in 1606, and he also printed 'The description of Mawooshen', though 'a written large Treatise of Mawauhen' was one of the items he had described as having been omitted, making it possible that he had longer and shorter versions of this exceptionally interesting but challenging account of the Eastern Abenaki territory from the Amerindian point of view. When he speaks of a journal of James Davies, captain of Fort St George, 1607, he has hitherto been thought to be alluding to the Journal which has survived; this is attributed in this volume to Captain Robert Davies, who piloted the *Mary and John* on her outward voyage, occupied the position of sergeant major briefly at the fort in 1607 and then commanded his ship on her homeward voyage. Colin Steele, in the *Hakluyt handbook*, I, 93–5, usefully enumerates the North Virginia items printed by Purchas from Hakluyt, but does not go into detail on those he omitted though he mentions that there were such (p. 83). The tragic loss of so much original material in a volume into which he had put so much that was already available in print and did not need reprinting is one of the darkest blots on Purchas' reputation, relieved only by the probability that he was running out of space, the printer's patience and money at the same time. That Hakluyt was collecting vigorously and comprehensively up to 1613 is certain, and it may well be that further items were added between then and his death and were amongst the papers Purchas acquired only after 1616.

THE 1602 VOYAGE

Our authority on the origins of the 1602 voyage is slight. Precisely why New England should then have attracted an English expedition is unknown. Some general considerations may be suggested. The reissue in 1600[1] of Hakluyt's narratives of the Gilbert venture of 1583, together with the last defeatist chapter of the Roanoke voyages, John White's on the 1590 venture, may have directed attention rather to the more northerly than the more southerly coast. The cessation of English ventures in the Gulf of St Lawrence after 1597, leaving it to the French,[2] and possible knowledge of French settlements on Sable Island (1598) and at Tadoussac (1600), could have aroused competitive desires to exploit the coasts immediately to the south of the main sphere of French activities as an alternative to the St Lawrence. The existence of a group of men, whose American preferences lay to the north rather than to the south, survived the death (in 1598) of Lord Burghley, its most prominent supporter.[3] It was represented, especially, by Edward Hayes who about 1592 or early in 1593 had written, apparently in association with Christopher Carleill, a long treatise[4] on the advantages of the country between 40° and 45° N. on the North American mainland. Hayes had some association with the 1602 voyage,[5] but how active he was in its inception cannot be established. Another anonymous

---

[1] *Principal navigations*, III, 243–95.
[2] See Quinn, *England and the discovery of America*, pp. 312–63.
[3] Ibid. pp. 316–18.
[4] *NAW*, III, 156–72. [5] See pp. 35, 140 below.

proponent of a similar policy left a comparable treatise, written about 1600, on the advantages of settlement in North America.[1] Whereas the Roanoke voyages had been advocated as a means of obtaining exotic and Mediterranean products, and the 'northern group' (if we may call them so) the products comparable with those of the Baltic, ships' stores in the main, this treatise advocated choice of a location for settlements with a climate and products as close as possible to those of England itself. Settlements, which were self-supporting, he thought, would be easiest where least adaptation was needed. This is, in essence, the emergence of the theory of planting a 'New England' in America. But the author is unknown, his influence incapable of being assessed and his connections with the 1602 venture not established. But at least such ideas were being ventilated before 1602. Knowledge of the French fur trade farther north may have been a significant influence. Richard Hakluyt is highly likely to have been concerned in the decision to make a voyage. He switched his emphasis from one part of North America to another in order to demonstrate all the incentives he could think of for English action on any part of the mainland. Whether or not he was a subscriber is not so easy to say in the absence of all direct evidence.

Bartholomew Gosnold came from a branch of the respected gentry family of Gosnold of Otley, Suffolk, and Warner F. Gookin was able to throw much light on his family background and fortunes,[2] but he learned too late of his privateering and ship-owning activities before his engagement in the 1602 voyage to North Virginia.[3] He suggests that Gosnold and the eventual narrator of the voyage, John Brereton, were in contact with Hakluyt, who lived part of each year at his parsonage at Wetheringsett, at no great distance from their homes, so that Hakluyt could have inspired both of them to go on a voyage to establish a trading post in and make an exploration of the still largely

[1] *NAW*, III, 172–5 (a commentary, it might appear, on the previous project).

[2] Warner F. Gookin and Philip L. Barbour, *Bartholomew Gosnold* (1963), especially pp. 10–48, 220–2, 253, 261. He was a pensioner at Jesus College, Cambridge, matriculating in 1597 (Venn, *Alumni cantabrigienses*, II, 242).

[3] Inventory of the *Diamond* of Hampton, Bartholomew Gosnold captain, Roger Newes master, taken at Penryn, 19 September 1599 (sugars, gold, civet, pearl, value £1645 16s 8d) P.R.O., HCA 24/67 (between numbers 5 and 6); letter from the earl of Nottingham, Lord High Admiral, to Dr Julius Caesar, 9 May 1600, instructing him to let Captain Gosnold and Captain Streynsham have commissions for their two ships and their pinnaces. He says 'They are wholle owners of theise vessells, which will tye them somewhat the more to their good behaviours, besides they have both of them bene formerlie att the seas, and noe complaintes have hitherto come against them, which is some testimonye of their honest carriages.' B.L. Additional MS 15208, ff. 510–11. Both of these documents were found by Professor K. R. Andrews and were made available by him.

unknown North Virginia. This is an attractive theory but no more. Research has not confirmed a firm link between the three men. What Gookin did establish was that through his mother-in-law, Martha Golding, Gosnold's wife Mary had many connections with prominent city merchant families, including Thomas Smith, already prominent in the Levant and East India Companies, and soon to be knighted by James I, and so could have introduced her husband into their circle. Whether Gosnold was the initiator of the expedition cannot be ascertained, and also whether the ship he commanded on the outward voyage, the *Concord*, was his own, has not been established. But it is difficult, when we examine the records of the voyage, to see him as the prime mover, who may rather have been Lord Cobham and his man, Bartholomew Gilbert.[1] Gookin also sees him as probably having known Gabriel Archer, possibly through overlapping with him at Cambridge and at the Inns of Court, though the chronology does not fit very well. Yet they were associates in the first Jamestown colony in 1606–7, where each played a prominent part for a time, and may indeed have known each other before 1602.[2] Gosnold's stay at the university may have been brief or longer – since he did not take his degree we have no way of knowing – but he had certainly studied some of the earlier voyages, especially that of Verrazzano, and is likely to have been led to participation in this one either by Hakluyt or by Hakluyt's works. He was willing to take risks and to stay over-winter in North America with a small party of sixteen men, but the theory that he was the sole begetter and financier of the expedition remains unproven, with the Cobham–Gilbert management having the slight benefit of the doubt as being the major factor in at least the practical working-out of the project. But Gookin, who made Gosnold his hero, and built him up as a plausible figure largely on the basis of placing him in successive genealogical networks, must be respected for what he did, and his work is worthy of continued consideration.

Of Gabriel Archer too there is little background information: we cannot say who inspired him to go on the voyage and to take on the tricky task of seconding and maintaining an experimental trading post (comparable with the French venture of 1600–1601 at Tadoussac which had failed) or who created his anterior interest in North America,

[1] Below pp. 34, 133–5, 143, 204–8.
[2] Gookin and Barbour, *Gosnold*, pp. 191–208; W. F. Gookin, 'The first leaders at Jamestown', *Virginia Magazine of History and Biography*, LVIII (1950), 181–93; P. L. Barbour, *The Jamestown voyages under the first charter*, I (1969), 2–3, 13, 16, 21, 46, 51, 80, 125–6, 170, 214–15, 217, 231–2; II, 378–9.

though he, like Gosnold, was to participate actively in the Jamestown voyage of 1606 and to have a longer association with the new Virginia colony.[1] That Bartholomew Gilbert[2] (like Gosnold and Archer designated as Captain though his role as such is not specified) was a major factor in the inception of the voyage is less doubtful. How much he was so of his own volition and how much of his master's, Lord Cobham, is less clear. Henry Brooke, 8th Lord Cobham,[3] can probably be seen as one principal instrument behind the expedition. Closely linked with Ralegh and frequently at Durham House with him, he would know very well of Ralegh's attempts to locate the Lost Colonists of 1587 and to develop a trade in sassafras and other valuable commodities with the more southerly shores of eastern North America. We know that Ralegh sent out two such ventures before 1602: it is likely, though direct evidence is lacking, that they were made in 1600 and 1601, and were under the command of Samuel Mace, as was the third in 1602.[4] Bartholomew Gilbert, a member of a prominent goldsmith's family in London and himself a member of the Goldsmiths' Company, had been involved in speculation in the produce of privateering voyages some years before. A possible theory of the origin of the voyage is that Cobham wished to find out for himself what Ralegh was acquiring from his American ventures, may indeed have been an investor in them, and so employed or incited Bartholomew Gilbert, who was in his service, to organise an expedition.[5] Cobham was a brother-in-law of Sir Robert Cecil from whom Hakluyt in 1600 had expected great things in the way of Virginia enterprises, but it might appear that Cecil knew nothing of it until *Concord* returned. Subsequent events indicate that immediate objectives were the acquisition of sassafras roots, branches and cedar wood, the former basically for medicinal uses, which Ralegh's small vessels had been searching for farther south. The origin of the plan for a trading post which[6] would

---

[1] Ibid. I, 3, 8, 80–102, 134, 170, 175, 179, 214, 218–24, 227–8, 212, 244; II, 253, 279–83, 322, 379, 382, 386, 394, 452, 454, 456, 465–8, 472–6. Archer was a pensioner of St John's College, Cambridge, *c.* 1591, and was admitted to Gray's Inn 15 March 1592, being described as of Mountnessing, Kent (Venn, I, 37).

[2] Gookin and Barbour, *Gosnold*, pp. 262–3.

[3] *DNB.* See pp. 133–5, 204–8 below for Bartholomew Gilbert.

[4] See Quinn, *England and the discovery of America*, pp. 401–3.

[5] Ralegh was in Weymouth in September 1601 (E. Edwards, *Life and letters of Sir Walter Ralegh*, II (1868), 240–1), and again in August 1602 (below, p. 205), probably in both cases in connection with voyages for commerce and discovery of his Lost Colonists (see Quinn, *England and the discovery of America*, pp. 445–7).

[6] Ibid. pp. 408, 413–16.

collect furs and other products over the winter is less clear. It looks very like an imitation of French theory and practice as exemplified in the Tadoussac venture of 1600–1601. It might be seen as having been injected into the enterprise at a rather late stage (by Hakluyt or by Hayes?) and that it did not command the interest or support of Gilbert to any great degree since he did not carry sufficient stores to make implementation possible. This was very much Gosnold's and Archer's pet project.[1] Gilbert appears to have organised the raising of money by a syndicate of adventurers, was himself an investor, and went on the expedition as its chief entrepreneur, being responsible for the victualling, the disposal of the cargo on its return, and the distribution of the proceeds amongst the adventurers. If this is what happened, then Cobham had gone behind Ralegh's back in intruding on a coast over which Ralegh still claimed monopoly rights under the 1584 charter.[2] The voyage was clearly made (from Ralegh's later reaction on his contacts with Gilbert after the Concord's return) without Ralegh's knowledge, but it is not impossible, or even unlikely, that one of his associates – Gookin thought Edward Hayes[3] – had an earlier unused licence from Ralegh to make an expedition to this coast, so that the element of double-dealing on Cobham's part (if our linking of him with it is correct) may not have been complete. This reconstruction is almost entirely the product of a series of statements in Ralegh's letter to Sir Robert Cecil on 21 August 1602[4] and is by no means clearly established, but it seems to make sense.

William Strachey, writing a decade later, says that Henry Wriothesley, earl of Southampton, was at least partly responsible for the inception of the voyage.[5] But he was in the Tower at the time, having been implicated with Essex in 1601 and was almost penniless. He would not have co-operated with Cobham who, with Ralegh, had been a prominent antagonist of Essex. This association, therefore, can be rejected even though his link with the 1605 expedition is very probable.

[1] Pp. 126–8, 153, 159.
[2] Ralegh's understanding was that so long as his Lost Colonists could be held to be alive in America (as they probably were) his rights under his 1584 charter, which otherwise would have expired in 1591, were valid, though this had not been tested in the courts and left openings for rival speculators to interlope. It may well have been argued that his charter did not apply by this time to what was being called North Virginia.
[3] Gookin and Barbour, Gosnold, pp. 174–5.
[4] See below, pp. 205–8.
[5] Historie of travell into Virginia Britania, ed. L. B. Wright and V. Freund (1953), pp. 150–1, and A. L. Rowse, Shakespeare's Southampton (1965), pp. 234–5, who does not, however, bring forward any evidence to support Strachey.

Since Robert Salterne of Bristol was on the voyage, as he was to be on Pring's the following year, it may point to Hakluyt having a hand in the expedition since it was largely he who was to bring the Bristol men into the Pring venture,[1] as he had inspired their support for Christopher Carleill nearly twenty years before.

A briefe and true relation. *1602*

Although Gabriel Archer's narrative is here printed first, the earliest account of North Virginia to appear in print, and the first published work to be devoted to what was to become New England was the pamphlet, *A briefe and true relation of the north part of Virginia.... Written by M. Iohn Brereton one of the voyage. Whereunto is annexed a treatise.... Written by M. Edward Haies, a gentleman of long service imploied in the like action* (London, at the expense of George Bishop, 1602, S.T.C. 3610: collation A–C^4 in fours).[2] This consisted of Brereton's much condensed account of Bartholomew Gilbert's recent voyage, which played down very much the reasons for not maintaining the post built on Elizabeths Isle and boosted the commodities to be found in the newly discovered Martha's Vineyard and the adjacent islands and mainland. At the head of Brereton's contribution there is a brief dedication to Sir Walter Ralegh (making amends for the expedition having been, from his point of view, an illegal one), and, on sig. B3 v, the addition of a brief note on Samuel Mace's 1602 expedition, made for Ralegh directly, in one of his attempts to combine trade with the Indians of the Carolina Outer Banks and locate the Lost Colony of 1587. The Hayes 'Treatise' promised in the title-page then follows, being neatly trimmed down to fill the remainder of the twenty-four page tract (sigs. B4–C4). The pamphlet was entered in the Stationers' Register on 27 October 1602 and must have been distributed in London and perhaps the southwest during November and December in order to prepare the way for more specific proposals to follow up the Gosnold venture. Few copies of this first edition have survived.

The first printing was soon exhausted, but it had aroused sufficient interest for it to appear shortly in a second, enlarged edition, under the same imprint,[3] but with a title which added 'With diuers instructions,

[1] See below, p. 214.

[2] Copies in Bodleian Library, Huntington Library, John Carter Brown Library and William L. Clements Library. The copy text was the John Carter Brown copy, collated with that at the Huntington.

[3] Copies in British Library (one imperfect), John Carter Brown Library, Harvard, Huntington Library, William L. Clements Library, Newberry Library. New York

of speciall moment, newly added in the second impression.' Bibliographers have usually considered this a second issue of the first edition, but it was in fact a new one, the original matter having been entirely re-set (S.T.C. 3611, collation A–F⁴ in fours). The doubling in size made it a more substantial piece of propaganda for a further venture and we may suggest that it was specifically designed for one already in contemplation. Though it contained the date '1602' this does not exclude the likelihood that it appeared early in 1603 and indeed this would appear likely, though it could have come out during the latter part of December. (While pamphlets usually followed calendar dating they did not invariably do so, and the publication of the book could be placed at any time up to March 24 in the next calendar year though February or March would appear too late.) By March Richard Hakluyt, in association with the Robert Salterne of Bristol, who had been with Gosnold, was busy raising support in Bristol (this time with Ralegh's blessing) for a further voyage. This was to be the Pring voyage which, it will be seen, abandoned the idea of occupying the fort on Elizabeths Isle and concentrated on grubbing up sassafras roots and cutting a few cedars on Cape Cod.[1]

There is no direct evidence that Hakluyt prepared the 1602 pamphlet. Either Brereton himself or Edward Hayes could have done so and there is no overt sign of any other hand. However, it may have been shaped by someone closer to Ralegh. Thomas Harriot had been involved both in the preparations for Mace's voyage and in clearing up the mess after Gosnold's return and his assistance may have been given to Ralegh in cutting and piecing the two items which made up the tract. There is no direct evidence of this. The inclusion of the piece on the Mace voyage is evidence that Ralegh supplied the material but the note is brief and impersonal.[2] The second edition is a different matter. Here Hakluyt most probably had a hand, either in selecting the additional material or trimming it down and inserting it himself, though if his energies were largely devoted to the Bristol venture he

Historical Society, New York Public Library, Princeton, Rosenbach Collection (Philadelphia), Philadelphia Public Library, Yale University Library. The copy text was that in the British Library, collated with that in the John Carter Brown Library. HN3366 is 19·95 cm tall and 15·15 cm broad. Probably 20 cm would be a tall copy. I am indebted to Miss Katherine Pantzer for her final list for the revised S.T.C.

The pamphlet was entered in the Stationers' Register (E. Arber, *A transcript of the registers of the Company of Stationers of London, 1554–1640 A.D.*, III (1876), 220):

Master Byssop. Entred for his copy in full court holden this day *A Discourse of the northe partes of Virginia* by Iohn Brierton *Anno Domini* 1602. October 27. vj d.

[1] It is unnecessary to repeat references which will be found in the notes to the text on pp. 214–30 below.   [2] Pp. 166–7 below.

may have left the materials to be fitted in by other hands so as to make the best use of the additional twenty-four pages.[1] That it was primarily devoted to publicity for the Bristol venture seems almost certain, but it may well have helped to arouse some further interest amongst the small but expanding group of 'Americans' in Court and City circles in the last months before the Queen died. If our reading of these circumstances is correct, Hakluyt did not at this time have the manuscript of the much fuller account of the Gosnold voyage by Gabriel Archer which Purchas was to print long after from Hakluyt's collections.[2]

John Brereton as narrator

The precise position of the two men John Brereton and Gabriel Archer who have left us accounts of the Gosnold voyage in 1602 is not easy in either case to specify. The Reverend John Brereton wrote the official version of the voyage which was twice published in 1602. This indicates that he was on the expedition primarily as its recorder, and secondarily, as its chaplain, though such a small company did not normally carry such an official. His presence, whatever additional tasks he had, shows that very considerable stress was put on the value of the observations to be obtained from the voyage. It was, therefore, at least as much an exploring as a trading mission.

We cannot very easily envisage the final journal which Brereton brought home. It must have been very much more detailed than what we are given and it may not have borne a very close relation to the surviving narrative. No trace of its existence after the return of the expedition has been found.

The narrative as we have it was probably prepared fairly soon after the return of the *Concord* in July 1602. About 3,500 words in length,[3] it was supplemented from his detailed records of the voyage by a list of commodities found in the country. When the various complications caused by Ralegh's intervention had been worked out, the narrative was cast into the form of a letter to Ralegh before being prepared for publication. *A briefe and true relation* was essentially a propaganda publication and the narrative of the voyage was, with little doubt, carefully gone over to see that it was clearly written, that it gave the kind of detail which was both attractive and useful in persuading readers to interest themselves further in 'the north part of Virginia', and at

[1] Pp. 180–203 below. [2] Pp. 112–37 below. [3] Pp. 143–61 below.

the same time did not convey too clear an idea of those aspects of the voyage which it might be useful to keep in reserve for the use of the promoters. We do not know who supervised this treatment of Brereton's work but the best guess might be Thomas Harriot. Whoever edited it is almost certain to have cut out carefully anything thought inappropriate for such a promotion tract as was envisaged.

In the narrative the *Concord* is taken briskly across the Atlantic without emphasising the voyage was difficult and long drawn out – exemplifying Hakluyt's notion that too much navigational detail was boring and unnecessary to the reader. Little attempt is made to help him to estimate where the first landing took place. On the other hand a vivid and effective picture of the semi-Europeanized Micmacs so unexpectedly encountered at Savage Rock is presented, so that human interest is rapidly injected into the narrative. The fishing prospects of Cape Cod Bay are briefly discussed, but little is said to specify Gosnold's visit to the Barnstable area which was so essential for the understanding of the later course of the voyage. The doubling of Cape Cod and the search for a channel into the interior and for an island potentially suitable for a trading post is perfunctorily told, until Brereton comes to a description of the small island (Capoag) he called 'Marthaes Vineyard'.[1] Here the shore visit is given in some detail. The reason is clearly that this island was thought at first to be a suitable site for settlement. The discovery that Capoag was adjacent to the island we call Martha's Vineyard and the latter was not part of the mainland, altered their intentions. Brereton gives no real information on the discovery of the larger island and of the transfer of the name Martha's Vineyard to it, consequently confusing subsequent commentators. He is interesting on the Indians met with in the course of the exploration but, again, does not become specific until he has Gosnold firmly installed on Elizabeths Isle (a combination, apparently of Cuttyhunk and Nashawena in the Elizabeth Islands) where it is decided to establish a post. What he does is to build up a picture of the island, its resources and potentialities which is attractive and well done. He gives a brief impression of a visit to the mainland across Buzzards Bay. His most interesting passages are on the Indians who came to inspect the visitors and trade with them on Elizabeths Isle. Thereafter, with only a cursory mention of the failure of the holding party to remain in the little fort which had been completed, he takes the *Concord* back again with little detail. The list of products which follows the narrative was somewhat

[1] P. 148 and see pp. 500–2 below.

elaborated, possibly from his own records, in the second edition which apparently followed shortly after the first.

What Brereton managed to put over in his brief account was that the voyage had been a relatively easy and also an interesting one. The emphasis on the natural resources of the coasts examined in America and on the character of the native peoples encountered is a very natural one for a tract the main purpose of which was propaganda for further trade and settlement. It is also very close to the formula that Hakluyt himself worked out for the presentation of voyage narratives. This is discussed in more detail in connection with Pring's voyage in 1603. Here we might consider either that Brereton was well briefed by Hakluyt before the narrative was written or that it was Hakluyt (rather than Harriot) who went over it and helped to reshape it into the form in which we now have it. But it seems less likely from the context. At the same time the narrative has a distinctive style and flavour of its own. The descriptions of the Indians in particular convey a strongly personal impression. As a piece of propaganda for the new coasts discovered in 1602 Brereton's brief narrative did effectively what was expected of it. For subsequent commentators it lacks significant details on the actual course of the expedition, has proved misleading in the past and difficult to interpret in detail down to this day. Indeed had it not been substantially supplemented by Gabriel Archer we should not be able to make very much sense of the course of the expedition at all.

The remaining contributions to the Brereton volume

The seven remaining items in the Brereton volume fall into two groups, the note on the Mace voyage of 1602 and the 'Treatise' by Edward Hayes which were contained in the first edition along with Brereton's narrative. The materials added to pad out the second edition are, the elder Hakluyt's 'Inducements' written in 1585 and summaries from the Gentleman of Elvas (1557) on Hernando de Soto, Laudonnière's *Histoire notable* (1586) on French Florida, Harriot's *A briefe and true report* (1588) on Ralegh's Virginia, and a miscellany mainly from Hakluyt's *Principal navigations*, III (1600), the last four pieces being almost entirely lists of commodities found or alleged to be found in some part of North America.[1] The first edition was mainly narrative, with accounts of the two voyages made in 1602, however inadequate, making up the bulk of the material but being extended in its range with a version of an

[1] Pp. 193–203 below.

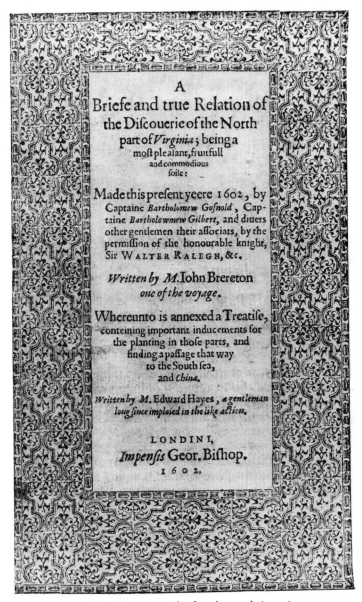

A

Briefe and true Relation of
the Difcouerie of the North
part of *Virginia*; being a
moſt pleaſant, fruitfull
and commodious
ſoile:

Made this preſent yeere 1602, by
Captaine *Bartholomew Goſnold*, Captaine *Bartholowmew Gilbert*, and diuers
other gentlemen their aſſociats, by the
permiſſion of the honourable knight,
Sir WALTER RALEGH, &c.

Written by M. Iohn Brereton
one of the voyage.

Whereunto is annexed a Treatiſe,
conteining important inducements for
the planting in thoſe parts, and
finding a paſſage that way
to the South ſea,
and *China.*

Written by M. Edward Hayes, *a gentleman*
long ſince imploied in the like action.

LONDINI,
Impenſis Geor. Biſhop.
1602.

Fig. 1. John Brereton. *A briefe and true relation.* 1602.

unpublished treatise written nearly a decade before. The second had nothing to add in the way of narrative, but contained an additional treatise, though one written nearly twenty years before, and snippets from narratives based on experiences of 1539–42, 1562–5, 1585–6, and 1584 – *circa* 1590. There were a few notes only in these which indicated the accession of material later than about 1586, while most had been previously published, and the novel items were given in a rather cryptic and non-self-explanatory fashion.[1]

The closest analogy to the 1602 volume in its second edition is the earliest compilation made by Richard Hakluyt, the younger, namely his *Divers voyages* of 1582.[2] This was a ragbag of information, narrative and analytical, on North America as it could be envisaged in England in 1581, and was not in its day very far from being comprehensive of all it was reasonable to include on the east coast, once Cartier's voyages had been published in English in 1580. In compiling the Brereton tract the editor or editors had a further major consideration to take into account. This was the existence of *Principal navigations*, the third volume of the second edition of which in 1600 contained all the narrative material on English contacts with eastern North America and a good deal on those of the French which had become available since 1582 and covering the period 1564–1597. The compiler could therefore assume that the serious reader of the compilation would go back to Hakluyt, so that 'the Booke of Discoveries' (*The principal navigations*) was several times mentioned in the book.[3] This meant that the compilers need not regard the lists they published as being more than rough indications, or we might say sales promotion lines, which would help carry the more solid parts of the volume, the narratives and the treatises. Together these were intended to show that voyaging was actively in progress (hence investments in future voyages were worth while) and that serious thought was being given to the problems and prospects of building up trade and colonies in North America (even if the treatises were rather out of date in certain respects). The summaries could help to convey the impression that there was a good deal of collateral data available which supported the rather meagre information on American products and potentialities given in the narratives and treatises. The general impression given by the volume in its larger form is that it was

[1] Pp. 201–3 below.
[2] See Quinn, *Richard Hakluyt, editor* (1967), the second volume of which prints the 1580 and 1582 texts in facsimile.
[3] See pp. 202–3, 210 below.

a rushed job. The first edition put out what was immediately available, since none of the items in it would take long to compile. The second was then hurriedly assembled from materials from other accessible sources and pushed into a continuation, much of it being in summary form, so as to be easily assimilated by intending subscribers to later voyages. The whole made up an adequate if rather clumsy piece of bookmaking, whose enduring value had much to do with the fact that it was the first of the independent publications of the new century which was wholly concerned with North America and was designed to encourage its exploitation by the English, and that it lay directly, with *Principal navigations*, III, in the sequence of publications and events which brought Englishmen finally to undertake the enduring colonisation of parts of North America. More particularly, it was the first publication whose focus was specifically on North Virginia.

While a firm conclusion on who did the work of compiling the two editions or even whether the material for the first edition was put together by the same hand that contributed the material for the second does not seem possible, the close association of Richard Hakluyt with both editions seems highly probable.[1] The method of compilation is largely his, though perhaps in a somewhat oldfashioned way, and it is clear that his library was at the disposal of the compiler or compilers. But it is hard to conclude that he made himself directly responsible for the editing of both editions. His fame, now that the second edition of his great collection was completed, was considerable, and the promoters of the venture could have greatly gained by the use of this name in the dedicatory epistle, if not on the title-page, if he had been prominently associated with it. Edward Hayes had been associated in one way or another with Hakluyt as far back as 1582, but he is not known to have been closely in touch with him in the years immediately before 1602: nonetheless he remains a possible candidate as the compiler, especially as he seems to have had in the years before about 1592 some material in his possession, deriving probably from Jean Noël of about 1587–8, which had been obtained by Hakluyt and presumably passed on to Hayes. Yet our anterior knowledge of Hayes might suggest that if he was the compiler he would have blown his own trumpet rather louder than was done in the little volume.[2] Thomas Harriot remains another probable candidate: he had been involved in the

---

[1] See pp. 139–41 below. The view expressed in Quinn, *Hakluyt handbook*, II, 514, was perhaps ultra-cautious.

[2] See Quinn, *England and the discovery of America*, pp. 227–45.

preparations for Mace's voyage and was busy on jobs for Ralegh arising out of Gosnold's expedition.[1] He could easily, with Hakluyt's encouragement, have put the materials together in a short time from the resources of Ralegh's library (which may well have contained a copy of Hayes' earlier treatise) and of Hakluyt's. But would he have given such a bald summary of his *Briefe and true report*, derived it is clear from the text printed by Hakluyt in 1600? The answer is probably in the negative. We are thrown back on Brereton as a probable protégé of Hakluyt who had known the great compiler and had learnt from him the narrative-paring which is well demonstrated – too well demonstrated perhaps – in the volume and also the craft of presenting other people's opinions and other people's specimen lists as a means of making more convincing a single brief narrative of one short, novel but not exceptionally exciting summer voyage. Our only question here is why Brereton does not appear again, later on, as a practitioner in this same art?[2] Perhaps this is because it was demonstrated from this book's lack of success to be a rather out-of-date type of production for a more sophisticated generation which could, in *Eastward Hoe* in 1605, laugh at such narratives and compilations[3] and needed authority, the backing of a great corporation like the Virginia Company under its 1606 and subsequent charters, to accept the importance of voyaging to and trading in Virginia north or south and to invest therein.

'A briefe note' on the Mace voyage needs little comment except to say that it was composed by someone with some contact with Sir Walter Ralegh and published with his approval.[4] It may be that its laconic form was dictated by Ralegh who wished to have only a limited amount of publicity for the voyage before he saw what the 1603 expeditions to both North and South Virginia would bring forth. The correct spelling of 'Hatarask' used throughout the 1600 volume of *The principal navigations* might suggest Hakluyt's hand here.[5] The 'Treatise' by Edward Hayes was a reasonably skillful abstract of the longer treatise

[1] Ibid. pp. 405–18.

[2] There seems no reason to deny, as Venn, I, 210, does, that John Brereton of Norwich, who had been to Norwich School and who matriculated at Cambridge from Caius College in 1589 is the man. *Visitations*, ed. Rye, p. 53, taken 1576, shows Cuthbert Brereton having a third son, John (there was a fourth). He was a scholar of Caius 1588–96, B.A. 1592–3, M.A. 1596, and ordained at Norwich in 1598. He was curate of Lawhall, Suffolk in 1598, and is found long after the 1602 voyage as rector of Brightwell, Suffolk. His dates would therefore be *c.* 1574–*c.* 1620 (cp. Gookin and Barbour, *Gosnold*, pp. 71–2).

[3] See Quinn, *England and the discovery of America*, p. 452.

[4] Pp. 166–7 below.

[5] See Quinn, *England and the discovery of America*, pp. 419–31.

now to be found as Cambridge University Library MS Dd.3.85, no. 4 now published in *New American World*.[1] Internal evidence shows that it was strongly influenced by Christopher Carleill and that it was written not long before the latter's death in 1593. As the 'Treatise' has some detail which differs from and adds to that contained in the earlier document, and as there is no sharp discrepancy in style, it would seem reasonable to assume that the revision and cutting was the work of Hayes himself – who was busily employed at this time in the debasement of the Irish currency – though it is possible that the editor had some responsibility in detail for preparing it for publication. Hayes was a promoter and sometimes, like others of his kind, says too much to be entirely convincing without backing up advertisement with sufficient information. If we discard his tendency to try to make all evidence, good and bad, work in favour of his schemes, there is shrewd observation and common sense to be found there as well as optimistic day-dreaming.[2]

What induced the editor to bring out of its long retirement the treatise which the elder Richard Hakluyt had devised in 1585 and which had not, in this form at least, been printed,[3] is less clear. It is full of practical observations by a man who had been in close contact with English merchants and their problems for many years before 1585 and who had been able to act as a consultant to a wide variety of them. But it was more than a little out of date. It reflected the information brought back from Roanoke Island by the reconnaissance voyage of 1584, but not the more mature data assembled by the colonists of 1585–6 much of which was summarized in turn by Thomas Harriot in 1588. It was not without value but it was not an effective or an up-to-date guide such as would be needed by serious investors and participants in further New England voyages. It was probably derived from Richard Hakluyt, the younger, who appears to have inherited his elder cousin's papers, but had not thought it necessary to include it in *Principal navigations*.

The compilations which conclude the little volume were inclined to give the impression, which was already a weakness of the *Divers voyages* in 1582, that all the commodities listed were to be found in

[1] First printed in *NAW*, III, 156–72. See Quinn, *England and the discovery of America*, pp. 239–40; for its similarity to Carleill's pamphlet of 1583 and the carrying over of his ideas cp. *NAW*, III, 27–34 and 156–72.

[2] Quinn, *England and the discovery of America*, pp. 233–4; and see his plans for Newfoundland in the 1580s, *NAW*, III, 124–38.

Pp. 180–93 below.

a single part of North America, instead of being scattered over enormous stretches of shore and interior. The reader, investor, adventurer in person was then left to put in his thumb and pull out any commodity he might be specially interested in, and convince himself that it could be found or grown in whatever area with which he was concerned, and in such quantities under such easy conditions as to make it inevitably highly profitable.[1] This may have been reasonably good promotion for the simple-minded, but it was a rather naïve way of handling a potential investing public which had by this time attained some degree of sophistication. The lists compiled from Laudonnière and Harriot need no comment: they could both have been compiled by any industrious reader of *Principal navigations*, III. The extracts from the Soto narrative of the Gentleman of Elvas, translated from a copy of the Evora edition of 1557 which was presumably in the possession of the younger Hakluyt are of more interest. It is the first we hear of Hakluyt having this book or even knowing about it as a source on the interior of North America. We may clearly presume that the translator and editor had access to Hakluyt's library where he saw this copy, but the translation is not similar to that which Hakluyt published as his own in 1609 when the Gentleman of Elvas appeared in the strange propagandist dress of *Virginia richly valued*.[2] Either Hakluyt had had an earlier try at translating it of which this was a sample or else, and more likely, the translation was done by the compiler of the volume. We have no information on whether Brereton or Hayes knew any Portuguese; Harriot is more likely to have done so. The miscellaneous notes at the end indicate that one important map, the Chamuscado map of 1585, which had been in Harriot's possession, was still being used for information on western North America and this is the last that has been heard of it.[3] The notes also contained a little more of the data on the Maritimes-St Lawrence area which we are inclined to associate with Jean Noël and to think of as having been brought back to England in 1588 by Hakluyt or obtained shortly thereafter through his French contacts.[4] There was, however, much information available in England from men who had sailed the waters of Newfoundland, the Gulf of St Lawrence, the Maritimes and possibly even the shores of New England which was not mobilised for

---

[1] Pp. 180–203.
[2] Pp. 193–5, 201; cp. the title-pages of the 1609 and 1611 editions in Quinn, *Hakluyt handbook*, pp. 524–7.
[3] Ibid. I, 50.   [4] P. 203 below.

the propagandist purpose of the Brereton volume. The holding back of more detailed information on the 1602 voyage and the substitution of this older, mainly literary, material showed that a substantial part of the information Archer and Gosnold wrote down about the voyage was regarded as a business secret not to be divulged prematurely to a curious and credulous investing public, even though the credulity of the public in this instance could have been, as already indicated, overestimated.

Gabriel Archer's narrative

Gabriel Archer's narrative, which has been printed here before Brereton's,[1] is the leading account of the Gosnold voyage, even though it was not published until more than twenty years after that of John Brereton. Considerable as the merits of Brereton's brief treatise were for the purposes of the two editions, it was not adequate as a factual account of what had taken place on the 1602 voyage, especially after subsequent voyages had created some sense of perspective about New England discovery and had brought out the seminal importance of what Gosnold had done which could scarcely be appreciated at the time.

We may take it as a reasonable hypothesis that when Hakluyt commenced to visualise the shape of a new section of voyage narratives to be added to his second edition series on North America he found Brereton alone inadequate for his purpose. We may also presume that he did not have available to him Brereton's complete journal from which much more detail could have been extracted. Gabriel Archer was closely associated with the Virginia plans of 1606 in which Hakluyt was very much involved, and so the two men would in all likelihood have come together then if they had not previously known each other. If Hakluyt did not know earlier that Archer had kept a separate journal of the voyage he learnt it then.

Archer's subsequent attempt at making a journal – 'A relatyon of the Discouery of our Riuer' (May–June 1607, on Christopher Newport's exploration of the James River) illustrates very well the sort of document he is likely to have put together in the course of Gosnold's voyage.[2] The 1607 document is a very detailed account of what happened from day to day, with many narrative incidents but little critical comment on the way. His 1602 journal was, we may assume,

[1] Pp. 114–38.
[2] A narrative, followed by two descriptive pieces almost certainly also by him. Barbour, *Jamestown voyages*, I, 80–98, with the other pieces following on pp. 98–104.

somewhat similar in character, but probably rougher and less comprehensive. It may have been difficult to read or to understand in some details at least after he brought it home. There is no suggestion that he intended it as anything more than a personal record, nor is there any proof that Hakluyt dictated the precise form in which he used his journal to complete the narrative. But Hakluyt had very definite ideas of what would and what would not fit into his voyage collections and we can be reasonably certain that Archer's was one of the narratives polished by himself which he handed over to Purchas when he felt he would not be able to complete the third edition of his great collection. How far, if at all, he tailored it to complement Brereton is not established and it may be that he did not curtail or modify it unduly, though the difficulty of reconciling certain aspects of the voyage in the two narratives suggests that some pruning was done.

The narrative as we have it is a valuable one. It contains a great deal of information which confirms and substantially expands what Brereton said or was made to say in 1602. It is crisply and economically written and, though it does not show such literary capacity as Brereton could demonstrate, it makes its points effectively and interestingly. What is also true, however, is that Archer involves himself and his readers in considerable ambiguity in the identification of a number of places touched on by Gosnold. Inability to give clear indications of a new coastline is a problem which presents itself acutely to anyone who is not an expert in navigation (as he clearly is not) and, in the absence of maps, is not unusual. The presentation of a fully intelligible narrative of a new coast for such a person is not always possible. While it might seem that Archer is unnecessarily obscure at times, Warner Gookin's view that he was intentionally cryptic and that matter had been eliminated from his account in order to make it too difficult for subsequent voyagers to repeat precisely Gosnold's voyage is almost certainly incorrect. It is not impossible that Hakluyt somewhat reshaped the narrative as Archer presented it to him, but there does not seem to be any evidence, apart from a slip in a direction taken, that there was deliberate alteration or suppression of matter from the journal since sense can be made of almost all of what Archer says, if with difficulty and with some residual ambiguities. What is true is that he was inconsistent in his treatment of his own material. At one time he is giving an item by item rendering of what he put in his journal, uninformed by any later knowledge which might have made his entries more intelligible, and examples of this are pointed out in the notes;

at other times he cheerfully anticipated events and explains his references. He is also, and this is primarily a stylistic trick, sometimes needlessly elliptical, and several of his sentences need careful unravelling, and cannot always be sorted out completely intelligibly. But if we take his narrative as one composed in this form at some distance from the events, and probably with some vagueness about the relations to each other of the various topographical features mentioned, we shall probably be on the right lines. When the composition could have taken place we do not know but it was before he left England on the Jamestown voyage with Newport late in 1606, and probably not too long after his return in 1602.

Archer's account of the outward voyage, though condensed, is explicit. He clearly had the use of the log and he employed it intelligently and made several sensible comments on the crossing. When he comes to comment on the coastal voyaging done by the *Concord* in New England he is, however, uneven. He gives a coherent account of the Maine landfall and of Gosnold's progress into Cape Cod Bay but he is needlessly obscure on what Gosnold actually did inside the Bay and is vague and unspecific about his course once he rounded and entered the Sounds to the South. He omits episodes mentioned by Brereton and he jumps from one place to another rather erratically. There is some indication that so far as the course through Nantucket Sound is concerned Archer was, in recollection, confused about precisely what was done, but if, at one point, we replace an 'E' with a 'W' in his narrative (a typical landsman's slip) it is possible to follow where they went and what was done. When he moves on to the Elizabeths Isle story he is much more specific, and his account can be followed, in spite of some ellipsis, quite easily. He does not spend much time on the homeward voyage but again he makes one or two intelligent comments on its course.

By and large Archer emphasised much the same kind of matter as Brereton had done. He gives some further interesting detail, for example, on the semi-Europeanized Micmac met at Savage Rock, so that his narrative here complements Brereton's very well. He gives us invaluable indications that Gosnold understood the layout of Cape Cod from his observations at the southern end of the Cape Cod Bay. His description of the Indians encountered on Lower Cape Cod is clear and specific. Like Brereton he makes a good deal of the small uninhabited island, called 'Marthaes Vineyard', where intensive prospecting as a possible site for a camp was done, which was evidently Capoag, the modern Cape Poge. Like him, too, he does not make it clear that when our Martha's Vineyard was recognised to be an island not a mainland the name was carried along to it. When he gets the *Concord* out into Vineyard Sound and in sight of the Elizabeth Islands he becomes much more effective. This may very well be because he had Elizabeths Isle and its immediate surroundings shown on some sort of sketch map in his journal. There may be traces of such a map, an extremely localised one, in the Velasco map of 1610. Brereton is more successful in conveying the character of the vegetation of Elizabeths Isle but Archer, for this period, concentrates on a day-to-day journal of events. As he was in charge of the building of the little fort and trading post on the island, he did not get a chance to do much exploring. His account of his brief excursion to the mainland with Gosnold is useful, though again there are some obscurities in the topographical description, but he does not mention the previous visit which Brereton and some of the men had made to the nearby shore a few days before. He gives a very good impression of what he and his men felt like when they were left on Elizabeths Isle for three days, while Gosnold was at Penikese, deprived of stores, nervous in the face of Indian threats. Thus he makes more intelligible than Brereton the reasons why it was decided to abandon the fort and sail home with only a few weeks' experience, not seven or eight months', of the southern New England shore, though the crucial factor was, it is clear, lack of stores to maintain sixteen men for that period. His references to various meetings with the Indians are lively but superficial, less careful and penetrating than Brereton's. He brings to life, without conscious effort, the circumstances of the English stay at the Elizabeth Islands but he does not summarize the resources they found, detail the character of the buildings erected on Elizabeths Isle, or make very clear precisely what furs were found in Indian possession and were traded from them.

The overall effect is that of a journal of a man of action, direct and practical, except in his incapacity to describe geographical features clearly, interested in what was being done, jocular in naming places, occasionally reflective. Brereton's approach is the more mature: Archer's the more specific. They complement each other to a considerable degree and, though of similar length and neither over 4,000 words, compress a substantial amount of information and comment into a short space. From Hakluyt's point of view they did very well in providing a brief section for his contemplated final collection. We would like to have had the originals of both journals rather than the edited versions, but we are most unlikely to find them, and are fortunate with these versions to be able to follow Gosnold, with whatever difficulty, as closely as we can.

Sir Walter Ralegh's letter

Ralegh's letter of 21 August 1602[1] forms an essential bridge between the voyage itself and the appearance of Brereton's *A briefe and true relation*. Ralegh maintained to Sir Robert Cecil, the principal secretary of state to whom, it will be remembered, Hakluyt dedicated the second edition of *The principal navigations*, that he had learned of the Gosnold–Gilbert voyage only when Gilbert brought a ship, presumably the *Concord*, to Weymouth, to sell sassafras and cedar trees, having already despatched most of the North Virginia cargo to London from Southampton. He offered to divide the cedar wood with Cecil and Nottingham, the lord high admiral, if they would have the cargo confiscated, and let him have the sassafras, more of which his own ship under Samuel Mace had just brought from South Virginia and delivered to him at Weymouth, while Thomas Harriot was also warned to track down the sassafras on his behalf in London. The next we learn, however, is that an agreement has been reached between the adventurers and Ralegh himself (though Gosnold says nothing of it in his letter to his father) that Brereton should publish his account of the voyage and other documents, including the brief note on Mace's voyage under Ralegh's sponsorship, thus signalising his taking over responsibility for the North Virginia voyages as well as those to South Virginia. At the same time, he hired Bartholomew Gilbert to command one of his own ships for a South Virginia voyage, on which Gilbert was to meet his death in 1603. The letter is typically arrogant and assertive. He clearly reckoned Cecil to be his friend, though he was soon to prove a deadly rival, and he reminded Cecil that the earl of Nottingham, the lord high admiral, had been an original adventurer in the 1585 venture and so a sharer in the monopoly control of North American voyages which he still claimed. Precisely what division of the spoils was contemplated or achieved we do not know. It seems likely that the furs and skins acquired were disposed of without his knowledge. Ironically, Ralegh's sassafras ventures left him with a glut on his hands which was not

[1] Pp. 205–8 below.

dispersed until after he had lost his monopoly and was a prisoner in the Tower under charges of treason.[1]

Bartholomew Gosnold's letter

Bartholomew Gosnold's own contribution to the documentation of his voyage is a single letter only, written to his father, Anthony Gosnold, early in September 1602.[2] It is clearly only a fragment of a correspondence and not the most important item, as it contains reference to an earlier letter in which he had told his father in some detail about what had been brought from New England in the *Concord*. This letter too was collected by Hakluyt for use in the never-completed third edition of 'The principal navigations' and came to be printed by Purchas. When and where Hakluyt obtained it, we have no knowledge, but it was perhaps about the time he got Archer's narrative, possibly 1605–6, or perhaps later, after Gosnold's death at Jamestown in 1607. It may well be that Hakluyt knew the elder Gosnold and obtained it directly from him. It does not appear that he ever got his hands on the earlier letter.

In it Gosnold confirms several statements made by Brereton about New England which might otherwise be called in question as mere propaganda. He testifies to the good climate, though he found spring to come there about a month later than in England, and he supposed that summer might continue longer also. The healthiness of the New England coast was demonstrated both by the fine physique of the Indians and also by the absence of sickness amongst the English visitors (thus comparing well with privateering voyages especially to the West Indies on which men frequently fell ill and died and of which he would have personal knowledge). He is evidently concerned to explain to his father why he did not bring back more sassafras. There was plenty to be had but his men were mostly engaged on the fort and in any case he had been warned that a cargo of more than a ton would glut the English market. Further, when they examined their stores they determined to get home as soon as possible as they were much less than had been anticipated: as it was they reached Portsmouth with their supplies completely exhausted. This last point would support the

---

[1] Quinn, *England and the discovery of America*, pp. 415–17, especially the letter of J. B. Zachelius to Sir Walter Ralegh, 10 July 1603.

[2] Pp. 208–11 below. What is known about Anthony Gosnold, a country gentleman, with lands in Clopton and Grundisburgh, Suffolk, is given in Gookin and Barbour, *Gosnold*, pp. 13–15.

reasons given by Brereton and Archer for the desertion of the fort and so help allay suspicions that something (an Indian attack for example) was being concealed. It leaves unsolved the important question of why the victualling was so mismanaged. The letter creates a good impression on the reader as an honest exposition of the conditions found by Gosnold and of the problems with which the adventurers had to contend. If it did not add very materially to the evidence otherwise available we can look at it best in the context of 1625 when Purchas printed it and when information on the Pilgrim colony was still limited. We can then see that it reinforced Archer (as well as Brereton) in accumulating evidence on a series of attractive locations in what was by that time known as New England, and was attracting attention from a variety of groups in England who were contemplating emigration to there for reasons of conscience or profit or both.

THE NARRATIVE OF THE PRING VOYAGE, 1603

This narrative was printed in 1625 by Samuel Purchas from the papers of Richard Hakluyt.[1] It had evidently, by internal evidence, been carefully prepared for publication by Hakluyt and was intended to go in, we may consider, almost unchanged into the projected third edition of 'The principal navigations'. If we ask who wrote the narrative we may seem to be on peculiarly unsure ground since the title 'A Voyage...under the command of me Martin Pring.' might seem to be conclusive evidence that it was written by Pring himself. But this seems unlikely once we examine the text since Pring is referred to as 'Master and chiefe Commander...a man very sufficient for his place,' and as 'our Captaine'.[2] In neither case is Pring likely to have written precisely in such terms. A simple explanation of the heading is that Hakluyt had it as 'under the command of one Martin Pring': Purchas or his printer got it wrong. Pring was a famous sea captain when Purchas was putting his *Pilgrimes* together, but he was almost unknown in 1603 when 'one' would have been appropriate. John Smith saw a version of the narrative before he put his *Generall historie* in print in 1624, that is before Purchas published it. He attributed it to Robert Salterne. Most of what Smith had before him was in the Purchas version: the one or two items it adds could have been derived by Smith from other sources than the narrative, while Smith was close enough to Purchas for many years before 1624 to have been allowed to see

---

[1] Pp. 214–28 below.　　　　　　[2] Pp. 214–15, 228–9 below.

the manuscript in his hands.[1] We know that Smith liked to have an author on whom to father his borrowings and he may have guessed that Salterne may have written it. There is however a possibility that he did so and that Smith knew this from Salterne himself. Salterne is referred to twice in the narrative. In one place he is said to have been on Gosnold's voyage of 1602 (and so had some qualification to be familiar with New England already), and is said to have accompanied Hakluyt and John Angell when they visited Ralegh to ask for permission to set out on the voyage. This reference does not argue against his having written the narrative: the other may, since it is a reference in the third person to a fruit found in New England 'a plant whereof...Master Robert Salterne brought to Bristol'.[2] He would scarcely write precisely like this about himself. We might say that Richard Hakluyt when licking the narrative into shape, which he almost certainly did, and not wishing for some reason to attribute it to Salterne, reworded it to read in this way. But Smith's attributions do not generally inspire confidence, and we have no confirmation that Salterne was, as Smith says he was, Pring's pilot and assistant on the voyage. Yet Salterne was not a wholly shadowy figure. He became a clergyman and retained his interest in and 'affection to Virginia', as he told Purchas who knew him, and if he could speak to Purchas he could have done so to Smith. If he wrote the narrative and if Purchas knew this it is very strange, however, that he should deny him the credit for authorship when he was putting the text in print. The Salterne attribution then is doubtful but not incredible.

As printed by Purchas it is indeed a very shapely piece of work of which its author need not have been ashamed. It is bright and interesting, gave a good, graphic description of a not too serious visit to Lower Cape Cod, and was a valuable advertisement – more valuable perhaps in 1603 than it was in 1625 – for the ease and interest and profit of a summer voyage to Massachusetts Bay.[3] It is certainly put together in the way that Hakluyt preferred to have narratives compiled. He was willing to print long and detailed journals of long and important voyages but for short episodes, and to some extent for extended expeditions as well, he liked to revise the reports he collected to fit a pattern of his own. That pattern we have seen emerging as *Principall navigations* of 1589 became *Principal navigations* of 1598–1600

[1] Pp. 229–30 below, from *The Generall historie of Virginia* (1624).
[2] P. 225.
[3] See pp. 212–14.

and we have already referred to it in connection with the 1602 materials.[1]

The Pring narrative conforms almost exactly to what we have come to see as a Hakluyt formula and there is little doubt that what we have is a Hakluyt-edited version of what could have been a longer and more diffuse document. It eliminates details of the ocean voyage but endeavours to make the landfalls vivid and interesting even, we might suspect, at the cost of a certain amount of suppression. It is strong in human interest. The seamen, their dogs and especially the Indians emerge vividly though they are lightly sketched. The Indians are treated not just as ethnological specimens but as lively human beings with whom effective contacts can be made. The main emphasis in the description of the land is on the natural resources of land and sea and on the advantages to be gained from their exploitation. The narrative is formed into a well written piece of travel literature, easy to read, well proportioned, without wearisome detail, and in particular with a decent reticence about the course and economics of the voyage which today we could do without. What Hakluyt intended in the way of publication for this document in 1603 we do not know. It would have proved useful ammunition for those who were urging the settlement of North Virginia. It could even have circulated in manuscript. Smith's acquisition of another version if he did not just see that which Purchas printed might lend a little support to this supposition.

FROM PRING TO WAYMOUTH

We have no materials for any New England voyages in 1604. We might surmise that Gosnold had been diverted from following up his 1602 voyage by Ralegh's intervention and his sponsoring of a Bristol venture in 1603, and he was not to reappear among the 'Virginians', as we may call the slowly growing band of enthusiasts for exploration and settlement in North America, until 1606. We may also surmise that the cargo of sassafras roots brought by Pring proved, like Ralegh's, to glut the market and so make a comparable voyage in the summer of 1604 unnecessary, while the other trade goods he brought may not have had sufficient value to justify another. The voyage may well have paid its way in the end but is unlikely to have made any substantial profit and so was not repeated since sassafras was unsaleable in any large

[1] See Quinn and Skelton, *Principall navigations, 1589*, I, li; Quinn, *Hakluyt handbook*, I, part ii, *passim*.

quantities, even though a number of important men in Bristol were to remain interested in North America and were to support later ventures there.

A new venture in 1605 was brought into being by the coalescing of two very different initiatives.[1] On the one hand some Devonians became interested in the possibilities of establishing fishing bases, summer or year-round ones, on the coasts and islands mentioned by Brereton and of which word must have reached them from Pring, so that they were prepared to venture on a prospecting voyage on the coast of North Virginia to discover whether the Gulf of Maine was, or was not, a continuation of or an addition to the Newfoundland fishing banks.[2] George Waymouth was available as the leader of such an expedition and among his supporters he had at Plymouth the former privateer William Parker, who was now a rich merchant, and another merchant, Thomas Love, whose associations with the western ventures run through from 1605 to 1607 though we know little else about him. The other movement for an exploratory voyage, but one which aimed not at fisheries but at a major landed colony, was inspired by Sir Thomas Arundell, a Catholic squire from Wiltshire, who had served the Holy Roman emperor with distinction against the Turks and had been made a Count by him, and who was now received at the English Court and was in favour with James I.[3] The earl of Southampton too had been brought out of prison and back to Court and it is probably true to say that he was, as Purchas stated, a sponsor of a western venture. This was very much a new-old one. Sir George Peckham and Sir Thomas Gerard, with whose families Arundell was acquainted, had planned in 1582–4 a great colony on the land round Verrazzano's 'Refugio', namely in southern New England, but this had been dropped through Spanish and Jesuit hostility and the unwillingness of a sufficiently large proportion of the loyal Catholic aristocracy and gentry to take the plunge involved in carrying out their plans for a society composed of great landed estates as proposed by the arch-land-speculator, Sir Humphrey Gilbert.[4] Many Protestant gentlemen too, a number of them younger sons, had been willing to associate themselves with the venture. It was only when the war was over and when Catholics might again be received at Court, even though the recusancy laws, which subjected

[1] P. 60 below.
[2] See Quinn, *England and the discovery of America*, pp. 168–82.
[3] Ibid. pp. 382–6.
[4] Quinn, *Gilbert*, II, contains all the documentation on the project. Two documents there (pp. 225–60) are now in the possession of the Public Archives of Canada.

them to fines and imprisonment for failure to attend the established church and for maintaining their own religious services, remained in force. We cannot tell precisely why this project revived after twenty years abeyance towards the end of 1604 or at the beginning of 1605. Arundell and his friends may have felt that James' tolerance was not to be relied on (and they were soon proved right), or that now peace had come an English Catholic community in America on oldfashioned paternal–feudal lines was at last possible. It may have been because their own clergy in England were hopelessly divided into factions, one urging a compromise with the Crown, the other (Jesuits) sticking to a hard line and working up, on its extreme fringe, to the Gunpowder Plot before the end of 1605. One line of pressure was to ensure some sort of home for the hundreds of English Catholics who had for long been in exile on the continent and had been serving in Spanish forces which were now to be or likely to be demobilised. We do not know how contact was made between them and the group around Arundell. All we can be sure of is that Tristram Winslade, a Cornish gentleman and veteran in the Spanish service, was working to organise such a migration. We have, however, only the dusty answer sent him by Father Robert Persons, rector of the English College at Rome, which represented the Jesuit view that Spain would massacre any English who tried to settle in America and that in any event they were traitors to the faith for attempting to opt out of the religious struggle in England. This squashed the continental approach flat, but Arundell and his friends were evidently less severely advised and were prepared to send George Waymouth out to look for land which would provide estates for Catholic and other gentlemen in a good climate and with limitless opportunities for both autonomy and self-aggrandisement. We can only guess how Arundell and Waymouth came together and conjoined the Plymouth and the Catholic objectives. The most likely explanation is that Waymouth had become known at Court when he presented his treatise on navigation, 'The Jewell of Artes' to King James in 1604 and that his contacts there put him in touch with Arundell. But Arundell wanted his own eyes and ears with the expedition and he sent James Rosier, a Cambridge graduate and recent Catholic convert, to report on the discovery of a suitable territory for his purpose, and also several other members of his household, including young Owen Griffin and a man named Booles.

There are apparently no surviving personal papers of Thomas, Lord Arundell of Wardour, and they are supposed to have perished in the destruction of Wardour Castle in the Civil War. A few of his estate papers still exist in the possession of his descendants at Hook Manor, Wiltshire, but they do not throw any light on the members of his household who took part in the 1605 voyage.

GEORGE WAYMOUTH AND JAMES ROSIER

George Waymouth

We can here make some diversion into the biographies of both George Waymouth and James Rosier. George Waymouth was a member of a family which had lived for a long time on the manor of Cockington in Devonshire under the aegis of the family of Carey of Cockington. His ancestors had been fishermen and tenants of the estate, but they had gradually emerged to some degree of independence in the lifetime of George's grandfather, William. It is from William's will, made in 1587, that we get a first clear picture of the family.[1] The eldest son was also William and in the will he was left most of the rather meagre possessions that the old man had, though they included the half share of a ship, the *Lyon*, worth £50, while young George, the younger William's second son, was to get the old man's chattels after the death of his elder son. It was George's father who began acquiring his own fishing vessels, launching out as he accumulated capital from fishing craft to ships, and finally to shipbuilding. It is highly probable that in the 1570s he was involved in the Newfoundland fishery and was sending his own ships there. We have no record of George's education: he probably attended a grammar school nearby as he wrote attractively and read widely. While he was growing up his father was branching out into building what were for the time substantial ships. For the *Judith*, 170 tons, in 1583, for the *Moyses*, 110 tons, in 1589, and for the *Crescent*, 250 tons, in 1594 he received royal subsidies at the rate of 5s. a ton. During this period it seems probable that George Waymouth was both learning the shipbuilder's trade and getting seagoing experience on his father's ships, and on those of others as well, perhaps especially in the Newfoundland fishery, since he emerges from his dimly understood period of apprenticeship as a fully-fledged authority on ships and the sea, and particularly on American waters. The elder Waymouth, William Waymouth of Cockington, merchant, subscribed as early as 1578 to an overseas venture when he put up some money, we do not

[1] Cockington Wills, Mallock MSS, Exeter City Library.

know how much, for Sir Humphrey Gilbert's voyage of that year and so he was carried over as a subscriber in the 1582–3 venture, though he may not have increased his contribution.

George Waymouth emerges as a protagonist of overseas voyaging some eighteen years after Gilbert's death, when he proposed to the recently organised East India Company that he should be put in command of a Northwest Passage venture to which they would contribute substantially. This was on 24 July 1601. After some discussions with the Russia or Muscovy Company, which had an interest in the area, this was agreed and on May 2 in the following year he left London with the *Discovery*, 70 tons, George Waymouth, captain, William Cobreth, master, and *Godspeed*, 60 tons, John Drew, master, with an experienced Muscovy Company agent, the Reverend John Cartwright, who had been as far east as Persia, as his mentor, as well as provisions for his thirty-four men for eighteen months.[1] He carried in a tin box a fine illuminated letter from Queen Elizabeth to the Emperor of China, with Latin, Italian and Spanish translations,[2] showing that the government regarded the mission as being a serious one. At sea Waymouth showed himself a very competent navigator. He managed, for example, to determine his latitude under unfavourable weather conditions, which was a tribute to his experience as well as to his skill. He usefully examined the Labrador coast and left some valuable original observations on it: in particular he showed that Hamilton Inlet penetrated well into the interior, but was not itself a channel through the mainland. He met uniformly poor weather, though he appears to have located the entry into Hudson Strait around Cape Chidley and, like other venturers into this area before and after, he was met with stout resistance to going any farther from his crew who eventually forced him, ignominiously, to turn back. His control over his men was not very effective and he showed little of that dogged tenacity and fanaticism which had distinguished the pioneer voyages of John Davis and was soon to bring Hudson to his death in his Northwest Passage search. The decision to return, however, was laid firmly on Cartwright's shoulders.

Waymouth set himself to complete a manual, which he may well

---

[1] *Cal. S.P. Colonial, East Indies, China and Japan, 1513–1616* (1862), pp. 128–38: a statement (p. xxxi) that he had put forward a Northwest Passage scheme as early as 1593 has not been substantiated. His own narrative is in Purchas, *Pilgrimes*, III (1625), 809–14, XIV (1906), 306–18.

[2] They were all formerly preserved, in their box, in the Lancashire County Record Office, Preston.

have begun some years before, 'The Jewell of Artes', which he proposed to present to King James in the hope of being supported by him in a further attempt to discover the Northwest Passage. This he did, first in a preliminary version (now in the Beinecke Library MS 565, Yale University)[1] and then in 1604 another (now B.L., Additional MS 19889)[2]. Both are in royal bindings of the period, though both somehow passed out of royal custody. The latter is a fine piece of work, well-written, comprehensive and illustrated with a remarkable series of drawings and volvelles. The largest section covers navigation instruments, a further one shipbuilding (his own family trade) and another 'Engines' (miscellaneous devices). But the final section has usually been taken to be simply a section on guns and fortifications of a general character. He has indeed much on plans for lighter guns and carriages, giving greater mobility, but it is clear that he intended his series of sections on guns, castles and fortified towns to be guides for the carrying through of an effective colonisation plan in North America, either connected with, or independent of, his Northwest Passage project. His introduction to the section strongly indicates that he had heard of the survival, or supposed survival, of Ralegh's Lost Colony since his devices are intended to provide means by which such a colony could be reinforced and defended. It is evident that he anticipated colonisation on a large scale, since many of his plans are very elaborate and envisage accommodation for a large number of settlers. His concept of large, urban nuclei for English settlements in North America is unique (except for one soldier's plan of 1585 prior to the Roanoke settlement which envisaged something similar if less elaborate) and his picture-plans of such settlements are of considerable theoretical, if less practical, importance. These town-plans are illustrated below for the first time.[3] This aspect of his work, however, explains why he was engaged both by the Plymouth merchants and by Sir Thomas Arundell as leader of an exploring expedition to North America in 1605. His conduct of this expedition and his actions after it had returned have already been discussed. It may perhaps be suggested that he expected to be asked to command one or other of the Virginia expeditions of 1606, in spite of his ties with the Zouche syndicate, and that the selection of other commanders, the young man Henry Challons and Thomas Hanham by the Plymouth division and of the experienced

[1] MS 565. (They are discussed in D. W. Waters, *The art of navigation in England* (1958), pp. 257–8, 295, 301, 304, 306–7.) See pp. 230–41 below.
[2] It is not known when they were separated from the royal collection.
[3] Figs. 9–14 below.

Christopher Newport by the Londoners, led him to dissociate himself from active involvement in the colonising enterprises which might have made his name.

Instead he involved himself in the underhand politics of the Virginia ventures. On 18 August 1607, Dudley Carleton wrote to John Chamberlain[1] that 'one Captain Waiman [an easy transposition of Waymouth] a speciall fauvrit of Sir Walter Copes was taken the last weeke in a port in Kent shipping himself to Spaine with intent as is thought to haue betrayed his friends and shewed the Spaniards a meanes how to defeat this Virginian attempt'. If this was Waymouth, and the association of his name with that of Cope, probably his principal contact at Court from 1604 onwards, makes it very likely, then Waymouth was evidently acting as a double agent, helping to expose the very active and partly successful Spanish espionage on the Virginia ventures. We might assume that Waymouth's task was to penetrate the spy-network which the Spanish ambassador was building up and reveal some, at least, of its members. That his name was divulged, even in a private letter and in ambiguous form, is most unlikely to have been intended. But virtual proof of this assumption is provided by the grant[2] to George Waymouth, on October 27 following, of a pension of 3s 4d a day, 'until such time as he shall receive from his Majesty some other advancement'. This would have brought him in a handsome £60 a year. We do not, however, yet know when he was next found employment, but it was evidently as a military engineer or as a consultant on such matters, though his shipbuilding business was evidently maintained. He is found again as the author of a manuscript, addressed to Prince Henry on familiar terms, entitled 'A Journall Relation of the seruice of the takinge of the toone & castle of Gulicke. this present yeare 1610. with a platt of the town and castle as it is againe to be fortified' (B.L. Royal MS 13. B. xxxiii).[3] It is dated in the dedication, December 13, 1610. Waymouth had accompanied Sir Edward Cecil, in command of two regiments, one English one Scottish, at the siege of Julich, where the British and Dutch (the French arriving too late for the action) took the heavily defended town from the Imperial forces which had seized it during a disputed succession. Waymouth signed the epistle to Prince Henry but the hand of the admirable narrative was a professional one, though the careful dispo-

---

[1] Carleton to Chamberlain, P.R.O., SP 14/28, 34.
[2] *Cal. S.P. Dom.*, *1603–10*, p. 377 (Privy Seal Docquet under date), Phineas Pett *Autobiography*, p. 72, says he was appointed 'Master Engineer' at the same salary.
[3] Vellum cover with Prince Henry's stamp.

sition diagrams and the final plan of the town were no doubt Waymouth's own. We next hear of him back in London at his own family trade when in 1611 the eminent London merchant, Sir James Bond, commissioned George Waymouth, gentleman, to build and equip a ship for him. He was to get together timber and all necessities to construct a vessel of forty tons, to make a voyage with twenty men for one year. He lived long enough to build at least one more ship and to earn the envy and hatred of a more famous shipbuilder, Phineas Pett, who maintains he was finally disgraced for his inadequacies. Waymouth certainly deserves more notice than he has hitherto received.[1]

James Rosier

Rosier has remained something of a mystery because there has been some doubt as to whether the Cambridge graduate, the recorder of the 1605 voyage, and the student at the English College at Rome, who became a Jesuit priest, can be the same man.[2] It now appears that they were and that the indications of Rosier's Catholicism, of which traces can be found in Purchas' extracts from his manuscript of the 1605 voyage, can be verified. Father Godfrey Anstruther, O.P. has found that a James Rosier and Dorothy Johnson were married at Winston, near Ipswich, in 1570 and that they had a son, James, who appears to have been the man in question and who was baptized there on 7 June 1573.[3] The elder James Rosier was a clergyman who became parson on 19 April 1579 of Sproughton, Suffolk (the transcript of the Sproughton Parish Register, 1540–1771, has him as 'Rose, p'son of Sproughton, 19 Apr. 1579'),[4] but it is clear from his dispute with Edmund Freke, bishop of Norwich, in 1579 that he was James Rosier.[5]

[1] Authorisation on Bond's behalf 'To all Christian people to whome these presents shall come', MS 9202, Rich (Duke of Manchester) Papers, Tracy McGregor Collection, Alderman Library, University of Virginia, Charlottesville; Pett, pp. 71–5.

[2] See *D.N.B.* (which gives 1575–1635 as his dates, the latter wholly on Cooper's authority), C. H. & T. Cooper, *Athenae Cantabrigienses*, III (1913), 18, Venn, *Alumni Cantabrigienses*, III, 488, also Henry Foley, *English records of the Society of Jesus*, I (1875), 196, who relied on a family transcript of the English College at Rome.

[3] Godfrey Anstruther, O.P., *The seminary priests*, II, 1603–1659 (1977), 272, from the Winston Parish register. We are grateful to Father Anstruther for his correspondence on this matter.

[4] Parish Register Transcripts, Suffolk, Ipswich Public Library. Venn, III, 488, has James Rosier, pensioner of St John's, Michaelmas 1559, later minister of Winston, Suffolk who is also certainly the same man.

[5] *Acts of the Privy Council, 1578–80*, pp. 286, 305; W. A. Copinger, *County of Suffolk*, V (1905), 15.

In the *Responsa Scholarum* of the English College at Rome,[1] James Rosier on 7 May 1608 declared he was born at 'Winton' near Ipswich and that he was about 32 years old (though in fact he would have been 34, almost 35), and that his father, a parson, had died when he was young. His mother was a Norfolk gentlewoman and he was brought up first at the house of her kinsman, Robert Wolfrestone, at Ipswich, and later in the household and with the children of Sir Philip Parker. He appears at Cambridge as a member of Pembroke College, where he proceeded B.A. in the year 1592–3 and M.A. in 1596, which his 1608 statement confirms.[2] After leaving the university he said that he became a member of the household of Sir Philip Woodhouse in Norfolk, and that under the influence of Edward Yelverton, Lady Woodhouse and her mother he became a Catholic about 1602.[3] In the *Visitations of Norfolk* of 1563, 1589 and 1613, Sir Philip Woodhouse of Kymberley Hall appears, whose wife had been 'Grysold, daughter of William Yelverton of Rougham, Norfolk', so that this seems confirmed. It might appear that he remained at Kimberley Hall for some years, his own family, including two brothers, dying off. Though he refers to a Catholic female cousin, all his other relatives remained Protestant. On becoming a Catholic he went to London and says that he entered the service of the noble Thomas Sackville. This must surely be Thomas Sackville, Lord Buckhurst, and Lord Treasurer, 1599–1608. With him he stayed two years before coming to Rome, which would make it the years 1606–8, which is possible even though Buckhurst was not himself a Catholic.[4] Thus he omits the years 1602–6 and says nothing of his association with Sir Thomas Arundell in 1605, and most probably earlier, neither does he mention his Virginian voyage nor the pamphlet published in his name. It is the omission of any reference to this episode in his long statement which has led his biographers, the latest, Godfrey Anstruther, among them, to doubt if the Catholic convert and priest could be the explorer. But when we look at the letter

---

[1] *The Responsa Scholarum of the English College, Rome.* Part I, 1598–1621, edited by Anthony Kenny (Catholic Record Society, LIV (1962)), pp. 206–7. A Sir Philip Parker of this date held various manors in Norfolk (Blomefield, *Norfolk*, x (1800), 295, 462).

[2] Venn, III, 488.

[3] *Visitations of Norfolk, 1563, 1589, 1613*, ed. Walter Rye (Harleian Society, XXXII (1891)), p. 322; he appears in F. Blomefield's *Norfolk*, II (1806), 376, 506, 536. Edward Yelverton was Lady Woodhouse's brother (*Visitations*, p. 328).

[4] If he was in Buckhurst's service immediately after his return from North Virginia, it may be that some of the statements attributed to him in his address to the reader (cp. p. 252) about his contacts with members of the privy council and court could have some substance.

which Father Robert Persons sent to Tristram Winslade in March 1605 we need not be surprised, since Persons was still rector of the English College when Rosier was admitted there and, in Persons' eyes, he would be regarded as a traitor to the faith for going to America even under the auspices of such a good Catholic as Arundell, and above all for letting his name appear on a pamphlet which showed that he was engaged in a major enterprise of a non-Catholic nature to encourage an English colony in North Virginia. Persons regarded all of America as Spanish, and the duty of all English Catholics, if they could, to stay at home, and certainly not go to America where Spaniards would, rightly, cut their throats.[1] Had he divulged his part in this venture, Rosier would never have been admitted to the English College. As it was, as an M.A. and reckoned to be well informed in philosophy and theology, he was rushed through the College in a mere eleven months and emerged on 18 April 1609 as Father James Rosier, S.J., though as the *Annales* of the College indicate, taking the pseudonym of Philip James, since he was intended for the English mission. Alas for his hopes, he died on the way at Loretto at what we take to be the age of 36.[2] If he was out of view in the vast household of the Lord Treasurer between 1606 and 1608 it is no wonder that we do not hear of him after the publication of his pamphlet, the precise form in which it was presented being probably somewhat disagreeable to him.

The Voyage, 1605: James Rosier, A true relation

Waymouth made a successful voyage. It seems likely that he, too, aimed to reach Verrazzano's 'Refugio' but he may not have have been wholly candid when he claimed to have been driven too far to the north, because it was there, at the limits of the shores touched by Pring, that fishing bases were most likely to be found and in Monhegan Island and the Georges Islands he found them. He confined his territorial explorations to one single water entry, the St George River, and it was this river, its valley and its upper reaches which were held out on his return as the ideal site for a mainland colony. The expedition was carried through with skill and speed between 5 March and 18 July 1605.

On their return Rosier and Waymouth each found a totally new

[1] See pp. 242-7.
[2] *Liber ruber venerabilis collegii anglorum de urbe*, edited by Wilfrid Kelly (Catholic Record Society, XXXVII (1940)), p. 153, gives his history while at the English College. Father Anstruther used both the *Responsa* and the *Liber ruber*.

situation. Arundell, since May Lord Arundell of Wardour, had been induced to take on the colonelcy of a recently embodied English regiment, hired to the administration of the Archdukes in the Spanish Netherlands, which was to absorb those English Catholic ex-members of the Spanish army who had hoped to go to America as well as any other Englishmen who cared to join it. Rosier was left with the task of finding such other backers at Court as Arundell had had. As a Catholic his own feelings would probably be to reject any more widely-based enterprise if it could be avoided, though he was to act, as we will see, as a witness to an agreement by which Waymouth was to be re-employed by an at least ostensibly non-Catholic group. However, with an initialed epistle to the reader in which he claimed a broad basis of support, including members of the privy council, for a further voyage, James Rosier's journal of the Waymouth voyage appeared sometime after October 30, as *A true relation of the most prosperous voyage made in this present year 1605, by Captaine George Waymouth* (London, at the costs of George Bishop, 1605, S.T.C. 21322, sig. A–E⁴ in fours).[1] Thereafter Rosier disappears from the Virginia story for reasons which have already been indicated. Nor can we say for certain how much he had to do with the preface and final text to which his name was put. This does not exclude the possibility that he worked for a time with Gorges at Plymouth on the five Eastern Abenaki Indians.

It is his narrative which gives us almost all our information on Waymouth's voyage but several changes in circumstance and perspective had to take place before it could get into print. We can think of Rosier's narrative emerging through three different stages. The first was his journal made at the time of the voyage, though perhaps elaborated in certain respects on his way home. It almost certainly contained substantially more detail on the voyage and the incidents therein, especially as regards observations of latitude and of navigational conditions, and also a large vocabulary of Indian words, completed after his return on the strength of his conversation with the five Indians captured by the expedition. No trace of this journal has been found and it may never have passed out of Rosier's possession. The second stage was his writing up of the journal for publication in the manuscript which passed first to Hakluyt and then after Hakluyt's death to Purchas.

[1] Copies in British Library, Glasgow University Library (Hunterian Collection). Folger, Huntington and Newberry Libraries, New York Public Library, Yale University Library.

We cannot tell, since Purchas abbreviated it to some extent, precisely what it contained that was not in the third version, but Purchas gave us enough to indicate the main points of difference.[1] It would be tempting to assign to Hakluyt the responsibility for the editing of the published version as he later owned the second, but there is no direct evidence that it was he, apart from its emergence from the hands of George Bishop, who published Brereton, and who had such close connections with Hakluyt earlier. References to Waymouth's forthcoming map and to the prognosis of future voyages, however, fit the text into a promotion pattern which is extremely complex and which is not clear to us from external evidence.[2]

Rosier is in many ways a good source and his is by far the most attractively written of our narratives.[3] He was an educated and intelligent man who depended a good deal on Captain Waymouth for his seaman's details of the voyage – as Waymouth was a serious sailor, interested in navigation, he mostly got them right. It is almost certain that Waymouth's log contained much of interest in the 'Remarks' added to the formal record of his ship's course. But Rosier supplied, himself, some valuable material on the natural history and resources of Mawooshen, as the Eastern Abenaki territory was known to its inhabitants, reported fairly fully on the Amerindians encountered, and attempted to collect an Eastern Abenaki vocabulary from such informants as he could get to listen to his signs and questions. There is little doubt that he modelled himself on Thomas Harriot, who had been the pioneer English surveyor of the North American scene in 1585–6 much farther to the south. He had not Harriot's intellectual drive or his extraordinary range of interests, was no land-surveyor and had no artist like John White, who partnered Harriot, to bring his pen pictures to life. Yet he did an able and effective job in co-operation with an exceptionally well informed commander so that what he has to say has some substantial value. Since we do not have his original

[1] The printed version and Purchas's version have been collated on pp. 251–304 below. For the first time they are printed in sequence in *NAW*, III, 365–91. Purchas of course contributed greatly to the value of his abbreviated version by including an Eastern Abenaki vocabulary and a list of sagamores (pp. 310–11 and Appendix, pp. 481–93).

[2] It is for this reason that we have postulated a first version, anterior to the autograph version which Hakluyt obtained and Purchas abbreviated in print, unless the exaggerations were concocted by himself and Waymouth and written down in this form on the voyage homewards. The difficulty in the way of accepting this is that they would conflict with the map which Waymouth was said to be preparing for eventual publication (in a geographical text it would seem) and so we must regard them primarily as a promotional device.   [3] Pp. 248–311.

journal we have to attempt to estimate how far he carried his observations in matters of detail. Neither do we have the detailed chart and the more general maps of the coastline which Waymouth, clearly, constructed.[1] What we have is what Rosier, his associates, his masters and his editor wished should be published about the voyage. This was a good deal but it was by no means the whole story, nor was it wholly true. Significant and deliberate alterations were made to distances with the purpose of enlarging the discoveries actually made by the expedition. This was conducted in a leisurely way and confined itself to the examination of islands and mainland within an area no greater than 20 miles by 10 (inflated to something like 60 miles by 15 to 20 miles in Rosier).[2] This blatant departure from accurate reporting must necessarily cast some doubt on the credibility of the remainder of the material Rosier gives. Some of his references to the St George River are dangerously inflated and are in many respects too big for the theme, yet his description of the country is accurate in the many respects in which it can be checked and is sometimes penetratingly so – and there does not seem to be any need to attack the bulk of what he presents as being in any direct way untrue.

The editor appointed, or who chose himself, Richard Hakluyt or another, then went through the manuscript to prepare it for the press. The alterations he made eliminated all references to latitude on the American coast in the vicinity of the discoveries made and also the vocabulary of Eastern Abenaki words, as not contributing to the publicity intended. Several references to Lord Arundell's association with the voyage, those, for example, indicating that it was two members of his household who were to be left behind to learn the Indian language, were eliminated. Also the name 'Insula Sanctae Crucis', given to Allen Island, was omitted as it might sound popish and stress the Catholic support for the voyage.[3] This, after the Gunpowder Plot of November 1605, might well be a fatal handicap to the success of a following venture, but it would apply even before that took place.

A few instances can be found of the suppression of a minor incident which might reflect unfavourably even if in a very small way on the efficiency of the members of the expedition, such as the admission that birds destroyed most of the seeds sown on Allen Island for growth tests. A number of details about the Indians are also eliminated. The Abenaki expression *Ho! Ho!*, for greeting and assent (rendered as 'oh, ho'),

---

[1] Pp. 252–3, 298–9.   [2] Pp. 289–90.   [3] P. 298.

'often repeated', as Rosier says, is cut out presumably because it sounded frivolous in English. The details of the Indian ceremony, conveying the impression that the participants felt a non-human entity was present and giving some indication of their regard for the heavenly bodies as gods, are removed, perhaps for ideological reasons perhaps, merely, because the detail given was thought to be excessive. All vague expressions about the natural resources of the area, as conveyed by the Indians, are eliminated: what is left is clear and definite. There are some problems on specific changes – in the Purchas version Indian bows are made from beech, in the printed tract from witch-hazel; in the first the two varieties of Indian dogs are 'like wolues' and 'like ours', respectively, and in the second 'like foxes' and 'like spaniels'.[1] In this case we may ask did the editor think he knew best, or did he refer them with the revised text to Rosier asking whether he had any second thoughts? The revised version was certainly tidier, if on a number of details less interesting. (How much more there was in the earlier version which Purchas did not give us, we cannot, of course, tell.)

Rosier's name was then put to a brief address to the reader in which was explained something of the purpose of the publication, admitted the suppression of some navigational details, but called attention to the detailed map which Waymouth had drawn (and which he intended to publish eventually), but all record of which has disappeared, and to his own Indian vocabulary, also left for another occasion. The latter, he said, consisted of four to five hundred words. Purchas, indeed, printed some eighty-five of them and they would appear, from what they specify, to be the words collected from the Indians by Rosier on the shore of Allen Island, an occasion which Rosier describes in his tract.[2] The list can be regarded as an integral part of the journal and of the manuscript passed on to Purchas by Hakluyt, and possibly all that was available in the way of an Indian vocabulary for Purchas to print.

If this is so, and if Rosier's assertion in his preface that he had collected some 500 Indian words is also correct, we have to consider what happened to this much larger and separate vocabulary. Rosier almost certainly compiled it for use on the next voyage which Waymouth started to plan but which never took place. It is clear that he collected much of it on the homeward voyage from the five Eastern Abenaki Indians who were brought back to England and of whom three were initially in the custody of Sir Ferdinando Gorges, though eventually

---

[1] Pp. 306–7.   [2] Cp. pp. 253, 273, 310.

joined by the other two. That Rosier had this vocabulary would thus be known to Gorges and may well explain his reference to such a list of Indian words in a context that makes more sense than the implication that Gorges himself had compiled it.[1] But whether Gorges only knew of it, had seen it but did not retain it in his possession is a matter for speculation. It is unlikely that he would have retained it immediately if Rosier intended to use it on the next voyage but it may have come into his possession later.

What is most significant is that the exaggeration of the area explored in America was contained in the first version and not in the second alone. Either it was a deliberate move on the part of the adventurers who invited Rosier to prepare the narrative, or else it was the result of a conspiracy between Waymouth and Rosier to inflate the amount of exploration done. We cannot tell for certain which was the case. The overriding of Waymouth's choice of the St George River in favour of the Kennebec River in 1607 as the site for the initial settlement, which was taken after the Hanham–Pring expedition of 1606 returned, may indeed suggest that the deception was Waymouth's and the adventurers'. Rosier and Waymouth might well have erred over their calculations of distances sailed and rowed but they would scarcely have been so largely out of scale. The sudden narrowing of the St George River into a small stream (at Thomaston) was not revealed and the deception of Rosier's narrative and, presumably, Waymouth's complicity can thus be most clearly demonstrated.

The introductory matter claims that the new venture, for which his tract is to be an advertisement, was backed not only by substantial gentlemen and merchants, but also by the King and by 'divers' members of his privy council. It is possible that Waymouth, himself, made some direct contact with the King, gave him a report of his discovery and received a measure of encouragement. Sir John Popham, amongst the privy councillors, Southampton probably, Nottingham possibly, could have given some measure of support. There is nothing to suggest Salisbury was involved and we do not know of others who at this time are likely to have been concerned in it. But the prefatory matter says specifically that it was not until the backing had been received that he, Rosier, was 'animated' to publish the account of the 1605 venture.

Attention is drawn in the preface to the dangers which have arisen because 'some foreign nation' has attempted (presumably through its

---

[1] See pp. 340–1 below.

ambassadors in England) to obtain information about Waymouth's voyage and had even attempted to acquire a map and to convey away the Indians brought from America for this purpose. No light can, so far, be thrown on these statements. French espionage was more likely, in this instance, than Spanish, but the latter is not entirely to be excluded.[1] Very slight suspicions may have been magnified in order to arouse nationalistic feeling in support of the new English venture, which provided backers with the excuse for suppressing information on the location of Waymouth's discoveries which might be even more valuable to a rival group of adventurers in the existing incoherent state of the Virginia plans.

The address to the reader was surprisingly vague about what precisely should be done by readers of his tract who might wish to participate in the new venture to follow up Waymouth's voyage. We may perhaps assume that it was circulated along with instructions (written or even printed) for would-be subscribers, or that it was pushed in some systematic way by participants who added it to their oral pleas for additional support. The author directed his attention especially to Londoners, telling them that many members of the *Archangell's* company were Thames-siders who could verify the report he made. He concluded with a religious appeal – with prayers for the conversion of the Indians – something of a routine exercise, but very much in line with Hakluyt's earlier propaganda for North American ventures. The tract contains no suggestion whatsoever that James Rosier was a Catholic and all the pious sentiments expressed in it – in very general terms – would fit an author who was a member of the Church of England with, or without, Puritan affiliations. The editing, after it left Rosier's hands, was thus very thorough.

The attempt to follow up the voyage: the Zouche enterprise

George Waymouth's first known commitment for a new voyage after his return, and his revelation that both good fishing and potentially profitable trade with the Indians were to be had on the Maine coast, was with a group of Plymouth merchants, William Parker, an important figure, Thomas Love, William Morgan and William Cam who may well have been the father of Thomas Cam, master's mate in the American voyage.[2] Waymouth undertook to carry out on their behalf

---

[1] Waymouth's later antics (pp. 61–2) may well have been associated with some such attempt. [2] Cp. pp. 257, 316.

a merchants' voyage in 1606. It does not seem that he found at Plymouth any willingness to embark on the colonisation venture for which his voyage had laid some foundations and it seems unlikely that any appreciable monetary support was forthcoming. Consequently, he went in search of further backers, and there is little doubt that he was eventually deserted by them and that this may have led to his retirement altogether from the Virginia venture. Meantime he found one in Sir John Zouche of Codnor in Derbyshire. Sir John's religious affiliations are not known but he is not considered to have been a recusant, though he had probably some encouragement from Arundell and other of the Catholic group at the time the agreement was signed. Later his brother-in-law, Edward, Lord Zouche, was to be his principal support. Consequently he was willing to make a bid for leadership of a colony in the area explored and extolled by Waymouth. The original document survives by which, on 30 October 1605, Waymouth agreed to turn over the land he had 'discovered' to Sir John Zouche as 'Lord paramount'.[1] Zouche was to equip two ships and provide 200 colonists for an expedition to be despatched before 30 April 1606. He undertook to pay Waymouth £100 towards his own costs. Consideration had to be given to the commitments Waymouth had already entered into at Plymouth. Zouche agreed that Waymouth could honour his contract and take under his wing the 'merchants voyage' already planned and carry it through in double harness with the colonising venture – which is doubtless why they deserted him later in 1606 in favour of a more promising enterprise since this arrangement was to be strictly limited to 1606 and was not to continue thereafter. Zouche most probably had in mind a permanent fishing and trading monopoly on the coast. He was to have the last word in deciding what was necessary for planting and fortifying the settlement, though Waymouth was to give him his loyal assistance. Zouche intended to accompany the colony, making choice of his own estate on his arrival. Waymouth was next to have choice of an estate and only then were the other colonists to make their selections.

This venture was very much in line with the much earlier one planned by Sir George Peckham and his associates in 1582–4, though on a less elaborate scale than theirs. It was, however, overturned almost at its inception by the revelation of the Catholic plot on November 4 which released a wave of repression and fear and made impossible any overt Catholic colonising attempt in the immediate future. How

---

[1] Pp. 314–17, 320–1, giving some particulars of its vicissitudes in ownership.

this affected the Rosier pamphlet and the project or projects associated with it we cannot say. From what ensued it may appear that the Zouche venture was allowed to simmer, while the main colonising objective was being diverted in other directions by those who had taken over Rosier's tract and put it into print.

What did ensue was a new body of support for a much more comprehensive venture. Much has been written about the circumstances under which Sir John Popham, chief justice of Common Pleas, became involved in the Virginia ventures but nothing is conclusively established except that he had, by the latter part of 1605, committed himself to the support of a systematic programme of colonisation. Almost all we know for certain of his motives is contained in a letter from Sir Walter Cope to Lord Salisbury which belongs to 1605 (i.e. to the year before 24 March 1606).[1] If we take this to have been written between mid-November 1605 and the end of January 1606 we shall probably be on fairly firm ground. Cope said that Popham's motives were primarily social – the finding of new opportunities and new homes for soldiers (officers and rank and file alike), unemployed now that the Spanish war was over, of unemployed but worthy citizens and of work-shy vagabonds. The problem presented by these groups (and, we may add, the Tudor fear of the masterless or restless man who could easily become a subversive element) had presented themselves to him in the courts. The interest he had developed had already made him 'affectionately bent to the plantation of Virginia' and in them 'he hath allredye taken greate paynes'. This last statement would imply that he had at least countenanced and at most supported financially Waymouth's voyage in 1605, though it may also mean that his concern stretched back further, perhaps to ventures of 1602 and 1603. His interest was now much more specifically aroused and he was prepared to support colonisation with the large subscription of £500 for each of the five years 1606 to 1610. The assurance of such a substantial subscription, in itself, was a very considerable step forward towards the implementation of a new Virginia voyage. We may ask if this was to be for a North Virginia expedition only? No conclusion can be given, but Popham's support in 1607 was firmly behind the northern part of the Virginia project and it is likely that his offer was designed in the first place to enable Waymouth's 1605 expedition to be followed up by a second reconnaissance and a subsequent settlement. Popham wished to have some formal encouragement in writing, either from

[1] Pp. 378–9.

72

Salisbury or from the privy council as a whole, so that he could assemble the various groups of gentlemen and merchants interested in North America for the concerted planning of an effective Virginia enterprise. From this movement was to emerge the Virginia Company Charter of 10 April 1606.

It is probable, however, that it is here that we should place the publication of James Rosier's *A true relation* which bore the date 1605, but which may have appeared either in December 1605 or January 1606. It is reasonably certain that it belonged to the period after the anti-Catholic scare which began on November 5, and so cannot have appeared before November at the earliest and most probably later still.[1] The Zouche project did not disappear but remained in limbo and it was August 1606 before Sir John got his passport to take the ships to sea (which he had undertaken to do by April) but after that all mention of his project is lost (except that the revived plan for 300 Catholic households to go to Virginia in June is likely to have been an attempt to put some backing into it).[2] It is strange that the Lord High Admiral, four months after the Virginia Company had been given a monopoly of western enterprises, should have given permission to Zouche to break it (even if he did not succeed in doing so).

THE VOYAGE OF THE *TRIALL*, 1606–1607

The voyage is not known, in its inception at least, to have anything to do with what had been attempted before.[3] It seems to have begun as an attempt by a group of members of the Fishmongers' Company of London, in a purely private speculation, to cash in on the news of new fishing grounds at and near Monhegan Island brought by Waymouth. A ship, the *Triall*, a substantial and well-armed vessel, and a master Arthur Chambers were engaged early in March, a month before the Virginia Company charter was granted. We know no more about the early plans since our main documentation comes from a later period when Chambers was found to have misused his trust. The ship did not set off until June and by that time an Irish dimension had been injected into her objectives. We have no information how this came about, but suspect that the initiative came from Sir Arthur Chichester,

[1] Pp. 250–3. [2] P. 318.
[3] Pp. 321–30, sample documentation; more is given in *NAW*, III, 396–402, which prints Roger Bamford's interrogatories and deposition in full. The details are in Quinn, 'The voyage of *Triall*, 1606–1607; an abortive Virginia venture', *American Neptune*, XXXI, 85–103.

lord deputy of Ireland, as a protégé of his, Sir Ralph Bingley who had been serving in Ireland, was sent over to London and on 28 May 1606 was given a passport, with Chambers as master, to command the *Triall*.[1] He then hurried back to Ireland to assemble an expedition which was already being prepared there, and picked up to accompany him a small vessel commanded by Rowland Bulkeley at Beaumaris, whose deposition, given in the High Court of Admiralty much later, supplies much of what we can add to the purser, Roger Bamford's, long story of the *Triall's* progress or lack of it.[2] We are still unable to tell whether Irish would-be settlers were to be brought to America to add another element to the Catholic colony which had been planned in England in 1605 or whether, from the beginning, Bingley, with Chichester's connivance, intended the assembly of the squadron, with the *Triall's* Virginia objective as cover, for a piratical venture against western European shipping. In any event his vessels soon separated on their own business (mostly robbery) and, eventually, Bingley took the *Triall* to sea ostensibly on a voyage to Virginia, early in 1607, claiming afterwards to have returned owing to shortage of provisions, as his lying letter in 1608 discloses, but in fact to attack peaceful shipping, mainly Spanish. The *Triall* was eventually recovered by her charterers and her owners, but the whole affair caused further friction between England and Spain and was even brought up in parliament. Bingley got away with his deceit under Chichester's protection.[3] The episode is of direct concern only marginally for this series of voyages so that the documentation has been kept to a minimum, but it illustrates that much more activity, including the Zouche enterprise, was going on after the charter had been granted than has hitherto been realised.

AFTER THE CHARTER OF 10 APRIL 1606, CONSTITUTING THE VIRGINIA COMPANY[4]

The Challons expedition

The documentation of the first expedition sent out by the Plymouth division to North Virginia is extensive but it is largely diplomatic and legal so is here confined to mainly narrative elements. In any event it never arrived in North Virginia. The narrative of John Stoneman, preserved by Hakluyt and printed by Purchas,[5] gives an account of

[1] P. 321.   [2] Pp. 322–8.   [3] Pp. 329–30.
[4] The charter and its effects on the North Virginia venture are discussed on pp. 376–7.
[5] Pp. 364–75.

the voyage, glossing over his defects as a pilot, or perhaps the instructions of his captain, a young Devonshire gentleman, Henry Challons, a protégé of Sir Ferdinando Gorges, in bringing the *Richard* so far south of the Canary Islands that she was unable to make her way through the doldrums and had to follow the southeast trades into the Caribbean. She was unfortunate enough, when almost clear of the Strait of Florida, to be involved with and captured by a small fleet of Spanish merchantmen from Santo Domingo in November 1606. Daniel Tucker in a narrative in the Cecil Papers at Hatfield[1] supplements and corrects Stoneman, while a series of depositions (only one, that of Nicholas Hind or Hine being given here) in the High Court of Admiralty, show how private and political pressure was attempted to get the Spanish government to release the vessel and her men. The main importance of the case is then a political one, not directly though indirectly, concerned with the voyage itself. This was significant for two reasons; firstly it was the initial enterprise of the Virginia Company after the charter was granted in April 1606; secondly it included two of the Indians taken in 1605 who were to direct the expedition to Pemaquid in Mawooshen, the first indication of the name of the Eastern Abenaki homeland, namely the area close to where Waymouth had been, though we cannot say certainly that it was the St George River so strongly advocated in the Rosier tract. The extensive diplomatic correspondence adds little more on these points, though many of the men got back either by slipping bail or by release in 1608, after punishment from which some died. The Spaniards seem to have taken little notice of the two Indians, one of whom appears to have died from wounds sustained at the time of the ship's capture, while the other, Assacomoit, by some means or other, made his way back eventually to Gorges at Plymouth, an interesting indication that the Indians were not, even in a complex European society, helpless savages. The *Richard* sank in the Guadalquivir. No compensation was ever paid for her so that the expedition was a dead loss to the Plymouth division, which was never well-financed in any event.[2]

[1] Pp. 360–3.
[2] A fuller selection of documents is given in *NAW*, III, 403–19, and the significance of the episode is discussed (with further references) in Quinn, 'James I and the beginnings of empire', *Journal of Imperial and Commonwealth History*, II (1974), 144–50.

The voyage of Thomas Hanham and Martin Pring, 1606

This voyage, begun in later September or early October and concluded towards the end of the year, is the most significant one on which our documentation is minimal, since the main source, the journal of Thomas Hanham, has not been seen since 1624. From mentions in 1614, 1622, 1625 and 1658 we can form some impression of its nature and importance but cannot resurrect it in any detail whatsoever. The ship, whose name is not known, was equipped by Sir John Popham at Bristol in order to mobilise the support of that city in an enterprise which the corporation of Plymouth had evidently hoped to dominate. The choice of Thomas Hanham was in line with Sir John's choice of a relative to command the colonising expedition of the following year. Thomas Hanham was his grandson, second son of the lawyer Thomas Hanham who had married Sir John's daughter Penelope, and lived at Dene, Wimborne, in Dorset. The younger Thomas was also a lawyer and had recently been made recorder of Bristol, not by any means a full-time post. He was to be guided by his master, the experienced Martin Pring, now one of Bristol's leading sailors. The ship expected to find Challons at Pemaquid or wherever nearby he had settled and brought out Nahanada, probably already sagamore of the Pemaquid band when taken in 1605, who was also, as John Smith was to testify later, a wise man. The voyage was direct and rapid and we must assume that the St George River was entered and discarded as a possible settlement site. The vessel then proceeded to explore other river entries on the Mawooshen coast and, probably with Nahanada's help, finally settled on the Kennebec, which would give an entry to a great system of inland waterways vital to Abenaki society and to presumably rich fur-trading areas. The explorers seem to have formed misleading concepts of the fertility of the land in the vicinity of the river. Hanham clearly made a fresh survey of the flora and fauna and collected additional words from the local language. The ship also entered a number of other rivers and harbours on the coast and made a chart of a wider area than Waymouth had done, before returning to England, to report that nothing but topographical knowledge had been obtained since there was no sign of Challons and they had, themselves, no authority to settle.[1] Everything else is lost except such information as may survive in the Velasco map of 1610.[2] Further sources on this voyage have been searched for in vain.

[1] Scraps of the story only are to be found on pp. 253, 337, 342, 348, 352, 364, below.
[2] Fig. 35.

The first colony on the Sagadahoc (Kennebec) River, 1607–1608

Once a point is reached where preparations are fully under way for a joint North and South Virginia venture, a charter for the dual London and Plymouth divisions was issued on 10 April 1606 and active preparations for both ventures were under way, the type of documentation changes. The formal documentation for the years 1606–8 covered both ventures and has already been edited by Philip L. Barbour in *The Jamestown voyages under the first charter* (1969) and the texts printed once again in *New American world*.[1] What remains specifically for the Plymouth division, concerned with the 'Second colonie' in North Virginia, is a smallish group of documents concerning the reactions of Plymouth to the proposed organisation of the royal council which would supervise the locally-based council. This was initially unfavourable as surviving documents show and the town rallied to its aid the Fort Major of Plymouth, Sir Ferdinando Gorges, since he had the ear, he hoped, of Lord Salisbury (as Sir Robert Cecil had now become), the lord treasurer, and who was the most powerful influence at the centre of government supporting the new venture. The Plymouth men were mollified when they were assured the royal council would act impartially between themselves and the London division and by the appointment in November 1606 of further representatives of western interests to the council.[2] We can sense from the beginning tension between Plymouth, which was merely a town, and Exeter and above all Bristol, which were old and proud cities. The corporation of Plymouth clearly regarded the venture as primarily its own and had to meet rebuffs from both Exeter and Bristol in the initial call for subscriptions,[3] though Bristol afterwards relented and agreed to collect a modest sum towards the setting up of the colony.[4] Thus far the documentation is adequate, but we are henceforth left with very little real information on how things were managed. So long as Sir John Popham was alive (until June 1607) the Plymouth men were content to leave the organisational drive largely in his hands and the preparations on the spot to his son Sir Francis Popham as treasurer of the division. But we cannot find that at any point a formally constituted council (though we hear incidentally of 'Committees' which suggests some sort of central organisation) with representatives of Bristol and of the west country gentry brought together with the representatives

[1] *NAW*, v, 191–232.
[2] Pp. 332, 376.
[3] Pp. 379–81.
[4] Pp. 381–3.

of the corporation of Plymouth and of the Popham family to plan the venture. On this the surviving documents give little or no aid, though they show Sir Francis Popham doing some preparatory work and bringing his father's ship, the *Gifte of God* and his father's cousin, George Popham, in as commander.[1]

But the centre of operations appears to have been the Fort where Gorges, though a member of the royal and not the local administration of that division at Plymouth, as he was at pains to point out, but a considerable subscriber, was the active agent in the preparations and remained so throughout the history of the venture, and particularly so after the death of Sir John Popham. He then seems to have taken over, with the approval or tacit consent of the corporation of Plymouth, the supplying and potential maintenance of the colony and his letters to Salisbury are our sole sources for the reactions of anyone in a controlling position in Plymouth to the news and products brought by the ships which returned respectively, in December 1607 and in February 1608, even though the Pophams, Lady Anne Popham and Sir John's heir, Sir Francis, treated the goods sent from the colony on their ship the *Gifte of God* as if they were their own personal property and were no concern of any company whatsoever.[2]

The preliminaries to the colonising voyage

The documentation of this stage in the organisation needs no special comment beyond what has already been given. The individual documents explain themselves. It is the gaps which are significant, notably the absence of any collections of private papers. There appears to be nothing surviving for either the Popham family or the Gilbert family for this period. The Seymour papers in the Devon County Record Office do not help as they are concerned solely with local military arrangements. Chance finds may, of course, emerge but extended searches have revealed nothing. If Plymouth has a few draft letters there is nothing about its financial commitments; if Bristol has left something about subscriptions (but not on how they were collected or for how long the collection was continued) we have nothing whatever in the way of correspondence. And valuable as Gorges' letters to Salisbury are, we would be very glad to be able to supplement them from his personal papers which are also lacking. But at the least this

[1] Pp. 332–3, 337, 341, 353, 377, 391, 464, *NAW*, III, 454–65 (details of Chancery cases).
[2] Pp. 458–65, *NAW*, III, 442–54 (with additional detail).

group of papers, together with the retention by the Corporation of Plymouth of the royal council's orders on how their colony should be organised, gives us an outline of how the venture got going.

The general accounts of the 1607 expedition

When we come to consider the documentation of the actual voyage of 1607, the history of the colony on the Kennebec, its explorations, its relations with the Eastern Abenaki and other Amerindian groups, we have no single coherent body of material. It has proved necessary to split it into three groups – the general accounts which attempt briefly to cover the whole field from 1606 to 1608, the single journal which we have of the 1607 colony in two versions and, finally, the incidental correspondence on the colony and court cases arising out of it.

In the first group a brief retrospect of the events of these years appeared in the pamphlet, apparently written by Sir Ferdinando Gorges, but put out by The President and Council of New England as *A briefe relation of the discovery and plantation of New England* in 1622. This states briefly what happened at Fort St George in 1607–8 and is useful in telling us a very little about the situation in 1608 which brought the colony to a close.[1] It seemed best to follow this by longer extracts from the tract which Sir Ferdinando Gorges wrote, late in his life, when he was in his seventies, surveying as he remembered them, and clearly with little documentation at his disposal when he was writing of his whole long experiences with New England, *A briefe narration of the original undertakings of the advancement of plantations into the parts of America*, which his grandson published in his memory with the date 1658.[2] It is a personal testament of how he became involved in the New England voyages from 1605 onwards, and contains a coherent if not always accurate account of the ventures from that year onward. It has been taken down to the point where he expresses his determination to carry on with the projects (as he did) after the collapse of the first colony in 1608. It does have some, if not a great deal of original value, particularly on the Hanham–Pring voyage of 1606, and also a little on the colonising venture itself.

Samuel Purchas included in his *Pilgrimage* (second and subsequent editions from 1614 to 1626), an invaluable brief commentary on the voyages of 1606–8.[3] It is exasperating in that it hints at how much riches were available to him, but he gives us only snippets. He gave in his

[1] Pp. 336–8.   [2] Pp. 338–47.   [3] Pp. 347–51.

margins references to the materials he had in hand. We might have expected some at least of them to appear in his *Pilgrimes* in 1625. He says he had prepared a number of them for the press, though on rather specious grounds – 'our voluminousnesse makes me afraid of offending nicer and queasier stomaches' – but probably because his printer was pressing him to finish off his vast fourth volume, he omitted all but the discourse on Mawooshen. Our gratitude for this must not dispel the sense of loss at such things as the omission of Thomas Hanham's journal of 1606 and Raleigh Gilbert's journal of 1607–8, which would have proved invaluable for our knowledge and understanding of the venture, as well as much other material. It is just conceivable that the letter from George Popham to Sir John Popham and Edward Seymour and those to Sir John Gilbert which he had, probably in copies, might turn up in some private collection. Extended searches for the letters and journals alike have proved wholly fruitless.

Finally, John Smith devoted a very brief retrospect to the period before his own expedition in 1614, in which he provides some useful data on the officials of the colony but dismisses the whole venture as a hopeless one from the start on account of the nature of the country where the settlement was located.[1]

THE BASIC JOURNAL OF THE COLONISING VOYAGE AND THE ESTABLISHMENT OF FORT ST GEORGE, 1607

William Strachey's version

We depend, in spite of the irony that more journals were kept than in any earlier English colonising episode, on a single document for giving us a consecutive account of the voyage to Mawooshen in North Virginia in 1607, telling us something about the settling in on the Kennebec River and of some exploration along the coast and up the river valley. This was a straightforward journal written by a skilled pilot and efficient observer, though without a great deal of insight, of what happened between the end of May and 6 October (or perhaps we should say the 8th though there are no entries, only a plan of that date). It has been attributed to James Davis, since Purchas mentions a journal by him, which he discarded in 1625, but there is no evidence that it was this journal. James Davis was commander of Fort St George and

---

[1] Pp. 353–4.

is very unlikely to have done the things recorded in the journal and, moreover, the first user of the Journal attributes it to 'Captain R. Davies'. Captain Robert Davies was sergeant major, a sort of military *aide* to the governor, though he piloted the *Mary and John* outward and was given command of her when he brought her safely home from the colony in December 1607. Certainly he reported to Sir Ferdinando Gorges on what had happened. The surviving copy of the journal, not quite complete, was found among Gorges' papers after his death in 1647 and Gorges himself, in the tract published in 1658 after his death relied on it for the few facts he gives about the first colony.[1] These details go most of the way towards establishing that it is the work of Captain Robert Davis or Davies, and this has been accepted by the present editors. They would prefer to write of him as Davis, in view of the almost invariable mispronunciation of the name outside Wales, but have kept Davies as it was used somewhat more frequently at the time.

The journal was found by B. F. de Costa and published by the Massachusetts Historical Society in 1880 from Lambeth MS 806, sect. 14, ff. 1–12, and subsequently by the Rev. Henry O. Thayer, *The Sagadahoc colony* (Portland: The Gorges Society, Publication 4, 1892). Already in 1849, R. H. Major, one of the founders of the Hakluyt Society, had published William Strachey's *The history of travaile into Virginia Britannia*, from British Museum Manuscript, Sloane 1622, as the sixth publication of the Society. The last chapter of this unfinished work was on the Sagadahoc colony and employed a version of the journal for this purpose. Strachey, it will be remembered, was sent in 1609 to Virginia as secretary of the Jamestown colony, but took more than a year to arrive, as he was shipwrecked on Bermuda on the way, but he stayed in Virginia for more than a year and returned to England about September 1611. One of his objectives, apparently fostered by the Company, was to draw up a history of what had happened so far. There seems reason to think that for this purpose the Company, now operating under its second charter of 1609, sent out to Strachey materials with which to develop his story. These appear (to the present editors at least) to have included the draft account of the resources of the Chesapeake area brought home by Captain John Smith in 1609 and, it is tempting to think, a copy of this journal which had been received from the Plymouth Company (or from the earl of Salisbury) as a record and explanation of part of the story of what had happened to the

[1] Cp. pp. 416–41, 343–5.

81

Plymouth division of the 1606 joint company. From these Strachey, during 1611 in Virginia and in England, after his return in 1611–12, developed a fuller version of the history on which he was engaged. The editors of the second published edition of Strachey, Louis B. Wright and V. Freund, who printed from the Princeton Manuscript which had originally belonged to the ninth earl of Northumberland (Hakluyt Society, 2nd series, CIII, 1953), considered Strachey had got well ahead with his work by the time of his return, and finished it during 1612.[1] The latter seems undoubted, but it would have given him time to have found Robert Davies' journal in England if he had not already received it in Virginia. His only contemporary reference is that some inhabitants of what we know as the Upper Cape and Martha's Vineyard, taken by Captain Edward Harlow in 1611, were being exhibited in London at the time he was putting the final polish to his work, namely in 1612.

Compared with the text of the journal which we have, Strachey's is a more polished performance. It is written as a continuous and on the whole effective narrative, leaving out a good deal of minor detail, but giving the main picture of the voyage and early settlement in the journal. There are two marks of difference. The first is the addition of a few sentences which suggests that the manuscript he had was somewhat fuller, and therefore different from the one Gorges had (unless the copyist, the otherwise unknown William Griffith, who preserved the Gorges text for us, omitted some things). The second is that where Griffith came to the end of the manuscript he copied there was an ugly break at the very point when the story of the interesting happenings of October 3 was being told. Strachey continued the use of his version of the journal to October 6, and the ship appears to have left on October 8. It is here printed for the first time from the third manuscript of Strachey's 'History', Bodleian Library, MS Ashmole 1758, ff. 65–73.[2] The Sloane MS of Strachey, alone of the three, has a number of roughly sketched coastal profiles as the Journal has (though there is one more in the Strachey MS and there are a few details not in the Journal), and these are lacking in both the Ashmole and Princeton MSS, though gaps are left for them to be drawn in. They are included below. Strachey, of course, was anticipated by Smith whose *Map of Virginia* had covered both narrative and description of the Jamestown colony. It had been published in Oxford, out of the way of the London

---

[1] *History of travell* (1953), p. xvii.
[2] Pp. 397–415.

Company with whom, by this time, Smith was not on the best of terms. Strachey was inhibited about finishing off his work, which looked in part as stolen from Smith (as in an indirect way it had been), unless he got a patron who would bear the cost and sponsor it. All three surviving manuscripts bear witness to his failure to do so. Nonetheless, in his dealings with the Davies journal Strachey showed that he could treat his sources well and he was the first to use it. Unfortunately he had no other sources to hand (he did not know Hakluyt, who had) to finish off the story of the northern colony in some detail to the end in 1608, so he added only a few perfunctory, though not incorrect, paragraphs after the journal ends.[1]

'The Relation of a Voyage unto New-England': Captain Robert Davies' Journal, 1 June–3 October 1607

The Lambeth MS as copied by William Griffith[2] has a title which would have been anachronistic at the time it was written and, as already stated, it lacked another leaf or two at the end, which Strachey had had. The copy appears to be a faithful one so far as can be judged. It will be seen that its discrepancies from Strachey's text are largely due (except for a few passages in Strachey) to the latter's compression of a journal into a literate account of a voyage. Davies was a thoroughly experienced pilot and had been piloting the *Mary and John* on her outward voyage, though it is clear that, on occasion, he did not see eye to eye with the master, whose name we do not know, or perhaps with her captain, Raleigh Gilbert. There is nothing vague or sloppy about the transatlantic narrative and the writer tries to liven a not very eventful voyage by elaborating an encounter with some Dutch ships at the Azores. The *Gifte of God* parted company, but they made their rendezvous very effectively at Waymouth's old anchorage, Georges Harbor. He does not go into the kind of detail that Rosier does or that Hanham probably did: the task of enumeration had been done. But he follows the coastline and its outstanding features (in the copied profiles as well as in words) faithfully. He made a good deal out of the failure of the ship to make the entry to the Kennebec at the first attempt and the dangers encountered before she got in, but he does not tell anything about the choice of the Kennebec rather than another river, about the choosing of a site, or about the ground where the fort was built. It was the lost journals of those on the *Gifte of God* which

[1] Pp. 414–15.   [2] Printed pp. 416–39.

would have told us about the reasons for Popham's choice (in our view it was based on the advice of Hanham and Pring). He repeatedly mentions the work proceeding on the fort, but does not convey a great deal of detail, though he makes it clear that work was put in hand at once to build a pinnace to demonstrate to the company in England that shipbuilding was feasible and easy. He is laconic but useful up to a point in relating what happened as they met different bands of the Eastern Abenaki Indians, records, but does not understand, their changes of mood and the alternations of suspicion and co-operation. He was at Raleigh Gilbert's side in the up-river expeditions which tell us something (though not perhaps as much as Champlain) about the river system of which the lower Kennebec formed part. He is most informative when he is sent to take the *Mary and John* exploring southwards into Casco Bay and he gives us for the first time some glimpses of the islands in the Bay. It might seem that Richmond Island, at the southern limit of the trip, attracted him most and that he would rather have had the colony situated there than on the Kennebec. Here and there he brings the landscape to life. After he returns he continues his account of river exploration and contacts with the Eastern Abenaki. He seems preoccupied with the building of a storehouse and chafes that it takes so long to get the *Mary and John*'s cargo shifted to it, as he has clearly been designated to command the ship homewards, taking with him samples of medicinal roots, probably some timber and a few odds and ends gathered on the journeys. He took also with him Dr Turner, the physician, who had need of medicines to bring out to Fort St George though we do not know if he ever returned.[1] The breaking off of this journal a few days before his departure on October 8 and its fortunate representation in Strachey, brings the story of the establishment of the colony to an end. If he continued it for the homeward voyage he did not bother to communicate it. Yet in giving an account of the colonising voyage it remains invaluable, wholesome, and explicit but limited in its range. On shipboard he did, however, carry John Hunt's plan of the fort as he saw it on 8 October 1608.

The incidental documents on the 1607–1608 colony

These are relatively few in number and they are poorly spaced over the life of the voyages and the settlement. George Popham, at his departure on his last voyage, expresses a fatal acceptance of his

[1] Pp. 334, 451.

inappropriate role.[1] Gorges, who takes the stage to keep Salisbury in the picture when the ships come in, discourses, when the *Mary and John* arrives, of the promise of the country but the poor performance of the settlers and the inflated plans (idle gossip perhaps) of young Gilbert. There is the pompous Latin of the only letter we have from the colony, that of the president to King James on 13 December 1607 (which Neil Cheshire newly translates),[2] telling tall tales of plants that never were and seas never to be sailed: poor windbag, he was to be dead within two months. When the second ship came in, the *Gifte* in February 1608, Gorges did not dare tell Salisbury she had brought back many of the settlers, but he did admit to the unseasonable cold they had suffered. The discoverers had not given place to effective explorers or tenacious settlers yet; he admitted it would take longer than he had thought, with less profit and more cold and other hardships to be borne.[3] But next month he assured Salisbury help was on the way, preparing to go soon, and more later.[4] Another year would, he was sure, work wonders. After that we have silence from the colony. The *Gifte*'s return was gone over and over in the High Court of Admiralty because her master had disposed of masts and spars at the Azores for food to keep his men alive, and the Pophams did not like it,[5] but the proceedings are spiced with a few glimpses of meetings and such like in the colony. The rest of the 1608 material is so sparse in the general accounts that we learn little of what happened in 1608. The death knell sounded in February 1609 when the royal council for Virginia wrote to the corporation of Plymouth[6] that now their venture was dead they might as well join, under a new charter, with the London venturers in what was to be the real Virginia, that on the Chesapeake.

The most important other materials are the plan and maps. The *Mary and John* carried a most detailed plan of Fort St George[7] which was completed on the day of sailing by a very competent draughtsman, otherwise unknown, John Hunt. This is analysed briefly in notes on pp. 441–2. That it found its way to Spain (and there seems little doubt that it was the original that did so), is a tribute to the capacity of Spanish intelligence sources. Not all the buildings shown by Hunt are likely to have been completed by October 8, but pole and frame construction would have enabled many of them to be rapidly framed and

[1] P. 446.
[2] Pp. 452–5.
[3] Pp. 445–8.
[4] Pp. 458–9.
[5] Pp. 459–65, *NAW*, III, 442–54.
[6] Pp. 466–8.
[7] Fig. 25, and pp. 441–2.

subsequently filled in with whatever kind of walling material was available from rushes, mud, lath-and-plaster, brick or even stone. Some of the ornamental features like the crenellated gates on the plan may well have been only concepts not achievements but there is every reason to believe the plan is basically correct. Whether the storehouse shown was the only one (Davies might suggest there was one nearer the landing place as a temporary shelter), and whether it was this or the much larger building on the plan which was destroyed by fire, or only part of it is not evident. What other buildings were destroyed or damaged at this time are not identified.

The remarkable map, known as the Velasco map,[1] a synthesis of English and French knowledge up to late 1610 (and a tribute to English espionage in obtaining Champlain materials), also ended up in Spain, sent there in February 1611. It contains much material derived from the voyages both of 1602 and of 1606–8 even if it is hard to disentangle them. The so-called Virginia Chart in the New York Public Library[2] has also got something for the 1606–8 expeditions. But there is no certainty that anything we have derives from Waymouth.

The 1607–8 colony assessed on the basis of its imperfect documentation

While we have a reasonable amount of information for the 1607 phase of the Sagadahoc settlement, if not enough to answer some essential questions about it, the documentation for the critical year of 1608, which would enable some systematic evaluation of its activities, problems and eventual failure, may never be filled since even modern archaeological techniques have failed to find any physical trace of its existence.

The colony must be looked on as an advance party who would establish a bridgehead from which effective settlement would be pursued while testing the resources of the country for exploitation of natural products, for agriculture and for trade with the natural inhabitants. Jamestown was of a very similar sort in 1607. The eventual aim, no doubt, was to transplant to this part of North America a slice of English society, men, women and children, having a community existence in a novel environment. A primary preoccupation in this was and continued to be the establishment of a substantial fort, capable of repelling attack by the French, which was feared and was, indeed, a possibility, and also of withstanding any hostile overtures by the

<hr>

[1] Figs. 34, 35, and pp. 520–4.   [2] See p. 527.

Indians. The personnel of the settlement was heavily biased on the military side – indeed George Popham's primary qualification was as a soldier – and the adequacy of the original settlement as a military post, at least until the end of 1607, is well borne out. Moreover, the settlers included good craftsmen, who could not only put up a considerable but flimsy and fire-prone village rapidly inside strong defences but also turn to such productive work as the building of the thirty-ton pinnace *Virginia*. But what else they could do is in doubt and must remain so.

The exploitation of timber was demonstrated in the token ship that was put in construction very early and in the cutting and hauling of a limited number of mast trees which again gave evidence of some value in the most obvious natural resources of the area – even if they had to be sold off in the Azores for food. There was a good deal of grubbing up of roots for presumed medicinal use: they were bitterly disappointed in not finding sassafras, though their first exploring expedition southward may have seen some growing on Richmond Island or nearby and in 1608 some further visits to the south could have been made, even if we have no evidence of them. The local produce which was brought back was the Green-brier, a Smilax, equated like its more southern relatives with the China root of medicinal commerce. But sassafras and china root and, perhaps, other plants of supposed medicinal qualities could not do more than form a subsidiary and marginally profitable return. The energies of others were employed mainly in exploration but they do not appear to have shown any great enterprise in this, nor to have covered any very large part of the areas of Mawooshen as sketched out for them by their Indian associates before they left England. Again, however, they may have been more energetic in 1608, after the snow and ice had cleared, than we have evidence for. Certainly, their failure, in spite of abortive attempts, to extend their reach even to Penobscot Bay in 1607, did not suggest they were capable of much, though the southern coastal expedition to Richmond Island was well managed, and their second venture up-river did take them an appreciable distance into the interior. For all that their search of the land, whether interior or coastlands, in 1607 was very much circumscribed by dilatoriness. They had no John Smith to lead exploring parties far afield in all sorts of weather – though Chesapeake Bay was easier to explore than Maine.

They did lay out garden plots outside the fort before early October but whether they planted anything in them or whether, if they did, anything survived the winter, we cannot say. There is no evidence that they reaped any crops, even garden crops, in 1608, but it must have become painfully clear that there was no extensive cultivable land anywhere in the vicinity of the fort. Agriculture, even if the forest was cleared, was impossible when rock lay so close to the surface except where there were marshes along the course of the river itself. The hopes entertained as a result, no doubt, of the favourable picture of meadow and potentially arable land created by Rosier's description, were seen very early to have been an almost total delusion, while the length and severity of the winter would have crushed any hopes of finding better conditions anywhere nearby. It may be remembered that the Eastern Abenaki captives who were so free with information on the river channels and the location and size of villages would have little to say about the fertility of the ground since, except for tobacco patches, they did not cultivate it or, if they did, it was in small areas well up the Penobscot Valley with which they and the settlers were not in contact. Fort St George was well placed for two things only, defence and the penetration of the river system. It could never become the mother town of a genuine agricultural settlement or even of a fishing colony. It could, however, become the base for a fur trade with the interior. It was as this alone that its potential must be judged, especially as they had sent home a substantial number of the settlers in December when weather became bad and stores ran low and was, therefore, capable of little more than acting as a trading post and having enough bodies to man the guns if external danger threatened.

Two things hampered the effectiveness of the colonists. One, already remarked on, was their initial inability to fathom the diplomacy of exchanges with the Indians, the other was the lack of commitment of the Indians to a systematic fur trade.

Calvin Martin, in his *Keepers of the game. Indian-animal relations and the fur trade* (1978), has thrown a great deal of light on the traditional symbiotic relationship which prevailed before white intervention between the northeastern Indians and the animals they hunted. This did not allow for any all-out slaughter of their mammalian friends, but only the culling for mutual benefit of a sufficient number of their bodies and pelts to enable the human community to endure. The gradual infiltration into this of white commercialism, with its demands for and payment for furs and skins, broke down this attitude, disrupted the Indian sense of unity with the non-human, living elements in his environment, and created in him a murderous hostility to the game he had hitherto regarded as part of a holistic system of mutual interdependence. How this happened is a complex process, not relevant to discuss in detail. But we may think of the Eastern Abenaki as being only on the fringes of white commercial influence, even though the French mart on the St Lawrence had been in existence for at least a generation and Champlain had brought it nearer at Ste Croix and Port Royal. Whether the tribal groups with which the English were in contact had come far enough along the commercial road is not clear from the evidence we have. The Micmac, clearly by this time, had been disoriented and had fitted themselves to the white men's demands by jettisoning much of their traditional outlook. Perhaps it would take some years yet before the traditional outlook of the Eastern Abenaki followed wholly the same route. Be that as it may, the prospects for a major fur trade on the Penobscot at this time do not appear to have been very good. Furs may well have been bought in some quantity in the summer but had there been a rapid flow of them to St George's Fort, we may be sure that it would not have been deserted in the autumn of 1608. If the surviving colonists insisted on returning, there should have been enough men available in the ships which came out with the stores – and probably reinforcements – to carry on over another season if the prospects were really good. Fur trading and fishing were to become mere seasonal occupations on the coast of Maine for many years.

The results of the colonial experiment in Maine were almost wholly negative. It was, it was concluded, no place to live the whole year round. There were no agricultural incentives whatever; no minerals had been found to justify enduring hardships to excavate them; the fur trade was not sufficient, as Champlain had already concluded for Acadia in 1607, to justify colonising enterprises that could not pay their way. Fishing was worth while, but it was seasonal only and could be combined with a seasonal fur trade. The area north of the Saco River was henceforth, until the 1620s, ruled out as even a location for year-round trading posts. In the light of what had been published about the 1602 voyage, and what circulated orally and in manuscript on it and on that of 1603, southern shores were more attractive in the area within the limits granted to the Plymouth Company. But fortunately it had not the money to try genuine colonising experiments there. Agricultural settlements in areas which at that time contained a numerous, settled Indian population would have made the insertion of any substantial English community virtually impossible without the assistance of either war or disease. No one could yet tell that disease would open the way for the Pilgrims and those who followed to provide cleared ground and scattered Indian remnants only. Englishmen had been enlightened by the explorations of the period 1602–8; they had not yet come to terms with the future New England as a location within which permanent settlement would be possible.

CULTURE CONTACTS AND ETHNOGRAPHIC EVIDENCE FROM THE NEW ENGLAND COAST

Archaeology and anthropology can provide much evidence about a dead culture but they cannot people it. It is when living records emerge that ethnohistory can begin. In a non-literate society, provided they are collected early enough, myths, legends and culture patterns which survive long enough to be recorded, can convey a great deal, but they are often lacking. Normally, the earliest records of contact with an external society, provided they were written down, supply what Dean R. Snow has, very usefully, termed 'the ethnohistoric baseline'.[1] For New England that baseline lies along the years 1524 to 1608, when the earliest European records of contacts with the Indians there appear.

Twelve Europeans have left some record or reference to Indians in this area between Rhode Island and Cape Breton before 1610. They are Giovanni da Verrazzano (1524),[2] John Walker (1580),[3] Simão Fernandes (1580),[4] Étienne Bellenger (1583),[5] John Brereton (1602),[6] Gabriel Archer (1602),[7] Martin Pring (1603),[8] James Rosier (1605),[9] Thomas Hanham (1606),[10] Samuel de Champlain (1604–7),[11] Marc Lescarbot (1606–7),[12] Robert Davies (1607),[13] with a few other scraps from 1607–8.[14] Some of the data supplied by these men is minimal in

[1] Dean R. Snow, 'The ethnohistoric baseline of the Eastern Abenaki', *Ethnohistory*, XXIII (1976), 291–306.
[2] Lawrence C. Wroth, *The voyages of Giovanni da Verrazzano, 1524–1528* (1970), pp. 140–1.
[3] Quinn, *Gilbert*, II, 309–10.   [4] Ibid. II, 282.
[5] Quinn, 'The voyage of Étienne Bellenger to the Maritimes, 1583: a new document', *Canadian Historical Review*, XLIII (1962), 328–53; *NAW*, IV, 306–8.
[6] Pp. 143–59 below.   [7] Pp. 112–38 below.
[8] Pp. 214–30 below.
[9] Pp. 251–309 below; another version in Purchas, *Pilgrimes*, IV (1625), 1558–62, *NAW*, III, 380–91.   [10] See p. 76 above.
[11] S. de Champlain, *Voyages* (Paris, 1613), pp. 7–159; *Works*, ed. H. P. Biggar, (1922), 234–469 (more on the Micmac than on others).
[12] M. Lescarbot, *Histoire de la Nouvelle France* (Paris, 1609); *Nova Francia*, ed. H. P. Biggar (1928), 7–330 (mostly on Micmac).   [13] Pp. 397–440 below.
[14] In what follows specific references to the text are not given (as they will be picked up in the index), while for simplicity spellings have been modernised.

content and significance; others, like Champlain's history or Rosier's account of the Waymouth voyage of 1605, are substantial contributions to history or descriptive scholarship. Though much of their contribution to ethnography has been assimilated in one form or another into the literature and has indeed become a classic part of it, it is worth reviewing, perhaps particularly by a historian, because of his emphasis on the sequence of events and the changing pattern imposed by time on intercultural relationships. To make a complete account of all these contributions might well be worth while: to do so here would not be practicable. It may be sufficient to go over the contributions of six of the English observers, Brereton, Archer, Pring, Rosier, Hanham and Davies to see to what extent they did or did not produce a coherent picture of Indian life, remembering the limitations of the opportunity they had to do it. Champlain lived for three winters on shore in this area; his work represents the Indians by one who knew them very well; he could note changes in language and the limitations of the interpreters he provided himself with; he could point to major subsistence changes, the absence of any large, observable cornfields north of Casco Bay, for example; but on the other hand he took the Indians largely for granted. He had described those of the St Lawrence valley in some detail in 1603 and was not primarily interested in minute accounts of their dress or their habits, even though he has left us much vital evidence embedded in his narrative.

The English observers were, like Verrazzano, educated men. Brereton, Rosier and Archer had been to a university, Archer as well to the Inns of Court: Pring may not have written the narrative of his own voyage, but whether he did or not it is an intelligent one. Each was a discoverer entirely new to America, so far as we know. They were therefore anxious to put down what they saw, rather than coming, with too strongly preconceived ideas about the Indians, to set them to rights or mould them into a European pattern. There are occasional hints of prejudice; there is an appreciable lack of comprehension of some of the things they saw; but there is also clearmindedness, a good capacity for understanding the exterior reality at least of what they saw; there is the desire to build up something of a humane picture of what the Indians were like so that those who sent them out to trade, to explore, or to prospect for sites for colonies should have some idea of what to expect. It is likely that they all had with them, in one of the four editions in which it had appeared, Thomas Harriot's *A briefe and true report of the new found land of Virginia* (editions of 1588, 1589, 1590,

1600), with its brief but sympathetic account of the Algonquian Indians seen farther south in what are now the North Carolina and Virginia coasts, and perhaps the illustrated pictures of them, with Harriot's notes, which had illuminated the 1590 edition.

There are considerable limitations on what these men saw or could see. They were on the North American coast for a period of a few weeks or months only in early summer – for the more extended stay of Hanham in 1606 and Davies in 1607 we have limited data only. For the most part the earliest visitors encountered the Indians not in their villages but in their summer fishing camps and expeditions to the offshore islands which were largely uninhabited during the winter months. They were therefore unable to observe or to describe many major aspects of Indian societal life. Their observations are confined to remarks on the behaviour of Indians with whom, for the most part, they were unable to speak, and in the description, often quite detailed, of the clothing and artifacts which these people had. Because their range was comparatively narrow it was all the more precise in regard to these objects. Sometimes, it is true, one wishes they had been just that little bit more precise or specific, but they were good at noticing and recording sizes and colours and shapes and relating them to similar or comparable objects in their own society. Rosier alone was able to do rather more, because he had with him on the homeward voyage and in England during the period before his tract, *A true relation of the most prosperous voyage made this present yeere by Captain George Waymouth in the discovery of the land of Virginia* (1605), appeared, the five Eastern Abenaki Indians seized near the opening of Penobscot Bay, who were taught some English and who supplied him with an extensive glossary of their own language. A shortened version of his longer manuscript and glossary appeared in 1625, but it did not contain all that he knew. Hanham had similar advantages. Davies did not exploit his contacts to any great effect.

A number of the descriptions of Indians and of the weapons and clothing became commonplace after Europeans had had fuller contacts with the Indians. At the same time it is always well to scrutinize even the most banal descriptions to see if there is not somewhere a hint of a culture trait which was rapidly modified by more penetrating and contaminating European contact. For many individual traits they provide the first and sometimes the only reference; for a number of artifacts, which were perishable, they give us the only clear descriptions from which we can reconstitute their appearance, valuable indicators of size, shape, colour, and articulation, even though modern ethno-graphers sometimes complain they are not precise enough, that, indeed, these observers were not equipped with the mental resources of twentieth century investigators. To the historian, as distinct from the social scientist, the narratives are significant examples of peoples of very different backgrounds and development – the aboriginal inhabitants having developed a society in most respects adequate for their own needs and exhibiting considerable complexity in structure, but still on the threshold of the age of metal; the Europeans, technologically advanced and culturally conditioned in a literate society, confident of their ability to expand into new territories, exploit their natural resources, trade with and possibly supplant existing human groupings there, but at this stage tentative, curious, empirical and pragmatic rather than aggressively imperialistic.

To add to the records of summer visits and tentative settlements recounted by Europeans, we have one exceptional record which derives from the Eastern Abenaki Indians, captured by George Waymouth in 1605 and associated with the English over the years following. It gives an outline sketch of the limits of and settlements (with names of native leaders – sagamores in this case) in one major grouping, the territory occupied by the Eastern Abenaki from the Saco River northward, approximately, to Mount Desert, known as Mawooshen, and domi-nated in some degree by a single leading sagamore, Bashabes. Had this been more than a topographical description, we should have a much more comprehensive picture of aboriginal society than Englishmen could give. As it is, largely through the efforts of Dean R. Snow, it is now possible to use it as a framework for ethnohistorical studies which have some relevance for a much wider area, particularly with regard to pre-epidemic Indian population.

The narratives cover two related but different culture complexes, the one primarily dependent on agriculture, the other on hunting, but with many shared characteristics.

The picture which we get from the views of the observers of southern New England Indians – the people encountered in Cape Cod Bay, and off the southern shore of Massachusetts (from people living there and also those coming to fish from what is now Rhode Island) – is one of a people (mainly of the Pockanoket nation) deferential to its sachems.[1] They appeared to have one for about every 50 males, though

---

[1] Salwen, in *Handbook*, p. 167, suggests that southern New England sachems had 'limited coercive power'.

this was in a fishing group which was not that of a typical year-round settlement,[1] but would have many men, few women, no young children. A reconstituted village group might then be of the order of 100–150 persons. The reception accorded to Bartholomew Gosnold and other Englishmen in 1602 provides us with a little insight into their own social practices. The Indian group sat down 'like greyhounds on their heels', and indicated to the Englishmen that they should do the same. The sachem received Gosnold's greetings impassively, and 'nothing moved or altered himself'. When Gosnold had done so he rose, delivered his own greeting, signalled to an attendant who handed him a beaver skin and then formally presented it to the visitor. Other contacts, apparently with a village community on the mainland shore, were less formal. Gosnold was greeted by women and children as well as some men. Over the weeks of contact the Indians made gifts of boiled fish, tobacco, furs, Indian hemp, dyed strings, chains (of wampum), deerskins, on one occasion a pipe and tobacco together,[2] while Gosnold responded on another occasion by the gift of a pair of knives. These episodes give only a few slight indications of communal characteristics and values.

The men are described as being swarthy in colour, specifically 'dark olive'. Some were 'tawny or chestnut', but this seems to have been the result of artificial colouring on the skin.[3] Some had thin black beards[4] – an unusual feature, since normally hair was carefully removed from the face. South of Cape Cod they were described as 'of stature much higher than we', but in Cape Cod Bay, towards the northern edge of the more southerly group, they are simply 'somewhat taller than our ordinary people'.[5] They were, south of Cape Cod at least, 'tall, big-boned', and 'strong, swift and well-proportioned': they were

[1] Women did more fishing and gathering of seafood than hunting, but fishing was, none the less, mainly a man's task, so that many women and most small children could be left in the villages during at least part of the fishing season in order to look after the growing crops and harvest them as they ripened. Driver and Massey, 'Comparative studies', p. 236.

[2] Cp. Salwen, in Handbook, p. 166, on aboriginal trade goods, especially wampum.

[3] The olive colour strongly suggests the application of oil or grease. The captives taken in Muscongus Bay in 1605 had well-greased bodies (p. 284 below). See N. N. Smith, 'Wabenaki use of grease and oils', Massachusetts Archaeological Society, Bulletin, xxi (1960), 19–21.

[4] Noticeable hair left on the face was exceptional. Rainey, 'Compilation', p. 18.

[5] The height indications in relation to that of the visiting Englishmen, 1602–8 (if 5 feet 7 inches to 5 feet 8 inches is taken as normal) are: south of Cape Cod 'much higher'; Cape Cod Bay 'somewhat taller'; Eastern Abenaki area 'not tall . . . in stature like us' though well up the Kennebec R. 'very strong and tall'.

also 'quick-eyed and steadfast in their look', intending no harm, as the English thought, timorous at first (one deserted his canoe which the Englishmen then appropriated). Later we hear of 'some of the meaner sort given to filching' or even being 'very thievish', while north of Cape Cod they were 'given to treachery'. Few women were seen, for reasons already suggested, in the fishing parties; in 1602, two women, mother and daughter it was thought, were shown off to the Englishmen, though the Indians warned the men not to touch them. In 1603 in Cape Cod Bay there seemed to be an attempt to segregate the women from the visitors. Children were probably met with in 1602 only briefly on the shore of Buzzards Bay; none are described in detail.

Indian women were described as 'clean and straight-bodied, with countenance sweet and pleasant' but 'low of stature...fat and well favoured', eyebrows, hair, clothing and the manner of wearing it like those of the men.

Nothing at all precise is said about houses[1] or villages, but gardens were seen in 1603 on Cape Cod Bay (Provincetown rather than Plymouth Harbor?). They were up to an acre in size, with some tobacco growing, and squashes with maize intermingled,[2] yet fish was, with deerflesh, the primary subsistence food – 'their own victuals were most of fish' though this of course was in early summer. The fish included some the Englishmen thought to be freshwater fish; crabs, turtles and snakes varied their diet.[3] Canoes south of the Cape were not described in detail: north of Cape Cod they were almost all bark canoes.[4] The description of one in Cape Cod Bay is an admirable example of what can be derived from such a narrative as Pring's:

[1] Brereton's 'a little old house, made of boughs, covered with bark', on Martha's Vineyard suggests a summer shelter only and is non-specific. So is his mention of a fish weir. Cp. Flannery, *Analysis*, p. 17.

[2] See H. C. Cutler, 'History and distribution of the cultured Cucurbits in the Americas', *American Antiquity*, XXVI (1961), 469–85; Eva L. Butler, 'A preliminary survey of Algonkian cultivation of Maize in southern New England', Massachusetts Archaeological Society, *Bulletin*, XXII (1948), 3–29; Salwen, in *Handbook*, pp. 164–5.

[3] Fishing on the seashore and, in winter, through the ice on rivers and lakes was important for subsistence; shellfish were collected and some smoked and dried for winter by inland parties as well as shoredwellers (oysters were the main shellfish eaten). See Driver and Massey, 'Comparative studies', p. 178; F. C. Speck and R. W. Dexter, 'Utilization of marine life by the Wampanoag Indians of Massachusetts', Washington Academy of Sciences, *Journal*, XXXVIII (1948), 257–65; Salwen, in *Handbook*, p. 162.

[4] While trade canoes of birch or elm bark later ran to as much as 40 feet long, pre-contact ones were 'certainly smaller and may have averaged less than half that length', Driver and Massey, 'Comparative studies', p. 289. See Rainey, 'Compilation', p. 22; Eva L. Butler and Wendell S. Hadlock, 'Uses of birchbark in the Northwest', Robert Abbé Museum, *Bulletin*, VII (1927); Salwen, in *Handbook*, pp. 163–4.

Their boats, whereof we brought one to Bristol, were in proportion like a wherry of the River Thames, seventeen foot long and four foot broad, and made of the bark of a birch tree, far exceeding in bigness those of England: it was sewed together with strong and tough osiers or twigs, and the seams covered over with resin or turpentine...: it was also open like a wherry, and sharp at both ends saving that the beak was a little bending roundly upward. And, though it carried nine men standing upright, yet it weighed not at the most above sixty pounds in weight.

Though he does not give any picture of the timber structure on which the bark was secured and did not know that the sewing cord was spruce root fibre, the description is in most respects a valuable one. The single-blade paddle[1] was also described: 'Their oars were flat at the end like oven peels, made of ash or maple and very light and strong, about two yards long.' The oven peel comparison would suggest that the paddle end, like a baker's shovel, was broad and probably squared off.

Indian weapons were primarily bows and arrows;[2] the hardwood selfbow, with three split feathers on the arrow[3] also emerges effectively together with the cane quivers:

Their weapons are bows of five or six foot long of witch-hazel or beech painted black and yellow, the strings of three twists of sinews, bigger than our bow strings. The arrows are of a yard and an handful [about 40 inches] not made of reeds, but of a fine light wood very smooth and round with three long and deep black feathers of some eagle, vulture, or kite, as closely fastened with some binding matter as any fletcher of ours can glue them on. Their quivers[4] are full a yard long, and made of long dried rushes wrought about two handfuls [about 8 inches] broad above and one handful beneath, with pretty works and compartments, diamondwise, of red and other colours.

No other weapons are indicated. No pottery was mentioned, and only one basket[5] on which boiled fish was presented, 'made of twigs not

[1] The single paddle was 'nearly universal', Driver and Massey, 'Comparative studies', p. 294.

[2] For the hardwood selfbow see Driver and Massey, 'Comparative studies', p. 351; Rainey, 'Compilation', pp. 25–6; S. L. Rogers, 'The aboriginal bow and arrow of North America and East Asia', *American Anthropologist*, new. ser., XLII (1940), 255–69; Salwen, in *Handbook*, p. 162 (citing the Pring description).

[3] Flannery, *Analysis*, p. 71, and see below pp. 221–2.

[4] On the quiver of 'woven rushes' see Flannery, *Analysis*, p. 72; and for its decoration, Willoughby, *Antiquities*, pp. 256–7 and fig. 135.

[5] For basketry distribution see Driver and Massey, 'Comparative studies', p. 322. There does not appear to be any agreement on precisely what kinds of wooden twigs were used in this area. Cp. Flannery, *Analysis*, p. 55; Willoughby, *Antiquities*, pp. 238–48. The use of Indian hemp (*Apocynum cannabium*), now accepted as native, for a seventeenth-century Connecticut basket is illustrated by Salwen, in *Handbook*, fig. 3, p. 163.

unlike our osier', which is of little descriptive value. 'Hemp' and flax 'not bright as ours', 'artificial [contrived or manufactured] strings coloured' (possibly moose hair work) give little impression of textile resources.[1] Dyes, too, though red, white and black are mentioned, are not further particularised. The Indians carried with them, in a deerskin purse at the girdles, a 'mineral stone' [iron pyrites] which they struck with a flat 'emery' stone tied to a little stick in order to make sparks fly on to touchwood to make fire. This percussion, strike-a-light, method of firemaking was a characteristic culture trait of this area and is well detailed.[2] Of their tobacco pipes we know that one was 'steeled with copper', the bowl probably being bound with sheet copper, but there is no indication if the bowl was stone or pottery.[3]

Bodypainting is mentioned, and in one case the painting of the whole face.[4] Hair was long and black, 'tied up behind in knots'; some with it 'braided in four parts and trussed up about their heads with a small knot behind'. No indications of shaving the sides of the head are given. In the hair were worn 'many feathers and toys [decorative trifles]'; in their knots 'they prick feathers of fowls in fashion of a coronet': one, probably a chief, had 'his head stuck with feathers in manner of a turkey cock's train' which gives rather the effect of a Plains Indian war bonnet,[5] so that the use of feathered headdresses was perhaps more profuse then than later. They used 'false beards' (masks), probably made from moose hair, for ceremonial purposes.[6] Their clothing was generally of deerskin, the girdles of deerskin or snakeskin, at which they hung their tobacco and mineral stone bags.[7] From the girdle depended the breechclout, 'a piece of leather drawn between their twists behind and before', which was said, on one occasion, to be black, namely dyed

[1] The most detailed study remains A. C. Whitford, 'Textile fabrics used in eastern aboriginal North America', American Museum of Natural History, *Anthropological Papers*, XXXVIII (1938), 1–22.

[2] The percussion method of firemaking depended largely on the accessibility of sulphide minerals. Driver and Massey, 'Comparative studies', p. 347; Flannery, *Analysis*, pp. 24–5.

[3] Cp. Driver and Massey, 'Comparative studies', pp. 263–4; Rainey, 'Compilation', p. 15. For this early use of copper see pp. 122, 150 below.

[4] Cp. Driver and Massey, 'Comparative studies', p. 326.

[5] The former indicates a circular arrangement of feathers stuck into the knot, the latter a circular arrangement of feathers round the whole head, requiring the use of an adhesive or the setting of the feathers in a band tied round the head. The latter appears almost like the later Plains Indian war bonnet. These variations are not allowed for in Driver and Massey, 'Comparative studies', p. 326, and see Rainey, 'Compilation', p. 25.

[6] Cp. Flannery, *Analysis*, pp. 52–3; Rainey, 'Compilation', p. 18.

[7] See Flannery, *Analysis*, pp. 40–1.

that colour.[1] The women may or may not have worn breechclouts: some did wear single apron skirts, 'aprons of leather skins before them, down to their knees', an exception apparently to the similarity of clothing between the sexes. Some women were wearing 'a bear's skin like an Irish mantle over one shoulder': some men wore furs round the neck.[2] The decorations specified are mostly copper, flat discs as ear-ornaments, other earrings, chains, and collars mainly of tubular beads, gorgets of several types. They also had copper cups and arrowheads, and probably brass as well as copper gorgets, at least in Cape Cod Bay.[3] Their dogs are described as 'like foxes, black and sharp nosed'.[4] The accurate capacity for linguistic imitation amongst the Indians is remarked. There is nothing on language, the Natick form of Algonquian being general throughout the area.

The totality is not of great value on the communal side though there are a few useful pointers on behaviour. The basic value is in building up a collective picture of the fishing parties during early summer and supplying a limited number of carefully observed features of dress, ornament, weapons, techniques and boats which help to strengthen and make more vivid the later descriptions of, for example, canoes, the appearance and techniques of making which are known from later examples, while there are also some useful indications which separate these people off from groups to the north of them. This latter point will appear when a similar account is given of the Eastern Abenaki Indians encountered in 1605–6.

The picture provided of the second cultural complex represented by the Eastern Abenaki[5] is in some respects rather less precise, but it is more valuable in the societal aspects, as James Rosier, our major informant, had the advantage of some discussions with captive Indians before he set out his descriptive material in print. The whole territory was known to them as Mawooshen and their head sagamore, Bashabes, had a measure of superiority or authority over the whole area. We know from Champlain that his main residence was at the head of Penobscot Bay, near the site of modern Bangor, but he seems to have spent some time

[1] Ibid. p. 16.

[2] Ibid. p. 43.

[3] On copper see pp. 98, 102, 109–11, 120, 122, 150, 154–6, 196, 198, 277, 287, 413.

[4] The small type of dog, mainly used as a pet and for a little hunting (for larger dogs among the Eastern Abenaki, see p. 348 below). Driver and Massey, 'Comparative studies', 283–4; G. M. Allen, 'Domesticated dogs of the American aborigines', Museum of Comparative Zoology, *Bulletin*, LXIII (1920), 431–517; Flannery, *Analysis*, pp. 32–3.

[5] Dean S. Snow, 'The ethnohistoric baseline of the Eastern Abenaki', *Ethnohistory*, XXIII (1976), 291–306; and Snow, in *Handbook*, pp. 137–42.

in the summer (he was there in July 1605)[1] in the vicinity of Owls Head near the southern entry to the Bay. He had recently been visited by Champlain, and sent to invite the Englishmen, too, to come to the mainland to trade for furs and tobacco, which they were afraid to do. Later some of the Englishmen encountered 283 Indians with arms and dogs, on the mainland (perhaps at Pemaquid Point), which sounds like a war party since they had no articles for exchange.

In physique the men are described as well-proportioned and 'well countenanced'. They were 'not very tall nor big, but in stature like us', rather jealous of their women, who were deferent to them and stood behind them when Englishmen were present. The women appear as 'well favoured in proportion of countenance, though coloured [painted] black, low of stature and fat'.[2]

The Indians showed a strong sense of hierarchy, respect for their sagamore and especially for war commanders: they went whale hunting under their 'king' – that is with their head sagamore (Bashabes) or a subordinate sagamore. On encountering an English party a sagamore gave a greeting oration ('Ho! Ho!' or 'Oh! Ho! often repeated'). The men treated Waymouth respectfully and referred to him as the 'bashabes', brought deerskins for him to use as mats, gave tobacco gifts, and on another occasion circulated pipes to be smoked by the English.[3] Visiting the ship, a group 'behaved...very civilly, neither laughing nor talking all the time, and at supper fed not like men of rude education', a condescending but not hostile account. The man chosen as a hostage, apparently a sagamore, 'utterly refused' to be such: the five captives brought to England had to be caught by force, though Rosier indicates that they were soon reconciled.

We have no useful descriptions of settlements and only one brief reference to housing. This is from Thomas Hanham,[4] and mentions 'houses built with withies and covered with mats, six or seven paces long'. Such would not be tepis but rectangular houses, though

[1] For Champlain's contact with Bashabes in 1604, see Champlain, *Works*, ed. Biggar, I (1922), 283–96.

[2] The 'low' stature and the fatness of the southern New England women had also been remarked on.

[3] See N. N. Smith, 'Smoking habits of the Wabenaki', Massachusetts Archeological Society, *Bulletin*, XVIII (1957), 76–7.

[4] Snow, in *Handbook*, pp. 139–40, says: 'Houses were either hemispherical with a circular floor plan, or pyramidal, in which case the floor plan could be square.' It would seem that these houses were of this type. He goes on to say: 'Houses were shingled with sheets of bark. There was a center post and a slab of rock to protect it from the adjacent fire. There were normally two doors, each covered by a deerskin. One was usually left open to provide an adequate draft for smoke exiting through a smokehole at the apex of the house.'

evidently not the barrel-roofed long house of the Iroquois and more southerly Algonquian groups. Maize,[1] 'pease'[2] (beans) and 'other pulse' were seen in use (maize bread was tried), but not growing. Most were probably imported from south of the Saco River. A tobacco patch had plants which were a foot high in June and were said to grow to three feet with a leaf some eight inches wide.[3] There is a good description of the birchbark canoe[4] 'strengthened with ribs and hoops of wood' and 'able to bear seven or eight people'. Their bows were described as being like English bows.[5] They were made of witch-hazel or beech, with a leather string, the bow not notched for the string but having holes at either end. The arrows were of the same woods or of ash, long, the arrows with three feathers tied on and notched at the end, the points,[6] double headed (or fanged) like harpoon heads, made from 'the long shankbone of a deer'. 'They have likewise darts,[7] headed with bone', these thrusting lances being possibly for use in whale killing as well as in hunting on land. For whale hunting[8] they used a harpoon,[9]

[1] There is still some ambiguity on whether the maize seen was grown by the Eastern Abenaki themselves or was traded in from south of the Casco River. Driver and Massey, 'Comparative studies', pp. 215–17, map 34, indicate the head of the Bay of Fundy as the northern limit on the east coast. Flannery, *Analysis*, pp. 5–7, 24–5 (largely on the basis of Champlain's observations) considered it was not grown at all north of Casco Bay (and it was not grown at this time by the Micmac). Later opinion (Snow, in *Handbook*, p. 138) is that a little was grown in the central part of the Kennebec basin but that some cultivated foodstuffs were traded up the coast in summer and autumn.

[2] Much the same can be said of the Common Bean, *Phaseolus vulgaris* L. Driver and Massey, 'Comparative studies', pp. 88–90, take its northern limit to be the same as that of maize.

[3] There is good evidence here that tobacco was grown in Eastern Abenaki territory, even though in general the limits were the same as those of maize and beans (cp. Driver and Massey, 'Comparative studies', pp. 88–90).

[4] The similarity of the canoe to that described for Cape Cod Bay is striking. Cp. Driver and Massey, 'Comparative studies', p. 289; Flannery, *Analysis*, pp. 58–9.

[5] Descriptions of bows demonstrate the familiarity of Englishmen with them (they may even have carried some). Though it is noted that while the bow of southern New England was strung with twisted sinew (pp. 220–1 above), here deer or moose leather was used. Notching of arrows and holes instead of notches on bows do not appear to have been remarked in other early accounts.

[6] Multiple points were not uncommon. Driver and Massey, 'Comparative studies', p. 353. Flannery, *Analysis*, 17–18 and Rainey, Compilation', p. 26, note the use of bone for arrowheads. Iron arrowheads, mentioned by Rosier also, are an indication of coastal trading from the French fur-trading area farther north.

[7] A 'long lance' was normal equipment for a hunter (Snow, in *Handbook*, p. 139). Fish spears were also used (cp. Driver and Massey, 'Comparative studies', pp. 189, 206, 357; Flannery, *Analysis*, pp. 17–18).

[8] Whale hunting in this area is not included in the mammal-hunting distribution-map in Driver and Massey, 'Comparative studies', p. 189. Cp. Glover N. Allen, 'Whales on the coast of New England', Boston Society of Natural History, *Memoirs*, VIII, pt. 2 (1916).

[9] Flannery, *Analysis*, p. 17, gives this as the earliest record of the use of the harpoon (ultimately derived from Eskimo) by an Algonquian people.

with a detachable bone head and a rope fastening. The strong rope,[1] 'great and strong of the bark of trees', attracted interest. They had a word for a fish-hook, for a knife and for an axe (or club, a tomahawk).[2] No utensils of pottery are mentioned though boiling could indicate its use, but bark berrying baskets were general – 'great cups,[3] made very wittily [skilfully] of bark, in form almost square', in which fruit was brought. Liquid dye, carried in bladders,[4] is described: they had a blue dye which interested the Englishmen, and had words for red and black paint.

They carried means of making fire rapidly and we later hear of their firesticks;[5] this would indicate the hand drill method. Pipes were made of clay, that is were made of pottery,[6] the only specific mention of it, and are described as black and short, while the short claw of a lobster[7] was also used on one occasion. They appear to have had reasonable quantities of tobacco. They ate fish, porpoise (probably), and dried whalemeat[8] boiled with beans and maize, and made bread from maize. Their captives tried to make the English believe, after they had seen cattle in England, that they 'made butter and cheese from the milk they have of the reindeer and fallow deer which they have tame as we have cows'.[9] The colour most frequently used for bodypainting[10] appears to have been black. On occasion they used face painting, 'very deep, some all black, some red, with stripes of excelling blue over their upper lips,

---

[1] Bark rope might be made from a number of trees, possibly elm in this case.

[2] The native tomahawk had a pick-like stone attached to a flattened and curved wooden handle (Driver and Massey, 'Comparative studies', p. 357), while the 'crooked knife' was a hafted beaver incisor (Snow, in *Handbook*, p. 139). For their words for fish-hook (bone), knife and axe see pp. 310, 492–3 below. The tools would soon be replaced by French axes and knives.

[3] Folded bark-containers, sewn with spruce or cedar roots (Snow, in *Handbook*, p. 139).

[4] Flannery, *Analysis*, p. 37, does not include this use of bladders as containers, though she did comment here on bark utensils.

[5] This method of fire-making was in use with the Abenaki (p. 278), the stick being rotated between the palms of the hands with the point on a stationary board or hearth. Driver and Massey, 'Comparative studies', p. 347.

[6] Usually pottery, mostly elbowed, and the only pottery object mentioned for this area. Driver and Massey, 'Comparative studies', pp. 262–3 and map 70; Flannery, *Analysis*, pp. 67–8.

[7] Rainey, 'Compilation', p. 23 says this is unique: it may have been intended as a joke.

[8] Dried whale-meat is not included in the subsistence lists in Snow, *Handbook*, p. 138, and Flannery, *Analysis*, p. 29. 'Whale' would, of course, include porpoise.

[9] Flannery, *Analysis*, p. 34, attempts to rationalize this but without success. It is a response given to a question which had no meaning for the person of whom it was asked. It was therefore answered as the questioner hinted it should be.

[10] See Flannery, *Analysis*, pp. 51–2.

nose and chin'. Long black hair characterized both men and women; It was said that married men, 'those that have wives', bind up their hair 'behind with a leather string in a long round knot'.[1] Some men were said to have naturally curly hair, an apparently anomalous feature. The basic piece of clothing was the breechclout,[2] here 'a piece of beaver's skin between their legs made fast about their waist', and apparently worn by women also. Mantles[3] were of 'beavers' skins or deerskins cast over them like a mantle and hanging down to their knees'. They were 'made fast together upon the shoulder with a leather string'. With them were associated sleeves[4] – 'some had sleeves and some had none' – indicating two sleeves as being usual where there were any, but not giving any information on how they were suspended. They had a word for 'a shirt or a coat' which might indicate some use of tailored garments.[5] They wore long leggings,[6] 'thin and soft'. Some male children wore nothing else except for the girdle to which the leggings were attached by straps. The tightly fastened girdle was,[7] in one case, 'decked about with little pieces of red copper'. This is the only reference to the metal in this area. Some men had birdskin head-dresses,[8] made of 'the white feathered skins of some fowl round about their head', made 'very cunningly of a substance like stiff hair, coloured red, broad and more than a handful [about four inches] in depth'.[9] This head-dress of dyed deer hair was probably a piece of

---

[1] See Rainey, 'Compilation', p. 18.

[2] Flannery, *Analysis*, pp. 40–1. The use of beaver-skin was characteristic of this Indian group.

[3] The fur robe was general in the East. Among Eastern Abenaki it was frequently a single covering tied over one shoulder and under the opposite arm. Driver and Massey, 'Comparative studies', p. 320; Snow, in *Handbook*, p. 141.

[4] Detachable sleeves of skin were frequently worn in cold weather, especially by women, the second being connected by a string passed over the shoulders. Driver and Massey, 'Comparative studies', p. 327; Flannery, *Analysis*, p. 42; Snow, in *Handbook*, p. 141.

[5] This suggests that a tailored, skin coat of some sort may also have been in use, but it is not confirmed from other early sources, though it was regularly used later. See Snow, in *Handbook*, p. 141, fig. 6.

[6] Leggings, like sleeves, were optional additions to the basic breechcloth and robe. They could be long enough to give the appearance of trousers. Their prominence in the dress of children helps to emphasise their protective character. See Driver and Massey, 'Comparative studies', p. 326; Flannery, *Analysis*, pp. 280–1; Snow, in *Handbook*, p. 141.

[7] Noted by Flannery, *Analysis*, p. 48; Rainey, 'Compilation', p. 19. It would normally be made of deerskin.

[8] 'White feathered bird skins' were sometimes worn by sagamores. Snow, in *Handbook*, p. 141. The bird may, in some cases, have been an egret.

[9] 'Sagamores sometimes wore coronets of red deer bristles' (Snow, in *Handbook*, p. 141). 'Sometimes a ruff or roach of animal hair was worn like a wig. This was often made of the white hair of a deer's tail dyed a brilliant red' (Driver and Massey,

chiefly insignia. The lesser sagamores, we are told, 'wear an ornament of white bone upon their foreheads'.[1] This 'bone' might be ivory or even bone, but it is most probably shell, white wampum obtained from southern New England, such 'bone' being specified for chains, bracelets and girdles, while they also have 'their skin garments sewn with them'. The bracelets of 'little white round bones, fastened together upon a leather string', were almost certainly discoidal wampum beads.[2] The 'jewels in their ears' were probably ear-ornaments of coloured stone. No special ornaments are specified for women, whose dress was said to be the same as that of the men. We hear of their 'dogs and wolves', which would suggest the use of both small and larger kinds of dogs. Hanham speaks of 'dogs like wolues, of colours black, white red, and grizzled'.[3] The broad pattern is one of a society oriented very much to hunting, though also involved in fishing and shore-gathering and only marginally, and in only a few places, agriculture.

One description of a communal activity builds up an effective picture of the Eastern Abenaki community in action. When whale came inshore, possibly the Right Whale, a tribal attack was decided.[4] The Indians made their way to the water under the direction of their 'king' or sagamore. We are told they go 'with a multitude of boats[5] and strike him with a bone made in fashion of a harping iron fastened to a rope, which they make great strong of the bark of trees, which they veer

---

'Comparative studies', p. 326). See also V. Kinietz, 'Notes on the roached head dress of animal hair among the North American Indians', Michigan Academy of Arts and Sciences, Arts and letters, Papers, XXVII (1940), 463–7. This may be the earliest mention of such an ornament.

[1] This might appear to be wampum rather than bone, but is not met with elsewhere as a sign of rank or distinction.

[2] The possession of chains (necklets), girdles (belts) and bracelets indicate the presence of substantial quantities of wampum. The cylindrical white beads, made from whelk shell, were imported from south of Cape Cod, and the black from quahog. While these did apparently travel by pre-contact trade routes (Salwen, in Handbook, p. 166), it would appear that bone, ivory and shell were all combined in the earliest contact references, even though the discoidal and cylindrical beads of wampum, proper, would be specially prized. The use of wampum appliqué on deerskin does not appear to be recorded earlier. F. G. Speck, 'The functions of wampum among the eastern Algonkians', American Anthropological Society, Memoirs, VI (1919), 3–71 (especially pp. 16–19) is still of value.

[3] 'Dogs were not used to pull or carry loads. They were kept for pets or for tracking game' (Snow, in Handbook, p. 139). But we have an emphasis on smaller dogs above (p. 98), and the 'dogs and wolves' would suggest they also had larger hunting dogs. This, perhaps requires further investigation. The references to their colour are also of interest.

[4] A sea-mammal hunt is not indicated by Driver and Massey, 'Comparative studies', pp. 171, 178 and map 11, south of Newfoundland.

[5] This use of the birch-bark canoe is, also, not indicated by Driver and Massey, p. 187.

out after him. Then all their boats come about him, as he riseth above water, with their arrows [and spears?] they shoot him to death. When they have killed him and dragged him to shore, they call their chief lords together and sing a song of joy[1] and those chief lords which they call 'sagamos' divide the spoils...give to every man a share, which pieces so distributed they hang up in their houses for provision and when they boil them they blow off the fat and put [it] to their peas, maize and other pulse which they eat'.[2] Their 'king' who accompanied them to the whale hunt was probably Bashabes himself and the 'chief lords' the leading sagamores of the bands who acknowledged him, but if this was so the whole venture must have been planned for a considerable time and involved the concentration of many hundreds of men from a dozen communal groups. It may, on the other hand, have been an activity of only one major group. In either event it ranked as a large-scale example of communal co-operation in hunting.

We have one other picture of a communal activity, the dance – the occasion not being known[3] – watched by the young Welshman Owen Griffin:

One among them (the eldest of the company as he judged) riseth right up, the rest sitting still, and suddenly cried 'Bowh waugh!' Then the women fall down and lie upon the ground and the men, altogether answering the same, fall a stamping round about with both feet as hard as they can, making the ground shake, with sundry loud outcries and change of voice and sound. Many take the fire sticks and thrust them into the earth and then rest silent a while. Of a sudden beginning as before, they look round about as if they expected the coming of something (as he verily supposed) and continue stamping till the younger sort fetch from the shore stones, of which every man took one, and first beat upon them with the fire sticks, then with the stones beat upon the ground with all their strength. And in this sort (as he reported) they continued above two hours.

This 'Ceremony of their Idolatry' was part of their animistic obser-vances, about which very little is known for this area, since later evidence is mainly from missionary sources. We are also told that: 'In the time of their "Pavose", our watch aboard were singing and they signed to him to do so, which he did, looking and lifting up his eyes

---

[1] A distinctive ceremony associated with whale-taking (first whale-taking?) is not indicated elsewhere. The magnitude of the operation, and the subsequent assembly of so many people, indicate that it was a very special occasion.

[2] The use of fat as seasoning is noted, for this occasion, by Flannery, *Analysis*, p. 22, but she does not comment on the whale-taking; see also N. N. Smith, *loc. cit.* (n. 180).

[3] See pp. 278–9 below.

to Heaven. Then they pointed to the Moon, as if they imagined he worshipped that, which, when he with signs denied, they pointed to the Sun rising, which he likewise disliked, lifting his hands again. Then they looked about as though they would see what Star it might be, laughing one to another.' There may have been something of mockery in this since Rosier is not unlikely to have tried to convey to them something of the nature of Christian religion, or they had had some inkling of it from or by way of the French. They appear to be stressing that their own veneration of the Moon and Sun was beyond the capacity of the Europeans to understand, as they, themselves, were unable to understand the concepts of Christianity. This may, however, be to read too much into a casual incident.

The cumulative impact of English and Indians, both in southern New England and in the Eastern Abenaki territory, was not great. The seizure of the five men by Waymouth and the subsequent cumulation of a large vocabulary of their language could have provided us with much more extensive information had anything like all of it survived, but the capture was not wholly without a cultural residue.

'The Description of the Countrey of Mawooshen' provided a different type of evidence than the contact narratives hitherto considered. According to Sir Ferdinando Gorges, it was composed shortly after he had acquired three of the five Eastern Abenaki Indians, brought back by Waymouth in July 1605. It is probable that on the formation of the Virginia Company in April 1606, if not before, the other two Indians also joined their fellows in Plymouth. The linguistic bridge could only have been broken quickly if James Rosier had been at Plymouth also for part of that time, since it was he who had compiled a list (and possibly a grammar) of this Algonquian dialect, and would have been needed to teach Nahanada, the Pemaquid sagamore, and the others, English as well as to gather detailed information from them. Assacomoit and Maneddo were despatched with Challons to 'Mawooshen' in July 1606 and it may be that the basic document had been hammered out by that time. It may also be that Nahanada, who left with Hanham and Pring about September, and was safely returned to his village and reinstated as sagamore, was the wise man who knew the country well enough to describe it. It had best be taken as a collective document, the primary agent in the mediation of which was probably Rosier, and that it was composed, basically as we have it, in the latter part of 1605 and the early months of 1606. It involved laying out in detail the river drainages between the Union River all the way southwards and westwards to the Presumpscot, with information on the location of twenty-one villages and twenty-three sagamores, with names for all the villages and all but one sagamore (some villages had two), together with estimates of adult male population for each, while a clear description is given of the complex Kennebec–Androscoggin drainages. The coast between ten of the drainages and well into the interior is said to be subject to Bashabes, a dominant (or at least highly-regarded) sagamore who was located on the Kenduskeag River, a tributary of the Penobscot, on the site of modern Bangor. This material, which Dean Snow has successfully analysed,[1] provides precisely the type of information which could only be gathered by English colonists after an extended stay in the country.

The collection by Rosier of some 500 words, of which some 85 have survived, also broke through the cultural as well as the linguistic barrier. It was possible for Hanham and Pring to explore late in 1606 with much (probably all) of this knowledge and form a basis on which a settlement could be established on the Kennebec in August 1607, which was to last for a little over a year. The lack of the crucial Hanham journal and of most of the journal material for the settlement on the Kennebec hampers our knowledge of Eastern Abenaki society at a vital point, so as to limit greatly our capacity to judge the nature and extent of the culture-contact between the two peoples, and to make conclusions on their precise nature virtually impossible to draw.

We have few of the no doubt innumerable notes of culture traits the lost journals held. We are told[2] that the Pemaquid band had a god called Tanto: 'So they call an evil spirit which haunts them every moon, and makes them worship him for fear. He commanded them not to dwell near or come among the English, threatening to kill some and inflict sickness on others beginning with two of the sagamore's [Nahanada's] children, saying he had power, and would do the like to the English the next moon, to wit in December.' This glimpse of animistic beliefs and shamanistic claims is tantalising. So is the mention of the ceremonial at and after a sagamore's death:[3] 'When a Sagamo dieth, they black themselves, and at the same time yearly renewe their great mourning with great howling: as they did for Kaskhurakeny who died the year before' – he may have been joint sagamore with Nahanada at Pemaquid. There is finally a brief indication of their

---

[1] See note p. 90 above. Dr Snow has also sent me several helpful letters. For the text see pp. 470–6 below.

[2] P. 350 below.   [3] P. 351 below.

cyclical pattern of living, a continued interest in their artifacts and an exceptional comment on their sexual cycle: 'The savages remove their dwellings in winter nearest the deer. They have a kind of shoes a yard long, fourteen inches broad, made like a racquet, with strong twine or sinews of a deer; in the midst is a hole wherein they put their feet, buckling it fast....In winter they are poor and weak, and do not company with their wives but in summer when they are fat and lusty.' 'Subsistence', Dean Snow tells us,[1] 'was based primarily upon an annual round of hunting and gathering. Spring was spent on the coast [as was much of summer]...The spring and summer diet was supplemented by various berries, cherries, grapes, and other wild fruits...Winter subsistence usually required frequent movement on snowshoes and toboggan [the latter not mentioned in English accounts].'

The indications of communal contacts are also scarce but would repay further study. Their communal reaction to the appearance of strangers was an automatic show of hostility. At Pemaquid, where Nahanada had been restored as sagamore the previous year, on the first coming of the English[2] – 'at our sight of them upon a howling or cry that they made they all presently issued forth towards us with their bows and arrows and we presently made a stand and suffered them to come near unto us', after which amicable relations were established. Even at a later visit on sight of the village 'presently Nahanada with all his Indians, with their bows and arrows in their hands came forth upon the sands'.

Once the English were established at Fort St George they would bring their canoes to the ship's side, come aboard briefly, but would not stay overnight (a memory of Waymouth's treachery in 1605 no doubt). What the English learned slowly and imperfectly was that market forces were not the primary impulses in exchanges of goods and that ceremonial exchanges must precede value for value bargaining. They did themselves much harm in refusing objects offered to them in exchange where these were not of good quality or were valued (in their eyes) too highly. In an expedition up the Kennebec they met[3] 'near fifty able men very strong and tall, such as their like they had not seen, all new painted and armed with their bows and arrows'. They refused to give them as much for their tobacco and skins in copper, beads and knives as they appeared to demand. In return for their

---

[1] Snow, in *Handbook*, p. 138.   [2] P. 426 below.   [3] Pp. 410–11 below.

discourtesy the Indians tried to trick them by ensuring their guns would not fire and behaved in a devious, semi-hostile manner, though doing them no harm. Gradually they learned the value of presents, sending such to Bashabes before attempting to make direct contact with him. One generous sagamore did indeed remove his robe and breechcloth and offered them as presents, desiring to be taken to England, but he was regarded as eccentric,[1] rather than as offering a ceremonial gift of valuable coat-beaver. By the time the Abenaki had prepared skins to dispose of in quantity in the summer of 1608 trading practices had evidently been worked out satisfactorily. There is too little evidence to allow for generalisations about the relationship in general of the colony and the inhabitants, but there was a strong element of mutual respect, though not much mutual or exclusive interdependence, since the Eastern Abenaki were already within the orbit of the French fur-trading zone, and had their other trading connections with southern New England groups from whom they obtained, chiefly, agricultural produce and wampum.

The fact that the Indians of southern New England had, from before Verrazzano's time, substantial quantities of copper which they transformed into a variety of decorative objects and, perhaps occasionally, into utilitarian ones, is undoubted. It has created a good deal of ambiguity in accounts of aboriginal artifacts from this region, since in them the historical and archaeological evidence has appeared to be at variance. In what are clearly precontact sites (though not older ones) no copper has been found. When it is found the assumption, based partly on the presumed incapacity of Indians to make sheet copper, which was so widely in use in beads and other ornaments, has led to the conclusion that all burials where such has been found are late and that, despite the historical evidence of the sixteenth century availability of copper, such sites must belong well into the seventeenth century when contact was being transformed into settlement. There has been no satisfactory elimination of the possibility of native copper being used, partly because so few attempts have been made at comparative analysis, which by modern scientific methods can differentiate copper of native and European origins provided the specimen has not decayed too far. It seems likely that small pieces of natural copper were recovered from time to time from riverine sources, but there has been no clear evidence that Lake Superior copper which was circulating so widely in the later Woodland Period reached New England, though

[1] Pp. 351, 413 below.

the percolation of small quantities cannot be wholly ruled out. There is some natural copper in the Connecticut Valley, but obscurity on this area and absence of evidence of its being worked and traded, make it a very dubious source. The one location adjacent to the Atlantic coast where natural copper was found was in the Minas Basin and nearby at Chignecto Head on the Bay of Fundy. Europeans were first excited about this and then discouraged at its limited character, but it remains the one pre-European source for the whole area east of the River St Lawrence, and it might appear to have been worked to some very limited extent by the Micmac before Europeans appeared.

The evidence of appreciable quantities of copper in the hands of New England Indians in 1524, 1602 and 1603, has been attributed in the past to European traders visiting the area almost as soon as it was discovered and bringing with them sufficient copper to lead to a substantial accumulation of it before 1524. Much historical work has been done on the exploratory voyages of the early sixteenth century, and the complete absence of evidence of systematic contact with southern New England before Verrazzano is striking. The failure of evidence of such contact to survive does not rule out the possibility that some contact did in fact take place, but that it could have been on such a scale as to produce the abundance of copper recorded by Verrazzano has remained and still remains very difficult to credit. Ethnographers have now recognised this difficulty to some extent and, by postulating pre-contact coastal trade, are able to indicate that the early appearance of copper in the sixteenth century in southern New England was achieved by the rapid passing of the results of early contacts with fishermen at Cape Breton and probably elsewhere in the vicinity, going back to about the end of the first decade of the century (our knowledge of the precise date of the first Breton contacts with this area are still rather nebulous but they appear to have been well established before 1511). Bert Salwen may be cited as giving views current in the 1970s,[1] when he says: 'European trade began quite early in the sixteenth century. Most of the earliest explorers of southeastern New England noted the presence of copper earrings, bracelets, pendants and breast-plates. The copper may have been obtained from early unrecorded European visitors to New England, but it seems more likely that it was first obtained by Maine and Nova Scotia Indians from European fishermen and fur traders and then travelled southwards down a well-established aboriginal coastal trading route.' This is acceptable as

[1] *Handbook*, p. 166.

a working hypothesis, though it might appear that the Maine Indians were by-passed by those from the Maritimes, since at the opening of the seventeenth century, the Eastern Abenaki seem to have been almost without copper. Micmac were vigorous traders and there is evidence that they had by the opening of the seventeenth century adopted European methods of sea transport (by the stealing of shallops) to reinforce their trade from, perhaps, the vicinity of the Saco River to Cape Ann, which had earlier been carried on in canoes. The supposition would be that they traded copper, certain furs and skins, and perhaps dried meat for wampum, corn, beans and tobacco with the Massachusetts and Pockanoket, and that from them copper was exchanged southward as far as Narragansett Bay at least. We might suggest that some small quantity of native copper from the Bay of Fundy may have been an ingredient in this trade in pre-contact times and that this explains why it so rapidly became a major item in trade after contact had been made with summer fishermen (who soon came to engage to a limited extent in fur trading as well) in the northern part of the Maritimes. It is still somewhat difficult to understand why so much copper was seen in southeastern New England whereas little notice was taken of its presence as Indian decoration north of Cape Cod. But the explanation of this may lie in the making of beads from whelk and quahog shells in quantity in southern New England and the disposal of wampum as an important item of pre-contact commerce all the way up the coast to the northeast, which would provide precisely the explanation why copper obtained in some quantity from Europeans came to rest in Pockanoket and possibly Narragansett hands quite early in the sixteenth century and certainly by the opening of the seventeenth. By the latter period the great summer fur-trading mart at Tadoussac was well established and European objects from it, of iron in greater quantity than copper, were finding their way southwards well beyond southern New England. There is a considerable speculative element in all this, which it is possible archaeology of the immediate pre- and post-contact periods will in time do something to clarify. We cannot, however, entirely eliminate the possibility that other sources of natural copper did not provide part of the southern New England supplies in the sixteenth and early seventeenth century. There may have been remnants of Archaic copper still extant from early grave sites: the Connecticut Valley, about which little is known for the immediate pre-contact period, may have had some natural copper which was being worked, and it is even possible that, intermediately, Lake Superior natural copper was reaching southern New England secondhand from the Iroquois who were the recipients of a certain amount of it even after French contact had brought European copper more readily to hand.

One of the principal problems with regard to New England copper was to find a site which had been properly excavated and which was marginally of the pre-contact and earliest contact period. Such a one appeared to be the Titicut site on the upper reaches of the Taunton River at Bridgewater, Massachusetts. Maurice Robbins excavated this site,[1] one where burials took place between about 1500 and about 1620, having been abandoned by 1621. A large number of tubular copper beads were found on this site which were deposited with the other finds at the Bronson Museum, Attleboro, Massachusetts. Dr Robbins, in discussion with me, considered that it would be worth while having a few of the beads tested, adequate methods of distinguishing European from native copper having then (1970) been developed. Six beads were selected for examination to destruction. Three were sent to the British Museum Laboratory, which reported that the specimens were too corroded for any testable metal to remain, so that no verdict could be given. The remaining three were submitted, through the courtesy of Mrs Waldo R. Wedel and the then chairman of the Department of Anthropology, Dr Clifford Evans, Smithsonian Institution, to Dr Robert M. Organ, Chief of the Conservation Analytical Laboratory, U.S. National Museum. In due course a report was made on the beads by Dr Organ and Dr Martha Goodway, dated 11 July 1973, which established, by analysis of one of the beads which contained sufficient sound metal, that the copper was undoubtedly European.[2] Dr Organ subsequently confirmed in conversation that he had little doubt that other copper material from the site would also be found to be European. The matter must rest there for the time being.

[1] 'The Titicut site', Massachusetts Archeological Society, *Bulletin*, xxviii (1967), 33–76.

[2] Report Cal. no. 1118, by Martha Goodway and R. M. Organ, Conservation Analytical Laboratory, U.S. National Museum, Washington D.C., 11 July 1973, to Clifford Evans, Chairman, Department of Anthropology.

CHAPTER I

GABRIEL ARCHER'S ACCOUNT OF CAPTAIN BARTHOLOMEW GOSNOLD'S VOYAGE TO 'NORTH VIRGINIA' IN 1602

Gabriel Archer's narrative of Bartholomew Gosnold's voyage to 'North Virginia' in 1602[1] is the first English account of an expedition which pioneered the way for all future voyages in this volume. Though it was not published until 1625, and John Brereton's account (pp. 143–59) appeared in 1602, it is different in character from the latter. It is a straightforward story with occasional comments, whereas Brereton's is mainly concerned to emphasise the material collected on the Indians and on natural products, with a much smaller narrative content. It was probably not published at the time because its specific detail would provide too clear an account of how access could be obtained to the shores of New England at a time when Ralegh and others were still uncertain what the next steps in its exploitation should be. The Pring voyage, one of those steps (pp. 214–28), was also kept out of print until 1625, apparently for similar reasons.

Archer indicates from the first that the expedition planned to establish a trading post at which 20 out of 32 persons forming the complement of the *Concord* would remain over the winter. The background to the making of such a decision remains obscure, but it was probably the result of information or rumours relating to the French fur trade along the northeastern coast of North America which suggested that the English could steal a march on the French by such an establishment. It is clear too that Gosnold, at least, wished to place the settlement at Verrazzano's site, Refugio (where he had remained for some tine in 1524, and which was in Narragansett Bay) (p. 210 below). The narrative gives brief but adequate details of the Atlantic crossing between 26 March and 14 May 1602, a reasonably good crossing during a period of mainly easterly winds. The arrival at Savage Rock (Cape Elizabeth or Cape Neddick) brought the Englishmen to the lands of the Massachusetts Indians but their first contact was with a Micmac-manned Basque shallop trading down from Newfoundland with southern New England. Archer gave a useful

---

[1] Only extant in Samuel Purchas, *Pilgrimes*, IV (1625), 1647–57 (XVIII (1906), 302–13), who had the manuscript from Richard Hakluyt's collection probably after he died in 1616 (see Quinn, *Hakluyt handbook*, I, 95). Archer is likely to have given it to Hakluyt at some time between his return in 1602 and his final departure for Virginia in 1609.

account of the exploration of Cape Cod Bay, but omitted Brereton's valuable information that, when Gosnold went ashore near modern Barnstable and surveyed the area to the south, he found the Upper Cape to be a peninsula, with islands lying to the south of it, to which he determined to go. Archer makes the rounding of Cape Cod and the entry into Nantucket Sound appear much easier than they can have been, even though he does, as Brereton does not, mention shoals at the entrance to the Sound. He records, again as Brereton does not, a meeting on the Upper Cape with Indians (probably Nausets of the Pockanoket tribe), and their willingness to barter skins and other 'trifles': he stresses particularly their possession of much copper. His account of the voyage along the south shore of the Upper Cape and then out into Nantucket Sound to circle round until they reached Capoag (Cape Poge), then an island, is difficult, but not wholly impossible, to follow. It was this island which Gosnold called Marthaes Vineyard, but he later extended the name to the much larger landmass to which it was almost joined to the west. As they sailed westward, what had appeared as a channel into the interior was now shown to be a chain of islands on their starboard side, while Marthas Vineyard itself appeared divided on the port side, with Gay Head standing out as a separate island. Contacts with Indians on the main island were brief but friendly: whether they were residents or a fishing party from the mainland is not clear. Gosnold now turned his attention to the outer chain of islands, and brought the *Concord* to anchor off the north shore of what he called Elizabeths Ile (now Cuttyhunk and Nashawena divided), and from which, to the north-east, extended a wide channel (Buzzards Bay) which might, it seemed, be the sought-for Refugio. (In fact on a clear day Cuttyhunk can be seen in the east from Point Judith at the entrance to Narragansett Bay, that is westwards from where they were lying). Indians came to vist them in small numbers. Gosnold decided, Archer tells us, to site the post on Elizabeths Isle, as a central point for trading purposes. His choice of an island on a lake on the island is described and it is made clear that Archer was to supervise the construction, while Gosnold explored the mainland, the northern shore of Buzzards Bay. The details of the construction of the building give some idea of its nature but not enough to avoid later controversy (pp. 504–9 below). The shallop was given a new keel and used for minor transport between the islands where sassafras and cedar trunks were cut and gathered. A considerable body of Pockanoket Indians, under a sachem, came to vist them, but, after exchanges of presents, they returned to the mainland. Meantime Gosnold had visited the northern shore of Buzzards Bay, and had come to the correct conclusion that it terminated some little way to the north, but he did not follow the coast far enough on his return southwestwards to reach Point Judith and to see Narragansett Bay spread out to the north (or if he did he kept the secret well). Clearly, Archer considered he was imposed on by being left too few men to finish the fort, and indeed on his final expedition Gosnold left them insufficient rations. Relations between Gosnold, who was to stay, and Bartholomew

Gilbert, who was to return, became bad when it became clear that the fort for twenty men was finished but there was, at most, six weeks', not six months', provisions to be left with them. This suggests that the holding party was expected to obtain some food locally as they were unlikely to be relieved for ten or eleven months. In the end it was decided (Brereton says the men decided for themselves) that they would all return. The voyage home was rapid and uneventful (18 June–23 July). Archer's narrative is literate and shows he was observant of natural resources and of Indian activities, but he was circumscribed in his view from Elizabeths Isle by his involvement at the fort and consequently his information on the exploring trips by Gosnold are brief and difficult to piece together. Generally, however, he conveys objectively what was seen and done, though he avoids making any assessment of future prospects for later expeditions. With the greater detail by Brereton on natural resources, the two narratives make up an adequate account of a voyage which demonstrated that in summer 'North Virginia' was easy of access and offered at least some prospects of exploitation, even if we do not learn that any major source of furs and skins was revealed. Cedar trunks and sassafras alone scarcely paid the costs of the expedition, to which Gosnold himself may well have been a substantial contributor.

---

1   The Relation of Captaine Gosnols Voyage to the North part of Virginia, begunne the sixe and twentieth of March, Anno 42.[1] Elizabethae Reginae 1602. and deliuered by Gabriel Archer, a Gentleman of the said Voyage.

The said Captaine did set sayle from Famouth,[2] the day and yeere aboue written accompanied with thirtie two persons, whereof eight Mariners and Saylers, twelue purposing vpon the Discouery to returne with the ship for England, the rest remayne there for population.[3] The fourteenth of Aprill following, wee had sight of Saint Maries an Iland of the Assoris.[4]

---

[1] '42' is a misprint for '44', the regnal year which began on 17 September 1601.

[2] We are not given any clear indication whether the ship originally sailed round from London, with the Londoners who included Gosnold, Archer and Bartholomew Gilbert, or whether they joined her at a western port, Dartmouth or even Falmouth. (Cp. p. 144, where Gosnold's oblique reference may be to a voyage beginning in the Thames.)

[3] The allocation of men as between mariners (8), settlers (12), including Gosnold and Archer, and adventurers (12), who included Brereton, Gilbert, Robert Salterne, and either Meriton or John Angell. It might appear that later it was decided 20 should settle, 8 manage the ship homeward and 4 adventurers only return (p. 159).

[4] For the course from Santa Maria on 14 April to 14 May we are dependent on Archer, whose account is close to the journal he made on board. They ran down the 37th parallel for 9 days, making 600 miles, about 66·5 miles a day. This, allowing 20 nautical miles to

The three and twentieth of the same, beeing two hundred leagues Westwards from the said Iland in the latitude of 37. degrees. The water in the mayne Ocean appeared yellow, the space of two leagues North and South, where sounding wyth thirtie fadome Line, wee found no ground, and taking vp some of the said water in a bucket, it altered not either in colour or taste from the Sea Azure. Ocean seeming yellow.

The seventh of May following, we first saw many Birds in bignesse of Cliffe Pidgeons, and after diuers other as Pettrels, Cootes, Hagbuts, Pengwins, Murres, Gannets, Cormorants, Guls, with many else in our English Tongue of no name.[1] The eight of the same the water changed to a yellowish greene, where at seuentie fadome we had ground. The ninth, wee had two and twentie fadome in faire sandie ground, hauing vpon our Lead many glittering Stones, somewhat heauie, which might promise some Minerall matter in the bottome, we held our selues by computation, well neere the latitude of 43. degrees.

The tenth wee sounded[2] in 27, 30. 37. 43. fadome: and then came to 108. some thought it to be the sounding of the Westermost end of Saint Johns Iland,[3] vpon this banke we saw sculs[4] of fish in great numbers. The twelfth we hoysed out halfe of our shallop, and sounding had then eightie fadome without any current perceiued by William Strete the Master, one hundred leagues Westward from Saint Maries til we came to the foresaid soundings continually passed fleeting by us Sea-Oare, which seemed to have their moueable course towards the North-east, a matter to set some subtle inuention on worke, for comprehending the true cause thereof. The thirteenth, wee sounded in Sea-Oare.

---

the degree, was a good average (Waters, *Art of navigation*, pp. 37, 64, 172). 100 miles might be regarded as a maximum. By May 23 they were evidently in an area of Yellow Green Algae, a combination of vegetable matter with plankton (cp. H. U. Sverdrup, M. W. Johnson and R. H. Fleming, *The oceans* (1942), pp. 295–302). From this point they evidently changed course northwestwards.

[1] The pigeon-like birds are non-diagnostic; his petrel probably Storm Petrel, *Hydrobates peligacus* (L.); his coot probably American Scoter, *Oidemia americana* Swainson (rather than American Coot, *Fulica americana americana* Gmelin); his hagbut (var. of hagdown) for the Greater Shearwater, *Puffinus gravis* (O'Reilly) but not found elsewhere so early; his penguins, Great Auks (p. 160); his murre Atlantic Murre, *Uria aalge aalge* (Pontoppidan); his gannet Gannet, *Morus bassanus* L.; his cormorant probably European Cormorant, *Phalocrocorax carbo carbo* (L.), and his gulls not specifically identifiable (Forbush and May, *Birds*, pp. 16, 87–8, 168–9, 12–13, 21–2, 22).

[2] Misprinted 'founded' for 'sounded'; corrected in *Pilgrimes*, XVIII (1906), 303. The soundings would fit a northwesterly course through the northern tip of Georges Bank into the Gulf of Maine. A closely similar series of depths can be seen between lat. 41° 23' N, long. 67° 10' W and lat. 42° 10' N, long. 68° 15' W (U.S.C. and G.S. Chart 70).

[3] 'I. S. Iohn' is still given for Nova Scotia on the Edward Wright map of 1599, which *Concord* is likely to have had on board, but there it lies along lat. 45° N.

[4] 'Sculs', schools.

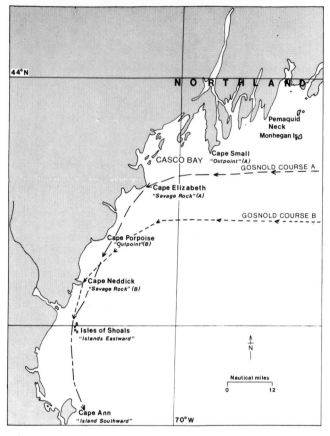

Fig. 2. *Concord*'s landfall, 14 May 1602. O.S.: alternative courses.

seuentie fadome, and obserued great beds of weedes, much woode and diuers things else floating by vs, when as we had smelling of the shoare,[1] such as from the Southerne Cape and Andulazia in Spaine.[2]

The fourteenth, about six in the morning we descried Land that lay North, &c. the Northerly part we called the North Land, which to

ll of the re.

---

[1] Inshore beds of seaweed, the movement of land-grown vegetable debris and the sensation of smelling the shore all indicate the *Concord* was now within the countercurrent in the Gulf of Maine (cp. Waters, *Art of navigation*, p. 257).

[2] The southern cape was Cape St Vincent, and the experience of the Andalusian shore indicates that Strete (or Archer) had been on the Mediterranean run before this voyage.

another Rocke[1] vpon the same lying twelue leagues West, that wee Sauage Rocke.
called Sauage Rocke, because the Sauages first shewed themselues there,
fiue leagues towards the said Rocke is an out Point of woodie ground,
the Trees thereof very high and straight, from the Rocke East
North-east.[2] From the said Rocke, came towards vs a Biscay shallop
with saile and Oares, hauing eight persons in it, whom we supposed
at first to bee Christians distressed. But approching vs neere, wee
perceiued them to bee Sauages. These comming within call hayled vs, Sauages.
and wee answered. Then after signes of peace, and a long speech by
one of them made, they came boldly aboord vs being all naked, sauing
about their shoulders certaine loose Deere-skinnes, and neere their
wastes Seale-skinnes tyed fast like to Irish Dimmie Trouses. One that
seemed to be their Commander wore a Wastecoate of blacke worke,
a paire of Breeches, cloth Stockings, Shooes, Hat, and Band, one or Their
two more had also a few things made by some Christians, these with behauiour.
a piece of Chalke described the Coast thereabouts, and could name
Placentia of the New-found-land, they spake divers Christian words,
and seemed to vnderstand much more then we, for want of Language
could comprehend. These people are in colour swart, their haire long
vp tyed with a knot in the part of behind the head. They paint their
bodies, which are strong and well proportioned.[3] These much desired
our longer stay, but finding our selues short of our purposed place, we

[1] Perhaps this should read 'North Land, which [extended] to another Rocke'. After
the fog had cleared (see Brereton, p. 144), the *Concord* would appear to have been on a
westerly course, seeing the Maine headlands from Pemaquid to Cape Small in an almost
continuous line of land, making up the 'North Land', our earliest descriptive name for
Maine.

[2] There is no certainty about the landfall. Cape Elizabeth (43° 34′ N, 70° 12′ W)
would fit in with the indications of a continuous northern shoreline, standing out effectively
from the sea and with an island in Casco Bay as 'the out Point of woodie ground'; Cape
Neddick (43° 10′ N, 70° 36′ W), some 25 miles farther south, which is not so prominent
from the sea but has Mount Agmenticus behind it, is the alternative, with Cape Porpoise
as the 'out Point'. Cape Neddick has been the favoured landfall (e.g. by S. E. Morison),
but John Bower who has sailed the coast repeatedly considers, with the editors, that Cape
Elizabeth is at least equally possible.

[3] The episode of the encounter with the Micmacs in a Basque shallop is annotated
from Brereton (pp. 145–6 below). Archer's additions to the Indians' equipment included
the information that one man's waistcoat was decorated with embroidery and that he wore
a hat and band. The trousers worn by one other is omitted, but hair knotted behind their
heads, the deerskin short mantles and the elaborated sealskin breechcloths (like Irish
half-trousers) are additions. Their naming of Placentia for Newfoundland and their use
of Christian words not understood (Basque?) fits in with their having been employed in
the fishery. Their capacity to draw an outline of the coast indicates that this was not the
first time they had been in this area (cp. Beck, *American Indians as sea fighters* (1959), pp.
16–17; Flannery, *Analysis*, p. 61).

set saile Westwards, leauing them and their Coast. About sixteene leagues South-west from thence, wee perceiued in that course two small Ilands, the one lying Eastward from Sauage Rock, the other to the Southwards of it,[1] the Coast we left was full of goodly Woods, faire Plaines, with little greene round Hils aboue the Cliffes appearing vnto vs, which are indifferently raised, but all Rockie, and of shining stones, which might haue perswaded vs a longer stay there.

The fifteenth day we had againe sight of the Land, which made a head being as wee thought an Iland,[2] by reason of a large sound that appeared Westward betweene it and the Mayne, for coming to the West end thereof, we did perceiue a large opening, we called it Shole-hope: Neere this Cape we came to Anchor in fifteene fadome, where wee tooke great store of Cod-fish, for which we altered the name, and called it Cape Cod.[3] Here wee saw sculs of Herrings, Mackerels and other small fish in great abundance. This is a low sandie shoare, but without danger, also wee came to Anchor againe in sixteene fadome, faire by the Land in the latitute of 42. degrees.[4] This Cape is well neere a mile broad, and lieth North-east by East. The Captaine went here ashoare and found the ground to be full of Pease, Strawberies, Hurtberies, &c. as then vnripe, the sand also by the shoare somewhat deepe, the firewood there by vs taken in was of Cypresse, Birch, Wich-hazell and

Shole-hope. (margin)

Cape Cod. (margin)

---

[1] Archer is not easy to follow. *Concord* would sail on so far westward as to keep land in view. If we take Cape Elizabeth as Savage Rock, the Isles of Shoals (at 42° 59′) would lie one point W and Cape Ann (which from the north has the appearance of an island) two points W (at 42° 41′), the second at about the distance of 48 miles. Since the Isles of Shoals are within 12 miles and Cape Ann within 30 from Cape Neddick, the observation (if Archer is to be relied on) strengthens the case for Cape Elizabeth as the first landfall.

[2] By now making her way southward, *Concord* would see the Provincetown–Truro area stand out, in the first place, as an island to the S.E. This area has moved substantially north and west since 1602, so that the configuration of Race Point and the spit enclosing Provincetown Harbor have considerably changed. It might seem that the entry was made into Provincetown Harbor, but it is possible from later indications that it was somewhat farther south and that *Concord* lay off Wellfleet Harbor (cp. Woodward and Wigglesworth, *Geography and geology of...Cape Cod* (1934), with W. M. Davis, *Geographical essays* (1909, repr. 1954), pp. 690–724; D. Johnson, *New England-Acadian shoreline* (1925), pp. 400, 405; B. B. Chamberlain, *These fragile outposts* (1964), pp. 121–7, 180–1, 211, 223–4, 269).

[3] The naming of Cape Cod was a permanent contribution, which John Smith was unable to displace, but whether Shole-hope (= shallow haven) was Provincetown Harbor (which has always seemed probable) or Wellfleet Harbor, is debatable. Only at the former was a depth of 15 fathoms possible. The first anchorage is ignored by Brereton.

[4] The second anchorage in Cape Cod Bay is implied as being near the first, but a depth of 16 fathoms cannot now be found off Barnstable Harbor (strongly indicated by Brereton (pp. 146–7)). Depths of 10–11 fathoms can be had about 2 miles offshore from Sandy Neck to the west of the opening of Barnstable Harbor, at a latitude of 41° 47′, thus fitting Brereton's 'within a league of the shore'.

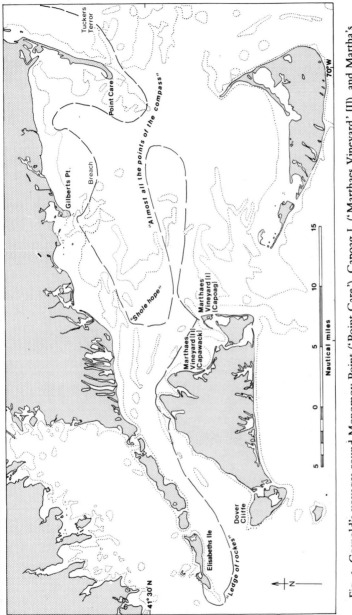

Fig. 3. Gosnold's voyages round Monomoy Point ('Point Care'), Capoag I. ('Marthaes Vineyard' [I]), and Martha's Vineyard ([II] also Capawack) and Cuttyhunk–Nashawena I. ('Elisabeths Ile').

Beech.[1] A young Indian came here to the Captaine, armed with his Bow and Arrowes, and had certaine plates of Copper hanging at his Eares,[2] hee shewed a willingnesse to helpe vs in our occasions.

The sixteenth, we trended the Coast Southerly,[3] which was all champaine and full of grasse,[4] but the Ilands somewhat wooddie.[5] Twelue leagues from Cape Cod, we descried a point, with some breach a good distance off,[6] and keeping our loffe to double it, wee came on

[1] While Brereton concentrated on topography, Archer dealt with the natural history. The beach peas, wild strawberries and the whortleberries will appear again (p. 160). The Canoe Birch, *Betula papyrifera*, Marsh, is rare here, but Yellow Birch, *B. lutea* Michx. and Gray or Poverty Birch, *B. populifolia* Marsh, are probable (Sargent, *Manual of the trees of North America*, 2nd ed. (1922), p. 207; Fernald, *Gray's Manual* (1950), 533–5; Gleason and Cronquist, *Manual* (1966), pp. 245–6. The American Witch Hazel, *Hamamelis virginiana* L., is not native to Europe. He may have meant the Hornbeam, in Europe *Carpinus betulus* L., in America *C. caroliniana* Walt. (or the northern variety *C. virginiana* (Marsh) Fern. Gerard, *Herball* (1597), p. 1296, says the 'Hornbeame tree, *Betulus siue Carpinus* is in some places called Witch Hazel'. For Cypress see above (p. 118). We may speculate whether Archer had not a copy of Gerard's *Herball*, bulky as it was, in his cabin.

[2] The disc-shaped copper ear-ornaments worn by this Pockanoket Indian of the Nauset band are not indicated elsewhere in this area. They were noted in F. G. Rainey, 'A compilation of historical data contributing to the ethnography of the Connecticut and south New England Indians', Conn. Arch. Soc., *Bulletin*, no. 3 (repr. 1956), p. 18. We may wonder what information he imparted and by what means. The authoritative study of this area is Bert Salwen, 'Indians of southern New England and Long Island', in Bruce Trigger, *The Northeast* (Handbook of the Indians of North America, general editor William T. Sturtevant, volume 15, Washington, D.C., 1978), pp. 160–76: subsequently referred to as Salwen. The copper problem is briefly dealt with on p. 109, the most probable explanation being that it was 'first obtained by Maine and Nova Scotia Indians from European fishermen and fur traders and then traveled southward down a well-established aboriginal coastal trade route'. This seems borne out by such evidence as we have, which puts the emphasis on Micmac waterborne traffic.

[3] Brereton ceases to be of value at this crucial stage of the voyage. The presumed course was northwards until Point Race was cleared, then E.S.E. along the outer shore of the Cape. Since the Outer and Inner Bars extend at least half a mile out to sea, Gosnold is likely to have kept well clear of them (cp. Chamberlain, *These fragile outposts*, pp. 248–51).

[4] While the Cape Cod Highlands are certainly not champaign country, open and level, B. B. Chamberlain says 'The plains of Eastham are mostly as flat as we should expect plains to be' (ibid. p. 129), so that Archer's description would apply from Nauset southwards only.

[5] Archer's woody islands have unfortunately disappeared. Nauset Island is shown inshore by Champlain (*Works*, ed. Biggar, I, p. lxxv). Webbs Island, cedar-covered, 5 to 9 miles S.E. of Chatham, was early deforested and swept away (prominent in map of New England, c. 1717 (Woodworth and Wigglesworth, *Geography and geology*, p. 7; Chamberlain, p. 131), with three small sandbanks ('The Seal Island') off its southern end John Seller, 'A mapp of New England' (State 1, J.C.B. and B.L., 1676; State 2, L. of C., 1680) shows a group of five islands, three close inshore, which B. B. Chamberlain (pp. 254–5) is inclined to accept as the lost islands.

[6] Monomoy Point, and the turning of it by Gosnold, is a problem. In modern times it is eroding on the west and building up on the east (Newton E. Chute, *Geology of the coast between Point Gammon and Monomoy Point* (1939), but such action has been punctuated

the sudden into shoale water, yet well quitted our selues thereof.[1] This breach wee called Tuckers Terror, vpon his expressed feare. The Point we named Point Care, hauing passed it wee bore vp againe with the Land, and in the night came with it anchoring in eight fadome, the ground good.[2] The seuenteenth, appeared many breaches round about vs, so as wee continued that day without remooue.

The eighteenth, being faire we sent forth the Boat to sound ouer a Breach, that in our course lay of another Point, by vs called Gilberts Point; who returned vs foure, five sixe and seuen fadome over.[3] Also a Discouery of Diuers Ilands which after prooued to bee Hils and

(margin notes) Tuckers Terror. Point Care.

(margin note) Gilberts Point.

(margin note) Diuers Ilands.

---

by devastating storms. Champlain's sketch (*Works*, I, pl. LXXVII) shows a long barrier beach curving round Chatham Harbor and Stage Harbor, but lying close inshore, but his text (pp. 407–8, 421) speaks instead of a sandy point extending S.S.E. for nearly 3 leagues and implying Monomoy Point already existed, though somewhat to the E. of its present position. *The Atlantic Neptune*, III (1781), pl. 29 (J.C.B. 116), has already a Cape Malabar or Sandy Point extending southwards 7 or 8 miles. We might guess the present southern tip of Monomoy Point (41° 33′ N, 70° 12′ W) was the highest position where a change of course to the W. could be made, and 12 leagues from the northern tip of Cape Cod a reasonable estimate. The main thesis in Gookin and Barbour, *Gosnold*, is that the 12 leagues should be measured from the tip of Monomoy Point, thus bringing *Concord* round Nantucket to the S. and allowing her to sail through Muskeget Channel between Muskeget I. and Chappaquiddick I. This is argued with skill and persistence, but absence of all mention of Nantucket and the unlikelihood that Archer referred to Monomoy Point as part of Cape Cod are weaknesses which may well be fatal. Here it is assumed Gosnold would enter Nantucket by the shortest route, as Champlain seems to do.

[1] *The English Pilot* (1706), pl. 11, shows a clear channel at 6 to 7 fathoms round its somewhat dubious representation of its Webbs Island–Monomoy Point–Seale Island complex between 41° 35′ and 41° 45′, but *The Atlantic Neptune*, III (1781), pl. 29 (J.C.B. 116), would place such a channel farther S. at 41° 26′. On U.S.C. & G.S. 1209 [now 13237] Pollock Rip Channel (41° 34′ N, 69° 55′ W) has 5 fathoms deepening to nearly 20 fathoms in Butler's Hole to the southwest, but is considered a dangerous entry. Since Champlain entered safely, without undue difficulty, in 1605, we might estimate there was sufficient water for a safe entry between about 41° 35′ and 41° 40′. If this is so Point Care would have been the southern tip of Monomoy Point, and Tuckers Terror a shoal somewhat to the east of it. Point Care has the obvious meaning of a place 'to take care' but it might also have been a pun of the name of a member of the company called Carey or Carew, while Tucker, of Tucker's Terror, was evidently named from the alarmed lookout man who panicked when he saw breaking water ahead.

[2] The land which they again approached was the mainland west of Stage Harbor, probably between it and Bass River, anchoring (if depths are comparable with this at present) about 4 miles south of Port Dennis in 6–8 fathoms. This was probably before nightfall on the 16th. On the 17th observations of the many 'breaches' in view to the south and west were made.

[3] Gilberts Point is most probably Point Gammon, 41° 36′ 30″ (his own figure of 41° 40′ is thus exceptionally accurate if this is so). The 'breach' sounded out before approaching now comprises Gazelle Rock, Senator Shoal, and Bishop and Clerks, permanent features of the Nantucket Sound, though probably modified in outline in course of time. Point Gammon now appears as a low extension of land into the sea.

Hummocks, distinct within the Land.[1] This day there came vnto the ships side diuers Canoas; the Indians apparelled as aforesaid, with Tobacco and Pipes steeled with Copper, Skins, artificiall strings and other trifles to barter, one had hanging about his necke a plate of rich Copper in length a foot, in breadth halfe a foot for a brest-plate, the Eares of all the rest had Pendants of Copper.[2] Also one of them had his face ouer painted,[3] and his head stucke with feathers in manner of a Turkey Cocks traine:[4] These are more timerous then those of the Savage Rocke, yet very theeuish.

The nineteenth, we passed ouer the breach of Gilberts Point in foure or fiue fadome, and anchored a league or somewhat more beyond it; betweene the last two Points are two leagues, the interim, along shoale water, the latitude here is 41. degrees two third parts.[5]

[1] Their perspective would apparently be towards the land between Hyannis Point and, possibly, Suconnesset Point on Upper Cape Cod.

[2] Their Indian contacts were likely to have been a Nauset band (though conceivably a fishing party from Narragansett Bay). No indication of numbers is given to enable a calculation of the size of the dug-out canoes to be made. The preparedness of the Indians to trade indicates previous contact with Europeans but none is documented for this area after Verrazzano (1524), but pre-contact trade in wampum as well as copper is stressed in Salwen, p. 166. Tobacco, dried leaves of *Nicotiana rustica*, may also indicate other trading contacts as do the pipes. Pipes, the mouthpieces of which were strengthened (steeled) with thin sheet copper, do not appear to be represented elsewhere. The skins were evidently few in number or were not considered valuable (so did not include beaver in any quantity). The manufactured 'strings' are not identifiable; they may have included dyed cordage adorned with stones, mussel pearls, or copper beads, or even porcupine quills: 'other trifles' does not suggest any specific objects but may have included dried fish or meat. This is the earliest copper gorget or breastplate met with in New England: examples in brass from the Fall River site (Willoughby, *Antiquities* (1935), pp. 233, 235, fig. 126h) and in copper (cut by an iron knife, in Peabody Museum, Harvard University) are thought to be later. Driver and Massey (A.P.S., *Transactions*, XLVII, pt. 2 (1957), p. 345) do not regard such plates as viable armour. Gorgets were worn by Carolina Algonquian Indians in 1585 and were believed to be in demand as trade goods by them in 1602 (cp. Quinn, *Roanoke voyages*, I (1955), 102, 438–40, *England and the discovery of America*, pp. 410–13). They were often later cut from copper cauldrons. Ear-pendants of copper have, also, not been met with earlier.

[3] Face-painting was common (see pp. 101–2; Willoughby, *Antiquities*, p. 282; Rainey, 'Compilation', p. 18) but the distinction between painting and tattooing (also common) is not made here.

[4] The chief has put on his head-dress of upright, turkey feathers, the earliest to be distinguished in this way (cp. Willoughby, *Antiquities*, p. 281).

[5] By the 19th sufficient soundings had been made to indicate what was probably a safe route westward into Nantucket Sound and then northward towards the mainland. Though from Monomoy Point to Point Gammon is more than 2 leagues (15 m. WNW), the latitude given is only about 4 minutes too high, but a course East by South from a position something less than three miles from Point Gammon would bring them back along the coast perhaps towards Stage Harbor. It is tempting to amend his reading to 'West and by South', since this would make sense of what has been a crucial passage, and since there was little point in returning eastward along the coast. A slip or misprint of this nature could easily have occurred.

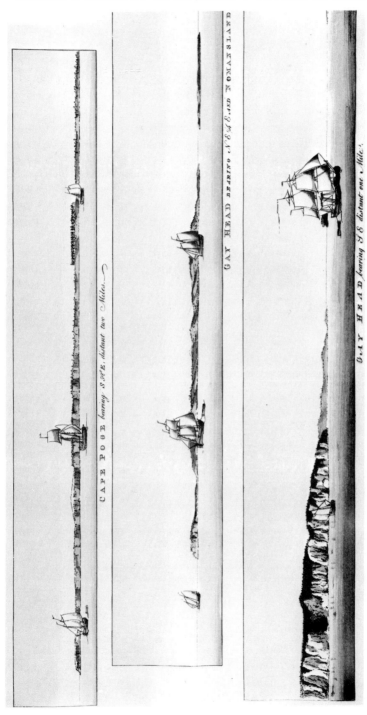

Fig. 4. Profiles of Cape Poge and Gay Head, 1776.

Pengwins   The twentieth, by the ships side we there killed Pengwins,[1] and saw
many sculs of fish. The Coast from Gilberts Point to the supposed Iles
lyeth East and by South. Here also we discoured two Inlets[2] which
might promise fresh water, inwardly whereof we perceiued much
smoake, as though some population had there beene: This Coast is very
full of people, for that as we trended the same Sauages still runne along
the shoare, as men much admiring at vs.

The one and twentieth, we went coasting from Gilberts Point to the
supposed Iles, in tenne, nine, eight, seuen, and six fadome close aboord
the shoare, and that depth lyeth a league off. A little from the supposed
Iles appeared vnto vs an opening, with which we stood iudging it to
bee the end of that which Captaine Gosnoll descrieth from Cape Cod,
and as hee thought to extend some thirtie or more miles in length, and
finding there but three fadomes a league off, we omitted to make
further discouerie of the same, calling it Shole-hope.[3]

From this opening the Mayne lyeth South-west, which coasting
along[4] we saw[5] a disinhabited Iland which so afterwards appeared vnto
Marthaes   vs: we bore with it, and named it Marthaes Vineyard, from Shole-hope
Vineyard.   it is eight leagues in circuit,[6] the Iland is fiue miles, and hath 41. degrees
and one quarter of latitude:[7] the place most pleasant; for the two and
twentieth, we went ashoare, and found it full of Wood, Vines,

---

[1] Penguins are Great Auks (see p. 162); 'sculs' again are schools.

[2] The two inlets, while not identifiable, could have been Cotuit Bay and New
Harbor.

[3] The point at which they found only 3 fathoms in depth (and which they named
Shole-Hope – again Shallow Haven) is not identifiable from modern charts.

[4] The coasting is likely to have taken *Concord* westward. The depths are right for
a short cruise round Poponesset Beach and the broken coast between there and Woods
Hole, together with a hazy view of Martha's Vineyard to the south, made up the 'Mayne'
and revealed the opening of Vineyard Haven. He adds to Brereton's information on what
Gosnold saw from the Barnstable Ridge (p. 146), namely an estimate of a thirty-mile
shoreline to the south of the supposed channel.

[5] It is necessary to interpolate a change of course to the southward, and not continued
coasting to the west. A turn across the opening to the S.E. seems essential if the sequence
adopted hereafter is correct.

[6] If Shole Hope is at 41° 36′ N, 70° 16′ W, then a circuit of eight leagues (Brereton
says 'not aboue sixe or seauen leagues from the maine' westward and then gradually
working round to the east would equate with Brereton on their sailing 'almost all the points
of the compasse' (p. 147). The location of an insular Cape Poge fits the picture of a search
for the southern shore of the supposed channel into the 'Mayne' which Vineyard Haven
seemed to be.

[7] Cape Poge (41° 25′ 24″ N, 70° 27′ W) best fits the first 'Marthaes Vineyard'. See
pp. 500–2 below. Gookin and Barbour, *Gosnold* suggest the 'Martha' is from Gosnold's
daughter, Martha, and possibly his mother-in-law Martha Golding (p. 133). The
'Vineyard' is from the grapes found on shore.

Gooseberie bushes, Hurtberies, Raspices, Eglentine, &c.[1] Heere we had Cranes, Hearnes, Shoulers Geese, and diuers other Birds[2] which there at that time vpon the Cliffes being sandie with some Rockie stones, did breed and had young.[3] In this place we saw Deere, heere we rode in eight fathome neere the shoare, where wee tooke great store of Cod, as before at Cape Cod, but much better.[4]

The three and twentieth wee weyed,[5] and towards night came to Anchor at the Northwest part of this Iland,[6] where the next morning offered vnto vs fast running thirteene Sauages apparelled as aforesaid, and armed with Bowes and Arrowes without any feare. They brought Tobacco, Deere skins and some sodden fish. These offered themselues vnto vs in great familiaritie, who seemed to be well conditioned. They came more rich in Copper then any before.[7] This Iland is sound, and hath no danger about it.

The foure and twentieth, we set saile and doubled the Cape[8] of

[1] Plant descriptions are vague, wood being probably simply undergrowth; vines, creeping plants, while raspberries, whortleberries and eglantine are likely to have been first guesses. He becomes more specific on the vegetation later (p. 128), since many plants were now only coming into leaf.

[2] Cranes, herons and geese appear below: Shoveller Duck, *Spatula clypeata* L., was in migration northward at just this time (Forbush and May, *Birds*, pp. 68–9).

[3] 21–22 April (1–2 May by modern reckoning) is early for seabirds to nest and hatch young for this area at present (cp. *Birds*, pp. 15–18).

[4] For deer see p. 163. *Concord* could ride comfortably at 8 fathoms, according to the modern chart, off the north shore of Cape Poge, the Des Barres chart showing 6 to 7 fathoms (*Atlantic Neptune*, III, pl. 31 (J.C.B. 116)), from which seabirds could be seen breeding on the cliff and from which cod could be caught on lines.

[5] Archer is describing a course along the north coast of the main island, to which the name Martha's Vineyard was then extended. The walk round Cape Poge Island on May 22 (pp. 500–2) would make it evident that this island, Chappaquiddick (if then separate) and the main island to the west were all probably insular and that the first assumption that they made up a mainland was mistaken. There is no need to assume any deliberate confusion (cf. Gookin and Barbour, pp. 128–30) in the extension of the name to the larger island, dominated by East Chop and West Chop as they proceeded westward, though making a diversion on the way (see p. 149) to the northern side of the channel, not noted by Archer.

[6] An anchorage in or off Lambert's Cove would provide good holding once West Chop had been passed (Brereton, p. 149, might indicate they anchored off West Chop). By this time Gosnold would have made a major and unfavourable discovery, namely that he was passing through a southwest trending passage (Vineyard Haven) not into the mainland but between two groups of islands.

[7] The Indians of Martha's Vineyard formed a distinct group though they could be reckoned as part of the Pockanoket tribe. The curiosity and the spontaneous gifts of tobacco, deerskins, and boiled fish were those apposite to visiting strangers and were not indications that they wished to trade. The emphasis on the richness if the copper they had, however, indicated that they were involved in the complex of operations (p. 109) connected with this metal. For additional information, culled in 1611, see p. 479 below.

[8] 'doubling' the Cape might suggest Gosnold came from the south (as some have argued) but its prominence in Vineyard Haven at the time justifies the expression.

Douer-cliffe-[1] sound.

another Iland next vnto it,[2] which wee called Douer Cliffe, and then came into a faire Sound, where wee roade all night, the next morning wee sent off our Boate to discouer another Cape, that lay betweene vs and the Mayne, from which were a ledge of Rockes a mile into the Sea, but all aboue water, and without danger, we went about them, and came to Anchor in eight fadome, a quarter of a mile from the shoare in one of the stateliest Sounds that euer I was in. This called wee Gosnolls Hope; the North banke whereof is the Mayne, which stretcheth East and West. This Iland Captaine Gosnoll called Elizabeths Ile, where we determined our abode: the distance betweene euery of these Ilands is, viz. from Marthaes Vineyard to Douer Cliffe, halfe a league over the Sound, thence to Elizabeths Ile one league distant. From Elizabeths Ile vnto the Mayne is foure leagues.[3] On the North side neere adioyning vnto the Iland Elizabeth, is an Ilet in compasse halfe a myle full of Cedars, by me called Hills Hap,[4] to the Northward of which in the mouth of an opening of the Mayne appeareth another the like, that I called Haps Hill, for that I hope much hap may be expected from it.[5]

Gosnolls Hope.

Elizabeths Ile.

Hills Hap.

Haps Hill.

    The fiue and twentieth, it was that we came from Gosnolls Hope. The six and twentieth, we trimmed and fitted vp our Shallop.[6] The seuen and twentieth, there came vnto vs an Indian and two women; the one we supposed to be his Wife, the other his Daughter, both cleane

---

[1] Gay Head stood out very much farther than at present (erosion and clay removal having been elements in this). Its prominence from the N shows in the profile in *Atlantic Neptune*, II (1780), (J.C.B. 127(3)) indicates this. The process is described by Johnson, *New England-Acadian shoreline*, pp. 403–4, and B. B. Chamberlain, *These fragile outposts*, p. 17, who remarks on the appositeness of the name 'Douer Cliffe' since Gay Head is also (if more highly coloured in its clays) of the same Cretaceous deposits as the Dover region.

[2] Archer emphasizes the insular character of Gay Head which would appear more likely from Elizabeths Isle. The half-a-league between Martha's Vineyard and Dover Cliff would represent the present Menemsha Bight (approx. 1 mile across), suggesting the present barrier beach was then absent or incipient only.

[3] The discovery and naming of Elizabeths Isle (Cuttyhunk–Nashawena) is discussed below pp. 503–4. From these the distance across Buzzards Bay to Gooseberry Neck from the western tip of modern Cuttyhunk is about 4½ miles: it may have been wider then owing to subsequent changes in the coastline.

[4] Hills Hap = Hill's Luck (or Fortune), probably being names for the lookout (cp. Haps Hill = Luck's Hill, his punning name (below p. 130)). The islet was Penikese, 41° 27' N,.70° 55' W.

[5] Hap's Hill was likely to have been West Island, which he would pick up at approximately lat. 41° 35', long. 70° 50', an effective landmark for the Acushnet River entrance and so a promise of a river access to the interior.

[6] Unmentioned since her use in Cape Cod Bay, she probably had been disassembled and, when employed again, it was with a fitted keel (Brereton, p. 130).

and straite bodied, with countenance sweet and pleasant. To these the Indian gave heedfull attendance for that they shewed them in much familiaritie with our men, although they would not admit of any immodest touch.

The eight and twentieth we entred counsell about our abode and plantation,[1] which was concluded to be in the West part of Elizabeths Iland. The North-east thereof running from out our ken. The South and North standeth in an equall Parallel. This Iland in the Westerside admitteth some Increekes, or sandie Coues, so girded, as the water in some places of each side meeteth,[2] to which the Indians from the Mayne doe oftentimes resort for fishing of Crabs. There is eight fadome very neere the shoare, and the latitude here is 41. degrees 10. minutes, the breadth from Sound to Sound in the Wester part is not passing a mile

Elizabeths Ile. in 41. degrees 10. minutes described.

[1] Modern Cuttyhunk and Nashawena made up the 1602 Elizabeths Isle. The decision to settle was probably based on grounds (1) of the favourable position of the island for further reconnaissance; (2) its central position for trade with the Pockanoket (though they would not have visited it in the winter); (3) for collection of cedar and sassafras from neighbouring sources. The choice of a site on an islet on a lake (instead of on the hill rising to 154 ft in the northeast of Cuttyhunk or comparable hills near the southern shore of Nashawena) was probably taken for its comparative ease of defence; its supply of fresh water (the Pond not yet having become brackish); the existence of timber on the islet; the ease with which boulders and timbers could be hauled over to the beach to the side of the Pond and thence to the islet; the probable intention to construct, eventually, some sort of drawbridge from the fort to the shore of the Pond.

The case for the union of the two islands, Cuttyhunk and Nashawena, separated by the narrow Canapitsit Channel, is a strong one. They are shown joined in *The English pilot. The fourth book* (1706), but separated later in the century (*American Neptune*, III (1781), pl. 29). Woodworth and Wigglesworth (*Geography and geology*, p. 318) regarded their earlier union as probable; Amelie F. Emerson (*Early history of Naushon Island*, p. 46) considered it as an inevitable deduction from the 1602 accounts. She estimated the circumference of both islands as between 12 and 14 miles (length $5\frac{1}{2}$ m, average width $\frac{3}{4}$ m. ranging from 600 to 2,000 yards). See also E. R. Mayhew, ed. *Martha's Vineyard*, pp. 155–6. An alternative view, that the 1602 island was Naushon appears in H. C. Wilson and W. C. Carr, 'Gosnold's Elizabeth's Isle; Cuttyhunk or Naushon?', *The American Neptune*, XXXIII (1973), 131–145, which is ingenious but unsuccessful.

Concord could anchor in from 7 to 12 fathoms, in a somewhat exposed anchorage, in Cuttyhunk Bay, close to the northern shore of the island. She would there have been accessible to the building operations in Gosnold Pond. She could, however, have worked her way between Cuttyhunk and Penikese to Cuttyhunk Harbor. But Archer gives a strong impression she remained at anchor to the north of the spit of land which lay between the sea and Gosnold Pond.

[2] 'increeks' were barrier beaches with breaches on the West part of Cuttyhunk (which now almost enclose the Pond), and those making up the long spit extending from Cuttyhunk Harbor towards Nashawena, some being apparently already covered at high tide (cp. fig. 29 and U.S.G.S. Cuttyhunk Quadrangle).

The position for Elisabeths Isle is actually 41° 25′ N, 70° 15′ W. The closeness of the estimation (41° 10′ N) gives confidence in other latitudes given. Here continuous observation was possible.

at most, altogether vnpeopled and disinhabited. It is ouer-growne with Wood and Rubbish,[1] viz. Okes, Ashes,[2] Beech, Wal-nut, Weech-hasle,[3] Sassafrage, and Cedars, with diuers other of vnknowne names. The Rubbish is wild Peaze, young Sassafrage, Cherie trees, Vines, Eglentine, Gooseberie bushes, Hawthorne,[4] Honisuckles,[5] with others of like qualitie. The herbs and Roots are Strawberies, Raspis, Ground Nuts, Alexander,[6] Surrin,[7] Tansie,[8] &c. without count. Touching the fertilitie of the soyle by our owne experience made, we found it to be excellent for sowing some English pulse it sprowted out in one fortnight almost halfe a foot. In this Iland is a stage[9] or Pond of fresh water, in circuit two miles, on the one side not distant from the Sea thirtie yards,[10] in the Centre whereof is a Rockie Islet, contayning neere

Fort begun. an Acre of ground full of wood,[11] on which wee beganne our Fort and

---

[1] Brereton's list of trees and plants (below pp. 160–4, where identifications are given) does not include the following names mentioned by Archer here; ash, witch-hazel, eglantine, hawthorn, honeysuckle, alexander and tansie.

[2] White Ash, *Fraxinus americana* L., Black Ash, *F. nigra* Marsh, and Red Ash, *F. pennsylvanica* Marsh (C. S. Sargent, *Manual of the trees of North America*, 2nd ed. (1944), pp. 841–6).

[3] Witch-hazel see p. 304 below.

[4] Hawthorn, *Crataegus*, numerous species and most abundant in eastern North America (C. S. Sargent, *Manual of the trees of North America*, 2nd ed. (1922) pp. 397–453).

[5] The two species most probably present are Blue Fly-honeysuckle, *Lonicera caerulea* Linn. and American Fly-honeysuckle, *L. canadensis* Marsh (Britton, *Manual*, 2nd ed. (1905), p. 876).

[6] Alexanders, Scotch Lovage, *Ligusticum scothicum* (Britton, *Manual*, 2nd ed. (1905), p. 683 and Fernald and Kinsey, *Edible Plants of Eastern North America* (1958) p. 295). This might have been confused with Seacoast Angelica, *Coelopleurum lucidum* (Fernald and Kinsey, p. 296).

[7] 'surrin', sorrel see p. 164 below.

[8] Tansy, *Tanacetum vulgare* Linn. was used as a condiment and cooked vegetable in England (Fernald and Kinsey, *Edible Plants* (1958), p. 362). Britton, *Manual*, 2nd ed. (1905), pp. 1016–17, says that *T. vulgare* was introduced from Europe. Could this have been like the Huron Tansy, *T. Huronense* Hutt. which is found in Maine and might perhaps have been seen in Massachusetts.

[9] 'stage', a misprint for 'stagne' (Lat. *stagnum*), a pool.

[10] The breaching of the barrier beach to the northwest of Gosnold Pond probably first during storms and later permanently, made the water first brackish and now salt. The barrier beach on the southwest has, however, built up substantially. The island, Gosnold Islet, is a little less than an acre in extent, and has for long been completely deforested. Woodward and Wigglesworth (p. 318) say, correctly, that the dimensions of the Pond given here are too large for the present body of water 'but the lake may have extended considerably farther north in 1602, the barrier beach on that side having since been driven in by erosion'. *The Atlantic Neptune*, III (1781), pls. 29, 32 (J.C.B. 116), shows a wider and unbroken barrier beach on the northwest and a longer and continuous pond (it is now divided).

[11] Woodworth and Wigglesworth, pp. 308–19, record the complete deforestation of the island. Visitors from 1797 onward found it treeless (p. 505).

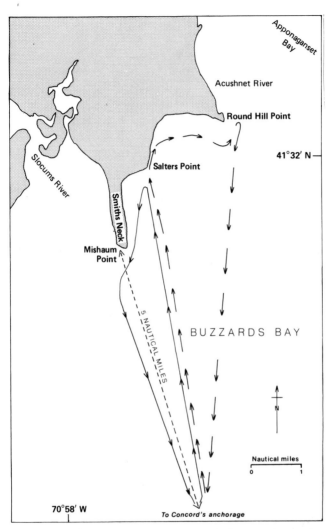

Fig. 5. Buzzard's Bay: the shallop's or light horseman's course.

place of abode, disposing it selfe so fit for the same. These Indians call Gold *Wassador*, which argueth there is thereof in the Countrey.[1]

The nine and twentieth, we laboured in getting of Sassafrage, rubbishing[2] our little Fort or Islet, new keeling our shallop; and making a Punt or Flat bottome Boate to passe to and fro our Fort ouer the fresh water,[3] the powder of Sassafrage in twelve houres cured one of our Company that had taken a great Surfet by eating the bellies of Dog-fish,[4] a very delicious meate.

The thirtieth, Captaine Gosnoll with diuers of his company went vpon pleasure in the shallop towards Hills Hap to view it,[5] and the Sandie Coue, and returning brought with him a Canoa that foure Indians had there left being fled away for feare of our English, which we brought into England.[6]

The one and thirtieth, Captaine Gosnoll desirous to see the Maine, because of the distance, hee set sayle ouer; where comming to anchor, went ashoare[7] with certaine of his companie, and immediately there presented vnto him men women and children, who with all curteous

[1] The form is taken from Lane's 1585 narrative, showing Archer to be familiar with (or to have had with him) Hakluyt's *Principal navigations*, III (1600), which Brereton also may have used (p. 203 below). The sound heard may have been similar. Natick has *wosittae*, bright, glistening (Trumbull, *Natick dictionary*, p. 193), agreeing with Cree *wasitao*, 'it is bright' (personal communication from P. L. Barbour). While the word may well have been used for copper, it had no connection with gold.

[2] 'Rubbishing' meant removing undergrowth (including sassafras roots and wood), and clearing stumps of trees to prepare a foundation for the fort. Whether or not a cellar of stone was constructed is discussed pp. 504–9 below.

[3] The use of a keel, and its replacement through damage, adds to our knowledge of the design of the shallop. This is missed in W. A. Baker, *Sloops and shallops* (1966), p. 19, though he thought some strengthening of keel and gunwales might have been done. The building of a flat-bottomed punt, to carry bulky materials to the islet, was an indication that the ships' carpenters were not fully employed on construction. It is possible that some prefabricated materials, doors, windows and the like, for the post were carried on shipboard.

We must assume that a forge and sawpit had been established on shore. If *Concord* was still riding off the north side of the Pond's barrier beach, these were probably situated there (she may have been eased into Cuttyhunk Harbor but this nowadays would be a somewhat risky proceeding though it could be done).

[4] Powdered sassafras root as a cure for colic is not well established.

[5] The Penikese expedition was primarily to cut cedar (some of it afterwards brought to England), and collect sassafras. Since deforestation the island has almost certainly become much smaller. His 'Sandie Coue' probably lay between the arms of the island (if it has retained its modern outline).

[6] This dugout canoe, brought to England, is not elsewhere mentioned. It must not have been of very large size (cp. H. P. Beck, *The American Indian as sea fighter*, pp. 10–11). The Indians must have escaped by swimming.

[7] Some of the approaches to the broad channel of Buzzards Bay would previously have been sounded so that *Concord* could be assured of sufficient water, though Gosnold probably used the light-horseman to approach the shore. Buzzards Bay later in the century

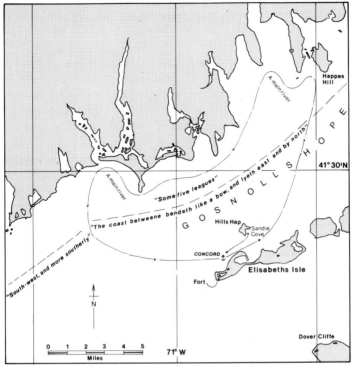

Fig. 6. Buzzard's Bay: *Concord*'s course.

kindnesse entertayned him, giuing him certaine skinnes of wilde beasts, which may be rich Furres, Tobacco, Turtles, Hempe, artificiall Strings coloured, Chaines, and such like things as at the instant they had about them. These are a faire conditioned people.[1] On all the Sea coast along The people.

---

developed a bad reputation, being described (from experiences of *c.* 1680) as 'a very foul Bay' (*The English pilot. The fourth book* (1706), p. 18). Archer (not Brereton) was present on this excursion. *Concord* is likely to have been taken NNE across Buzzards Bay to Haps Hill (above), probably West Island, just beyond the Acushnet River entrance and a useful landmark for it, so that the 'Maine' would be in the vicinity of Clarks Point or Sconticut Point.

[1] The group of Indian families may have had a village nearby (since he does not mention houses) and had come to the shore to welcome the strange ship. Their lavish gifts without, it seems, insistence on trade, compare with the limited ceremonial gift-making already experienced at Cuttyhunk (p. 122). It seems possible they were Narragansett, rather than Pockanoket. They had already established some degree of dominance over the Pockanoket (centred round modern Bristol) and their collecting area overlapped with theirs (cp. M. Robbins, 'Indians of the Old Colony', Mass. Arch. Soc., *Bulletin* XVII (1956), 59–74;

we found Mussell shells that in colour did represent Mother-of-pearle, but not hauing meanes to dredge, could not apprehend further knowledge thereof.[1] This Maine is the goodliest Continent that ever we saw, promising more by farre then we any way did expect:[2] for it is replenished with faire fields, and in them fragrant Flowers, also Medowes, and hedged in with stately Groues, being furnished also with pleasant Brookes, and beautified with two maine Riuers that (as wee iudge) may haply become good Harbours, and conduct vs to the hopes men so greedily doe thirst after.[3] In the mouth of one of these Inlets or Rivers lieth that little Ile before mentioned, called Happes Hill, from which unto the Westermost end of the Maine, appearing where the other Inlet is,[4] I account some fiue leagues, and the Coast betweene bendeth like a Bow, and lyeth East and by North.[5] Beyond these two Inlets[6] we might perceiue the Mayne to beare vp South-west, and more

Goodly Countrey.

H M. Chapin, *Sachems of the Narragansetts* (1931), pp. 6–9). Emphasis on their physique, manners and temperament suggest the latter (cp. Roger Williams, *A key* (1643)). On their expansion at the expense of the Pockanokets see Salwen, p. 171. Unidentified furs, tobacco, turtles do not leave room for further comment. The 'strings' (and presumably the 'artificial strings') are discussed above, p. 97. The Hemp is of more interest. Indian Hemp in the varieties *Apocynum cannabium* L. and *A. sibiricum* Jacq. was most commonly used for nets, lines, ropes, and twined baskets (Fernald, *Gray's manual* (1950), p. 1169; Salwen, p. 162). Among other fibrous plants, Leatherwood, *Dirca palustris* L., provided tough bark for thongs, as did Basswood, *Tilia americana* L. (Fernald, *Gray's manual*, pp. 1044, 999; Gleason, II, 572, 523).

[1] The Mussel shells were from the common mussel (cp. p. 165).

[2] The varied and effective coastline to be seen on the voyage proved a legitimate pointer towards later, long-term settlement, more so than the shores previously examined. This character much of it has retained.

[3] Archer's indications are too limited to make wholly positive claims for the locations reached. Once *Concord* was in the main channel and proceeding northeastwards up Buzzards Bay West Island stands out as a landmark. The perspective between the Elizabeth Islands and the mainland would appear too close as he proceeded up the Bay, so that he would gradually become aware that this was not a strait but an entry into the land, only.

[4] West Island would stand out as a guide to position. Gosnold would first see the Acushnet River estuary receding into the land to the N. As he neared the island the narrow gap between it and Sconticut Neck, indicating a passage into the interior, would become evident, though only after passing Clark Point would the direction of the river, to the northwest, become apparent. It is not clear that he entered the river, but he is likely to have put ashore on either Sconticut Neck or West island to assess the quality of the land at close quarters.

[5] As he stood off from West Island the impression that the coast 'bendeth like a Bow, and lyeth East and by North' became evident, giving an effect of a shore, divided by many inlets but generally curving round from northeast to southwest.

[6] His major inlet some 15 miles southward may have been round Sakonnet Point. It seems likely that if he sailed down midchannel to a point some 6 or 7 miles south of his accustomed anchorage north of Cuttyhunk he would have seen the point and its turning clearly enough to assume the existence of another major inlet, in this case Narragansett

Southerly.[1] Thus with this taste of Discouery, we now contented our selues, and the same day made returne vnto our Fort, time not permitting more sparing delay.

The first of Iune, we employed our selues in getting Sassafrage, and the building of our Fort.[2] The second, third and fourth, we wrought hard to make readie our house for the prouision to bee had ashore to sustaine vs till our ships returne. This day from the Mayne came to our ships side a Canoa, with their Lord or chiefe Commander,[3] for that they made little stay only pointing to the Sunne, as in signe that the next day hee would come and visit vs, which hee did accordingly.

The fifth, wee continued our labour, when there came vnto vs ashoare from the Mayne fiftie Sauages, stout and lustie men with their Bowes and Arrowes, amongst them there seemed to be one of authoritie, because the rest made an inclining respect vnto him. The ship was at their comming a league off,[4] and Captaine Gosnoll aboord, and so likewise Captaine Gilbert, who almost neuer went ashoare, the

---

Bay, Verrazzano's *Refugio*, which it was his principal object to find. This cannot be stated with absolute assurance since Archer's data is limited and his assessment of distances not necessarily to be relied on. Nevertheless, from a point in mid-channel south of West Island or the mouth of the Acushnet R. a direct course of 15 miles would bring him within sight of Sakonnet Point and enable him to ascertain that another major inlet existed immediately beyond it.

[1] The southwestward trend of the coast from point to point – Smiths Neck, Gooseberry Neck, Sakonnet Point – would be clearly visible (already Sakonnet Point could have been seen from the highest point of Cuttyhunk Island in conditions of moderate visibility). From his turning point he ought to have been able to see something of Point Judith (15 to 21 miles away and well to the south). If he worked well out to sea on his way back to Cuttyhunk he might even have caught from the crow's-nest a glimpse of Block Island (though this is purely conjectural). We can take the point that the mainland at extreme distance 'bore up more Southerly'.

[2] Preoccupation with the 'house' (above pp. 128–9) indicated that Gosnold contemplated getting *Concord* on her way as early as possible, probably to secure her return by the autumn. Otherwise he could have contemplated a fuller and more leisurely review of the mainland shore.

[3] The sachem's regalia revealed his status. If he was the Pockanoket (Wampanoag) ruling Sachem he was probably the father of the well-known Ousamequin (Massasoit), but it is possible he was Canonicus (b. *c.* 1565), sachem of the Narragansett (at this time probably in association with his brother Mascus), (cp. H. M. Chapin, *Sachems of the Narragansetts*, pp. 5–9). Though he may have been a lesser dignitary, the sustained activities of the Englishmen, especially in building on the island, would have probably required the attention of one or other major sachems.

[4] *Concord* was riding in mid-channel, about halfway between Cuttyhunk and the mainland, having put ashore Archer and some others but having most of the company on board, 23 out of his 32 men (preparatory, perhaps, to making a further exploration to the south). With Gosnold was Captain Bartholomew Gilbert, hitherto unmentioned but commemorated in Gilberts Point (fig. 3), but who is said to have almost never gone ashore. Perhaps the implied sneer is a sign of dissension.

company with me only eight persons. These Indians in hastie manner came towards vs, so as we thought fit to make a stand at an angle betweene the Sea and a fresh water, I mooued my selfe towards him seuen or eight steps, and clapt my hands first on the sides of mine head, then on my breast, and after presented my Musket with a threatning countenance, thereby to signifie vnto them, either a choice of Peace or Warre,[1] whereupon hee vsing me with mine owne signes of Peace, I stept forth and imbraced him, his company then all sate downe in manner like Grey-hounds vpon their heeles with whom my company fell a bartering.[2] By this time Captaine Gosnoll was come with twelue men more from aboord, and to shew the Sauage Seignior that he was our Captaine, we receiued him in a guard, which he passing thorow, saluted the Seignior with ceremonies of our salutations, whereat he nothing mooued or altered himselfe. Our Captaine gaue him a straw Hat and a paire of Kniues, the Hat awhiles hee wore, but the Kniues he beheld with great maruelling, being very bright and sharpe, this our courtesie made them all in loue with vs.[3]

The sixt being raine, we spent idlely aboord.[4] The seuenth, the Seignior came againe with all his troupe as before, and continued with vs the most part of the day, we going to dinner about noone,[5] they sate with vs and did eate of our Bacaleure[6] and Mustard, dranke of our Beere, but the Mustard nipping them in their noses they could not indure: it was a sport to behold their faces made being bitten therewith.

[1] Archer was disconcerted by the arrival of a fleet of canoes with their sachem and 50 men. His action in taking protective precautions (so far as possible) and his diplomatic reactions to the Indians' present show him to have been resourceful (though it is his own account). That the Indians were equipped for trading is evident from their earliest actions after friendly relations had been established.

[2] Driver and Massey, 'Comparative studies', Amer. Phil. Soc., *Transactions*, XLVII (1957), 342–4, indicate that presentation of furs and skins for sale in any quantity (since they required previous processing to make them saleable) suggests that there was already an established coastal trade with Indians and possibly Europeans.

[3] The narrative of the confrontation of the two leaders is well, if briefly, told. The acceptance and brief wearing of the hat was a concession by the chief, whose own headdress (which he may have had to remove) was a sign of his office. The success of the shining knives indicates the continued desire of the Indians to acquire effective iron tools and weapons.

[4] The fort was evidently considered ill equipped for overnight occupation and we must assume the men were rowed out to *Concord*. Had she been anchored in Cuttyhunk Harbor (as is possible if not documented) access to and from her would have been easier.

[5] Dinner was in the open air, with English and Indians mingling freely. Archer's use of 'Seignior' for the sachem indicated he was regarded as the dominant authority in his tribal area.

[6] 'Bacaleure' (Bacalao) was sun-dried cod from Newfoundland. Strong mustard helped to make stale food tolerable.

In time of Dinner the Sauages had stolne a Target wherewith acquainting the Seignior, with feare and great trembling they restored it againe, thinking perhaps we would have beene reuenged for it, but seeing our familiaritie to continue,[1] they fell a fresh to roasting of Crabs, Red Herrings,[2] which were excceding great, ground Nuts,[3] &c. as before. Our Dinner ended, the Seignior first tooke leaue and departed, next all the rest sauing foure that stayed and went into the Wood to helpe vs digge Sassafrage,[4] whom we desired to goe aboord vs, which they refused and so departed.[5]

The eighth wee diuided the victuals, viz. the ships store for England, and that of the Planters, which by Captaine Gilberts allowance could be but six weekes for six moneths, whereby there fell out a countrouersie, the rather, for that some seemed secretly to vnderstand of a purpose Captaine Gilbert had not to returne with supplie of the issue, those goods should make by him to be carried home. Besides, there wanted not ambitious conceits in the mindes of some wrangling and ill disposed persons that ouerthrew the stay there at that time, which vpon consultation thereof had, about fiue dayes after was fully resolved all for England againe.[6] There came in this interim aboord vnto vs, that stayed all night, an Indian, whom wee vsed kindly, and the next day sent ashoare hee shewed himself the most sober of all the rest, wee

Their purpose of stay broken off.

---

[1] Minor misunderstandings over the mustard and the filching of a small target were soon smoothed over since each party was nervous of the other but neither wished to be considered potentially hostile.

[2] Red Herrings imply alewife (or shad) dried to a dark brown colour over a fire in the Indian manner.

[3] Ground nuts may have been *Apios tuberosa* L. (but this may be too far north for it. Fernald and Kinsey, *Edible plants*, pp. 252–5, and Yanovsky, *Food plants*, p. 37, deal with it and with other tuberious plants for which the Indians foraged. Salwen comments on the scarcity of early evidence of wild plant use, p. 162.

[4] The departure of the chief, with his 45 men, and the leaving of 4 others to assist the English with collecting sassafras, suggests some arrangement with Gosnold (made by signs presumably) that they would co-operate in trading, the English promising knives and the like for Indian help as well as for furs in prospect.

[5] The caution of the Indians in showing unwillingness to board might be an indication that there had been earlier kidnappings (but may have been simply fear of entering such a strange contraption).

[6] The division over supplies brings Gilbert out of his obscurity. It seems clear that once the initial exploration was done and the post built, he took over as captain of the *Concord*, while Gosnold reverted to being commander of the land party only. Gilbert offered only 6 weeks' (instead of 6 months') stores, but with the understanding that he could come back within something like that time which, Archer said, the men would not credit. Gilbert was indeed being generous on what could be spared since, in fact, the ship was badly undervictualled and unable to spare more than this amount at most. We may take it that the main division was over going or staying and the decision to go was at least almost unanimous.

held him sent as a Spie. In the morning he filched away our Pot-hookes, thinking he had not done any ill therein;[1] being ashoare wee bid him strike fire, which with an Emerald stone (such as the Glasiers vse, to cut Glasse) he did. It take it to be the very same that in Latine is called *Smiris*, for striking therewith vpon Touch-wood that of purpose hee had, by meane of a mynerall stone vsed therein sparkles proceeded and forth with kindled with making of flame.[2] The ninth, wee continued working on our Store-house for as yet remayned in vs a desired resolution of making stay.[3] The tenth, Captaine Gosnoll fell downe with the ship to the little Ilet of Cedars, called Hills happe, to take in Cedar wood,[4] leauing mee and nine more in the Fort, onely with three meales meate, vpon promise to returne the next day.

The eleuenth, he came not, neither sent, wherevpon I commanded foure of my companie to seeke out for Crabbes, Lobsters, Turtles &c. for sustayning us till the ships returne, which was gone cleane out of sight, and had the winde chopt up at South-west, with much difficulty would shee haue beene able in short time to haue made returne.[5] These foure Purveyers, whom I counselled to keepe together for their better safety diuided themselues, two going one wayes and two another, in search as aforesaid. One of these petie companies was assaulted by foure Indians, who with Arrowes did shoot and hurt one of the two in his side, the other a lusty and nimble fellow, leapt in and cut their Bow-strings whereupon they fled.[6] Being late in the euening, they were driuen to lie all night in the Woods, not knowing the way home thorow

Sauage assault.

---

[1] The first Indian to come on board *Concord* may indeed have been a spy. He could have had previous contact with Europeans. They appear to have overlooked his filching of their pothooks. They may in ordinary usage have been the S-shaped hooks on which pots were hung but were more probably just simply large fish hooks.

[2] Indian strike-a-light techniques appear to have varied somewhat from place to place. 'Smiris' (from a Greek word) is a synonym for emery, given by O.E.D. from 1610, and merely meant a rough-grained stone from which, with another suitable-shaped striker or still harder stone, he could set touchwood (decayed woody matter as tinder) alight. Flannery, *Analysis*, pp. 34-5.

[3] The party in favour of staying was still, under Gosnold's orders, continuing with the construction of the post, which must have been almost completed.

[4] The cedar laden at Penikese was intended at this time for transport to England, not for the fort, and was brought back, though most was apparently consumed as firewood on the return voyage (see p. 207 below).

[5] Gosnold's (or Gilbert's) retention of all food and stores on shipboard shows that he feared mutiny if he divided his resources. It also indicates that he had probably decided to abandon the fort, though he clearly wished to leave it in such shape that it could be subsequently reoccupied.

[6] The Indian attack may have been from a band distinct from that with whom they had formally established trading relations. Its psychological effect on those who expected to be left in the fort may have been a factor in the decision not to stay.

the thicke rubbish, as also the weather somewhat stormie. The want of these sorrowed vs much, as not able to coniecture any thing of them vnlesse very euill.

The twelfth, those two came vnto vs againe, whereat our ioy was encreased, yet the want of our Captaine, that promised to returne, as aforesaid, strooke vs in a dumpish terrour, for that hee performed not the same in the space of almost three dayes. In the meane wee sustayned our selues with Alexander and Sorrell pottage, Ground-nuts and Tobacco, which gaue nature a reasonable content.[1] Wee heard at last, our Captaine[2] to lewre vnto vs,[3] which made such musike as sweeter neuer came vnto poore men.

The thirteenth, beganne some of our companie that before vowed to stay, to make reuolt: whereupon the planters diminishing, all was giuen ouer.[4] The fourteenth, fifteenth, and sixteenth wee spent in getting Sasafrage and fire-wood of Cedar,[5] leauing House and little Fort[6] by ten men in nineteene dayes sufficient made to harbour twenty persons at least with their necessary prouision.

The seuenteenth, we set sayle, doubling the Rockes of Elizabeths Iland, and passing by Douer Cliffe, came to anchor at Marthaes Vineyard being fiue leagues distant from our Fort, where we went ashoare, and had young Cranes, Herneshowes, and Geese, which now were growne to pretie bignesse.[7]

[1] For the commodities see for alexanders p. 128, for sorrel and ground-nuts (of which some were to be found on the island), pp. 163–4.

[2] We do not know whether Gosnold was delayed by rough seas or whether he made a further, unrecorded reconnaissance. It is just possible that he did so, but if he discovered the entrance to Narragansett Bay he made no further use of the discovery (and the balance is probably against his having made the discovery).

[3] Lure, used of the falconer's call to his hawk, but here probably a trumpet call.

[4] Archer's nine men, after their desertion and trouble with the Indians, probably led the resistance to continuing the settlement. If the majority of them refused, this explains why the settling party was reduced from 20 to 12 (p. 159).

[5] The equipping of the fort with supplies of sassafras and cedar (if they were for store and not for freight) indicates that Gosnold planned to return later in the year, or in the following season, so as to place 20 men in the post.

[6] For the 'House and little Fort', see pp. 504–9.

[7] The course homeward is clear enough. From the Cuttyhunk roadstead *Concord* sailed round the W end of the Sow and Pigs shoal, picked up Gay Head and, turning it, anchored off the southern shore E of Nashaquitsa Cliffs, and sending ashore to hunt cranes, herons and geese at what are now Chilmark Pond and Tisbury Great Pond. They were probably then inlets. Barrier beaches, cutting off the ponds from the sea, have built up from the erosion of more than 1,000 feet from Nashaquitsa Cliffs (cp. Woodworth and Wigglesworth, *Geography and geology*, pp. 133–5); beaches were almost complete, apart from one break, when the charts for *The American Neptune*, III (1781), pls 29, 32 (J.C.B. 117) were compiled in 1775–6.

Returne.   The eighteenth, we set sayle and bore for England, cutting off our Shalop,[1] that was well able to land fiue and twenty men, or more, a Boate very necessary for the like occasions. The winds doe raigne most commonly vpon this coast in the Summer time Westerly. In our homeward courses wee obserued the foresaid fleeting weeds to continue till we came within two hundred leagues of Europe.

The three and twentieth of Iuly[2] we came to anchor before Exmouth.[3]

[1] Cutting loose the shallop indicated that superfluous lading (now that a cargo of sassafras and cedar as well as a dugout canoe was on board) was being dispensed with. Archer's praise for the shallop as an instrument for the transport of 25 or more men and so an effective tool for exploration, is valuable (Baker, *Sloops and shallops*, p. 19, found her capacity rather exceptional).

[2] Their arrival after thirty-six days with the help of the westerlies compares favourably with their longer passage outward (pp. 114–16).

[3] From Exmouth, where some of her men and probably part of her cargo were landed, *Concord* went on, possibly to Dartmouth, and then to Portsmouth, Southampton and Weymouth (pp. 159, 205, 211).

CHAPTER II

JOHN BRERETON, *A BRIEFE AND TRVE RELATION OF THE DISCOVERIE OF THE NORTH PART OF VIRGINIA*. 1602

This small book, which went into two editions within a few months on account of its novelty was the first account ever to be published about the region which we now call New England and which is here referred to, for the first time, as 'North Virginia'. The only exception, and it is a partial one is the Verrazzano letter on his 1524 voyage, published first in Italian in 1556. Nearly eighty years later the English expedition under Bartholomew Gosnold went out to attempt to retrace Verrazzano's steps over part of his route, which had brought him to a temporary, safe anchorage and resting place at Narragansett Bay. When Gosnold returned from his voyage on 23 July 1602, he soon found himself involved in a legal tangle with Sir Walter Ralegh out of which he and his companions extricated themselves by promising to dedicate the published narration of the voyage to the holder of the charter of 1584 and this dedication was duly placed in the little volume which followed (pp. 142–4). He had at his disposal a considerable amount of data on the voyage, a detailed account by Gabriel Archer, which has been discussed, and a journal kept by the Reverend John Brereton which could, alternatively, be used. The voyage, it was intended, should be used as a propaganda lever to create a new English drive towards the exploration and colonisation of North America which had lain virtually dormant for fifteen years. The device chosen was that employed by Richard Hakluyt the younger in his first book, *Diuers voyages concerning the discouerie of America*, exactly twenty years before, namely to combine narrative with propaganda, so as to build up a picture of this newly explored part of eastern North America in a much wider context, since Ralegh had already begun to plan a revival of the Roanoke ('South Virginia') project and was inspired to knit in with the new 'North Virginia' exploration. The mystery of its editorship has been discussed (pp. 36–8, 43), but the inspiration was clearly Ralegh's. In these circumstances a short narrative was all that was necessary to introduce the new volume, and Brereton's was chosen for this purpose, duly trimmed to convey in a lucid but severely edited form the essentials of the attempt to explore the land lying between 41 and 43 degrees North. Some 4,000 words was enough. Within this space Brereton, who was probably chaplain to the voyage and also its official recorder conveyed effectively the speed and assurance with which the *Concord* crossed the Atlantic between 26 March and 14 May, passed lightly over the voyage down the southern shore of Maine and into Cape Cod Bay, and then concentrated on the passage to the islands south of Cape Cod, the advantages of which as an advanced trading (and settlement) base were stressed. The choice of Elizabeths Isle (Cuttyhunk–Nashawena) is justified for its central position in relation to the larger islands and to the mainland. The friendliness of the Indians, their potential as a market and the attractiveness of the terrain are highlighted. The abandonment of the post on Elizabeths Isle is placed at the door of the men who refused to stay and is justified cautiously by indicating the small numbers available to man the post. Without overt propaganda, every indication is given that the post might easily be reoccupied and that new explorations would be profitable and also lay a basis for settlement in climatic and environmental circumstances favourable to Englishmen. But if we had Brereton alone, without Archer, we would know much less about the voyage than we do, even if, between them, they have left problems of detail which have not yet wholly been resolved.

The volume then continued, significantly enough, with a brief, up-to-the-minute report of a voyage made on Ralegh's behalf to 'South Virginia' where the emphasis again was on trade, and a cursory and ineffective search for the Lost Colonists of 1587. It was followed by a treatise by Edward Hayes, stressing the merits of settling in latitudes south of those favoured by the French (namely the St Lawrence River) but north of 'South Virginia'. This was not new but was pared down from a longer discourse which Hayes had composed (apparently in association with Christopher Carleill) about 1592, and for which Hakluyt had provided some materials. Hayes was known as the reporter of Gilbert's voyage of 1583 and for long an enthusiast for Newfoundland, which he renounced in this document as unsuitable for settlement. This was thought sufficient to circulate amongst those who might be interested in the revival of English trading and settling on North American shores. It was evidently an immediate success and was soon out of print. The promoters had it reset, and in this second edition doubled its size. The editions were entirely propagandist and were almost totally divorced from the voyage itself. They began with a treatise by the elder Richard Hakluyt, dead since 1591. It was said to have been written in 1585 recommending settlement between 40 and 42 degrees North, and composed as part of the preparations for the Virginia voyage of that year, the precise latitudinal location of whose settlement had evidently not been finalised. Nearly twenty years old, it was partly out of date but contained commonsense advice about the preparation of a settlement, proving that the bias, implicit in the first edition that not merely trading but settlement was intended, was now being intensified. The remaining additions were lists of commodities which had been remarked as growing or obtainable over a wide area of North America in the sixteenth century, by Hernando de Soto (through the narrative of the Gentleman of Elvas), by René de

Laudonnière (from the 1586 history), by Thomas Harriot (from his 1588 pamphlet), and several final pages, perhaps newly written by Richard Hakluyt, perhaps by Hayes with Hakluyt's help, providing some further miscellaneous data on North America with stress being laid on alleged finds of minerals, precious and otherwise, but containing one or two valuable new items. The book in its first edition was a reputable enough attempt to revive English interest in North America by emphasis on the 'North Virginia' voyage and other relevant (or nearly-relevant) material. The second edition was a blatant piece of propaganda, assembling data from sources which were not only out-dated but largely irrelevant to any attempts that might be made to explore 'North Virginia' further or to revive the examination of 'South Virginia'. It aimed at producing support for American settlement but by means which we can perceive as entirely lacking in scruple. Whether we should wholly lay the responsibility on Ralegh or not, the lack of respect for the intelligence of intending investors and settlers was not uncharacteristic of him. The solid and novel item remained the brief, (and on the whole clear and objective) narrative by John Brereton.

———————————

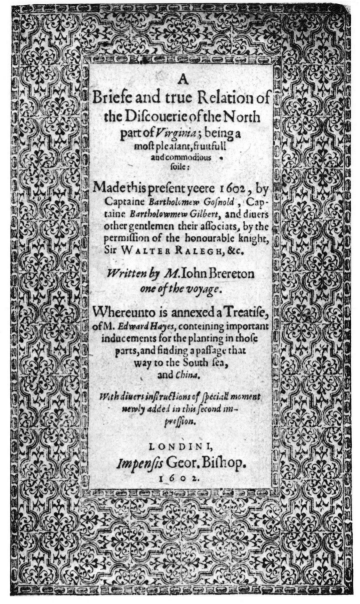

A

Briefe and true Relation of
the Difcouerie of the North
part of *Virginia*; being a
moft pleafant, fruitfull
and commodious
foile:

Made this prefent yeere 1602, by
Captaine *Bartholomew Gofnold*, Captaine *Bartholowmew Gilbert*, and diuers
other gentlemen their affociats, by the
permiffion of the honourable knight,
Sir WALTER RALEGH, &c.

*Written by M.*Iohn Brereton
one of the voyage.

Whereunto is annexed a Treatife,
of M. *Edward Hayes*, conteining important
inducements for the planting in thofe
parts, and finding a paffage that
way to the South fea,
and *China*.

With diuers inftruttions of fpeciall moment
newly added in this fecond im-
preffion.

LONDINI,
Impenfis Geor. Bifhop.
1 6 0 2.

Fig. 7. John Brereton. *A briefe and true relation.* 1602.

2 A BRIEFE AND TRVE RELATION OF THE DIS-COVERIE OF THE NORTH PART OF VIRGINIA;

being a most pleasant, fruitfull and commodious soile: made this present yeere 1602, BY Captaine Bartholomew Gosnold, Captain Bartholomew Gilbert, and diuers other gentlemen their associats, by the permission of the honourable knight, Sir Walter Ralegh, &c. Written by M. Iohn Brereton one of the voyage. Whereunto is annexed a treatise, of M. Edward Hayes, conteining important inducements for the planting in those parts, and finding a passage that way to the South sea, and China. With diuers instructions of speciall moment newly added in this second impression.

LONDINI,

Impensis Geor. Bishop.[1]

1602.

TO THE HONOVRABLE, SIR WALTER RALEGH, KNIGHT, CAPTAINE OF HER Maiesties Guards, Lord Warden of the Stanneries, Lieutenant of Cornwall, and Gouernour of the Isle of Iersey.[2]

[1] The copy text used is that of the second edition in the British Library (303 . d . 27(1)). Fig. 7 shows the title page of the second B.L. copy G 7124. The statement that it is a 'second impression' has confused commentators. It is not a reissue of the first edition with additional matter and therefore an 'impression' but a complete resetting of the first edition and therefore a new edition. The collations with the first edition are made from the John Carter Brown Library copy compared with that in the Huntington Library. The latter shows a few minor variations such as are not unusual between different copies of the same edition, but no substantive differences have been found. Collations of copies in the John Carter Brown Library and the two Huntington Library copies of the second edition have not disclosed variations in readings.

The heading of the first edition reads: 'To the honourable Sir WALTER RALEGH, Knight, *Captaine of her*/ Maiesties Guards, Lord Warden of the/ Stanneries, Lieutenant of *Cornwall*, and/ Gouernour of the Isle/ of *Iersey*. (Fig. 1).

[2] Ralegh's permission for the voyage, which he held contravened his 1584 patent, had not been obtained before the expedition left. The circumstances under which he and the participants were reconciled and the dedication permitted are discussed on pp. 34–5, 205–8.

Honourable sir, being earnestly requested by a deere friend,[1] to put downe in writing, some true relation of our late performed voyage to the North parts of Virginia; at length I resolued to satisfie his request, who also emboldened[2] me to direct the same to your honourable consideration; to whom indeed of duetie it perteineth.

May it please your Lordship therefore to vnderstand, that vpon the sixe and twentieth of March 1602, being Friday, we went from Falmouth, being in all, two & thirtie persons, in a small barke of Dartmouth, called The Concord,[3] holding a course for the North part of Virginia:[4] and although by chance the winde fauoured vs not at first as we wished, but inforced vs so farre to the Southward,[5] as we fell with S. Marie,[6] one of the islands of the Açores (which was not much out of our way) but[7] holding our course directly from thence, we made our iourney shorter (than hitherto accustomed) by the better part of a thousand leagues, yet were wee longer in our passage than we expected;[8] which happened, for that our barke being weake, we were loth to presse her with much saile; also, our sailers being few, and they none[9] of the best, we bare (except in faire weather) but low saile; besides, our going vpon an vnknowen coast, made vs not ouer-bolde to stand in with the shore, but in open weather; which caused vs to be certeine daies in sounding, before we discouered the coast, the weather being by chance, somewhat foggie. But on Friday the

They fel with S. Marie, one of the Açores.

---

[1] The 'deere friend' could well have been Richard Hakluyt, but this is not certain (see Quinn, ed. *Hakluyt handbook*, II, 574), and he could, as well, have been either Thomas Harriot, who was acting for Ralegh after August 1602, or Edward Hayes who had close associations with the compilation of the volume (pp. 37, 43).

[2] First ed. 'imboldened me'.

[3] The *Concord* of Dartmouth has not otherwise been traced. As 'a small barke' she might be larger than a pinnace and smaller than a ship, but barks of from 12 to 50 tons existed at the time and we might guess at a tonnage of about 30 tons. What is known of barks is set out in William A. Baker, *Colonial vessels* (Barre, Mass., 1962), pp. 78–110. Departure late in March was usual for ships bound for Newfoundland, since easterly winds then usually prevailed.

[4] This is the first case where the usage 'the North part of Virginia' replaces the older Norumbega for what, after 1616, was known as New England.

[5] The indication may be that she met NE rather than E winds.

[6] Santa Maria, lat. 36° 58′ N, long. 27° 7′ W.

[7] First ed. 'yet'.

[8] To attempt to sail due west a little to the north of the Azores was something of a novelty (Newfoundlanders tried to turn to the north west). Gosnold was fortunate in being driven southwards and also in picking up good enough winds to take him westwards to the North American mainland without being becalmed (cp. D. W. Waters, *Art of navigation*, p. 257).

[9] First ed. 'noue'.

fourteenth of May,[1] early in the morning,[2] wee made the land,[3] being full[4] of faire trees, the land somewhat low, certeine hummocks or hilles lying into the land, the shore full of white sand, but very stony or rocky. And standing faire alongst by the shore, about twelue of the clocke the same day, we came to an anker, where eight[6] Indians, in a Baske-shallop with mast and saile,[7] an iron grapple, and a kettle of Copper,[8] came boldly aboord vs, one of them apparelled with a wastcoat and breeches of blacke serdge, made after our sea-fashion, hose and shoes on his feet; all the rest (sauing one that had a paire of breeches of blue cloth) were naked.[9] These people are of tall stature, broad and grim visage, of a blacke swart complexion, their eie-browes painted white; their weapons are bowes and arrowes.[10] It seemed by

They discouered land the 14. of May.

Eight[5] Indians come aboord of them.

The description of them.

---

[1] First ed.'fourteenth'. A landfall on the 49th day after leaving England was more than was taken by subsequent expeditions, though Brereton's excuses appear valid.

[2] First ed. 'we'.

[3] Brereton suggests the *Concord* was well inshore when land was sighted at (according to Archer) about 6 a.m. Archer also indicates it lay towards the south, and that they reached Savage Rock after six hours sailing (making at least 18 nautical miles). It would fit a landfall at, say, Cape Small (43° 10′ N, 69° 50′ W) and a landing at Cape Elizabeth, somewhat better than a landfall at Cape Elizabeth and a landing at Cape Neddick (cp. fig. 1).

[4] First ed. B.L. 'ful', Hn. 'full'.   [5] First ed. 'Six'.

[6] First ed. J.C.B. 'six': HN copy 'sixe'.

[7] The episode is a graphic indication of the spread of European culture-contacts down the east coast. Micmac Indians were apparently employed to assist French Basque cod fishermen in the Cape Breton area (and possibly also in southern Newfoundland). The man, fully dressed in the serge waistcoat and breeches (probably made of English serge), and with stockings and shoes (and speaking, Archer says (p. 117) some French words), is likely to have been an experienced employee. That he and his associates should not only have stolen a shallop (cp. Quinn, 'Voyage of Étienne Bellenger', p. 341), but have known how to sail it some hundreds of miles southward, argues a degree of sophistication not elsewhere documented, but probably not unique. It is likely also that they were coming to trade with the Massachusetts and other tribes for furs (cp. p. 109), which would be re-sold to Europeans farther north. When the Micmac referred to Placentia they were not necessarily speaking about the bay and famous beach site of that name in Newfoundland but about the whole island, *Plisantik*, in French of the time *Presentic*, being their name for Newfoundland (John Hewson, 'Micmac placenames in Newfoundland', *Regional Language Studies: Newfoundland*, no. 8 (15 Aug. 1978), p. 15).

[8] First ed. 'copper'. Cauldrons or kettles, used for oil-extraction, were chiefly prized by the Indians as sources of ornaments and weapons and were acquired in trade or robbery for such purposes. French explorers frequently had cauldrons stolen (Champlain, *Works*, I (1922), 353–4; Lescarbot, *History of New France*, II (1911), 277), while Wood (*New Englands prospect* (1634), p. 67) says the Indians of the Massachusetts Bay area 'have large kettles which they traded for with the French long since, and doe still buy from the English', indicating that some were retained intact and were used for cooking.

[9] First ed. 'all naked'.

[10] First ed. 'arrowes: it'. The picture of Micmac individuals is valuable, their height, grim expression, dark complexion (aided by sun and oil), and the white-painted eyebrows (an unusual culture-trait) made up a clear impression (cp. Wallis, *Micmacs*, passim).

some words and signes they made, that some Basks or of S,[1] Iohn de Luz, haue fished or traded in this place, being in the latitude of 43. degrees.[2] But riding heere, in no very good harbour,[3] and withall, doubting the weather, about three of the clocke the same day in the afternoone we weighed, & standing Southerly off into sea the rest of that day and the night following, with a fresh gale of winde, in the morning we found our selues embaied[4] with a mightie headland; but comming to an anker about nine of the clocke the same day, within a league of the shore, we hoised out the one halfe of our shallop, and captaine Bartholmew Gosnold, my selfe, and three others, went ashore, being a white sandie and very bolde shore; and marching all that[5] afternoone with our muskets on our necks, on the highest hilles which we saw (the weather very hot) at length we perceiued this headland to be parcell of the maine, and sundrie Islands lying almost round about

Their first
landing.

[1] First ed. 'S.' has a full stop instead of a comma. St Jean-de-Luz, Basses Pyrénées, 43° 23′ N, 1° 39′ W, was the leading fishing port (though its harbour was not good) of the French Basque country. Whether or not French Basque ships came as far south as this to fish (on the Georges Bank) and to trade, is not yet corroborated, but it is not improbable.

[2] First ed. '43' has no full stop. Cape Elizabeth is at 43° 40′ N, 69° 15′ W and Cape Neddick at 43° 9′ N, 70° 11′ W, each within the range of accuracy to be expected of latitude observations taken at sea.

[3] The harbour at Cape Elizabeth (between High Head and Richmond Island) and that to the north of Cape Neddick were each adequate for a small vessel but neither was well-protected. During her three-hour stay the *Concord* is unlikely to have landed men or perhaps even launched her boat.

[4] First ed. 'embayed'. Sailing southwards, well off-shore, with a NE or N wind, Gosnold is likely to have had a clear night, if not a moon, and so could make an average of some 4 knots, perhaps a little more. The great headland within which they were embayed was Cape Cod, distinguished by its length and curvature rather than its height. Archer suggests they made an initial landing some way south of the curved headland (Wellfleet Harbor perhaps), and Brereton that they sailed directly to the southern limit of Cape Cod Bay, anchoring in the vicinity of Barnstable. On a direct course Cape Elizabeth to Race Point is some 85 miles, and from Cape Neddick almost 70. At between 4 and 5 knots a margin of 72 to 90 miles over the 18 hours would make either feasible.

[5] First ed. 'afternoon'. Gosnold's sally on dry land remains conjectural. If he landed on Barnstable Harbor and walked inland, perhaps by way of Mill Creek to avoid marshes, he would reach the high Barnstable Ridge about a mile and a half from the shore. If he worked his way westwards to the highest point, Shoot Flying Hill (200 feet at 41° 41′ N, 70° 21′ W) he could see, especially if he or his men ascended the higher trees, a substantial part of Nantucket Sound. To the south-west he would see Vineyard Sound appearing as, apparently, a wide channel into the mainland (made up of the mainland peninsula and the Elizabeth Islands on the northern side, and of Martha's Vineyard, including West Chop and East Chop, to the south). On a clear day, to the south and south-east, he could get a sharp indication of Capoag (Cape Poge then an island), Muskeget and possibly a suggestion of Nantucket (if not this then a sun-glint from sandy shores or a bank of haze suggesting further islands in this direction), though frequently there is nothing to be seen. Shoot Flying Hill was the suggestion of Warner Gookin (Barbour and Gookin, *Gosnold*, pp. 99–101), but a site nearer Barnstable Harbor on the ridge, using a high tree, would

it:[1] so returning (towards euening) to our shallop[2] (for by that time, the other part was brought ashore and set together) we espied an Indian, a yoong man,[3] of proper stature, and of a pleasing countenance; and after some familiaritie with him, we left him at the sea side, and returned to our ship; where, in fiue or sixe houres absence, we had pestered our ship[4] so with Cod fish, that we threw numbers of them ouer-boord againe: and surely, I am persuaded that in the moneths of March, April, and May, there is vpon this coast, better fishing, and in as great plentie, as in Newfound-land: for the sculles of Mackerell, herrings, Cod, and other fish, that we daily[5] saw as we went and came from the shore, were woonderfull; and besides, the places where we tooke these Cods (and might in a few daies haue laden our ship) were but in seuen fadome[6] water, and within lesse than a league of the shore: where, in Newfound-land they fish in fortie or fiftie fadome water, and farre off. From this place, we sailed round about this headland, almost all the points of the compasse, the shore very bolde: but as no coast is free from dangers, so I am persuaded, this is as free as any.[7] The land somwhat lowe, full of goodly woods, but in some places

Marginal notes: Another Indian. / An excellent Cod fishing. / A great headland. / Many faire Islands.

---

bring a similar result. The observers do not appear to have used a compass from their lookout point. The continuance of the ridge to the east with the northward trend of Lower Cape Cod, would be clear, as the narrative indicates.

[1] The description is too vague to add much to the crux of what was and was not seen from the ridge (cp. pp. 496–8).

[2] The half-shallop, which carried the shore party, would have been the fore part between 12 and 15 feet long with an exceptionally broad stern. She would be awkward to row. Her counterpart would be squared off at both ends, though with a somewhat narrowed stern. The two parts were bolted together and fitted with mast and keel, to make a vessel of some 25 to 30 feet in length. See for shallop, Baker, *Sloops and shallops* (1966), pp. 18–19 and *Colonial vessels*, pp. 56–51, and his 'Gosnold's shallop', *American Neptune*, XXXIV (1974), 234–42, which is not, however, a satisfactory reading of the evidence.

[3] First ed. 'Yong',; Hn. 'Yong'. The Indian was presumably a member of the Nauset band of the Pockanoket tribe, the first New England inhabitant to be encountered.

[4] First ed. 'ship' is followed by a comma. While Gosnold and his party spent 5 or 6 hours on shore, another party was preparing the shallop and the remainder took the *Concord* to sea to fish. If she sailed to the eastward from Barnstable Harbor she would have found bottom at 20 to 25 feet and had a good chance of making a satisfactory catch of cod. This would fit Brereton's mention of fishing in 7 fathoms within three miles of the shore.

[5] First ed. 'dayly'.

[6] First ed. 'faddome'.

[7] First ed. 'any; the'. Brereton avoids description of the crucial issue of the nature of and time taken for the voyage round Cape Cod and the arrival of the *Concord* in Nantucket Sound. Gookin believed excisions were made to render it difficult for others to follow the course in detail. (Barbour and Gookin, *Gosnold*, pp. 184–6), and see the discussion of Archer below. The dangerous seas breaking on the east shore of the Cape would be compounded by the still more treacherous shoals off Monomoy Point.

plaine.[1] At length we were come amongst many faire Islands, which we had partly discerned at our first landing; all lying within a league or two one of another, and the outermost not aboue sixe or seuen leagues from the maine: but comming to an anker vnder one of them,[2] which was about three or foure leagues from the maine, captaine Gosnold, my selfe, and some others, went ashore, and going round about it,[4] we found it to be foure English miles in compasse, without house or inhabitant, sauing a little old house made of boughes, couered with barke,[5] an olde piece of a weare of the Indians, to catch fish,[6] and one or two places, where they had made fires. The chiefest trees of this Island, are Beeches and Cedars;[7] the outward parts all ouergrowen with lowe bushie trees, three or foure foot in height, which beare some kind of fruits, as appeared by their blossomes;[8] Strawberries,[9] red and white, as sweet and much bigger than ours in England:[10] Rasberies,[11] Gooseberies,[12] Hurtleberies,[13] and such an[14] incredible store of Vines, aswell in the wooddie part of the Island, where they run vpon euery tree, as on the outward parts, that we could not goe for treading

The first Island called Marthaes vineyard.[3]

Beeches. Cedars.

Vines in abundance.

---

[1] First ed. 'plaine: at'. The 'faire Islands' seen from the Barnstable Ridge are not specified in detail apart from the relative distances between them (3 to 6 miles) and the farthest 18 to 21 miles from the mainland (Monomoy Point?).

[2] First ed. 'comming to an anker vnder one of them'. The argument that this was an insular Cape Poge is developed on pp. 500–2. The distance of 9 to 12 miles from the mainland is a useful specific point.

[3] On the name see p. 124.

[4] The circumambulation of the little island of Capoag (p. 124) by Gosnold, Brereton and others would have given them a reasonable impression of the vegetation to be found on the other islands of Nantucket and Vineyard Sounds.

[5] This suggests a conical shelter. Driver and Massey, *A.P.S. Transactions*, XLVII (1957), 295, assign the crude conical type to the area north of Cape Cod.

[6] The earliest mention of a fish-weir for this area (cited in Flannery, *Analysis*, p. 17), but the precise character of which is unspecified.

[7] The description of the vegetation of the then Cape Poge island (Capoag) is also appropriate to that of modern Martha's Vineyard. Beech, *Fagus grandifolia* Ehrh., and 'cypress', Red Cedar, *Juniperus virginia* L., would be the most prominent trees.

[8] The bushes are not sufficiently differentiated for identification.

[9] First ed. 'strawberries'.

[10] First ed. 'England' followed by a comma. Strawberry, *Fragaria virginiana* L., ripe and unripe; larger than English wild strawberry (on account of more sun at lower latitude?).

[11] Raspberry, *Rubus strigosus* Michx.

[12] Some variety of sp. *Ribes*: gooseberries are European in origin, cp. pp. 163–4 below.

[13] Varieties of sp. *Gaylussacia*, huckleberries (or possibly gen. *Vaccinium*, blueberries, etc.)

[14] First ed. 'such' followed by a semi-colon. Vines, to the English visitor, were grape vines. Several species of these are likely to have been seen, including Summer-grape, *Vitis aestivalis* Michx., the fruit on which would be already visible. Other climbers may well be included (as in American usage) in his class of vines.

vpon them: also, many springs of excellent sweet water, and a great standing lake of fresh water, neere the sea side, an English mile in compasse,[1] which is mainteined with the springs running exceeding pleasantly thorow the wooddie grounds which are very rockie. Here are also in this Island, great store of Deere,[2] which we saw, and other beasts, as appeared by their tracks; as also diuers fowles, as Cranes, Hernshawes, Bitters, Geese, Mallards, Teales, and other fowles, in great plenty;[3] also, great store of Pease,[4] which grow in certeine plots all the Island ouer. On the North side of this Island we found many huge bones and ribbes of Whales.[5] This Island, as also all the rest of these Islands, are full of all sorts of stones fit for building; the sea sides all couered with stones, many of them glistring[6] and shining like minerall stones, and verie rockie: also, the rest of these Islands are replenished with these commodities, and vpon some of them, inhabitants; as vpon an Island to the Northward, and within two leagues of this;[7] yet wee found no townes, nor many of their houses, although we saw manie Indians, which are tall big boned men,[8] all naked, sauing they couer their priuy parts with a blacke tewed skin, much like a Black-smiths[9] apron, tied about their middle and betweene their legs behinde: they gaue vs of their fish readie boiled, (which[10] they carried in a basket made

Springs. A Lake.

Deere. Other beasts. Cranes. Hernshawes. Bitters. Geese. Mallards. Teales.

[1] At the eastern side of modern Cape Poge Pond the former freshwater pond has long been salt and has long been assimilated into it; there is no reason why this should not have been entirely fresh in 1602; the size is appropriate.

[2] Deer, *Oedicoeleus virginiana* L.

[3] For the birds see pp. 160, 162–3. Now mainly Blackbacked Gulls which nest in great numbers.

[4] The ubiquitous Beach-pea, *Lathyrus maritimus* (L) Bigel.

[5] Not surprising since several species of whale frequented Vineyard Sound and Nantucket Sound: the accumulation was probably one from natural deaths since no evidence of early European whaling in this region has so far been found.

[6] First ed. 'glistering'. Mostly glacial erratics. The island is mainly composed of Quaternary materials and would not produce many boulders and stones.

[7] Brereton creates topographical difficulties by his failure to be more specific, moving from the first landing on Cape Poge Island, named Marthaes Vineyard, to the larger island, the present Martha's Vineyard, to which the name was extended since they were virtually continuous. 'Island to the Northward' is probably West Chop (part of Martha's Vineyard) and northeast at about 6 miles from the anchorage off Cape Poge, though the anchorage may have been a little farther to the west (cp. figs 3–4).

[8] Compare other comments on the tallness of the Indians (p. 94), who were on fishing and gathering expeditions and did not live near the coast (or indeed, necessarily, on the island).

[9] First ed. 'Black-smithes'. The small beaver-skin breechclout was, characteristically, worn by both sexes (Willoughby, *Antiquities*, p. 280; pp. 97–8, 149), but a blacksmith's apron would be a rectangular piece of leather, reaching some way down the thigh, and might suggest rather an apron-skirt, not typical of this area.

[10] First ed. 'boiled (which'. Possibly, from the season, alewife or shad.

of twigges, not vnlike our osier)[1] whereof we did eat, and iudged them

Tabacco.

to be fresh water fish: they gaue vs also of their Tabacco, which they drinke greene,[2] but dried into powder, very strong and pleasant, and much better than any I haue tasted in England: the necks of their pipes are made of clay hard dried, (whereof[3] in that Island is great store both red and white) the other part is[4] a piece of hollow copper, very finely closed and semented together.[5] Wee gaue vnto them certeine trifles,

Elizabeths Island.

as kniues, points, and such like, which they much esteemed.[6] From hence we went to another Island, to the Northwest of this, and within a league or two of the maine, which we found to bee[7] greater than before we imagined, being 16. English[8] miles at the least in compasse; for it conteineth many pieces or necks of land, which differ nothing from seuerall Islands, sauing that certeine banks of small bredth, do, like bridges, ioine[9] them to this Island. On[10] the outsides of this Island are many plaine places of grasse, abundance of Strawberies & other

Wheat, Barley, and Oats sowed, came vp nine inches in fourteene daies.

berries before mentioned. In[11] mid May we did sowe in this Island (for a triall) in sundry places, Wheat, Barley, Oats, and Pease, which in

---

[1] A willow-twig basket seems probable (several species of *Salix* are available). The earliest surviving basket from the Narragensett-Wampanoag area dates from about 1675, but is made of basswood bark and cornhusk (in R.I. Hist. Soc., John Brown House, Power St., Providence, cp. R.I. Hist. Soc., *Collections*, XVIII (1925), 23–5).

[2] The English at this time spoke of 'drinking' tobacco: 'greene' does not imply it was taken undried but that the leaf in drying has remained green (a modern category of tobacco, an inferior grade, retains the name). Rainey 'Compilation', p. 15, notes the powdering of the leaf, not specifically remarked in other early sources.

[3] First ed. 'dried (whereof'. The necks are presumably the bowls of the pipes and the upper part of the stem made, as he says, from clay.

[4] First ed. 'part, is'. The fine sheet-copper (or brass) cylinder was presumably the mouthpiece, normally of wood, but perhaps in such cases sheathed in copper. Surviving examples (in R.I. Hist. Soc. collection) lack the copper mouthpiece, and are shown in Willoughby, *Antiquities*, p. 182, fig. 104 b, 184 (mentioning the 1602 descriptions), 228, 231; Rainey, 'Compilation', p. 15; Flannery, *Analysis*, pp. 167–8). It is not certain that Archer (p. 122) is describing precisely the same sort of pipe.

[5] First ed. 'together: we'.

[6] First ed. 'Elizabeths Island'. Here the presents of knives and tags were in return for their gift of fish and were not in trade.

[7] First ed. 'be'. This is his only description of the passing of Gay Head and the crossing of Vineyard Haven to the newly named Elizabeths Isle (cp. p. 126, figs. 3–4).

[8] First ed. '16 English'. The circuit is approximately that of today's Cuttyhunk and Nashawena (p. 000).

[9] First ed. 'do like bridges ione'. The outer shores of Gosnolds Pond for example and the long spit which joined (it is maintained) the two islands now separated by the narrow and shallow Canapitsit Channel (cp. p. 127).

[10] First ed. 'Island: on'.

[11] First ed. 'mentioned: in'. It might appear that the woodland was concentrated in the central, higher parts of the then joined Cuttyhunk and Nashawena.

fourteene daies were sprung vp nine inches and more. The[1] soile is fat and lustie,[2] the vpper crust of gray colour; but a foot or lesse in depth, of the colour of our hempelands in England; and being thus apt for these and the like graines; the sowing or setting (after the ground is clensed)[3] is no greater labour, than if you should set or sow in[4] one of our best prepared gardens in England. This Island is full of high timbred Oakes,[5] their leaues thrise so broad as ours; Cedars, straight and tall; Beech, Elme, hollie, Walnut trees in aboundance,[6] the fruit as bigge as ours, as appeared by those we found vnder the trees. which had lien all the yeere vngathered; Haslenut trees, Cherry trees, the leafe, barke and bignesse not differing from ours in England, but the stalke beareth the blossoms[7] or fruit at the end thereof, like a cluster of Grapes, forty or fifty in a bunch; Sassafras trees great plentie all the Island ouer, a tree of high price and profit; also diuers[8] other fruit trees, some of them with strange barkes, of an Orange colour, in feeling soft and smoothe like Veluet: in the thickest parts of these woods, you may see a furlong or more round about. On the Northwest side of this Island, neere to the sea side, is a standing Lake of fresh water, almost three

Oakes.
Cedars.
Beech. Elme.
Hollie,
Walnut trees.
Cherry trees.

Sassafras trees.
Diuers other trees.

[1] First ed. 'more: the'. Such 'trials' of seed were frequent practice but this was the first known in New England: germination was evidently rapid. The total period available was 25 May–17 June, a maximum of 24 days, and a notional average growth of 9 inches would not be exceptional.

[2] First ed. 'lustie; the vpper crust, of gray, colour'. A humus layer of 12 inches would now only be found in very sheltered parts of the island: it could be expected, for example, on Naushon where part of the primary forest survives to protect it. The subsoil is a coarse glacial drift (Woodworth and Wigglesworth, pp. 306, 316–17).

[3] First ed. 'cleansed'. Hemp and flax would make considerable demands on the soil and would not be suitable for insular cultivation. The first step in the 'cleansing' process was removal of sassafras, cedar and 'rubbish' by the expedition.

[4] First ed. 'sowe'.

[5] First ed. 'timbred Oaks'. The larger leaves might possibly suggest Northern Red Oak, *Quercus borealis* Michx.

[6] First ed. 'Cedars, strait and tall; Beech, Elme, Hollie, Walnut trees in abundance.' Red Cedar, Beech, American Elm (probably), American Holly, and Butternut or White Walnut seem probable identifications. Supplies of desiccated untouched fruit from the previous year probably resulted from the lack of any permanent Indian population.

[7] First ed. 'blossomes'. Hazel bushes are probable; the cherries may not be as clearly diagnostic but the bunched flowers (and fruit) suggest Choke Cherry, *Prunus virginia* L. or Black Cherry *P. serotina* Ehrh. Lyte, *Herbal* (1578), p. 843, describes cherries in this way: 'Besides these kinds [single fruited ones] there are Cherries that grow, three, fower, and five vpon a stem, and also that hang in clusters like grapes.' It seems probable Archer (or Meriton, pp. 160, 162) carried a herbal (Gerard's, Lyte's, or both).

[8] First ed. 'also, diuers'. The tree with orange bark and a smooth 'Velvet' feel may very well be a dogwood, *Cornus* fam., not a fruit tree.

English miles in compasse,[1] in the middest whereof stands a plot of woody[2] ground, an acre in quantitie or not aboue: this Lake is full of small Tortoises,[3] and exceedingly frequented with all sorts of fowles before rehearsed, which breed, some low on the banks, and others on low trees[4] about this Lake in great aboundance, whose yong[5] ones of all sorts we tooke and eat at our pleasure: but all these fowles are much bigger than ours in England. Also, in euery Island, and almost in euery part of euery Island, are great store of Ground nuts, fortie together on a string, some of them as bigge as hennes egges; they grow not two inches vnder ground: the which nuts we found to be as good as Potatoes.[6] Also, diuers sorts of shell-fish, as Scalops,[7] Muscles, Cockles, Lobsters, Crabs, Oisters, and Wilks, exceeding good and very great. But not to cloy you with particular rehearsall of such things as God & Nature hath bestowed on these places, in comparison whereof, the most fertil part of al England is (of it selfe) but barren; we went in our light-horsman from[8] this Island to the maine, right against this Island some two leagues off,[9] where comming ashore, we stood a while like men rauished at the beautie and delicacie of this sweet soile; for besides diuers cleere Lakes of fresh water (whereof we saw no end) Medowes very large and full of greene grasse; euen the most woody[10] places (I speake onely of such as I saw) doe grow so distinct and apart, one tree

Side notes:
A lake three miles about.
Small Tortoises.
Abundance of fowles, much bigger than ours in England.
Ground nuts.
Shell-fish.
The exceeding beautie of the maine land. Great Lakes. Large medowes

---

[1] Cp. fig. 29. It is impossible to estimate the circumference of Gosnolds Pond at this time, but 3 miles in 1602 does not appear excessive, though Woodworth and Wigglesworth, p. 318, considered it too great.

[2] First ed. 'wooddie'. Archer had considerable clearing to do on Gosnolds Isle (p. 128).   [3] Tortoises are noted on p. 161.

[4] First ed. 'lowe on the banks, and others on lowe trees'. Equating sizes between varying species is not a fruitful pursuit.

[5] First ed. 'abundance, whose yoong'. For hatching seabirds on Cape Poge see p. 125.

[6] Clearly *Apios tuberosa*, but with what sort of potatoes is he comparing them? Only sweet potatoes were available in England at the time, except in experimental gardens such as Gerard's. Could Brereton have had experience of *Solanum tuberosum* in southern Europe? But his reference, in a popular tract, would there appear meaningless.

[7] First ed. 'Scallops'. Atlantic Deep-sea Scallop, *Placopecten majellanicus* Gmelin (Abbott, *Marine shells*, p. 144), if not simply clams.

[8] First ed. 'fro'. The light-horseman here is the name given to the ship's boat, as distinct from the larger shallop: it would be about 15 ft long. The precise form of boat which led it to be given this name is not known (cp. Quinn, *Roanoke voyages*, I, 247, 271–2, 286).

[9] This was clearly a different expedition made by Gosnold to West Island in the shallop at the end of the month. It might appear that late on the 24th or early on the 25th a brief excursion to the mainland to the north was made of which Archer says nothing. A six-mile row would bring them ashore between Round Hill Point and Mishaum Point (on Smith's Neck), but no certainty can be obtained about this.

[10] First ed. 'wooddy'. First ed. also adds additional side note 'large medowes'.

from another, vpon greene grassie ground, somewhat higher than the
Plaines, as if Nature would shew her selfe[1] aboue her power, artificall.
Hard by, we espied seuen Indians, and cumming[2] vp to them, at first
they expressed some feare; but being emboldned by our curteous[3]
vsage, and some trifles which we gaue them, they followed vs to a necke
of land, which we imagined had beene seuered from the maine; but[4]
finding it otherwise, we perceiued a broad harbour or riuers mouth,
which ranne vp into the maine: and because the day was farre spent,
we were forced to returne to the Island from whence we came, leauing
the discouery[5] of this harbour, for a time of better leasure. Of[6] the
goodnesse of which harbour, as also of many others thereabouts, there
is small doubt, considering that all the Islands, as also the maine (where
we were) is all rockie grounds and broken lands. Now the next day,
we determined to fortifie our selues in a little[7] plot of ground in the
midst of the Lake aboue mentioned, where we built an house, and
couered it with sedge, which grew about this lake in great aboundance;[8]
in building whereof, we spent three weeks and more: but the second
day after our comming from the maine, we espied 11 canowes[9] or boats,
with fiftie Indians in them, comming toward vs from this part of the
maine, where we, two daies before landed;[10] and being loth they should
discouer our fortification, we went out on the sea side to meete[11] them;

Margin notes: Seuen Indians. · A broad riuer. · A good harbour. · The English house. · Eleuen canows with fiftie Indians in them.

[1] First ed. 'herselfe'. Brereton's lyrical impression of the N. shore of Buzzards Bay may be taken as genuine (if a little inflated).

[2] First ed. 'Indians; and comming.'

[3] First ed. 'coutreous'. A casual party for whom he gives no details on the differentiation of sexes. If all males they were probably hunting rather than gathering.

[4] First ed. 'maine: but'. A landing near Salters Point and a short walk to Smiths Neck (probably then almost an island), ending at Mishaum Point and revealing the entry to Slocums River is possible. Alternatively, working eastward from Salters Point the point of land would be Round Hill Point (not now likely to be taken for an island), but opening a view of Apponaganset Bay and the wider expanses of the Achushnet River estuary.

[5] First ed. 'discouerie'.

[6] First ed. 'leasure: of'. The next expedition was on May 31. (p. 130).

[7] First ed. 'in the little'.

[8] First ed. 'abundance'. Brereton uses house for the structure being built on Gosnolds Isle, where Archer uses 'storehouse' and 'fort' (pp. 136, 128). Any stout-culmed sedge, skilfully chosen and applied, would be adequate for roofing.

[9] First ed. 'Nine canoas' in margin; '9 canowes' in text. This may be the correct number. Archer does not refer to this visitation on the 29th. The smaller number would be adequate for a party of 50: there is no doubt that these were all men, that they had come to confirm the friendly contact made on the 27th with Brereton and that they were prepared to trade.

[10] First ed. 'before, landed'.

[11] First ed. 'meet'. They probably met them on the barrier beach at the S.W. end of Cuttyhunk. The Indians would be able to see building activity from any point of this shore but not be able to obtain any detail of it, as the structures had made little progress.

and comming somewhat neere them, they all sat downe vpon the stones, calling aloud to vs (as we rightly ghessed) to doe the like,[1] a little distance from them: hauing sat a while in this order, captaine Gosnold willed me to goe[2] vnto them, to see what countenance they would make; but as soone[3] as I came vp vnto them, one of them, to whom I had giuen a knife two daies before in the maine, knew me, (whom I also very wel remembred) and smiling vpon me, spake

Their captaine.

somewhat vnto their lord or captaine, which sat in the midst of them, who presently rose vp and tooke a large Beauer skin from one that stood about him and gaue it vnto me, which I requited for that time the best I could:[4] but I,[5] pointing towards captaine Gosnold, make signes vnto him, that he was our captaine, and desirous to be his friend, and enter league with him, which (as I perceiued) he vnderstood, and made signes of ioy: whereuppon[6] captaine Gosnold with the rest of his companie, being twenty[7] in all, came vp vnto them; and after many signes of gratulations (captaine Gosnold presenting their Lord with certaine[8] trifles which they wondred at, and highly esteemed) we became very great friends, and sent for meat aboord our shallop, and gaue them such meats as we had then readie dressed, whereof they misliked nothing but our mustard, whereat they made many a sowre face. While we were thus mery,[9] one of them had conueied a target of ours into one of their canowes, which we suffered, onely to trie whether they were in subiection to this Lord to[10] whom we made signes (by shewing him another of the same likenesse, and pointing to the

---

[1] Indians were accustomed to arranging a formal meeting in this manner.

[2] First ed. 'go'.

[3] First ed. 'as assoone'. Brereton's earlier contact indicates that the men he met contacted their village (or hunting-gathering group) and so set them on their way to meet the visitors.

[4] The formal gift of a beaver skin, and Brereton's return of something he had, represented the ceremonial exchange of gifts prior to beginning serious business.

[5] First ed. 'I pointing'. It is unlikely that this was as high-ranking a sachem as the one who came on the later visit (pp. 133–4).

[6] First ed. 'whereupon'.

[7] First ed. 'twentie'. The remaining 12 were presumably on board *Concord* or the shallop: he, himself, had been laying out the outlines of the fort.

[8] First ed. 'Their L. with certeine'. Gosnold took over the ceremonial requital for which Brereton had been inadequately prepared.

[9] First ed. 'wee were thus merry'. Archer places the episode of the mustard on the later occasion. The shallop was evidently lying close to shore off the barrier beach and food for the men working on the islet fort had been prepared for them.

[10] First ed. 'this L. to'. This episode is also placed later by Archer (p. 135). Indian pilfering is later recorded by Champlain, *Works*, ed. H. P. Biggar, I (1922), 353–4, 357; Lescarbot, *History*, ed. W. L. Grant and H. P. Biggar, II (1911), 325–7.

canow)[1] what one of his companie had done: who suddenly expressed some feare, and speaking angerly to one about him (as we perceiued by his countenance) caused it presently to be brought backe againe. So the rest of the day we spent in trading with them for Furres,[2] which are Beauers, Luzernes, Marterns, Otters, Wild-cat skinnes, very[3] large and deepe Furre, blacke Foxes, Conie skinnes, of the colour of our Hares, but somewhat lesse, Deere skinnes, very large, Seale skinnes, and other beasts skinnes, to vs vnknowen. They haue also great store of Copper, some very redde, and some of a paler colour; none of them but haue chaines, earings,[4] or collars of this mettall: they head some of their arrowes herewith much[5] like our broad arrow heads, very workmanly made. Their chaines are many hollow pieces semented together, ech piece of the bignesse of one of our reeds, a finger in length, ten or twelue of them together on a string, which they weare about their necks:[6] their collars they weare about their bodies like bandelieres

Seuerall sorts of Furres.

Red Copper in abundance.

Chaines.

Collars.

---

[1] First ed. 'canowe'.

[2] The chief's action was clearly taken not only to show his authority but to prevent any spoiling of the trade for which he had come.

[3] First ed. 'skinnes very'. The accumulation of so many dressed skins shows extensive preparation for the market, strengthening the impression that the Massachusetts and Narraganset Bay Indians were well accustomed to commerce in furs and skins. It is, perhaps, significant that the knowledge of this rich purchase should have, at the beginning at least, been concealed from Sir Walter Ralegh (cp. pp. 204–8).

Beaver; if we are to distinguish 'Luzarnes' and 'Wild-cat' this must be Puma; Muskrat; Otter; Bobcat; though perhaps this is the Puma; Black Fox; Northern Cottontail, and varying Hare; Northern Virginia and the White-tailed Deer (or perhaps Elk or even Moose); Harbor Seal (and perhaps other seal species). This covers most of the major land mammals, so that it seems scarcely worth while speculating what the others might be. See below p. 160.

[4] First ed. 'earrings'. Light and dark copper cannot be seen as diagnostic.

[5] First ed. 'herewith, much'. Copper points are known from specimens in Rhode Island Historical Society (R.I. Hist. Soc., *Collections*, XVII (1925), 29), at the Peabody Museum, Andover, Mass., and the Bronson Museum, Attleboro, Mass. The use of copper for arrowheads and drinking cups may antedate its use as ornament (Driver and Massey, *A.P.S. Transactions*, LXVII (1957), 345–7).

[6] Chains (round the waist) and collars (tight to the neck) would compare in style with later wampum necklets and belts. It has proved difficult to date tubular copper beads. Examples are in Rhode Island Hist. Soc., Providence and see R.I. Hist. Soc., *Collections*, XIX (1926), p. 127, XXVII (1934), 45; Bronson Museum, Attleboro, Mass. (specimens from there $\frac{3}{4}$ inch to $2\frac{1}{2}$ inches long, being described in Mass. Arch. Soc., *Bulletin* XX; Peabody Museum of Archeology, Andover, Mass. A few cylinder beads about $\frac{5}{8}$ inch long were found at the Lagoon Pond site on Martha's Vineyard, *The Dukes County Intelligencer*, I (1959), pl. IX, 'Preliminary report on the Lagoon Pond site', Mass. Arch. Soc., *Bulletin*, XVIII (1957), 59–61, and one at the Squibnocket Cliff site (D. S. Byers and F. Johnson, *Two sites on Martha's Vineyard* (1940), pp. 52 (pl. VI, no. 21), 53, 94). Those submitted to analysis have so far proved to be of European copper (but this raises problems of sources and chronology; see p. 111). It may yet be established that some native copper, perhaps even

a handfull broad, all hollow pieces, like the other, but somewhat
shorter, four[1] hundred pieces in a collar, very fine and euenly set
together. Besides these, they haue large drinking cups made[2] like

Drinking cuppes of Copper.

sculles, and other thinne plates of copper,[3] make much like our
boare-speare blades, all which they so little esteeme, as they offered their
fairest collars or chaines, for a knife or such like trifle, but we seemed
little to regard it; yet I was desirous to vnderstand where they had such
store of this mettall, and made signes to one of them (with whom I

Mines of Copper.

was very[4] familiar) who taking a piece of Copper in his hand, made
a hole with his finger in the ground, and withall pointed to the maine
from whence they came. They strike fire in this manner; euery one
carrieth about him in a purse of tewd[5] leather, a Minerall stone (which

Minerall stones. Emerie stones.

I take to be their Copper) and with a flat Emerie Stone (wherewith
Glasiers cut glasse, and Cutlers glase blades)[6] tied fast to the end of a
little sticke, gently he striketh vpon the Minerall stone, and within a

---

in thin sheet form, was used before the fur trade began. Brereton's description is very
valuable for its detail.

[1] First ed. 'foure'. There is confusion between chains and collars. This could be a
series of successive rows of copper beads set below one another to make up something like
a breastplate, or it could be a belt hung over one shoulder and hanging down the sides
(but perhaps containing several rows of beads, as he says, like a bandolier).

[2] First ed. 'cups. made'. Drinking cups like skullcaps might parallel the headcovering
of hammered sheet copper from the Fall River burial (though this is appreciably later).
Willoughby, *Antiquities*, pp. 236, 241. He also (pp. 232, 236) reports the finding at
Winthrop, Mass., of parts of a copper vessel 'evidently formed from a circular piece of
sheet copper by laying it over a block with a depression on its surface, and beating it with
a hammer of stone or other material having a convex face'.

[3] First ed. 'Copper'. Broad-based, elongated, curved and pointed objects like
boar-spears (though they would be of steel) were probably gorgets for hanging from the
neck since a copper gorget, shaped somewhat like this, and pierced, was found at the
Titicut, Mass. site (M. Robbins, 'Some Indian burials from Southeast Massachusetts', Mass.
Arch. Soc., *Bulletin*, XXI (1959), 26).

[4] First ed. 'verie'. Probably the Indian who recognised him from the previous
meeting. Brereton is inquiring about sources of copper (or gold). This inquiry may explain
the interpolation out of context by Archer of the sentence 'These Indians call Gold
Wassador which argueth there is thereof in the Countrey' (p. 130).

[5] First ed. 'maner'; 'tewed'. The equipment for the percussion (strike-a-light)
method of fire-making comprised two lumps of stone, iron pyrites or felsite or one of these,
and flint for striking sparks, together with touchwood ('spunk') dry rotten wood (often
from black birch) the whole contained in a skin pouch hung from the girdle. Driver and
Massey (*A.P.S. Transactions*, XLVII (1957), 347-8) regard this as a northern (Micmac) trait,
Cape Cod and southern Mass. being its extreme limits. It is not known from Narragansett
Bay and so might point to these being Massachusetts Indians. It might also support the
association of Micmacs and Basques in the southern New England fur trade (suggested
above, p. 109). Brereton's is an excellent account.

[6] Compare Archer's '*smiris*' (p. 136), where he is less explicit on the equipment.

stroke or two, a sparke falleth vpon a piece of Touchwood (much like our Spunge in England) and with the least sparke he maketh a fire presently. We had also of their Flaxe, wherewith they make many strings and cords, but it is not so bright of colour as ours in England:[1] I am perswaded they haue great store growing vpon the maine, as also Mines and many other rich commodities, which we, wanting both time and meanes, could not possibly discouer. Thus they continued with vs three daies, euery night retiring them selues[2] to the furthermost part of our Island two or three miles from our fort: but the fourth day they returned to the maine, pointing fiue or six[3] times to the Sun, and once to the maine, which we vnderstood, that within fiue or six daies they would come from the maine to vs againe: but being in their canowes a little from the shore, they made huge cries & shouts of ioy vnto vs; and we with our trumpet and cornet,[4] and casting vp our cappes into the aire, made them the best farewell we could: yet six or seuen of them remained with vs behinde, bearing vs company euery day into the woods, and helpt vs to cut and carie our Sassafras, and some of them lay aboord our ship.[5] These people, as they are exceeding courteous, gentle of disposition, and well conditioned, excelling all others that we haue seene; so for shape of bodie and louely fauour, I thinke they excell all the people of America;[6] of stature much higher than we; of complexion or colour, much like a darke Oliue; their eie-browes and haire blacke, which they weare long, tied vp behinde in knots, whereon they pricke feathers of fowles, in fashion of a

Flaxe.

Indians apt for seruice.

Sassafras.

A goodly people, & of good conditions.

---

[1] Probably Indian hemp, or, less likely, their native flax (cp. p. 164).

[2] First ed. 'themselues'. This strengthens the position that modern Cuttyhunk and Nashawena were then joined. Cuttyhunk is not so large as this and their 2 or 3 miles would have brought them on to what is now Nashawena.

[3] First ed. (Huntington Library copy) 'sixe'. The 4th day would be June 1. They would thus reckon to return on 6 or 7 June.

[4] For what was probably the use of the trumpet by the ship (see p. 137); the cornet may have been for their entertainment but it may also have been used as a call sign from shallop to ship.

[5] Archer (p. 134) put the staying of the Indians to help as occurring on 7 June, and the number as 4, saying they would go on board ship. The aid of 6 or 7 would have been considerable, given the amount of work to do in construction and the unwillingness, as Gosnold reported (p. 210) of the Englishmen to collect too much sassafras (cp. also p. 206). These particular men did stay on shipboard.

[6] This description of the Indian is somewhat idealised, but expressive. Their height was clearly substantially higher than that of the English (which was probably in the 5 ft 6 in–5 ft 8 in range). Their dark olive complexion was partly the result of oil and remnants of artificial colouring. Their long hair, tied in knots and stuck with feathers, is attested by others but is not unfortunately illustrated.

crownet: some of them are blacke thin bearded;[1] they make beards of the haire of beasts: and one of them offered a beard of their making to one of our sailers, for his that grew on his face, which because it was of a red colour, they iudged to be none of his owne.[2] They are quicke eied, and stedfast in their looks, fearelesse of others harmes, as intending none themselues; some of the meaner sort giuen to filching, which the very name of Saluages (not weighing their ignorance in good

Their apparell. or euill) may easily excuse:[3] their garments are of Deere skins,[4] and some of them weare Furres round and close about their necks. They pronounce our language with great facilitie; for one[5] of them one day sitting by mee,[6] vpon occasion I spake smiling to him these words: How now (sirrha)[7] are you so saucie with my Tabacco? which words (without any further repetition) he suddenly spake so plaine and distinctly, as if he had beene a long scholar in the language. Many other

Their women. such trials we had, which are heere needlesse to repeat.[8] Their women (such as we saw) which were but three in all, were but lowe of stature, their eie-browes, haire, apparell, and maner of wearing, like to the men, fat, and very well fauoured, and much delighted in our company;[9] the

---

[1] The retention of any facial hair is unusual. Wood, *New Englands prospect* (1634), p. 64, says 'you cannot move them to weare it on their chinnes, where it no sooner growes, but it is stubbed up by the rootes'.

[2] It seems possible the Indians were tying their roached head-dresses of animal hair dyed red (cp. p. 97) round their faces to simulate (and mock) the English. Wood (p. 64) found Indians so hostile to beards that 'they call him an English mans bastard that hath but the appearance of a beard'.

[3] Earlier they were thieves who had to be made to return what they had taken (p. 154): Brereton attempts to explain their lack of respect for property by their lack of Christian standards.

[4] These were deerskin mantles, passed under the right arm and fastened over the left shoulder, leaving an arm exposed which was covered with a lynxskin muff in winter (Willoughby, *Antiquities*, p. 280: Wood, *New Englands prospect*, p. 65). The fur necklet is likely to have been fur of a smaller animal, and neither would be worn in summer except on ceremonial occasions.

[5] 'for [to] one of them' is required.

[6] First ed. 'me'. Capacity for linguistic imitation seems to have been common, but whether the Micmac first met with (pp. 117–18) were speaking Basque or imitating Basque words is uncertain.   [7] First ed. 'sirha'.

[8] Brereton is passing over the return of the Indians and dealings with them on 5 and 7 June, having we suspect already inserted incidents from the later meetings into his account of the earlier meeting. That this took place is clear from Archer's account of his isolation at the fort during Gosnold's absence, whereas he was close to hand on the earlier occasion.

[9] First edition 'compane'. The women almost certainly came on the later visit. They would be kept on shore earlier until firm and friendly trading relations had been established. The similarity of the dress of men and women is well attested. Their relative height is, unfortunately, not indicated.

men are very dutifull towards them. And truely, the holsomnesse and temperature of this Climat, doth not onely argue this people to be answerable to this description, but also of a perfect constitution of body, actiue, strong, healthfull, and very wittie,[1] as the sundry toies of theirs cunningly wrought, may easily witnes. For the agreeing of this Climat with vs (I speake of my selfe, & so I may iustly do for the rest of our company)[2] that we found our health & strength all the while we remained there, so to renew and increase, as notwithstanding our diet and lodging was none of the best,[3] yet not one of our company (God be thanked) felt the least grudging or inclination to any disease or sicknesse, but were much fatter and in better health than when we went out of England. But after our barke had taken in so much Sassafras, Cedar, Furres, Skinnes, and other commodities,[4] as were thought conuenient; some of our company that had promised captaine Gosnold to stay, hauing nothing but a sauing voyage in their minds, made our company of inhabitants (which was small enough before) much smaller; so as captaine Gosnold seeing his whole strength to consist but of twelue men, and they but meanly prouided determined to return for England,[5] leauing this Island (which he called Elizabeths Island) with as many true sorrowfull eies, as were before desirous to see it. So the 18. of Iune,[6] being Friday, we weighed, and with indifferent faire winde and weather came to anker the 23 of Iuly, being also Friday (in all, bare fiue weeks) before Exmouth.

The goodnesse of the Climat.

Their return.

> Your Lordships[7] to command,
> Ihon Brereton.

[1] Witty here means intelligent and skilful.

[2] First ed. 'companie'. Gosnold (p. 210) was later also to stress the healthiness of the climate.

[3] The shortness in the stores was evident while they were still constructing the fort.

[4] We hear a good deal about sassafras and cedar once *Concord* got to England (pp. 205–8 below) but nothing of the furs.

[5] There is an element of confusion about the reason for not staying. Archer makes it clear that Gilbert was now in command of *Concord* and withheld supplies (wisely as it turned out). Gosnold's position was ambiguous: he desired to stay but was not prepared to force his men to take risks. As Archer makes clear, some distrusted Gilbert's promises to return as soon as possible (p. 137), and as others wanted their share of the proceeds of what they had got ('a saving voyage') the project was given up on 13 June. What Brereton does not say is that the fort was completed after this, before 17 June when they sailed, so that Gosnold's intention to return, if possible, is clear.

[6] First ed. no stop after '18'. They left on the 17th and rounded Gay Head on the 18th.

[7] His 'Lordship' is evidently Ralegh.

159

A briefe Note of such commodities as we saw in the country, notwithstanding our small time of stay.

Trees.

Sassafras trees, the roots whereof at 3.s. the pound are 336.l the tunne.[1]

Cedars tall and straight, in great abundance.[2]

Cypres trees.[3]

Oakes.[4]

Walnut trees great store.[5]

Elmes.[6]

Beech.[7]

Hollie.[8]

Haslenut trees.[9]

Cherry trees.[10]

Cotten trees.[11]

Other fruit trees to vs vnknowen.

The finder of our Sassafras in these parts, was one Master Robert Meriton.[12]

Fowles.

Eagles.[13]

Hernshawes.[14]

Cranes.[15]

Bitters.[16]

Mallards.[17]

Teales.[18]

Geese.[19]

Pengwins.[20]

Ospreis and Hawks.[21]

Crowes.[22]

Rauens.[23]

Mewes.[24]

Doues.[25]

Sea-pies.[26]

Blacke-birds with carnation wings.[27]

Beastes[28]

Deere in great store, very great and large.[29]

Beares.[30]

Luzernes.[31]

Blacke Foxes.[32]

Beauers.[33]

Otters.[34]

Wilde-Cats, very large and great.[35]

Dogs like Foxes, blacke and sharpe nosed.[36]

Conies.[37]

Fruits, Plants, and Herbs.

Tabacco, excellent sweet and strong.[38]

Vines in more plenty than in France.[39]

Ground-nuts, good meat, & also medicinable.[40]

Strawberries.[41]

Raspeberries.[42]

Gooseberries.[43]

Hurtleberries.[44]

Pease growing naturally.[45]

Flaxe.[46]

Iris Florentina, whereof apothecaries make sweet balles.[47]

Sorrell,[48] and many other herbs wherewith they made sallets.

Fishes.

Whales.[49]	Rockefish.[58]
Tortoises, both on land and sea.[50]	Doggefish.[59]
Seales.[51]	Lobstars.[60]
Cods.[52]	Crabbes.[61]
Mackerell:[53]	Muscles.[62]
Breames.[54]	Wilks.[63]
Herrings.[55]	Cockles.[64]
Thornbacke.[56]	Scallops.[65]
Hakes.[57]	Oisters.[66]

Snakes foure foot in length, and sixe inches about, which the Indians eat for daintie meat, the skinnes whereof they vse for girdles.[67]

Colours to die with, red, white, and blacke.[68]

Mettals and Stones.

Copper in great abundance,[69]	Stones of a blue metalline colour, which we take to be Steele oare.
Emerie stones for Glasiers & Cutlers.	Stones of all sorts for buildings.[70]
Alabaster very white.	
Stones glistering and shining like Minerall stones.	Clay, red & white, which may proue good Terra Sigillata.[71]

[1] White Sassafras, *Sassafras albidum* (Nutt.) Nees. For its use as food, drink and medicine *see* Fernald, Kinsey and Rollins, *Edible plants of eastern North America* (1958), pp. 209–11; Charles Manning and Merrill Moore 'Sassafras and syphilis' in *New England Quarterly*, IX (1936), 473–5. For prices see pp. 160, 206 below.

[2] White Cedar, Arbor Vitae, *Thuja occidentalis* L. but possibly also Atlantic White Cedar, *Chamaecyparis thyoides* (L.) BSP.

[3] Common Juniper, *Juniperus communis* L. which in America is only occasionally tree-like and 10–20 feet tall. This could have been the Atlantic White Cedar or the Red Cedar, *J. virginiana* L. For other junipers see Hyland and Steinmetz, *The Woody Plants of Maine* (1944), pp. 3–4.

[4] See p. 259 below.

[5] White Walnut or Butternut, *Juglans cinerea* L. is the most common species in eastern North America. The Black Walnut, *J. nigra* L. may have been more widely distributed at this time since it was valued by the Indians as an important source of food.

[6] American Elm, *Ulmus americana* L. and possibly Slippery Elm, *U. rubra* Muhl, but Cork or Rock Elm, *U. Thomasi* Sarg. is less likely.

[7] Beech, *Fagus grandifolia* Ehrh.

Notes for pp. 160–161

⁸ American Holly, *Ilex opaca* Ait most nearly resembles the European holly. The Black Alder or Winterberry, *I. verticillata* (L.) Gray. var. *fastigiata* (Bickn.) Fern. is a holly found growing on wet sands near the sea in this New England area.

⁹ Hazel-nut, *Corylus americana* Walt. Some of the hickories may also be included, possibly Shagbark, *Carya ovata* (Mill.) K. Koch and Pignut, *C. ovalis* (Wang.) Sarg.

¹⁰ Beach Plum, *Prunus maritima* March, Choke Cherry, *P. virginiana* L., Black Cherry, *P. serotina* Ehrh, Pin-cherry, *P. pensylvanica* L.f. and possibly also Service Berry, *Amelanchier canadensis* (L.) Medic. These are generally of shrubby habit and will grow especially in burnt clearings and other disturbed habitats.

¹¹ Balsam Poplar or Taccamahac, *Populus balsamifera* L. is a possibility or the Cottonwood, *P. deltoides* Marsh may have been present.

¹² Besides adding a name to the few known members of the *Concord's* company this suggests that Robert Meriton was an apothecary or apothecary's servant sent to collect medicinal plants. If so he may have contributed significantly to the record of the natural resources of the islands. If he was not, his ability to identify sassafras could have come from having been on one of the Roanoke voyages or some later sassafras hunting expedition.

¹³ Bald Eagle, *Haliaeetus leucocephalus leucocephalus* (Linnaeus).

¹⁴ Great Blue Heron, *Ardea herodias herodias* Linnaeus, Black-crowned Night Heron, *Nycticorax nycticorax hoactli* (Gmelin), Eastern Green heron, *Butorides virescens virescens* (Linnaeus) and possibly Yellow-crowned Night Heron, *Nyctanassa violacea violacea* since 'the tendency of young herons in America to migrate northward in summer is well known'.

¹⁵ Of the Whooping Crane, *Grus americana* (Linnaeus), now in danger of extinction, this comment is made, 'a search through the writings of the early explorers and settlers on the Atlantic coast leads to the belief that this great bird was once a transient there, and was at least an occasional visitor to some New England States' (Forbush and May, p. 155). The Sandhill Crane, *G. canadensis tabida* (Peters), was also seen in migration in New England before settlement drove it west.

¹⁶ American Bittern, *Botaurus lentiginosus* (Montagu), and possibly Eastern Least Bittern, *Ixobrychus exilis exilis* (Gmelin).

¹⁷ Common Mallard, *Anas platyrhynchos platyrhynchos* Linnaeus. For other ducks see p. 305 below.

¹⁸ Green-winged Teal, *Nettion carolinense* (Gmelin) would certainly be seen in migration and Blue-winged Teal, *Querquedula discors* (Linnaeus) which breeds in Maine and Rhode Island.

¹⁹ American Brant, *Branta bernicla hrota* (Müller) winters on the Atlantic coast from Massachusetts to Florida migrating north from February to March in increasing numbers. Some of the Common Canada Goose, *B. canadensis canadensis* winter in Martha's Vineyard and elsewhere in Massachusetts and begin migration from there in late February and March. White-fronted Goose, *Anser albifrons albifrons* (Scopoli) could also have been seen.

²⁰ The penguins were specimens of the Great Auk, *Alca impennis* Linn., then prevalent on the New England shores and known to English Newfoundland fishermen who used them for food. Instead of Gilbert Point, 'C. Penquin' appears to mark this point on the Velasco map of 1610 (cp. p. 523). Great Auk, *Plautus impennis* (Linnaeus); Forbush & May, *Birds of Eastern and Central North America*, pp. 241–2; Great Auk, *Pinguinus impennis* (Linnaeus), W. E. Godfrey, *Birds of Canada* (1966), p. 195.

²¹ Sharp-shinned Hawk, *Accipiter velox velox* (Wilson), Eastern Red-tailed Hawk, *Buteo borealis borealis* (Gmelin), Marsh Hawk, *Circus hudsonius* (Linnaeus) and other species. American Osprey, *Pandion haliaetus carolinensis* (Gmelin).

[22] Eastern Crow, *Corvus brachyrhynchos brachyrhynchos* Brehm, with Fish Crow, *C. ossifragus* Wilson for southern Connecticut, Buzzards Bay and Cape Cod.

[23] Northern Raven, *Corvus corax principalis* Ridgway.

[24] Black-backed Gull, *Larus marinus* Linnaeus, Herring Gull, *L. argentatus smithsonianus* Coues, Laughing Gull, *L. atricilla* Linnaeus, and at this time, before settlement, Ring-billed Gull, *L. delawarensis* Ord, would seem to be the most common of the gulls.

[25] Eastern Mourning Dove, *Zenaidura macroura carolinensis* (Linnaeus).

[26] American Oyster-catcher, *Haemotopus palliatus palliatus* Temminck.

[27] Eastern Red-wing, *Agelais phoeniceus phoeniceus* (Linnaeus).

[28] A. K. Keith, *The Mammals of Martha's Vineyard* (Dukes County Historical Society, Edgartown, 1969) is a useful checklist. But some of the furs and skins came from animals not known to have reached the island.

[29] White-tailed Deer, *Dama virginiana*, the subspecies for the northern area being *D. v. borealis* (Miller).

[30] Black Bear, *Ursus americanus*, the most likely being *U. americanus americanus* Pallas.

[31] As Brereton makes a distinction between luzernes and wild-cats the former would most probably be the Lynx, *Lynx canadensis* with the Bobcat, *Felis rufa* or *Lynx rufus*, or even the Puma, see above p. 155.

[32] Gray Fox, *Urocyon cinereoargenteus*, the species most common to eastern New England being *U. cinereoargenteus borealis* Merriam, and *U. cinereoargenteus cinereoargenteus* (Schreber).

[33] Beaver, *Castor canadensis acadicus* V. Bailey and Doutt ranges from eastern Canada to Connecticut.

[34] River Otter, *Lutra canadensis canadensis* Schreber for the northern area, with *L. canadensis laxatina* occuring south from Connecticut.

[35] Wilde-cats see n. 31 above, and pp. 170, 225 below. This does sound like the Puma.

[36] Dogs like foxes, pp. 306–7.

[37] Marsh rabbit, *Sylvilagus palustris palustris*, Eastern Cottontail, *S. floridanus hitchensi*, New England Cottontail, *S. transitionalis* (Bangs) are indicated for New England.

[38] Tobacco, *Nicotiana rustica* L., the common Indian-cultivated variety; cp. Driver and Massey 'Comparative studies' (pp. 260–2, map 67). It was not greatly appreciated in England.

[39] Fox Grape, *Vitis labrusca* L. the common wild grape of the northeast and the species which has contributed to the parentage of many cultivated varieties. Summer Grape, *V. aestivalis* Michx, spreads north into Massachusetts and is found on Martha's Vineyard and Cape Cod.

[40] Groundnuts, *Apios americana* Medic. This plant was held in high repute by the Indians and the early colonists as a valuable food. (Fernald, Kinsey and Rollins, *Edible Plants of Eastern North America* (1958), pp. 252–4.)

[41] Strawberry, *Fragaria virginia* Duchesne, including *F. canadensis* (Michx) Fern.

[42] The genus Rubus includes raspberries, blackberries, dewberries and cloudberries. In England in the sixteenth century the genus was covered by the name Bramble while Raspberry, *Rubus Idaeus*, was the cultivated berry. This raspberry, now *R. idaeus* L., was introduced from Europe into America and naturalized but the native American species closely resembled it and was related to *R. strigosus* Michx. The most common tall Blackberry in the northeast is *R. allegheniensis* Porter, with many variants as the species hybridizes freely. It is therefore not possible to say what species of Rubus they found growing there but it is interesting that they should use the name of the more desirable raspberry to describe them.

43 Wild Gooseberry, *Ribes cynosbati* L. Ribes includes currants as well as gooseberries and Archer is probably using the name to cover currants, such as Wild Currant, *R. triste* Pall and Wild, Black Currant, *R. americanum* Mill. Rosier does distinguish gooseberries and currants (see below p. 308).

44 Low Sweet Blueberry, *Vaccinium angustifolium* Ait, and Blue Huckleberry, *V. vacillans* Torr are typical of the northeastern states. As this species hybridizes freely precise identification would be misleading. A useful general comment is given in Fernald, Kinsey and Rollins, *Edible Plants of eastern North America* (1958), pp. 315–16.

45 Beach Pea, *Lathyrus japonicus* Willd. and *L. maritimus* (L) Bigel. The two North American plants var. *glaber* (Ser.) Fern. and var. *pellitus* (Fern.) Gl. vary in abundance between the New England coast and the Great Lakes, and would be the ones most commonly found on the shore. Another widely distributed species both in N. America and Eurasia found on shores and wet meadows is the Marsh Vetchling, *L. palustris* L.

46 *Linum virginianum* L., *L. intercursum* Bickn. and *L. striatum* Walt. var. *multijugum* Fern. are the native flax plants most common in this region, and are very like the European plant.

47 Not in first edition. Iris Florentina, *Iris florentina* Linn. is not native to Britain or to North America. It has a white flower and its aromatic root, orris root, was used for making sweet waters and powders. The plant with a superficial resemblance in America is the Sweet Flag, *Acorus calamus* L. which belongs to the arum family but has an aromatic root. See above pp. 20–1.

48 'This was almost certainly some of the species of Dock rather than *Oxalis*, the Wood Sorrel. Both Lyte and Gerard follow Dioscorides in having a section for the Docks called Sorrel. Gerard distinguishes sorrel from the dock as having leaves winged at the base where they spring from the stem (*Herball*, pp. 319–21). Of the native American Docks the most probable are Golden Dock, *Rumex maritimus* L. which is also widely distributed in Europe, Seashore Dock, *R. persicaroides* L., both growing along the coast of New England, and Water Dock, *R. orbiculatus* Gray. There are many species of sorrel in America the most common in the northeast being *Oxalis stricta* L.

49 Whales, see p. 307 below.

50 The description is too vague for any identification to be possible. The Snapping Turtle, *Chelydra serpentina serpentina* Linn. and Box Turtle, *Terrapene carolina carolina* Linn. are the most likely. They could have been Sea Turtles, possibly Loggerhead Turtle, *Caretta caretta caretta* (Lin.) though this is less likely. (Cp. C. H. Pope, *Turtles of the United States and Canada* (1939), pp. 72–83, 138–47, 278–86; A. F. Carr, *Handbook of Turtles* (1952), pp. 61–9, 116–35, 382–93.)

51 Harbor Seal, *Phoca vitulina* Linn. with possibly Harp Seal *P. groenlandica* Erxleben and Hooded Seal, *P. cristata* Nilsson (cp. Allen, 'List of the *Mammalia*', *Fauna of New England*, pt. 3 (1904), pp. 20–1).

52 Cod, *Gadus calarias* Linn. as in European waters.

53 Mackerel, *Scomber scombrus* Linn. and Club Mackerel, *Pneumatophorus colias* (Gmelin) both as in European waters.

54 No bream as such are found off New England. Probably some of the Porgies are meant, Scup, *Stenotomus versicolor* (Mitchill), being the more likely though Sheepshead, *Archosargus probatocephalus* (Walbaum) is possible.

55 Herring, *Clupea harengus* Linn. as in Europe, together with species of a similar character including Alewife, *Pomolonus pseudoharengus* (Wilson) and Blueback (Summer Herring), *P. aestivalis* (Mitchill), and possibly – though rather large and distinctive to be identified as herring – Shad, *Alosa sapidissima* (Wilson). Cp. Wood, *New Englands prospect* (1634), p. 34, 'The Herrings be much like them that be caught on the English coasts. Alewives be a kind of fish which is much like a Herring, which in the latter end of Aprill

Notes for pp. 160–161

come up the fresh Rivers to Spawne...The Shaddes be bigger than the English Shaddes and fatter.'

[56] Thorny Skate, *Raia radiata* Donovan, also in European waters.

[57] Silver Hake, *Merluccius bilinearis* (Mitchill); *see also* Whiting below p. 307. White Hake, *Urophycis tensus* (Mitchill) and Squirrel Hake, U. chuss (Welbaum) are probably all included.

[58] It is not quite clear whether the Sea Basses or Rockfishes (or both) are meant. The Rosefish, *Sebastes marinus* (Linn.), occurs in European waters and is the more likely for Maine. It is, with the Sea Bass, *Centropristes striatus* (Linn.), likely south of Cape Cod.

[59] The only member of the shark family mentioned in this group of narratives, Spiny Dogfish, *Squalus acanthias* Linn., as in European waters.

[60] First ed. 'Lobster'. Lobster, *Homarus americanus* Milne Edwards (Mary J. Rathbun, 'List of the *Crustacea*', *Fauna of New England*, pt, 5 (1905), p. 18).

[61] Rock Crab, *Cancer irroratus* Say, Green Crab, *Carcinides maenas* (Linn.), and Spider Crab, *Libinia emarginata* Leach (M. J. Rathbun 'List of the *Crustacea*', *Fauna of New England*, pt. 5 (1905), pp. 8, 9, 12), are found all along the New England coast. The Blue Crab, *Callinectes sapidus* Rathbun is found only south of Cape Cod (ibid., p. 9).

[62] Blue Mussel, *Mytilus edulis* Linn., Northern Horse Mussel, *Modiclus* (or *Valsella*) *modlicus* Linn. and Hooked Mussel, *Brachicontes recurvus* Dafinesque (cp. R. Tucker Abbott, *American Seashells* (1954), pp. 303, 351, 354).

[63] Common Northern Buccinum (as in Europe), *Buccinum undatum* Linn., and also the Channeled Whelk, *Busycon canaliculatum* Linn. are the most common species in this area. (Cp. R. Tucker Abbott, *American Seashells* (1954), pp. 225, 236.)

[64] Morton's Egg Cockle, *Laevicardium mortoni* Conrad, and Iceland Cockle, *Clinocardium ciliatum* Fabricius are both present (cp. R. Tucker Abbott, *American sea shells* (1954), pp. 400, 408). Wood, *New Englands prospect* (1634), p. 35, however describes the clam as 'a shelfish not much unlike a cockle', while Josselyn, *New-Englands rarities* (1672), pp. 36–7, describes the shell from which the Indians make wampum (quahog) as 'a kind of Coccle', so that Brereton's 'cockles' are quite likely to be clams.

[65]. Rough (or Bay) Scallop, *Aequipectum irradians* (Lamarck). He may also have seen shells of the Atlantic Deep-sea Scallop, *Placopecten magellanicus* Gmelin. (Cp. R. Tucker Abbott, *American Seashells* (1954), pp. 366–8.)

[66] Oyster, *Crassostrea virginica* Gmelin (cp. R. Tucker Abbott, *American Seashells* (1954), p. 375).

[67] For snake-eating see Flannery, *Analysis*, p. 25.

[68] 'Colours...black', not in 1st ed.

[69] No sources of native copper could have been discovered within the area the expedition covered.

[70] See pp. 109–11. It seems pointless to discuss the other minerals mentioned since the whole area from the tip of Cape Cod, southwards and westwards along the southern coast of Massachusetts is covered with glacial drift (except for Cretaceous outcrops at Gay Head) and in this any kind of erratic may be found, while there are clay-beds widely dispersed. See Barbara B. Chamberlain, *These fragile outposts* (1964), *passim* and map at p. 72. The *Terra Sigillata* is a myth (cp. Quinn, *Roanoke voyages*, I, 208, 328).

[71] 'Which...Sigillata', not in 1st ed.

A briefe Note[1] of the sending another barke this present yeere 1602.[2] by the honorable knight, SIR WALTE[R][3] RALEGH for the searching out of his Colonie in Virginia.

Samuel Mace of Weimouth,[4] a very sufficent Mariner, an honest sober man, who had beene at Virginia twise before, was imploied thither by Sir Walter Ralegh, to finde those people which were left there in the yeere 1587.[5] To whose succour he hath sent fiue seuerall times at his own charges.[6] The parties by him set foorth, performed nothing; some of them following their owne profit elsewhere; others returning with friuolous allegations.[7] At this last time, to auoid all excuse,[8] he bought a barke, and hired all the company for wages by the moneth: who departing from Weimouth in March last 1602,[9] fell fortie leagues to the Southwestward of Hatarask,[10] in thirtie foure

---

[1] Reprinted by Purchas, *Pilgrimes*, IV (1625), 1613, without significant variants.

[2] First ed. '1602, by the honourable'.

[3] First ed. 'Walter'. Final 'R' omitted in second.

[4] Samuel Mace of Weymouth, Dorset (on whom there appears to be nothing whatever in the Weymouth Borough Records), was master of the *Brave* of the Isle of Wight in 1590 (P.R.O., H.C.A. 13/29, 24: see Quinn, *Roanoke voyages*, II, 564). He was concerned in the Ralegh-Keymis Guiana voyages of 1594–6, but no clear evidence on his Virginia voyages before 1602 is available, though it appears likely that they took place in 1600 and 1601, respectively. See Quinn, *England and the Discovery of America* (1973), pp. 202–14.

[5] On the Lost Colonists see Quinn, *Roanoke voyages*, II, *passim*, and *England and the discovery of America* (1979), pp. 432–81.

[6] The voyages of 1588 and 1590 are well documented (Quinn, *Roanoke voyages*, II, *passim*). Ralegh's intention of calling at Virginia on his way back from Guiana in 1595 was not implemented (*Discoverie of Guiana* (1596), p. 5). Since the five occasions apparently included 1602 it seems least unlikely that the missing voyages were in 1600 and 1601.

[7] The attempts in 1588, 1590, and 1602 (but see pp. 204–6 below) were not frivolous. If Mace had been involved in any of them the wording casts some reflection on his ability.

[8] It may be that on one or more occasions Ralegh had tried to divert privateers, as in 1590, to call at Roanoke Island on their way home, and that they failed to do so.

[9] First ed. '1602': second edition '1602', which by strict English usage could extend up to 24 March the following year, though the use of the calendar year, especially with Hakluyt, was common, and is here intended.

[10] 'Hatarask' was the name given, 1584–90, to the island which extended northwards in the Carolina Outer Banks from modern Cape Hatteras to what is now Oregon Inlet but it also, and especially after 1586, meant the entry through the Banks somewhat to the north of the modern Oregon Inlet. Search for the Lost Colonists there had failed in 1590: it might have been more logical if Mace had been directed to Chesapeake Bay where the colonists intended to go in 1587. A distance of 40 leagues, 120 nautical miles, to a latitude of approximately 34° N. would bring a landfall between Cape Fear and Cape Lookout, possibly a little nearer to the latter, but no great accuracy can be inferred from the indications.

degrees or thereabout;[1] and hauing there spent a moneth;[2] when they came along the coast to seeke the people, they did it not, pretending that the extremitie of weather and losse of some principall ground-tackle, forced and feared them from searching the port of Hatarask, to which they were sent. From that place where they abode, they brought Sassafras,[3] Radix Chinae or the China root,[4] Beniamin,[5] Cassia, lignea[6] & a rinde of a tree more strong than any spice as yet knowen,[7] with diuers other commodities,[8] which hereafter in a larger discourse may come to light.[9]

A Treatise, conteining important inducements for the planting in these parts, and finding a passage that way to the South sea and China.[10]

[1] Mace may have gone the long way out by way of the Caribbean, or directly westward from Madeira as Grenville did in 1586. If he left England about 20 March he would arrive by the longer route about 1 June, and if he left for England about 1 July he could have got to Weymouth between 15 and 20 August where Ralegh met him (cp. p. 205 below). Rough weather on this coast in early summer (indeed in almost any season) would not be unlikely: there were no sheltered harbours outside the Banks.

[2] The expedition was equipped to dig out roots, etc. and had copper gorgets and other articles for trade (see Quinn, *England and the Discovery of America*, pp. 411–12), though we do not know that Indians were encountered. The stormy Outer Banks, especially, near modern Cape Hatteras gave them an excuse for not anchoring off Hatarask if they lacked sufficient anchors.

[3] *Sassafras albidum* (Nutt.) Nees, cp. pp. 224–5: '...they cast foorth a moste sweete smell, so that at the beginning when they saw them first, they thought they had beene trees of Cinamon.' (Gerard, *Herball* (1597), p. 1341.)

[4] *Smilax pseudochina* L. or related Woody Smilax, see pp. 196, 437 below.

[5] Benjamin is possibly Wild Spicebush, *Lindera Benzoin* (L) Blume (Fernald, *Gray's Manual* (1950), p. 678; Gleason and Cronquist, *Manual* (1963), p. 322). Cp. the almond benjamin, *Belzuinum mandolato*, a gum resin from Sian and Baros, in Hakluyt, *Principall navigations* (1589), p. 219.

[6] First ed. 'cassia lignea'. There is no tree-like cassia in North America, It is probably Sweet Gum, *Liquidambar styraciflua* (Gleason and Cronquist, *Manual*, p. 364). Cp. Gerard, *Herball* (1597), p. 1349, on the Cinnamon Tree, 'it is called of some Cassia, and Cassia lignea, but vnproperly'.

[7] This is quite probably Sweet Bay, *Magnolia virginiana* L.

[8] Nothing is known of the other commodities brought back.

[9] No such additional narrative has come to light.

[10] The heading is completely reset in the same words from the first edition, though Huntington 2 has 'see'. The document is essentially an abstract (with a few additions) of 'A discourse conserning a voyage intended for the planting of chrystyan religion and people in the Northwest regions of America', prepared by Edward Hayes in 1592 or 1593 (Cambridge University Library, MS Dd. 3. 85, no. 4). Published for the first time in *N.A.W.*, III (1979), pp. 156–72.

Temperate
Climats.

The voiage which we intend, is to plant Christian people and religion[1] vpon the Northwest countries of America,[2] in places temperat and well agreeing with our constitution, which though the same doe lie betweene 40. and 44. degrees[3] of latitude, vnder the Paralels of Italy and France,[4] yet are not they so hot; by reason that the suns heat is qualified in his course ouer the Ocean, before he arriueth vpon the coasts of America,[5] attracting much vapour from the sea: which mitigation of his heat, we take for a benefit to vs that intend to inhabit there; because vnder the Climat of 40 degrees, the same would be too vehement els for our bodies to endure.[6]

Her Maiesties
title.

These lands were neuer yet actually possessed by any Christian prince or people, yet often intended to be by the French nation, which long sithence had inhabited there, if domesticall warres had not withheld them:[7] notwithstanding the same are the rightfull inheritance of her Maiestie,[8] being first discouered by our nation in the time of King Henrie the seuenth, vnder the conduct of Iohn Cabot and his sonnes:[9] by which title of first discouery, the kings of Portugall and Spaine doe holde and enioy their ample and rich kingdomes in their Indies East and West; and also lately planted in part by the Colonies sent thither by the honourable knight, Sir Walter Ralegh.[10]

[1] First ed. '&'. The East India Company was at this time reviving the idea of voyaging to the East by way of a Northwest Passage, to which George Waymouth led an unsuccessful expedition in 1602 (*Calendar of State Papers, Colonial, East Indies, China and Japan, 1513–1616*, pp. 128–38). Compare the sequence with that of the elder Hakluyt below p. 181. The Cambridge version has a preliminary chapter on the need for missions (*NAW*, III, 158).

[2] 'Northwest' is used as meaning Northwest of Europe, i.e. Northeast North America. Cp. a discourse of *circa* 1593–7 (P.R.O., C.O. 1/1,9 in *NAW*, III, 172–5), which has the same confusing usage.

[3] First ed. 'do lie betweene 40 & 44 degrees'.

[4] First ed. 'Italie & France'.

[5] Hayes is still taking a Ptolemaic view of the cosmos, with his Sun going round the earth (cp. his views in 1583, Quinn, *Gilbert*, II, 405).

[6] A typically English – perhaps Liverpudlian – reluctance to admit that even southern Europe had a summer climate bearable for Englishmen.

[7] One major incentive to renewed English enterprise in North America had been increased activity there by France after the signing of the Treaty of Vervins in 1598 with Spain.

[8] The English challenge to Spain had more often been on the basis of effective occupation than of prior discovery, though the latter had been used by Hakluyt (notably in his 'A particuler discourse', in 1584; Taylor, *Hakluyts*, II; *NAW*, III, 71–123).

[9] Hayes had 'John Cabot the father, and Sebastian his sonne' in his 1583 narrative (*NAW*, IV, 23), but not in his Newfoundland treatise of 1586 (B.L., Lansdowne MS 100, f. 83; *NAW*, III, 125).

[10] The colonies of 1585, 1586, and 1587, the last of which was assumed to be still in being. This is not in C.U.L. MS Dd. 3. 85, no. 4; *NAW*, III, 156–72; cp. Quinn, *England and the discovery of America*, pp. 432–81.

The course vnto these countreys, is thorow the Ocean, altogether free from all restraint by forren princes to be made; whereunto other our accustomed trades are subiect; apt for most winds that can blow, to be performed commonly in 30 or 35 daies.[1] The coast faire, with safe roads and harbors for ships: Many riuers.

These lands be faire and pleasant, resembling France, intermedled with mountaines, valleys, medowes, woodlands, and champians. The soile is exceeding strong, by reason it was neuer manured; and will be therefore most fit to beare at first, Rape-seeds, Hempe, Flax, and whatsoeuer els requireth such strong soile. Rape-oiles, and all sorts of oiles, will be very commodious for England, which spendeth oiles aboundantly[2] about Clothing and Leather-dressing. In like sort, Hempe and Flax are profitable, whether the same be sent into England, or wrought there by our people; Oad also will grow there aswell or better than in Terçera.

The Saluages weare faire colours in some of their atire,[3] whereby we hope to finde rich dies and colours for painting.

The trees are for the most part, Cedars, Pines, Spruse, Firre and Oaks[4], to the Northward. Of these trees will be drawen Tarre and Pitch, Rosen, Turpentine, and Soapeashes:[5] They will make masts for the greatest shippes of the world: Excellent timbers of Cedar, and boords for curious building.[6]

Margin notes: A commodious and safe course. Riuers. Fertile lands. Rape oiles. Dies.

---

[1] C.U.L. MS Dd. 3. 85, no. 4 (*NAW*, III, 159), has 'commonly in 30 dayes or vnder', though his own voyage to Newfoundland took 51 days in 1583 (Quinn, *Gilbert*, II, 380).

[2] First ed. 'abundantly'. Vegetable oils (e.g. rape oil from Rape, *Brassica campestris* L.), textiles for ropes and sails (notably Hemp, *Cannabis sativa* L. and Flax, *Linum usitatissimum* L.) and dyes (including Woad, *Isatis tinctoria* L.) were amongst the Eurasian plants sought in vain by the English in North America. These plants were hard on the soil and woad had been forbidden to be grown in England in 1585. Their cultivation in America offered an incentive both to settlers and to investors in settlement. Rape (not rape oil), flax, hemp, but not Terceira woad are mentioned in C.U.L. MS Dd. 3. 85, no. 4, *NAW*, III, 159.

[3] J.C.B. and Huntington have 'attire'. Most expeditions noted the evidence of dyestuffs in Indian bodypaint and decorated objects since the cloth trade required new sources of colours: such colours were remarked by Hakluyt (1582), Bellenger (1583), Harriot (1588) and Brereton (above p. 161).

[4] 'Fyrr, pyne & cedar', in C.U.L. MS Dd. 3, 85, no. 4, *NAW*, III, 159. His cedar was a member of the Cypress family. He could have seen the Juniper, *Juniperus communis* L. in Newfoundland in 1583, while it is just possible that there were specimens of the White Cedar, *Thuja occidentalis* L. there present as well (cp. Gleason and Cronquist, *Manual*, pp. 30–1). He would also know the Red Cedar, *J. virginiana* L. was brought from Roanoke Island in 1584 and later (Quinn, *Roanoke voyages*, I, 95, 97, 364).

[5] First ed. 'Soapeashes. They'.

[6] 'curious' here means exotic. Huntington has 'buildings'. Pitch, tar, resin, and turpentine were all primary necessities for ships' stores, potash for soapmaking, essential

Minerals.
Copper.

The cliffes vpon the coasts and mountaines euery where shew great likelihood of Minerals. A very rich mine of Copper is found, whereof I haue seene proofe; and the place described.[1] Not farre from which there is great hope also of a Siluer mine. There be faire quarries of stone, of beautifull colours, for buildings.[2]

Grapes.

The ground bringeth forth,[3] without industrie, Pease, Roses, Grapes, Hempe, besides other plants, fruits, herbs and flowers, whose pleasant view and delectable smelles doe demonstrate sufficiently the fertility[4] and sweetnesse of that soile and aire.

Beasts.

Beasts of many kindes; some of the bignesse of an Oxe, whose hides make good buffe:[5] Deere, both red and of other sorts in aboundance:[6] Luzerns, Marterns, Sables, Beauers, Beares, Otters, Wolues, Foxes, and Squirrels, which to the Northward are blacke, and accounted very rich furres.[7]

Fowles.

Fowles both of the water and land, infinit store and varietie; Hawks both short and long winged, Partriges[8] in abundance, which are verie

---

in the cloth industry. There appears to have been increased competition in the Baltic (from the Dutch) for these commodities and especially for good mast timber, which North America could, all early observers were sure, supply most satisfactorily.

[1] This is evidently drawn from his experience in Newfoundland in 1583 but 'cliffes' did not appear in C.U.L. MS Dd. 3. 85, no. 4, *NAW*, III, 159. On copper and silver resources believed to be present see pp. 202–3, 348 below.

[2] First ed. 'buldings'.   [3] First ed. 'forth without'.

[4] First ed. 'fertilitie'. A vaguely generalized paragraph: even his mention of individual plants is unsystematic. Beach-peas, wild roses and nettles (for hemp) he could have seen at St John's in 1583, grapes not.

[5] First ed. 'Buffe'. C.U.L. MS Dd. 3. 85, no. 4 (*NAW*, III, 159–60), has 'Somme of the Bygnes of an oxe...not much vnlyke the Buffel'. Parkhurst had reported buffalo from Newfoundland in 1578, Gilbert had had news of comparable large skins from the mainland in 1580, while Hayes in 1583 had reports of 'buffaloes or a beast it seemeth by the track and foote very large in manner of an oxe' (Hakluyt, *Principall navigations* (1589), pp. 676, 689; Quinn, *Gilbert*, II, 310). Hayes may well have had news of the buffalo on the mainland but he had no data to distinguish between the other large beasts of the mainland and islands, moose and caribou (only the latter being in Newfoundland).

[6] First ed. 'abundance'.

[7] First ed. 'Furres'. *Lynx canadensis canadensis* Kerr, in Newfoundland and the mainland, Bobcat, *Lynx rufus rufus* (Schreber), probably on mainland only (cp. Hall and Kelson, *Mammals*, II, 971). His 'Marterns' are Fisher, *Mustela vison* L. or possibly Muskrat, cp. p. 155 above. There are no northern black squirrels. It is possible he heard of or saw skins of the Fox Squirrel with men who had been to trade for furs in the St Lawrence since the Fox Squirrel, *Sciurus niger niger* L. has, as its northern limit, the southern shores of the Great Lakes from which its skins could have been traded. (Cp. Hall and Kelson, *Mammals*, I, 387–8).

[8] First ed. 'Partidges', 'very', 'aswell'. Hayes was no ornithologist but his observations probably reflect what he remembered of what he saw in 1583. His blackbird would be Rusty Blackbird, *Euphagus carolinus* (Müller), but there is no bird now in Newfoundland more like a canary than the Yellow Warbler, *Dendroica petechia* (L.) (Godfrey, *Birds of Canada* (1966), pp. 358, 326).

great, and easily taken. Birds great and small some like vnto our Blacke-birds, others like Canarie-birds: And many (as well birds as other creatures) strange and differing from ours of Europe.

Fish, namely Cods, which as we encline more vnto the South, are more large and vendible for England and France, then the[1] Newland fish. Whales and Seales in great abundances.[2] Oiles of them are rich commodities for England, whereof we now make Soape, besides many other vses. Item, Tunneys, Anchoues, Bonits, Salmons, Lobsters, Oisters hauing Pearle,[3] and infinit other sorts of fish, which are more plentifull vpon those Northwest coasts of America, than in any parts of the knowen world. Salt is reported to be found there, which els may be made there,[4] to serue sufficiently for all fishing.

So as the commodities there to be raised both of the sea and land (after that we haue planted our people skilfull and industrious) will be Fish, Whale and Seale oiles, Soape ashes and Soape, Tarre and Pitch, Rosen and Turpentine, Masts, Timber and boords of Cedars, Firres, and Pines, Hempe, Flaxe, Cables and Ropes, Saile-clothes, Grapes, and Raisens and Wines, Corne, Rape-seeds & oiles, Hides, Skinnes, Furres, Dies and Colours for painting, Pearle, Mettals, and other Minerals. *Commodities in generall.*

These commodities before rehearsed, albeit for the most part they be grosse,[5] yet are the same profitable for the State of England specially, aswell in regard of the vse of such commodities, as for the imploiment also of our people and ships; the want whereof, doth decay our townes *Imploiment of our people, and repairing decaied ports.*

---

[1] First ed. 'than'. Evidence on cod off the mainland coast was new in 1602 (p. 118 above). He could perhaps have taken something from Richard Fisher who fished in 1593 off the Nova Scotia coast (Hakluyt, *Principal navigations* (1600), 193), though it is just possible he had information on earlier English fishing pioneers in the Gulf of Maine. The paragraph is not in C.U.L. Ms Dd. 3. 85, no. 4 (*NAW*, III, 160).

[2] First ed. 'abundance'. For the search for animal oils see Quinn, *England and the discovery of America*, pp. 320–21.

[3] He does not mention lobsters in C.U.L. MS Dd. 3. 85, no. 4 (*NAW*, III, 160), but all are in his 1583 reports except anchovy and tuna. Anchovies are not now recorded for Newfoundland (Jordan and Evermann, *Checklist* (1896), pp. 284–6), while the oyster now appears only on the southern shores of the Gulf of St Lawrence (J. Stafford, *The Canadian Oyster* (1913), pp. 8–9). Did Hayes have an opportunity before 1583 of meeting Englishmen who had been in the Gulf of St Lawrence (Edward Cotton appears to have been there in 1579 or 1580, see *England and the discovery of America*, p. 315), or, later on, fishermen who had before 1602 caught anchovies off Cape Cod or farther south?

[4] Hayes is not clear: salt 'found' would presumably be rock salt; salt which could be 'made' would depend on climate and suitable beaches (cp. pp. 188, 216–17).

[5] 'slight' commodities were those of small bulk and high value; 'gross' commodities were those of high bulk and small unit value. Hayes is hoping that with the access of 'gross' commodities from North America to her markets she would attract the bulk of the fur and fishing produce of America also and make her the great entrepôt for American trade. He does not indicate how he would dispossess French and Basques of their established trade (in 1586 he would have taxed them, B.L. Lansdowne MS 100, ff. 83–94, *NAW*, III, 128).

and ports of England, and causeth the realme to swarme full with poore and idle people.[1]

The trade to Newfoundland shalbe remoued to vs.

These commodities in like sort, are of great vse and estimation in all the South and Westerne countreys of Europe; namely, Italie, France and Spaine: for the which all nations that haue beene accustomed to repaire vnto the Newfound-land for the commoditie of fish and oiles alone, will henceforward forsake the Newfound-land, and trade with vs, when once we haue planted people in those parts: by whose industrie shall be prouided for all commers, both fish and oiles, and many commodities besides, of good importance & value.

Spanish commodities.

Then will the Spaniards and Portugals bring vnto vs in exchange of such commodities before mentioned, Wines, Sweet oiles, Fruits, Spices, Sugars, Silks, Gold and Siluer, or whatsoeuer that Europe yeeldeth, to supply our necessities, and to increase our delights.[2]

English commodities.

For which Spanish commodities and other sorts likewise, our merchants of England will bring vnto vs againe, Cloth, Cattell, for our store and breed,[3] and euery thing els that we shall need, or that England shall haply exchange for such commodities.

Vent of our Cloth.

By this intercourse, our habitations will be made a Staple of all vendible commodities of the world, and a meanes to vent a very great quantitie of our English cloth into all the cold regions of America extended very farre.[4]

Intercourse will soone be had with other nacions.

This intercourse also will[5] be soone drawen together by this reason: That neere adioining vpon the same coasts of Newfound-land, is the greatest fishing of the world; whether[6] doe yeerely repaire about 400 sailes of ships, for no other commoditie than Fish and Whale-oiles. Then

[1] Unemployment had loomed large in Hakluyt's 'A particuler discourse' in 1584 (Taylor, *Hakluyts*, II, 233–9), but whether it was still a major factor in 1602 is not clear – war had influenced trades in ways difficult for a contemporary to calculate. He seems to be saying the import of 'gross' commodities to England would be worthwhile for social if not for market reasons. Did he then anticipate state subsidies to make such trade viable?

[2] The possibilities of diverting more Mediterranean commodities to England by these means were not grounded on serious argument.

[3] First ed. 'breed; and'.

[4] The final result would thus be an adequate export of manufactured articles, supplies of livestock etc. to the colony so as to boost its resources both for capital investment and consumption outlay. Hayes' criterion seems to have been that the blanket was mightier than the sword. One function of colonies was, as he indicates on p. 177 below, to act as way stations for the assumed Pacific trade.

[5] First ed. 'wil'.

[6] First ed. 'whither'. In 1592 he has '3 or 400 Sayles', (C.U.L. MS Dd. 3. 85, no. 4; *NAW*, III, 161) and in 1586 'not fewer than 400 sayle' (B.L. Lansdowne MS 100, ff. 83–94; *NAW*, III, 128). See Quinn, *North America* (1977), pp. 528–9. We have no information on what Hayes based his computation.

forasmuch as merchants are diligent inquisitours after gaines, they will soone remooue their trade from Newfound-land vnto vs neere at hand, for so great increase of gaine as they shall make by trading with vs.[1] For whereas the voyage vnto the Newfoundland is into a more cold and intemperate place, not to be traded nor frequented at all times, nor fortified[2] for securitie of the ships and goods;[3] oft spoiled by pirats or men of warre; the charges great for salt; double manning and double victualling their ships, in regard that the labor is great and the time long, before their lading can be made readie: they cary outwards no commodities for fraight; and after sixe moneths voyage, their returne is made but of Fish and Oiles.[4]

Incommodities in the Newland trade.

Contrariwise, by trading with vs at our intended place, the course shalbe in a maner as short; into a more temperate and healthfull climat; at all times of the yeere to be traded; harbors fortified to secure ships and goods; charges abridged of salt, victualling and manning ships double: because lading shall be prouided vnto their hands at a more easie rate than themselues could make it. They shall carry fraight also outward, to make exchange with vs; and so get profit both waies: and then euery foure moneths they may make a voyage and returne, of both fish and oiles, and many other commodities of good worth.[5]

Commodities by hauing trade with vs.

These reasons aduisedly waighed,[6] shall make our enterprise appeare

Note.

[1] He ignores the potential friction between seasonal fishermen and resident colonists such as was to bedevil Newfoundland's early colonial history and which would emerge if the colony did attract merchants from England.

[2] First ed. 'not'. In 1583 Hayes had backed Newfoundland as a main colonial centre for English enterprise (Quinn, *Gilbert*, II, 404–9) and continued to do so in 1585–6 (B.L. Lansdowne MS 37, ff. 166–7; MS 100, ff. 83–94; *NAW*, III, 124–38): by 1592 he had become converted to a mainland site farther south (C.U.L. MS Dd. 3. 85, no. 4, *NAW*, III, 156–72) though he did not there attack Newfoundland's climate. This he now proceeds to do. What brought the shift is not clear: it may have been the influence of Christopher Carleill whose views can be traced in the Cambridge MS. Hayes had proposed the fortification of Newfoundland in 1586 (B.L. Lansdowne MS 100, ff. 83–94, *NAW*, III, 138), but had changed his mind on its practicability by 1592.

[3] First ed. 'goods, oft'. Attacks by English privateers had taken place in 1582 (Quinn, *Gilbert*, I, 85) and 1585 (Quinn, *Roanoke voyages*, I, 171–3, 234–47; *NAW*, IV, 13–44), and had been stepped up against the Portuguese in 1585 (Ibid., 47–52) the Basques and French 'Leaguer' vessels after 1588 (see Ibid., 53–5, 78–9, 108–18).

[4] Freedom to organise the fishery in Newfoundland and freedom to make high profits were important to the fishermen: profitable outward cargoes would not have seemed to them to offset the time involved in offloading or the lack of freedom which colonial regulation would involve.

[5] Theoretically to link outward trade in fish and agricultural produce with imports of necessities and luxuries for a colony was sensible. In the end New England colonists succeeded in doing so. In Newfoundland the fishery was so highly specialised that any intrusion of other commercial interests would force a reorganisation which would prove, as it did in Newfoundland, unpalatable to the fishermen. [6] First ed. 'weighed'.

easie, and the most profitable of the world, for our nation to vndertake. The reasons we chiefly relie vpon are these, namely.[1]

1. Those lands which we intend to inhabit, shall minister vnto our people, the subiect and matter of many notable commodities.
2. England shall affoord vs people both men, women and children aboue 10000, which may very happily be spared from hence to worke[2] those commodities there.
3. Newfound-land shall minister shipping to carrie away all our commodities, and to bring others vnto vs againe for our supplie.[3]

An easie enterprise, and great reward. Now two of these reasons are already effected vnto our hands: that is to say: The place where we shall finde rich commodities, and ships to vent them. It remaineth only for our parts, to carrie and transport people with their prouisions from England, where the miserie and necessitie of manie crie out for such helpe and reliefe.

The English nation most fit for discoueries. This considered, no nation of Christendom is so fit for this action as England, by reason of our superfluous people (as I may tearme them) and of our long domesticall peace.[4] And after that we be once 200 men strong, victualled and fortified,[5] we can not be remooued by as many thousands.

For besides that, we haue seene both in France and the Low-countreys, where 200 men well fortified and victualled, haue kept out the forces both of the French & Spanish kings, euen within their owne kingdomes: it shall be[6] also a matter of great difficulty, to transport an army ouer the Ocean with victuals and munition, and afterwards to abide long siege abroad, against vs fortified within, where the very elements and famine shall fight for vs, though we should lie still and defend onely.[7]

[1] First ed. 'these: namely'.

[2] First ed. 'work'. In 1592 (C.U.L. MS Dd. 3. 85, no. 4, *NAW*, III, 164) he stated this proposition in general terms but later mentioned 'yea 20 thousand of our spare people', including women and children, who could be released. (On the background to this see Carl Bridenbaugh, *Vexed and troubled Englishmen* (1968), revised 1971, *passim*.)

[3] Hayes is hardly consistent or logical. He expects to by-pass Newfoundland and concentrate the fishery in association with the mainland colony and also expects the fishing vessels designed for Newfoundland to bring out colonists and their supplies.

[4] While England had had substantial peace at home she had been at war with Spain since 1585 and was substantially committed in Ireland from 1594 onwards.

[5] The figure of 200 represents only the initial colony envisaged by Hayes in 1592 (C.U.L. MS Dd. 3. 85, no. 4, *NAW*, III, 166-7), but it is retained by his editor here as giving some idea of what was thought to be the size of a feasible colony in 1602.

[6] First ed. 'shalbe'.

[7] He does not face up to the threat which Spain could pose (as she did to the French in Florida in 1565) to a mainland colony where she thought her vital interests were threatened.

The Saluages neither in this attempt shall hurt vs, they being simple, naked and vnarmed, destitute of edge-tooles or weapons; whereby[1] they are vnable either to defend themselues or to offend vs: neither is it our intent[2] to prouoke, but to cherish and win them vnto Christianitie by faire meanes; yet not to trust them too far, but to prouide against all accidents.

The Saluages vnable to defend or offend.

Then to conclude, as we of all other nations are most fit for a discouery and planting in remote places;[3] euen so, vnder the heauens there is no place to be found so conuenient for such a purpose; by reason of the temperature, commodities, apt site for trade, & repaire thither already of so many ships, which in any other frequented[4] countrey, can not be procured in a mans age, nor with expense of halfe a million.

So as the onely difficultie now, is in our first preparation to transport some few people at the beginning; the charges whereof shall be defraied by our first returne,[5] of fish and some commodities of Sassafras, Hides, Skinnes and Furres, which we shall also haue by trading with the Saluages. The proofe of which commodities shall incourage our merchants to venter largely in the next. The supplie shall easily and continually be sent by ships, which yeerely goe from hence vnto the Newfound-land and vs; and the intercourse & exchange we shall haue with all nations repairing thither, shall store vs with aboundance[6] of all things for our necessities and delightes. Which reasons if[7] they had

This action but set on foot, will goe forward of it selfe.

Ouersight in choice of a new habitation.

[1] First ed. 'whereby'. Hayes had no contact at all with the Beothuk Indians of Newfoundland in 1583 (Quinn, *Gilbert*, II, 581) so that all his knowledge was at secondhand, mostly by way of Hakluyt, *Principal navigations*, III (1600). In 1583 (C.U.L. MS Dd. 3. 85, no. 4; *NAW*, III, 167–72) he writes of 'The naturall inhabitants are savage. Simple, naked and unarmed people. destitute of edge tooles and weapon. whearby they shalbe unable to defend themselves, or to offend us.'

[2] First ed. 'neither is our intent'. On his native policy compare Peckham, 1583 (Quinn, *Gilbert*, II, 450–8), the elder Hakluyt (below p. 188), and the younger Hakluyt (Taylor, *Hakluyts*, II, 214–18, 257, 503). The last wrote, in *Virginia richly valued* (1609), sig. A4 'To handle them gently; while gentle courses may be found to serue, it will be without comparison the best: but if gentle polishing will not serue, then we shall not want hammerours and rough masons enow, I meane our old soldiers trained vp in the Netherlands, to square and prepare them to our Preachers hands'.

[3] Hayes' nationalist confidence in the fitness of England to dominate North America is interesting. In the second chapter of C.U.L. MS Dd. 3. 85., no. 4; *NAW*, III, 158) he had stressed the god-given character of English enterprise in America.

[4] First ed. 'vnfrequented'. This is more specifically focused on the problems of a 1602 settlement than the more diffuse matter of C.U.L. MS dd. 3. 85, no. 4 (*NAW*, III, 156–72), on this point, but his reliance on English fishing vessels for outward carriage to the colony and on foreign vessels for luxuries had appeared in his projects advocating Newfoundland colonization in 1585–6 (B.L. Lansdowne MSS 37 and 100, cp. *NAW*, III, 124–38).   [5] First ed. 'returne of.'

[6] First ed. 'abundance'.   [7] First ed. 'delights, which reasons, if'.

beene foreseene of them that planted in the South part of Virginia (which is a place destitute of good harbours, and farre from all trade) no doubt but if they had settled[1] neerer vnto this frequented trade in the Newfound-land, they had by this time beene a flourishing State, and plentifull in all things; who also might then haue made way into the bowels of that large continent, where assuredly we shall discouer very goodly and rich kingdomes and cities.

A matter of importance for England. It may also seeme a matter of great consequence for the good and securitie of England; that out of these Northerly regions we shall be able to furnish this realme of all maner of prouisions for our nauies; namely, Pitch, Rosen, Cables, Ropes, Masts, and such like; which shall be made within those her Maiesties owne dominions, by her owne subiects, and brought hither thorow the Ocean, free from restraint of any other prince;[2] whereby the customes and charges bestowed by our merchants (to the inriching of forren Estates) shall be lessened, and turned to the benefit of her Highnesse and her deputies in those parts: which also shall[3] deliuer our merchants from many troubles & molestations which they now vnwillingly indure in our East trades; and shall make vs the lesse to doubt the malice of those States whom now we may not offend, lest we should be intercepted of the same prouisions, to the weakening of our nauie, the most roiall defence of this noble realme.[4]

Of a conuenient passage and trade into the
South Sea, vnder temperate regions part
by riuers, and some part ouer land,
in the continent of America.

I Will adde hereunto[5] an assured hope (grounded vpon infallible

---

[1] First ed. 'setled'; 'a very flourishing'. This criticism of Ralegh's sponsoring of the Roanoke colonies in 1584–7 appeared in C.U.L. MS Dd. 3. 85, no. 4 (NAW, III, 163), only in a sidenote. He implies here that the Lost Colony need not have been deserted if it had been located nearer Newfoundland.

[2] He takes up more specifically than in 1593 (C.U.L. MS Dd. 3. 85, no. 4; NAW, III, 156–72) the 'troubles and impositions' involved in the Baltic trade. There had been in the meantime new problems with the London Steelyard and consequently less easy relations with the Hansards trading in the Baltic (see E. P. Cheyney, History of England from the defeat of the Armada to the death of Queen Elizabeth, I (1914), 478–9, 492–7).

[3] First ed. 'shal'. He puts his finger on the problem of the Eastland trade in indicating that it was, so far, a natural monopoly with no real alternative sources of supply for naval stores: hence the strategic potential of an American source if only for bargaining with Danes, Swedes and Hansards.

[4] See p. 43 above. Hayes is being at his most topical and promotional.

[5] First ed. 'heereunto'.

reasons)[1] of a way to be made part ouerland,[2] & part by riuers or lakes, into the South seas vnto Cathay, China, and those passing rich countreys, lying in the East parts of the world: which way or passage (supposed to be beyond the vttermost bounds of America, vnder the frozen Zone) is neuerthelesse, held by the opinion of many learned writers and men of iudgement now liuing, to be in these more temperate rigions;[3] and that the same shall neuer be made knowen, vnlesse we plant first; whereby we shall learne as much by inquisition of the naturall inhabitants, as by our owne nauigations. I will not herein[4] relie vpon reports made in the French mens discoueries; that the sea which giueth passage vnto Cathay, extendeth from the North, neere vnto the riuer of Canada, into 44 degrees, where the same of the Saluages is called Tadouac.[5]

Neither vpon the discoueries of Iaques Noel, who hauing passed beyond the three Saults, where Iaques Cartier left to discouer, finding the riuer of S. Laurence passable on the other side or branch; and afterwards, vnderstood of the inhabitants, that the same riuer did lead into a mighty[6] lake, which at the entrance was fresh, but beyond, was bitter or salt; the end whereof was vnknowen.

Omitting therefore these hopes, I will ground my opinion vpon reason and nature, which will not faile.

For this we know alreadie, that great riuers haue beene discouered a thousand England miles into that continent of America; namely, that

---

[1] The 'infallible reasons' appear in a somewhat different context in C.U.L. MS Dd. 3. 85, no. 4; *NAW*, III, 171.

[2] First ed. 'made, part ouer land'.

[3] First ed. 'regions'. He is concerned to stress, if rather indirectly, that what he advocates is not the old Northwest Passage around America but one through the continent using lakes and portages rather than a continuous water channel.

[4] First ed. 'heerein'.

[5] The classical Northwest Passage of the academic geographers was assumed to lie well to the North of 60°. Hayes realised that intimate local knowledge gained from the Indians, such as Cartier obtained, could provide effective keys to the geography of the interior, but he wholly miscalculated in thinking this could extend the Europeans' knowledge to the Pacific. He was not to be the last to do so.

[6] First ed. 'inhabitants that'; 'leade'; 'mightie'. The Jacques Noël letters of 1587 (printed by Hakluyt, *Principal navigations*, III (1600), 236–7) recorded the existence of a 'great Lake' (Lake Ontario) beyond the St Lawrence Rapids near Montreal, but there is nothing about the character of the lake. Expeditions beyond the Lachine rapids probably took place in 1583 or 1584. The inference that further Noël material was available by 1602 is inescapable (see the Wright map in Hakluyt, II (1599)), but this entry may specifically raise the question whether Jacques Noël or his sons Michael and Jean did not reach Lake Ontario later in 1587 or subsequently, even though competitors evidently prevented their exploitation of the new route (Quinn, *North America* (1977), p. 468).

of S. Laurence or Canada.[1] But not regarding miles more or lesse, most assuredly, that and other knowen riuers there doe descend from the highest parts or mountaines, or middle of that continent, into our North sea. And like as those mountains doe cast from them, streames into our North seas; euen so the like they doe[2] into the South sea, which is on the backe of that continent.

A large course of a riuer thorow a mightie continent, produceth a portable riuer.

For all mountaines haue their descents toward the seas about them, which are the lowest places and proper mansions of water: and waters (which are contained in the mountaines, as it were in cisternes) descending naturally, doe alwaies resort vnto the seas inuironing those lands: for example; From the Alps confining Germanie, France, and Italie, the mighty riuer Danubie[3] doth take his course East, and dischargeth into the Pontique sea:[4] the Rhine, North, and falleth into the Germane sea: the Rhosne,[5] West, and goeth into the Mediterran sea: the Po, South, is emptied into the Adriatick or gulfe of Venice.[6] other instances may be produced to like effect in Africk; yea, at home amongst the mountaines in England.

Seeing then in nature this can not be denied, and by experience elsewhere is found to be so, I will shew how a trade may be disposed more commodiously into the South sea thorow these temperate and habitable regions, than by the frozen Zones in the supposed passages of Northwest or Northeast:[7] where, if the very moment be omitted of the time to passe, then are we like to be frozen in the seas, or forced to Winter in extreame cold and darkenesse like vnto hell: or in the midst of Summer, we shalbe in perill to haue our ships ouerwhelmed or crusht in pieces by hideous and fearefull mountaines of yce floting vpon those seas.

Therefore foure Staple-places must be erected, when the most short and passable way is found: that is to say, two vpon the North side,

---

[1] Cartier's penetration from the entry of the Strait of Belle Isle to Montreal was approximately 1,000 miles.

[2] First ed. 'there doe'; 'do'; 'do'. The discourse on watersheds is sensible if elementary. His problem was that he envisaged the Appalachian chain (of which he could only be partly aware) as the probable watershed between the Atlantic and Pacific whereas it was such only between the Atlantic and the Mississippi–Missouri basin.

[3] First ed. 'conteined'; 'mightie riuer Daunbie'.

[4] Black Sea. In C.U.L. MS Dd. 3. 85, no. 4 (*NAW*, III, 170), he has 'the Sea Euxinus'.

[5] Rhône.

[6] First ed. 'Venice. Other'.

[7] His promotional voice is less strident in C.U.L. MS Dd. 3. 85, no. 4 (*NAW*, III, 170), where he says 'we may certainly conclude.'.

at the head and fall of[1] the riuer; and two others on the South side, at the head and fall also of that other riuer.

Prouided, that ships may passe vp those riuers vnto the Staples, so farre as the same be nauigable into the land; and afterwards, that boats with flat bottomes may also passe so high and neere the heads of the riuers vnto the Staples, as possibly they can, euen with lesse than two foot water, which can not then be far from the heads;[2] as in the riuer of Chagre.[3]

That necke or space of land betweene the two heads of the said riuers, if it be 100 leagues (which is not like) the commodities from the North and from the South sea brought thither, may wel be carried ouer the same vpon horses, mules or beasts of that countrey apt to labour (as the elke or buffel) or by the aid of many Saluages accustomed to burdens; who shall stead vs greatly in these affaires.[4]

It is moreouer to be considered, that all these countreys do yeeld (so farre as is knowen) Cedars, Pines, Firre trees and Oaks, to build, mast, and yeard ships; wherefore we may not doubt, but that ships may be builded on the South sea.

Then as ships on the South side may goe and returne to and from Cathay, China, and other most rich regions of the East world in fiue moneths or thereabouts; euen so the goods being carried ouer vnto the North side, ships may come thither from England to fetch the same goods, and returne by a voyage of foure or fiue months vsually.

So as in euery foure moneths may be returned into England the greatest riches of Cathay, China, Iapan, and the rest which[5] will be

---

[1] First ed. 'fal'. It might be thought that Hayes had a specific river (or rivers) in mind or wished to give that impression. He has shifted his advocacy from permanent, self-perpetuating and exporting settlements to transit ports – two on the Atlantic side, two on the Pacific – so that the two projects are not mutually exclusive. They reflect Hayes' characteristic inability to avoid overelaboration in his projects.

[2] Hayes evidently knew nothing of the Fall Line or the complications it could present for inland navigation over the greater part of the interior of eastern North America by such unportable vessels as he proposed.

[3] Chagres, Panama. For its use by the Spaniards see Hakluyt, *Principal navigations*, III (1600), 458, 556.

[4] He cheerfully envisaged a portage of some 300 miles (in C.U.L. MS Dd. 3. 85, no. 4; *NAW*, III, no. 364, he went as far as 600 miles). To raise such a major difficulty and then discard it so lightly is typical of his promotional technique.

[5] First ed. 'great riches...the rest, which'. Hayes could pick up a certain amount on the Manila galleon from the narratives of the Cavendish voyage (Hakluyt, *Principall navigations* (1589), 812–13, *Principal navigations*, III (1600), 815–17), and he may well have heard some gossip as well, but he was not accurately informed about the time it took for the return trip (cp. C. L. Schurz, *The Manila galleon* (1938), *passim*).

Spices, Drugges, Muske, Pearle, Stones, Gold, Siluer, Silks, Clothes of gold, & all maner of precious things, which shall recompense the time and labour of their transportation and carriage, if it were as farre and dangerous as the Moores trade is from Fess and Marocco (ouer the burning and moueable sands, in which they perish many times, and suffer commonly great distresses) vnto the riuer called Niger in Africa, and from thence, vp the said riuer manie hundred miles; afterwards ouer-land againe, vnto the riuer Nilus; and so vnto Cairo in Egypt, from whence they returne the way they came.[1]

Or if it were a voyage so farre as our merchants haue made into Persia, euen to Ormus, by the way of the North, through Russia into the Caspian sea, and so foorth, with paiment of many tolles. But this passage ouer and thorow the continent of America,, [sic] as the same shall be alwaies vnder temperate and habitable climats, and a pleasant passage after it hath beene a little frequented: euen so it must fall out much shorter than it seemeth, by false description of that continent, which doth not extend so farre into the West, as by later nauigations is found and described in more exquisit charts. Besides that, the sea extends it selfe into the land very farre in many places on the South side; whereby our accesse vnto the South ocean, shall be by so much the shorter.　　　　　　FINIS.

[The second edition continues from here.]

Inducements[2] to the liking of the voyage intended towards Virginia in 40. and 42. degrees of latitude, written 1585. by M. Richard Hakluyt the elder, sometime student of the Middle Temple.

[1] There is something on the desert trade in Hakluyt, *Principal navigations*, II (1599), 188, but he may well have had other oral sources (cp. E. W. Bovill, *The golden trade* (2nd ed. 1965), pp. 120–31, for the problems Europeans had in trying to locate the Bure (and Bambuk and Lodi) sources of the caravan trade in gold: the Ashanti source was the only well-known one.

[2] This begins the additional matter from the second edition. Reprinted in Taylor, *Hakluyts*, II (1935), 327–38, with a few notes. It seems likely that this was an extended version of a shorter tract prepared late in 1583 or early in 1584 to accompany David Ingram's *A true discourse* in print. It is found so associated in B.L., Sloane MS 1447. Though we know the Ingram tract was printed with date 1583 (which could mean up to March 1584), no copy has survived (Quinn, *Roanoke voyages*, I, 4–5). The present tract bears clear internal evidence that it was written after the return of Barlowe from the Roanoke Island reconnaisance in September 1584 and could have been completed within the following six months. We have two problems: was the heading with '40. and 42. degrees' as the limits to which it refers present in 1585 or was it added later? And secondly were other

[1] The glory of God by planting of religion among those infidels.

2   The increase of the force of the Christians.

3   The possibilitie of the inlarging of the dominions of the Queenes most excellent Maiestie, and consequently of her honour, reuenues, and of her power by this enterprise.

4   An ample vent in time to come of the Woollen clothes of England, especially those of the coursest sorts, to the maintenance of our poore, that else sterue or become burdensome to the realme: and vent also of sundry our commodities vpon the tract of that firme land, and possibly in other regions from the Northerne side of that maine.

5   A great possibilitie of further discoueries of other regions from the North part of the same land by sea, and of vnspeakable honor and benefit that may rise vpon the same, by the trades to ensue in Iapan, China, and Cathay, &c.

6   By returne thence, this realme shall receiue (by reason of the situation of the climate, and by reason of the excellent soile) Oade, Oile, Wines, Hops, Salt, and most or all the commodities that we receiue from the best parts of Europe, and we shall receiue the same better cheape, than now we receiue them, as we may vse the matter.[1]

7   Receiuing the same thence, the nauie, the humane strength of this realme, our merchants and their goods shal not be subiect to arrest of ancient enemies & doubtfull friends, as of late yeeres they haue beene.

8   If our nation do not make any conquest there, but only vse trafficke and change of commodities, yet by meane the countrey is not very mightie, but diuided into pety kingdoms, they shall not dare to offer vs any great annoy, but such as we may easily reuenge with sufficient chastisement to the vnarmed people there.[2]

9   Whatsoeuer commodities we receiue by the Steelyard merchants,

---

internal alterations made before it was published in 1602? Internal evidence indicates the limits it was meant for as between 34° and 40° which is what we would expect in 1584–5. We have no specific indication of its provenance though the younger Richard Hakluyt inherited a number of his elder cousin's papers when he died in 1591. For what is known of the elder Hakluyt see Parks, *Hakluyt* and Taylor, *Hakluyts*, and Quinn, ed., *The Hakluyt handbook*, 2 vols., 1974, I, 8, 133, 160, 224, 254, 265, 294, II, 345, 363–4, 307–8, 373–4, 376, 415, 423, 435, 596. The setting of the tract may perhaps be best understood in the context of Carol Shammas 'English commercial development and American colonization 1560–1620', in Andrews, Canny and Hair, *The Western enterprise* (1978), pp. 151–74.

[1] The emphasis on Mediterranean products is one indicator that the original limits proposed were 34–40° N.

[2] Hakluyt is much less committed to a colonisation programme than Hayes.

or by our owne merchants from Eastland, be it Flaxe, Hempe, Pitch, Tarre, Masts, Clap-boord, Wainscot, or such like; the like good may we receiue from the North and Northeast part of that countrey neere vnto Cape Briton, in returne for our course Woollen clothes, Flanels and Rugges fit for those colder regions.[1]

10 The passage to and fro, is thorow the maine Ocean sea, so as we are not in danger of any enemies coast.

11 In the voyage, we are not to crosse the burnt Zone, nor to passe thorow frozen seas encombred with ice and fogs, but in temperate climate at all times of the yeere: and it requireth not, as the East India voiage doth, the taking in of water in diuers places, by reason that it is to be sailed in fiue or six weeks; and by the shortnesse, the merchant may yeerely make two returnes (a factory once being erected there) a matter in trade of great moment.

12 In this trade by the way in our passe to and fro, we haue in tempests and other haps, all the ports of Ireland to our aid, and no neere coast of any enemy.

13 By this ordinary trade we may annoy the enemies to Ireland, and succour the Queenes Maiesties friends there, and in time we may from Virginia yeeld them whatsoeuer commoditie they now receiue from the Spaniard; and so the Spaniards shall want the ordinary victual that heertofore they receiued yeerely from thence, and so they shall not continue trade, nor fall so aptly in practise against this gouernment, as now by their trade thither they may.[2]

14 We shall, as it is thought, enioy in this voyage, either some small Islands to settle on, or some one place or other on the firme land to fortifie for the saftie of our ships, our men, and our goods, the

---

[1] The Hanseatic merchants of the London Steelyard (to 1598), and the English Eastland Company. Between them they had supplied vital maritime stores for England. A main purpose of the 1602 ventures (according to the selection of documents printed in 1602 at least) was the location and exploitation of alternative American resources for such commodities.

[2] He is one of the few Elizabethan writers to reflect on the effects of transatlantic establishments on Ireland though Ireland was often in the minds of same men who were active in Irish and American affairs (cp. Quinn, *Elizabethans and the Irish*, N. P. Canny, *The Elizabethan conquest of Ireland* (1976), and Andrews, Canny and Hair, *The westward enterprise* (1978), passim). Hakluyt saw American colonies as a means and a reason for developing Irish ports to protect ships going to and from Virginia and also give these ports a new concern with the Atlantic trade and wean them from an old dependence on Iberian commerce, thus 'annoying' the Spaniards and also the French. Virginia could then supply Ireland with American commodities she would otherwise have to get by way of Spain. The narrower economic nationalism of the later acts of trade is not here in view.

like whereof we haue not in any forren place of our trafficke, in which respect we may be in degree of more safetie, and more quiet.

15   The great plentie of Buffe hides,[1] and of many other sundry kinds of hides there now presently to be had, the trade of Whale and Seale fishing, and of diuers other fishings in the great riuers, great bayes, and seas there, shall presently defray the charge in good part or in all of the first enterprise, and so we shall be in better case than our men were in Russia, where many yeeres were spent, and great summes of money consumed, before gaine was found.[2]

16   The great broad riuers of that maine that we are to enter into so many leagues nauigable or portable into the maine land, lying so long a tract with so excellent and so fertile a soile on both sides, doe seeme to promise all things that the life of man doth require, and whatsoeuer men may wish, that are to plant vpon the same, or to trafficke in the same.

17   And whatsoeuer notable commoditie the soile within or without doth yeeld in so long a tract that is to be carried out from thence to England, the same riuers so great and deepe, do yeeld no small benefit for the sure, safe, easie and cheape cariage of the same to shipboard, be it of great bulke or of great weight.

18   And in like sort whatsoeuer commoditie of England the Inland people there shall need, the same riuers doe worke the like effect in benefit for the incariage of the same, aptly, easily, and cheaply.

19   If we finde the countrey populous, and desirous to expel vs, and iniuriously to offend vs, that seeke but iust and lawfull trafficke, then by reason that we are lords of nauigation, and they not so, we are the better able to defend our selues by reason of those great riuers, & to annoy them in many places.[3]

20   Where there be many petie kings or lords planted on the riuers sides, and by all likelihood mainteine the frontiers of their seuerall territories by warres, we may by the aide of this riuer ioine with this king heere, or with that king there, at our pleasure, and may so with a few men be reuenged of any wrong offered by any of them; or may, if we will proceed with extremitie, conquer, fortifie, and plant in soiles most sweet, most pleasant, most strong,

[1] See pp. 170, 306, 348 for problems of distinguishing buffalo, moose and elk hides.

[2] Cp. T. S. Willan, *The early history of the Russia Company, 1555–1603* (1956), pp. 48–156.

[3] On the right of the English to lawful trade with the native inhabitants see Sir George Peckham in 1583, Quinn, *Gilbert*, II, 450–1, *NAW*, III, 43–8.

and most fertile, and in the end bring them all in subiection and to ciuilitie.

21 The knowen abundance of Fresh fish in the riuers, and the knowen plentie of Fish on the sea coast there, may assure vs of sufficient victuall in spight of the people, if we will vse salt and industrie.

22 The knowen plentie and varietie of Flesh, of diuers kinds of beasts at land there, may seeme to say to vs, that we may cheaply victuall our nauies to England for our returnes, which benefit euery where is not found of merchants.

23 The practise of the people of the East Indies, when the Portugals came thither first, was to cut from the Portugals their lading of Spice: and heereby they thought to ouerthrow their purposed trade. If these people shall practise the like, by not suffering vs to haue any commoditie of theirs without conquest, (which requireth some time) yet may we mainteine our first voyage thither, till our purpose come to effect, by the sea-fishing on the coasts there, and by dragging for pearles, which are said to be on those parts; and by returne of those commodities, the charges in part shall be defraied: which is a matter of consideration in enterprises of charge.

24 If this realme shall abound too too much with youth, in the mines there of Golde, (as that of Chisca[1] and Saguenay) of Siluer, Copper, Yron, &c. may be an imployment to the benefit of this realme; in tilling of the rich soile there for graine, and in planting of Vines there for Wine; or dressing of those Vines which grow there naturally in great abundance, Oliues for Oile; Orenge trees, Limons, Figs and Almonds for fruit; Oad, Saffron, and Madder for Diers; Hoppes for Brewers; Hempe, Flaxe; and in many such other things, by imploiment of the soile, our people void of sufficient trades, may be honestly imploied, that els may become hurtfull at home.[2]

25 The nauigating of the seas in the voyage, and of the great riuers there, will breed many Mariners for seruice, and mainteine much nauigation.

26 The number of raw Hides there of diuers kindes of beasts, if we shall possesse some Island there, or settle on the firme, may

---

[1] Chisca as a gold source goes back to Soto, see p. 201 below.

[2] Cp. Hayes, p. 171 above. He concentrates on more southerly commodities, making it evident that the document was composed, as we now have it, for the Virginia voyage of 1585. Woad, obtained at this time mainly from southwestern France and from the Atlantic islands (in Iberian hands), was essential for the production of dyed broadcloths, and for the still infant 'new draperies'.

presently imploy many of our idle people in diuers seuerall dressings of the same, and so we may returne them to the people that cannot dresse them so well; or into this realm, where the same are good merchandize; or to Flanders, &c. which present gaine at the first, raiseth great incouragement presently to the enterprise.

27 Since great waste Woods be there, of Oake, Cedar, Pine, Wall-nuts, and sundry other sorts, many of our waste people may be imployed in making of Ships, Hoies, Busses and Boats; and in making of Rozen, Pitch and Tarre, the trees naturall for the same, being certeinly knowen to be neere Cape Briton and the Bay of Menan, and in many other places there about.

28 If mines of white or gray marble, Iet, or other rich stone be found there, our idle people may be imployed in the mines of the same, and in preparing the same to shape, and so shaped, they may be caried into this realm as good balast for our ships, and after serue for noble buildings.

29 Sugar-canes may be planted aswell as they are now in the South of Spaine, and besides the imploiment of our idle people, we may receiue the commodity cheaper, and not inrich infidels or our doubtful friends, of whom now we receiue that commoditie.

30 The daily great increase of Woolles in Spaine, and the like in the West Indies, and the great imploiment of the same into Cloth in both places, may mooue vs to endeuour, for vent of our Cloth, new discoueries of peopled regions, where hope of sale may arise; otherwise in short time many inconueniences may possibly ensue.[1]

31 This land that we purpose to direct our course to, lying in part in the 40 degree of latitude,[2] being in like heat as Lisbone in Portugall doth, and in the more Southerly part as the most Southerly coast of Spaine doth, may by our diligence yeeld vnto vs besides Wines and Oiles and Sugars, Orenges, Limons, Figs, Resings,[3] Almonds, Pomegranates, Rice, Raw-silks such as come from Granada, and diuers commodities for Diers, as Anile and Cochenillio,[4] and sundry other colours and materials. Moreouer,

---

[1] After the peace Spanish clothing industries were to decline and Spanish wool to come to England to be used in the 'new draperies'; elsewhere in Europe cloth production was to grow and become much more competitive.

[2] There was in 1585, so far as we know, no 40° objective. This figure could have survived from the 1583–4 version (see above pp. 180–1), or have been inserted in 1585 to cover longer-term prospects. It was of course appropriate, more so than some other items in the document, to what was being contemplated in 1602–3.   [3] Raisins.

[4] Anil, from the indigo bush, and cochineal, the insect used for dyeing found on the Nopal Cactus. Both, at this time, were produced in the Iberian empires.

we shall not onely receiue many precious commodities besides
from thence, but also shal in time finde ample vent of the labour
of our poore people at home, by sale of Hats, Bonets, Kniues,
Fish-hooks, Copper kettles, Beads, Looking-glasses, Bugles,[1] & a
thousand kinds of other wrought wares, that in short time may
be brought in vse among the people of that countrey, to the great
reliefe of the multitude of our poore people, and to the woonderfull
enriching of this realme. And in time, such league and entercourse
may arise betweene our Stapling seats[2] there, and other ports of
our Northern America, and of the Islands of the same, that
incredible things, and by few as yet dreamed of, may speedily
follow, tending to the impeachment of our mightie enemies, and
to the common good of this noble gouernment.

The ends of this voyage are these:	1. To plant Christian religion. } Or, to doe all three.[3]
	2. To trafficke.
	3. To conquer.

To plant Christian religion without conquest, will bee hard.
Trafficke easily followeth conquest: conquest is not easie. Trafficke
without conquest seemeth possible, and not vneasie. What is to be done,
is the question.[4]

If the people be content to liue naked, and to content themselues
with few things of meere necessity, then trafficke is not. So then in
vaine seemeth our voyage, vnlesse this nature may be altered, as by
conquest and other good meanes it may be, but not on a sudden. The
like whereof appeared in the East Indies, vpon the Portugals seating
there.

If the people in the Inland be clothed, and desire to liue in the
abundance of all such things as Europe doth, and haue at home all the
same in plentie, yet we can not haue trafficke with them, by meane
they want not any thing that we can yeeld them.

Admit that they haue desire to your commodities, and as yet haue
neither Golde, Siluer, Copper, Iron, nor sufficient quantitie of other

---

[1] Long cylindrical beads. They were not unlike those made from copper by the
Indians of New England (cp. p. 107).

[2] Stapling seats were the ports or internal distribution centres for collecting local
goods and distributing imported ones.

[3] Compare the emphasis in Hayes (pp. 171–4 above).

[4] These aphorisms were perhaps intended to be developed further in a longer version
of the tract which was never completed. On their own they stand out a little starkly.

present commoditie to mainteine the yeerely trade: What is then to be done?

The soile and climate first is to be considered, and you are with Argus eies to see what commoditie by industrie of man you are able to make it to yeeld, that England doth want or doth desire: as for the purpose, if you can make it to yeeld good Wine, or good Oile, as it is like you may by the climat, (where wilde Vines of sundry sorts doe naturally grow already in great abundance) then your trade may be mainteined. But admit the soile were in our disposition (as yet it is not) in what time may this be brought about? Meanes to breed a speedie trade.

For Wine this is to be affirmed, that first the soile lying in 36 or 37 degrees in the temperature of South Spaine, in setting your Vine-plants this yeere, you may haue Wine within three yeeres. And it may be that the wilde Vines growing there already, by orderly pruning and dressing at your first arriuall, may come to profit in shorter time.

And planting your Oliue trees this yeere, you may haue Oile within three yeeres.

And if the sea shores be flat, and fit for receipt of salt water, and for Salt making, without any annoy of neere freshes, then the trade of Salt onely may mainteine a yeerely nauigation (as our men now trade to the isle of Maio, and the Hollanders to Terra Firma neere the West end of the Isle of Margarita.)[1]

But how the naturall people of the countrey may be made skilfull to plant Vines, and to know the vse, or to set Oliue trees, and to know the making of Oile, and withall to vse both the trades, that is a matter of small consideration: but to conquer a countrey or prouince in climate & soile of Italie, Spaine or the Islands from whence we receiue our Wines & Oiles, and to man it, to plant it, and to keepe it, and to continue the making of Wines and Oiles able to serue England, were a matter of great importance both in respect of the sauing at home of our great treasure now yeerely going away, and in respect of the

[1] Maio, Cape Verde Islands. If this passage was indeed written in 1585 it is a very early indication of Dutch penetration into the Spanish Indies. The references we have are to development of salt collection and other activity associated with it at Margarita and elsewhere in the southern Caribbean in the 1590s (cp. Engel Sluiter, 'Dutch–Spanish rivalry in the Caribbean, 1594–1609', *Hispanic American Historical Review*, XXVIII (1948), 165–96; K. R. Andrews, *English privateering voyages*, pp. 38, 384, and *The Spanish Caribbean, 1530–1630* (1978), pp. 178–81, putting the first known independent voyage as 1593). One would suspect, therefore, that this was an interpolation subsequent to the death of the author in 1591, though it does not seem easy to establish it as such.

annoyance thereby growing to our enemies. The like consideration
would be had, touching a place for the making of Salt, of temperature
like those of France, not too too colde, as the Salts of the Northern
regions be; nor too too firy, as those be that be made more Southerly
than France. In regard whereof, many circumstances are to be
considered; and principally, by what meane the people of those parties
may be drawn by all courtesie into loue with our nation; that we
become not hatefull vnto them, as the Spaniard is in Italie and in the
West Indies, and elswhere, by their maner of vsage: for a gentle course
without crueltie and tyrannie best answereth the profession of a
Christian, best planteth Christian religion; maketh our seating most
void of blood, most profitable in trade of merchandise, most firme and
stable, and least subiect to remooue by practise of enemies. But that
we may in seating there, not be subiect wholly to the malice of enemies,
and may be more able to preserue our bodies, ships, and goods in more
safetie, and to be knowen to be more able to scourge the people there,
ciuill or sauage, than willing to offer any violence. And for the more
quiet exercise of our manurance of the soiles where we shall seat, and
of our manuall occcupations, it is to be wished that some ancient
captaines of milde disposition and great iudgement be sent thither with
men most skilfull in the arte of fortification; and that direction be taken
that the mouthes of great riuers, and the Islands in the same (as things
of great moment) be taken, manned, and fortified; and that hauens be
cut out for safetie of the Nauie, that we may be lords of the gates and
entries. to goe out and come in at pleasure, and to lie in safetie, and
be able to command and to controle all within, and to force all forren
nauigation to lie out in open rode subiect to all weathers, to be dispersed
by tempests and flawes, if the force within be not able to giue them
the encounter abroad.

[1] The Red Muscadell grape, that bishop Grindall procured out of
Germanie;[1] the great White Muscadell; the Yellow grape: the cuts
of these were woont yeerely to be set at Fulham; and after one
yeeres rooting to be giuen by the bishop, and to be sold by his

A gentle course best to be held.

---

[1] Edmund Grindal had spent Queen Mary's reign in Germany, mainly in the
Rhineland, as an exile. He evidently brought vines from there or had others sent over and
developed them in the gardens of Fulham Palace, where he lived as Bishop of London,
1559–70, and the grapes from which he presented annually to the Queen (John Strype,
Life of Grindal (1820), p. 216). He moved to York as archbishop and subsequently to
Canterbury, his last years being ones during which he was in disgrace with the Queen (he
died in 1583). It might seem from the way Hakluyt refers to the garden and its management
that Grindal may have continued to rent it after Fulham Palace had ceased to be his home,
though this has not been confirmed. It may be that his successors in London, Edwin Sandys
(1570–77) and John Aylmer (1579–94), and their gardeners continued to dispose of cuttings.

gardener. These presently prouided, and placed in earth, and many of these so rooted, with store of cuts vnrooted besides, placed in tubbes of earth shipped at the next voyage, to be planted in Virginia, may begin Vineyards, and bring Wines out of hand.[1]

2 Prouision great of wilde Oliue trees may be made out of this citie[2] so then to be caried, to encrease great store of stocks to graffe the best Oliue on: and Virginia standing in the same degree that The Shroffe[3] the Oliue place doth in Spaine, we may win that merchandise, graffing the wilde.

3 Sugar-canes, if you can not procure them from the Spanish Islands, yet may you by your Barberie merchants procure them.

4 There is an herbe in Persia, whereof Anile is made, and it is also in Barbarie: to procure that by seed or root, were of importance for a trade of merchandise for our clothing countrey.[4]

5 Oad by the seeds you may haue; for you may haue hundreds of bushels in England, as it is multiplied: and hauing soile and labor in Virginia cheape, and the Oad in great value, lying in small roome, it will be a trade of great gaine to this clothing realme: and the thing can not be destroyed by Saluages. The roots of this you may haue in plenty and number comming in the trade: so this may grow in trade within a yeere ready for the merchant.

6 Figge trees of many good kinds may be had hence in barrell, if now presently they be prouided; and they in that climat will yeeld noble fruit, and feed your people presently, and will be brought in frailes[5] home as merchandise, or in barrell, as Resings also may be.

[1] This technique was tried, though without success, in the Virginia voyage of 1585 when sugar canes and other plants were brought to Roanoke Island. As they were probably mostly unsuited to this latitude it is not surprising we hear nothing of how they fared. Dry vats were coffer-like containers which could, if necessary, be covered by lids.

[2] The introduction and growth of olive trees in London gardens does not seem to be otherwise recorded. They do not appear, for example, in B. D. Jackson, ed., *A catalogue of the plants cultivated in the garden of J. Gerard in the years 1596–1599* (1896). The original title was *Catalogus arborum, fruticum, ac plantarum tam indigenarum quam exoticarum in horto J. G....nascantium* (1596).

[3] 'The Shroffe' ought to be identifiable but it has eluded definition. The word would seem to be sharif, but direct Arabic survivals were not too common in Spain (cp. *Principall navigations* (1589), p. 907 (Shersbonare), 920 (sharif)).

[4] The passage should be compared with the elder Hakluyt's notes to a factor at Constantinople in 1582 (Taylor, *Hakluyts*, I, 1935) in which he outlines the introduction of new plants into Europe and advocates further activity in the field. Both Hakluyts seem to have left garden cultivation experiments to others, men like Gerard and Garth, with whom they were friendly.

[5] Rush baskets.

7   Sawed boords of Sassafras and Cedar, to be turned into small boxes for ladies and gentlewomen, would become a present trade.[1]

8   To the infinite naturall increase of Hogs, to adde a deuice how the same may be fed by roots, acornes, &c. without spoiling your corne, would be of great effect to feed the multitude continually imployed in labour:[2] and the same cheaply bred and salted, and barrelled there and brought home, will be well solde for a good merchandise; and the barrels after, will serue for our home Herring-fishing: and so you sell your woods and labour of your cooper.

9   Receiuing the saluage women and their children of both sexes by courtesie into your protection,[3] and imploying the English women and the others in making of Linnen, you shal raise a woonderfull trade of benefit, both to carie into England and also into the Islands, and into the maine of the West Indies, victuall and labour being so cheape there.

10 The trade of making cables and cordage there, will be of great importance, in respect of a cheape maintenance of the Nauie that shall passe to and fro; and in respect of such Nauie as may in those parties be vsed for the venting of the commodities of England to be brought thither. And Powldauies, &c. made for sailes of the poore Saluages, yeeld to the Nauie a great helpe, and a great gaine in the trafficke.[4]

But if seeking reuenge on euery iniurie of the Saluages we seeke blood & raise war, our Vines, our Oliues, our Figge trees, our Sugar-canes, our Orenges and Limons, Corne, Cattell, &c. will be destroyed, and trade of merchandise in all things ouerthrowen; and so the English nation there planted and to be planted, shalbe rooted out with sword and hunger.[5]

----

[1] For the use of cedar and sassafras wood see pp. 206–7. He is probably basing his remarks on samples brought by Barlowe in September 1584.

[2] The supply of cheap labour involved exploiting the Indians as an agricultural labour force. The intention was not usually made as explicit as it is here.

[3] The expectation of using Indian women and children in a domestic textile industry is another indication of how he saw the colonising process in terms of labour exploitation.

[4] This is not pellucidly clear, but seems to mean that poldavys, a type of coarse canvas developed in Brittany and used for sailcloth, would be manufactured by Indians working under supervision of colonists.

[5] Caution in using violence to the Indians, the injunction to treat them gently, the insistence on settling and trading (by force if necessary), Christianisation, and the exploitation of men, women and children to work for the colonists make up a coherent if not wholly self-consistent policy.

Sorts of men which are to be passed
in this voyage.

1 Men skilfull in all Minerall causes.

2 Men skilful in all kinde of drugges.

3 Fishermen, to consider of the sea fishings there on the coasts, to be reduced to trade hereafter: and others for the fresh water fishings.

4 Salt-makers, to view the coast, and to make triall how rich the sea-water there is, to aduise for the trade.

5 Husbandmen, to view the soile, to resolue for tillage in all sorts.

6 Vineyard-men bred, to see how the soile may serue for the planting of Vines.[1]

7 Men bred in the Shroffe in South Spaine, for discerning how Oliue trees may be planted there.[2]

8 Others, for planting of Orenge trees, Figge trees, Limon trees, and Almond trees; for iudging how the soile may serue for the same.

9 Gardeners, to prooue the seuerall soiles of the Islands, and of our setling places, to see how the same may serue for all herbs and roots for our victualling; since by rough seas sometimes we may want fish, and since we may want flesh to victuall vs, by the malice of the naturall people there: and gardeners for planting of our common trees of fruit, as Peares, Apples, Plummes, Peaches, Medlers, Apricoes,[3] Quinces for conserues, &c.

10 Lime-makers, to make lime for buildings.

11 Masons, Carpenters, &c. for building there.

12 Bricke-makers and Tile-makers.

13 Men cunning in the art of fortification, that may chuse out places strong by nature to be fortified, and that can plot out and direct workemen.

14 Choise Spade-men, to trench cunningly, and to raise bulwarks and rampiers of earth for defence and offence.

15 Spade-makers, that may, out of the Woods there, make spades like

[1] To bring experienced *vignerons*, recourse would have to be had to the continent. This course was adopted later by the Virginia Company though without conspicuous success.

[2] Hakluyt is evidently writing before the economic break between England and Spain in May 1585, but he does not show much realism in expecting that Spaniards would (or would be allowed) even in peaceful circumstances to come to an English colony in America. This is evidence of a certain lack of political sophistication on his part.

[3] Apricots.

those of Deuonshire,[1] and of other sorts, and shouels from time to time for common vse.

16 Smithes, to forge the yrons of the shouels and spades, and to make blacke billes and other weapons, and to mend many things.

17 Men that vse to breake Ash trees for pike-staues, to be imploied in the Woods there.

18 Others, that finish vp the same so rough hewd, such as in London are to be had.

19 Coopers, to make caske of all sorts.

20 Forgers of pikes heads and of arrow heads, with forges, with Spanish yron, and with all maner of tooles to be caried with them.

21 Fletchers, to renew arrowes, since archerie preuaileth much against vnarmed people: and gunpowder may soone perish, by setting on fire.

22 Bowyers also, to make bowes there for need.

23 Makers of oares, since for seruice vpon those riuers it is to great purpose, for the boats and barges they are to passe and enter with.

24 Shipwrights, to make barges and boats, and bigger vessels, if need be, to run along the coast, and to pierce the great Bayes and Inlets.[2]

25 Turners, to turne targets of Elme and tough wood, for vse against the darts and arrowes of Saluages.

26 Such also as haue knowledge to make targets of horne.

27 Such also as can make armor of hides vpon moulds, such as were woont to be made in this realme about an hundred yeeres since, and were called Scotish iacks:[3] such armor is light and defensiue enough against the force of Saluages.

28 Tanners, to tanne hides of Buffes,[4] Oxen, etc. in the Iles where you shall plant.

29 White Tawyers[5] of all other skinnes there.

30 Men skilfull in burning of Sope ashes, and in making of Pitch, and Tarre, and Rozen, to be fetched out of Prussia and Poland, which are thence to be had for small wages, being there in maner of slaues.

The seuerall sorts of trees, as Pines, Firres, Spruses, Birch and others, are to be boared with great augers a foot or halfe a yard aboue the ground, as they use in Vesely towards Languedock[6] and

---

[1] The special characteristics of Devonshire spades have not been established.

[2] Compare Hayes (above p. 179) on the need for flat-bottomed boats for the transit trade he envisaged.

[3] Jacks were sleeveless jackets of Spanish leather, quilted and sometimes plated with iron.   [4] Cp. on buff hides p. 170.

[5] White tawyers made alum-dressed leather.

[6] Vézelay, department of Yonne, *en route* to Languedoc.

neere Bayona in Gascoigne:[1] and so you shall easily and quickly
see what Gummes, Rozen, Turpentine, Tarre, or liquor is in them,
which will quickly distill out cleerely without any filthie mixture,
and will shew what commoditie may be made of them: their
goodnesse and greatnesse for masts is also to be considered.

31   A skilfull painter is also to be caried with you, which the Spaniards
vsed commonly in all their discoueries to bring the descriptions
of all beasts, birds, fishes, trees, townes, &c.[2]

A briefe note[3] of the corne, fowles, fruits and beasts of the Inland of Florida on the backeside of Virginia, taken out of the 44 chapter of the discouery of the said countrey, begun by Fernando de Soto gouernour of Cuba, in the yeere of our Lord 1539.

The bread which they eat in all the land of Florida, is of Maiz, which
is like to course Millet.[4] And in all the Islands and West Indies from
the Antiles forward there is this Maiz.

Likewise in Florida there be many Wallnuts,[5] Plummes, Mulberies,
& Grapes. They sowe their Maiz, and gather it, euery man his owne
croppe. The fruits are common to all men, because they grow
abundantly in the fields without planting or dressing. In the mountaines
there grow Chestnuts; they are somewhat smaller than the Chestnuts
of Spaine, which are called Collarínnas.[6] From Rio Grande toward the
West, the Walnuts are differing from the other; for they are softer and

---

[1]   Bayonne in Gascony.

[2]   This prescription may have led to the bringing of John White to Roanoke Island
in 1585. For the background to the use of painters in discovery voyages see Hulton and
Quinn, *American drawings of John White*, I, 29–36; Andrews, Canny and Hair, *The western
enterprise 1480–1650* (1978), pp. 14–16, 195–201. F. Chiapelli, ed., *First images of America*,
I (1976), 417–54. Spanish 'painters' were primarily cartographers.

[3]   The note is a slightly contracted translation of Fidalgo Delvas, *Relaçam verdadeira
dos trabalhos q̃ hõ gouernador dõ Fernãdo d'Souto* (Evora, Andree de Burgos, 1557),
ff. clxxix–clxxx. The chapter appeared in the translation of Richard Hakluyt the younger,
Virginia richly valued by the description of the maine land of Florida her next neighbour
(F. Kyngston for M. Lownes, 1609), pp. 178–9. The translation here printed was done from
Hakluyt's copy (see p. 201 below), but it is not the same as Hakluyt's. The best modern
edition is by James Alexander Robertson, Gentleman of Elvas, *True relation of the hardships
suffered by Governor Fernando de Soto* (2 vols., De Land, Florida, 1932–3), the text of his
translation being reprinted in *NAW*, II, 97–158.

[4]   'milho Zaburo', coarse millet, Robertson, II, 311.

[5]   'nozes', translated also as 'walnuts' by Hakluyt and Robertson.

[6]   'colbarinhas', ignored by Hakluyt and Robertson: not identified, but may be
associated with *chola*, a leguminous plant.

round like bullets. And from Rio Grande toward Puerto del Spirito Santo Eastward, for the most part they are harder. And the Trees and Nuts are like in fashion vnto those of Spaine. There is in all the countrey a fruit which groweth vpon an herbe or plant[1] like to the herbe called Dogs-tongue, which the Indians doe sowe. The fruit is like vnto the

These may be the Tunas. Peres Rial:[2] it is of a very good rellish, and of a pleasant taste. Another herbe groweth in the fields, which beareth a fruit neere the ground like to a Strawberie, very pleasant in taste. The Plummes are of two sorts, red and gray, in fashion and bignesse of Walnuts, and haue three or foure stones in them.[3] These are better than any in Spaine, and they make better Prunes of them. The want of dressing is perceiued only in the Grapes: which although they be great, yet they haue a great kernell. All the rest of the fruits are very perfect, and lesse hurtfull than those of Spaine.

The beasts of Florida. There are in Florida many Beares, Lions, Stags, Roebucks, Wild-cats, and Conies.[4]

There be many Wild-hennes as bigge as Peacocks,[5] small Partridges like those of Africa, Cranes, Ducks, Rolas, Blackbirds, and Sparrowes. There be certaine Blacke birds bigger than Sparrowes[6] and lesser than Stares.[7]

There be Sore-hauks, Faulcons, Gosse-hauks,[8] and all fowles of pray that are in Spaine.

The Indians are well proportioned. Those of the plaine countreys are taller of stature, and better proportioned than those of the mountaines. Those of the Inland are better furnished with corne and wealth of the country, than those of the sea coast. The countrey on

[1] 'a plant like to Ligoacan' (Hakluyt, p. 178). The piece on the Dogs-tongue is an interpolation: it seems unjustified. The Dogs-tongue is a borage, *Cynoglossum officinale* (cp. Gerard, *Herball* (1597), p. 659). This is either the avocado (Sp. *aguacate*) (Robertson, II, 395) or much more probably (as the editor's sidenote, his second thoughts perhaps, may infer), a cactus, Prickly Pear, *Opuntia*, several sp.

[2] 'peros reaos', royal pear (Robertson, II, 311). The sidenote associates them with 'Tunas', Spanish *tunel*, the prickly pear.

[3] 'como madrohosa', persimmon (see Robertson, II, 375).

[4] 'Beares and Lyons, Wolues, Deere, Dogges, Cattes, Marterns and Conies', Hakluyt, p. 179. This version omits wolves, has both deer and roebucks, and does not translate 'adites' which is 'jackals' in Robertson, II, 312.

[5] The first item is really peafowls (though probably intended for turkeys), and the last three 'turtledoves, thrushes, and sparrows', (Robertson, II, 312).

[6] The black bird is Brown-headed Cowbird, *Molothrus pecoris ater ater* (Boddaert) (C. S. Robbin (et al.), *Birds of North America*, (1966), p. 282; Forbush and May, *Birds*, pp. 477–8). This is only slightly smaller than the starling (7 inches instead of 7½ inches).

[7] 'Stares' are starlings.

[8] 'goshawks, falcons, sparrowhawks', (Robertson, II, 312).

the sea coast toward the gulfe of Mexico is barren and poore, and the people more warrelike.[1] The coast beareth from Puerto del Spirito Santo vnto Apalache, and from Apalache to Rio de Palmas almost from East to West; from Rio de Palmas vnto Noua Hispania it runneth from North to South. It is a gentle coast, but it hath many sholds and bannks or shelues of sand.

A Note of such commodities as are found in Florida next adioning vnto the South part of Virginia, taken out of the description of the said countrey, written by Mounsieur Rene Laudonniere, who inhabited there two Sommers and one winter.[2]

The countrey of Florida is flat, and diuided with diuers riuers, and therefore moist, and is sandy towards the sea-shore. *The trees of Florida.*

There groweth in those parts great quantitie of Pyne trees, which haue no kernels in the apples that they beare.[3]

Their woods are full of Oakes, Walnut trees, blacke Cherrie trees. Mulberie trees, Lentiskes which yeeld Masticke,[4] and Chestnut trees, which are more wilde than those of France.

There is great store of Cedars, Cypresses, Baies, Palme trees, Grapes: *Good Grapes.* There is there a kind of Medlars, the fruit whereof is better than that of France, and bigger. There are also Plumme trees, which beare very faire fruit, but such as is not very good.

There are Raspesses, and a little bery which we call among vs Blues,[5] which are very good to eat.

There grow in that countrey a kinde of Rootes, which they call in their language Hazes,[6] whereof in necessities they make bread.

---

[1] 'the Countrie along the sea coast is barren and poore', (Hakluyt, p. 179).

[2] From René de Laudonnière, *Histoire notable de la Floride* (Paris, 1586), translated by Richard Hakluyt as *A notable historie containing foure voyages made into Florida* (1587) and reprinted by him in *Principal navigations*, III (1600), 301–60. The passage is largely taken from *A notable historie* (1587), pp. 2–2v.; *Principal navigations*, III, 505–6. The French is *Histoire notable*, ff. 3–4, the best edition of which is by Susanne Lussagnet, *Les français en l'Amérique pendant la deuxième moitié du XVIᵉ siècle*, II (1958), 27–200, which has valuable notes. See also *NAW*, II, 281–307, 319–61.

[3] The French has 'prunes', which Mlle Lussagnet suggests is a misprint for 'pignes', pine-nuts (*Fr. en Amér.*, II, 40n).   [4] 'which yeald Masticke', is added.

[5] Fr. 'bleues'. Mlle Lussagnet points out that in French Canada 'bleues' are Blueberries and other species of *Vaccinium*, which would appear to be appropriate since at least three species extend down into this area (cp. Gleason and Cronquist, *Manual*, pp. 532–5).

[6] Fr. 'Hasse', the Muskhogean transliteration of which cannot be suggested.

There is also the tree called Esquine,[1] (which I take to be the Sassafras) which is very good against the pocks and other contagious diseases.

The Beasts of Florida.

The Beasts best knowen in this countrey are Stagges, Roes, Deere, Goates, Leopards, Ownces, Lucernes, diuers sorts of Woolues, wilde Dogges, Hares, Connies, and a certeine kinde of beast that differeth little from the Lion of Africke.[2]

The Fowles of Florida.

The Fowles are Turkie Cocks, Partridges, Perrots, Pigeons, Ring-doues, Turtles, Blacke birds, Crowes, Tarcels, Faulcons, Leonards,[3] Herons, Cranes, Storkes, wilde Geese, Mallards,[4] Cormorants, Herne-shawes, white, red, blacke, and gray, and an infinit sort of all wildfoule.

There is such aboundance of Crocodiles, that oftentimes in swim-ming, men are assailed by them: Of serpents there are many sorts.

Gold and Siluer.

There is found among the Sauages good quantitie of Gold and Siluer, which is gotten out of the ships that are lost vpon the coast: Neuerthelesse they say, that in the mountains of Apalatcy, there are mines of Copper, which I thinke to be Gold.[5]

Store of dies and colours.

There is also in this countrey, great store of Graines and Herbes, whereof might be made excellent good dies and paintings of all kinde of colours.

They sowe their Maiz or Corne twice a yeere, to wit, in March and in Iune: and all in one and the same soile: The said Maiz from the time that it is sowed, vnto the time that it is gathered, is but three moneths in the ground. They haue also faire Pumpions and very good Beanes:

Oile in Florida.

They haue certeine kinds of oile, wherewith they vse to annoint themselues.[6]

---

[1] 'which I take to be the Sassafras' is added: there is no qualification either in the French or in Hakluyt's translation. Mlle Lussagnet points out (*Fr. en Amèr.*, II, 41n) that Esquine is the China Root, here *Smilax pseudochina* L., and associated species of the Woody Smilax (see Quinn, *Roanoke voyages*, I, 348, and pp. 167, 437, 449).

[2] Fr. 'Cerfs, Biches, Cheureux, Dains, Ours [omitted above], Leopards, Loups, Ceruiers, Onces' (f. 2v), Hakluyt having 'Stags, Hinds, Goats, Deere, Beares, Leopards, Ownces, Luserns' (f. 2). The phrase about the Lion is added.

[3] Fr. 'Laniers' (f. 3v); Hakluyt, 'Laynerds' (f. 2), a kind of falcon.

[4] Fr. 'Canars' only.

[5] Cp. John Sparke on his 1565 visit with Hawkins – 'As for mines either of gold or siluer, the Frenchemen can heare of none they haue vpon the Island [i.e. the Florida peninsula], but of copper'. (*Principal navigations*, III (1600), 519; *NAW*, II, 368). But the Le Moyne engraving gave wider credence to this belief. See P. H. Hulton, *The work of Jacques Le Moyne*, I, 215, II, pl. 133.

[6] The final paragraph is made up of later references in the book.

A briefe extract of the merchantable commodities found in the South part of Virginia, ann. 1585. and 1586.[1] Gathered out of the learned worke of master Thomas Herriot, which was there remaining the space of eleuen moneths.

Silke of Grasse, or Grasse-silke, the like whereof groweth in Persia, whereof I haue seene good Grograine made.

Worme-silke.

Flaxe and Hempe.

Allom.

Wapeih a kinde of earth so called by the naturall inhabitants, very like to Terra Sigillata, and by some of our Physitions found more effectuall.

Pitch, Tarre, Rozen, and Turpentine: there are those kinds of trees that yeeld them aboundantly and in great store.

Sassafras, called by the inhabitants Wynauk: of whose soueraigne and manifold vertues, reade Monardes the Phisician of Siuile,[2] in his booke entituled in English: The ioyfull newes from the West Indies.

Cedar.

Vines of two sorts.

Oile: there are two sorts of Wall-nuts, both holding oile. Furthermore, there are three seuerall kindes of Berries, in the forme of Oake Acornes, which also by the experience and vse of the inhabitants, we finde to yeeld very good and sweete Oile. There are also Beares, which are commonly very fat, and in some places there are many, their fatnesse because it is so liquid, may well be termed Oyle, and hath many speciall vses.

Furres.

Ottars, Marternes, and Lucernes.

Deere skinnes.

---

[1] From Thomas Hariot, *A briefe and true report of the new found land of Virginia* (1588), conscientiously summarized from the fourth printing in Richard Hakluyt, *Principal navigations*, III (1600), 266–80; *NAW*, III, 139–55. The notes from the editions in D. B. Quinn, *Roanoke voyages*, I (1955), 317–89, and D. B. and A. M. Quinn, *Virginia voyages from Hakluyt* (1973), pp. 150–57, are not repeated here.

[2] 'the Phisician of Siuile' is added (cp. Quinn, *Roanoke voyages*, I, 329). Nicolás Monardes, *Primera y segunda y tercera partes de la historia natural...de nuestras Indias* (Seville, 1574), which appeared as *Joyfull newes out of the newe founde worlde*, trans. John Frampton (1577; 1580 with addition; 1596 with further additions), for which see *Joyfull newes*, ed. Stephen Gaselee, 2 vols (1924), I, v.

Ciuet Cattes.

Iron.

Copper. The foresaid Copper, we also found by triall to hold Siluer.

Pearle. One of our company, a man of skill in such matters, had gathered together from the Sauages, aboue fiue thousand.

Sweet Gummes of diuers kinds, and many other Apothecary drugs.

Dies of diuers kinds.

There is Shoemake, well knowen and vsed in England for blacke; the seed of an herbe called Wasebur, little small rootes called Chappacor, and the barke of a tree called by the inhabitants, Tangomockonomindge, which Dies are for diuers sorts of red.

Commodities in Virginia, knowen to yeeld victuals.

Pagatowr or Mays, which is their principall corne.

Okindgier, called by vs Beanes.

Wickonzour,[1] called by vs Pease.

Macocquer, called by vs, Pompions, Mellons, & Gourds.

An herbe which in Dutch is called Melden, being a kinde of Orage, &c.

An herbe in forme of a Marigold, sixe foot in height, taken to be Planta Solis.

Vppowoc, or Tabacco, of great estimation among the Sauages.

Rootes

Openauck,[2] a kinde of Rootes of round forme, as bigge as Wall-nuts, some farre greater. Monardes calleth them Beades, or Pater nostri of Sancta Helena, and master Brereton Ground Nuts.

Okeepenauk, are Rootes of round shape found in dry grounds, the inhabitants vse to boile and eat many of them.

Tsinaw, a kind of Roote much like vnto that which in England is called the China Roote, brought from the East Indies.

Coscushaw, a Roote taken to be that which the Spaniards in the West Indies, doe call Cassauy.

Habascon, a Roote of hot taste, almost of the forme and bignesse of a Parsnep.

Leekes differing little from ours in England.

Fruites.

Chestnuts there are in diuers places great store, vsed diuers waies for food.

---

[1] Hariot spells it 'Wickonzòwr'.　　　　[2] Hariot spells it 'Openauk'.

Walnuts there are two kinds, and of them infinit store in many places, where are very great woods for many miles together, the third part of the trees are Walnut trees, they vse them for meate, and make a milke of them of verie pleasant taste, and holesome.

Medlers, a kinde of very good fruit, they are as red as cherries, and very lushous sweet.

Mutaquesunnauk,[1] a kinde of pleasant fruit, almost of the shape and bignesse of English Peares, but they are of a perfect red colour, as well within as without, they grow on a plant whose leaues are very thicke and full of prickles, as sharpe as needles: some, which haue been in Noua Hispania, where they haue seene that kinde of red Die of exceeding great price, which is called Cochenile, to grow, do describe his plant right like vnto this of Mutaquesunnauk: howbeit the Cochenile is not the fruit, but a graine found on the leaues of the plant, and stricken off vpon sheetes, and dried in the sunne.

These plants are called Tunas also, whereof there be three sorts: that which beareth no fruit.[2] bringeth foorth the Cochenile.

Grapes there are of two sorts, which I mentioned in the merchantable commodities.

Strawberies there are, as good and as great as in any English garden.

Mulberies,
Apple-crabbes,   } such as we haue in England.
Hurts, or Hurtleberies,

Sacquenummener a kinde of berries almost like vnto Capers but somewhat greater, which grow together in clusters vpon a plant or hearbe that is found in shollow waters, being boiled eight or nine houres according to their kinde, are very good meat and holsome, otherwise if they be eaten, they will make a man for the time franticke or extremely sicke.

A Reed which beareth a seed almost like vnto our Rie or Wheat and being boiled is good meat.

In our trauells in some places, we found wilde Pease like vnto ours in England, but that they were lesse, which are also good meat.

A kind of Berry like vnto an Acorne, of fiue sorts, growing on seuerall kindes of trees: the one sort is called Sagatemener, the second, Osamener, the third Pummuckoner. the inhabitants vse to dry them vpon hurdles like Malt in England. when they vse them, they first water

---

[1] This is Hakluyt's spelling (III (1600), 273): Hariot's is 'Metaquesúnnauk', (see Quinn, *Roanoke voyages*, I, 351).

[2] The side note is slightly modified from Hakluyt's – 'There are iii. kinds of Tunas wherof that which beareth no fruit bringeth foorth the Cochinillo' (III (1600), 273). This established that Hakluyt's text was used. Although it was not the Nopal Cactus on which the Cochineal insect feeds, it was the not dissimilar cactus, the Prickly Pear (*Opuntia* sp.).

them till they be soft, and then being sod, they make loues of bread of them. of these three kindes also the inhabitants doe vse to make sweet oile.

The fourth sort is called Sapummener, which being boiled or perched be like vnto rosted Chesnuts; of this sort they make bread also.

The fift sort is called Mangummenauk, the very Acorne of their kind of Oake; being dried as the rest, and after watered, they boile them, and their seruants, and somtimes the chiefe themselues eate them with their fish and flesh.

Beasts.

Deere, vp into the countrey very great, and in some places, great store.

Conies, of a gray colour like vnto hares: they make mantles of the furre or flue of their skinnes.

Saquenuckot and Maquowoc, two kindes of small beasts greater then Conies, which are very good meat.

Squirels, which are of a gray colour, we haue taken and eaten.

Beares, which are of blacke colour. They are good meat. And being hunted they climbe vp into trees and are killed by the Saluages with their arrowes, and sometimes by vs with our Caliuers.

The Lion is sometimes killed by the Saluages and eaten. Woolues or Wooluish dogges.

I haue the names of eight and twenty sorts of beasts dispersed in the maine, of which their are onely twelue kindes by vs as yet discouered.

Fowle

Turkie cocks and Turkie hennes, Stock-doues, and Partriges, Cranes, hernes, and in Winter great store of Swannes, and Geese.

There are also Parrots, Falcons, and Marlin haukes.

Of all sorts of foules I haue the names in the countrey language of fowrescore and sixe.

Fish.

Sturgions, Herrings, Porpoises, Troutes, Rayes, Oldwiues, Mullets, Plaice, and very many other sorts of very excellent fish.

Seacrabs, Oisters, great, small, round, long: Muscles, Scalops, Periwincles, and Creuises.

Seekanauk, a kinde of crustie shell-fish, which is good meate, about a foot in bredth, hauing a crusty taile, many legges like a Crabbe, and her eyes in her backe. They are found in shallowes of water, and sometimes on the shore.

Tortoises both of land and sea kinde; they are very good meate and their egges also:

Certaine briefe testimonies touching sundry rich mines of Gold, Siluer, and Copper, in part found and in part constantly heard of, in North Florida, and the Inland of the Maine of Virginia, and other countreys there vnto on the North part neere adioining, gathered out of the works, all (one excepted) extant in print, of such as were personall trauellers in those countries[1]

1   In the second relation of Iaques Cartier the 12 chapter he reporteth that he vnderstood by Donnacona the king of the countrey, and others, that to the Southwest of Canada there are people clad with cloth, as the French were, very honest, and many inhabited townes, and that they haue great store of Gold and red Copper, &c.[2]   *I take these to be the people toward Cibola, clad in mantels of cotten.*[3]

2   In the discouery of the Inland of Florida farre to the North begun by Fernando de Soto, gouernour of Cuba in the yeere 1539. (and to be seene in print in the hands of Master Richard Hackluyt)[4] The Indians in many places farre distant the one from the other gaue them often and certaine aduertisement, that beyond the mountaines Northward there were mines of Gold at a place called by them Chisca, and some shewed the maner which the Indians vsed in refining the same.[5] This place in mine opinion cannot be

[1] The main printed work relied on is Hakluyt, *Principal navigations*, III (1600).
[2] Ibid. III, 225.
[3] The side note is not taken directly from Hakluyt but appears to be based on passages from Alarcón's report (Ibid., III, 452).
[4] The indication that Hakluyt in 1602 had a copy of the Evora edition of the Gentleman of Elvas, 1557, is significant. He did not use it as late as 1600 so he may have recently acquired it, and he was to complete and publish his translation by 1609 (p. 193 above). The editor clearly had access to Hakluyt's library.
[5] Hakluyt discussed Chisca, mentioned by Soto, as a gold-source in the dedication to *Virginia richly valued* (1609), sig. A2v–A3. It was supposed to lie to the west of the Mississippi.

farre from the great riuer[1] that falleth into the Southwest part of the Bay of Chesepioc.[2]

3 The Indians enformed Mounsieur Rene Laudonniere in Florida,[3] that there were mines of red mettall, which they call in their language Sieroa Pira,[4] in the mountaines of Apalatcy, which vpon triall made thereof by the French was found perfect Gold, as appeareth Pagina 352. In the third volume of the English voiages, and in the same relation there is very often mention of Siluer and excellent perfect and faire perles found by the french in those parts.

4 In the late discouerie of New Mexico made by Antonio de Espeio on the backe side of Virginia[5] extant in Spanish and English in the third volume of the English voyages paginis 303. &c.[6] there is mention of rich Siluer mines (and sometimes of Gold in aboundance) eleuen or twelue times found as they trauelled Northward, by men very skilfull in minerall matters, which went in the voyage for that purpose. The large description and chart of which voyage containing great numbers of townes and diuers great riuers discouered in that action made in Mexico by Francisco Xamuscado 1585 being intercepted afterward by the English at sea, we haue in London to be shewed to such as shall haue occasion to make vse of the same.[7]

5 The constant report of many of the Saluages to the worshipfull Master Ralfe Lane then gouernour of the English colonie in

---

[1] The great river is the James. Knowledge about it in printed sources was confined to what little of it was shown in the De Bry version (1590) of John White's map (see Hulton and Quinn, *American drawings of John White*, I (1964), 136–7, II, 122) which is only its mouth. It seems not unlikely that Hayes had heard about it from some member of the party which in 1585–6 wintered near the Chesapeake Bay (Quinn, *Roanoke voyages*, I, 244–6). If so it is a valuable link between the Roanoke and the Jamestown voyages. The informant could have been Thomas Harriot: we know of no extant written source.

[2] The myth of the nearness of the Pacific to the Atlantic (in spite of Coronado and Soto) was present in Ralph Lane's Roanoke River story (Ibid., I, 264), and inspired a number of attempts to pierce the interior beyond the Fall Line in the Virginia colony after 1607.

[3] From *A notable historie* (1587), reprinted in *Principal navigations*, III (1600), 352.

[4] Susanne Lussagnet (*Fr. en Amèr.*, p. 171n), following Albert S. Gatschet, 'The Timucua language', American Philosophical Society, *Proceedings*, XVII (1878), 468, indicates that 'pira' means 'red' or 'yellow'.

[5] From 'El viaje que Hizo Antonio de Espejo en el anno de ochenta y tres', first published separately by Hakluyt in Paris in 1586, and here taken from *Principal navigations*, III (1600), 383–96, see Quinn, *Hakluyt handbook*, II, 468–9. [6] A misprint for '393'.

[7] The Francisco Chamuscado chart of 1585 has unfortunately disappeared: this was the 'secret mappe of those partes made in Mexico the yeere before [1585] for the king of Spain, (which originall with many others is [1599] in the custodie of the excellent Mathematician M. Thomas Hariot)' (Hakluyt's dedication, *Principal navigations*, II (1599), sig. ★2v). This might suggest that the compiler had access to Harriot's collections also and that the map was still in his possession (see D. B. Quinn, *England and the discovery of America*, pp. 416–17).

Virginia of the rich mine of Wassador or Gold at a place by them named Chaunis Temoatam, twentie daies iourney ouerland from the Mangoaks, set downe by himselfe at large in the first part of his relation of the said countrey of Virginia, extant in the third volume of the English voyages pagina 258.[1] is much to be regarded and considered by those that intend to prosecute this new enterprise of planting nere vnto those parts.

6   I could giue large information of the rich copper mine in the East side of the Bay of Menan within 30 or 40. leagues to the Southwest of Cape Breton, whereof I my selfe haue seene aboue an hundred pieces of the copper, and haue shewed some part thereof to diuers knightes of qualitie, as also of Salt as good as that of Buruage in France, found neere that Bay, and could make proofe of the testimonie of the Saluages touching a Siluer mine in another Bay within two or three leagues to the west of the aforesaid Bay of Menan: But I reserue a further relation heereof to a more conuenient time and place.[2]

7   Yf it please any man to read the Summarie of Gonsaluo de Ouiedo extant in part in the English decads,[3] of the voyage of Sebastian Cabote along this coast of Virginia and Norumbega:[4] And the short relation of Iohn de Verarsana, which ranged the said coast long after him in the yeere 1524. which is also to be seene in the third volume of the English voyages pagine 298.[5] he shall finde often mention of rich Minerals and store of excellent copper, which so long agoe they saw among the Saluages, they being the first knowen Christians that euer saw those coasts. So that it were more than wilful madnesse to doubt of rich mines to be in the aforesaid countreys.[6]

FINIS

[1] From *Principal navigations*, III (1600), 257–9.

[2] This is material not previously published, some of it from Bellenger (*NAW*, IV, 306–8, v), but some not. Is the 'I' Hakluyt, Harriot or Hayes? Hayes is slightly the more probable.

[3] Francisco González de Oviedo, *Sumario* (1527), partly translated in Richard Eden, *The decades of the newe worlde or West India* (1555), ff. 173v–214.

[4] See *Principal navigations*, III (1600), 6–9, and cp. Quinn, *England and the discovery of America*, pp. 136–44, *North America* (1977), pp. 114–35. The words 'this coast of Virginia and Norumbega', is the editor's addition.

[5] Giovanni da Verrazzano, 'The relation...1524', was first translated by the younger Hakluyt for *Divers voyages* (1582), second numeration, sig. A1–E1, and reprinted in *Principal navigations*, III (1600), 295–300. See *NAW*, I, 281–9.

[6] The last promotional sentence might perhaps be thought characteristic of Edward Hayes. Cp. p. 43 above.

CHAPTER III

CONTEMPORARY CORRESPONDENCE ON THE 1602 VOYAGE

Whatever circumstance or persons led to the initiation of the Gosnold voyage, it had been begun without any reference to Sir Walter Ralegh, nor was there any obvious necessity for him to have been involved. He had shown no public interest in Virginia since 1589, except for a single reference in his Guiana tract of 1596, however much he may have been working in secret (since 1599 perhaps) to establish contacts with the Lost Colonists of 1587, though the first, unsuccessful, voyage to the Carolina Outer Banks that we know of was that of Samuel Mace in 1602. He now maintained that since the Lost Colonists must still be regarded as living, his monopoly over English voyages to North America had not expired, as it should have done, in 1591 but was still operative. When he discovered in August 1602 that Bartholomew Gilbert had been trying to sell sassafras brought home from 'North Virginia' in July at various southern ports, and had encountered him at Weymouth, he wrote to Sir Robert Cecil to invoke his and the earl of Nottingham's help in confiscating the sassafras (and indeed setting Thomas Harriot to work in London to intercept a cartload coming from Southampton) for his own use. His arrogant letter does, however, indicate that that he was again regarding North America as a serious field for enterprise. He wished to stop Gilbert, but he soon changed his policy in his dealings with Gilbert and his associates, arranging, in some way, for the publication of the results of their voyage (and of his own southern venture) as if both had been conducted under his auspices. He thus, indirectly, declared his interest in the exploration and eventual settlement of 'North Virginia' as well as 'South Virginia', though he engaged Gilbert to make a voyage for him in the latter direction in 1603. The little book addressed to him which emerged (from these decisions) is discussed above, though we cannot say how or why Brereton was chosen to set out the narrative with which it began. He does not appear in Ralegh's letter, nor, strangely, does Bartholomew Gosnold, the captain of the *Concord* (unless we regard him as having been susperseded by Gilbert on the homeward run by earlier arrangement, since Gosnold was to have remained at the trading post and would not therefore be expected to continue his command of the vessel after she left to return to England).

In contrast to the dogmatic assertions and pragmatic action brought out in Ralegh's letter of August 17, Gosnold's letter to his father on September

7, is placid and unconcerned. He had written earlier, in a letter now lost, to give a brief account of the cargo brought back. He now writes in a leisurely way about the climate of 'North Virginia', noting its later spring, and indicating that he had been influenced by the English version of Verrazzano's letter in Hakluyt's *Principal navigations* (III (1600), 295–307). He indicates also that too much sassafras could easily be a drug on the market, as indeed it was to prove (Quinn, *England and the discovery of America*, pp. 415–16). He also made it clear that no holding party could have been left behind, since they had barely enough food on board to see them home. His glossing over of the Ralegh affair and his failure to mention anything about the impending publication on the voyage might suggest that he had retired to the sidelines and had refused to be embroiled in the politics or even the economics of the voyage's aftermath. Both letters do, however, throw light on the voyage as well as on what happened after the *Concord* returned.

---

3 21 August 1602. Sir Walter Ralegh to Sir Robert Cecil[1]

S*i*r, wheras I wrate vnto yow in my last[2] y*t* I was Gon*n* to weymouth to speak*e* with a pinnes of myne arived from virginia[3] / I found this bearer Captayn Gilbert[4] ther also who went on*n* the same voyage butt myne fell 40 leaugs to the west of it, & this bearer as mich to the east, so as neather of them spake with the peopell,[5] butt I do sende bothe the barks away agayne having saved the charg in sarsephraze woode,[6] butt this bearer bringinge svme 2200 waighte to hampton his adventurers

---

[1] Holograph. Hatfield House, Cecil Papers 94/160 (first printed in Edward Edwards, *The life of Sir Walter Ralegh with his letters*, II (1866), 251–2). I am indebted to Pierre Lefranc for a correct transcript. See Gookin and Barbour, *Gosnold*, pp. 167–71.

[2] Ralegh's earlier letter to Cecil has not been found.

[3] For Samuel Mace's voyage of 1602 see pp. 166–7 and Quinn, *England and the discovery of America*, pp. 405–18.

[4] After arrival at Exmouth, and possibly a brief call at Dartmouth, *Concord* had gone to Portsmouth (where Gosnold perhaps disembarked), and then to Southampton where most of the sassafras was put on shore, before reaching Weymouth about 31 July or 1 August. It would seem that Gilbert was made to carry the letter to Cecil and to explain himself.

[5] Mace's landfall was in the region of Cape Lookout or a little farther south (just north of 34°), *Concord's* was at approximately 43° (Cape Small is at 43° 20′), extending down to perhaps 41° 10′ (Elizabeths Isle being at 41° 20′). Gosnold was not concerned with searching for Ralegh's Lost Colonists.

[6] Ralegh had *Concord* arrested, had taken steps to impound sassafras still at Southampton, was on the track of that sent to London, and had taken Gilbert (and *Concord*) into his service to go in 1603 to Chesapeake Bay. He had covered the cost of Mace's voyage from sassafras already sold (most probably not at such prices as 10 to 20 shillings a pound).

have taken away their parts & brought it to lvndvn[1] / I do therfore humble pray yow to deale with my L: Admirall[2] for a letter to make seasure of all y^t which is cume to lvndvn ether by his L: octoretye, or by the Judge[3] because I have a patent y^t all shipps & goods ar confiscate y^t shall trade ther without my leve / & wheras sarsephraze was worth 10^s, 12^s, & 20^{s}[4] apound before Gilbert returned his cloying of the markett will overthrow all myne & his owne also[5] / he is contented to have all stayde, not only for this present, butt being to go agayne others will also go & distroy the trade, which otherwize would yeild 8, or 10, for on in certenty, & a returne in xx[6] weekes / I desire butt right herein, & my L: Admirall I hope will not be a hinderance to a matter of trade gravnted by the great seale of Inglande, his L: havinge also freedvme & an interest in the countrye[7] / a man of my Lords of hampton arested a part of Gilberts for the xths / I hope my L: will not take it belonging not vnto hyme,[8] having also hyme sealf poure

[1] Ralegh's patent of 25 March 1584 was due to expire on 24 March 1591 unless he had established a settled colony before then. The Lost Colony, unseen since 1587, gave him a tenuous (but apparently accepted) hold on his monopoly to all English voyages to North America, apart from Newfoundland. The confiscation clause (Quinn, *Roanoke voyages*, 1, 84) covered 200 leagues north and south of the established colony, so that on a latitude reckoning (alone) he was within his rights in dealing with Gilbert as he did. His strategy was to take over public responsibility for the voyage, allow or inspire the compilation of Brereton's tract, and, since it was apparently successful, to promote a second edition. By 1603 he expected to have created a renewed interest in both South Virginia (where his Lost Colonists were, most probably, still established) and the newly named North Virginia explored by Gosnold and Gilbert.

[2] Charles Howard, earl of Nottingham, lord high admiral. Ralegh had written to Thomas Harriot to track down sassafras already despatched from Southampton. Harriot made these notes of the letter (B.L. Additional MS 6789, f. 514): 'Sir Walter Ralegh. / Sassafras come to London in Carte. / remembrances to arest.' (Quinn, *England and the discovery of America*, p. 414).

[3] Judge of the High Court of Admiralty in London: by this time he was Sir Thomas Crompton.

[4] Ralegh has written superscript '6' for superscript 's' in all cases. He is claiming a 20 week voyage would produce an 800 to 1,000 per cent profit if interlopers were kept out.

[5] Brereton's estimate of 3s as the going price makes Ralegh's figures look highly suspicious. Gosnold (p. 210) maintained that more than one ton would break the market.

[6] 'wayghtes' crossed out.

[7] This is evidence of Nottingham's financial association with Ralegh in the Roanoke ventures since 1585, indicating the existence of some continuing syndicate (or one which could be revived). An island was called after the admiral in 1585 (Quinn, *Roanoke voyages*, 1, 283).

[8] The Queen's customers would take 5 per cent poundage on imported goods from *Concord*, but the admiral's official had intervened to take the additional half per cent the lord high admiral got from prize goods and had impounded part of the cargo when he was not satisfied the goods were obtained in legitimate trade.

to trade ther by his interest, & it were pitty to overthrow the enterprize for I shall yet live to see it an inglishe nation[1] / ther was also brought 26 sedar trees by Gilbert[2] which on staplyne of dartmouth hath[3] / if my L: will vouchsauf to write to C: Harris to seaze them, we will part them in three parts,[4] to seele cabin neats & make bords, & many other delicate things[5] / I beseich yow vouchsauf to speak to my L: I know his L: will do mee right herein / I for hast have not written / for if a stay be not made it wilbe spent & sold into many hands//. this bearer cap: Gilbert who is my L: Cobhames man, will find out wher it is / hee came to mee with your post letter / it is he by a good token y[t] had the great deamonde[6] / I beseich yow favor our right, & yow shall see what a pretty, honorabell, & sauf trade we[7] will make/

yours ever to serve yow
W Ralegh

I hope yow will excuse my cumbersvme letters & sutes / it is your destiney to be trobled with your frinds & so must all men bee / butt what yow thinck vnfitt to be dvn for mee, shall never be a quarrell ether internall or externall, I thanck yow evermore for the good, &

---

[1] Ralegh's expressed confidence in the eventual successful colonisation of North America is frequently cited, but ironically he was prevented by imprisonment in July 1603 from taking any part in it.

[2] The 26 cedars represented part (or all) of those cut on Penikese on 10–12 June (p. 130).

[3] It is not clear whether *Concord* entered Dartmouth (her home port) to dispose of the timber or whether her purchaser came down to Exmouth to buy it. Christopher Staplyn, merchant of Dartmouth, has not been identified.

[4] Christopher Harris of Dartmouth was a vice-admiral of Devon, representing the lord high admiral's interests there. Ralegh is offering to divide this part of the cargo between himself, Cecil and Nottingham.

[5] Cedar of Lebanon (*Cedrus lebani*) was prized 'to ceil [line] cabinets and to make boards and other delicate things' because of its attractive odour and its insect-repelling qualities. It was expected that North American Red Cedar would have similar qualities: it was already known to Ralegh from Roanoke Island.

[6] Bartholomew Gilbert was (needless to say) no relative of Sir Humphrey Gilbert or of Ralegh. He was a London goldsmith of somewhat doubtful reputation, thought to have been concerned in dealing in a major diamond from the Portuguese carrack, *Madre de Deus*, taken in 1592, for which he was for a time imprisoned, 1594–5 (Hist. MSS Comm., *Cecil MSS*, v (1894), 33, 38–9, 68, 94, 280–4). How long and in what capacity he had served Henry Brooke, Lord Cobham (arrested 1603) is not known, nor is his record of previous experience at sea. (Cp. Gookin and Barbour, *Gosnold*, pp. 167–33.) If Gilbert had taken a previous letter from Ralegh to Cecil, he was clearly known in some capacity to both of them, but it may have been some time previous so that Ralegh is careful to remind Cecil who Gilbert was.

[7] 'We' inserted above the line. Ralegh is anxious to involve Cecil directly in subsequent North American ventures.

what cannot be effected farewell hit / if wee cannot have what wee would, mee thinck it is a great bounde to finde a frinde y^t will strayne hyme sealf in his frinds cause in what soever as this world fareth/[1]

wemouth this 21 of august:

Gilbert went without my leve & therefore all is confiscate, & he shall have his part agayne/.[2]

[Endorsed:]
[1.] To the right honorabell Sir
      Robert Cecyll knight
      principall Sacritorye G[3]
[2.] 1602
      August 21
      Sir Walter Raleigh to my master[4]

---

4   7 September 1602 Bartholomew Gosnold to Anthony Gosnold[5]

Master Bartholomew Gosnolds Letter to his Father, touching his
first Voyage to Virginia, 1602.

My duetie remembred, &c. Sir, I was in good hope that my occasions would haue allowed mee so much libertie, as to haue come vnto you before this time; otherwise I would haue written more at large concerning the Countrie from whence we lately came, then I did: but not well remembring what I haue already written (though I am assured

---

[1] The postscript indicates how anxious Ralegh was to stress his need for and appreciation of Cecil's friendship and protection: he was soon to be disillusioned by Cecil's part in his downfall in 1603.

[2] Ralegh stresses again that all cargoes brought from North America should come to him alone (if he then gave part to Nottingham and Cecil that was another matter): he wanted Cecil's great authority as Secretary to be placed behind Ralegh's agents who were searching for the sassafras in London.

[3] In Ralegh's hand.

[4] In the hand of one of Cecil's secretaries. A seal below.

[5] Purchas, *Pilgrimes*, IV (1625) 1646 (XVIII (1906), 300–2), which came from Hakluyt's collections, though it is not marked as such in his contents list. Hakluyt is very likely to have known the Gosnolds of Netherhall, Otley, Suffolk. Anthony Gosnold, the recipient, was born about 1535 and so would have been about 67 years old (cp. Gookin and Barbour, *Gosnold*, pp. 14–16, 32–4).

that there is nothing set downe disagreeing with the truth)[1] I thought it fittest not to goe about to adde any thing in writing, but rather to leaue the report of the rest till I come my selfe; which now I hope shall be shortly, and so soone as with conueniency I may. In the meane time, notwithstanding whereas you seeme not to be satisfied by that which I haue already written, concerning some especiall matters. I have here briefely (and as well as I can) added these few lines for your further satisfaction: and first as touching that place where we were most resident, it is in the Latitude of 41. degrees, and one third part; which albeit it be so much to the Southward, yet is it more cold then those parts of Europe, which are scituated vnder the same paralell: but one thing is worth the noting, that notwithstanding the place is not so much subiect to cold as England is, yet did we finde the Spring to be later there, then it is with vs here, by almost a moneth: this whether it hapned accidentally this last Spring to be so, or whether it be so of course, I am not very certaine;[2] the latter seemes most likely, whereof also there may be given some sufficient reason, which now I omit: as for the Acornes we saw gathered on heapes, they were of the last yeare, but doubtlesse their Summer continues longer then ours.[3] We cannot gather by any thing we could obserue in the people, or by any triall we had thereof our selues; but that it is as healthfull a Climate as any can be.

[1] The text of his first letter to his father (probably a brief note on his arrival at Exmouth) is not known to have survived. It is strange that though the *Concord* arrived at Portsmouth on 27 July, he had not had leisure to write to his father fully before 7 September, six weeks later. He was almost certainly involved in the intervention of Ralegh at the beginning of August and the consequent legal complications about the disposal of sassafras, but says nothing about them (they seem mainly to have concerned Bartholomew Gilbert in any case). William Gosnoll, a relative, was Lord Cobham's lawyer in 1603 (Hist. MSS Comm., *Cecil MSS*, XV (1930), 272 *passim*) and may have helped clear him and Gilbert of the infringement problem while it, and Ralegh's dealings with Gilbert at Weymouth (pp. 205–8), opened the way for the publication of the Brereton tract, with its Ralegh dedication. He was clearly hoping to get away from London to Suffolk shortly.

[2] He has some genuine concern for the climate of New England and is here the first to express it. Placing Elizabeths Isle as 41° 20′ (roughly in the latitude of Barcelona or Rome, cp. p. 168), he is interested to find it a little colder than Europe would have been in comparable places at this time and also, in spite of lower latitudes, to have its spring something like a month later. This, he recognised, might not be a typical year, but it represents the first glimpse of an eastern-oriented, continental climate which was to give rise to misunderstandings later. He admitted that summers might, as they do, last longer. He had tried to find out something more but achieved no enlightenment through lack of effective communication with the Indians. His comments show him able to absorb geographic information in an open-minded way.

[3] Acorn heaps were collected by Indians for tanning and food. With walnuts and chestnuts they were dried and stored for food. They 'could be turned, by thorough boiling, into a palatable dish' (Salwen, in *Handbook*, p. 162).

The Inhabitants there, as I wrote before, being of tall stature, comely proportion, strong, active, and some of good yeares, and as it should seeme very healthfull,[1] are sufficient proofe of the healthfulnesse of the place. First, for our selues (thankes be to God) we had not a man sicke two dayes together in all our Voyage; whereas others that went out with vs, or about that time on other Voyages (especially such as went upon reprisall) were most of them infected with sicknesse, whereof they lost some of their men, and brought home a many sicke, returning notwithstanding long before vs.[2] But Verazzano, and others (as I take it, you may reade in the Booke of Discoueries)[3] doe more particularly intreate of the Age of the people in that coast.[4] The Sassafras[5] which we brought we had vpon the Ilands: where though we had little disturbance, and reasonable plenty: yet for that the greatest part of our people were imployed about the fitting of our house,[6] and such like affaires, and a few (and those but easie labourers) vndertooke this worke, the rather because we were informed before our going forth, that a tunne was sufficient to cloy England) and further, for that we had resolued upon our returne, and taken view of our victuall, we iudged it then needefull to vse expedition; which afterward we had more certaine proofe of; for when we came to an anker before Portsmouth, which was some foure dayes after we made the land, we had not one Cake of Bread, nor any drinke, but a little Vinegar, left:[7] for these and

---

[1] Like his associates he was impressed by the height and physique of the Indians (Pockanoket but perhaps especially the Narragansett if he encountered any) and also with the sight of some longlived Indians as an indication of a healthy climate.

[2] Though food was not plentiful he was able to report a healthy crew. It appears that *Concord*, perhaps commencing her voyage from London, was in company with privateers down and some way out from the English Channel. Gosnold had made contact with some of their men since he returned and found (not surprisingly) that in tropical latitudes sickness has affected them (he probably had had personal experience of this in the West Indies in 1599 (p. 32).

[3] He assumed his father had read Verrazzano's letter in its English dress in Hakluyt (*Principal navigations*, III (1600), 295–300) and had probably studied the book with him before he left (even perhaps taking a copy with him).

[4] Verrazzano's reference to the age of the Indians he met on Narragansett Bay is in Hakluyt, III, 298–9.

[5] He indicates that sassafras in some quantity could be had on the islands. His men, like himself, did not work hard as they knew a ton would glut the English market (cp. p. 206).

[6] He indicates that much of their time was spent on the fort (though he gives no hint on whether he hoped to go out again to occupy it): in fact it was the team of 8 or 9 men under Archer who did almost all the work. The 'such like affaires' included exploration: he does not claim to have found Verrazzano's Refugio but he does not eliminate the possibility that he recognised Narragansett Bay for what it was.

[7] Realisation of the inadequacy of their stores, he gives as the reason for their return. It might appear they got no fresh supplies at Exmouth or Dartmouth in July, since their

other reasons, we returned no otherwise laden then you haue heard.[1]
And thus much I hope shall suffice till I can my selfe come to giue you
further notice, which though it be not so soone as I could have wisht,
yet I hope it shall be in conuenient time.[2] In the meane time crauing
your pardon, for which the urgent occasions of my stay will pleade,
I humbly take my leaue. 7. Septemb. 1602.[3]

Your dutifull Sonne,

BARTH. GOSNOLD.

---

arrival on 27 July, without food or drink, would stretch them to the limit. He had evidently
been fortunate in his rapid crossing.

[1] He evidently detailed their cargo in his previous letter. We could do with
information on what value the furs proved to have and what became of the canoe and
Indian curios they brought home.

[2] He is trying to allay what he felt would be his father's anxiety if he stayed away
from home much longer.

[3] The letter was almost certainly written from London.

CHAPTER IV

MARTIN PRING'S VOYAGE TO 'NORTH VIRGINIA' IN 1603

This voyage was a direct follow-up of the Gosnold expedition of 1602. Like it, the Pring expedition was a commercial one, aiming at collecting sassafras and other medicinal plants, and examining the possibilities of trading with the Indians for furs.

Pring proved a very competent navigator and organiser. His exploration of the Maine coast was more comprehensive than that of Gosnold but was brief and a preliminary only to the discovery of a place where a summer trading centre might be established. (In contrast to 1602, no plans were made for wintering.) Pring and his associates were set on doing this inside the great bay, Cape Cod Bay, which lay well to the south, as those who were on the earlier voyage could inform them, of the Savage rock which was Gosnold's first stopping point. This has for a long time been taken to be on Plymouth Harbor, the location of the 1620 Pilgrim colony. But a close examination of both text and topography indicates that it is considerably more likely to have been on Lower Cape Cod itself, in the vicinity of modern Provincetown, and this has been taken as the site of the enclosed camp which Pring created, even if the identification lacks complete certainty.

The inception of the voyage is of some interest. It was the first since the efforts of the younger Richard Hakluyt and Christopher Carleill in 1583–4 to involve the city merchants of Bristol in a purely North American enterprise (though some merchants were concerned with attempts to open the Gulf of St Lawrence to English enterprise in the 1590s). Moreover, Richard Hakluyt, by this time a prebendary of both Bristol Cathedral and of Westminster Abbey, was the main inspirer and organiser of the voyage. He had evidently maintained his contacts with Bristol merchants, even if he had taken little part in the Cathedral Chapter. It was also carefully licensed by Sir Walter Ralegh, whose discovery that Gosnold had gone without his licence in 1602 had caused some difficulty. It was influenced, though to what extent we cannot estimate, by the Brereton pamphlet of 1602 and, indeed, the second edition of this may have helped to recruit subscribers to the voyage as well as to indicate the type of product which might entice the Indians to trade (and we have a long list of commodities brought for this purpose). Robert Salterne of Bristol was the main person link between the two expeditions, but the financing of the voyage may well have been organised by John Whitson, Mayor of Bristol, after whom they named Cape Cod Bay. The use of two vessels, the *Speedwell* of some

50 tons and a smaller bark (or pinnace), the *Discoverer* (26 tons), with 43 persons in all, suggests that the lessons of the previous year in not having enough men or adequate shipping for exploration had not been lost. The new information acquired on the Maine coast may well have been greater than is given in the narrative, which concentrates on the location of the trading camp and the activity carried on there. From Savage Rock (again probably Cape Elizabeth) the ships soon entered Cape Cod Bay, in which they found a harbour with a protecting sandspit 'winding in compasse like the shell of a Snaile' and with a good anchorage. At no great distance from this they constructed a camp, a fenced barricade, probably with an outer defensive ditch. This would have been easy to make since there was plenty of timber and the soil was light and sandy. They had with them, to protect them from the prospective customers, two powerful mastiffs. They were soon joined by bands of Indians. These were most probably members of the Massachusetts tribe, who had come over for summer fishing and gathering on Cape Cod, rather than the Pamet Indians (part of the Pockanoket tribe) whom Champlain was soon to meet at Stage Harbor. They came and went, offered ceremonial gifts of tobacco, and were presented with some of the least valuable merchandise as gifts. We are not told that there was, in fact, any significant trading for furs and skins, though the narrative may not tell all. The main emphasis on the economic side of the venture is on removing sassafras, roots and all, from the sandy soil, sending a cargo of it home by the *Discoverer* before the end of July, and implying that by 9 August they had also laden the *Speedwell* with the same commodity. Before they left an apparently hostile demonstration by Indians took place but was not pressed to an attack. The narrative is especially valuable for accurate details of Indian cultural characteristics and artifacts and contains the fruit of accurate observation also of natural resources, while the usual (but short-term) growing tests were made. Lower Cape Cod did not offer any great variety of vegetation or soil. As the return voyage took only five weeks and ended safely at Bristol on 2 October, we are left with several weeks unaccounted for, so that further exploration may have been done which does not figure in the narrative. We may conclude that the sassafras brought home was sufficient to glut the market for several years and this may well have discouraged further voyages for summer trading. It is clear too that many of the trade goods were brought back, since furs in quantity were not available in spite of reports of what the French had been able to acquire farther north the same year. Champlain, like Pring, was to find that southern New England was no place for such exchanges (see D. B. Quinn, 'The preliminaries to New France. Site selection for the fur trade by the French, 1604–1608', *Wirtschaftskräfte und Wirtschaftswege. Festschrift für Hermann Kellenbenz*, ed. Jürgen Schneider, IV (Nürnberg, 1978), 9–25). The Pring voyage was a valuable indication that summer trading or exploration of 'North Virginia' was a feasible proposition, but that it pointed towards settlement rather than commerce. The publication of the narrative only in 1625 (though it may well

have circulated in Bristol in manuscript) limited its value to later explorers. By 1625 much of the ground had been covered again several times. If the Indians were from the Massachusetts tribe the description of culture traits has a special interest since the tribe was decimated by disease before settlement on their territory began in 1620.

---

5   A Voyage set out from the Citie of Bristoll at the charge of the chiefest Merchants and Inhabitants of the said Citie with a small Ship and a Barke for the discouerie of the North part of Virginia,[1] in the yeere 1603. Vnder the command of me Martin Pringe.[2]

Vpon many probable and reasonable inducements, vsed vnto sundry of the chiefest Merchants of Bristoll, by Master Richard Hakluyt Prebendary of Saint Augustines the Cathedrall Church of the said Citie,[3] after diuers meetings and due consultation they resolued to set forth a Voyage for the farther Discouerie of the North part of Virginia. And first they sent the said Master Hakluyt accompanied with one Master Iohn Angell, and Master Robert Saltern (which had beene in the said Discouerie the yeere before with Captaine Bartholomew Gosnold) to obtaine permission of Sir Walter Raleigh (which has a most ample Patent of all those parts from Queene Elizabeth) to entermeddle and deale in that action. Leaue being obtained of him vnder his hand and Seale, they speedily prepared a small ship called the Speed-well in burthern about fiftie tunnes, manning the same with some thirtie men

Master Salterne yet liueth neither is his zeale dead to this action. He is now a Minister and hath both by hand and writing to mee testified his affection to Virginia.

---

[1] Samuel Purchas, *Pilgrimes*, IV (1625), 1654–6 (XVIII (1905), 322–9). This was obtained from Richard Hakluyt's papers.

[2] Though ascribed to Pring himself and undoubtedly based on his journal the version has been extensively edited. It is argued above that it was rewritten for Hakluyt's proposed edition of *Principal navigations* on lines he, by then, considered appropriate to voyage narratives, namely the omission of maritime detail and of irrelevant chronological material, and concentration on economic and ethnographic information. It might be argued that Brereton's narrative was edited on similar principles (pp. 40, 54–5) but we have no information that it passed through Hakluyt's hands.

[3] Hakluyt's contacts with Bristol can be traced in Quinn, ed. *Hakluyt handbook*. His active association went back at least to 1583 (I, 277); he was a prebendary of the Cathedral from 1586 (I, 288); he was active on behalf of Bristol trade with the Gulf of St Lawrence, 1591–6 (and perhaps later); after Gosnold's voyage of 1602 he took up with Sir Walter Ralegh the possibility of a Bristol expedition to North Virginia, and appears to have visited Bristol specially to forward the project. He accompanied two possible sponsors, John Angell and Robert Salterne – the latter having been with Gosnold – to obtain Ralegh's permission, which it is indicated was formally granted, *c*. Dec. 1602–Jan. 1603.

and Boyes, wherein went for Master and chiefe Commander in the
Voyage one Martin Pring, a man very sufficient for his place, and
Edmund Iones his Mate, and Robert Salterne aboue mentioned, as their
chiefe Agent, with a Barke called the Discouerer, of six and twentie
tunnes or thereabout,[2] wherein went for Master William Browne, and
Samuell Kirkland his Mate,[3] both good and skilfull Mariners, being
thirteene men and a Boy in all in that Barke.[4] The aforesaid ship and
Barke were plentifully victualled for eight monethes,[5] and furnished
with slight Merchandizes thought fit to trade with the people of the
Countrey, as Hats of diuers colours, greene, blue and yellow, apparell
of coarse Kersie and Canuasse readie made,[6] Stockings and Shooes,
Sawes, Pick-axes, Spades and Shouels, Axes, Hatchets, Hookes, Kniues,

Master Pring
whose Voyage
to the East
Indies are in
the former
Tome.[1]

[1] Purchas notes that by 1624 (or 1625) Richard Salterne was in holy orders. His cross
references to Pring's East Indian Company service, 1613–20, is to *Pilgrimes*, IV (1905), 214,
256, 420, 540, 547, 567, 572; V (1905), 1–63, 71.

[2] *Speedwell* at 50 tons was 'a small ship'; *Concord*, possibly not much less was 'a small
bark'; *Discoverer*, at 26 tons, was 'a Barke', but would usually be described as a pinnace.
The terms may not be Pring's own. Two ships could be more useful than one, though
the small shallop had proved valuable for exploration to Gosnold. *Discoverer* could act her
part.

[3] For Pring see pp. 53–5. Salterne (or Saltren) was an active merchant in Bristol at the
time, but his later clerical career has not been traced. Nothing has so far been found on
Edmund Jones, William Browne and Samuel Kirkland.

[4] A total complement of some 44 being higher and with more allowance for
mischances than Gosnold's 32. Equipping the vessels would take at least a month, possibly
a little more. The initial licence may go back to the beginning of the year when the second
edition of Brereton would be in circulation (pp. 36–7).

[5] Since Gosnold's expedition had been undervictualled (pp. 159, 210), it was a wise
precaution to provision the ships for somewhat more than they might need (since no colony
was contemplated).

[6] In 'A particuler discourse' (*Discourse of Western Planting*), ch. 4, Hakluyt in 1584
referred to the distressed state of the English cloth and associated trades. The list of trade
goods only partly reflects this preoccupation (conditions had changed in 20 years): hats,
made-up clothes of coarse kersey and canvas, stockings, thread represent the only textiles:
shoes would seem an unnecessary inclusion. Mostly, tools and weapons figure in the
list – saws, pickaxes, spades, shovels, axes, hatchets (many useful in enabling the English
to get Indian aid to extract sassafras roots and cut timber), hooks (sickles), knives, scissors,
hammers, nails, chisels, fish-hooks (all metal tools Indians were anxious to acquire even
if not for their uses in England); bells, beads, bugles (long, glass beads), looking glasses,
thimbles, pins, needles (all 'toys', worthless but decorative objects for which Indians might
give more than their value in furs, though they soon became selective, stressing beads
particularly). We would like quantities, but the list is useful, especially if compared with
the Anglo-French cargo of *Castor and Pollux* of 1604 (listed by her Spanish captors in 1605,
in *NAW*, v, 125), where tools and weapons figure almost exclusively for an intended trade
between modern S. Carolina and the Bay of Fundy. The absence of copper and brass
suggests they expected the Indians to have enough already. The expression 'slight
merchandises' was used in contrast to her 'gross' merchandises and applied to materials
of small bulk and relatively high value.

Sizzers, Hammers, Nailes, Chissels, Fish-hookes, Bels, Beades, Bugles, Looking-glasses, Thimbles, Pinnes, Needles, Threed, and such like. They set saile from Kingrode[1] the twentieth day of March.

We set saile from Milford Hauen[2] (where the winds had stayed us a fortnight,[3] in which space we heard of Queene Elizabeths death[4]) the tenth of Aprill 1603. In our course we passed by the Iles of the Açores, had first sight of the Pike,[5] and afterward of the Iland of Cueruo and Flores, and after we had runne some five hundred leagues, we fell with a multitude of small Ilands on the North Coast of Virginia, in the latitude of 43. degrees, the [   ][6] of Iune, which Ilands wee found very pleasant to behold, adorned with goodly grasse and sundry sorts of Trees, as Cedars, Spruce, Pines, and Firre-trees.[7] Heere wee found an excellent fishing for Cods, which are better then those of New-found-land, and withall we saw good and Rockie ground to drie them vpon:[8] also we see no reason to the contrary, but that Salt may bee

Marginal notes:
April 10.
1603.

They discouer many Ilands.

Good fishing place.

[1] The Kingroad was the roadstead of Bristol, at the mouth of the Avon.

[2] Milford Haven, Pembrokeshire, was a good harbour and a last haven for vessels unable to get clear for an Atlantic voyage until they reached Ireland.

[3] Strong westerlies blowing up the Bristol Channel in March and April do occur, though easterlies are more common at that time: perhaps the ship set sail a few days too late to catch them.

[4] News of Queen Elizabeth's death on 24 March probably reached them about 1 April or a little later.

[5] Sailing west by Pico, Corvo and Flores (lats. 38° 30' to 35° 50' N, long. 28° to 31° W) would put them on a more northerly course than that followed by *Concord* (pp. 114–15): it may well be that they then ran down the latitude of 40° and turned a little northward when dead reckoning suggested they might be near the American coast.

[6] The gap for the precise date may simply represent the inability of the printer to read the figure (it could, however, have been left in the MS by Hakluyt to be filled in later).

[7] That they made their landfall in the vicinity of the opening of Penobscot Bay is highly likely, and so the islands are likely to be those standing out in the Bay. But any identifications of islands off the Maine coast at this period is liable to error. The islands in the group, dominated by Vinalhaven (Southern Fox Island) and North Haven Island (Northern Fox Island) were known as Fox Islands since about 1680, when the charts in *The English pilot. The fourth book* (1706) were made, and in *The Atlantic Neptune*, III (1781) (J.C.B. 112), but over the past century the name Fox Island has attached itself to a smaller island in the group. This led H. S. Burrage, *English and French voyages* (1906), p. 345, to identify this island with Pring's. However, the outer group, centering round Matinicus Island (lat. 43° 51' N, long. 68° 54' W) may appear more likely. Even so, Pring's 43° is considerably at fault. No islands at this latitude, or within the 20' or 30' (which would be a normal limit of inaccuracy) can be located. The island at the southwest end, off which they anchored, could nevertheless have been Matinicus, with Fox I. (as Ragged I.) to the south.

Red Cedar, *Juniperus virginiana* L.; Spruce, probably *Picea glauca* (Moench) Voss; Pine, possibly White Pine, *Pinus strobus* L. (as the most striking of the genus); fir (if specific), *Abies balsamea* (L.) Mill. (Cp. pp. 161.)

[8] Familiarity with the process of preparing dried cod in Newfoundland on the part of some members of the expedition can be assumed. Cod can be dried directly on rocks

made in these parts, a matter of no small importance.[1] We sayled to
the South-west end of these Ilands, and there rode with our ships vnder one of the greatest. One of them we named Foxe Iland, because we found those kind of beasts thereon.[2] So passing through the rest with our Boates to the mayne Land, which lieth for a good space North-east and South-west, we found very safe riding among them, in sixe, seuen, eight, ten and twelue fathomes. At length comming to the Mayne in the latitude of 43. degrees and an halfe, we ranged the same to the South-west.[3] In which course we found foure Inlets, the most Easterly whereof was barred at the mouth, but hauing passed over the barre, wee ranne up into it fiue miles, and for a certaine space found very good depth, and comming out againe, as we sailed South-westward, wee lighted vpon two other Inlets, which vpon our search we found to pierce not farre into the Land, the fourth and most Westerly was the best, which we rowed vp ten or twelue miles.[4]

    In all these places we found no people, but signes of fires where they had beene.[5] Howbeit we beheld very goodly Groues and Woods[6]

Foxe Iland.

---

but the turning operations made the use of flakes (platforms with a surface of twigs over a framework of boughs) more efficient.

[1] Salt-pans in Maine would have been impracticable from frequent rain showers, but salt boiling would have been practicable though expensive in time and fuel.

[2] Prevalence of the Gray Fox, *Urocyon cinereoargenteus* Merriam (Hall and Kelson, *Mammals of North America*, pp. 855, 861), on a single island has not been accounted for.

[3] The general trend of the coast, complicated by offshore islands and deep inlets, is approximately NE–SW from Owls Head, southwestward.

[4] A boat passage across the mouth of Penobscot Bay would have found depths of this order (with occasional deeper stretches). An exploration of the mainland southwestwards from Owls Head (43° 5′) would make sense. The expenditure of three weeks in exploring from Penobscot Bay (if this landfall is correct) to Savage Rock, where Gosnold had spent 36 hours on a shorter stretch, means that the editor has removed much navigational detail and made determination of the inlets seen very difficult, if not impossible, to identify. Jeremy Belknap (*American biography*, II (1798), 126) jumped as far east as the Saco River (barred), Kennebunk, York and Piscataqua Rivers, and Burrage (*Early English and French voyages*, p. 346) can do no better. From Owls Head westward Pemaquid Point becomes the first prominent terminus for a wide inlet, Muscongus Bay, and with the Damariscotta River as the first, barred entry. Neither Boothbay nor the Sheepscot River could easily be missed and might be taken together or separately, according as to whether the mouth of the Kennebec (Sagadahoc) River was identified or not (its entry being covered from the ocean by Seguin Island) as the third. This is approximately the view taken in Maine Historical Society, *Collections*, 1st ser. VII (1876), 293, and more knowledgeable on the appearance of the coast than most. The fourth would then be in the Casco Bay area; New Meadows River or Falmouth Harbor if we take Cape Elizabeth to be Savage Rock or the Saco river if we prefer Cape Neddick.

[5] The absence of Indians might seem to have been a temporary removal from their coastal fishing grounds (which they would frequent for most of the summer) for a brief but profitable fishing season at the falls of the rivers in the interior (Eva L. Butler and Wendell Hadlock, *A preliminary survey of the Munsungan–Allagash waterways* (1962), p. 2).

[6] The penetration of either the Kennebec or a branch of Casco Bay would have given

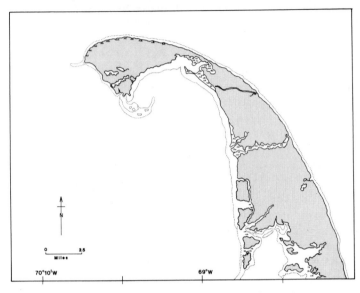

Fig. 8. Cape Cod, 1776. Pring's Cape Cod, 1603?
Des Barres, *Atlantic Neptune.*

replenished with tall Okes, Beeches, Pine-trees, Firre-trees, Hasels,
Wich-hasels and Maples. We saw here also sundry sorts of Beasts, as
Stags, Deere, Beares, Wolues, Foxes, Lusernes, and Dogges with sharpe
noses. But meeting with no Sassafras,[1] we left these places with all the
Sauage Rocke. foresaid Ilands,[2] shaping our course for Sauage Rocke, discouered the
yeere before by Captaine Gosnold,[3] where going vpon the Mayne we

---

Pring the first glimpse of the interior, and indicated strongly its forested character. We
do not know of any earlier Englishman who had done this in New England.

[1] The run of trees seen, oaks, beech, pine, fir, hazel, witch hazel (if he could identify
it), and maple gives a fair impression of the tree cover. His list of animals seen is surprisingly
large, deer, bear, wolves, foxes, lynx. The 'dogges with sharp noses', if they were not
raccoons, were domesticated Indian dogs, indicating that the strangers were being watched
even if the Indians did not reveal themselves. The northern limit of sassafras is effectively
the Mass. state line.

[2] In describing the ships' run when he had turned southward from the Maine coast
Pring is giving confusing directions as he sailed along southern Maine, New Hampshire
and Massachusetts. His 'North side', where Gosnold had found the Micmac visitors in 1602
is in fact the west, while his 'South side' is really the east. Where Gosnold went was north
of Cape Cod; where Pring went was south of Cape Cod.

[3] He does not help us to decide whether Gosnold's Savage Rock was Cape Elizabeth or
Cape Neddick. The fact that he encountered Massachusetts Indians there is not developed
(though it was also perhaps a primary contact for the English): the failure to find sassafras

found people, with whom we had no long conuersation, because here ·People.
also we could find no Sassafras. Departing hence we bare into that great
Gulfe which Captaine Gosnold ouer-shot the yeere before, coasting and ·Great Gulfe.
finding people on the North side thereof. Not yet satisfied in our
expectation, we left them and sailed ouer, and came to an Anchor on
the South side in the latitude of 41. degrees and odde minutes: where
we went on Land in a certaine Bay, which we called Whitson Bay,[1] ·Whitson Bay.
by the name of the Worshipfull Master Iohn Whitson then Maior of
the Citie of Bristoll, and one of the chiefe Aduenturers,[2] and finding
a pleasant Hill thereunto adioyning,[3] wee called it Mount Aldworth, ·M. Aldworth.
for Master Robert Aldworths sake a chiefe furtherer of the Voyage,
aswell with his Purse as with his trauell.[4] Here we had sufficient
quantitie of Sassafras.[5]

At our going on shore, vpon view of the people and sight of the
place, wee thought it conuenient to make a small baricado to keepe
diligent watch and ward in, for the aduertizement and succour of our
men, while they should worke in the Woods.[6] During our abode on

---

is not surprising in view of the latitude. The expedition was primarily a trading one, with
sassafras as one of its main economic incentives (in spite of the 1602 glut of the market).

[1] Traditionally, since 1878, the harbour he entered has been taken to be Plymouth
Harbor: W. F. Gookin queried this before his death in 1952, and I echoed the query. Our
results are given in 'Martin Pring at Provincetown?' *New England Quarterly*, XL (1967),
79–91, and asserted more positively in my *England and the discovery of America*, pp. 423–7,
where it is maintained that Provincetown Harbor is the more likely location. The first clue
is the misdirection; the second is that the hook of the Cape has changed, as sand from Race
Point has drifted to Sandy Point, as is shown in the Velasco and Smith maps (apart from
later ones) making the shape more consistent with Pring's description (it is still called 'the
Hook of the Cape'); the third is that the depth of the entry fits Provincetown Harbor ('one
of the best harbors on the Atlantic Coast', *U.S. Coast Pilot* 2 (1978 ed.), p. 91); it has a
suitable hill (or hills) such as the one referred to; the camp Pring made may be the one
found by the Pilgrims in 1620. Plymouth's priority appears most unlikely.

[2] John Whitson was a powerful figure in Bristol and his backing was important for
the voyage. It was natural that a place should be named for him. There is a brief study
of his contribution to Bristol mercantile and civic life in Patrick McGrath, *John Whitson
and the merchant community of Bristol* (Bristol Historical Association, 1970), and an engraved
portrait in John Whitson, *A pious meditation...with additional memoirs*, ed. John Eden
(Bristol, 1829).

[3] '41. degrees and odde minutes' is loose. Purchas used this narrative in his *Pilgrimage*,
2nd ed. (1614), p. 755 (and subsequently) as 'one and forty degrees twenty five minutes'.
The location is 42° 5′ N, 70° 18′ W.

[4] Robert Aldworth was a Bristol merchant with a wide range of overseas interests.
He was later to involve himself in East India Company affairs, see p. 383 below. Mount
Aldworth could well have been Monument Hill (80 feet), so closely associated with the
Pilgrim landing.   [5] Sassafras grows freely on the west side of the Lower Cape.

[6] This enclosure is described in a little more detail below (p. 227). It is tentatively
identified with the 'old Fort or Palizis' which H. M. Dexter worked out to have been near
the mouth of the Pamet River (probably at this time accessible to *Speedwell*, and probably

The people
visit them.

shore, the people of the Countrey came to our men sometimes ten, twentie, fortie or threescore, and at one time one hundred and twentie at once.[1] We vsed them kindly and gaue them diuers sorts of our meanest Merchandize. They did eat Pease and Beanes with our men. Their owne victuals were most of fish.[2]

The Sauages
take great
delight in
musick.

Dances.

We had a youth in our company that could play vpon a Gitterne,[3] in whose homely Musicke they tooke great delight, and would giue him many things, as Tobacco, Tobacco-pipes, Snakes skinnes of sixe foot long, which they vse for Girdles, Fawnes skinnes, and such like,[4] and danced twentie in a Ring, and the Gitterne in the middest of them, vsing many Sauage gestures, singing Io, Ia, Io, Ia, Ia, Io: him that first brake the ring, the rest would knocke and cry out vpon.[5] Some few of them had plates of Brasse a foot long, and halfe a foote broad before their breasts.[6] Their weapons are Bowes of fiue or sixe foot long of Wich-hasell, painted blacke and yellow, the strings of three twists of

Weapons.

---

on Corn Hill (just over 100 feet). He was able, in his edition of *Mourt's relation or Journal of the plantation at Plymouth* (Boston, 1865), to follow the activities in unsurpassed, and apparently very accurate, detail. (Cp. William Bradford, *History of Plymouth Plantation*, ed. C. W. Ford, I, 165.) There were, of course, opportunities for other traders to have established similar protective enclosures between 1604 and, say, 1616.

[1] The Indians who came to them were a band of Massachusett or Nauset Indians but perhaps joined for the summer shore gathering season by Indians from the mainland. Their numbers, 100 to 120, made Pring's security measures understandable.

[2] Initial exchanges were of a ceremonial character. The primary commercial activity was digging up sassafras roots (the trunks and at least the stripped bark are likely to have been taken also).

[3] The gittern, or cithern, was a guitar-like instrument with wire strings, played with a plectrum.

[4] The attraction was of a type of instrument unknown to the Indians as well as its music. The gifts were those appropriate to an English leader (or other Indian chief) so that his status was possibly equated with that of a shaman. Tobacco, tobacco pipes, skins of young deer are closely paralleled with those offered to Gosnold on Martha's Vineyard, though there the snakeskin girdles were 4 ft 6 in in length (the 6 ft ones being almost certainly from the Black Snake). (Cp. Rainey, 'Compilation', p. 16.)

[5] The circular dance, the rejection of the men who broke the ring, and the cry do not seem to be paralleled in other New England accounts. The chant was apparently io–ia–io–ia–ia–io. The dance performed for Poutrincourt on the St John River in 1606 was similarly accompanied by an Indian 'qui dansoit chantant yo, yo, yo le fit approcher' (M. Lescarbot, *History of New France*, I (1911), 561, 330). This suggests that this type of dance and chant was characteristic of a number of northeastern Algonquian tribes.

[6] This is the first clear mention of brass rather than copper plates (though Brereton has noted darker and lighter metal). Gorgets of this size made from plate brass were clearly the result of continued contact with Europeans. Their significance was as ceremonial insignia not armour and they have been found in New England graves of what are considered to have been later periods (Flannery, *Analysis*, pp. 18–19). There are elaborate early brass pendants from Rhode Island in the Heye Museum of the American Indian, New York.

sinewes, bigger then our Bow-strings.[1] Their Arrowes are of a yard and an handfull long not made of Reeds, but of a fine light wood very smooth and round with three long and deepe blacke feathers of some Eagle, Vulture, or Kite, as closely fastened with some binding matter, as any Fletcher of ours can glue them on.[2] Their Quiuers are full a yard long, made of long dried rushes wrought about two handfuls broad aboue, and one handfull beneath with prettie workes and comparti-ments. Diamant wise of red and other colours.[3]

We carried with us from Bristoll two excellent Mastiues of whom the Indians were more afraid, then of twentie of our men. One of these Mastiues would carrie a halfe Pike in his mouth.[4] And one Master Thomas Bridges a Gentleman of our company accompanied only with one of these Dogs, and passed six miles alone in the Countrey hauing lost his fellowes, and returned safely.[5] And when we would be rid of the Sauages company wee would let loose the Mastiues, and suddenly with out-cryes they would flee away. These people in colour are inclined to a swart, tawnie, or Chestnut colour, not by nature but accidentally,[6] and doe weare their haire brayded in foure parts, and

The great vse of Mastiues.

[1] Specimens were probably acquired from the Indians to enable such a 'good description [Rainey's description, 'Compilation', pp. 25–6] to be made'. The use of black-and yellow-painted witch hazel (or other) wood, 5 to 6 ft long (surviving late-seventeenth-century specimens are in the 5 ft range, p. 96), the twisted sinew bowstrings (not elsewhere specified; probably deer sinews), and the mention of their greater thickness than English strings, all demand sound observational skill. Salwen, (in *Handbook*, p. 163), uses this description as the basic source of information for bows and arrows.

[2] The radial-flighted arrow is characteristic of this region. This involved the application of two or three (most usual) or four half-feathers to the end so that each radiates from the centre of a circle formed by the cross-section of the shaft (Driver and Massey, *A.P.S. Transactions*, XLVII (1957), 351–2; Flannery, *Analysis*, p. 71). The Bald Eagle (rather than a vulture or hawk) is likely to have supplied the feathers: the adhesive would have been fish glue. A yard and a handful was 40 in.

[3] The description of the tapered rush-woven quiver is a most valuable one, indeed unique (Flannery, *Analysis*, p. 72). With a length of 3 ft, tapering down from 8 in to 4 in diameter, they could hold a substantial number of arrows. Diamond-shaped designs (here red and other colours) are typical of the more northern Algonquian tribes (many are found depicted on inscribed rocks). There does not appear to be evidence of what varieties of the genus *Juncus* were used.

[4] Hakluyt in 1584 (Taylor, *Hakluyts*, II, 351) advocated the use of mastiffs as guard dogs and as aggressive weapons as the Spanish did. Ralph Lane had two at Roanoke until he was obliged to eat them in 1586 (Quinn, *Roanoke voyages*, I, 267, 272). The strength of this specimen is evident from his ability to carry a half-pike (some 7 to 8 ft long) in his mouth. Cp. p. 227.

[5] This is the first record of the penetration of the New England interior on foot. Was it that of the Lower Cape or inland Massachusetts:

[6] Pring is the first to attribute much of the Indians' colour to the use of body-oil, paint and the summer sun. The natural skin-colour was more a yellowish white.

trussed vp about their heads with a small knot behind:[1] in which haire of theirs they sticke many feathers and toyes for brauerie and pleasure. They couer their priuities only with a piece of leather drawne betwixt their twists and fastened to their Girdles behind and before:[2] whereunto they hang their bags of Tobacco.[3] They seeme to bee somewhat iealous of their women, for we saw not past two of them,[4] who weare Aprons of Leather skins before them downe to the knees,[5] and a Beares skinne like an Irish Mantle over one shoulder.[6] The men are of stature somewhat taller then our ordinary people, strong, swift, well proportioned,[7] and giuen to treacherie, as in the end we perceiued.

The fashion of their boats.

Their Boats, whereof we brought one to Bristoll, were in proportion like a Wherrie of the Riuer of Thames,[8] seventeene foot long and foure foot broad, made of the Barke of a Birch-tree, farre exceeding in bignesse those of England:[9] it was sowed together with strong and

[1] Four-part hair plaiting and the piling of the plaits on the crown does not appear elsewhere in the early narratives, though the knot (or bun) at the back does (cp. p. 97). Use of some turkey feathers was usual, but not 'toys' (trinkets). The shaman of the Carolina Algonquians wore a bird attached to the side of the head (Hulton and Quinn, *American drawings of John White*, II, pl. 48).

[2] The skin (beaver usually) breech-clout is described elsewhere (pp. 97–8). The girdles were often of snakeskin.

[3] The tobacco bag does not appear in other early narratives but it was an obvious amenity analogous directly with the strike-a-light pouch (p. 97). Willoughby (*Antiquities*, pp. 253–5) identified a small woven basket or bag of textile material as probably a tobacco bag (c. 1650, in possession of Conn. Hist. Soc.).

[4] Whether women were kept out of the way of the white men or were simply left behind in the villages while parties such as this went to fish or trade is not clear (cp. pp. 94–5).

[5] This seems a clear indication of the use by women of the single apron-skirt, rather than a breech-clout (cp. p. 149). The women of the Carolina Outer Banks wore either a single or a double apron-skirt (Hulton and Quinn, *American drawings of John White* (1964), II, pls. 32, 36, 38).

[6] Bearskin mantles in summer appear exceptional; they were usually of deerskin. The Irish mantle was a long, fringed blanket-like garment of coarse woollen cloth, so it may be that the mantle was made up of skins cut and sewn into rectangular shape and fringed at the edges. For the use of Irish analogies for American Indian dress and customs see Quinn, *Elizabethans and the Irish* (1966), *passim*.

[7] Physical qualities of the Indians observed in 1602, 1603 and 1605 are very similarly described (p. 222).

[8] Thames wherries carried one to four passengers besides the two watermen (a contemporary engraving, copy in the Folger Library, Washington, D.C., shows one such in the water near the Tower of London).

[9] Canoe birch, *Betula papyrifera* Marsh would grow here to sufficient size for the skin to be used for sizeable birch-bark canoes. The dimensions are fairly large, 17 ft by 4 ft, and weighing 60 lb. Basswood fibre rather than willow twigs was later normally used for sewing, but the use of spruce gum for sealing continued. The open waist and pointed ends are characteristic but the up-curved bow (but not stern) was perhaps a local feature.

tough Oziers or twigs, and the seames couered over with Rozen or
Turpentine little inferiour in sweetnesse to Frankincense, as we made
triall by burning a little thereof on the coales at sundry times after our
comming home: it was also open like a Wherrie, and sharpe at both
ends, sauing that the beake was a little bending roundly vpward. And
though it carried nine men standing vpright, yet it weighed not at the
most aboue sixtie pounds in weight, a thing almost incredible in regard
of the largenesse and capacitie thereof.[1] Their Oares were flat at the
end like an Ouen peele, made of Ash or Maple very light and strong,
about two yards long, wherewith they row very swiftly:[2] Passing vp
a Riuer we saw certaine Cottages[3] together, abandoned by the Sauages,
and not farre off we beheld their Gardens and one among the rest of
an Acre of ground, and in the same was sowne Tobacco, Pompions,
Cowcumbers and such like;[4] and some of the people had Maiz or Indian
Wheate among them. In the fields we found wild Pease, Strawberries

---

E. S. Dodge and W. Hadlock, *A canoe from the Penobscot River* (Salem, Mass. 1951?),
describe a later specimen; E. L. Butler and W. Hadlock, *Uses of birchbark in the northeast*
(Robert Abbe Museum, *Bulletin*, VI, Bar Harbor, Me., 1957) give valuable technical details.
Distribution of types is covered in Driver and Massey, *A.P.S. Transactions*, XLVII (1957),
288, 290–1. The dug-out canoes were also used north of Cape Cod but the birch-bark canoe
rarely south of it (Salwen, pp. 163–4). Canoes were brought to London by Gosnold in 1602
(dug-out, p. 130); and by an unknown in 1603 (almost certainly dug-out, Quinn, *England
and the discovery of America*, pp. 419–31), so this may possibly have been the first birch-bark
canoe seen in Bristol (they had seen a kayak in action in 1577).

[1] The Pring account should be compared with Rosier's. In some respects they are
complementary (p. 269).

[2] The canoe paddle is not elsewhere described in these narratives. It was probably
made of ash or maple. It did not apparently have the Micmac crutch-handle (cp. Driver
and Massey, 'Comparative studies', pp. 293–4), since the oven peel, a baker's shovel, had
a broad flat disc at one end but no crutch as a handle.

[3] 'Cottages' does not appear accurately to describe the round type of house, but rather
the longhouse. Both Nauset Harbor and Stage Harbor in Champlain's sketches (*Works*,
I, 358, 421) show a mixture of round and the 'rectangular barrel-roofed houses' not usually
found north of Cape Cod Bay (Driver and Massey, 'Comparative studies', pp. 298–300).
Salwen distinguishes domed from barrel-vaulted wigwams (*Handbook*, p. 164). The empty
house meant that the occupants were at the beaches gathering seafood unless it was deserted
after the death of the occupant.

[4] 'Pompions and Cowcumbers' were different varieties of squashes. Field Pumpkin,
Cucurbita pepo L. and Gourd, *Lagneraria ciceria* L. (edible when young), with young plants
described as cucumbers (cp. W. W. Robbins, *Botany of crop plants* (3rd ed. 1931), pp. 574–93;
L. H. Bailey, *Manual of cultivated plants* (1924), pp. 733–5; E. Yanovsky, *Food plants of the
North Americans* (1936), p. 59). For cultivation in this area see Willoughby, 'House and
gardens of the New England Indians', *American Anthropologist*, n.s., VIII (1906), 115–32,
Antiquities, pp. 297–8; A. B. Stout, 'Vegetable food of the American Indian', New York
Botanic Garden, *Journal*, XV (1914), 50–60.

very faire and bigge, Goose-berries, Raspices, Hurts, and other wild fruits.[1]

Having spent three Weekes vpon the Coast[2] before we came to this place[3] where we meant to stay & take in our lading, according to our instructions giuen vs in charge before our setting forth, we pared and digged vp the Earth with shouels, and sowed Wheate, Barley, Oates, Pease, and sundry sorts of Garden Seeds, which for the time of our abode there, being about seven Weeks, although they were late sowne, came vp very well, giuing certaine testimonie of the goodnesse of the Climate and of the Soyle.[4] And it seemeth that Oade,[5] Hempe, Flaxe, Rape-seed and such like which require a rich and fat ground, would prosper excellently in these parts. For in diuers places here we found grasse aboue knee deepe.

As for Trees the Country yeeldeth Sassafras a plant of souereigne

[1] Most probably Beach Pea, *Lathyrus maritimus* L.; the strawberries do not present any problem of identification nor do the raspberries while the 'hurts' were blueberries, but there is some question about gooseberries (cp. Salwen, p. 162, and p. 308 below). The intermingling of maize and cucurbits was characteristic of Indian garden plots.

[2] The account of the exploration of the shores of Massachusetts Bay is much curtailed, apparently the work of the editor, and we thus miss much specific detail on the course of the voyage. The exploration gave Pring much advantage when he came to explore the coast in more detail in 1606 with Thomas Hanham, though again we lack details (cp. pp. 348, 352 below).

[3] The argument is put forward by D. B. Quinn (and W. F. Gookin), 'Martin Pring at Provincetown, 1603', *New England Quarterly*, XL (1957), 79–91, and is stated somewhat more positively in *England and the discovery of America* (1974), p. 426. It depends partly on the entrance to the harbour 'curving like a snail' which it certainly did on early maps, the existence of deep water close inshore, which makes Provincetown an exceptionally good anchorage; the character of the vegetation by classical accounts such as that of Thoreau; and the discovery by the Pilgrims in 1620 of a 'small barrico' which might appear to be the remains of Pring's stockade in 1603 (see especially *Mourt's relation or journal of the plantation at Plymouth*, ed. H. M. Dexter (Boston, 1860), pp. 3, 23, which covers the ground minutely). The older view that it was Plymouth Harbor was argued by B. F. DeCosta, 'Gosnold and Pring, 1602–1603', *New England Historical and Genealogical Register*, XXXII (1878), 79–80.

[4] Growth-testing for a period of seven weeks was much more effective than the two weeks or so which were all that Gosnold or Waymouth could spare (pp. 128, 264). Peas and garden seeds would make good progress in this time so as to indicate their full ripening period, while grain (wheat, barley and oats) would make a respectable showing.
Seven weeks from the date of departure brings us back from August 8 or 9 to June 21 or 22. Allowing 21 days for exploration, as indicated, we are left with a sailing time of 52 or 53 days from Milford Haven.

[5] Misprinted 'oats' (Purchas, XVIII (1906), 327). One of the problems with Woad, *Isatis tinctoria* L., Hemp, *Cannabis sativa* L., Flax, *Linum isitatissum* L., and Rape, *Brassica nepus* (if Charlock, *Sinapis arvensis* L. is not meant) is that all of them speedily impoverished the soil and were grown somewhat reluctantly by English farmers: thus an American location offered long-term advantages (cp. L. H. Bailey, *Manual of cultivated plants* (1924), 313, 329, 440, 504–5, and Quinn, *Roanoke voyages*, I, 335–6). Woad, extensively used for dyeing, was largely obtained from France and from the Azores.

vertue for the French Poxe, and as some of late haue learnedly written good against the Plague and many other maladies;[1] Vines, Cedars, Okes, Ashes, Beeches, Birch trees, Cherie trees, bearing fruit whereof wee did eate, Hasels, Wich-hasels, the best wood of all other to make Sope-ashes withall, Walnut-trees, Maples, holy to make Bird-lime with,[2] and a kind of tree bearing a fruit like a small red Peare-plum with a crowne or knop on the top (a plant whereof carefully wrapped up in earth, Master Robert Salterne brought to Bristoll).[3] We found also low trees bearing faire Cheries. There were likewise a white kind of Plums[4] which were not growne to their perfect ripenesse. With diuers other sorts of trees to vs vnknowne.

The Beasts here are Stags, fallow Deere in abundance, Beares, Wolues, Foxes, Lusernes,[5] and (some say) Tygres,[6] Porcupines,[7] and Dogges with sharpe and long noses,[8] with many other sorts of wild beasts, whose Cases[9] and Furres being hereafter purchased by exchange may yeeld no smal gaine to vs. Since as we are certainly informed, the

[1] For the Monardes references see above pp. 197–8. Monardes continued to be published up to 1596. Plague broke out in London in 1603 and proved devastating but Pring is not likely to have known of this before he left. We have not traced any publication between 1600 and 1603 which recommended sassafras as a specific against plague.

[2] This is an excellent conspectus of the natural plant resources. For vines, cedars, oak, beech, hazel, walnut, cherry see Brereton, pp. 160–5; for ash, birch (and Pring's own canoe reference), witch-hazel (hornbeam), see Archer, p. 128; for maple and holly see Waymouth, pp. 304–9.

[3] The 'red Peare-plum' a specimen of which Robert Salterne, acting apparently as cape merchant of the expedition, took back to Bristol, is a genuine mystery and has puzzled every American authority we have asked. Service Berry or Shad bush, *Amelanchier canadensis*, unknown in England, is worth considering. Fernald and Kinsey (*Edible plants*, pp. 230–31) give Indian pear as an alternative name and describe it as having berries on slender stalks, round to pear-shaped, red, becoming purplish or blue-black, with the conspicuous 5 toothed 'blossome' (calyx lobes) at the summit. Thoreau (*Cape Cod*, II (1865), 105) says it was known in this area as the Josh-pear (see p. 23). Another possibility is the Prickly Pear, *Opuntia compressa* (Salisb.) Macbr. but this was known already (as the Tuna, pp. 23, 194 above).

[4] Here almost certainly Beach Plum, *Prunus maritima* Marsh, the fruit of which is almost white.

[5] For deer, bear, fox and luzerne (lynx), see Brereton, pp. 160, 163; for wolf, see Waymouth, p. 306. Deer formed the main source of animal food (Salwen, *Handbook* p. 161).

[6] The 'Tygres' are rumoured Mountain Lion, *Felis concolor* L., or Puma.

[7] For porcupines see Waymouth, p. 306.

[8] The smallish, long-nosed Indian domestic dogs were frequently encountered. If Indians were not seen with them they were not far away; though it is just possible he thought raccoons were dogs.

[9] 'cases' were pelts or skins. It seems unlikely that Pring was able on this occasion to obtain any considerable quantity of skins or furs, though he probably got enough to convince him that a market could be built up for them; his main concentration was on sassafras.

Frenchmen brought from Canada the value of thirtie thousand Crownes in the yeere 1604. almost in Beuers and Otters skinnes only.[1] The most vsuall Fowles are Eagles, Vultures, Hawkes, Cranes, Herons, Crowes, Gulls, and great store of other Riuer and Sea-fowles.[2] And as the Land is full of Gods good blessings, so is the Sea replenished with great abundance of excellent fish, as Cods sufficient to lade many ships, which we found vpon the Coast in the moneth of Iune, Seales to make Oile withall,[3] Mullets,[4] Turbuts,[5] Mackerels, Herrings, Crabs, Lobsters,[6] Creuises,[7] and Muscles with ragged pearles in them.[8]

Barke sent home.

By the end of July we had laded our small Barke called the Discouerer, with as much Sassafras as we thought sufficient, and sent her home into England before, to giue some speedie contentment to

[1] This item is clearly added by the editor of the narrative and indicates that the revision (by Hakluyt or another) was made late in 1604 or in 1605. The source of the information is not known, but Hakluyt had old connections in France who could have passed on the information to him. It has nothing directly to do with Pring's voyage except to add a propagandist element to it.

[2] For the eagle, hawk, crane, heron, crow, gull (mew), see Brereton, pp. 160, 162–3; for the vulture see above, p. 221. There is no mention of the kite which was noted by Brereton.

[3] For cod and seal see Brereton, pp. 161, 163. The value of mammalian oil for the European economy is stressed in Quinn, *England and the discovery of America*, pp. 320–1, *North America from earliest discovery to first settlements*, pp. 128, 352, 362, 420, 523 (for cod liver oil; train oil), 465, 518, 520, 521 (whale oil). Seal oil was prized by the Indians (*Handbook*, p. 162).

[4] Common Mullet, *Mugil cephalus* Linn., as in European waters, subsequently uncommon north of Cape Cod. (Bigelow and Schroeder, *Fishes of the Gulf of Maine* (1953), pp. 305–6; Kendall, 'List of the *Pisces*', *Fauna of New England*, pt. 8 (1908), pp. 67–8). Indian concentration on fish and crustacea is stressed by Salwen, p. 162.

[5] Pring's Turbot probably overlaps with Rosier's plaice and sole (p. 308 below). It could well be the Sand Flounder, *Lophopsetta maculata* (Mitchill), nearest to the European Turbot (Bigelow and Schroeder, *Fishes of the Gulf of Maine* (1953), pp. 29–94; Kendall 'List of the *Pisces*', *Fauna of New England*, pt. 8 (1908), p. 150), but it could also be the Halibut, *Hippoglossus hippoglossus* (Linn.) of European and American waters. (Bigelow and Schroeder, pp. 247–8; Kendall, pp. 145–6). Cp. Wood, *New Englands prospect* (1634), pp. 33–4, 'The Hollibut is not much unlike a pleace or Turbut, some being two yards long and one wide, and a foot thicke; the plenty of better fish makes these of little esteeme, except the head and finnes, which stewed or baked is very good; these Hollibuts be little set by while Basse is in season'.

[6] For mackerel, herring, crab, lobster see Brereton, pp. 161, 164–5. It was Waymouth, however, who drew attention to the teeming lobster population of Maine waters (pp. 264, 283, 307).

[7] Probably a fresh-water Crayfish, *Cambarus bartonii* (Fabricius), (M. T. Rathbun, 'Lists of the *Crustacea*', *Fauna of New England*, pt. 5 (1905), pp. 18–19), or a littoral Shrimp, *Palaemonetes vulgaris* (Say), (Ibid. p. 25).

[8] Blue Mussel, *Mytilus edulis* Linn. and Northern Horse Mussel, *Modiolus* (or *Valsella*) *modiolus* Linn. (cp. R. Tucker Abbott, *American Seashells* (1954), pp. 354, 351). Rosier was later (p. 307) to call attention to the not very valuable or numerous pearls, and to make too much of them.

the Aduenturers: who arriued safely in Kingrode aboue a fortnight before vs.[1] After their departure we so bestirred our selues, that our shippe also had gotten in her lading, during which time there fell out this accident. On a day about noone tide while our men which vsed to cut downe Sassafras in the Woods[2] were asleepe, as they vsed to doe for two houres in the heat of the day, there came downe about seuen score Sauages armed with their Bowes and Arrows,[3] and enuironed our House or Barricado, wherein were foure of our men alone with their Muskets to keepe Centinell, whom they sought to haue come downe vnto them, which they vtterly refused, and stood vpon their guard. Our Master likewise being very carefull and circumspect having not past two with him in the shippe put the same in the best defence he could, lest they should haue inuaded the same, and caused a piece of great Ordnance to bee shot off, to giue terrour to the Indians, and warning to our men which were fast asleepe in the Woods: at the noyse of which Peece they were a little awaked, and beganne a little to call for Foole and Gallant, their great and fearefull Mastiues, and full quietly laid themselves downe againe, but beeing quickned vp eftsoones againe with a second shot they rowsed vp themselues, betooke them to their weapons and with their Mastiues, great Foole with an halfe Pike in his mouth drew downe to their ship: whom when the Indians beheld afarre off, with the Mastiue which they most feared, in dissembling manner they turned all to a iest and sport, and departed away in friendly manner:[4] yet not long after, euen the day before our departure, they set fire on the Woods where wee wrought, which wee did behold to burne for a mile space,[5] and the very same day that wee

Danger of the Sauages.

[1] The device of sending the *Discoverer* home as soon as she had got a cargo of sassafras was a sound one. Pring would know that Ralegh had sent out Bartholomew Gilbert (and possibly Samuel Mace as well) to search the Chesapeake Bay area and to bring home sassafras (Quinn, *England and the discovery of America*, p. 447). An early arrival of his cargo would secure a good price.

[2] Despite the dangers of a glut in sassafras (see pp. 206, 210) above, Pring persisted in filling the vessel with roots and branches.

[3] We have no information on who these Indians were, though it is not unlikely they were from a major village of the Pockanoket (Wampanoag) tribe: the Nausets' bands were much smaller. They could be Massachusetts from across Cape Cod Bay. The surrounding of the palisade by 140 men did not necessarily mean hostility though it did involve suspicion. Had they wished to attack they could easily have set the enclosure on fire. The request to have the guards from the camp come down to them may have been for the purpose of parleying with them.

[4] Pring, with so few men in fort and camp, was in a difficult position. The warning shot and the letting loose of the two formidable mastiffs were sufficient to divert them. The Indians turned off the occasion as mere gestures, but the encounter is vividly presented.

[5] The burning of the woods was a warning that they could, if they wished, make short work of the English party. At this stage, however, the Indians would be preparing

weighed Anchor, they came downe to the shoare in greater number, to wit, very neere two hundred by our estimation, and some of them came in their Boates to our ship, and would haue had vs come in againe: but we sent them backe, and would none of their entertainment.[1]

About the eighth or ninth of August, wee left this excellent Hauen at the entrance whereof we found twentie fathomes water, and rode at our ease in seuen fathomes being Land-locked, the Hauen winding in compasse like the shell of a Snaile, and it is in latitude of one and forty degrees and fiue and twentie minutes.[2]

This by the way is not to be forgotton, that our Captaine fell so much to the Northward because he would find high grounds, where commonly the best Hauens are: which also fell out to his expectation.[3] We also obserued that we could find no Sassafras but in sandie ground.[4] In our returne we brought our selues into the latitude of eight and thirtie degrees about the Açores for certaine causes,[5] and within fiue weekes space came from our Port of Virginia, into the Soundings of England, but there being long encountred with Easterly winds, we came at length into Kingrode, the second of October 1603.[6] The Discouerer was out fiue moneths and an halfe.[7] The Speedwell was out sixe moneths vpon the Voyage.

---

to return from their shore gathering to their villages for harvest, and one reason for firing the woods may have been their customary clearing of them in readiness for their winter hunting, the next occasion on which such a concentration might be in this district.

[1] Once again the actions of the Indians are ambiguous. Did they wish to allay the fears of the Englishmen and induce them to trade (we hear of no exchanges), or did they intend to lure the vessel back to attack her? Their rejection by Pring and his dubious report of their intentions probably prevented other such summer expeditions being made in following years even if this one achieved its object with little difficulty.

[2] This fits Provincetown Harbor excellently. The precise position of modern Provincetown is 42° 4' N, 70° 11' W.

[3] Pring's search for good harbours is given as his reason for the coasting of Maine, where indeed they were plentiful. The Roanoke experiment had shown that there were considerable stretches of coast farther south where good harbours were scarce.

[4] The observation that sassafras prefers a sandy habitat is a sound one. For this the Lower Cape was excellent: 'but' appears as 'brit' in 1625.

[5] We are not told why they sailed down to 38°, but a likely reason was to be near supplies of food and firewood in the Azores if they were needed. Pring may also have hoped to pick up a Spanish prize as the war was not yet over.

[6] A voyage of 35 days net to the mouth of the English Channel was good sailing. We do not learn precisely how long they were delayed before they could make their way up the Bristol Channel.

[7] The *Discoverer* therefore arrived about 19 September.

6   1603. Brief narrative of Pring's voyage, attributed to Robert Salterne[1]

A Voyage of Captaine Martin Pring, with two Barks from Bristow, for the North part of Virginia. 1603.

By the inducements and perswasions of *Master* Richard Hackluite, *Master* Iohn Whitson being Maior, with his brethren the Aldermen, & most of the Merchants of the Citie of Bristow, raised a stock of 1000 l.[2] to furnish out two Barkes, the one of 50. tuns, with 30. men and boyes, the other 26. tuns, with 13. men and boyes, having Martin Pring an vnderstanding Gentleman, and a sufficient Mariner for Captaine, and Robert Salterne his Assistant, who had bin with Captaine Gosnoll there the yeare before for Pilot. Though they were much crossed by contrary windes vpon the coast of England, and the death of that ever most memorable miracle of the world, our most deare soveraigne Lady and Queene Elizabeth: yet at the last they passed by the westerne Isles, and about the 7. of Iune, fell vpon the north part of Virginia, about the degrees of fortie three. Where they found plentie of most sorts of fish, and saw a high country full of great woods of sundry sorts.[3] As they ranged the coast at a place they named Whitson Bay,[4] they were kindly vsed by the Natiues, that came to them, in troupes, of tens, twenties, & thirties, and sometimes more.[5] But because in this Voyage for the most part they followed the course of Captaine Gosnoll,[6] and haue made no relation but to the same effect he writ before, we will thus conclude;

---

[1] John Smith, *The generall historie of Virginia* (1624), p. 18; *Works*, ed. E. Arber (184), p. 336. He attributes his information to Robert Salterne, but as usual this must be taken with some caution.

[2] The raising of £1,000 for the expedition is not found elsewhere. The size of Pring's vessel (50 tons), the information that Salterne was Pring's 'Assistant', whatever that might mean, is useful: he appears to have acted as cape merchant. Smith was aware of the initial difficulty of the vessels in leaving the Bristol Channel and the approximate time of their arrival (7 June, not in Purchas), to make a landfall about 43° N.

[3] Smith, by the time he wrote, had himself explored the 'high country' and found plenty of timber and fish.

[4] The name Whitson Bay, for the mayor of Bristol, John Whitson, did not survive for long.

[5] He is very vague about the Indians. Perhaps on their exploration of the Maine coast they had more varied and friendly contacts than they had on the Lower Cape.

[6] Pring's route was very different from that of Gosnold in that he made no attempt to round Cape Cod and Monomoy Point and so revisit the Elizabeth Islands.

Lay hands vnto this worke with all thy wit,
But pray that God would speed and perfit it.[1]

Robert Salterne.

[1] As usual a verse tag, appropriated by Smith from another source, is appended above the nominal contributor of the section, Robert Salterne. Taken from Fotherby, *Atheomastix*, p. 282, and derived from Pythagoras (communication from P. L. Barbour).

CHAPTER V

PRELUDES TO THE WAYMOUTH VOYAGE OF 1605

George Waymouth's 'The Jewell of Artes'

After his return from his unsuccessful voyage in 1602, George Waymouth sat down to prepare a treatise which would convince the new king of his learning, ingenuity and technical skill so that he would again be employed on voyages of discovery. With much labour two copies were prepared, each with many illustrations and volvelles. He presented the first version to the king (with a dedication) probably early in 1604 and the fuller one later in the year (after peace with Spain had been signed on 19/29 August). Both have survived in their royal bindings, showing they were incorporated in James I's library. The earlier copy which is now MS 565 in the Beinecke Library, Yale University (formerly in the Henry C. Taylor Collection, no. 10, bequeathed to the University in 1971) is bound in brown calf, gilt, with the arms of James I. The other is British Library, Additional MS 19889, acquired at auction in the mid-nineteenth century (15 June 1854) in an elaborate royal binding, and it too was apparently in the royal collection. The volume is an outstanding summary of the arts and crafts which an ambitious would-be commander at sea and leader of a voyage of discovery could master, and has been praised as such by Dr D. W. Waters in his *Art of navigation in England* (1958). Besides its exposition of the navigational arts, it also made substantial contributions to both military engineering and to shipbuilding. Its precise significance has not yet been adequately assessed.

It has not been hitherto realised that the volume, which was primarily intended to win back for him a place at the head of a Northwest Passage expedition such as he had failed, for sufficient reasons, to carry forward in 1602, was also a blueprint for a colonial settlement or settlements in North America – probably fortified by reports of the continued survival of the Lost Colonists of 1587, which appear to have reached London in 1603. He therefore included in his book, on the assumption that such settlements should be enlarged and extended, numerous plans for castles and, more significant, the first town plans for English colonial settlements in North America to survive. Because these have been considered to be part of the military engineering aspect of his volume, they have been overlooked in relation to English colonising projects in North America. They are, however over-elaborate they may seem in practice, of considerable significance in the development of concepts of nucleated settlement in English North America and fit into a hitherto unrecognised gap in the formative period discussed by Professor John W. Reps in his researches into the conception and realisation of the town in early modern North America (*The making of urban America* (1965)). Only the briefest extracts, together with the reproduction of the town plans on a small scale can be given here, but what Waymouth says clearly demonstrates why he could be considered a suitable commander for an expedition to explore the possibility of large-scale English settlement in North Virginia in 1605. The whole volume demands further examination and, if possible, publication – though the latter, in view of the number of coloured plates and the complex volvelles involved and also, it must be admitted, a certain unevenness in scale and quality between successive sections, would be a complex and expensive project to undertake. The extracts given, however, form an essential preliminary to the materials on the voyages of 1605.

---

7   The Iewel of Artes

The preface

[f. 6] It were muche to be wished that all those that doe vndertake to make Discouery of any straunge cuntries or passages: had some skill in all these artes comprehende in this my present booke, as first in the Instrumentes of nauigation they ought to know both the making and vse of so many as is possible, for if they knowe not howe theire instrumentes ought to be made, then may they be so faultie as they shall not be any thing profited by them. for if in all occupations they vse to say that good tooles doe make a good woorke man; howe much rather in him which affourdeth more honoure, wealth, and comoditie: vnto this famous Ilande: then any trade in all the land besides may I truly say that good instrumentes make a good nauigator. with out the which it is impossible for hym to doe any good in performance of any profitable voyage at sea: in discouering of straung countries, or passages againe if they be neuer be exactly made yett if seamen want skill howe to vse them as haue them: for what can profitt him that knoweth not howe to vse it: wherefore I say it is verry necessarie that hee be skillfull in both. neigther is it sufficient that they be skillfull in some fewe, but (as I sayde before) in as many as possibly he can that is euen in all for there be many Instrumentes that will not / yea verry fewe that wil serue [f. 7] In all places, nor at all tymes: but that some times they must vse one and some time other: secondly it were requisite they had knowledge in buildinge of shippes, not only to the ende they might by there experience know howe to direct the shipwrightes in building there shippes most fitt and comodious for theire intended discouery, but allso if in case theire shippes in their voyage should be frozen vpp in the Ice (as some haue beene) or by any other misffortune lost, that then they might be able giue order to theire companies howe to make newe eyther of the same timber if it may be gotten out (as perhaps much may) though the shipp cannot be gotten out whole, or elles of other timber where they may most conueniently gett it when they are landed, a further opportunity to attempt it, of which he is confident of success.]

[In the volume itself he proceeds to describe and illustrate successively the topics he has enumerated in the preface: instruments and their use (the longest section); shipbuilding, which is practical but somewhat brief and cursory; 'engines' (devices for escape and attack, which are not very numerous or convincing); ordnance, with many illustrations of his lighter carriages and the guns to be mounted on them; castles, a long series [ff. 205v–246], and, finally, town plans for fortified settlements [ff. 246v–251r]. On f. 202 he has a short introduction to the last two sections.]

[f. 201] The fifte booke concering [sic] fortification
[f. 202] ...All though to many men it may seeme A vaine thing to bestowe any time in the practice of fortification. in respect of the generall peace that England nowe enioyeth...yett might the practise of fortification nowe, as necessarilie be imployed in the land of florida in those partes there of which longe haue beene in possession of our English nation, as it hathe here to fore been in this our famous kingdome, for that countrie being as but weakely planted with the English, and they more weakely defended from the in vasions of the heathen, Amongst whom they dwell or subiect vnto manifolde perills, and dangers whereas it being so fruitful A soyle. so [f. 203] abounding with woodes. so goodlie riuers, and thinges necessarie for fortifica-tion . if sufficient numbers of industrious and paine full men were there in imploied, and suche as would willinglie vndertake the same . those partes I say might easilie be fortified . and well planted , with the Englishe, which by the blessing of god, might become A mightie people allso, to the increasment of gods church by conuerting many heathen to the faythe of christ by the preaching of the gospell to them and to the great profite and commoditie of this lande by the continuall traffique that might be had in to those partes if it were so inhabited, and fortified. by meanes whereof the finding of the norwest passage, might greatlye

be furdered with many other commodities (which for breuities sake I willinglie omitt) for all which considerations not with standing this may be a meanes for them to escape, when as other wise they might perishe, and vtterly ouerthrowe theire voyage. thirdly they ought to haue knowledge in making of Engines for in such voyages (comonly) they carry but smale store of men because they cannot bestowe much victaile for them : and there fore ought to vse all possible meanes, to preserue both them selues, and theire companies not only from rouers, pirates and men of warre at sea : but allso from the furie of the sauages on lande, where with many strannge contries are replenished and by whose rages [f. 8] And crueltie many christans haue lamentably beene destroyed. fourthly. being landed, in any strannge cuntrie among the sauages it is good that they be skillfull in surueying that theire by they may make choyce of the most fitt and comodious place they can attayne for their better safetie./ fiftly hauing surueyed the lande and found a fitt place for theire purpose they ought to be skillfull in fortification, that theire by they might be the better secured from their enimies, and defended from the extremities of the weather by which meanes allso many men haue pettifullie perished in heathen contries. sixthly it is most needefull that they be expert in gunners arte where by they may not only be able to defend them selues from rouers and pyrates in theire discouery att sea, but allso when they may haue fortified them selues at land, if by necessitie they be there vnto enforced . and seauenthly be cause theire companies are comonly smale (as I sayd before) and that the ordinance nowe vsed is somewhat combersome to be handled by fewe men, I haue theire fore sett downe the manner of making of a more exclent kinde, with their carriages, and other necessaries belonging vnto them, which in such voyages or any other may be very comodious to as many as wil vse them, not only in theire sayling at sea, but allso being fortified att lande if at any [f. 9] Time it so happen for that in such necessities comonly the strength of theire men is decayed, or else some of them lost, and perished : or both. and theire fore had they more neede to be easied so much as is possible'. [He goes on to say that 'while I endeauored the best meanes I can for the furtherance of Discoueries, and passages', yet he is mainly concerned to justify his actions in 1602 on his Northwest Passage voyage and to plead] for I haue though[t] good to shew by. // Demonstrations. the most commodious and fittest figures and shapes to be vsed as well in building of townes by making their streets faire, and large : and fitt for the defence of there inhabitantes , and by fortifying About the same with walles, and bullwarkes ; as howe by the degrees of a circle to make the bullwarkes proportionall to any figure , or shape required and defensice [*sic*] [f. 204] Defensicene [*sic*] for the same. such as in A royall frontire are necessarie both with flanckes to defend there ditches . and eares to defend their flanckes . and all so the manner howe to laye the foundation of any castle or forte and to builde vppon the same proportionallie some of whose ditches are to be defended by their flanckes as those whiche are farre distant Assunder, and other some has their vaultes as those which are neere together . and finallie . how to be seige any towne . castle or forte: and howe to defende any towne, castle, or fort : besieged : and all which demonstrations are so plaine for euery sencible man to vnderstand , that I shall not neede to make any longer discourse of them . but refer you to the viewe of them in order as the[y] follow / which who so euer by dilligent viewing shall perfectlie vnderstand , may knowe howe to drawe out the forme, or figure , of A towne, castle, or forte eyther with right, circuler, or Irregular Angles : in anny scituation what so euer.

[f. 246v] The demonstration of the foundation and bullwarkes of a towne, whose ditches are defended by there flanckes / and there streetes are straight with a skale to measure euery parte therof /

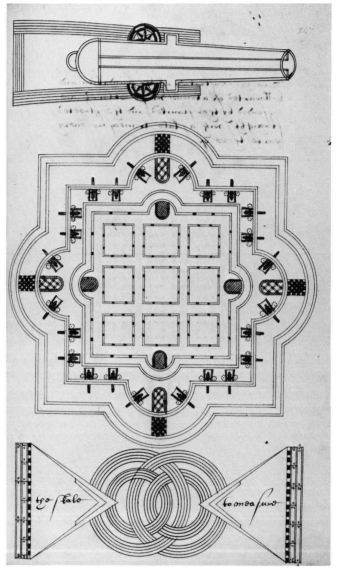

Fig. 9. 1604. George Waymouth. Plan for colonial town in North America.

[f. 247v] The demonstration of the foundation and bullwarkes of a
towne whose ditches are defended by ther flanckes / and the streetes
straight with a skale to measure euery parte there of

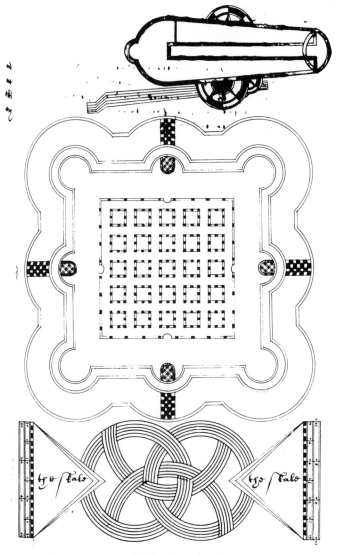

Fig. 10. 1604. George Waymouth. Plan for colonial town in North America.

[f. 248v] The demonstration of the foundation and bullwarkes of a towne whose ditches are defended by there flanckes / and the streetes are strayt , with a skale to measure euery parte there of /

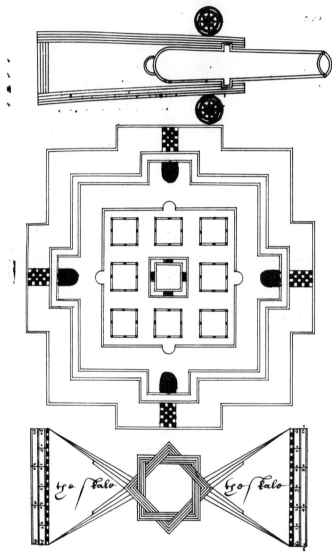

Fig. 11. 1604. George Waymouth. Plan for colonial town in North America.

[f. 249v] The demonstration of the foundation and bullwarkes of a towne whose ditches are defended by those vaultes, and the streetes circuler, with a skale to measure euery parte there of/

Fig. 12. 1604. George Waymouth. Plan for colonial town in North America.

[f. 250v] The demonstration of the foundation and bullwarkes of a towne whos ditches are defended by their vaultes / and the streetes circuler with the / skale to measure euery parte there of /

Fig. 13. 1604. George Waymouth. Plan for colonial town in North America.

[f. 251v] The Demonstration of the foundation and bullwarkes . of a towne whose ditch are [*sic*] defended by their vault / and the skale to measure euery parte there of / whose streetes ar straight.

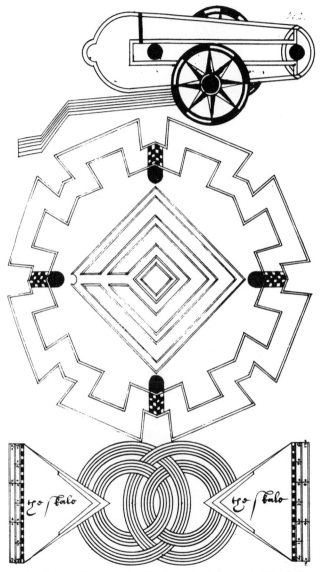

Fig. 14. 1604. George Waymouth. Plan for colonial town in North America.

8 8/18 March 1605. The Reverend Robert Persons S.J. to Tristram Winslade[1]

Peace came rather suddenly between England and Spain in the Treaty of London in August 1604, the negotiation of which had looked like being bogged down for a long time by conflicting claims. After nearly twenty years of war there remained many problems to be clarified. Was English trade (or piracy or a combination of both) to be permitted in the Caribbean? Was England to be obstructed in her efforts, begun again before 1604, to explore eastern North America as a prelude to settlement? Time was to show that these issues could not rapidly be settled (my paper 'James I and the beginnings of empire in America', *The Journal of Imperial and Commonwealth History*, II (1974), 135–52, discusses some of them; K. R. Andrews, *The Spanish Caribbean*, *1530–1630* (1978), pp. 198–223, others). But the problem of what to do with refugees from the Elizabethan régime in Spanish territory was a pressing one, especially English Catholics in the Spanish army now due for demobilisation.[2] We do not know when projects of reviving plans for transplanting English Catholics to colonise North America, dormant for over twenty years, were revived, but the moving spirit was apparently Sir Thomas Arundell, who rapidly won his way into the good graces of King James. He was also *persona grata* with Spain, since for his services to the Hapsburg emperor in wars with the Turks he had been made a Count of the Holy Roman Empire. It was probably he (though we have no direct evidence on this) who got in touch with English Catholic soldiers serving in the Spanish Netherlands, who were due to be disbanded, and suggested that, instead of applying for permission to return to England, they join in the proposed Catholic colony in North America, presumably going directly from the Continent to there. Tristram Winslade, a veteran exile, seems to have taken on the task of recruiting men, but also of gaining permission from both officials of the Catholic Church and of the Spanish monarchy.[3] Our only document is the answer to him of the rector of the English College at Rome, Father Robert Persons (or Parsons),

[1] Stonyhurst College, MS Anglia III, no. 53, a contemporary copy not in Persons' hand. It was published in Thomas Hughes, *History of the Society of Jesus in North America*, Documents, I (1908), 3–5. This transcript was made by Miss P. Renold, secretary of the Catholic Record Society and permission to publish it was received from the Rev. H. Chadwick, S.J., sometime Librarian of Stonyhurst College on behalf of the Rector. J. G. Shea used it (without reference to his source) in *The Church in the Colonies, 1531–1763* (1886), pp. 24–8, and his accurate transcript is in J. G. Shea MSS, no. 88–9, Georgetown University Library.

[2] The treaty of London between England and Spain had brought war to an end on 19 August 1604 (though it was not ratified until June 1605). Very soon after the treaty was signed plans for English exiles in the Spanish service to return to their English allegiance were under discussion.

[3] Tristram Winslade was a Cornish gentleman, long in the Spanish military service, and a pensioner of Philip III (see Quinn, *England and the discovery of America*, 383–6).

S.J.,[1] and this is wholly hostile to Englishmen of any sort intruding on the Spanish empire, which included in his view North America. The church would listen but with hesitation; the Spanish monarchy would refuse. The project in its continental context was dropped, but Arundell went ahead with James's blessing (he created him Lord Arundell of Wardour in May) and sent out George Waymouth's expedition, which has left us a major narrative. The English refugees were dealt with in a rather different way. The Spaniards disliked the continued presence of English regiments on the Dutch side in the continuing war; an arrangement was made by which an English regiment would be formed of such Catholics and others who would serve in it and so counterbalance for Spain the English forces on the other side. In the end Lord Arundell was weaned from his own American plans by being offered and accepting the colonelcy of the new regiment. Waymouth returned to find his primary sponsor diverted to another project and area (pp. 70–3 above). Persons' reply to Winslade is, however, a key document in understanding continental attitudes to English voyages to and colonies in North America.

My judgement about transferringe Englishe Catholiques to the Northern partes of America for inhabitinge those partes and convertinge those barbarous people to Christianitie.

The intention of the author and the good and godly endes proposed by hime and diverse good particularities of meanes and helpes whereby to arive to those endes discreetly and piously put downe, I like very well, but yet for the execution and puttinge in ure the enterpriz it self I find many great difficultyes which seeme to me scarsly to be superable as amonge others these that folowe.

First for England it self it is very likely that the kinge and his counsel will never allowe of it apprehendinge the same as not onely dishonorable to them but dangerous also, dishonorable in that they should force so many of thire naturall subjects to flie and abandon theire owne countrey in respect of persecutione: dangerous in that those men goinge abroad with averted minde might joyne together ether before theire goinge to the Indies or after and returne uppon them havinge theire kinsfolk and frends at home to joyne with them and then the kinge and counsell being against it, yt moste needs folowe that nonn shall have license to goe forth, nonn to sell their lands, nonn to make over money, and

---

[1] Robert Persons or Parsons (Persons is probably correct but Parsons was more frequently used in his own time and later), 1546–1610, rector of English College at Rome, 1597–1610, and the leading pro-Spanish Jesuit among the English exiles.

the like. All which the Author himself doth graunt; and owt of this one head will growe many and great difficulties or rather impossibilities.[1]

Secondly for the Catholiques to be drawne to the enterpriz will be a very hard matter for that the better and richer sort in respecte of theire wealth and commodities at home and of the love of the countrey and feare of the state will disdayne commonly to heare of such a motione, and the poore sort without the riche will be of smal importance, besides that they doe depende wholy of the riche and of thire counsell, and the difficultie of gettinge out will be common to all.[2]

Thirdly I doe persuade myself that if this proposition should be begune or imparted to any Prince abroade without communicatinge the same first in England it would be verie ill taken by the Catholicks generally as a matter soundinge to thier discredite and contempte to have as it were theire exportation to barbarous people treated with Princes in thire name without theire knowledge and consent, the Hereticks also would laughe and exprobrate the same unto them as they did when Sir George Peckhame and Sir Thomas Gerrarde about XX yeares gone should have made the same viage to Nerembrage by the Queene and counsells consent with some evacuatione of Papistes as then they called them which attempte became presently most odiouse to the Catholicke partie.[3]

Fourthly it may be more then probablie thought that this attempt may be very prejudiciall to the increase of Catholicke religione in

[1] Persons was very much out of touch with realities in England. James had welcomed a number of leading Catholics to his Court, including Sir Thomas Arundell, and was, it was soon to appear, not at all unwilling that they should create an overseas bridgehead in North America. His apprehensions about obtaining the release of English Catholics – especially loyalist gentlemen – from England were unfounded. We have no evidence that James, however, looked with favour on sending former soldiers in the Spanish forces to retirement across the ocean. They might, as Persons felt, be considered to be of doubtful loyalty. On the other hand, from James's point of view, they might be just the entering wedge into the Spanish monopoly which he hoped for after the treaty.

[2] Clearly, in 1604–5 some English Catholic gentry were prepared to move with their tenants to North America, as Arundell established, and the project to bring them continued to revive after 1605, p. 318.

[3] In 1582–4 a serious attempt to plan Catholic colonies in America was undertaken, but fell through partly through the death at sea of their first inspirer, Sir Humphrey Gilbert, but also through opposition from Spain and, most likely, from Persons and other exiles (in 1582 Persons was in Spain trying to persuade Philip II to invade England). The leading exiles indeed regarded any attempt by English Catholics to go to America (or probably even to Ireland) as the desertion of their posts as instruments of the reconversion of England to the Roman faith. (See Quinn, *Gilbert*, passim, and *England and the discovery*, pp. 368–82.)

England not onely by decresinge the number of Catholicks there and thireby discouragine the rest, and makinge them more contemptible to thire adversaryes [p. 2] but also by exasperatinge the kinge and estate against them as unquiet and practizing people, and so by restrayninge there goinge out and in, the entrance of Priests and comminge of scholars to the Seminaries would be more narrowly looked unto under that pretence Priests also could not find sufficient harbour in England and other such like things would probable folowe.[1]

Fifthly for foren partes princes and kingdome there doe offer themselves no lesse or fewer difficulties, for first wither and to what place or porte shall come that first come out of England, to witt the first 1000 of diverse sorts of husband men laborers and craftesmen required by the Author, and so supposinge they might gette forth freely how shall they be mantayned and where untill thire passaige be redy, for noe prince will easely admitte 1000 strangers into his countrey together without jelosy especially if they shall offende also thereby the king and state of England.[2]

Sixthly I doe see a mighty difficultie in behalfe of the Kinge of Spaine and his counsell who are soe jelouse that noe strainge nation take footinge in any part of the Indyes,[3] as not any particular man lightly though he have lived never so longe in Spayne canne gette licence once to goe thither but by great sute and surties and then may we imagine what they will thinke of the going thither of a whole natione, which may in time uppon many occasions of state or otherwise being [overwritten, but not crossed out: 'become'] thire enimyes though they be Catholicke, nether is it sufficient to say that those partes are not presently occupied by the Spaynairds for they will answere, they may be in time and that it is noe reason if a man have a pallace with a hundred chambers and doe occupie but 10 for the presente that a

---

[1] The point that if Catholic gentry moved away there would be less cover for missionary priests is an obvious one from Persons' point of view, but if Catholic gentry could emigrate and take their priests with them the perspective might appear somewhat different.

[2] This is obscure on account of the absence of Winslade's own plan. Persons assumes that the rank and file of the proposed colony would have to come to some continental country first before going to America. It is very unlikely that Winslade meant this. He is more likely to have expressed some doubt whether the English authorities would welcome the temporary return of former exiles from the continent to England *en route* to America.

[3] Here Persons has his strongest point. From 1603 onwards Spain set her face steadily against any encroachment into the Indies, and was to try to press James to withdraw his support from the Virginia Company from 1606 onwards (Quinn, 'James I', pp. 139–52).

strainger enter uppon the rest and say that the other useth them not, the care of the Spaniards is that noe other European natione have footinge in that continent beside them selves where a fleet may reste and refreshe or fortifie her self againste the rest of the Indies possessed by them and for this cause they made such haste and put them selves to such laboure and charges to extinguishe the Frenchmen that were in Nova Francia, and the like noe doubt would they doe to the Englishe if they should goe thither without theire licence the which to obtaine I hould it for impossible yet may it be attempted if any man will take it in hand.[1]

And hereupon seventhly it followeth that wee shall have very litle hope to deale with his heighnes or withe the Archeduke of Flanders or any other Prince of Italy that is frend to the Kinge of Spaine except first the saide Kinge be delt withall.[2]

The collections also to be made aboute the world for furnishinge the enterprice would have very doubtfull eventes in my opinione and perhapps offende not onely the Kinge of England but the Catholiks also to be spoken of in pulpitte for such a jorney for that the people would not soe much looke into the laste end of convertinge those barbarouse people as into the first apprehensione of thire flight.[3]

Finally what thire successe would be amongst those wilde people wilde beasts unexperienced ayre unprovided lande God onely knoweth, yet as I sayd the intention of convertinge those people liketh me soe well and in soe [p. 3] high a degree as for that onely I would desire my self to goe in the jorny shuttinge my eyes to all other difficulties if it were possible to obtayne it but yet for others also wee moste looke to all other necessary circumstances whereof the first of moste importance are in my opinion that the matter be broken in England and Spaine wherein for many reasons I may not be the broaker but if those ii were once optayned I would then be willing to doe in Rome

[1] The massacre of the French in Florida in 1565. In 1605 Spaniards were still ready to take English and French prisoners (and hand them over to Indian mercies) if they were found trading well outside the limits of effective Spanish occupation in North America. (See Quinn, 'An Anglo-French "Voyage of Discovery" to North America in 1604–5 and its sequel', *Miscellanea Charles Verlinden*, II (1974), 514–34; *NAW*, v, 108–27.

[2] The support of the Archduke Albert, co-ruler of the Spanish Low Countries, could prove valuable but would be unlikely to be worth much against an absolute Spanish veto.

[3] Winslade had evidently hoped the missionary objective might appeal to Catholics on the continent and lead to public appeals for funds being successful. This was certainly naive since the religious orders, let alone the papacy, would insist on direct control of any such missions, and James was most unlikely to tolerate this. Persons' point about such an appeal discrediting English Catholicism was perhaps less cogent.

what lieth in me and this is all that I canne say in this matter. Christ Jesus keepe you in health this 18th of March 1605.[1]

Endorsed: A Copye of F. Persons answere to Mr. Winslade touching Norimbega.

[1] Persons did not rate the chances of conversion of North American Indians highly, but his avowed desire to see conversion begun (and thus giving him one point of sympathy with Winslade) is clearly sincere. He undertook that if the plan survived opposition in England and Spain he would speak up for it in Rome, but this was clearly cool comfort at the most for Winslade; so much so that he gave up the plan, retired to the English college at Douai and died there in 1606. The Jesuit Order was to change its mind 1632–4 when it agreed to invest in and send priests and missionaries to help found Maryland under Lord Baltimore.

CHAPTER VI

JAMES ROSIER, *A True Relation*. 1605

James Rosier's true relation stands in time at a crucial point in English concern with 'North Virginia' and even with eastern North America as a whole. It was a clear, literate and informative report of a successful summer expedition to a part of the American coast on which nothing had hitherto been printed. It certainly had a substantial degree of influence on the crucial events of 1606, on which our knowledge is still incomplete. It was, cautiously and non-specifically, a prospectus for the follow-up of Waymouth's voyage which he arranged with Sir John Zouche of Codnor on 30 October 1605 (pp. 314–17), and envisaged royal interest, support from privy councillors and courtiers for some enlargement of this project. Over the winter of 1605–6 the pamphlet attracted much attention. We can see in it the direct inspiration of the London fishmongers' involvement in the *Triall* project in February and March 1606. It, more vaguely on our present knowledge, set going some moves in Ireland for participation in the *Triall* venture which were under way before the end of May 1606 (pp. 321–30). It is likely to have both attracted and repelled the Plymouth merchants' group, and a landed gentleman with a Plymouth base (as governor of the fort there), Sir Ferdinando Gorges, who acknowledged the Waymouth voyage and the Indians brought back as his primary inspiration to take part in American exploration and settlement (p. 340). We can see that the Plymouth merchants who had backed Waymouth in part could have been dissatisfied with the limitation of their monopoly of fishing under the Zouche–Waymouth agreement, and so left them open to influence by Gorges and the Lord Chief Justice, Sir John Popham, to detach themselves from a venture which had still (we must assume) some Catholic backing. The hopes which the pamphlet expressed of having exclusive support at Court for a large 'north Virginia' enterprise were undercut, among other things, by the broader movement with which Robert Cecil, earl of Salisbury, Sir Thomas Smith, the East India and Levant Company merchant, Sir Walter Cope and others were concerned to make the main drive for settlement to 'South Virginia', thus diverting attention from the 'north Virginia' project. Lord Zouche had evidently emerged as a leading figure in the Waymouth–Zouche enterprise, and Sir John Popham as the backer of a Plymouth enterprise. They were old antagonists, having had a fierce disagreement about certain competing limits of legal jurisdiction between Wales and England in 1604. It is perhaps worth speculating that Popham, together with the intransigence of the Zouche group about Plymouth fishing prospects, detached the Plymouth men from the earlier scheme. This was one factor, most probably, in the fusion of the London and Plymouth groups under the Virginia Company charter of 10 April 1606, and their agreement to operate separately in the southern and northern areas respectively. At the same time the Fishmongers' *Triall* venture (with its Irish affiliations) and also the Zouche project (though robbed of the services, we think, of both Waymouth and Rosier by the summer of 1606) were allowed to go ahead, since their inception had preceded the creation of the Virginia Company's monopoly. For both these ventures the pamphlet is likely to have remained an instrument for obtaining subscriptions, even if neither succeeded, and it is likely also to have greatly encouraged the Plymouth division of the Virginia Company by its dual emphasis on fishing and settling. It may well have continued to do so during the course of the Plymouth Company venture, and even after its failure, because it was, with the Brereton pamphlet, the only piece of printed publicity in England for English ventures to 'North Virginia' until the appearance of John Smith's *A description of New England* in 1616. It occupies, therefore, a very significant place in the annals of English North American voyaging and is a key text in the early literature of what John Smith made more widely known as New England.

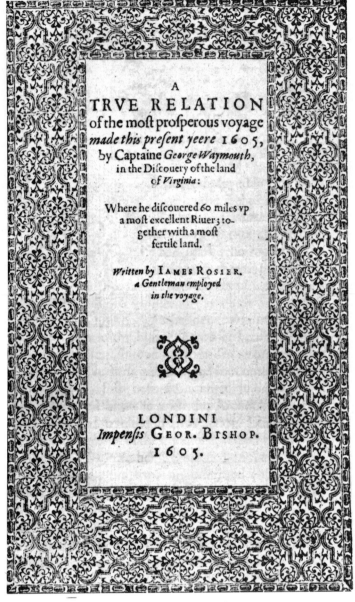

A

TRVE RELATION

of the moſt proſperous voyage
made this preſent yeere 1605,
by Captaine *George Waymouth,*
in the Diſcouery of the land
of *Virginia:*

Where he diſcouered 60 miles vp
a moſt excellent Riuer; together with a moſt
fertile land.

Written by IAMES ROSIER.
*a Gentleman employed
in the voyage.*

LONDINI
Impenſis GEOR. BISHOP.
1605.

Fig. 15. James Rosier. *A true relation.* 1605.

9 A TRVE RELATION[1] of the most prosperous voyage made this present yeere 1605, by Captaine *George Waymouth*, in the Discouery of the land of *Virginia:*[2] Where he discouered 60 miles vp a most excellent Riuer;[3] together with a most fertile land. *Written by* Iames Rosier, *a Gentleman employed in the voyage.*[4]

LONDINI
Impensis GEOR. BISHOP. 1605.[5]

TO THE READER.

Being employed in this Voyage by the right honourable Thomas Arundell Baron of Warder,[6] to take due notice, and make true report of the discouery therein performed: I became very diligent to obserue (as much as I could) whatsoeuer was materiall or of consequence in the businesse, which I collected into this briefe summe, intending vpon our returne to publish the same. But he soone changed the course of

[1] The title-page is a characteristic production by George Bishop, and uses the same woodcut border as he did for the Galvão, *The discoueries of the world* (1601), in Hakluyt's translation (S.T.C. 11543; Quinn, *Hakluyt handbook*, II, 522–3. His close association (since 1589) with Hakluyt's publications and those of his friends may give rise to the suspicion that Hakluyt was the editor of the text for publication (especially since he is known to have owned the manuscript), but this cannot be clearly established.

[2] It may be worth while stressing that the voyage is here described as being directed to 'Virginia', not to 'the North part of Virginia' as with Brereton. It may be that by the time publication took place the editor's mind was focused on a united effort to settle 'Virginia' as a whole (as the charter of 10 April 1606 envisaged).

[3] The river entry, stressed in the title-page, would have seemed especially attractive to Hakluyt (whose influence may be seen in the instructions given to Christopher Newport in 1606), but which was (as is shown below) quite misleading in its alleged '60 miles'.

[4] We do not know enough about Rosier to be able to say if his claim to be 'a Gentleman' rested on birth or solely on his Cambridge degrees which would entitle him to the appellation (see p. 63 above).

[5] As always, 'this present yeere 1605' and the date '1605' could mean anything up to 24 March 1606, but the chances are that it was put in print shortly after the Waymouth–Zouche agreement, which Rosier witnessed, on 30 October 1605 (pp. 314–17 above), though it is exceptional in not pleading for subscribers for a further voyage. It could, however, be later and would have been of value in convincing the Plymouth associates of the Virginia Company to take part in a joint venture to North and South Virginia in 1606. Short pamphlets usually, if not invariably, took the calendar year for their dating.

[6] Rosier is frank about his employment by Sir Thomas Arundell, Count of the Holy Roman Empire, at his departure but created on 4 May 1605 Baron Arundell of Wardour in the County of Wiltshire when the expedition was at sea. He asserts his task was to act as observer and reporter of the voyage: in practice he acted as cape merchant as well. He says nothing of the Roman Catholic backing, as such, of the voyage, though this would be known to many of his readers through Arundell's openly Catholic allegiance.

251

his intendments; and long before our arriuall in England had so farre engaged himselfe with the Archduke, that he was constrained to relinquish this action.[1] But the commodities and profits of the countrey, together with the fitnesse of plantation, being by some honourable Gentlemen of good woorth and qualitie, and Merchants of good sufficiency and iudgement duly considered, haue at their owne charge (intending both their priuate and the common benefit of their countrey) vndertaken the transporting of a Colony for the plantation thereof;[2] being much encouraged thereunto by the gracious fauour of the Kings Maiesty himselfe, and diuers Lords of his Highnesse most Honourable Priuie Councell.[3] After these purposed designes were concluded, I was animated to publish this briefe Relation, and not before;[4] because some forrein Nation (being fully assured of the fruitfulnesse of the countrie) haue hoped hereby to gaine some knowledge of the place, seeing they could not allure our Captaine or any speciall man of our Company to combine with them for their direction, nor obtaine their purpose, in conueying away our Saluages, which was busily in practise.[5] And this is the cause that I haue neither written of the latitude or variation most exactly obserued by our

[1] The circumstances under which Arundell switched from being the would-be leader (we think) of English Catholic exservicemen and others to America to being the commander of an officially-recognized mercenary English regiment in the service of the Archdukes is described on p. 65 above: details will be found in G.E.C., *Complete peerage*, I, 263–4.

[2] Here, if anywhere, the Waymouth–Zouche contract might specifically have been mentioned. Perhaps it was not yet thought politic to bring its existence to public notice as the Plymouth interests had not yet been engaged (and may have rejected their minor part in it) 'honourable Gentlemen' and 'Merchants of good sufficiency and iudgement' being considered generalizations.

[3] We have no information under what circumstances the possibility of following up the voyage was brought before the king and certain privy councillors. It was of some significance that the king was already acquainted with Waymouth; Salisbury, and Nottingham, with Cumberland, were survivors of the western advocates of the war period; Northumberland had close personal links with Arundell; Northampton's and Suffolk's Catholic sympathies may have linked them with him; Zouche was certainly involved in some measure (see p. 71), but any more precise identifications would be risky, particularly as we are uncertain how merchant opinion at this moment regarded colonial ventures, even if, shortly after, it was to be drawn in behind them.

[4] The passage is obscure but implies a later rather than an earlier publication (but how late?).

[5] The foreign nation is likely to have been France rather than Spain, though surviving diplomatic correspondence seems to afford no clue to the alleged subornation of Waymouth (but see p. 61) or the attempt to get possession of the Indians. De Monts had almost certainly sent home news of their capture and of Champlain's information regarding the activities of an English ship on the Maine coast which he had garnered from the Eastern Abenaki of the Penobscot area.

Captaine with sundrie instruments,[1] which together with his perfect Geographicall Map of the countrey, he entendeth hereafter to set forth.[2] I haue likewise purposedly omitted here to adde a collection of many words in their language to the number of foure or fiue hundred, as also the names of diuers of their gouernours, aswell their friends as their enemies; being reserued to be made knowen for the benefit of those that shal goe in the next Voyage.[3] But our particular proceedings in the whole Discouerie, the commodious situation of the Riuer, the fertilitie of the land, with the profits there to be had, and here reported, I refer to be verified by the whole Company, as being eye-witnesses of my words, and most of them neere inhabitants vpon the Thames.[4] So with my prayers to God for the conuersion of so ingenious and well disposed people, and for the prosperous successiue euents of the noble intenders the prosecution thereof, I rest.[5]

Your friend I.R.[6]

A true relation. of Captaine George Waymouth his Voyage, made this present yeere 1605: in the Discouerie of the North part of Virginia.[7]

[1] Waymouth's treatise on navigation and shipbuilding, 'The Iewell of Artes', B.L., Add. MS 19889, had been dedicated to the King in 1604. Waters (*English navigation*, p. 258) considers the Taylor version in the Beinecke Library, Yale University, to be the earlier one. It does indeed convey an impression of expertise in nautical matters. On pp. 298–9 Rosier does give some emphasis to Waymouth's observations of latitude.

[2] No trace of the map itself has been found. It is likely that it was used (and corrected) by Hanham and Pring in 1606, and it may have left traces on maps such as the so-called Virginia chart and the Velasco map (pp. 520–7), but this is pure conjecture, except that later maps almost eliminate the St. George River as worthy of consideration, though they note the Georges Islands and Monhegan.

[3] A small number of words was printed by Purchas from the manuscript he had. It may well be that some of the information on persons and places in the 'Mawooshen' document was already assembled by Rosier (cp. pp. 470–6, below). A vocabulary of as many as 500 Abenaki words would have been of great linguistic value; those which survive have, Dr P. L. Barbour has shown, revealed much that is of interest.

[4] The Thames-side seamen appealed to as witnesses is a novel feature. It might suggest that a broader public appeal, beyond the aristocracy and merchant community, was being contemplated.

[5] Rosier's pious sentiments were not sectarian and could be, at this stage, as appropriate to a Catholic as to a member of the Established Church.

[6] 'Your friend' is a pleasingly intimate touch.

[7] We have here a pointer to 'the North part of Virginia' lacking in the title-page. For the narrative we have a truncated version of Rosier's own manuscript, as Purchas acknowledges (see Quinn, *Hakluyt handbook*, I, 95). Purchas, *Pilgrimes*, IV (1625), 1659–67; XVIII (1906), 335–59, is headed 'Extracts of a Virginian Voyage made An. 1605. by Captain George Waymouth, in the Archangell. Set forth by the Right Honorable Henry Earle of South-hampton, and the Lord Thomas Arundel, written by James Rosier.' This indicates

Vpon Tuesday the 5 day of March, about ten a clocke afore noone, we set saile from Ratcliffe,[1] and came to an anker that tide about two a clocke before Grauesend.[2]

From thence the 10 of March being Sunday at night we ankered in the Downes:[3] and there rode til the next day about three a clocke after noone, when with a scant winde we set saile; and by reason the winde continued Southwardly, we were beaten vp and downe: but on Saturday the 16 day about foure a clocke after noon we put into Dartmouth Hauen, where the continuance of the winde at South & South-west constrained vs to ride till the last of this moneth. There we shipped some of our men, and supplied necessaries for our Ship and Voyage.[4]

Vpon Easter day we put to sea.

Our Companie 29 persons.

Vpon Easter day, being the last of March, the winde comming at North-North-East, about fiue a clocke after noone we wayed anker, and put to sea, In the name of God, being well victualled and furnished with munition and all necessaries: Our whole Company being but 29 persons; of whom I may boldly say, few voyages haue beene manned

---

(1) that the original MS was longer, as it also differed from the printed version of 1605 but Purchas did not print it all; (2) that the ship was the *Archangell*, information not found elsewhere but almost certainly in the original MS, and while there was a privateer the *Archangel* of London, captain Michael Geare, in the Caribbean in 1602–3, her rating of 365 tons would seem to be too high for Waymouth's ship (29 being a small crew for such a vessel though not impossibly so), and there was also an (unrated) *Archangel* of Portsmouth about this time (K. R. Andrews, 'English voyages to the Caribbean, 1596 to 1604', *William and Mary Quarterly*, XXX (1974), 250–2; R. G. Marsden, 'English ships in the reign of James I', Royal Hist. Soc., *Trans.*, n.s., XIX (1905), 314); (3) Southampton's later link (from 1609) with the Virginia Company is undoubted but biographers are somewhat sceptical of his earlier concerns with America, though if the MS recorded him as a sponsor he undoubtedly was so. Otherwise Purchas (if he added the heading) tended to inaccuracy and is therefore not a wholly reliable authority; (4) the form of Lord Arundell of Wardour's name looks more like one given by Purchas than by Rosier. In this edition substantive statements from Purchas have been added in footnotes. The two versions are printed consecutively, for the first time, in Quinn, *New American world*, III, 365–91. Purchas alone prints the valuable, if incomplete, vocabulary (p. 310, below).

¹ Ratcliffe on the Essex side was a favoured starting place for London ships, where many of the Thames-side sailors of whom he has written (p. 253) lived.

² Gravesend, on the Kent side, was where the Thames pilot was dropped, another pilot taken on board, and late-comers had a chance (often a last one) to board.

³ Pilotage beyond the Downs was not necessary, but winds often held ships for a considerable time there. *Archangell* was lucky and well-sailed to get to Dartmouth in eleven days at this time of year.

⁴ Waymouth, a Devon man, had evidently arranged to have men he knew and stores he could rely on shipped from the safe anchorage of Dartmouth. The 15 days spent there may indicate support for the venture from neighbouring families, such as that of Sir John Gilbert of Greenway, but a good wind was the prime consideration for leaving.

forth with better Sea-men generally in respect of our small number.[1]

Munday the next day, being the first of Aprill, by sixe a clocke in the morning we were sixe leagues South-South-East from the Lizarde.

At two a clocke in the afternoone this day, the weather being very faire, our Captaine for his own experience and others with him sounded, and had sixe and fiftie fathoms and a halfe. The sounding was some small blacke perrie sand, some reddish sand, a match or two,[2] with small shels called Saint Iames his Shels.[3]

Sounding.

The foureteenth of Aprill being Sunday, betweene nine and ten of the clocke in the morning our Captaine descried the Iland Cueruo: which bare South-West and by West, about seuen leagues from vs: by eleuen of the clocke we descried Flores to the Southward of Cueruo, as it lieth: by foure a clocke in the afternoone we brought Cueruo due South from vs within two leagues of the shore, but we touched not, because the winde was faire, and we thought our selues sufficiently watered and wooded.[4]

We fell with the Ilands of Azores.

Heere our Captaine obserued the Sunne, and found himself in the latitude of 40 degrees and 7 minutes: so he iudged the North part of Cueruo to be in 40 degrees.[5]

After we had kept our course about a hundred leagues from the Ilands, by continuall Southerly windes we were forced and driuen from the Southward, whither we first intended.[6] And when our Captaine

---

[1] Names of passengers will be found in the narrative in one or other version but we must take Rosier's word, and the successful conduct of the voyage, for his approval of the seamen in general terms, rather than by specific identifications, though some had been with Ralegh on his Guyana voyage of 1595 (p. 292 below).

[2] 'match' is a misprint for 'mathes', worms (cp. Hakluyt, *Principall navigations* (1589), p. 312).

[3] Sand containing what appeared to be small gem-like particles. The St James's shells were small scallops. The soundings indicate he had not yet left the continental shelf.

[4] It is interesting that (unlike Gosnold) he should not have felt he needed water and firewood at the Azores: the *Archangell* was evidently well found.

[5] At 2 leagues north of Corvo he would be in approximately lat. 39° 42′, and so his observations were (at 40° 7′) 35′ too high. His later observations were not much more accurate (cp. p. 258).

[6] The easterly and southeasterly winds which had brought them easily to the Azores, gave place to southerly winds. Waymouth, we might think, had aimed at a crossing by sailing down the 40th parallel. This would have brought him well to the north of the voyages in search of the Lost Colonists and equally well south of the 1602–3 North Virginia ventures, and so opened up the coastline between the Delaware and Narragansett Bay (a task left to Hudson in 1609). It would have left open the question whether, after making such a landfall, he would explore to the N or to the S in order to find a location for

by long beating saw it was but in vaine to striue with windes, not knowing Gods purposes heerein to our further blessing,[1] (which after by his especiall direction wee found) he thought best to stand as nigh as he could by the winde to recouer what land we might first discouer.[2]

Munday, the 6 of May, being in the latitude of 39 and a halfe[3] about ten a clocke afore noone, we came to a riplin, which we discerned a head our ship, which is a breach of water caused either by a fall, or by some meeting of currents, which we iudged this to be;[4] for the weather being very faire, and a small gale of winde, we sounded and found no ground in a hundred fathoms.

Munday, the 13 of May, about eleuen a clocke afore noone, our Captaine, iudging we were not farre from land, sounded, and had a soft oaze in a hundred and sixty fathomes.[5] At fowre a clocke after noone we sounded againe, and had the same oaze in a hundred fathoms.[6]

From 10 a clocke that night till three a clocke in the morning, our Captaine tooke in all sailes and lay at hull,[7] being desirous to fall with

---

his colony. A further approach to Verrazzano's *Refugio*, this time from the south, is not ruled out in view of the Catholic interest dating from 1582–3 in that area (Quinn, *England and the discovery of America* (1974), pp. 370–81).

[1] The note of pious resignation to God's will, sounded here, may appear Puritan rather then Roman Catholic.

[2] Observations at sea were not usually accurate. His lat. 40° 7′ was actually most probably 39° 42′ so that a run 'southwards' to his 39° 30′ would involve his running down the latitude on a steady westerly course, but if his rate of error for Corvo (40° 7′ for 39° 47′) was maintained he would indeed have come down as far as about 39° 15′, which, extended westwards, would bring him approximately to Delaware Bay. It may well be that he hoped to arrive somewhat to the south of the lowest latitude reached by Gosnold, about 41° (cp. p. 127 above).

[3] As Waymouth, however, decided to let the prevailing winds carry him northwards, it seems likely that between May 6 and May 13 he attained a considerably higher latitude. A north-westerly course until he was a little north of lat. 42° and a westerly course along, say, 42° 20′ N (just north of Georges Bank which extends from lat. 40° 30′ to 42° 3′ N, long. 66° to 69° W) would best fit the picture which his subsequent soundings reveal. It is unfortunate that once he had turned northwards some indication of the latitude achieved by May 13 was not indicated.

[4] An effect caused by cross-currents or tides, not necessarily indicative of an approaching shore.

[5] Waymouth had now been at sea for thirty days since sighting Corvo, a very slow rate of progress, indicating a sustained attempt to sail into the wind before submitting to being carried north-westwards. A sequence of soundings between 100 and 200 fathoms seems possible only north of Georges Bank.

[6] Soundings of 100 fathoms and more would be possible only if he was north of lat. 42° (and perhaps long. 69° 30′ or thereabouts).

[7] Hull-to or a-hull, lying athwart the wind, with very little canvas set.

the land in the day time, because it was an vnknowen coast, which
it pleased God in his mercy to grant vs, otherwise we had run our ship
vpon the hidden rockes and perished all. For when we set saile we
sounded in 100 fathoms: and by eight a clock, hauing not made aboue
fiue or six leagues, our Captaine vpon a sudden change of water
(supposing verily he saw the sand) presently sounded, and had but fiue
fathoms.[1] Much maruelling because we saw no land, he sent one to
the top, who thence descried a whitish sandy cliffe,[2] which bare
West-North-West about six leagues off from vs:[3] but comming neerer
within three or fowre leagues, we saw many breaches still neerer the
land:[4] at last we espied a great breach a head vs al along the shore,
into which before we should enter, our Captaine thought best to hoise
out his ship boate and sound it.[5] Which if he had not done, we had
beene in great danger: for he bare vp the ship, as neere as he durst after
the boat: vntill Thomas Cam, his mate, being in the boat, called to
him to tacke about & stand off, for in this breach he had very showld
water, two fathoms and lesse vpon rockes, and sometime they supposed
they saw the rocke within three or fowre foote, whereon the sea made
a very strong breach: which we might discerne (from the top) to run

[1] Sudden shoaling, from 100 fathoms to 5 fathoms within 15 miles is out of the
question in 'possible' latitudes except to the eastwards of the Cape Cod peninsula unless,
indeed, Waymouth is still farther north. A conventional reading of his course as directed
to Nantucket Shoals is possible only if Rosier is putting feet for fathoms (in which case
the *Archangell* would probably have gone aground), or else the use of the lead-line was
wildly inaccurate. (It was possible for the lead to be carried well above the sea-floor, while
it may have been possible to miscalculate the amount of line run out – normally from
barrels each containing 100 fathoms). A final possibility is that Rosier is deliberately confusing the trail (see below pp. 288–97). It seems simplest to work on the figures he gives.
[2] Since the eighteenth century, before charts with accurate soundings were available,
it has been customary to take the light-coloured cliffs of Sankatty Head as Waymouth's
landfall. On what he says it is much more likely to have been one of the higher parts of
Cape Cod, and the cliffs the hills ranging between Eastham and Truro as the most likely
alternative. It is not possible to suggest a specific spot, especially when we consider that
the headland might be, say, Cape Ann, still farther to the North and to the West. All we
can say is that it is most unlikely to have been anywhere south of Chatham: and is more
likely to have been farther N on the Lower Cape.
[3] A WNW bearing would fit in with the suggested approach to Cape Cod, or to
Cape Ann.
[4] If the argument of the previous paragraphs is to be sustained, Waymouth must have
been driven southward again (or he had attempted to correct his course in that direction).
Clearly his position now can only be south and southeast of Nantucket on the edge of
the Nantucket Bank (if it has not shifted radically).
[5] Leading with his boat in an area where he was subject to broken and shoaly water
was the device of a cautious captain (and master), but it was only possible in calm and
moderately clear weather.

along as we sailed by it 6 or 7 leagues to the Southward. This was in
the latitude of 41 degrees, 20 minuts:[1] wherefore we were constrained
to put backe againe from the land: and sounding, (the weather being
very faire and a small winde) we found our selues embaied with
continuall showldes and rockes in a most vncertaine ground, from fiue
or sixe fathoms, at the next cast of the lead we should haue 15 & 18
fathoms. Ouer many which we passed, and God so blessed vs, that we
had wind and weather as faire as poore men in this distresse could wish:
whereby we both perfectly discerned euery breach, and with the winde
were able to turne, where we saw most hope of safest passage. Thus
we parted from the land, which we had not as much before desired,
and at the first sight reioiced, as now we all ioifully praised God, that
it had pleased him to deliuer vs from so imminent danger.[2]

Heere we found great store of excellent Cod fish, and saw many
Whales,[3] as we had done two or three daies before.

We stood off all that night, and the next day being Wednesday; but
the wind still continuing between the points of South-South-West, and
West-South-West: so as we could not make any way to the Southward,
in regard of our great want of water and wood (which was now spent)
we much desired land, and therefore sought for it, where the wind
would best suffer vs to refresh our selues.[4]

Thursday, the 16 of May, we stood in directly with the land, and
much maruelled we descried it not, wherein we found our sea charts
very false, putting land where none is.'[5]

Friday, the 17 of May, about six a clocke at night we descried the

[1] The latitude reading would leave him only a little south of east from Nantucket
but if his error is constant he would be more likely to be farther south and on the fringes
of the Nantucket Bank.

[2] Clearly he despaired of making any progress westward at this latitude and turned
away most reluctantly (strengthening the impression that a possible objective was
Narragansett Bay), and once more made his way northwards.

[3] Waymouth is an early observer of whales in considerable number outside the
Nantucket Bank, while Brereton and Archer had recorded many bones of whales inside
Nantucket Sound. The concentration of cod was less unusual.

[4] Waymouth was, frankly, going round in circles: progress southwards against such
winds as he describes was simply not possible.

[5] Purchas (*Pilgrimes*, IV (1625), viii, 1659, XVIII (1906), 337; *NAW*, III, 382) has side
note 'Sea-charts false'. In the text he adds 'for though we bare in directly with it according
to them: yet in almost fifty leagues we found none'. No sea charts of the coast made prior
to 1605 now survive from English sources. He clearly relied, we must suppose, on a chart
made on the Gosnold voyage in 1602 (some traces of which survive most probably in the
Velasco map of 1610, see pp. 520–5): it is possible too that Pring made a sea chart on his
1603 voyage and that this too was in Waymouth's hands.

land, which bare from vs North-North-East;[1] but because it blew a great gale of winde, the sea very high, and neere night, not fit to come vpon an vnknowen coast, we stood off till two a clocke in the morning, being Saturday: then standing in with it againe, we descried it by eight a clocke in the morning, bearing North-East from vs. It appeared a meane high land, as we after found it, being but an Iland of some six miles[2] in compasse, but I hope the most fortunate euer yet discouered. About twelue a clocke that day, we came to an anker on the North side of this Iland, about a league from the shore.[3] About two a clocke our Captaine with twelue men rowed in his ship-boat to the shore, where we made no long stay, but laded our boat with dry wood of olde trees vpon the shore side, and returned to our ship, where we rode that night.[4]

The description of the Iland.

This Iland is woody,[5] growen with Firre, Birch, Oke and Beech, as farre as we saw along the shore;[6] and so likely to be within. On

[1] Purchas (*Pilgrimes*, IV (1625), 1659, XVIII (1906), 338) has side note 'Land descried'. Waymouth had been giving way before the wind for more than 24 hours so that he was well to the north of his position reached when he had first sighted land at Cape Cod. His approximate position was 43° 40′ N 69° 20′ W having sailed across Georges Bank, part of it for the second time.

[2] Purchas (*Pilgrimes*, IV (1625), 1659, XVIII (1906), 338) has side note 'Saturday wee made the land'. Monhegan, with its attendant island Manana I., stands up prominently from the sea (which is why it became such a favourite landmark for later navigators), the central point reaching 178 ft and the N end averaging well over 100 ft.

[3] Purchas (*Pilgrimes*, IV (1625) viii, 1660, XVIII (1906), 338; *NAW*, III, 382) has side note 'Our Captaine named this S. Georges Iland.' The naming of the island after St George, as the patron saint of England, is not surprising, though perhaps the continued use of the saint's name shows a certain lack of originality, but there may well have been the desire also to mark in a secondary way the name of the discoverer (cp. the naming of Elizabeths Isle above, p. 126).

[4] It is probable that the men pulled into Monhegan Harbor, lying between Manana I. and Monhegan, where the ledges are low and access to the wooded interior most easy, though even now on the wooded north shore the forest comes very close to the sea.

[5] Monhegan has lost some of its major tree species but it is still well covered with characteristic vegetation. Besides the standard authorities, F. Hyland and F. H. Steinmetz, *The woody plants of Maine* (Orono, Me., 1944), is specially helpful in locating the probable species to be found on this and other offshore islands.

[6] White Pine, *Pinus strobus* L. was probably the species then as now most prominent, varied with Red Pine, *P. resinosa* Ait. and Pitch Pine, *P. rigida* Mill., together with Fir, *Abies balsamea* (L.) Mill.; Gray Birch, *Betula populifolia* Marsh is now commonest on the coast, varied with Canoe Birch, *B. cordifolia* Marsh, and Yellow Birch, *B. lutea* Michx.; the oaks have now disappeared from the Monhegan woods, having been removed for shipbuilding and not reinstated. White Oak, *Quercus alba* L. and Northern Red Oak, *Q. borealis* Michx. are likely to have been the most common species; beech (American Beech, *Fagus grandifolia* Ehrh.) was formerly one of the most significant elements in the forest cover of the island which is not (or rarely) now found (Hyland and Steinmetz, p. 15).

the verge grow Gooseberries, Strawberries, Wild pease, and Wild-rose bushes.[1] The water issued foorth downe the Rocky cliffes in many places: and much fowle of diuers kinds breed vpon the shore and rocks.[2]

While we were at shore, our men aboord with a few hooks got aboue thirty great Cods and Hadocks, which gaue vs a taste of the great plenty of fish which we found afterward wheresoeuer we went vpon the coast.[3]

From hence we might discerne the maine land from the West-South-West to the East-North-East, and a great way (as it then seemed, and as we after found it) vp into the maine we might discerne very high mountaines, though the maine seemed but low land;[4] which gaue vs a hope it would please God to direct vs to the discouerie of some good; although wee were driuen by winds farre from that place,

---

[1] Gooseberries create something of a difficulty since none would be in fruit. Hyland and Steinmetz (pp. 19–20) do not suggest the Prickly Gooseberry, *Ribes cynosbata* L. would be present in this area, while the Smooth Gooseberry, *R. hirtellum* Michx., while present, would not have the characteristic prickles. All we can say is that one of a number of species of *Ribes* (including their later 'Currants') suggested gooseberry bushes; Strawberry, *Fragaria virginiana* Duchesne would be recognisable, but *Waldsteinia*, not a strawberry, has very similar foliage; great banks of Beach Pea, *Lathyrus maritima* (L.) Bigel, then as now, would decorate the shoreline just above high water; *Rosa nitida* Willd., *R. palustris* Marsh and *R. carolina* L. would be present (Hyland and Steinmetz, pp. 29–30).

[2] Cormorants, gulls, especially the Greater Black-backed Gull, and puffins are now most prominently in evidence. At this time, at the nesting season, there were probably more species present.

[3] Cod (up to 40 pounds weight) and large haddock can still be taken off the north shore.

[4] Waymouth was clearly very fortunate in getting such good visibility for his first view of the Maine coast. His viewpoint was either the highest point of the island (where the lighthouse stands), not too far from the southern end of the island which rises to 178 ft, and could have been augmented by another 100 ft from a suitable tree on the summit: alternatively it could have been from Seal-ledge Hill (140 ft) to the northeast. There is no land WSW nearer than Seguin I. and Cape Small, nor NNE than Vinalhaven (Fox I.). Pemaquid Point would stand out clearly northwest and Matinicus I. northeast. The main mass of land would lie north, with small islands (Burnt I. in particular) shrouding the channel to and up the St George River. The 'very high mountains' need not have been more than the Camden Hills, rising to 650 ft, at distances from 20 to 25 miles. Waymouth could not assess the distance at which they lay nor distinguish between high hills some little way into the interior from the high mountains much farther inland. The hills appear grey and distant against the greener vegetation of the coast. It is possible, however, that the Union Mountains (1,000–1,300 ft) visible on a clear day at a range of 30–35 miles behind the hills and somewhat to the west, could have added to his impression. Maine historians have frequently discussed whether he might have seen the White Mountains (Mt Washington, 6,288 ft, in particular), but this is highly unlikely though it has been known to be occasionally possible. It is not here necessary to conclude that he saw anything beyond the Camden Hills. (Cp. Rosier, *A true relation*, ed. H. S. Burrage, pp. 96–100 (where his sketch-profile made in 1885 is given); Marion Jaques Smith, *A history of Maine* (1949), pp. 25–7.)

whither (both by our direction and desire) we euer intended to shape the course of our voyage.[1]

The next day, being Whit-Sunday;[2] because we rode too much open to the sea and windes,[3] we weyed anker about twelue a clocke, and came along to the other Ilands more adioyning to the maine, and in the rode directly with the mountaines, about three leagues from the first Iland where we had ankered.[4]

When we came neere vnto them (sounding all along in a good depth) our Captaine manned his ship-boat and sent her before with Thomas Cam one of his Mates, whom he knew to be of good experience, to sound & search betweene the Ilands for a place safe for our shippe to ride in; in the meane while we kept aloofe at sea, hauing giuen them in the boat a token to weffe in the ship,[5] if he found a conuenient Harbour; which it pleased God to send vs, farre beyond our expectation, in a most safe birth defended from all windes, in an excellent depth of water for ships of any burthen, in six, seuen, eight, nine, and ten fathoms vpon a clay oaze very tough.[6]

[1] We have here the most explicit mention of Waymouth's objective, though it is negative rather than positive in form. It was clearly well below his observed latitude of 40° N. at the Azores (p. 256 above), and was therefore also very much to the south of Gosnold's observed latitude of 41° 40′ N for the Elizabeth Isles (p. 127 above). Since we hear nothing of an attempt to find Ralegh's lost colonists, in pursuit of which Bartholomew Gilbert had been lost in 1603, we may take it that the objective was probably not Roanoke Island or Chesapeake Bay, even though this is not certain. Gilbert had sailed along the shore first northwards to just over 40° N and southwards to, it would be presumed, about 37° N, where he was thought to have been killed. It seems most likely that Waymouth intended to examine the coast northwards from about 37° or 38° to the place where Gosnold had intended to establish his post (Cuttyhunk).

[2] Sunday 19 May.

[3] With freshening winds from the North-east or South-west Waymouth would experience fairly rough seas off the North coast of Monhegan and would be in danger of being driven on to the rocks and islet (Manana I.) off the North-west shore of the island.

[4] Sailing North from the island (or a point to the East) Waymouth would reach in less than six (nautical) miles sailing the channel between Allen Island (to port) and Burnt Island but avoiding the Dry Ledges, where he would at once find shelter. 'Three leagues' for two is the first clear exaggeration of distance in the narrative, and is minimal. On a northerly course the Camden Hills would remain clearly visible to the look-out throughout the passage.

[5] The tribute to Thomas Cam's experience is probably well-deserved, though he has not been traced earlier. The ship's boat in which he was leading is, with little possibility of doubt, that referred to later as the light-horseman. The token by which he was to wave the ship into a suitable harbour when he found one was, almost certainly, a brightly coloured flag, perhaps Arundell's own standard.

[6] This was the narrow but deep channel between the Dry Ledges and Burnt Is. Purchas, *Pilgrimes* IV (1625), 1661, XVIII (1905), 339, *NAW*, III, 382, adds '...where is good moring, euen on the Rockes vpon the Cliffe side.' This would certainly be true of the north shore of Allen Island.

We all with great ioy praised God for his vnspeakable goodnesse, who had from so apparent danger deliuered vs, & directed vs vpon this day into so secure an Harbour: in remembrance wherof we named it Pentecost-harbor,[1] we arriuing there that day out of our last Harbor in England, from whence we set saile vpon Easterday.[2]

About foure a clocke, after we were ankered and well mored, our Captaine with halfe a dozen of our Company went on shore to seeke fresh watering, and a conuenient place to set together a pinnesse, which we brought in pieces out of England: both which we found very fitting.

Vpon this Iland, as also vpon the former, we found (at our first comming to shore) where fire had beene made:[3] and about the place were very great egge shelles bigger than goose egges,[4] fish bones, and as we iudged, the bones of some beast.

Heere we espied Cranes stalking on the shore of a little Iland adioyning; where we after saw they vsed to breed.[5]

Whitsun-munday, the 20 day of May, very early in the morning, our

---

[1] Purchas, *op. cit.*, gives a somewhat enlarged version: 'We all with great admiration praised God, who had from so apparent danger miraculously deliuered vs, and directed vs vpon this day (vpon which he sent the chief promised Director of all goodnesse vnto his Apostles and Disciples) into such a place, wherof here before we reade none to haue made either description or relation, and then which neither our selues could wish, or Nature affoord more secure. In remembrance whereof, our Captaine named it Pentecost Harbour.'

Georges Harbor, the traditional place of entry, was later used as a sheltering-place by sailing vessels, and lies with Allen I. to the south, Benner I. to the west and Davis I. to the north. In the entrance channel, where the *Archangell* is thought to have anchored there are depths of 42 and 72 feet with hard ground. *The U.S. Coast Pilot*, sect. A (1950), p. 250, says 'the best water is in mid-channel, in entering the thoroughfare from northeastward. Entering from southwestward, the south side should be favoured'. To the southeast lie Little Burnt and Burnt Is., and in discussions with Rear-Admiral (retd.) William F. Royall, the alternative anchorage a little way to the southeast, in the roadstead between Allen and Burnt Is. was suggested. Though not protected from southerly winds, it offered more freedom of movement, and safety from possible contact with a rock in the Harbor. My view is that Waymouth anchored in the Harbor while he was engaged in exploring the Georges Islands but may well have used the roadstead for periods when he might need to set sail or anchor when he was exploring further afield.

[2] The voyage thus took from 31 March to 20 May. Fifty days' sailing was perhaps a reasonable, though not exceptionally rapid, time for a westward voyage at this time. We should add ten days to these dates to give the Gregorian dating and so keep in mind what is said about plant-growth and faunal activity.

[3] An Indian hearth site has been found on Monhegan Is. (information from Wendell S. Hadlock) and others would be expected on the Georges Islands. These would constitute evidence of summer fishing sites used by the Eastern Abenaki bands from the mainland. There was no permanent Indian occupation of the islands.

[4] Shells and bones of the Great Auk, *Plautus impennis* (Linn.) would remain from Indian use of the bird for food, and are frequently found on coastal sites on the mainland (information from Wendell S. Hadlock).

[5] For Cranes see p. 305 below.

262

Captaine caused the pieces of the pinnesse to be carried a shore,[1] where while some were busied about her, others digged welles to receiue the fresh water, which we found issuing downe out of the land in many places. Heere I can not omit (for foolish feare of imputation of flattery) the painfull industry of our Captaine, who as at sea he is alwayes most carefull and vigilant, so at land he refuseth no paines; but his labour was euer as much or rather more than any mans: which not only encourageth others with better content, but also effecteth much with great expedition.[2]

In digging we found excellent clay for bricke or tile.[3]

The next day we finished a well of good and holesome cleere water in a great empty caske, which we left there.[4] We cut yards, waste trees, and many necessaries for our ship,[5] while our Carpenter and Cooper[6] laboured to fit and furnish forth the shallop.

This day our boat went out about a mile from our ship, and in small time with two or three hooks was fished sufficiently for our whole Company three dayes, with great Cod, Haddocke, and Thornebacke.[7]

We fished.

[1] Purchas, following on the mention of the carrying ashore of the shallop on 20 May, adds: 'This day our pinnace was fitted together and lanched, in small time.' (*Pilgrimes*, IV (1625), 1660, XVIII (1906), 339; *NAW*, III, 382.) This might indicate that she was also a two-piece vessel bolted together (cp. p. 126), and strengthened with a keel and pieces along the gunwales. But since Rosier refers to her subsequently as a pinnace it may be that she was larger than the shallop used by Gosnold (and cut away as he left the Elizabeth Islands (p. 138 above).

[2] The tribute to Waymouth is flattering indeed, but was in the original MS and was not added in the printed version to inflate his merits.

[3] As the islands are principally composed of glacial debris this would not have been difficult. Boulder clay covers a substantial part of Allen, Davis and Burnt Islands. Purchas, *Pilgrimes*, IV (1625), 1660, XVIII (1906), 339; *NAW*, III, 382) says: 'In digging (amongst other things) we founde in some places (and not deepe) clay ground, blue, red and white, to make Bricke or Tile, fit for building.' There is no evidence that Waymouth might advocate settlement on the small islands but they would serve, as Monhegan was to do, as summer bases for fishing vessels.

[4] The practice of completing a well by inserting a barrel or cask at the bottom was usual in the early 17th century. Examples have been found at Jamestown. The Roanoke settlers did so in an attempt to store water – probably rainwater – on Roanoke Island (Quinn, *Roanoke voyages*, II, 811, now relocated): There was, on 25 August 1970, a good natural spring on the east side of Allen I. not far from the anchorage.

[5] Waymouth was laying in spare timber for his return journey. He had experience in 1602 of the damage that the westerlies could do to spars and rigging. Waist-trees were spars stowed along the ship's waist.

[6] Both carpenter and cooper were essential members of the crew of a sailing vessel of the time, the cooper being necessary to fashion and knock up barrels not only for water but for carrying wet-fish if they could be taken.

[7] Waymouth took every opportunity of trying out the possibilities for fishing since this was the principal preoccupation of his Plymouth backers. Cod and haddock were everywhere: the thornback was the Spiny Skate, *Raia radiata* Donovan (W. C. Kendall, *An annotated catalogue of the fishes of Maine* (1944), p. 13).

Abundance of
many good
fishes.

And towards night we drew with a small net of twenty fathoms very nigh the shore: we got about thirty very good and great Lobsters,[1] many Rockfish, some Plaise, and other small fishes called Lumpes,[2] verie pleasant to the taste: and we generally obserued, that all the fish, of what kind soeuer we tooke, were well fed, fat and sweet in taste.

Wednesday, the 22 of May, we felled and cut wood for our ships vse, cleansed and scoured our wels,[3] and digged a plot of ground, Corne sowed. wherein, amongst some garden seeds, we sowed peaze and barley, which in sixteen dayes grew eight inches aboue ground; and so continued growing euery day halfe an inch, although this was but the crust of the ground, and much inferior to the mould we after found in the maine.[4]

Friday, the 24 of May, after we had made an end of cutting wood, and carying water aboord our shippe,[5] with foureteene Shot and Pikes we marched about and thorow part of two of the Ilands;[6] the bigger of which we iudged to be foure or fiue miles in compasse, and a mile broad.[7]

The profits and fruits which are naturally on these Ilands are these:

[1] This appears to be the earliest specific reference to the presence, in quantity, of *Homerus americanus* Milne Edwards, in Maine waters.

[2] Rockfish were Sea Bass (Cunners), *Tautogobabrus adspersus*; plaice were flounders or dabs, probably here Sand Flounder, *Lophopsetta maculata* Mitchill (Kendall, pp. 70–1); Lump, *Cyclopterus lumpus* L. as in European waters.

[3] More than one well was now in operation.

[4] Purchas, *Pilgrimes*, IV (1625), 1660, XVIII (1906) 340; *NAW*, III, 383) has 'where in among some Garden seeds (which most the birds destroyed) we set Pease and Barley'. Growth tests were usual on such expeditions (pp. 128, 150–1, 213, 224): Rosier is perceptive in comparing the thin soil of the islands with the thick humus of parts of the mainland.

[5] Purchas (*Pilgrimes*, IV (1625), 1660, XVIII (1906), 340; *NAW*, III, 383) adds: 'All the next day [Thursday, 22 May] we labored hard to make vp our wood [here for firewood], because our Captaine intended not to spare, or spend any more time in that of our Voyage. This day our Boat fished againe as before, because wee still were much refreshed with the fresh fish.' The modern tree cover is almost wholly spruce, but the islands have been cut over frequently, and there may have been at this time more variety in available timber.

[6] This rather pretentious exercise was intended to provide some disciplined activity in a rough American terrain (later it was to be employed on the mainland) for men long cooped up on shipboard. The fourteen men were clearly the 'soldiers' of the expedition and may not have included any seamen or craftsmen. The march would further provide evidence of the variety of rock formations, fertile ground and range of vegetation, while it would also establish that no Indians were concealed on the island.

[7] Allen Island is about 2,900 yards in length and about 950 yards at its greatest breadth, so that a circuit of 4 to 5 miles seems reasonable. Benner Island was nearest but small and scarcely worth (one would think) the trouble of perambulating. Burnt Island, across the channel to the south, would provide a better test as it is larger than Allen (about 1,250 yards long by 1,350 yards on average).

All along the shore and
some space within,
where the wood
hindereth not, grow
plentifully.[1]

{ Rasberries.
Gooseberries.
Strawberries.
Roses.
Currants.
Wild-vines.[2]
Angelica.[3]

The fruit of
the Ilands.

Within the Ilands growe
wood of sundry sorts,
some very great, and
all tall:[4]

{ Birch.
Beech.
Ash.
Maple.
Spruce.
Cherry-tree.
Yew.[5]
Oke very great and good.[6]
Firre-tree, out of which

---

[1] Plants of a number of these species would be only in bloom or have immature fruit just beginning to set at this time, and there is no reason to believe that Rosier could thus distinguish between different species of *Rubus* and *Ribes*. His raspberry may indeed be Red Raspberry, *Rubus strigosus* Michx., and his currants, Wild Black Currant, *Ribes americanum* Mill, but his gooseberry is most likely an invention (cp. p. 260 above); he may have been misled by the spines of the Swamp Currant, *Ribes lacustre* (Pers.) Poir (cp. Hyland and Steinmetz, *Woody plants of Maine* (1944), pp. 19–20). For strawberries and wild roses in the area see p. 260 above.

[2] Here he is using the words in the European rather than the modern American sense to mean grape vines. The Northern Fox Grape, *Vitis labrusca* L. and *V. riparia* Michx. (possibly var. *V. novae-angliae* Fern.) Hyland and Steinmetz, pp. 19–20, (qualified in Gleason and Cronquist, *Manual*, p. 460).

[3] Seacoast Angelica, *Angelica lucida* L. (also *Coelopleurum Gmelini* (D.C.) Ledeb.), or (if a seacoast location is known for it) Purple Angelica, *A. atropurpurea* L. Rosier would have been familiar with related species in Europe whose roots and young shoots were candied (Fernald, Kinsey and Rollins, *Edible plants of eastern North America*, 2nd ed. (1957), pp. 685–6).

[4] The coniferous forest association type vegetation, characteristic of the islands, was originally dominated by the Red Spruce, growing closely in exposed situations which, as it decayed, gave way in many locations to a more varied forest cover, with the Balsam Fir, *Abies balsama* (Linn.) Mill. especially, Canoe Birch, *Betula papyrifera* Marsh, White Spruce, *Picea glauca* (Moench) Voss, Mountain-Ash, *Pyrus americana* (Marsh) D.C., Mountain Maple, *Acer spicatum* Lam., Alder, *Alnus mollis*, Fernald and others, and American Yew, *Taxus canadensis* Marsh, with a few other species, entering and finally establishing an equilibrium, undisturbed until the period of white settlement unless modified locally by Indian burnings (not probable on these islands). The ecological picture accords in general with that indicated by Rosier. (Cp. Albert F. Hill, 'The vegetation of the Penobscot Bay region, Maine,' Portland society of Natural History, *Proceedings*, III (1923), 339–43; Hyland and Steinmetz, *Woody plants of Maine*, pp. 1–2, 12–13, 27, 41.)

[5] Ash, Spruce, Cherry and Yew are added to those noted for Monhegan (pp. 259–60 above). We can add to species already mentioned the White Ash, *Fraxinus americana* Linn

issueth Turpentine[1] in so maruellous plenty, and so sweet, as our Chirurgeon[2] and others affirmed they neuer saw so good in England. We pulled off much Gumme congealed on the outside of the barke, which smelled like Frankincense. This would be a great benefit for making Tarre and Pitch.

We stayed the longer in this place, not only because of our good Harbour (which is an excellent comfort) but because euery day we did more and more discouer the pleasant fruitfulnesse; insomuch as many of our Companie wished themselues setled heere, not expecting any farther hopes, or better discouery to be made.[3]

Pearle.

Heere our men found abundance of great muscels[4] among the rocks; and in some of them many small Pearls: and in one muscell (which we drew vp in our net) was found fourteene Pearles, whereof one of prety bignesse and orient:[5] in another aboue fiftie small Pearles: and if we had had a Drag,[6] no doubt we had found some of great valew, seeing these did certainly shew, that heere they were bred: the shels all glistering with mother of Pearle.

(perhaps with Mountain-ash); the Black Spruce, *Picea mariana* (Mill.) BSP (to the Red and White Spruces); the Beach Plum, *Prunus maritimus* Marsh (for his Cherry); and possibly the Creeping Juniper, *Juniperus horizontalis* Moench (to add to his Yew) (cp. Hyland and Steinmetz, *Woody plants of Maine*, pp. 52, 2, 26, 4).

[6] Purchas (*Pilgrimes*, IV (1625), 1660, XVIII (1906), 340; *NAW*, III, 383) adds: 'Oake great and firme, with so fine graine and colour, as our Captaine, and men of best experience, had neuer seene the like.' The emphasis on the Oaks – of special interest to English explorers for their use in ship construction – suggests they were better developed on Allen Island than on Monhegan. Northern Red Oak, *Quercus borealis* Michx. would probably be the most prominent species (cp. Hyland and Steinmetz, *Woody plants of Maine*, pp. 15–16).

[1] Balsam Fir as well as the spruces would show resinous accretions on the bark.

[2] Unfortunately the name of the surgeon of the expedition is not known. It would be valuable to know what other reactions he had to the natural products of Maine and how far he assisted Rosier in identifying particular species.

[3] The preference for an island site follows the pattern of the Gosnold expedition on which some of Waymouth's men had been. Seeing them only in May and June they can scarcely have had much idea of how exposed they were to wind and how isolated they could be in winter weather. It is ironic that almost at this very time the Sieur de Monts and Champlain were dismantling their island site (Ste Croix) for Port Royal, because it had proved virtually untenable in an admittedly unusually bad northeastern North American winter.

[4] The Common Mussel, *Mytilus edulis* L. is still the most common shell-fish on the islands, and indeed the whole area. The size is not now exceptional. Pearls, mostly small and irregular in shape, are found in them, up to half a dozen at least in some specimens. They are frequently found in Indian shell-mounds. Though the shell shines, it is too fragile to be of much use: mother of pearl was made from the shells of the fresh-water mussel. (Information from Wendell S. Hadlock.)

[5] 'orient' here is 'having the lustre of a pearl from the Orient', an earlier use in this sense than is recognised in the *O.E.D.*

[6] Here probably an oyster-dredge (a frame of iron with a net attached) is meant.

Wednesday the 29 day,[1] our shallop being now finished, and our Captaine and men furnished to depart with hir from the ship: we set vp a crosse on the shore side vpon the rockes.

Thursday, the 30 of May, about ten a clocke afore noon, our Captaine with 13 men more, in the name of God, and with all our praiers for their prosperous discouerie, and safe returne, departed in the shallop:[3] leauing the ship in a good harbour, which before I mentioned, well mored, and manned with 14 men.[4]

This day, about fiue a clocke in the afternoone, we in the shippe espied three Canoas comming towards vs, which went to the iland adioining, where they went a shore, and very quickly had made a fire, about which they stood beholding our ship: to whom we made signes with our hands and hats, weffing vnto them to come vnto vs,[6] because we had not seene any of the people yet. They sent one Canoa with three men, one of which, when they came neere vnto vs, spake in his language very lowd and very boldly: seeming as though he would know why we were there, and by pointing with this oare towards the sea, we coniectured he meant we should be gone.[7] But when we shewed

---

[1] Purchas (*Pilgrimes*, IV (1625), 1661, XVIII (1906), 341; *NAW*, 383) omits 'Wednesday...rockes.' His version already has the shallop launched on 20 May. If so a further nine days would not be necessary to fit her out (cp. pp. 146–7 where the 1602 shallop was assembled in a single day). Had she been carried in a number of pieces, instead of two, the delay would be intelligible. It is impossible to know which version to accept.

[2] The cross erected in 1905 to mark the tercentenary of Waymouth's voyage is located on a small point inside the harbour. As it was visible to the *Gifte of God* in 1607 when she was riding about 1½m. to the north (H. O. Thayer, *The Sagadahoc Colony*, pp. 53–4; H. S. Burrage, *English and French voyages, 1534–1610* (1907), p. 406), it was almost certainly in a prominent position, probably on the cliff at the northeast extremity of Allen I., overlooking the channel. A comparable commanding position on the north end of Burnt I. would be impossible to find though it could conceivably have been located at the north tip of Little Burnt I. The cross may well have been made of wood gathered on the spot, along with the second later erected on the mainland (pp. 512–13 below). It must have been of substantial character to have been in good shape two years later: it was not apparently heard of subsequently.

[3] The accommodation of 14 men in the shallop gives some indication of her size. Since there were 29 members of the expedition, Rosier is excluding himself when he says that only 14 were left on the ship. It is surprising that he should not have been chosen to accompany the reconnaissance expedition. It may be that he was felt to be needed to command the vessel in Waymouth's absence. But the completeness of his narrative is limited by this omission.

[4] If we assume that *Archangell* was moored in Georges Harbor close to Allen I. then the adjoining island was Benner I.: if, as is less likely, she was moored off Burnt I., the adjoining island would be Little Burnt I.

[5] This fishing party of Eastern Abenaki Indians evidently arrived in ignorance of the English presence.

[6] Here 'weffing' is simply waving (usually it involves the use of a flag).

[7] This episode is the first evidence of English contact with the Eastern Abenaki and

them kniues and their vse by cutting of stickes[1] and other trifles, as combs and glasses, they came close aboard our ship, as desirous to entertaine our friendship. To these we gaue such things as we perceiued they liked, when wee shewed them the vse: bracelets, rings, peacocke-feathers, which they stucke in their haire, and Tabacco pipes.[2] After their departure to their company on the shore, presently came foure other in another Canoa: to whom we gaue as to the former, vsing them with as much kindnes as we could.

three sorts of colours of painting

The[3] shape of their body is very proportionable, they are well countenanced, not very tal nor big, but in stature like to vs:[4] they paint their bodies with blacke, their faces, some with red, some with blacke, and some with blew.[5]

Their clothing and buskins.

Their clothing is Beauers skins, or Deares skins, cast ouer them like a mantle, and hanging downe to their knees, made fast together vpon the shoulder with leather: some of them had sleeues, most had none:[6]

---

is important for ethnographic detail. The leader of the Indian party may have been a village sagamore. He was making a characteristic greeting oration and his gesticulation is more likely to have been a question whether they had come from the sea rather than a possessive and dismissive assertion.

[1] This was to assume the Indians wholly ignorant of iron knives. This seems most unlikely (cp. Snow, in *Handbook*, p. 139). On the other hand this did not minimize their attractiveness: demand for additional iron was to continue for many years.

[2] The stock of trade goods indicated here is interesting. Knives were of substantial value. Combs, looking-glasses, bracelets and rings (of brass?), peacock feathers, and tobacco pipes were mostly of small value to Europeans, but were expected to be of more account to the Indians likely to be encountered. Certainly the peacock feathers would be particularly attractive as ornaments. The English tobacco pipes would be regarded as a novelty also. This is the first case where the latter are known to have been used in trade. It is argued in Quinn, *Roanoke voyages*, I, 345–6, that pipes made in England subsequent to 1586 owed something to North Carolina Algonkian types. In nearly twenty years, however, many variations in the clay pipe had developed there so that the idea of shipping them back to North America as trade goods would be both ingenious and feasible. The ease with which presents were accepted might suggest some familiarity already with European goods, but probably by way of Micmac traders.

[3] The description which follows is one of the most detailed that we have of the appearance and dress of the Eastern Abenaki of the period.

[4] The Eastern Abenaki, unlike many Indian groups of the time, are not regarded as being on the average a good deal taller than Englishmen (cp. p. 99). See W. W. Howells, 'Physical types of the Northeast', in F. Johnson, ed, *Man in northeastern North America* (1946), p. 170.

[5] 'Facial and body painting was frequent' (Snow, p. 141). The black was usually soot (possibly occasionally sumac); the red was (typically) red ochre, Bloodroot, *Sanguinaria canadensis* L., or Partridge-berry, *Michellia repens* L. Authorities are somewhat evasive about the origin of the blue. Black and red were, according to Champlain (*Works*, I, 306), normal for the whole coast of Nova Scotia-Cape Cod. Yellow is mentioned for Cape Cod (I, 356).

[6] 'A single covering tied over one shoulder and under the opposite arm was common' (Snow, p. 141). Often these were made of beaver-skins laced together; otherwise they were

some had buskins[1] of such leather tewed: they haue besides a peece of Beauers skin between their legs, made fast about their waste, to couer their priuities.[2]

They suffer no haire to grow on their faces,[3] but on their head very long and very blacke,[4] which those that haue wiues, binde vp behinde with a leather string, in a long round knot.[5]

They seemed all very ciuill and merrie: shewing tokens of much thankefulnesse, for those things we gaue them.[6] We found them then (as after) a people of exceeding good inuention, quicke vnderstanding and readie capacitie.[7]

Their Canoas are made without any iron, of the bark of a birch tree, strengthened within with ribs and hoops of wood,[8] in so good fashion, with such excellent ingenious art, as they are able to beare seuen or eight persons, far exceeding any in the Indies.[9]   Their boats.

---

deerskin or moose hides (the latter dressed on both sides and sometimes decorated with painted designs): the leather shoulder-thongs are also noted by Lescarbot (*Works*, III, 132). The sleeves were a moveable accessory (Snow, p. 141; Flannery, *Analysis*, p. 42). Purchas (*Pilgrimes*, IV (1625), 1661, XVIII (1906), 341; *NAW* III, (1979), 383), adds: 'Some weare the haire of their skins outward, some inward.'

[1] Buskins were leggings of dressed skin, probably attached to the moccasins at the ankle (their distribution extended southwards to Massachusetts and possibly Connecticut, cp. Driver and Massey, 'Comparative studies,' p. 318; Rainey, p. 16). Like the sleeves they were not an invariable part of the costume.

[2] The beaverskin breechclout was used by both sexes (cp. pp. 97–8, 276). This is the only early reference for the Eastern Abenaki.

[3] Hairlessness (achieved by plucking) was often remarked on (cp. p. 94).

[4] There is no mention here of shaving the sides of the head, but the long hair is normally noted (cp. pp. 97, 276).

[5] A specific manner of dressing their hair confined to married men is not recorded elsewhere for this region. If it is correct, the information was clearly conveyed to Rosier after he was able to make linguistic contact with the Indians. Purchas (*Pilgrimes*, IV (1625), 1661, XVIII (1906), 341; *NAW*, III, 383), omits the mention of the married men and has: 'They suffer no hairs to grow vpon their faces, but vpon their head very long and very blacke, which behind they binde vp with a string on a long round knot, some of them haue haire all curled naturally,' the latter feature not appearing in other accounts.

[6] The present-giving would normally be received civilly. Purchas (*Pilgrimes*, IV (1625), 1661, XVIII (1906), 342; *NAW*, III, 383) adds: 'which they expresse in their language by these words, oh, ho, often repeated' (cp. pp. 220, 278).

[7] Rosier is anxious to convey that further visitors will find the Indians reasonable and intelligent persons.

[8] As two canoes were brought back, Rosier knew them as well as Pring (p. 222). He pays attention to their internal framing. Purchas (*Pilgrimes*, IV , 1661, XVIII, 342; *NAW*, III, 383) has 'made of the barke of Beech', an obvious misprint.

[9] Purchas (*Pilgrimes*, IV, 1661, XVIII, 342; *NAW*, III, 383–4) has: 'as our men that had been often in the Indies, said they farre exceeded any that euer they had seen'. This is somewhat ambiguous since in the Caribbean they would have seen only dugout canoes, or indeed had they been with Gosnold in 1602 (though occasionally birchbark canoes were

One of their Canoas came not to vs, wherein we imagined their women were: of whom they are (as all Saluages) very iealous.[1]

When I signed vnto them they should goe sleepe, because it was night, they vnderstood presently, and pointed that at the shore, right against our ship, they would stay all night: as they did.[2]

The next morning very early, came one Canoa abord vs againe with three Saluages, whom we easily then enticed into our ship, and vnder the decke: where we gaue them porke, fish, bread and pease, all which they did eat: and this I noted, they would eat nothing raw, either fish or flesh.[3] They maruelled much and much looked vpon the making of our canne and kettle,[4] so they did at a head-peece and at our guns, of which they are most fearefull, and would fall flat downe at the report of them.[5] At their departure I signed vnto them, that if they would bring me such skins as they ware I would giue them knives, and such things as I saw they most liked, which the chiefe of them promised to do by that time the Sunne should be beyond the middest of the firmament; this I did to bring them to an vnderstanding of exchange, and that they might conceiue the intent of our comming to them to be for no other end.[6]

About 10 a clocke this day we descried our Shallop[7] returning

---

brought south of Cape Cod). Had any been with Pring in 1603 they would have seen canoes of almost identical construction. On the details of construction Fanny Eckstorm, *Handicrafts of Maine* (1932), pp. 55–64, is still one of the fullest and best authorities.

[1] Women came with their men on shore gathering expeditions; male protective attitudes towards them had already been shown in the course of the Gosnold expedition (pp. 126–7, 158–9).

[2] In Waymouth's absence Rosier is evidently in command of the ship and takes the initiative in using sign language to communicate. The Indians were quick to respond.

[3] Salt pork, wet-salted or dried cod, ship's biscuit, and dried peas, the staple of the ship's diet, could not have been attractive raw: cooked, they would not differ so markedly from the meat and fish stews which the Indians ate.

[4] The ignorance of metal containers (they used sewed bark ones which held liquids) would indicate that this group had no previous direct contact with European ships. Metal cans and the large iron pot (or cooking kettle) would thus appear strange and interesting to them (though perhaps rather for the metal they contained than for their use).

[5] The headpiece was probably a complete helmet, still regarded as the definitive head-protector and used even in the Virginia colony (one was found by Noel Hume at Martins Hundred in 1977). The novelty of gun-fire is another pointer away from previous direct contact with Europeans.

[6] The mechanism of such an elaborate series of signs is not easy to work out, but it was apparently effective. Indian procedures were of course to precede trade with a ceremonial interchange of gifts, and this the English did not fully understand. Trading was not novel to the Indians and it is probable that the meal they were given was taken as an adequate preliminary to commercial exchange.

[7] Purchas (*Pilgrimes*, IV (1625), 1661, XVIII (1906), 342; *NAW*, III, 384) has: 'our Pinnace'.

towards vs, which so soone as we espied, we certainly coniectured our Captaine had found some vnexpected harbour, further vp towards the maine to bring the ship into, or some riuer; knowing his determination and resolution, not so suddenly else to make return: which when they came neerer they expressed by shooting volleies of shot; and when they were come within Musket shot, they gaue vs a volley and haled vs, then we in the shippe gaue them a great peece and haled them.[1]

Thus we welcomed them, who gladded vs exceedingly with their ioiful relation of their happie discouerie, which shall appeare in the sequele. And we likewise gaue them cause of mutuall ioy with vs, in discoursing of the kinde ciuility we found in a people, where we little expected any sparke of humanity.[2]

Our Captaine had in this small time discouered vp a great riuer,[3] trending alongst into the maine about forty miles.[4] The pleasantnesse whereof, with the safety of harbour for shipping, together with the fertility of ground and other fruits, which were generally by his whole company related, I omit, till I report of the whole discouery therein after performed. For by the breadth, depth and strong flood, imagining it to run far vp into the land, he with speed returned, intending to flanke his light horsman for arrowes, least it might happen that the further part of the riuer should be narrow, and by that meanes subiect to the volley of Saluages on either side out of the woods.[5]

[1]. Waymouth had been away little over twenty-four hours during which time he had evidently been sailing throughout: his unexpected return and the boisterousness of his reception suggests that those left on the ship had been somewhat nervous at being left behind.

[2] Rosier's expectation that the Indians would show no 'spark of humanity' reflects the total ignorance of Indian society shown by the English and also reflects strongly their assumption of cultural superiority. Precisely why his expectations should have been set quite so low is not explicable on the evidence we have at present, but the fishing party already met with would fail to illustrate many Eastern Abenaki culture traits.

[3] It must seem that Waymouth had sailed directly up the St George River, which they were soon to re-enter and re-explore. If he landed at the head of the broad estuary (see p. 292) he may well have hit the important canoe-carry from the vicinity of modern Thomastown across the neck to Penobscot Bay, used by the Indians to save themselves the long haul round by Owl's Head. (Information from Wendell S. Hadlock.) The marking of this trail implied an intention to reinspect it, and this was done during the subsequent march inland in this vicinity when, as it says below (p. 272), the objects had disappeared.

[4] This 40 mile figure is to reappear again for the much shorter St George River passage, but the actual length is less than half of this. The question is did the exaggeration begin with Waymouth's reconnaissance in the shallop or did it enter into Rosier's narrative as a propaganda element from the earliest drafts of his report?

[5] If he penetrated to the head of the estuary near modern Thomaston, Waymouth knew that the subsequent course of the river was narrow. His insistence on preparing the light-horseman for its exploration strongly suggests that he did so. Flanking the boat involved placing light wooden sidings on her, with openings for the rowers, to protect

Vntill his returne, our Captaine left on shoare where he landed in a path (which seemed to be frequented) a pipe, a brooch and a knife, thereby to know if the Saluages had recourse that way, because they

Trifles left on shore.

could at that time see none of them, but they were taken away before our returne thither.

I returne now to our Saluages, who according to their appointment about one a clocke, came with 4 Canoas to the shoare of the iland right ouer against vs, where they had lodged the last night, and sent one Canoa to vs with two of those Saluages, who had beene a bord, and another, who then seemed to haue command of them:[1] for though we perceiued their willingnesse, yet he would not permit them to come abord: but he hauing viewed vs and our ship, signed that he would go to the rest of the company and returne againe. Presently after their departure it began to raine, and continued all that afternoone, so as they could not come to vs with their skins and furs, nor we go to them.[2] But after an howre or there about, the three which had beene with vs before came againe, whom we had to our fire and couered them with our gownes. Our Captaine bestowed a shirt vpon him, whom we thought to be their chiefe, who seemed neuer to haue seene any before; we gaue him a brooch to hang about his necke,[3] a great knife, and lesser kniues to the two other, and to euery one of them a combe and glasse, the vse whereof we shewed them: whereat they laughed and tooke gladly; we victualled them, and gaue them aqua vitae,[4] which they tasted, but would by no meanes drinke; our beueridge[5] they liked well, we gaue them Sugar Candy, which after they had tasted they liked and desired more, and raisons which were giuen them; and some of euery thing they would reserue to carry to their company. Wherefore we pittying their being in the raine, and therefore not able to get themselues victuall (as we thought) we gaue them bread and fish.[6]

The intent of our kind vsage of the Saluages

Thus because we found the land a place answereable to the intent

---

the men on board from arrows. The use of the word in this particular sense is not illustrated earlier.

[1] We have no indication of whether he was a village sagamore or other elder.

[2] The party had come to trade but we are not told whether, in return for what they were given, they had produced any furs on the first occasion of their coming aboard, most probably not. [3] Brooch is clearly here a necklet.

[4] Any unrectified spirit; here a crude brandy.

[5] Beer, probably small beer made on board ship, or possibly cider.

[6] While the Indians would expect and appreciate hospitality they may, by the time they left the ship, have felt the Englishmen had been overdoing it.

of our discouery, viz, fit for any nation to inhabit, we vsed the people with as great kindnes as we could deuise, or found them capable of.

The next day, being Saturday and the first of Iune, I traded with the Saluages all the fore-noone vpon the shore, where were eight and twenty of them:[1] and because our ship rode nigh, we were but fiue or sixe: where for kniues, glasses, combes and other trifles to the valew of foure or fiue shillings, we had 40 good Beauers skins,[2] Otters skins,[3] Sables,[4] and other small skins, which we knewe not how to call. Our trade being ended, many of them came abord vs, and did eat by our fire, and would be verie merrie and bold, in regard of our kinde vsage of them.[5] Towards night our Captaine went on shore, to haue a draught with the Sein or Net. And we carried two of them with vs, who maruelled to see vs catch fish with a net.[6] Most of that we caught we gaue them and their company. Then on the shore I learned the names of diuers things of them: and when they perceiued me to note them down, they would of themselues, fetch fishes, and fruit bushes, and stand by me to see me write their names.[7]

We traded with the Saluages.

[1] The 28 Indians kept together in case of treachery from the whites, but this was probably a customary method in exchanges with other Indian bands.

[2] Rosier, acting as cape merchant, had his trade goods in a box and presumably offered one or more objects for each skin. The Indians did not necessarily require to trade on a one-for-one basis. 48 skins of *Castor canadensis* Kuhl was not a large number by French standards of trade but promising from the English point of view, as indicating there might be many more later. (That is on the assumption that the '40' excluded the other skins.)

[3] *Lutra canadensis* (Schreber) Sabine.

[4] Here Pine Martern, *Mustela americana* Thurton, and probably Fisher, *M. pennanti* Erxleben. There is a useful regional list in Glover M. Allen, 'List of the Mammalia', *Fauna of New England*, pt. 3 (Boston, 1904), pp. 26–7: we have no clue as to what the unidentified skins might be, though they could well have included raccoon and skunk. It is clear that the possession of a reasonable quantity of dressed skins for trade indicated that they were well accustomed to exchange procedures but, if Rosier interpreted their reactions correctly, not directly with Europeans but with Micmac.

[5] Trading was accomplished with some formality; informal friendly relations could now be resumed.

[6] Waymouth would be using a net such as that described by Richard Carew, *The suruey of Cornwall* (1602): 'The Sayne is a net, of about fortie fathome in length, with which they encompasse a parte of the Sea and drawe the same on land by two ropes, fastned at his end, together with such fish, as lighteth within his precinct.' He probably went to one of the islands with an open beach and some distance from the ship. The Indians used handnets, but would never have had experience of this type of fishing. Fishweirs may not have been used by the Eastern Abenaki.

[7] Purchas *Pilgrimes*, IV (1625), 1661, XVIII (1906), 342; *NAW*, III, 383, omits: 'Then on the shore...write their names.' The language exercise is the first on which we have direct evidence. We cannot be sure whether or not Rosier was using a dictionary and placing the words he heard against English equivalents where this was possible. It seems more likely that he was simply making notes and putting down the words phonetically – not an easy thing to do with Algonquian languages. The Indians were quick to understand

Our Captaine shewed them a strange thing which they woondered at. His sword and mine hauing beene touched with the Loadstone,[1] tooke vp a knife, and held it fast when they plucked it away, made the knife turne, being laid on a blocke, and touching it with his sword, made that take vp a needle, whereat they much maruelled. This we did to cause them to imagine some great power in vs: and for that to loue and feare vs.[2]

When we went on shore to trade with them, in one of their Canoas I saw their bowes and arrowes, which I tooke vp and drew an arrow in one of them, which I found to be of strength able to carry an arrow fiue or sixe score stronglie:[3] and one of them tooke it and drew as we draw our bowes, not like the Indians.[4] Their bow is made of Wich Hazell, and some of Beech in fashion much like our bowes,[5] but they want nocks,[6] onely a string of leather put through a hole at one end,

Their bowes and Arrowes.

Their Bowes.

---

what he was trying to do and their co-operation was rapid and apparently effective (what words we have were no doubt corrected to some extent by the Indians they brought back to England before he incorporated them in his list, of which we have only a small part (p. 310)). Thomas Harriot must have done much the same thing, but he had in many cases John White standing by to make a sketch of the object described, while he, already in 1585–6, understood and could speak some Algonquian (Quinn, *Roanoke voyages*, I, 52, 356, 358–9, 389; *England and the discovery of America*, pp. 407, 411, 413); it has subsequently become known that a manuscript volume of the language, for which he had devised a special orthography, was in the possession of Sion College until it was destroyed in the Fire of London, as appears from the MS catalogue of the original library (which included a copy of his printed *A briefe and true report* (1588) as well).

[1] Carried on all ships to remagnetise the compass.

[2] Rosier could be using love and fear with a religious meaning, a combination of affection with reverence and awe, implying that they wished to suggest to the Indians that their power was godlike. This is an example of European superiority playing on the superstitious fears of presumably ignorant natives.

[3] Rosier had evidently some experience of archery and would recognise 100–120 yards as a good range of fire for English bows.

[4] The English method was to raise the bow deliberately to the shoulder, sight and release the arrow, while the Indians shot rapidly from as near the position of rest of the bow as possible, i.e. from the waist or a little lower, without sighting. Rapidity of fire at a nearby target was their normal objective, but their skill in shooting at a distance by this method was also considerable. It is interesting how rapidly the Indians took to imitating the English method, which would seem slow and clumsy to them, though they may have been impressed by its accuracy.

[5] Rosier probably meant the Hornbeam, or Wych Elm (above p. 220); the American species, a distinctive one, was *Hammamelis virginiana* L. and would not be suitable. Beech, *Fagus grandifolia* Ehrh. is quite possible. Fanny Eckstorm (*Handicrafts*, p. 12), considered Rock Maple, *Acer saccharinum* L. or White Ash, *Fraxinus americana* L. as more usually employed. She describes an early Penobscot bow in the Heye Museum of the American Indian, New York, as being 4 ft 8 in long, and up to $\frac{7}{8}$ in thick, with a flat back and a rounded fore-surface, though she does not identify the wood.

[6] Nocks are notches cut in the wood for the bowstring to reduce fraying: the Indians secured it to holes at either end of the bow.

and made fast with a knot at the other. Their arrowes are made of the same wood, some of Ash, big and long, with three feathers tied on, and nocked very artificiallie: headed with the long shanke bone of a Deere, made very sharpe with two fangs in manner of a harping iron.[1] They haue likewise Darts,[2] headed with like bone,[3] one of which I darted among the rockes, and it brake not. These they vse very cunningly, to kill fish, fowle and beasts.

Arrowes.

Their Darts

Our Captaine had two of them at supper with vs in his cabbin to see their demeanure, and had them in presence at seruice: who behaued themselues very ciuilly, neither laughing nor talking all the time, and at supper fed not like men of rude education, neither would they eat or drinke more than seemed to content nature;[4] they desired pease to carry a shore to their women, which we gaue them, with fish and bread, and lent them pewter dishes, which they carefully brought againe.

In the euening another boat came to them on the shore, and because they had some Tabacco, which they brought for their owne vse,[5] the other came for vs, making signe what they had, and offered to carry some of vs in their boat, but foure or fiue of vs went with them in our owne boat: when we came on shore they gaue vs the best welcome

Tabacco excellent.

---

[1] Purchas (*Pilgrimes*, IV (1625), 1661, XVIII (1906), 343; *NAW*, III, 384) has: 'Their Arrowes are of much greater size then our and longer, feathered with three feathers tyed on, and nocked very artificially, headed with a long shanke bone of a Deere, made very sharpe, and some Iron heads, with two fangs in manner of a harping Iron.' The three-feathered fighting was done where possible with feathers of the Bald Eagle, *Halaieetus leucocephalus leucocephalus* (Linn.) Boie., or otherwise with those of the Crow, *Corvus brachyrynchos* C. L. Brehm. The use of iron points at this stage is not surprising. We are still ignorant of how much (or how little) European contact there had been with the area southward from the Penobscot before 1602 (p. 90). However, Micmac contacts with French fishermen and fur traders farther north were of long standing and their coastal trading extended along the whole of the Maine coast (p. 110). Even if they were often at enmity with the Eastern Abenaki, periods of friendly contact were not unknown (Champlain could use Micmac interpreters, 1604–7). There was also the possibility of iron being traded through from the trading-mart at Tadoussac on the St Lawrence. Rosier is the first to note the careful nocking of the base of the arrow.

[2] Small throwing spears, with similar points to those used in arrows, were widely used. (Cp. for use among the Carolina Algonquians, Quinn, *Roanoke voyages*, I, 350.) To Englishmen familiar with Ireland they would appear very similar to the Irish throwing darts.

[3] Wendell S. Hadlock, 'Bone implements from shell heaps around Frenchmen's Bay, Maine', *American Antiquity*, VIII (1943), 341–53, gives the fullest series of simple and serrated points. The names 'harpoons', 'Spears' and 'arrowheads' have all been used for the serrated points: the smaller serrated points seem best described as arrows, the larger as harpoons.

[4] The careful copying of white demeanour in eating, and so on, did not reflect Indian passivity, but their capacity, when it suited them, for imitation.

[5] The sending for the tobacco to the shore showed that they had an encampment or village nearby. It also signified that their trading session was at an end and that ceremonial proceedings, marking the closer association with the Englishmen, were now beginning.

they could, spreading fallow Deeres skins for vs to sit on the ground by their fire, and gaue vs of their Tabacco in our pipes,[1] which was excellent, and so generally commended of vs all to be as good as any we euer tooke, being the simple leafe without any composition,[2] strong, and of sweet taste: they gaue vs some to carry to our Captaine, whom they called our Bashabes:[3] neither did they require any thing for it, but we would not receiue any thing from them without remuneration.

Heere we saw foure of their women, who stood behind them, as desirous to see vs, but not willing to be seene:[4] for before, whensoeuer we came on shore, they retired into the woods, whether it were in regard of their owne naturall modestie, being couered only as the men with the foresaid Beauers skins,[5] or by the commanding iealously [sic][6] of their husbands, which we rather suspected, because it is an inclination much noted to be in Saluages;[7] wherfore we would by no meanes seeme to take any speciall notice of them. They were very well fauored in proportion of countenance, though coloured blacke,[8] low of stature, and fat,[9] bare headed as the men, wearing their haire long:[10] they had two little male children of a yeere and half old, as we iudged, very fat and of good countenances, which they loue tenderly, all naked, except their

The description of their Woman and Children.

[1] The tobacco, *Nicotiana rustica* L., was grown in small patches round the villages by the men. When used on such an occasion it was in the nature of a social ceremony, bidding the participants to co-operate. The English were quite unaware of this ceremonial pattern and simply regarded the tobacco as another commodity. (Cp. T. H. Goodspeed, *The genus Nicotiana* (1954)).

[2] What precisely the type of 'composition' (pressing, possible use of molasses and saltpetre, and so on) employed in England at the time, actually was, does not appear to be clearly understood.

[3] Fanny Eckstorm's view (in her *Old John Neptune* (1945), p. 76) that Bashabes was the name of an individual and not a title borne by the ruling chief of the Eastern Abenaki, is now accepted (Snow, in *Handbook*, pp. 140–1). Yet the use of the term here does seem to connote an office rather than a person, if it could be applied to Waymouth, as the 'Bashabes' of the English expedition: it must therefore have been used by analogy.

[4] The shyness and reticence of the women is not wholly different from the experience of Gosnold in southern Massachusetts (pp. 126–7), though cp. Quinn, *Roanoke voyages*, *passim*, where the women of the Carolina Algonquian group were usually willing to appear before Englishmen without hesitation).

[5] That is they were wearing the beaver-skin breechclout.

[6] A misprint for 'iealousy'.

[7] Rosier's generalisation is not likely to have been based on any wide experience.

[8] The black colour is something of a puzzle. He may mean they were wearing black bodycolour, but more likely he means they were very dark in appearance rather than black, from the combined effects of animal oil, old bodycolour and sunshine.

[9] The rather short, fat and well-featured women provide a significant addition to our knowledge of the appearance of the Eastern Abenaki.

[10] We are not told how the long hair was arranged.

legs,[1] which were couered with thin leather buskins tewed,[2] fastened with strops to a girdle about their waste, which they girde very streight,[3] and is decked round about with little peeces of red Copper;[4] to these I gaue chaines and bracelets, glasses, and other trifles which the Saluages seemed to accept in great kindnesse.

At our comming away, we would haue had those two that supped with vs, to go abord and sleepe, as they had promised: but it appeared their company would not suffer them.[5] Whereat we might easily perceiue they were much greeued: but not long after our departure, they came with three more to our ship, signing to vs, that if one of our company would go lie on shore with them, they would stay with vs.[6] Then Owen Griffin (one of the two we were to leaue in the Country,[7] if we had thought it needfull or conuenient) went with them in their Canoa, and 3 of them staied aborde vs, whom our whole company very kindly vsed. Our Captaine saw their lodging prouided, and them lodged in an old saile vpon the Orlop:[8] and because they

[1] The detailed descriptions of the children are not paralleled in other very early narratives.

[2] The dressed, deerskin leggings were not clothing but protection from thorn and brushwood in the undergrowth.

[3] The fastening by deerskin straps to a deerskin girdle is unique. The tight girdles were characteristic of the men also.

[4] The small pieces of red copper decorating the girdle are the only indications given by either Rosier (or Champlain) that the Eastern Abenaki used copper ornaments. These are likely to have been pieces of natural copper obtained from the streams, rather than traded metal. On the other hand it seems likely that an occasional copper knife, obtained by trade or in war with the Micmac, was in use by this time.

[5] It is not clear precisely why the two men were not permitted by their fellows to remain on shipboard. It may be that already some suspicions of English intentions to remove one or more of them had begun to circulate.

[6] The arrangement for an exchange would seem to imply that caution was their motive.

[7] Purchas (*Pilgrimes*, IV (1625), 1662, XVIII (1905), 344; *NAW*, III, 384–5) has: 'Our Captaine would command none: but Griffin, one of them we were to leave in the Countrey, by their agreement with my Lord the Right Honorable Count Arundell (if it should be thought needefull or convenient) went with them in their Canoe.' A sidenote adds 'We brought them home again.' This passage is of interest. Rosier is referring to Sir Thomas Arundell as a Count of the Holy Roman Empire (which he became in 1595) and not as Lord Arundell of Wardour, which he had become when the expedition returned. This would suggest that the Purchas MS was composed on shipboard, before the arrival in England. The choice of someone who was almost certainly a Welshman, who spoke Welsh, may have been due to the fiction, already current, that Indians spoke a kind of Welsh. Arundell's plan to leave two men behind to live with the Indians (as the Jamestown settlers were to do with Thomas Savage) indicates how closely he was involved in providing instructions for the Waymouth venture. All this is covered up (as are the Catholic objectives) in the printed version.

[8] Though originally the lower or lowest deck, 'orlop' simply means here 'deck'.

much feared our dogs, they were tied vp whensoeuer any of them came abord vs.[1]

The ceremonies of the Saluages in their idolatry.

Owen Griffin, which lay on the shore, reported vnto me their maner, and (as I may terme them) the ceremonies of their idolatry: which they performe thus. One among them (the eldest of the Company, as he iudged) riseth right vp, the other sitting still, and looking about, suddenly cried with a loud voice, Baugh, Waugh: then the women fall downe, and lie vpon the ground, and the men all together answering the same, fall a stamping round about the fire with both feet, as hard as they can making the ground shake, with sundry out-cries, and change of voice and sound. Many take the fire-sticks and thrust them into the earth, and then rest awhile: of a sudden beginning as before, they continue so stamping, till the yonger sort fetched from the shore many stones, of which euery man tooke one, and first beat vpon them with their fire sticks, then with the stones beat the earth with all their strength. And in this maner (as he reported) they continued aboue two houres.[2]

[1] We have hitherto heard nothing of dogs brought with them. If Pring's example was followed they were probably mastiffs and no doubt as such terrifying to the Indians whose own dogs were small and not fierce.

[2] Purchas (*Pilgrimes*, IV (1625), 1662, XVIII (1906), 344–5; *NAW*, III, 385), has a version which varies in detail and adds a few significant touches. 'Griffin which lay on Shoare, reported vnto me their manner, and (as I may tearme them) the Ceremonies of their Idolatry, which they performe thus. One among them (the eldest of the company as he iudged) riseth right vp, the rest sitting still, and sodainely cryed, Bowh, waugh; then the women fall downe, and lye upon the ground, and the men altogether answering the same, fall a stamping round about with both feete as hard as they can, making the ground shake, with sundry loud outcries, and change of voyce and sound; many take the fire stickes and thrust them into the earth, and then rest silent a while, of a sudden beginning as before, they looke round about, as though they expected the comming of something (as hee verily supposed) and continue stamping till the yonger sort fetch from the Shoare Stones, of which euery man take one, and first beate vpon them with the fire sticks, then with the Stones beate the ground with all their strength: and in this sort (as he reported) they continued aboue two houres. In the time of their Pauose, our watch aboord were singing, and they signed to him to doe so, which he did, looking and lifting vp his hands to heaven: then they pointed to the Moone, as if they imagined hee worshipped that, which when he with signes denied, they pointed to the Sunne rising, which he likewise disliked, lifting vp his hands againe, then they looked about, as though they would see what Starre it might be, laughing one to another.'

The description of the dance is masterly and gives a detailed account of its sequence especially when read in the Purchas version. Rosier had no concept of its significance and, indeed, little is known of its precise relevance, except that it may have been intended to ward off any harm the foreigners might possibly do them. Something is known of their religious practices: see F. G. Speck, 'Penobscot shamanism', American Anthropological Association, *Memoirs*, VI, no. 4 (1919). A wooden drum maul (of natural hardwood birch) for keeping time on a wooden drum for dancing, is shown in Eckstorm, *Handicrafts*, plate II.

After this ended, they which haue wiues take them apart, and
withdraw themselues seuerally into the wood all night.

The next morning, assoone as they saw the Sunne rise, they pointed
to him to come with them to our shippe: and hauing receiued their
men from vs, they came with fiue or sixe of their Canoas and Company
houering about our ship, to whom (because it was the Sabbath day)
I signed they should depart,[2] and at the next Sun rising we would
goe along with them to their houses: which they vnderstood (as we
thought) and departed, some of their Canoas coursing about the Iland,
and the other directly towards the maine.

This day, about fiue a clocke after noone, came three other Canoas
from the maine, of which some had beene with vs before; and they
came aboord vs, and brought vs Tabacco, which we tooke with them
in their pipes,[3] which were made of earth, very strong, blacke, and short,
containing a great quantity:[4] some Tabacco they gaue vnto our
Captaine, and some to me, in very ciuill kind maner. We requited them
with bread and peaze, which they caried to their Company on shore,
seeming very thankefull. After supper they returned with their Canoa
to fetch vs a shore to take Tabacco with them there; with whom six
or seuen of vs went, and caried some trifles, if per-aduenture they had
any trucke, among which I caried some few biskets, to try if they would
exchange for them, seeing they so well liked to eat them. When we
came at shore, they most kindly entertained vs, taking vs by the hands,
as they had obserued we did to them aboord, in token of welcome,
and brought vs to sit downe by their fire, where sat together thirteene
of them.[5] They filled their Tabacco pipe, which was then the short claw
of a Lobster,[6] which will hold ten of our pipes full, and we dranke of

---

[1] This is the only other reference in these documents to sexual practices amongst the
Indians. Copulation after a major dance-ceremony seems likely.

[2] The appearance of the Indians in numbers indicates they wished to build up on the
acquaintance made the previous day. Their exclusion by the English must have seemed
rude and incomprehensible. The use of the term 'the Sabbath day' and the cessation from
labour indicates a Puritan, rather than Catholic, atmosphere on board.

[3] The additional canoes contained newcomers and they had to go through ceremonial
tobacco-taking as well as the others who had been there for some time.

[4] Short, black, clay pipes are unknown in this area so that Rosier is confusing their
short stone pipes, with hollow, detachable mouth-pieces of wood, for pottery ones
(Eckstorm, *Handicrafts of Maine*, pp. 15–16).

[5] The convivial party on shore with thirteen of the male Indians did not have any
ceremonial connotations and was primarily social. 'Drinking' tobacco was still the normal
expression for smoking.

[6] The large tobacco pipe made from a lobster claw, used for handing round the circle
for communal use, is not recorded elsewhere (Flannery, *Analysis*, p. 23).

their excellent Tabacco as much as we would with them; but we saw not any great quantity to trucke for;[1] and it seemed they had not much left of old, for they spend a great quantity yeerely by their continuall drinking: and they would signe vnto vs, that it was growen yet but a foot aboue ground, and would be aboue a yard high, with a leafe as broad as both their hands.[2] They often would (by pointing to one part of the maine Eastward) signe vnto vs, that their Bashabes (that is, their King) had great plenty of Furres, and much Tabacco.[3] When we had sufficiently taken Tabacco with them, I shewed some of our trifles for trade; but they made signe that they had there nothing to exchange; for (as I after conceiued) they had beene fishing and fowling, and so came thither to lodge that night by vs:[4] for when we were ready to come away, they shewed vs great cups made very wittily of barke, in forme almost square,[5] full of a red berry about the bignesse of a bullis,[6] which they did eat, and gaue vs by handfuls; of which (though I liked not the taste) yet I kept some, because I would by no meanes but accept their kindnesse. They shewed me likewise a great piece of fish, whereof I tasted, and it was fat like Porpoise;[7] and another kinde of great scaly fish, broiled on the coales, much like white Salmon, which the

The dwelling of Bashabesis Eastward from ye great River.

A red berrie which they feede on.

---

[1] Rosier as cape-merchant was prepared to trade with the Indians for tobacco if they had no furs to offer. The growth of sufficient for their own purposes alone and not for trade is characteristic.

[2] Sign language was now sufficiently advanced to allow a fairly accurate indication of the development of the tobacco patches to be indicated.

[3] It is not surprising that Bashabes on the 'Great River', the Penobscot, should have had considerable quantities of tobacco as he maintained his dominance largely by the kind of diplomacy which required many ceremonial meetings. It may well be, however, that a formal tribute in tobacco was rendered to him by the villages.

[4] This party of Indians had come down to the shore from the interior to join those who had been fishing and gathering there. It is not surprising that they had nothing to trade.

[5] The square waterproof cups of birch bark strip, sewn with spruce root thread, were and remained a characteristic of Eastern Abenaki craftsmanship. There are a number of specimens (though none going back to the seventeenth century) in the Abbe Museum, Bar Harbor. (Cp. Eckstorm, *Handicrafts*, p. 11, plate XXII; Louise D. Rich, *The coast of Maine* (1956), pp. 14–15, and for the generality of their use Flannery, *Analysis*, pp. 27, 36; Rainey, 'Compilation', p. 24; Willoughby, *Antiquities*, p. 295; *Handbook*, p. 139.)

[6] Bullace, a wild plum of southern England, larger than a sloe. In June if these were plum-like fruits they are likely to have been berries preserved from the previous year or, more likely, the Service Berry, *Amelanchier canadensis* as it hangs on the bushes over the winter in some cases (above p. 225).

[7] It may well have been porpoise, most likely the Harbor Porpoise, *Phocaena phocaena* (L.), which averages only some 4½ ft, or other species (Slijper, *Whales*, pp. 199–200). Eckstorm, *Handicrafts*, p. 15, says porpoise oil continued to be stored by the Abenaki. The Harbor Porpoise was also used for oil by the Micmac (Nicolas Denys, *Description and natural history of the coast of North America* (Acadia), ed. W. F. Ganong (1908), p. 351).

Frenchmen call Aloza,[1] for these they would haue had bread;[2] which I refused, because in maner of exchange, I would alwayes make the greatest esteeme I could of our commodities whatsoeuer; although they saw aboord our Captaine was liberall to giue them, to the end we might allure them still to frequent vs. Then they shewed me foure yoong Goslings,[3] for which they required foure biskets, but I offered them two; which they tooke and were well content.

We had yong Goslings of the Saluages.

At our departure they made signe, that if any of vs would stay there on shore, some of them would go lie aboord vs: at which motion two of our Company stayed with them, and three of the Saluages lodged with vs in maner as the night before.[4]

Early the next morning, being Munday the third of Iune, when they had brought our men aboord, they came about our ship, earnestly by signes desiring that we would go with them along to the maine, for that there they had Furres and Tabacco to traffique with vs.[5] Wherefore our Captaine manned the light-horseman with as many men as he could well, which were about fifteene with rowers and all;[6] and we went along with them. Two of their Canoas they sent away before, and they which lay aboord vs all night, kept company with vs to direct vs.[7]

June 3.

This we noted as we went along, they in their Canoa with three oares, would at their will go ahead of vs and about vs, when we rowed

Their Canoa outrowed vs.

---

[1] 'Aloza' sounds more like Spanish Basque than French: the word could well have been picked up by a member of the ship's company who had fished at Newfoundland. Shad, *Alosa sapidissima* (Wilson), was running up the Maine rivers at this time. (Cp. Kendall, *Fishes of Maine*, pp. 27–8; N. Denys, *Description and natural history*, pp. 351, 563 (*Aloze*)).

[2] In the absence of home-grown cereals, bread of any sort was a luxury to the Indians.

[3] These were probably young Canada Geese, *Branta canadensis* L. Bartering for such small objects and Rosier's reluctance to give them what they asked, must have helped to characterize the English as tough and inconsiderate traders, though the Indian taste for ship's biscuit is hard to understand.

[4] Once again exchange of personnel provided a means of learning something of the Indian way of life. Purchas (*Pilgrimes*, IV (1625), 1662, XVIII (1906), 346; *NAW*, III, 185) adds: 'at which motion Master Booles, seruant to the Right Honorable Count Arundell, being desirous to see the manner of the foresaid Ceremonies, staied with them, and had Griffin with him', adding the sidenote: 'Master Booles lay a shoare, and Griffin'. The first name of Booles is not known, but his presence and his preselection for this task again emphasizes Arundell's role in planning the expedition.

[5] The signs may or may not have been what Waymouth and Rosier thought them to be but, if he interpreted them correctly, trading techniques were already well known to them.

[6] A good indication of the capacity of the type of ship's boat known as a light horseman. If she was light she was also large, and could accommodate four oarsmen a side.

[7] The willingness of the Indians to stay on board overnight indicates some considerable degree of trust had been established.

with eight oars strong; such was their swiftnesse, by reason of the lightnesse and artificiall composition of their Canoa and oares.

When we came neere the point we[1] saw their fires, where they intended to land, and where they imagined some few of vs would come on shore with our merchandize, as we had accustomed before; when they had often numbred our men very diligently, they scoured away to their Campany, not doubting we would haue followed them. But when we perceiued this, and knew not either their intents, or number of Saluages on the shore, our Captaine, after consultation, stood off, and wefted[2] them to vs, determining that I should go on shore first to take a view of them, and what they had to traffique: if he, whom at our first sight of them seemed to be of most respect among them,[3] and being then in the Canoa, would stay as a pawne for me. When they came to vs (notwithstanding all our former courtesies) he vtterly refused; but would leaue a young Saluage; and for him our Captaine sent Griffin in their Canoa, while we lay hulling a little off.[4] Griffin at his returne reported, they had there assembled together, as he numbred them, two hundred eighty three Saluages, [with] euery one his bowe and arrowes, with their dogges, and wolues which they keepe tame at command,[5] and not any thing to exchange at all; but would haue drawen vs further vp into a little narrow nooke of a riuer, for their Furres, as they pretended.[6]

283 Saluages.

[1] Are we correct in thinking that the trading area was Pemaquid Point or is it more likely to have been a site near the opening of St. George River? Champlain's Bedabedec (*Works*, I, 286–7, 297) is likely to have been the latter: later relationships with the Pemaquid community might point to it.

[2] Waymouth's fear of treachery is evident. But his signal to them with a flag ('wefting') may have seemed ambiguous. (Cp. Champlain's boldness in September 1604 in confronting Bashabes (*Works*, I, 293–7).)

[3] He was probably the sagamore (Nahanada, even) of the band and insisted on making his own terms in regard to hostages. Once again the transmission of messages of this sort raises questions on how, precisely, it was done.

[4] The willingness to exchange only young men as hostages argues some degree of mistrust, but also a limited and cautious degree of mutual respect. The role of Griffin was to pick up as much of the language as he could as well as to act as a scout.

[5] The sight of 283 Indian men (how was Griffin able to count them so precisely?) with their arms and dogs was certainly an alarming one. We have no explanation of the size of this assembly. It certainly involved men from a considerable number of villages and was perhaps a war and trading party assembled by Bashabes, who may himself have been present. On the analogy of his dealings with Champlain in 1604, his intentions should have been friendly, but the obvious differences between the English and the French, and the comparative lack of confidence on the part of the former may indeed have led him to contemplate an attack.

[6] The indication that the trading place was at a nearby site may have been genuine none the less. If we are concerned with Bedabedec, it was probably made up of the triangle

These things considered, we began to ioyne them in the ranke of other Saluages, who haue beene by trauellers in most discoueries found very trecherous: neuer attempting mischiefe, vntill by some remisnesse, fit opportunity affoordeth them certaine ability to execute the same.[1] Wherefore after good aduice taken, we determined so soone as we could to take some of them, least (being suspitious we had discouered their plots) they should absent themselues from vs.[2]

Tuesday, the fourth of June, our men tooke Cod and Hadocke with hooks by our ship side, and Lobsters very great: which before we had not tried.[3]

Fish in the Harbour.

About eight a clocke this day we went on shore with our boats, to fetch aboord water and wood,[4] our Captaine leauing word with the Gunner in the shippe, by discharging a musket, to giue notice if they espied any Canoa comming: which they did about ten a clocke.[5] He therefore being carefull they should be kindly entreated, requested me to go aboord, intending with dispatch to make what haste after he possibly could.[6] When I came to the ship, there were two Canoas, and in either of them three Saluages; of whom two were below at the fire, the other staied in their Canoas about the ship; and because we could not entice them abord,[7] we gaue them a Canne of pease and bread, which

---

formed by Roose Point, Mosquito Island, and Marshal Point within which there was a number of small coves.

[1] Waymouth's reaction that treachery was intended and that he must break off contact reflects his uncertainty in dealing with Indians. Purchas supports him in his suspicions but he is editing Waymouth after the Virginia rising of 1622. His side-notes are: 'Savages assembled in a trecherie', and 'Disposition of Sauages in the Virginian Massacre, & other their dealings found too true' (*Pilgrimes*, IV (1625), 1663, XVIII (1906), 347; *NAW*, III, 386).

[2] Waymouth's party made no attempt to make further contact and returned to the ship. The absence of any show of hostility would suggest he was mistaken. But Rosier's admission that from this time on he planned treachery against them by seizing some of their members represents a sharp shift in attitude which had hitherto been well-disposed and generous.

[3] Seeing that some of the men must have been aware of practices in the Newfoundland fishery it is surprising that fishing over the side had not been earlier attempted. The side-note stresses the location as 'in the Harbour' which suggests Pentecost Harbor rather than an anchorage off Burnt I. (cp. pp. 511–13).

[4] This shore visit was merely to the well(s) and woodland of Burnt I.

[5] Waymouth did not anticipate Indian hostility in this setting. Any large flotilla of canoes could be seen at a distance. On the other hand he wished to cultivate relations with the fishing and gathering parties as they appeared.

[6] Rosier was sent to deal with the Indians when the signal was given.

[7] Of the six Indians, two had come below deck to the firebox in the forecastle. The reluctance of the others to join them may have been due to some lingering suspicion (well justified) of English intentions.

they carried to the shore to eat. But one of them brought backe our Canne[1] presently and staid abord with the other two; for he being yoong, of a ready capacity, and one we most desired to bring with vs into England, had receiued exceeding kinde vsage at our hands, and was therefore much delighted in our company.[2] When our Captaine was come, we consulted how to catch the other three at shore, which we performed thus.

Our manner of taking the Saluages.[3] We manned the light horseman with 7 or 8 men, one standing before carried our box of Marchandise, as we were woont when I went to traffique with them, and a platter of pease, which meat they loued: but before we were landed, one of them (being too suspitiously fearefull of his owne good) withdrew himselfe into the wood. The other two met vs on the shore side, to receiue the pease, with whom we went vp the Cliffe to their fire and sate downe with them, and whiles we were discussing how to catch the third man who was gone, I opened the box, and shewed them trifles to exchange, thinking thereby to haue banisht feare from the other, and drawen him to returne:[4] but when we could not, we vsed little delay, but suddenly laid hands vpon them. And it was as much as fiue or sixe of vs could doe to get them into the light horseman. For they were strong and so naked as our best hold was by their long haire on their heads:[5] and we would haue beene very loath to haue done them any hurt, which of necessity we had beene constrained to haue done if we had attempted them in a multitude, which we must and would, rather than haue wanted them, being a matter of great importance for the full accomplement of our voyage.[6]

[1] Here a substantial vessel, of metal or wood, for holding liquids.

[2] We cannot say who he was, but the most anglicized by 1607 was Skidwarres.

[3] The elaborate description of the trick played to catch the remaining Indians shows that Rosier regarded it as his own major achievement. The location is more likely to have been Allen I. or perhaps Benner I. both of which have some elevation (and perhaps had more then): Davis I., which the Indians did use, had less height and cover.

[4] The sixth Indian must have had some slight reason to suspect English intentions. After all the English were acting a part and may not have been entirely convincing. His suspicions cannot, however, have been sufficient to make him warn his companions.

[5] The struggle between the boat's crew and the two captives indicates the physical vigour of the Indians: seizure of their scalp-locks must have convinced them they were to be sacrificed.

[6] This capture of this party of Pemaquid Indians, including their sagamore Nahanada, was intended to provide a means of learning their language and the nature and resources of their country. It was to prove in many ways an effective instrument, but one which by its very nature left behind a lasting suspicion of the English, which may well have prejudiced the eventual attempted settlement of 1607–8.

Thus we shipped fiue Saluages, two Canoas, with all their bowes and arrowes.[1]

The next day we made an end of getting our wood aboord, and filled our empty caske with water.[2]

Thursday, the 6 of Iune, we spent in bestowing the Canoas vpon the orlop safe from hurt, because they were subiect to breaking, which our Captaine was carefull to preuent.

Saturday, the eight of Iune (our Captaine being desirous to finish all businesse about this harbour) very early in the morning, with the light horseman, coasted fiue or sixe leagues about the Ilands adioining, and sounded all along wheresoeuer we went. He likewise diligently searched the mouth of the Harbour, and about the rocks which shew themselues at all times,[3] and are an excellent breach of the water, so as no Sea can come in to offend the Harbour. This he did to instruct himselfe, and thereby [be] able to direct others that shall happen to come to this place. For euery where both neere the rocks & in all soundings about the Ilands, we neuer found lesse water than foure and fiue

We caught fiue Saluages, two Canoas and their bowes and arrowes.

Soundes about the rocks and mouth of the Harbour.

---

[1] Purchas (*Pilgrimes*, IV (1625), 1663, XVIII (1906), 347; *NAW*, III, 386) reads: We shipped him [the third captive], and four others, two Canoas, with all their Bowes and Arrowes, which is the chiefe substance [= resources] they posesse.' Stowing two birch-bark canoes on the deck would not have been an easy matter because of their combined bulk and fragility (for the bringing of other canoes see pp. 130, 222). The sixth Indian who escaped was evidently soon rescued and spread the news of the kidnapping far and wide. On July 31 (July 21 by English reckoning), Champlain, at the mouth of the Kennebec R., was informed by the chief Arrassoc of the capture. 'En l'attendent [another chief Sasinous] il vint à nous vn capitaine appelé Anassou pour nous voir, laquel traicta quelque peu de pelleterie; & fismes alliance auec luy. Il nous dit qu'il y auoit vn vaisseau à dix lieues du port que faisoit pesche de poisson, & que ceux dedans auoient tué cinq sauuages d'icelle riuiere, soubs ombre d'amitié: & selon le façon qu'il nous despeignoit les gens du vaisseau, nous les iugeasmes estre Anglois, & nommasmes l'isle où ils estoient la nef [Monhegan I.]: pour ce que de loing elle en auoit le semblance' (Samuel de Champlain, *Les voyages* (1613), sig. M3v, p. 94; *Works*, I (1922), 364–5).

[2] The kidnapping represented the third stage in the mission, the first to reconnoitre, the second to test the temper of the Indians (which was judged uncertain at the least). Preparing water and wood supplies to bring them back to England was the last but one. this was to be a detailed survey of the entry into the country discovered by Waymouth, the St George River.

[3] The rocks which show themselves at all times could well be the Dry Ledges in the channel between Allen and Burnt Islands, but they do not protect the anchorage between the islands to the north of them from southerly or southwesterly gales and there is no protection from the north. The narrow channel between Allen and Benner Islands, also rock infested and with a narrow passage, is a better protection for Georges Harbor, which, however, remains vulnerable from northeast and northwest though to a lesser degree. Had Rosier given us a single indication of the direction the continued ambiguity about the anchorage might have been resolved.

fathoms, which was seldome; but seuen, eight, nine and ten fathoms is the continuall sounding by the shore. In some places much deeper vpon clay oaze or soft sand: so that if any bound for this place, should be either driuen or scanted with winds, he shall be able (with his direcions) to recouer safely his harbour most securely in water enough by foure seuerall passages,[1] more then which I thinke no man of iudgement will desire as necessarie.

Vpon one of the Ilands (because it had a pleasant sandy Coue[2] for
A Ponde of fresh Water.
small barks to ride in) we landed,[3] and found hard by the shore a pond of fresh water, which flowed ouer the banks, some what ouergrowen with little shrub trees, and searching vp in the Iland, we saw it fed with a strong run, which with small labour, and little time, might be made to driue a mill. In this Iland, as in the other, were spruce trees[4] of excellent timber and height, able to mast ships of great burthen.

Great plenty of Cod fish.
While we thus sounded from one place to another in so good deepes, our Captaine to make some triall of the fishing himselfe, caused a hooke or two to be cast out at the mouth of the harbour, not aboue halfe a league from our ship, where in small time only, with the baits which they cut from the fish and three hooks, we got fish enough for our

[1] The 'foure seuerall passages' into Georges Harbor can easily be defined. One, from the southwest between Benner I. and Allen I. is shallow (13 ft); one from the east deep (35 ft at least); one from the northwest between Benner and Davis Islands (22 ft), and one from NNE between Davis I. and an outlying rock (21 ft). As for the anchorage between Allen and Burnt Islands, the entrance from the northwest between Davis and Allen Islands has 33 ft, that from the north 38 ft at least; that from the east the same, and that from the south 52 ft. The maximum depths are virtually the same (76 and 75 ft respectively), in neither case at any great distance from shore. Once more a single indication of direction could have resolved a continuing ambiguity. How accurate the soundings were, of course, cannot be precisely determined. The whole operation well demonstrates Waymouth's assiduity and skill as a navigator. He was now determined that his description of how access could be gained to his chosen river should be as foolproof as possible. He was to demonstrate this further by his final observation (p. 298).

[2] The 'pleasant sandy Coue' would best fit the northwest side of Burnt I. If this is so it would help to place the anchorage in Georges Harbor as it is evidently not the island, or the part of the island, where the ship was moored. The absence of a pond at present but the continued existence of a spring (or springs) would seem to fit the situation. The pond on the east side of Allen I. (p. 263 above) is not now associated with a sandy cove, though again changes in the shoreline features may possibly have altered the disposition of sand and rock quite substantially.

[3] In the absence of Waymouth's chart (p. 299) it is not possible to trace precisely the course of Archangell into the somewhat congested entrance to Georges River. The landing may have been made on the south shore of Hopper Island which would stand across their course. No personal investigation of spring sources has been made.

[4] On the White Spruce see p. 265. This is the first specific mention of the value of the tall trees for masts. They were to be utilised by the 1607–8 settlers as such (pp. 448, 459–60). The location would appear to have been on the north or more sheltered side of the island.

whole Company (though now augmented) for three daies.[1] Which I omit not to report, because it sheweth how great a profit the fishing would be, they being so plentifull, so great, and so good, with such conuenient drying as can be wished, neere at hand vpon the Rocks.[2]

This day, about one a clocke after noone, came from the Eastward two Canoas abord vs, wherein was he that refused to stay with vs for a pawne,[3] and with him six other Saluages which we had not seene before, who had beautified themselues after their manner very gallantly, though their clothing was not differing from the former, yet they had newly painted their faces very deep, some all blacke, some red, with stripes of excellent blew ouer their vpper lips, nose and chin. One of them ware a kinde of coronet about his head, made very cunningly, of a substance like stiffe haire coloured red, broad, and more then a handfull in depth, which we imagined to be some ensigne of his superioritie: for he so much esteemed it as he would not for any thing exchange the same.[4] Other ware the white feathered skins of some fowle, round about their head,[5] iewels in their eares,[6] and bracelets of little white round bone,[7] fastned together vpon a leather string. These made not any shew that they had notice of the other before taken, but

Their Ornaments of gallantnesse.

[1] They had now 34 mouths to feed and, by implication, the captive Indians were not refusing food.

[2] Good fishing obtained off all the islands outside the river channel and the suggestion of drying cod on the smooth rock faces near the sea was soon to be followed up on Monhegan I. (and possibly other islands). If the rocks were not adequate, the erection of flakes, as in Newfoundland, could then easily be resorted to.

[3] The presence of the Indian who had escaped, who was from the Pemaquid village, suggests that he had taken refuge with another village to the eastward and enlisted their sagamore to support his renewal of contact with the English. The description which follows, giving details of ceremonial painting etc., is of some considerable ethnographic importance.

[4] He is a sagamore wearing a coronet of red deer bristles. Naturally he would not surrender what was, in effect, his badge of office. It is typical of the lack of consideration for Indian custom that the English should have expected him to do so. See *Handbook*, p. 141.

[5] A coronet of white bird feathers was in use by their chiefs (*Handbook*, p. 141). Though gull feathers could be used the plumes of the Common Egret, *Casmeralius albus* L. is likely in this case.

[6] The 'jewels' are likely to have been polished shell or bone (which were sometimes combined with a little copper. Tubular shell beads may or may not have been used.

[7] The bracelet was certainly much more than an ordinary wrist ornament. Purchas (*Pilgrimes*, IV (1625), 1663, XVIII (1906), 347; *NAW*, III, 387) adds the description that they were a 'handfull in breadth' and 'which he so esteemed, as he would not for any trucke exchange the same'. This suggests a form of wampum girdle, normally worn round the shoulders as a scarf or else round the waist, a mark of distinction and highly prized. It would probably be already made of tubular beads of clam shell (Quahog, *Vebus mercenaria* L.). (Cp. Roger Williams, *A key*, ch. 24); 'Máchequoce, a Girdle; which they made curiously of one, two, three, four and five inches thickness and more...which...they weare about their middle and as a scarfe about their shoulders and breasts'. This example may have been less elaborate in form than later wampum belts but it served the same function.

we vnderstood them by their speech and signes, that they came sent from the Bashabes,[1] and that his desire was that we would bring vp our ship (which they call as their owne boats, a Quiden)[2] to his house, being, as they pointed, vpon the main towards the East, from whence they came, and that he would exchange with vs for Furres and Tabacco. But because our Company was but small, and now our desire was with speed to discouer vp the riuer, we let them vnderstand, that if their Bashabes would come to vs, he should be welcome, but we would not remoue to him.[3] Which when they vnderstood (receiuing of vs bread and fish, and euery of them a knife) they departed;[4] for we had then no will to stay them long abord, least they should discouer the other Saluages which we had stowed below.[5]

We went vp with our ship into the Riuer.[6]

Tuesday, the 11 of Iune, we passed vp into the riuer with our ship, about six and twenty miles.[7] Of which I had rather not write, then

[1] It is not clear whether this royal command that they should bring their ship to trade was to be at a shore residence near the entrance to Penobscot Bay or to Kenduskeag itself, his chief village, at the head of the tidewater of the Penobscot River.

[2] Purchas has 'bring up our ship (which they call a Quiden). 'Quiden' is in the list (p. 310): the correct form being aqwíden (p. 492).

[3] The invitation to trade was attractive. Purchas put their refusal 'but because we had no desire to discouer any further that way, and now making what speed we could vp the Riuer, wee let them vnderstand....' The expedition was indeed missing its major chance of exploring Mawooshen (and so anticipating Champlain in effective European contact with Bashabes), but its members were basically unwilling to trust their ship within reach of a major group of Indians. The presence of their captives on board put them in a position when they could scarcely accept the invitation yet, diplomatically, it was probably an item of considerable importance in the failure of English influence to develop satisfactorily in this area. In this the French were much more successful.

[4] The presents were adequate for the non-ranking visitors but a distinctive gift should have been given to the sagamore as Bashabes' representative, and probably some individual present sent to Bashabes himself. The ceremonial aspect of gift-making was still not appreciated.

[5] It seems surprising that the imprisoned Indians did not make contact by signs or shouting with the visitors. The whole invitation by Bashabes could, indeed, have been a plot to get *Archangell* into his power and so rescue them. At the same time the simple-minded version by Rosier may be true.

[6] The high point of the expedition was the exploration of St George River. It was also the area on which least reliance is to be laid on Rosier's account. His exaggerations may have arisen from simple-mindedness (but the rest of the narrative does not indicate this), but most probably from his determination to assert (with no doubt Waymouth's authority behind him) that their discovery was of a major river and settlement area. This was unfair to their sponsor and could have been fatal if his plans had developed.

[7] Even if we make the starting point Georges Harbor, the distance traversed northwards to Hooper Point where the entrance to the river becomes clear is only 4 nautical miles. From there the course upstream is northeast and the channel narrows at Fort Point, some 6 nautical miles farther on, which might appear to be a reasonable estimate of the distance made before anchoring for the night. A carefully charted progress of 10 miles, with some allowance for deviations from the mid-channel course, would appear reasonable. The exaggeration of this distance to 26 miles is clearly deliberate.

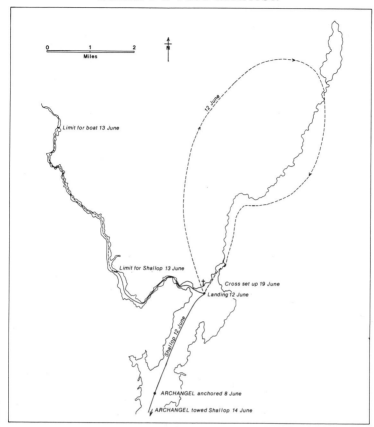

Fig. 16. George Waymouth's searches on the St George River, June 1605.

by my relation to detract from the worthinesse thereof. For the Riuer, besides that it is subiect by shipping to bring in all traffiques of Marchandise, a benefit alwaies accounted the richest treasury to any land: for which cause our Thames hath that due denomination, and France by her nauigable Riuers receiueth hir greatest wealth; yet this place of it selfe from God and nature affoordeth as much diuersitie of good commodities, as any reasonable man can wish, for present habitation and planting.[1]

---

[1] The 26 miles of June 11 are overlapped by the nearly 40 of June 12, so that the total distance he indicates from Georges Harbor to the limit of the exploration is somewhere between 40 and 66 miles. The approximate figures are Georges Harbor to Hooper Point 4 m., Hooper Point to Fort Point 6 m., Fort Point to modern Thomaston 4 m., modern Thomaston to modern Warren 6 m., which makes about 20 nautical miles in all. No clear ratio between the real distances and the imagined ones can be discerned.

The first and chiefest thing required, is a bold coast and faire land to fall with; the next, a safe harbour for ships to ride in.

The first is a speciall attribute to this shore, being most free from sands or dangerous rocks in a continuall good depth, with a most excellent land-fall, which is the first Iland we fell with, named by vs, Saint Georges Iland.[1] For the second, by iudgement of our Captaine, who knoweth most of the coast of England, and most of other Countries,[2] (hauing beene experienced by imployments in discoueries and trauels from his childhood) and by opinion of others of good iudgement in our shippe, heere are more good harbours for ships of all burthens, than England can affoord, and far more secure from all winds and weathers, than any in England, Scotland, France or Spaine.[3] For besides without the Riuer in the channell, and sounds about the ilands adioining to the mouth thereof, no better riding can be desired for an infinite number of ships. The Riuer it selfe as it runneth vp into the main very nigh forty miles[4] toward the great mountaines, beareth in bredth a mile, sometimes three quarters, and halfe a mile is the narrowest, where you shall neuer haue vnder 4 and 5 fathoms water hard by the shore, but 6, 7, 8, 9, and 10 fathoms all along,[5] and on both sides euery halfe mile very gallant Coues, some able to conteine almost

The profits of the Riuer.

The breadth of the Riuer.

[1] Monhegan Island. Rosier is writing about the calmest and most temperate part of the year. However attractive the coast is at this time much of what he has written is sheer propaganda based on no more than a superficial knowledge of an area of extreme climate on which his remarks are mostly misleading. He may have contributed substantially to the misunderstandings and sufferings of the Sagadahoc colony of 1607–8.

[2] As we are ignorant of George Waymouth's career before 1602 (when he made his Northwest Passage voyage), Rosier may be exaggerating his commander's reputation.

[3] Purchas (*Pilgrimes*, IV (1625), 1664, XVIII (1906), 350; *NAW*, III, 387) adds: 'or any other part hitherto discouered, wherof we haue receiued any relation'.

[4] Purchas in 1613 added to the exaggeration already engaged in by Rosier. In his *Pilgrimage* (1st ed. 1613), p. 632 (followed in subsequent editions of 1614, p. 755, 1617, p. 938, and 1626, p. 829) he stated: 'Captain George Waymouth made thither a prosperous voyage, and discoured threescore miles vp a most excellent Riuer. His voyage was set forth in print by Iames Rosier'. Though before 1624 he acquired a manuscript of Rosier's relation he made no alteration to his statement. He either misread Rosier's length of the St George River ('nigh forty miles') or else he added his estimate of the distance between Monhegan (his St Georges I.) and the mouth of the river. In this case Rosier is not responsible for error added to error. While careful examination of all channels and inlets from Allen I. to the head of the broad estuary at modern Thomaston may have produced a voyage of 40 miles, the estuary itself is not more than 12 miles at most in length; as for 'the great mountains', the hills of a few hundred feet high are all that could be seen from a vessel sailing upstream (cp. p. 260).

[6] The channel of the St George River is a deep one and as far as Fort Point also wide. Depths of over 60 ft are general as far almost as Watts Point and they reduce to 30 ft only some 2 m. south of Thomaston and then to some 15 ft at Thomaston. The channel is not now dredged and these depths may not have varied very much since 1605 except for some silting near the head of the channel.

a hundred saile, where the ground is excellent soft oaze with a tough clay vnder for anker hold, and where ships may ly without either Cable or Anker, only mored to the shore with a Hauser.[1]

 It floweth by their iudgement eighteen or twenty foot at high water.[2]

 Heere are made by nature most excellent places, as Docks to graue or Carine ships of all burthens:[3] secured from all windes, which is such a necessary incomparable benefit, that in few places in England, or in any parts of Christendome, art, with great charges, can make the like.[4]

 Besides, the bordering land is a most rich neighbour trending all along on both sides, in an equall plaine, neither mountainous nor rocky, but verged with a greene bordure of grasse, both make tender vnto the beholder of hir pleasant fertility, if by clensing away the woods she were conuerted into meddow.[6]

[Side-notes:] The ground soft oaze and clay. What flowe of water. Dockes to graue and carine ships. The Land.[5]

[1] The continuing names Deep Cove, Turkey Cove, Teal Cove, Maple Juice Cove, Otis Cove, Watts Cove, Hyler Cove – indicate the validity of this observation. They are mostly shallow and many dry out at low tide. Their interest to the explorers is that they provided access for potential settlers to a substantial range of land which could then focus upon the river. The sequence of 'good anchorage' and 'soft bottom' will be found in *U.S. Coast Pilot. Atlantic Coast, Section A* (1950), pp. 250–2, for a number of the coves and parts of the channel. Considerable depths close to the shore are found in the Narrows and between Watts Point and Fort Point.

[2] Purchas (*Pilgrimes*, IV (1625), 1664, XVIII (1906), 350; *NAW*, III, 387) has 'sixteene or eightene foot at a high water'. This illustrates well the continuing progress of exaggeration between the initial draft and the published version. The range of spring tide at modern Rockland, just outside the entrance to Penobscot Bay, is 11 ft and a figure of 10 ft to 12 ft would be considered maximal by modern residents in the area.

[3] Rosier is correct in this. Ship and boat building was carried on in the early nineteenth century, both in the wide estuary from Port Clyde at its mouth and Thomaston at its head, and also in the narrow part of the upper river almost as far as Warren (though floating vessels down from the latter through what is now a narrow rocky stream cannot have been easy).

[4] After the shipbuilding piece Purchas (*Pilgrimes*, IV (1625), 1664, XVIII (1906), 350; *NAW*, III, 387) has 'can make the like'.

[5] Purchas (Ibid.) has 'It yeeldeth plentie of Salmons, and other fishes of great bignesse, and assuredly great probabilitie of better things to be found, seeing about the Ilands wee had such certaine hope of Pearle and Oare. Besides all these commodities innative to this Riuer, the bordering Land is a most rich neighbour...' and adds the side-note 'Salmons and store of fish'. 'Innative' is an old word for native. We have hitherto heard of the (valueless) mussel pearls, but nothing of ore. This passage was thus wisely omitted from the printed version.

[6] It is difficult to estimate the appearance of the land in 1605. Major clearings for Indian villages where corn was not grown are improbable: on the other hand some meadow land (and swamp mistaken for meadow) may have been seen, more especially to the east, between St George River and Penobscot Bay. But the greater part of the shores and inland from them was heavily wooded and was chiefly prized for its heavy timber cover in the nineteenth century, so that the task of clearing timber was much heavier than he could envisage and the average quality of the soil much lower. Albert F. Hill, 'The vegetation of the Penobscot Bay region, Maine,' Portland Natural History Society, *Proceedings*, III (1923), 305–438, says that 'Evidences of the nature of the original climax forest which formerly existed in this region are very meagre.... There can be no doubt, however, but

The Wood.

The wood she beareth is not shrubbish fit only for fewell, but goodly tall Firre, Spruce, Birch,[1] Beech, Oke, which in many places is not so thicke, but may with small labour be made feeding ground, being plentifull like the outward Ilands with fresh water, which streameth downe in many places.

As we passed with a gentle winde vp with our ship in this Riuer, any man may conceiue with what admiration we all consented in ioy. Many of our Company who had beene trauellers in sundry countries, and in the most famous Riuers, yet affirmed them not comparable to this they now beheld. Some that were with Sir Walter Ralegh in his

The riuer preferred before Orenoque: and why.

voyage to Guiana,[2] in the discouery of the Riuer Orenoque, which echoed fame to the worlds eares, gaue reasons why it was not to be compared with this, which wanteth the dangers of many Shoules, and broken ground, wherewith that was incombred. Others before that notable Riuer in the West Indies called Rio Grande;[3] some before the Riuer of Loyer, the Riuer Seine, and of Burdeaux in France;[4] which although they be great and goodly Riuers, yet it is no detraction from them to be accounted inferiour to this, which not only yeeldeth all the foresaid pleasant profits, but also appeared infallibly to vs free from all inconueniences.

I will not prefer it before our riuer of Thames, because it is Englands[5] richest treasure; but we all did wish those excellent Harbours, good deeps in a continuall conuenient breadth, and small tide gates, to be aswell therein for our countries good, as we found them here (beyond our hopes) in certaine, for those to whom it shall please God to grant this land for habitation; which if it had, with the other inseparable adherent commodities here to be found; then I would boldly affirme

---

that deciduous forests of the climax type [Canadian Transition Zone of the Transition Forest Region] were once widespread...the first settlers found huge forests of beech, maple, hemlock, spruce, pine and oak' (p. 326).

[1] Purchas (*Pilgrimes*, IV (1625), 1664, XVIII (1906), 350; *NAW*, III, 387) misprints 'birds' for 'Birch'. The main species noted above are there though maple is omitted and hemlock would not be differentiated.   [2] In 1595. Who they were is unknown.

[3] How much would be known by any Englishman of the modern Rio Grande (or perhaps the Mississippi is implied) is impossible to say. Perhaps this was simply a flight of fancy.

[4] Loire, Seine and Garonne. Purchas (*Pilgrimes*, IV (1625), 1664, XVIII (1906), 351; *NAW*, III, 388), has: 'Others preferred it farre before that notable Riuer in the West Indias, called Rio Grande: some before the Riuers of Burduua, Orleance and Brest in France, Naunce, and the Riuer of Rhoane.' It might be gathered from this that Rosier had himself little precise knowledge of French rivers.

[5] Purchas (Ibid.) reads 'because it is Natale solum, Englands richest treasure', and adds the tag in the margin 'Nescio qua Natale solum. &c [dulce diue Cunctas ducit]' (Ovid, *Epistulae ex Ponto*, 1.3.35).

it to be the most rich, beautifull, large & secure harbouring riuer that the world affoordeth.[1]

Wednesday, the twelfth of Iune, our Captaine manned his light-horseman with 17 men, and ranne vp from the ship riding in the riuer[2] vp to the codde[3] thereof, where we landed, leauing six to keepe the light-horseman till our returne. Ten of vs with our shot, and some armed, with a boy to carry powder and match, marched vp into the countrey towards the mountaines,[4] which we descried at our first falling with the land. Vnto some of them the riuer brought vs so neere, as we iudged our selues when we landed to haue beene within a league of them:[5] but we marched vp about foure miles in the maine, and passed ouer three hilles: and because the weather was parching hot, and our men in their armour not able to trauel farre and returne that night to our ship, we resolued not to passe any further, being all very weary of so tedious and laboursome a trauell.[6]

In this march we passed ouer very good ground, pleasant and fertile, fit for pasture, for the space of some three miles, hauing but little wood, and that Oke like stands left in our pastures in England, good and great fit timber for any vse. Some small Birch, Hazle and

Side note (right margin): We marched vp into ye land about 4 miles.

Side note (right margin): Good pasture.

---

[1] Purchas (*Pilgrimes*, IV (1625), 1664, XVIII (1906), 351; *NAW*, III, 388) adds: '...for if man should wish, or Art inuent, a River subiect to all conueniences, and free from all dangers, here they may take a view in a Plat-forme framed by nature, who in her perfection farre exceedeth all Arts inuention.'

[2] We have suggested Fort Point as the approximate limit to which Waymouth is likely to have taken the *Archangell*, but it could well have been somewhat below or somewhat above this limit.

[3] The 'codde' of the river is the circular bay on which modern Thomaston lies.

[4] The Camden Hills would appear to come closer as the boat ascended the river but would almost disappear by the time they reached the head of the bay.

[5] It seems not unlikely that they ran their boat at high water up to Mill River and set out up its west bank (instructing their boat to make its way upstream so that they could make contact with it later). They would then have walked inland on the low limestone plateau (long exploited for lime and cement) where the forest cover was thin. They would then encounter a small spur which would bring them above the 100 ft contour and enable them to glimpse some higher ground inland. It might be expected to provide a view of Rockland Harbor and West Penobscot Bay beyond. This is however masked by other high ground at this point. Turning west they could easily cross the stream and reach two further hills of some 200 ft before reaching the channel of Oyster River which is likely to have been the river mentioned by Rosier, and from which they would soon return to the St George River. This reconstruction is largely conjectural but it meets most of the specific requirements of the narrative. (It is based largely on the intimate local topographical knowledge of Wendell S. Hadlock and on visits to the area with him.) It appears they were looking for the Indian 'carry' across the neck to Penobscot Bay.

[6] The progress of the armour-burdened party over this not very exciting terrain has its comic aspects, since helmets and body armour would soon fatigue strong men. The general aspect of the country is roughly as is described here but the element of exaggeration continues to be present.

Brake, which might in small time with few men be cleansed and made good arable land:[1] but as it now is will feed cattell of all kindes with fodder enough for Summer and Winter. The soile is blacke, bearing sundry hearbs, grasse, and strawberries bigger than ours in England. In many places are lowe Thicks[2] like our Copisses of small yoong wood. And surely it did all resemble a stately Parke, wherein appeare some old trees with high withered tops, and other flourishing with liuing greene boughs.[3] Vpon the hilles grow notable high timber trees, masts for ships of 400 tun:[4] and at the bottome of euery hill, a little run of fresh water: but the furthest and last we passed, ranne with a great streame able to driue a mill.[5]

Deere. Hares. Hogges.

We might see in some places where fallow Deere and Hares had beene,[6] and by the rooting of ground we supposed wilde Hogs had ranged there, but we could descrie no beast, because our noise still chased them from vs.[7]

We were no sooner come aboord our light-horseman, returning towards our ship, but we espied a Canoa comming from the further part of the Cod[8] of the riuer Eastward, which hasted to vs; wherin, with two others, was he who refused to stay for a pawne: and his comming was very earnestly importing to haue one of our men to go lie on shore with their Bashabes (who was there on shore, as they signed)[9] and then the next morning he would come to our ship with many Furres and Tabacco. This we perceiued to be only a meere deuice to get possession of any of our men, to ransome all those which we had taken, which their naturall policy could not so shadow, but we did easily discouer and preuent. These meanes were by this Saluage

[1] Oak, birch and hazel (or hickory) would be general: the area of the treeless parts is debatable: 'brake' might be general for either rough brushwood or specific for Bracken Fern, *Pteridium aquilinum* (L.) Kuhn, which covers much of the hill slopes.

[2] Thickets.

[3] The description fits an area of climax forest, where tree-cover was uneven. Otherwise the factors stressed are indications of good observation.

[4] The area was to be famous for pine masts in later times.

[5] Perhaps the Oyster River (see p. 293).

[6] For deer and hares see p. 306.

[7] Any disturbance of the ground was done by deer and may represent places where stags had fought.

[8] This was where there was a 'carry' for Indian canoes.

[9] Purchas (*Pilgrimes*, IV (1625), 1665, XVIII (1906), 353; *NAW*, III, 388) has: '...and his comming was very earnestly importuning to haue one of our men to goe lye with their Bashabe or Captaine (as they now tearmed him) who was there ashoare (as they signed) and then the next morning...'. They had evidently picked up the English 'captain' as a term of authority, accorded to Waymouth, and transferred it to their own leader.

practised, because we had one of his kinsemen prisoner, as we iudged by his most kinde vsage of him being aboord vs together.[1]

Thursday, the 13 of Iune, by two a clocke in the morning (because our Captaine would take the helpe and aduantage of the tide) in the light–horseman with our Company well prouided and furnished with armour and shot both to deffend and offend; we went from our ship vp to that part of the riuer which trended Westward into the maine,[2] to search that: and we carried with vs a Crosse, to erect at that point, which (because it was not daylight, we left on the shore vntill our returne backe; when we set it vp in maner as the former.[3] For this (by the way) we diligently obserued, that in no place, either about the Ilands, or vp in the maine, or alongst the riuer, we could discerne any token or signe, that euer any Christian had beene before; of which either by cutting wood, digging for water, or setting vp Crosses (a thing neuer omitted by any Christian trauellers) we should haue perceiued some mention left.

We set vp another crosse.

But to returne to our riuer, further vp into which we then rowed by estimation twenty miles,[4] the beauty and goodnesse wherof I can not by relation sufficiently demonstrate. That which I can say in generall is this; What profit or pleasure soeuer is described and truly verified in the former part of the riuer, is wholly doubled in this; for the bredth and depth is such, that any ship drawing 17 or 18 foot water, might haue passed as farre as we went with our light-horsman, and by all our mens iudgment much further, because we left it in so good

Conueniency of transportation.

---

[1] Rosier's suspicions may or may not have been justified. Bashabes may, indeed, have been in the neighbourhood. Clearly the Indian who had escaped then was able to communicate with the English and may have learned a few words from them, while Rosier also by this time would have known some Algonquian. Precisely how well they understood each other is difficult to assess. It may be that here, once again, an opportunity for trade and for contact with Bashabes was passed over for lack of trust (though certainly the Indians did not have much reason to trust the English).

[2] After ignoring the Indians the expedition turned from the wide estuary, trending roughly from south to north, averaging some 990 yards in width, to the westward course of the river where at full tide the width in one place reaches 250 yards but in general is about 100 yards, while some six miles from modern Thomaston, at modern Warren, falls prevent any further penetration by boat.

[3] The cross was probably left on shore on the north bank at the point where the estuary ends and the narrow channel to the west begins. There is a small elevated point here from which a cross could be seen from some distance downstream. The cross itself cannot have been too large if it was conveyed by the ship's boat: it would, of course, be constructed of timber and nothing is ever heard of it again.

[4] The degree of exaggeration is now clear, since in this case the 20 miles is no more than 6.

depth and bredth;[1] which is so much the more to be esteemed of greater woorth, by how much it trendeth further vp into the maine: for from the place of our ships riding in the Harbour at the entrance into the Sound, to the furthest part we were in this riuer, by our estimation was not much lesse than threescore miles.

From ech banke of this riuer are diuers branching streames into the maine, whereby is affoorded an vnspeakable profit by the conueniency of transportation from place to place, which in some countries is both chargeable, and not so fit, by cariages on waine,[2] or horsebacke.

Heere we saw great store of fish, some great, leaping aboue water, which we iudged to be Salmons.[3] All along is an excellent mould of ground. The wood in most places, especially on the East side, very thinne, chiefly oke and some small yoong birch, bordering low vpon the riuer; all fit for medow and pasture ground: and in that space we went, we had on both sides the riuer many plaine plots of medow, some of three or foure acres, some of eight or nine: so as we iudged in the whole to be betweene thirty and forty acres of good grasse, and where the armes run out into the Maine, there likewise went a space on both sides of cleere grasse, how far we know not, in many places we might see paths made to come downe to the watering.

Meddow and Grasse.

The excellencie of this part of the Riuer, for his good breadth, depth, and fertile bordering ground,[4] did so rauish vs all with variety of pleasantnesse, as we could not tell what to commend, but only admired; some compared it to the Riuer Seuerne, (but in a higher degree) and we all concluded (as I verily thinke we might rightly) that we should neuer see the like Riuer in euery degree equall, vntill it pleased God we beheld the same againe. For the farther we went, the more pleasing it was to euery man, alluring vs still with expectation of better, so as our men, although they had with great labour rowed long and eat nothing (for we carried with vs no victuall, but a little

[1] Purchas (*Pilgrimes*, IV (1625), 1664, XVIII (1906), 350; *NAW*, III, 387), has: 'sixteene or eighteene foote at a high water'. This illustrates well the continuing progress of exaggeration between the initial draft and the published version. Depths in the upper stretch fall from 18 ft at the western turn to 2 ft within 2 miles, with a spring tide range of 12 ft or 13 ft.

[2] By carriage on a wain or farm cart.

[3] Salmon, *Salmo salar* L., may indeed have been in the river (recorded in 1851), but since they were not positively identified this guess is of little value. Other more likely fish to have been running at this time were Alewife, *Pomolobus pseudoharengus* (Wilson) and *P. aestivalis* (Mitchill), and Shad, *Alosa sapidissima* (Wilson). (Kendall, *Fishes of Maine*, passim.)

[4] The limitations of the 'fertile bordering ground' have already been indicated, though no precise estimate of the relationship between uncleared climax forest and of open ground (much of which was lightly-covered rock or marsh) can be attempted.

cheese and bread) yet they were so refreshed with the pleasant beholding thereof, and so loath to forsake it, as some of them affirmed, they would haue continued willingly with that onely fare and labour 2 daies; but the tide not suffering vs to make any longer stay (because we were to come backe with the tide) and our Captaine better knowing what was fit then we, and better what they in labour were able to endure, being verie loath to make any desperate hazard, where so little necessitie required, thought it best to make returne, because whither we had discouered was sufficient to conceiue that the Riuer ran very far into the land. For we passed six or seuen miles,[1] altogether fresh water (whereof we all dranke) forced vp by the flowing of the Salt:[2] which after a great while eb, where we left it, by breadth of channell and depth of water was likely to run by estimation of our whole company an vnknowen way farther: the search whereof our Captaine hath left till his returne, if it shall so please God to dispose of him and vs.[3]

For we hauing now by the direction of the omnipotent disposer of all good intents (far beyond the period of our hopes) fallen with so bold a coast, found so excellent and secure harbour, for as many ships as any nation professing Christ is able to set forth to Sea, discouered a Riuer, which the All-creating god, with his most liberall hand, hath made aboue report notable with his foresaid blessings, bordered with a land, whose pleasant fertility bewraieth it selfe to be the garden of nature, wherin she only intended to delight hir selfe, hauing hitherto obscured it to any, except to a purblind generation, whose vnderstanding it hath pleased God so to darken, as they can neither discerne, vse, or rightly esteeme the vnualuable riches in middest whereof they live sensually content with the barke and outward rinds, as neither knowing the sweetnes of the inward marrow, nor acknowledging the Deity of the Almighty giuer: hauing I say thus far proceeded, and hauing some of the inhabitant nation (of best vnderstanding we saw among them) who (learning our language) may be able to giue vs further instruction, concerning all the premised particulars, as also of their gouernours, and gouernment, situation of townes, and what else shall be conuenient,

We were loath to leaue this Riuer.

---

[1] After rowing a mere 6 miles they would be unable in any case to proceed farther unless they portaged their boat over the falls, which mark the head of the tidal stream.

[2] The phenomenon of fresh water taking the place of salt at the surface of a river at ebb tide is not unusual, but it is a transitory one.

[3] Purchas (*Pilgrimes*, IV (1625), 1665, XVIII (1906), 355; *NAW*, III, 389) adds: 'And as our Captaine verily thought (although hee then concealed it) might possibly make a passage into (or very nigh) the South Sea: which hee neither had commission nor time now to search.' This was omitted in the printed version. Waymouth, as an experienced navigator, can have thought no such thing.

which by no meanes otherwise we could by any obseruation of our selues learne in a long time:[1] our Captaine now wholy intended his prouision for speedy returne. For although the time of yeere and our victuall were not so spent, but we could haue made a longer voyage, The cause of our speedy returne. in searching farther and trading for very good commodities, yet as they might haue beene much profitable, so (our company being small) much more preiudiciall to the whole state of our voyage, which we were most regardfull now not to hazard.[2] For we supposing not a little present priuate profit, but a publique good, and true zeale of promulgating Gods holy Church,[3] by planting Christianity, to be the sole intent of the Honourable setters foorth of this discouery; thought it generally most expedient, by our speedy returne, to giue the longer space of time to make prouision for so weighty an enterprise.

Friday, the 14 day of Iune, early by foure a clocke in the morning, We ankered at the mouth of the Riuer. with the tide, our two boats, and a little helpe of the winde, we rowed downe to the riuers mouth and there came to an anker about eleuen a clocke. Afterward our Captaine in the light horseman searched the sounding all about the mouth and comming to the Riuer, for his certaine instruction of a perfect description.[4]

The next day, being Saturday, we wayed anker, and with a briese from the land, we sailed vp to our watering place, and there stopped, went on shore and filled all our empty caske with fresh water.[5]

Our Captaine made his certaine obseruation. Our Captaine vpon the Rocke in the middest of the harbour obserued the height, latitude, and variation exactly vpon his instruments.[6]

[1] Having got his eloquent but absurd peroration off his chest, Rosier now turns to practical matters. The Indians brought back were indeed eventually able to give 'The description of the Countrey of Mawooshen' (pp. 470–6), which, however, was of no assistance to English settlement.

[2] Waymouth had in fact exhausted the possibilities of the limited part of Maine he had chosen to examine (Monhegan, the Georges Islands, and the St George River). Had he wished he could have gone on westwards (as Hanham and Pring were to do in 1606) to make some more wide-ranging survey and find much more dramatic and enticing rivers to investigate.

[3] In the printed version 'Gods holy Church' would imply the Church of England, even if the major purpose of the expedition was to find a site for a Roman Catholic colony.

[4] Already Waymouth had examined the mouth of the estuary with some care. At this time we can assume he made a detailed chart of its depths and hazards.

[5] On Allen Island. Purchas (*Pilgrimes*, IV (1625), 1666, XVIII (1906), 355; *NAW*, III, 390) has the side note (taken from the manuscript): 'The Iland where we watered is named Insula Sanctæ Crucis, because there wee set our first Crosse.' This would fit in with the draft Rosier prepared for Arundell and has a suitable Catholic orientation. The name never reappears in any other context.

[6] The rock in the middle of 'Pentecost Harbour' (Georges Harbor) is unnamed in U.S.C.G.S., Chart 1209, but it would probably be adequate for his purpose. He wished to get away from the ship where a certain amount of iron on board could affect his magnetic observations. Here he is carrying out an exercise to demonstrate his practical command

1. Astrolabe.[1]   4. Crosse staffe.[4]
2. Semisphere.[2]   5. And an excellent compasse[5]
3. Ringe instrument.[3]   made for the variation.

The certainty whereof, together with the particularities of euery depth and sounding, aswell at our falling with the land, as in the discouery, and at our departure from the coast;[6] I refer to his owne relation in the Map of his Geographicall description, which for the benefit of others he intendeth most exactly to publish.[7]

---

of the theoretical knowledge shown in 1604 in his treatise 'The Jewell of Artes' (B.L., Additional MS 19889.)

[1] The sea or mariner's astrolabe was long and heavy, being perforated to reduce resistance to the wind. The illustration in William Bourne, *A regiment of the sea* (1574), reprinted in Bourne, *A regiment of the sea*, ed. E. G. R. Taylor (1963), p. 207, is graduated only in degrees so that minute intervals had to be estimated. R. G. Gunther, *Astrolabes of the world* (1932; reprinted 1976), pp. 529–33, shows how attempts were made to provide small intervals of 15' and even 6' during the period from about 1616 onward. Waymouth may already have had such an improved device.

[2] 'Semisphere' is not found elsewhere, and is probably a slip for 'Hemisphere'. Frobisher in 1576 had a 'Hemispherium' and an example by Humphrey Coles, dated 1582, is in St Andrews University. It was used for problems relating to the position of the sun at various periods, and is discussed in Edward Wright, *Description and vse of the spheres* (1613) (cp. D. W. Waters, *Navigation in England* (1958), pp. 144, 530). A navigational notebook of c. 1616, sold at Sothebys on 24 July 1978 (no. 97), now in B.L., contained a treatise 'The use of the hemisphere in plaine' giving examples of its use. Again Waymouth may have had with him an instrument designed or modified by himself.

[3] Presumably one of the new sea rings, a set of astronomer's rings fixed above a large mariner's compass, too elaborate to be used at sea (E. G. R. Taylor, *The haven finding art* (1956), p. 227).

[4] The cross-staff or forestaff was the simple working instrument for taking the height of the Pole Star. It was also used for taking the elevation of the sun at noon but was unsatisfactory for this and by 1605 had been largely replaced by the back staff (or Davis staff) which enabled the sun to be observed indirectly (see E. G. R. Taylor and M. Richey, *The mathematical seaman* (1962), pp. 37–40). It is probable that a Davis staff was used on this occasion.

[5] The azimuth compass or compass of variation was by this time well-developed with 'a graduated brass rim or sight-rule turning on this rim. The object was to get a precise magnetic bearing of the sun for comparison with its true bearing... the sailor was furnished, towards the close of the sixteenth century, with a table of true amplitudes' (Taylor and Richey, p. 33).

[6] Purchas (*Pilgrimes*, IV (1625), 1666, XVIII (1906), 355–6; *NAW*, III, 390) adds: 'The latitude he found to be 43. degrees 20. minutes, North [the actual latitude is approximately 43° 52' N, longitude 69° 19' W]. The variation, 11. degrees 15. minutes, viz. one point of the Compas Westward. And it is so much in England at Lime-house by London, Eastward.' This last statement is cited from William Bourne, *A discourse of the variation* (1581) (cp. Waters, *Navigation in England*, p. 258). The recording of the precise ascertained latitude in the printed version would be at variance with the policy of secrecy set out in the preliminaries (pp. 252–3).

[7] Unfortunately Waymouth neither published his detailed map, nor has any trace of its influence been identified on subsequent charts, though presumably it was available to Hanham and Pring in 1606, since it is evident that their lost chart had a considerable

The temperature of the Climate (albeit a very important matter) I had almost passed without mentioning, because it affoorded to vs no great alteration from our disposition in England;[1] somewhat hotter vp into the Maine, because it lieth open to the South, the aire so wholesome, as I suppose not any of vs found our selues at any time more healthfull, more able to labour, nor with better stomacks to such good fare, as we partly brought, and partly found.

Sunday, the 16 of Iune, the winde being faire, and because we had set out of England vpon a Sunday, made the Ilands vpon a Sunday, and as we doubt not (by Gods appointment) happily fell into our harbour vpon a Sunday; so now (beseeching him still with like prosperity to blesse our returne into England our country, and from thence with his good will and pleasure to hasten our next arriuall there) we waied Anker and quit the Land vpon a Sunday.[2]

Tuesday, the 18 day, being not run aboue 30 leagues from land, and our Captaine for his certaine knowledge how to fall with the coast, hauing sounded euery watch, and from 40 fathoms had come into good deeping, to 70, and so to an hundred:[3] this day the weather being faire, after the foure a clocke watch, when we supposed not to haue found ground so farre from land, and before sounded in aboue 100 fathoms, we had ground in 24 fathomes. Wherefore our sailes being downe, Thomas King boatswaine, presently cast out a hooke, and before he iudged it at ground, was fished and haled vp an exceeding great and well fed Cod: then there were cast out 3 or 4 more, and the fish was so plentifull and so great, as when our Captaine would haue set saile, we all desired him to suffer them to take fish a while, because we were so delighted to see them catch so great fish, so fast as the hooke came downe: some with playing with the hooke they tooke by the backe, and one of the Mates with two hookes at a lead at fiue draughts together

---

amount of detail (cp. p. 253). Waymouth in compiling his map would have needed not only his own observations but the record of soundings which the master would have had and the detailed log of the latter stages of the voyage. Whether Rosier and others were able to assist with shore profiles and other visual aids we do not know.

[1] The island temperatures would indeed be comparable to those of England but the mainland would be (at times) hotter, the temperatures reaching about 85 °F.

[2] The superstition that there was something specially auspicious in sailing on a Sunday has not hitherto been encountered. It would run counter to Puritan views at least.

[3] Purchas (*Pilgrimes*, IV (1625), 1666, XVIII (1906), 356; *NAW*, III, 390) has: 'Tuesday the eighteenth day of Iune, being not runne aboue fiue and thirty leagues from Land, and our Captaine for his certaine knowledge how to fall with the Coast, hauing sounded euery watch, and from fifty fathom had come in good deeping to seuenty, and so to an hundred.'

haled vp tenne fishes; all were generally very great, some they measured to be fiue foot long, and three foot about.[1]

This caused our Captaine not to maruell at the shoulding, for he perceiued it was a fish banke;[2] which (for our farewell from the land) it pleased God in continuance of his blessings, to giue vs knowledge of: the abundant profit whereof should be alone sufficient cause to draw men againe, if there were no other good both in present certaine, and in hope probable to be discouered. To amplifie this with words, were to adde light to the Sunne: for euery one in the shippe could easily account this present commodity; much more those of iudgement, which knew what belonged to fishing, would warrant (by the helpe of God) in a short voyage with few good fishers to make a more profitable returne from hence than from New-found-land: the fish being so much greater, better fed, and abundant with traine; of which some they desired, and did bring into England to bestow among their friends, and to testifie the true report.[3]

After, we kept our course directly for England & with ordinary winds, and sometime calmes, vpon Sunday the 14 of July about six a clocke at night, we were come into sounding[4] in our channell, but with darke weather and contrary winds, we were constrained to beat vp and downe till Tuesday the 16 of July, when by fiue a clocke in the morning we made Sylly;[5] from whence, hindered with calmes and small winds, vpon Thursday the 18 of July about foure a clocke after noone, we came into Dartmouth: which Hauen happily (with Gods gracious assistance) we made our last and first Harbour in England.[6]

Further, I haue thought fit here to adde some things worthy to be

Margin notes: A fishing banke. We came into sounding.

---

[1] Great cod at least approaching these dimensions were occasionally caught off Monhegan I. down to the twentieth century.

[2] This would appear to be the 'S Georges Banck' of the Velasco Map (p. 523) lying immediately south of Penobscot Bay, and associated with an island which is perhaps a duplicate of 'I. St George' (Allen I.) lying off the St George R. It is likely to be Jeffreys Bank, 43° 35' N, 68° 40' W, and this would place Waymouth on a southeasterly course from Monhegan I., which seems probable. The whole of the Gulf of Maine is, however, a great fishing bank of varying depths (see Henry B. Bigelow, 'Physical oceanography of the Gulf of Maine'. U.S. Board of Fisheries, *Bulletin*, XL, part 2 (1928), 520).

[3] The cod fishery, which attracted a number of vessels each summer from 1608 onward, was the principal achievement of the Waymouth expedition. It may also have been a main stimulus in getting the Plymouth merchant support for the colonising venture of 1607.

[4] A crossing from Maine to the mouth of the English Channel by the 27th day was very expeditious. Rosier was anxious to stress the ease of the voyage outward and returning. Waymouth was, indeed, very fortunate.   [5] The Scilly Isles.

[6] The *Archangell* was later brought round to Plymouth and London, but it would appear that such West Country men as were on board left her at Dartmouth.

regarded, which we haue obserued from the Saluages since we tooke them.

First, although at the time when we surprised them, they made their best resistance, not knowing our purpose, nor what we were, nor how we meant to vse them; yet after perceiuing by their kinde vsage we intended them no harme, they haue neuer since seemed discontented with vs, but very tractable, louing, & willing by their best meanes to satisfie vs in any thing we demand of them, by words or signes for their vnderstanding: neither haue they at any time beene at the least discord among themselues; insomuch as we haue not seene them angry, but merry;[1] and so kinde, as if you giue any thing to one of them, he will distribute part of euery one of the rest.

We haue brought them to vnderstand some English, and we vnderstand much of their language; so as we are able to aske them many things. And this we haue obserued, that if we shew them any thing, and aske them if they haue it in their countrey, they will tell you if they haue it, and the vse of it, the difference from ours in bignesse, colour, or forme: but if they haue it not, be it a thing neuer so precious, they will denie the knowledge of it.[2]

They haue names for many starres, which they will shew in the firmament.[3]

They shew great reuerence to their King, and are in great subiection to their Gouernours:[4] and they will shew a great respect to any we tell them are our Commanders.

[1] The culture-shock of their captivity on the Indians must have been considerable but there is no doubt that kindness and an easy voyage at sea, together with the care which Rosier undoubtedly took to establish a linguistic bridge between him and them, did bring the five captives into a co-operative frame of mind. They were, however, to show that at no time were they subservient to their English masters and followed their own interests at a later date as opportunity offered.

[2] Rosier's description of the cross-cultural fertilisation sequence is very interesting as it is the only one (except for hints in Harriot's *Brief and true report*) of the process as attempted by the English. The one most important aspect of it was that those Englishmen brought into contact with the captives formed a good impression of their intelligence (which they were to show in various ways in later years). This meant that for at least the activities of of the Plymouth Company, 1606–8, there was no underestimation of Indian capacities, intellectual or practical. On the other hand it is clear that mutual comprehension was not always perfect and that Rosier was somewhat naive in his comments.

[3] This is virtually the only reference to Indian star-knowledge for this area.

[4] The respect shown for Bashabes and for their own sagamores is interesting. In the one case it shows that the Penobscot high chief was an effective authority over the Eastern Abenaki at this time, and on the other that their sagamores were chosen and obeyed primarily for their achievements rather than their lineage (cp. *Handbook*, pp. 140–1).

They shew the maner how they make bread of their Indian wheat,[1] and how they make butter and cheese of the milke they haue of the Rain-Deere and Fallo-Deere, which they haue tame as we haue Cowes.[2]

They haue excellent colours. And hauing seene our Indico, they make shew of it, or of some other like thing which maketh as good a blew.[3]

Indico and other excellent colours in the countrey.

One especiall thing is their maner of killing the Whale,[4] which they call Powdawe; and will describe his forme; how he bloweth vp the water; and that he is 12 fathoms long; and that they go in company of their King with a multitude of their boats, and strike him with a bone made in fashion of a harping iron fastened to a rope, which they make great and strong of the barke of trees, which they veare out after him: then all their boats come about him, and as he riseth aboue water, with their arrowes they shoot him to death;[5] when they haue killed

Their killing of the Whale.

---

[1] Here they are misleading Rosier. The coastal Eastern Abenaki at this time grew no maize, as Champlain makes clear. But it is possible a little was grown in the middle reaches of the Kennebec R. (p. 100), while they knew of it and may at times have obtained some from the corn-growers of the Saco R. If they misled Rosier about having corn with which to make bread it was possibly because he wished to have this kind of information and they gave him what he wanted.

[2] The Indians did not domesticate deer and this is either a lie or a complete misunderstanding. Flannery, *Analysis*, p. 34, thinks they may have been speaking about the 'use of deer grease or suet which was used like butter'.

[3] The problem of blue dyes has been mentioned above. Fannie H. Eckstorm, 'The handicrafts of the modern Indians of Maine', Abbe Museum, *Bulletin*, III (1932), 24, considered that blue dyes were obtained from a species of *Viburnum*, which she calls the wild raisin', and also from Bristly Sarsaparilla, *Aralia hispida* Vent., a perennial herb of the Ginseng family, but more work needs to be done on this subject.

[4] There is a considerable controversy on whether or not the Eastern Abenaki could and did kill whale, apart from using stranded whales and porpoises cast up on the shore. On the other hand, with possession of seaworthy boats and bone harpoons, they were as well equipped (almost) to do so as the Eskimo. If they did so their quarry was the Right Whale, *Eubalaena glacialis* Bonnet, whose average length is 48 feet (8 not 12 fathoms long). Basque whalers had dealt with this type of whale with very little better weapons for centuries before the discovery of America. Of course they might more easily have dealt with members of the Porpoise family. Cp. Everhard J. Slijper, *Whales*, trans. A. J. Pomerans (1962), pp. 199–200 (where details of whale and porpoise on this coast are given).

[5] Fannie H. Eckstorm, in Louis C. Hatch, ed., *Maine: a history* (5 vols., N.Y., 1919), I, 57, strongly supports the whale-hunting picture given here. She cites harpoons with single and multiple points, twisted leather thongs for tying points to harpoons and ropes to their handles, and a strong cord made from the bark and roots of various conifers, which when twisted would make adequate rope. Basswood, *Tilia americana* L., also produced a bark from which strong cords could be made. Philip F. Purrington, of the Old Dartmouth Historical Society Whaling Museum, New Bedford, Mass. (in a letter of 11 Sept. 1975) expresses considerable scepticism about the capacity of any New England Indians to take whale. He says that the Right Whale moved down the New England coast from early November to January and northwards again between March and May but was too powerful to be killed. He does not find any artifacts of the New England Indians suitable

him & dragged him to shore,[1] they call all their chiefe lords together,[2] & sing a song of ioy: and those chiefe lords, whom they call Sagamos, diuide the spoile, and giue to euery man a share, which pieces so distributed they hang vp about their houses for prouision:[3] and when they boile them, they blow off the fat,[4] and put to their peaze, maiz, and other pulse,[5] which they eat.

A briefe note of what profits we saw the
Countrey yeeld in the small time of
our stay there.

TREES.	Beech.[8]
Oke of an excellent graine, strait, and great timber.[6]	Birch, very tall & great; of whose barke they make their Canoas.[9]
Elme.[7]	Wich-Hazell.[10]

for the capture of whales or any skeletal whale parts in Indian sites, nor does he think the dugout canoe suitable for whaling. In this he is qualified for the Indians of southern New England, *Handbook*, p. 162. The position of the Abenaki and Micmac Indians was still more favourable. They had suitable weapons and the much more substantial and manoeuverable birch-bark canoes which made whaling possible, though attacks on *Eubalaena glacialis* would remain highly dangerous unless, and if, the whale were stranded.

[1] The whole story of the whale-chase, many canoes, harpooning, followed by a multiple arrow attack, and the dragging of the animal ashore, is so circumstantial that it cannot be dismissed.

[2] The assembly of the high chief, Bashabes, and the village sagamores to divide the whale is an interesting example of the co-operative character of Eastern Abenaki society, even though it was primarily a hunting and gathering one and very mobile.

[3] The division of the whale meat (and fat) by households is interesting: the meat would be dried and retained for use as pemmican on hunting expeditions.

[4] Seasoning cooked food with whale fat was one way of making palatable their boiled food, which consisted of wild plants and roots, together with deer and other meat (cp. Flannery, *Analysis*, p. 22). Whale blubber may also have been used for oiling human and animal skin.

[5] There were, so far as is known, no cultivated maize, peas, or other vegetables in this area, so that Rosier is again being somewhat misled. Imports from the south are possible on rare occasions (tobacco alone was generally grown).

[6] The emphasis on the Oaks – of special interest to English explorers for their use in ship construction – suggests that they were better developed on Allen I. than on Monhegan. Northern Red Oak, *Quercus borealis* Michaux would probably be the most prominent species.

[7] American Elm, *Ulmus americana* Linn. and possibly Slippery or Red Elm, *U. rubra* Muhl (*U. fulva* Michx.); less likely Rock or Cork Elm, *U. Thomasi* Sarg. (*U. racemosa* Thomas).

[8] Beech, *Fagus grandifolia* Ehrh.   [9] Canoe Birch, *Betula papyrifera* Marsh.

[10] Hornbeam, *Ostrya virginiana* (Mill) K. Koch. *Purchas*, IV (1625), 1666; XVIII (1906), 357. *NAW*, III, 390) has 'Nut-hasle, Hasle' for these two items.

TREES.	Many fruit trees, which
Hazell.[1]	we knew not.
Alder.[2]	
Cherry-tree.[3]	FOWLES.
Ash.[4]	Eagles.[10]
Maple.[5]	Hernshawes.[11]
Yew.[6]	Cranes.[12]
Spruce.[7]	Ducks great.[13]
Aspe.[8]	Geese.[14]
Firre.[9]	Swannes.[15]

[1] Hazel-nut, *Corylus americana* Watt.

[2] Green Alder, *Alnus crispa* (Ait.) Pursh with var. *mollis* Fern. at low altitudes, and Speckled Alder, *A rugosa* (DuRoi) Spreng.

[3] Beach Plum, *Prunus maritima* Marsh, along with Pin Cherry, *P. pensylvanica* Linn. f., Wild Plum, *P. nigra* Air, Common Choke Cherry, *P. virginiana* Linn. cp. Hyland and Steinmetz, *Woody plants of Maine*, pp. 26–7.

[4] White Ash, *Fraxinus americana* Linn (to go with the Mountain Ash).

[5] Red Maple, *Acer rubrum* L., White or Sugar Maple, *A. saccharum* Marsh and possibly on the St George river *A. saccharinum* L., the River Maple. Striped Maple or Moosewood, *A. pensylvanicum* L. is doubtful on the coast.

[6] American Yew, *Taxus canadensis* Marsh, a straggling bush also known as Ground Hemlock, and possibly the Creeping Juniper, *Juniperus horizontalis* Moench.

[7] White Spruce, *Picea glauca* (Moench) Voss. with a dwarf form in exposed habitats, forma *parva* (Vict.) Fern & Weath; Black Spruce, *P. mariana* (Mill.) BSP and possibly, although a mountain species, Red Spruce, *P. rubens* Sarg.

[8] Big-tooth Aspen, *Populus grandidentata* Michx, Quaking Aspen, *P. tremuloides* Michx., Balsam, *P. tacamahacca* Mill and Balsam Poplar, *P. balsamifera* L.

[9] Balsam Fir, *Abies balsamea* (L.) Mill and in exposed places a low or prostrate shrub, forma *hudsonia* (Jacques) Fern. & Weath. White Pine, *Pinus Strobus* L., Red Pine, *P. resinosa* Ait, Pitch Pine, *P. rigida* Mill and possibly the smaller Jack Pine, *P. Banksiana* Lamb. *Purchas*, IV (1625), 1667, XVIII (1906), 357, *NAW*, III, 390, has 'Fir in great abundance'.

[10] Bald Eagle, *Haliaeetus leucocephalus leucocephalus* (Linnaeus).

[11] Great Blue Heron, *Ardea herodias herodias* Linnaeus, and Black-crowned Night heron, *Nycticorax nycticorax hoactli* (Gmelin).

[12] Whooping Crane, *Grus americana* (Linnaeus): Sandhill Crane, *G. canadensis tabida* (Peters).

[13] Common Mallard, *Anas platyrhinchos platyrhinchos* Linnaeus, Common Black Duck, *A. rubripes tristis* Brewster, the 'Wild Duck' of New England, and Red-legged Black Duck, *A rubripes rubripes* Brewster are the most likely. Other kinds of water fowl were probably included among the ducks such as the mergansers, especially American Merganser, *Mergus merganser americanus* Cassin and Red-breasted Merganser, *M. serrator* Linnaeus.

[14] American Brant, *Branta bernicla hrota* (Müller) and Common Canada Goose, *B. canadensis canadensis* (Linnaeus).

[15] Whistling Swan, *Cygnus columbianus* (Ord), once so abundant in migration along New England coasts that 'many a lake, swamp or point of land received its name from them'. Trumpeter Swan, *C. buccinator* Richardson may also have been seen as it was also abundant before settlements. As a freshwater fowl it would probably not be found off the coast.

FOWLES.	BEASTS.
Penguins.[1]	Raine-Deere.[7]
Crowes.[2]	Stagges.[8]
Sharks.[3]	Fallow-Deere.
Rauens.[4]	Beares.[9]
Mewes.[5]	Wolues.[10]
Turtle-Doues.[6]	Beauer.[11]
Many birds of sundrie colours.	Otter.[12]
	Hare.[13]
Many other fowls in flocks, vnknowen.	Cony.[14]
	Hedge-Hoggs.[15]
	Polcats.[16]
	Wilde great Cats.[17]
	Dogges: some like Wolues, some like Spaniels.[18]

[1] Great Auk, *Plautus impennis* (Linnaeus). See above pp. 162, 262.

[2] Eastern Crow, *Corvus brachyrhynchos brachyrhynchos* (Brehm).

[3] For 'Shaggs'? Cormorant, *Phalacrocorax carbo carbo* (Linnaeus) and Double-crested Cormorant, *P. auritus auritus* (Lesson) are both present on the coast of Maine either in migration or in colonies off the coast.

[4] ·Northern Raven, *Corvus corax principalis* Ridgway. Purchas, iv (1625), 1667, xviii (1906), 357, *NAW*, iii, 390, adds 'Kite, Soga'. As a single word it has an Indian meaning of 'Cormorant', but see p. 25 above.

[5] Black-backed Gull, *Larus marinus* Linnaeus, the Herring Gull, *L. argentatus smithsonianus* Coues and probably Glaucous Gull, *L. hyperboreus* Gunnerus. Before settlement and during migration other gulls may well have been present at this time.

[6] Passenger Pigeon, *Ectopistes migratorius* (Linnaeus), now extinct; possibly also Mourning Dove, *Zenaidura macroura carolinensis* (Linnaeus).

[7] Caribou, *Rangifer tarandus* especially *R. t. caribou* (Gmelin) ranges southward as far as Maine, New Hampshire, Vermont and the Connecticut Lakes; possibly Moose, *Alces alces americana* (Clinton) is not distinguished here as elk. See pp. 170, 350. Purchas, iv (1625), 1667, xviii (1906), 357, *NAW*, iii, 390, has 'Deere red and fallow'.

[8] White-tailed Deer, *Dama virginiana*, *D.v. borealis* (Miller); possibly the Wapiti, *Cervus canadensis canadensis* although it occurs mostly in the interior. See below p. 348.

[9] Black Bear, *Ursus americanus*.

[10] Gray Wolf, *Canis lupus lycaon* (Schreber) as the northeastern species.

[11] Beaver, *Castor canadensis acadicus*.

[12] River Otter, *Lutra canadensis canadensis* Schreber.

[13] Hare, *Lepus americanus struthopus* Bangs; Snowshoe Rabbit, *L. americanus viriginianus* Harlan.

[14] Marsh Rabbit, *Sylvilagus palustris palustris*, Eastern Cottontail, *S. floridanus hitchensi*, New England Cottontail, *S. transitionalis* (Bangs).

[15] Porcupine, *Erethizon dorsatum dorsatum* (Linnaeus).

[16] Striped Skunk, *Mephitis mephitis nigra* (Peale and Palisot de Beauvois).

[17] Mountain Lion or Puma, *Felis concolor couguar* Kerr, also the lynx, *Lynx canadensis canadensis* Kerr, and the bobcat, *Lynx rufus gigas* Bangs.

[18] On this valuable reference to Indian dogs see E. M. Butler and W. S. Hadlock, 'Dogs of the northeastern woodland Indians', Mass. Arch. Soc., *Bulletin*, x (1949), 17–35, and for other early references see P. Hulton and D. B. Quinn, *The American drawings of*

FISHES.	Lobster great.[9]
Whales.[1]	Crabs.[10]
Seales.[2]	Muscels great, with pearles
Cod very great.[3]	in them.[11]
Haddocke great.[4]	Cockles:[12]
Herring great.[5]	Wilks.[13]
Plaise.[6]	Cunner fish.[14]
Thornebacke.[7]	Lumps.[15]
Rockefish.[8]	Whiting.[16]

John White, I (1964), 87. Purchas, IV (1625), 1667, XVIII (1906), 357, *NAW*, III, 391, has 'Dogs some like Foxes, some like our other beasts the Sauages signe vnto vs with hornes and broad eares; which we take to be Olkes or Loshes.' The latter would appear clearly to be Moose, *Alces alces americana* (Clinton), whether it is also implied above or not.

[1] The most common species in Maine waters are Fin Whale, *Balaenoptera physalus* (Linn.) True, Blue Whale, *B. musculus* (Linn.) True, Sperm Whale, *Physeter macrocephalus* Linn., Hump-back Whale, *Megaptera nova-angliae* (Borowski), and Pilot Whale, *Globicepahala melaena* (Traill) De Kay, though other species may also have been seen (cp. Allen, 'List of the *Mammalia*', *Fauna of New England*, pt. 3 (1904), pp. 1–3; E. J. Slijper, *Whales* (1962), 417–20). Purchas, IV (1625), XVIII (1906), 357, *NAW*, III, 390, adds 'Porpoise'. Rosier's editor evidently decided that 'Porpoise' was superfluous. He would have seen the Common Harbor Porpoise, *Phocaena phoecaena* (Linn.) Jordan, Common Dolphin, *Delphinus delphis* Linn., and probably the Bottle-nosed Porpoise, *Tursiops truncatus* (Montagu) True (cp. Allen, 'List of the *Mammalia*', *Fauna of New England*, pt. 3 (1904), pp. 6–7; Slijper, *Whales* (1962), pp. 419–20).

[2] Harbor Seal, *Phoca vitulina* Linn.; possibly Harp Seal, *P. groenlandica* Erzleben and Hooded Seal, *P. cristata*.   [3] Cod, *Gaduс calarias* Linn.

[4] Haddock, *Melanogrammus aeglefinnus* (Linn.), as in European waters.

[5] Herring, *Clupea harengus* Linn. (see its inclusion by Kendall in *Catalogue of the fishes of Maine* (1914), though not in 'List of the *Pisces*', *Fauna of New England*, pt. 11 (1909), p. 38); Alewife, *Pomolobus pseudoharengus* (Wilson). We might also add Shad, *Alosa sapidissima* (Wilson), distinguished by its greater size from the herring.

[6] Plaice here are probably the Sand Flounder, *Lophopsetta maculata* (Mitchill), the markings on which would suggest the European plaice or, alternatively, the Summer Flounder, *Paralichthys dentatus* (Linn.).   [7] Thorny Skate, *Raia radiata* Donovan.

[8] Possibly here Sea Bass, *Roccus lineatus* (Bloch).

[9] Lobster, *Homarus americanus* Milne Edwards.

[10] Rock Crab, *Cancer irroratus* Say, with Green Crab, *Carcinides maenas* (Linn.) and Spider Crab, *Libinia emarginata* Leach, and possibly other species, would have been noticed (cp. M. J. Rathbun, 'List of the *Crustacea*', *Fauna of New England*, pt. 5 (1905), pp. 8–15).

[11] Common Mussel, *Mytilus edulis* Linn. (Johnson, 'Mollusca', *Fauna of New England*, pt. 13 (1915), p. 32. Pearl in this mussel is not normally prominent.

[12] Morton's Egg Cockle, *Laevicardium mortoni*, Conrad, and *Clinocardium ciliatum* Fabricius.

[13] Common Northern Buccinum, *Buccinum undatum* Linn., and Channeled Whelk, *Busycon canaliculatum* Linn.

[14] The English Gilthead or Cunnerfish is represented by Cunner, *Tautogolabrus adspersus* (Walbaum) and Tautog, *Tautoga onitis* (Linn.).

[15] *Cyclopterus lumpus* Linn., as in European waters. Purchas, IV (1625), XVIII (1906), 358, *NAW*, III, 391, has 'Lumpe-fish'.

[16] Whiting would most likely be young specimens of Silver Hake, *Merluccius bilinearis* (Mitchill).

FISHES.

Soales.[1]

Tortoises.[2]

Oisters.[3]

FRUITS, PLANTS and HERBS.

Tabacco, excellent sweet and strong.[4]

Wild-Vines.[5]

Strawberries.[6]

Raspberries[7]

Gooseberries[8]

Hurtleberries[9] } abundance.

Currant trees[8]

Rose-bushes.[10]

Peaze.[11]

Ground-nuts.[12]

[1] Soles. The Hogchoker, *Achirus fascietus* Lacépède, is nearest to the European sole and is found close inshore, especially in brackish water, though uncommon north of Cape Cod. Three of the other American Flounders are more likely, Smoothback Flounder, *Lophopsetta putnami* (Gill), Winter Flounder, *Pseudopleuronectes americanus* (Walbaum) and Witch Flounder, *Glyptocephalus cynoglossus* (Linn.). Purchas, IV (1625), 1667, XVIII (1906), 358, *NAW*, III, 391, omits 'Soales'.

[2] Purchas, IV (1625), 1667, XVIII (1906), 358, *NAW*, III, 391 has 'the Sauages signe vnto vs that they haue Tortoise very great'. Large sea turtles are rare visitors. Possible are Common Snapping Turtle, *Chelydra serpentina serpentina* Linn. (C. H. Pope, *Turtles of the United States and Canada* (1939), pp. 72–83; A. F. Carr, *Handbook of Turtles* (1962), pp. 61–69); Wood Turtle, *Clemmys insculpta* (Le Conte), Pope, pp. 92–9 (Carr, pp. 118–126); Spotted Turtle, *C. guttata* (Schneider), Pope, pp. 85–92 (Carr, pp. 113–118).

[3] Oyster, *Crassostrea virginica* Gmelin (R. Tucker Abbott, *American seashells* (1954), p. 375).

[4] Tobacco, *Nicotiana rustica* L. See above pp. 160, 163.

[5] Here he is likely to be using the words in the English rather than the modern American sense to mean Grapes; the alternatives would be Northern Fox Grape, *Vitis labrusca* Linn. or the New England (or Pilgrim) Grape, *V. novae-angliae* Fernald (cp. Hyland and Steinmetz, *Woody plants of Maine*, pp. 19–20).

[6] Strawberry, *Fragaria virginia* Duchesne, including *F. canadensis* (Michx) Fern.

[7] Raspberry, *Rubus Idaeus*.

[8] With the plants in bloom or with fruit just beginning to set in mid-May Rosier might not have differentiated too closely between various species of *Ribes*. Wild gooseberries are Dogberry, *Ribes Cynosbati* L., and *R. hirtellum* Michx. Wild Black Currant, *R. americanum* Mill. could be the currant tree along with *R. triste* Pall and Swamp Black Currant, *R. lacustre* (Pers.) Poir but the Swamp Currant is prickly and could have been identified as a gooseberry. It is not frequent on the coast. (cp. Hyland and Steinmetz, *Woody plants of Maine* (1944), pp. 19–20).

[9] They would have seen a number of species of Vaccinia, certainly the Low Sweet Blueberry, *Vaccinium angustifolium*; probably Swamp Blueberry, *V. corymbosum* Linn and Black Highback Blueberry, *V. atrococcum* (Gray) Heller, as well as the Cranberry, *V. macrocarpon* Ait, the fruit of which would not yet be clearly distinguishable from the Blueberry. (cp. Hyland and Steinmetz, *Woody Plants of Maine*, pp. 50–52). They may have received dried berries from the Indians.

[10] *Rosa virginiana* Mill and other species.

[11] Beach Pea, *Lathyrus maritimus* (L.) Bigel and possibly Marsh Vetchling, *L. palustris* L. Purchas, IV (1625), 1667, XVIII (1906), 398, *NAW*, III, 391, has 'Pease, which the Sauages signe to be very great in the Maine'. Beans are likely to have been cultivated by the Saco River Indians, but not farther north.

[12] Groundnuts, *Apios americana* Medic.

FRUITS, PLANTS & HERBS.
Angelica, a most soueraigne
  herbe.[1]
An hearbe that spreadeth
  the ground, & smelleth
  like Sweet Marioram,
  great plenty.[2]

Very good Dies, which
  appeare by their
  painting; which they
  carrie with them in
  bladders.[3]

The names of the fiue Saluages which we brought home
into England, which are all yet aliue, are these.

1. Tahánedo, a Sagamo or Commander.[4]
2. Amóret[5] ⎫
3. Skicowáros[6] ⎬ Gentlemen.
4. Maneddo[7] ⎭
5. Sassacomoit, a seruant.[8]

[1] *Angelica lucida* L. or *A. atropurpurea* L., the latter being very similar to the species with which Rosier was familiar in Europe whose roots and young shoots are candied (cp. Fernald, Kinsey and Rollins, *Edible plants of eastern North America* (2nd ed., 1958), pp. 685–6). Asa Gray suggests Wild Sarsaparilla, *Aralia nudicaulis* L. (Morton, *New English Canaan* (1637) ed. 1883) and the Fernald, *Gray's Manual* (1950), p. 1077 comments 'The long horizontal aromatic roots are a substitute for officinal Sarsaparilla'. (But see p. 334.)

[2] As Rosier indicates, this was not Camomile or Marjoram, neither of them native to America. The native wild Basil, *Satureja vulgaris* (L.) Fritsch var. *neogaes* Fern. grows on shores as well as in woods.   [3] Dyes are discussed on p. 268 above.

[4] Purchas (*Pilgrimes*, IV (1625), 1667, XVIII (1906), 359; *NAW*, III, 391) has: 'Bdahanedo, brother to the Bashabes'. It is not at all clear that he was Bashabes' brother, though it is not impossible: he was certainly sagamore of the Pemaquid village community. He fell to Sir John Popham's share of the human spoils and was brought back to the village by Hanham and Pring in 1606 (F. Gorges, *Brief narration* (1658), p. 8 (as Dehamda)), and as Nahaneda was in close relationship with the 1607–8 colony, Raleigh Gilbert referring to him as 'Cheefe Comander' (p. 426). John Smith met him in 1614 (*The description of New England* (1616), pp. 45–6), and describes him as 'Dohannida, one of their greatest Lords', who proved most co-operative.

[5] 'Amooret, his [Bdahanedo's] brother,' according to the Purchas version. This is not confirmed. He is not found named elsewhere, but it is not unlikely that if he was brother to the sagamore he, too, was sent back in 1606.

[6] 'Sickaworrowse', according to Purchas. He was one of those who came into the possession of Sir Ferdinando Gorges (*Brief narration*, pp. 3–8, as Skettawarroes, Skitwarres and Sketwarrers). He was brought back to his village (as Skidwarres or Skidwares) by Raleigh Gilbert in the *Mary & John* in 1607 and insisted on remaining at Pemaquid (pp. 403–5).

[7] 'Maneduck' in Purchas. He came into Gorges' possession (Gorges, *Briefe narration* (1658), p. 3) as 'Manida', and was sent out with Challons (Purchas, IV, 1832, XIX (1906), 284; *NAW*, III, 404), as 'Mannido'. He appears in [F. Gorges], *A briefe relation of the discovery and plantation of New England* (1622), sig. B1*v*. as 'Manedy'. He disappears entirely from view and may have died of wounds in Spain.

[8] 'Satacomoah' in Purchas. He was taken over by Gorges and was sent on the Challons voyage in 1606 and was captured by the Spaniards (see deposition of John

10 Additions by Purchas to the printed Rosier narrative, containing the word list and list of sagamores of the Eastern Abenaki.

Words which I learned of the Sauages, in their Language.[1]

Sunne or Moone, Kesus. Cod-fish, Biskeiore. A fish with hornes, Manedo. Lobster, Shoggah. Rock-fish, Shagatocke. Cockle-fish, Hesucke. Muskell, Shoorocke. Cunner-fish, Tattaucke. Crabbe, Wussorasha. Porpoise, Muscopeiuck. Plaise, Anego. Tortoise, Romcaneeke. Pease, Vshcomono. Tobacco, Tomoch. A leafe, Mebeere. A weed, Cashterush. A Firre tree, Seteock. A stone, Nabscurr. A Bowe, Shoanor. An Arrow, Tobood. Barke of a tree, Mashquere. Water, Shamogoon. Sand, Cheemuck. Crowe, Cagagoose. Haire, Messer or Meris. A beard, Nicowur. A Beare, Rogsoo. Beauer, Paneah. Otter, Nymemano. Rat, Sanuke. Polcat, Pocamka. Cat, Pushuck. Fallow Deere, Coribo. Hogge, Madoso. Red Deere, Moosurr. They tell vs of other beasts, which they call, Tasquus, Pisho, Narsim. Teeth, Ibider. A hand and finger, Breeche. A Naile of the hand, Cushe. A legge, Codd. A foot, Musseete. Plum-tree, Epsegan. Strawberry, Pishoa. Gooseberry, Shewanor. Cherry tree, Espegononino. Corant tree, Asheemena. Rashberrie, Kiskeemy. A lippe, Metoan. Fire, Squida. The maine Land, Bemoquiducke. Sea, Shoubbe. Father, Wado. Sonne, Vsto. Wane of the Sea, Toboogg. Pitch and Tallow, Poco. Wilde Rose, Minusheck. Birch, Pasquar. Sword, Edagawancke. Mountaine, Machoucke. Winde, Puckchawsen. Bloud, Pagâgocun. Red Paint, Woroman. Blacke Paint, Cogosho. A Dogge, Remoose. A Ship or Boat, Quiden. An Oare, Wuttohoganor. A Garnepo Fly, Chussuah. Bread, Paune. Raine, Soogoran. A nose, Peech-ten. An Axe or Hatchet, Tomaheegon. A Knife, Quodogon. Oake, Askabesse. White Bone, whereof they haue Chaines, Girdles, Bracelets, Speesone. The Cheeke, Canoah. A Shirt or Coat, Tenoganuke. The Chinne, Queh. An Eye, Sheesuck. Eylid, Momon. Forehead, Scottoquah. An Eare, Fawwucke. A fish-hooke, Makeecon. A Rainbow, Shomogon.

Stoneman in Purchas (*Pilgrimes*, IV (1625), 1832, XIX (1906), 284; *NAW*, III, 406), where he is called 'Assacomoit'). He is also mentioned (as 'Assecumet') in *A brief relation of...New England* (1622), sig. B1 *v*. He was eventually recovered by Gorges, though under what circumstances we do not know (Gorges, *Briefe narration* (1658), p. 14, who had confused him (on p. 3) with Tasquantum). It might appear that the description of him as a servant implies he was a war prisoner of the Pemaquid village.

[1] The wordlist is dealt with by Dr P. L. Barbour in Appendix I.

The Names of their chiefe Gouernours, whom they call Sagomoh.

1. Bashabez.[1] 2. Abatuckquishe.[2] 3. Bdahanedo, one of them we haue.[3] 4. Abokeesussick.[4] 5. Shurokinit.[5] 6. Psaheno.[6] 7. Mentoelmet.[7] 8. Ageemohuck.[8] 9. Mawermet.[9] 10. Chanacoboin.[10] 11. Amilquin.[11] 12. Muasacoromoneete.[12] These dwell vpon the Maine, and weare an ornament of white bone vpon their head; and Chaines, and Bracelets, and Girdles, and haue their skinne garments laced with them.[13]

The Names of our Virginians.[14] Bdahanedo, Brother to the Bashabes.[15] Amooret, his Brother.[16] Satacomoah. Maneduck. Scikaworrowse.

[1] For Bashabes, the high chief of the Eastern Abenaki see pp. 98–9. Snow (in *Handbook*, pp. 140–1) says he was succeeded by Asticou in 1614 or 1615.

[2] Possibly Baccatusshe of the 'Description', p. 475.

[3] This is Nahanada, sagamore of Pemaquid, see p. 309.

[4] Abochigishic of the 'Description', p. 476, and Abecogissick of 'The Names of the Rivers', p. 477.

[5] Not found elsewhere.

[6] Not found.

[7] Mentaurmet of the 'Description', p. 473, and Mentoermit of 'The Names of the Rivers', p. 480.

[8] Not found.

[9] Abermot of the 'Description', p. 471, and Abermite of 'The Names of the Rivers', 477, see p. 344.

[10] Not found.

[11] Amniquin of the 'Description', p. 473, and Amenqum of 'The Names of the Rivers', p. 477; Amenquin, pp. 351, 413.

[12] Not found.

[13] The insignia of the sagamores, a white bone on the head (or a worked shell?), chains, bracelets and girdles of, presumably, wampum beads, is not otherwise detailed.

[14] For the five see pp. 309–10 above.

[15] Nahanada was not, apparently, the brother of Bashabes. When the brother comes ˒to the Kennebec he is described as such and is with Nahanada who is not.

[16] Amoret is not elsewhere described as Nahanada's brother.

CHAPTER VII

ABORTIVE NORTH VIRGINIA
PROJECTS, 1605–1607

Orthodox accounts of the inception of English settlement under the Virginia Company charter of 10 April 1606, which gave the joint London and Plymouth divisions a monopoly of English rights to North America between 36° and 45° N, make no allowance for ventures pursued, even if not to success, after the grant of the charter. They do not provide any significant material on exploration, but they provide some insight into the people and their objectives who concerned themselves with North America, as well as highlighting the high degree of efficiency of the 'South Virginia' voyages and even those to 'North Virginia' under the Plymouth division as well. It has been suggested that if Rosier's tract, *A true relation*, provided an incentive for bringing 'North Virginia' into the Virginia Company's orbit, it did not stand in the way of, or impede other ventures, or plans for ventures, quite outside the framework of the charter.

The Waymouth–Zouche Venture (*Documents nos 10–14*)

The agreement between Sir John Zouche of Codnor and George Waymouth follows on from those by Sir Humphrey Gilbert and continued in many Stuart grants after 1620. The absolute proprietorship of the grantee was to be assured (even if he was undoubtedly only a figurehead for others), Waymouth was to be assured of secondary landed benefits and his merchant supporters in Plymouth were to be offered only a single year's monopoly of fishing and trading. The following of this agreement by Rosier's *A true relation* seemed to indicate substantial progress toward the development of a gentry (including Catholic gentry) and merchant association, but the process was stopped for many months by the reaction against the Catholics following the Gunpowder Plot of 5 November 1605 and by the gradual emergence of wider plans for eastern North America as a whole. It was only after the grant of the Virginia Company charter that the project was revived. These events may have prevented Waymouth (if he had continued to serve in the project) from having two ships prepared by 30 April 1606. It was not until late June that fresh Catholic appeals to send a colony to Virginia were made to the crown. We may surmise that they were associated with the Zouche scheme and that they were approved in principle some time during July, though at present neither assumption can be firmly established. At some time during late spring or summer Lord Zouche had offered to stand surety for his brother-in-law and distant cousin, Sir John Zouche, so that a passport could be issued. Pressure was put on the Lord High Admiral, Nottingham, to grant the permission necessary, but for 'some private reasons' (p. 319) he did not give way until 13 August. The bond under which Lord Zouche became responsible for the good behaviour of Sir John's 'two shippes & a Pinnace' was issued the following day (and was probably accompanied by a passport). The delay evidently proved fatal to the Zouche project, even though the ships were probably ready, as permission had been delayed until an expedition was no longer practicable. The plan aborted, at least partly owing to administrative obstruction at a high level.

The Triall *and its associated ventures* (Documents nos. 15–20)

Basically the *Triall* venture was a simple one, the hiring of a ship for nine months to exploit the fishing and drying facilities revealed by Rosier's *A true relation* and, no doubt, verbal information from Thames–side sailors whom Rosier mentions. The sponsors were London fishmongers, and the evidence on the venture is chronicled in D. B. Quinn, 'The voyage of Triall 1606–1607: an abortive Virginia venture', *American Neptune*, XXXI (1971), 85–103 (while selected documents appear in *NAW*, III, 396–402). The charter was from 10 March 1606 to 9 December 1606, with Arthur Chambers as master and Roger Bamford as purser. The examination of Bamford on 3 September 1607 (*NAW*, III, 397–402; briefly extracted on pp. 328–9 below) reveals that the voyage beginning only in June, was mismanaged to his own benefit by Chambers who proceeded incredibly slowly to the southwest, embezzling the ship's stores as he went. In the meantime the promoters had approached or been approached by Sir Ralph Bingley, a soldier serving in Ireland, to join the venture to one he was promoting there (under, we surmise, the protection of Sir Arthur Chichester, lord deputy of Ireland). Consequently in the passport of 28 May 1606 for the *Triall* to make a voyage to Virginia 'to search for new trades' Bingley was named captain, with Chambers as master. Bingley had evidently come to London to make final arrangements for the conjunction of the two enterprises. On his way back he collected some men to bring to Ireland to serve on the voyage and persuaded Rowland Bulkeley of Beaumaris to accompany him to Ireland where he was assembling a squadron for a Virginia voyage. Lying off Drogheda, Bulkeley found the vessels to consist of *Dragon* (300–400 tons), Sir John Ferne, owner, *Greyhound* of Bridgwater (200 tons), Henry Thynne, owner and captain, and *Triall* (160 tons), Sir Ralph Bingley captain, Arthur Chambers, master. This was in late July or August. Before October Bingley had in practice abandoned the Virginia enterprise, and his squadron dispersed, except for the *Triall* and Bulkeley's pinnace. After some misadventures the ships reached Kinsale before the end of 1606 (protests against the misuse of the *Triall* having reached London in October and proceedings begun to recover the ship). In December Bingley was associating with known pirates on the south coast of Ireland, but when he sent in a force to cut off and rob a small vessel in Cork Harbour on 20 December 1606 he still maintained he was bound for Virginia (p. 322). It was probably in January 1607 that Bingley set sail. His final apologia (pp. 329–30) maintained he was bound for Virginia but had to turn back through lack of victuals. Bulkeley later learned, correctly, that he had been accompanied by the notorious pirate Captain Isaack and sailed for the Spanish coast where they took two or three Spanish ships and brought them to Kinsale or other Irish ports (p. 327). On 3 November 1606 the *Triall's* owners had obtained an admiralty warrant to recover the ship and to arrest Bingley and Chambers: the recovery of the *Triall* was eventually secured but it was not until September 1607 that civil action was taken against Chambers, and Bamford was able to make his deposition on the sorry story. Before that, on 15 June 1607, Sir Francis Bacon had accused Bingley in parliament of committing piracy under the guise of making an expedition to Virginia and so prejudicing England's relations with Spain (p. 328). Criminal proceedings had been taken against him in the High Court of Admiralty in 1607 and Bulkeley gave his damning deposition on 29 April 1607, though in further proceedings on 25 June and 7 July Bingley was cleared of piracy charges, through the influence of Sir Arthur Chichester, and the connivance of Salisbury, Bingley was allowed to place on record a lying exculpatory letter to the latter, 5 April 1608 (pp. 329–30) putting his case for a genuine attempt at a Virginia voyage early in 1607, which was given over through stress of weather and lack of provisions, and this was virtually the end of the matter. Bingley was later to receive rewards of land and office from Chichester in return, with little doubt, for a share in the spoil. So it is little wonder Virginia, 'North Virginia' in particular, had got a bad name by the time of the return of the Plymouth settlers from the Kennebec before the end of 1608.

The Waymouth–Zouche Venture

11   30 October 1605. Agreement between George Waymouth and Sir John Zouche[1]

Articles of Agreement Indented made and agreed vpon the Thirtiethe

[1] Counterpart of indenture. Formerly in P.R.O., Gifts and Deposits, Duke of Manchester Papers, PRO 30/15, 2, no. 203; sold in New York at Parke-Bernet Galleries, *The American papers of Sir Nathaniel Rich, property of his Grace the tenth duke of Manchester*, 5 May 1970, p. 80, no. 60; purchased by Messrs Fleming, New York, resold to Tracy W. McGregor Collection, Alderman Library, University of Virginia Library, Charlottesville. Printed by Alexander Brown, *Genesis*, I, 32–5; reprinted by permission of the University of Virginia Library.

daie of October[1] In the yeeres of the Reigne of our Sovereigne Lord Iames by the grace of God kinge of England Scotland Fraunce and Ireland defender of the faith &c. That is to saie of England Fraunce and Ireland the third and of Scotland the Nyne and thirtieth Betweene the Righte worshipfull Sir Iohn Zouche of Codnor[2] in the County of Darby knight on the one parte, and Captayne George Waynmouth [sic][3] of Cockington in the County of Deuon gentleman on the other parte   For and Concerninge a voiage, intended to be made vnto the land commonly called by the name of Virginia vppon the Continent of America.

Firste on the parte and behalfe of the said Sir Iohn Zouche.[4] It is Covenaunted and agreed, That he shall at his owne proper Costes and Charges, sett forth two shipps fitted, prepared and furnished with all necessaries of victuall provision munition, and two hundreth able and sufficient men,[5] that is to saie of such trades and artes as are fitting for a plantation and Colonie, before the last daie of Aprill nexte cominge[6] after the date hereof. Item it is covenaunted and agreed that he, the said Sir Iohn, shall in present paymente give and deliver vnto the said Captayne George Waymouthe the somme of one hundreth poundes of lawfull English money within twenty one[7] dayes next after

---

[1] 'Thirtieth' and 'Codnor' inserted in reddened ink by Zouche. Waymouth had returned from the Maine coast three months earlier on July 18 (p. 301). Sir John Zouche of Codnor, a distant relative of Lord Zouche, lord president of the Council of Wales and the Marches since 1602, and probably a nominee for the Zouche interests and those who were backing them (the Zouches are not known to be Catholics but were themselves apparently acting as a front for some of the Catholic gentry formerly associated with Lord Arundell). For Sir John Zouche (1559–1610) see C. Kerry, 'Codnor Castle and its ancient owners', Derbyshire Archaeological and Natural History Society, *Journal*, XIV (1892), R. J. Burton, 'Zouche of Codnor', *ibid.* XXI (1909), 358; for Edward, eleventh Lord Zouche (1556–1625), Penry Williams, *The Council of Wales and the Marches under Elizabeth I* (1958), pp. 360–1 and Christopher Hussey, *Parham Park* (1950), p. 22, plates 11–12.

[2] 'Zouche' and 'Codnor' are inserted by Zouche himself. The insertions indicate that Waymouth's agent who drew up the draft was not certain of the names of the parties, or that it was intended to keep them secret from him. As this counterpart does not bear Waymouth's signature, it appears the transaction was managed for him by his representatives, William Rigges and James Rosier.

[3] Waynmouth, Weymouth, Wainman and other variations were used for George Waymouth's name (cp. pp. 58–62).   [4] Zouche again inserts his surname.

[5] The total costs of equipping 200 colonists for an indefinite stay in America and providing shipping and other necessities would be high, probably at least in the region of £4,000 to £5,000. Compare the costs of equipping privateering vessels in K. R. Andrews, *Elizabethan privateering* (1964), pp. 32–50. Colonising was perhaps twice to thrice as expensive in the initial stages.

[6] 30 April 1606, or a little earlier if possible, would be suitable for a voyage to the coast of Maine.

[7] The advance or earnest to be paid to Waymouth was thus to be delivered before 20 November 1605. The 'twentie one' is in Zouche's hand.

the date of theis presentes in Consideration of his travell and paynes
to be taken in and about the saide voyage and for his own Charge
defrayinge. Item that whereas the said Captayne George Waymouth
hath heretofore ingaged himself by band and Covenauntes, made
betweene him and William Parker,[1] Thomas Love,[2] [William] Came,[3]
and William Morgan of Plymouth[4] marchauntes to carry them with
their shippinge and provision (accordinge to the Tenour of such
Covenauntes of Agreementes as are made between him and them) to
the saide lande of Virginia, there to fishe, traffick and to doe what els
shalbe fittinge for a Marchantes voyage. He, the said Sir Iohn Zouche,
shall suffer and by all meanes permitt the said Merchauntes to make
their trade for what Commodities soever without anie hindraunce or
disturbance of his parte or any of his followers vnnder his Commaund
for the space of one wholle yeere nowe next Comminge, and not after.[5]
Item it is Covenaunted and agreed that he, the said Sir Iohn Zouche,[6]
beinge Cheife Commaunder shall allowe and giue vnto the said
Captaine George Waymouth the next place of Commaunde vnto
himselfe aswell at sea as at land. Item, if it soe please God to prosper
and blisse the said intended voiage and the actions of the same, that
thereby the lande aforesaid shalbe inhabited with our English Nation,
and according to polliticque estate of Goverment proportion of lande

<hr/>

[1] Captain William Parker of Plymouth, captain of the *Prudence* in privateering
ventures to the Caribbean, 1598 and 1600 (K. R. Andrews, 'English voyages to the
Caribbean, 1596 to 1604: an annotated list', *William and Mary Quarterly*, XXXI (1974), 246,
249). On 13 November 1605 Parker deposed in the High Court of Admiralty (P.R.O.,
HCA 1/46) that he built the ship *Prosperous* and later sold a one-third part to Thomas Love
and William Cann [Cam] of Plymouth. He made voyages with her in 1602 and early in
1603, and off the Spanish coast attacked and removed some provisions from a flyboat of
Rotterdam, bound with corn for Spain. He took her and sent her home. He was named
as one of the petitioners for the northern (Plymouth) company in the Virginia Company
charter of 12 April 1606 and took part in the preparation of the Kennebec River colony
of 1607–8.

[2] Thomas Love was a merchant and shipowner of Plymouth (n. 1), and was employed
by the town of Plymouth to go to London to discuss the affairs of the North Virginia
venture, so that he was clearly a subscriber to that venture (p. 384 below).

[3] This was probably the shipowner of Plymouth mentioned in n. 1. Thomas Cam,
who was master's mate on the *Archangell* (pp. 257, 261) may have been his son.

[4] William Morgan has not yet been identified as a Plymouth merchant.

[5] Clearly Waymouth had, when he set out in 1605, an agreement with a number
of Plymouth merchants to make a reconnaissance for a fishing bank or base, as well as his
contract with Sir Thomas Arundell to search for a site for a colony: we do not know
whether these were separate or combined undertakings. Zouche was prepared to honour
the agreement for a monopoly of trade and fishing with the Plymouth group for one year
only (which perhaps is one reason why the group combined with the Londoners in the
1606 Virginia charter and abandoned the Zouche venture).

[6] 'Zouche' again inserted in his own hand.

be allotted to such as shalbe transported thither to inhabit   That then after the said Sir Iohn shall haue made his choise and assumed vnto his possession in manner of Inheritaunce such quantitie of lande as the said Sir Iohn shall thinck good.[1] Then he the said Captayne George Waymouth and his Assignes shall and maie make his or their next choise of lande for his or their possession and plantacion. To holde the same in tenure of him the said Sir Iohn as Lorde Paramount which said lande soe by the said Captayne George Waynmouth to be chosen shall discend to his heires or assignes, or shalbe vppon reasonable consideracions to his or their vses imployed or disposed   And in like manner on the behalfe of the said Captayne George Waymouth it is agreed that he shall with his best indeavoure Councell and aduise, be helpinge aydinge and assistinge to the Said Sir Iohn for the furnishinge and settinge forth of the said voyage. Item that hee the said Captaine George Waymouth shalbe readye to goe with him the said Sir Iohn in the said voiage at such tyme as is lymitted or before, if conveniency shall require and all thinges necessary fitted in readines, vnlesse he shalbe by sicknes or other such visitation hindred   And that when they shalbe arrived vppon the land aforesaid, he shall with his best arte furtheraunce and indeavour, be assistinge to the said Sir Iohn for his plantation and fortification, and what els shalbe thought fittinge and necessary by the said Sir Iohn. And that the said Captayne George Waymouth shall not be aydinge and assistinge by person or direction to any other in or for the said pretended lande or voiage without the Consent or allowance of the said Sir Iohn.[2]

In Witness whereof the parties abouenamed to theis present Articles Indented interchangeably haue sett their handes and seales the daye and yeare first aboue wrytten.

Iohn Zouche[3]

Memorandum. Theise words by the said Sir Iohn Zouche were interlyned before the Sealynge.

---

[1] Zouche had no previous experience that we know of acting in a position of command, but he was determined to preside in person in the establishment of the settlement and have first choice of land for himself. His proprietorial plans were similar to those of Sir Humphrey Gilbert in 1582-3.

[2] Waymouth was to be second in command of the settlement and to have second choice of land for himself. His experience would be essential to the inexperienced Zouche. The last sentences tie in Waymouth in every way so as to prevent any independent action on his part. It may be that they proved too rigorous, as he appears to have retired early from the venture and somehow got out of his obligations.

[3] Holograph signature.

Sealed and deliuered in the presence of

| William Rigges[1] | Robert frayt |
| Iames Rosier[2] | Inno Sanger[3] |

12   19 June 1606. William Udall to the earl of Salisbury[4]

[Udall tells Salisbury that 'the secular priests and Lay Catholics' have offered James I guarantees of their loyalty and of their anxiety to have the Jesuits expelled from England.[5] He continues:]

The other offer, by way of Suite is That his Maiesty may be pleased to Graunt Licence to three Hundred Catholic Housholds at theyre owne cost & Charges, to depart this Land to inhabit Virginia to hold such part as shalbe allotted to them, for his Maiestie and his Successors, with and vppon such Conditions as his Maiestye with the Aduise of his Counsell shall sett downe,[6] so that they be not agaynst theyre Consciences, with this prouiso that no one Houshold shalbe admitted into that viage which is Conuicted and might thereby Hinder any Commoditye due to his Maiestye.... This 19 of Iune.[7]   Yours Honors most Deuoted

William Vdall

[1] William Rigges was apparently acting for Waymouth (and could have been a lawyer), but has not been identified.

[2] James Rosier, acting for Waymouth. This is his only known signature. Whether his account of the 1605 voyage was published before or after this indenture was completed is not known. If it was after, it is perhaps surprising that it did not make a direct appeal for support for Zouche.

[3] The last two names apparently sign as Zouche's witnesses. Brown, *Genesis*, I, 35, gives the second as Timothy Sanger. The signature is indifferently written: the Christian name appears to be 'Inno' for John or Jonathan and the surname could be 'Langer', though it is more probably 'Sanger'. Neither has been identified.

[4] Manuscripts of the Marquess of Salisbury, Hatfield House, CP 192/96 (Hist. MSS Comm., *Cal. Cecil MSS*, XVIII, 13). Extract (a more extended version in *NAW*, III, 393).

[5] This may be seen as an indication of continued Catholic interest in an autonomous North American settlement, in circumstances when resentment against the Gunpowder Plot was just beginning to die down. It can plausibly be associated (but not definitively linked) with the continuance of the Zouche project, the delay in approving which may reflect continuing doubts about the wisdom of encouraging Catholic emigration. Even if no proof has been found that the Zouche project was still partly a Catholic one, circumstances would point this way in view of the letter.

[6] These conditions may point to those at which Arundell was aiming in 1605. They may well have included a willingness to take the oath of allegiance without also taking the oath of supremacy, which few could bring themselves to do as it involved a partial repudiation of papal authority.

[7] Udall wrote again to Salisbury on 28 June (CP 116/123, *Cal. Cecil MSS*, XVIII (181–2), *NAW*, III, 393) to say the offer 'the priestes and Lay Catholics' had made was now being sponsored by John Digby at Court (this was the future first earl of Bristol who

13   17 January 1609. Pedro de Zúñiga to Philip III[1]

They are likewise negotiating with the Baron of Arundell,[2] who is the one took the regiment to Flanders, that he should engage to go with 500 Englishmen, and with as many Irishmen to settle in Virginia, to fortify themselves there, and to take the necessary supplies, so as to put it in the best state of defence.[3] He has asked for two things: First, a patent by this king, and secondly, money.[4] So far they have told him that, as to a patent, they dare not give it to him, and as to the other, they have none.

14   13 August 1606. Charles Howard, earl of Nottingham, Lord High Admiral, to Sir Thomas Crompton, judge of the High Court of Admiralty[5]

Sir,

I have bene much laboured to geve Sir Iohn Zouch leave to passe away with his shippes in his intended voyage for Virginea, whome for some private ressons knowne to myselfe I have thought good to staye. And now being sattisfied in some things whereof I stood before ielous, I am content to geve him power to passe so that my Lord Zouch will become bound in a bond of a thousand pounds,[6] vppon this condicion

---

was rising in James's favour and was shortly after knighted and launched on his long diplomatic career, so that if he sponsored the Catholic request in 1606 it did not hurt his later prospects).

[1] Simancas, Archivo General, Estado 2585, f. 85; translated in Brown, *Genesis*, I (1890), 198.

[2] Lord Arundell of Wardour, There is no confirmation of this from any English source.

[3] It might appear they were being suggested for northern Virginia, to take over Fort St George and hold it against the French, if indeed there is anything in the story. Zúñiga may well have been ignorant of the evacuation of Fort St George.

[4] The suggestion that Arundell wanted a separate patent strongly suggests a North Virginia destination. A licence had been granted to Lord Zouche as late as August 1606 (pp. 320–1) and was not out of the question for North Virginia if it were not for the negotiations already nearly complete for the reorganisation of the Virginia Company and the vested interests which Sir Francis Popham, Gorges, etc. had acquired in North Virginia in the meantime.

[5] The original of this has not been seen, but is now buried in the HCA records. It was printed with the attached bond (following) by J. F. Jameson, 'Notes and queries', *Virginia Magazine of History and Biography*, XIX (1911), 195–6; reprinted *NAW*, III, 394. Jameson's reference was to an old numeration, not since traced, in P.R.O., HCA, Miscellaneous 1140.

[6] Lord Zouche relinquished his position as president of the Council of Wales and the Marches on 14 June 1607, but retained his position as privy councillor. He was evidently

that Sir Iohn Zouch shall not in thole discourse of his voiage comitt any act ether preiudicial to the State of England or dishonorable to the peace and amitie which His Maiestie hath now with forrain Princes: Thus having delivered vnto you my pleasure herein I pray you to hasten his despatching according to these directions. And so I rest your very loving frend,

Nottingham

At Grenewich this 13th of August, 1606.[1]

[*Addressed*:] To my very loving friend Sir Thomas Crompton Knight, Iudge of the Admiralty.

[*Endorsed*:] My Lord Admirall for takinge band of my Lord Zouche for the good behaviour of Sir Iohn Zouche his companye and shipps bound for Virginea with the band taken here and enclosed.

15   14 August 1606. Bond and obligation by Lord Zouche in £1,000 for good behaviour of Sir John Zouche and his two ships in their voyage to Virginia.[2]

The bond provides that Edward Lord Zouche of Harningworth, Northamptonshire, should be bound in the sum of £1,000 to Charles, earl of Nottingham, his attorney, heirs and successors, on behalf of himself, his heirs and successors to observe the conditions attached. 14 August 1606.

'The Condition of this obligation is such That whereas Sir Iohn Zouch

---

not sufficiently influential there to override the 'reasons' which prevented Nottingham, his fellow-councillor, from granting an earlier release to Sir John Zouche's ships. His wife, Eleanora, was a sister of Sir John Zouche of Codnor (who died in 1610), but they had lived apart for many years, though this did not prevent him from sponsoring his distant cousin's American venture. He was to be active in the council of the Virginia Company from 23 May 1609, after the Zouche venture had foundered. (Cp. G.E.C., *Complete peerage*, XII (pt. ii), 949–52, and R. J. Burton, 'Zouch of Codnor', Derbyshire Archaeological and Natural History Society, *Journal*, XXXI (1909), 35–8.)

[1] The long delay in permitting the Zouche vessels to depart for Virginia could have been occasioned by some opposition to their going now that the Virginia Company had been chartered (though an earlier post-charter permit had been issued, p. 321). It may also have been delayed pending a resolution on whether Catholics should be permitted to participate (though there is no evidence either way on their continued association with the project, it seems likely they were still concerned in the venture). It is clear too that Nottingham was concerned there should not be attacks on Spanish vessels by the intending colonists as Nottingham had been in Spain in 1605 and knew how touchy the Spaniards were.

[2] P.R.O., HCA 14/39, 239 (draft); also with the previous item from another copy.

knight[1] is licensed to passe vppon an intended viadge for Virginia with two shippes & a pinnace and their Captaines, Masters and companyes Yf therefore the said Sir Iohn Zouch and company or eany of them shall not duringe the said viadge committ eany acte eyther preiudiciall to the state of England or dishonorable to the peace and amity which his maiesty nowe hath with forraine princes in eany sorte or condition that then this obligation to be void &c.'

16   28 May 1606. Draft passport for Sir Henry [= Ralph] Bingley and Arthur Chambers to take the *Triall* on a voyage to Virginia.[2]

The earl of Nottingham, as Lord High Admiral, understands that Lewes Owyn, gent., William Lancaster, gent., William Angell and John Halsey, fishmongers, are the owners of a ship called the *Triall* which has been chartered to go, under the command of Sir Henry [= Ralph] Bingley, on a maritime expedition to the parts of Virginia to search for new trades (*pro navali expeditione ad partes Virginae pro novo commertio deligendo*), it being agreed that Sir Henry Bingley shall be captain of the ship and Arthur Chambers master. They are to be assisted and not impeded in their voyage. 28 May 1606.

[*Endorsed*:] 'Lewes Owyn Esquire William Lancaster esquire William A[ngell] & Iohn Halsey Fishmongers owners of the Triall [of] London of 160 tonne where Sir Raph Bingley Knight goeth Captaine for Virginia/Arthure [Chambers] master.'

The *Triall* and its Associated Ventures

17   3 November 1606. Commission for the arrest of the flyboat *Triall* and of Sir Ralph Bingley captain, and Arthur Chambers master[3]

[1] The long delay may have finally exhausted the patience of Sir John Zouche and his former partner, George Waymouth, while the Plymouth merchants were already busy in the North Virginia project of the Virginia Company at Plymouth. August was much too late for a voyage to Maine to be begun, and we can only conclude that the delay in receiving permission was fatal to the enterprise of which we hear no more.

[2] Abstract. P.R.O., HCA 14/38, 6. The existence of a draft is normally evidence that the passport was in fact issued. It may be noted that it was issued after the grant of the Virginia Company Charter on 10 April 1606 and before the similar passport, on more stringent terms, to Sir John Zouche on 14 August 1606 (p. 319).

The clerk was evidently incorrectly informed of Sir Ralph Bingley's name and gives it as 'Henry', although the endorsement, in a very similar hand, correctly uses 'Raph'.

[3] P.R.O., HCA 14/38, 65, draft (imperfect), Latin. Translated abstract.

The earl of Nottingham, as Lord High Admiral, issues his commission for the arrest of a certain ship called 'A Fliebote *alias* The Triall',[1] together with her captain, Sir Ralph Bingley, and her master Arthur Chambers, at the suit of Lewes Owen, William [Lancaster], William Angel and John Halsey, citizens and fishmongers of London, and that Bingley and Chambers shall appear before the court in the borough of Southwarke to answer charges made by the complainants. 3 November 1606.

18   3 January 1607. Richard Roche, sovereign of Kinsale, asks assistance in recovering a pinnace and goods taken by Sir Ralph Bingley's men.[2]

To all people to whom thease [presents] shall Com Richard Roche [Beynge] the Sofferainge of the Towne [of kensal] within the Realme of Irelaund Sendeth greeting. Knowe yee that the said Richard Roche [at the] request of Thomas Farris & Iohn Quyne of the Cittie of Corck and Richard Nagle of [the Cittie (?)] aforesaid marchauntes, Doe hereby testifie and beare withnes that vppon the seventine Daie of the moneth of December last past before the Date hereof one Sir Rallfe byngleigh of Flyntshire[3] within the Realme of England knight beinge att kensale aforesaid In a Shippe of his Called the Tryall of london bounde for the laund of Vyrgynia, and oute of the harbour of kensale aforesaid Certaine of the said Sir Rallfe his Companie to the nomber of eight or nyne men and a boy went in the longe bote of the Said Shippe into the harbour of Corck aforesaid three leagues distaunce in warlyke manner with armour and weapons and theire the 20th of the foresaid moneth of December haue taken a Pynnas of the bourden of seven or eight tonnes or thereaboutes hauinge abourde the said Pynnas, twoe pypes of Cannarie wynes, seven hocsetes [hogsheads] of gascon wyne, fowre hocsettes and one barrell of salt, a Trowncke, three Cheastes wherein there was a fedder bedde, Certain Woullen Cardes, a sute of apparrell, and other mercerye wares and goodes, beinge the true and

---

[1]   The vessel is cited by type as a flyboat in case her name should be changed in the course of the charter. Though technically a flyboat was a broad-beamed cargo-carrier of Dutch design, the term was used loosely in England at this time. No precise definition of contemporary English usage has been found.

[2]   P.R.O., HCA 14/39, 196. Copy of a circular letter sent by Roche, sovereign (= chief officer) of Kinsale. He had evidently recently succeeded Jeffrey Galway as Sovereign (*The council book of Kinsale*, ed. R. Caulfield (1879), pp. xxxi–xxxii).

[3]   It is worth noting that Bingley is described as 'of Flyntshire' and that he was then in his ship, the *Triall* of London, allegedly 'bounde for the land of Vyrgynia'.

proper goodes of the aboue named Thomas Farris, Iohn Quyne, and Richard Nagle aforesaid   And in takinge of the said Pynnas did wound beate and batter most Cruelly the Company of the said Pynnas.[1] And nowe forasmuch as the said marchauntes beinge the true owners aswell of the said Pynnas as Also of all the goodes and ladinge aforesaid, And nowe mynded to followe and poursue theire said Pynnas and goodes into Englaund and els wheare. I haue therefore thought good hereby to testifie the trueth toutchynge the Premisses. And also to praie and desire all and singuler his maiestes officers, mynysters and lovinge Soubiectes to whom itt shall appertain[in]ge to be as well ayding, healpinge, and assystinge the said marchauntes or any of them that so shall followe the said Pynnas and goodes to recouer & take againe the said Pynnas and goodes & enny parte thereof that they or enny of them shall so happen to Fynde as also to arest staye and ymprison the said malleFactours and euerie or enny of them to be fourthcominge to answer for so greate a myschyfe accordinge to equitie and Iustice.

In testimonie whereof I the said Soffreing of Kensale haue herevnto sett my seale of office and Subscribed my name the iij[th] of Ianuarij 1606.

Richard Roche
Sofferainge of Kynssall

19   29 April 1607. Deposition of Rowland Bulkeley of Beaumaris.[2]

Die mercurij 29 [Aprilis] 1607

Rowland Buckley[3] of Bewmaris in Angleseye gentleman aged xxiij yeares or thereaboutes sworne and examined before master Doctor Houe deputy to Sir Thomas Crompton knighte Iudge of the Admiralty as concerninge the viadge intended by Sir Raffe Bingley knighte and his associattes sayth by chardge of his oath, that this examinate at midsomer last came to Chester with a smale pinnace of xxx tonnes which was bought of master Banninge[4] of London with intente to make

---

[1] Rowland Bulkeley later described this seizure (p. 326).

[2] P.R.O., HCA 1/46, under date, taken in the course of criminal proceedings (not proceeded with), against Sir Ralph Bingley.

[3] Correctly 'Bulkeley'. He was evidently a member of the prominent landed and merchant family, Bulkeley of Baron Hill by Beaumaris, Anglesey, and was, perhaps, a younger son of Sir Richard Bulkeley (d. 1621) or other near relative (see Aled Eames, *Ships and seamen of Anglesey* (Llangefni, 1973), pp. 35—6).

[4] Probably Paul Bayning (d. 1616), head of the important merchant and privateering London firm (see Andrews, *Elizabethan privateering*, pp. 109—10).

a viadge in trade to the Indies for tobacco[1] and for that purpose this examinate came to Chester to buy iron ware at the faire there to cary for the Indies. And sayth that Sir Raffe Bingley beinge then in Chester[2] bound over for Ireland hired this examinate to cary him and his men to Ireland in the said pinnace and aggreed with him to give him xiiij pounds for his and his mens passage. And as this examinate and his men beinge fyve in number were on theire viadge betwixte Chester and Ireland in transporting over the said Sir Raffe Bingley & his men Sir Raffe advertised this examinate that he was bound for Virginia & had his shipping in Ireland appointed for that viadge[3] & so persuaded this examinate & his men that they consented to goe with him   And comminge into Ireland, there were thre ships in the bay of Tredath[4] called the Dragon of London sometymes the Bevis of Southampton[5] belonginge to Sir Iohn Ferne knighte,[6] The Triall of London belonginge to master Angell & others[7] & the Greyhound of Bridgwater apperteyninge to Sir Henry Thyn[8] which were appointed to goe for Virginia vnder the commaund of the said Raffe Bingley as yt was given out,[9] And within fore dayes after this comminge to Ireland as aforesaid the Dragon and the Greyhound wente away the one for the strayghtes [i.e. the Mediterranean] & the other for England as he heard. And

---

[1] Trade in tobacco in the Caribbean was beginning but was still mixed up with piracy against Spanish ships.

[2] If Bingley had been in London at the end of May, his appearance at Beaumaris with five men to reinforce the *Triall* would be intelligible.

[3] This is the clearest statement of Bingley's alleged objective, not only intending to take the *Triall* but other shipping on a Virginia voyage.

[4] The roads off Drogheda.

[5] *Bevis* of Southampton, alias the *Dragon* (300 or 400 tons), on West Indian privateering voyage, 1596–7 (Andrews, 'English voyages to the Caribbean', p. 245; Marsden, 'English ships in the reign of James I', pp. 315, 337, 339.

[6] Sir John Ferne of St Gabriel Fenchurch, London (Quinn, 'Voyage of *Triall*', p. 91).

[7] *Triall* of London, correctly assigned to ownership of William Angell and others (ibid. p. 87), rated at 160 tons. Andrews, 'English voyages to the Caribbean', p. 248, has a *Trial* of London (100 tons) active in the Caribbean, 1599–1600, which may be the same since ratings were often guesses.

[8] *Greyhound* of Bridgwater (200 tons) (Marsden, 'English ships in the reign of James I', pp. 321, 336). Henry Thynne, knighted 23 July 1606, second son of the second marriage of Sir John Thynne the elder of Longleat, later of Kingwood, Wiltshire (Quinn, 'Voyage of *Triall*', p. 91).

[9] A squadron consisting of the three ships mentioned, with Bulkeley's pinnace, would have formed a suitable force for a Virginia expedition, intended for colonisation, and equipped to meet French or Spanish opposition. It may well be that in June Bingley's plans were genuinely intended to bring an expedition to Virginia. If so he changed them almost immediately after Bulkeley's arrival, but no reason can be suggested. None of these vessels is known to have engaged in open piracy against Spain after 1604 though our information is still incomplete.

before there departure thence this examinate vnderstood by the master
and company of the Dragon that Sir Raffe Bingley was determined
to goe for the Abbay of St Nicholas in Russia to make spoile thereof
as they sayd was given out by one Captaine Hoorde who was the
plotter of that viadge as him self reported, and for that cause the Dragon
& the Greyhound lefte him the said Sir Raffe Bingley, and so this
examinate also intended,[1] and as he was goinge away in his said pinnace
Sir Raffe sente xx or xxx of his men on borde this examinates pinnace,
and deteyned both the pinnace and this examinate & his men beinge
six in number & would not suffer them to departe, but carried both
the Triall and this examinates pinnace to Clantarf poole[2] in the River
of Dublyn where the shipp was trimmed, and sente the pinnace to a
towne called Bullick or Bluicke,[3] havinge a smale creeke to be trimmed
& kepte there   And in this tyme, the purser of the Triall beinge Master
Angell his man made a peticion to the Lord Deputy of Ireland
complayninge that the tyme was expired for the which Sir Raffe had
hired the said shippe and that yt was not his masters intention the shipp
should be imployed further & desired that the shipp mighte be stayed
and Sir Raffe Bingley not to be suffered to proceede to sea therein. And
this examinate heard say the said peticion was returned to Raffe Bingley
to answere howe beit he knoweth Sir Raffe had vnderstandinge thereof
for that this examinate heard Sir Raffe Bingle [sic] grevously threaten
him the said purser called Roger Bamford[4] as he remembrethe, and
that he would hange him for yt, & from that tyme Sir Raffe kepte
the said purser as a prisoner & would not suffer him to goe out of the
shippe   And after the shipp was trimmed wente by lande to Kinsale
to one Captaine Isaack a pirate[5] who was come in thither and had
promised Sir Raffe moneyes to victuall him out as yt was reported,

[1] The dispersal of the vessels, the *Dragon* for the Mediterranean, the *Greyhound* for
England, and Bingley's alleged plan to make a piratical attack on Archangel (an absurd
rumour), together with the seizure of the pinnace suggests the abandonment of the original
Virginia project. Possibly support from intending colonists in Ireland proved not to be
forthcoming if, that is, it had ever been canvassed.
[2] Clontarf Pool, on the north side of Dublin Bay, where for a time the *Triall* also
lay.
[3] Bullock Harbour, Dalkey, co. Dublin, a small inlet on the south side of Dublin
Bay.
[4] Roger Bamford's petition that the *Triall* was being misemployed was probably
made in late September or early October, since by November proceedings were being taken
to recover the ship even though the time charter had not expired. Chichester, the lord
deputy, as Bingley's secret backer, was not likely to help.
[5] Captain Isaack, the notorious pirate, who was to accompany Bingley early in 1607
on his alleged 'Virginia' voyage. The other pirate captains have not yet been fully
investigated and they are not pursued here.

and gave order for his shipp & pinnace to goe about to meete him there, and as they were goinge aboute a storme hapned wherein the shipp spente her maste and putt into Waterford from where word was sente over lande to Sir Raffe Bingley, who togeather with one Captaine Swedon who was consorted with Captain Isaack came to Waterford, and having no other meanes to maste his shippe, solde this examinates pinnace contrary to this examinates will to make money to mast the said shippe & there this examinate would have gon from Sir Raffe Bingley but was kepte by his order on shipp bord & not suffered to goe on lande but was caried in the shippe to Kinsale where the said Captaine Isaack was, having in his company one Captaine Davis, and Captaine Thomas Coward, & Captaine Henry Duffeld Captaine Sweden & Captaine Thompson with many others to the number of xxx or xl men who had brought in thither a Frenche shippe with Spanishe woole and other goodes and had victualed out the said French shippe againe for a man of warre before this examinate came to Kinsale. And sayth that Captaine Isaack and the other Captaines aforesaid were full of gold and had xxv peeces of english coine very plentifullye And sayth that whiless this examinate was deteyned on borde the Triall aforesaid, Captaine Coward came on bord to Sir Raffe Bingley and tolde him there was a Dunkerker in Corck havon & wisshed him to man out his longe boat to take her, and there vppon the longe boate was manned out & one Arthure Chambers of London was sente captaine, & the said Coward, & one Captaine Rainbowe with aboute xxx men accompanied them to take the said shippe, And comminge to Corck, the said shipp which was sayd to be a Dunkerker, was an englishe shipp belonginge to master Sweete and was gott above Halebowlinge Forte that the said Captaines could not take her for feare of the Forte, And missinge theire purpose the said Captaines Coward Chambers Rainbow & the reste, saving nyne men & a boy, beinge the ginge of the boat, lefte the boate & wente overland from Corck to Kinsale and after they were gon, the said ginge or mariners lefte in the said boate tooke an irishe shipp of Kinsale laden with salte & six tonnes of wines sack clarett & white with certaine Trunckes with apparell which was said to belonge to Sir Thomas Roper, & caried yt into Siverne Water where they sold the said goodes & afterwardes tooke other barkes in Siverne, & robbed many people, as this examinate heard, & by a storme they were putte into Cardiffe, where two were apprehended & the reste escaped, As namely Richard Brian of Minied in Somersettshire &

Thomas Persivall of Clay in Norff[olk] & a boy called Francys were apprehended. Martin Chesshire of Eastsmithfeild Iohn Sloe of South Hampton, Xpofer Belman of Lyme, Iosephe Smith of Lyme George Goddyn and Iohn Battle of London, Iohn Swetemann of Dover were they that escaped. And sayth that this ex*amina*te before the sending of the said boate manned to take the Dunkerker as is aforesaid, spiinge his tyme when S*ir* Raffe Bingley was ashore at Kinsale at Captaine Henry Duffealds house, gott a shore into Kensale and the same nighte wente to Corck, for that S*ir* Raffe hearing that this ex*amina*te was come on shore, sente him worde to goe on bord againe or otherwise he would send some to carry him on bord, & then he would vse him as he should deserve & therefore fearing he should be forced to goe to sea with him he wente to Corcke & from thence to Dungarvan where he mett with the Irishe man who lost his barck & wares aforesaid called Richard Nagle who tould this ex*amina*te how he was spoyled[1] and from Dungarvan this ex*amina*te gott passage in a boate of Pattrick Gosse bound for Bristoll & having byn thre dayes at sea putt in with Ilfordcomb & puttinge thence to goe for Bristoll were driven to Cardiff, where the said Richard Nagle found his boate & the said Richard Brian and Thomas Persevall & the boy in prison, with whom this ex*amina*te there spake & they told him the names of the rest that had byn with them at the said robbery whom he knew for that he had byn before with them in the Triall as ys aforesaid   And sayth that of late this ex*amina*te mett with one Adam Duglas in Ratcliff, where he lieth at the Bell beinge a scottishman & one of the company of Captaine Isaack, who told this ex*amina*te that S*ir* Raffe Bingley with his company in the Triall consorted with Captaine Isaack wente to sea from Kinsale to the quost of Spaine where they tooke two or thre spanishe ships with theire ladinges, and haue sente them to Kinsale or some other porte thereaboutes[2]

And he also told this ex*amina*te that Captaine Isaack of late within this moneth pursued a French shipp into Falmouthe Havon & would have taken her there but that the Sheriffe of the Shire as he termed him gott a company of men togeather & reskued the Frenche shippe. And shortly after Captaine Isaack came ashore to iustify him self that

---

[1] This was the vessel seized by Bingley on 20 December 1606 as described by Richard Roche, pp. 322–3.

[2] Bingley's raid on the coast of Spain, in company with Isaack, was the aborted 'Virginia' voyage he later claimed to have made (p. 330).

he mente not to meddle with the said frenche shippe, & so wente a hunting with the sheriffe & lay at his house or a shore with him & the nexte day the sheriffe apprehended Captaine Isaack and an other Captaine one of his company & kepte them a day or two and then tooke two hundreth pounds in money of them & lett them goe.

Rowland Bulk[e]ley.

20   15 June 1607. Sir Francis Bacon's statement in the House of Commons[1]

Sir Francis Bacon, reporting to the House of Commons on 15 June 1607 on the complaints of English merchants against Spanish interference with their trade and cruel treatment of individuals, and counter complaints of the Spanish ambassador about English piratical activities, said 'the offences and scandals of some had made this point worse then it was; in regard that this very last voyage to Virginia, intended for trade and plantation where the Spaniard has no people nor possession, is already become infamed for piracy: Witness Bingley, who first insinuating his purpose to be an actor in that worthy action of enlarging trades and plantations, is become a pirate, and hath been so pursued as his ship is taken to Ireland, though his person is not in hold.'[2]

21   13 September 1607. Deposition by Roger Bamford on the abortive voyage of the *Triall* to Virginia, 1606–7[3]

[1] James Spedding, *Letters and life of Sir Francis Bacon*, III (1868), 353–4; J. F. Stock, *Proceedings and debates of the British parliaments respecting North America*, I (1924), 8–18; brief summary and modernised quotation.

Bingley, a *protégé* of Sir Arthur Chichester, lord deputy of Ireland, had apparently some standing in England or Bacon would scarcely have referred to him in these terms.

Bacon's speech was noted in general terms in *The parliamentary diary of Robert Bowyer*, ed. D. H. Willson (1931), p. 336. The issue arose at a very awkward time in the English government's relations with Spain over access to the Indies and, indeed, to Virginia in particular (see Quinn, 'James I and the beginnings of empire in America', *Journal of Imperial and Commonwealth History*, II (1974), 135–52, and pp. 355–6 below).

[2] This is the only evidence that the voyage was intended for plantation and not merely trade and fishing. It is still impossible to tell from the surviving evidence how far the initial plans went beyond the immediate objectives of the London fishmongers.

[3] P.R.O. HCA 24/72, 97, interrogatories; HCA 13/9, 3 September 1607, deposition. The long deposition by Roger Bamford, purser of the *Triall*, is printed in full in *NAW*, III, 397–402, and is here only briefly summarised. It is somewhat disingenuous as he does not indicate that at Dublin Bingley took over the ship in spite of his protests and that Chambers agreed to take her to Kinsale before she was dismasted. Nor is he specific either about what happened at Kinsale and Cork (as Rowland Bulkeley testified), nor does he state how the ship was recovered and brought back to London. The explanation here is, probably, that civil damages were being sought against Chambers and that criminal acts were being glossed over. Bamford's own defence of his owners' ship was, probably, also somewhat intermittent. The deposition forms the core of Quinn, 'The voyage of *Triall* 1606–1607: an abortive Virginia venture', *American Neptune*, XXXI (1971), 85–103.

Roger Bamford, servant of William Angell, deposed that the ship *Triall* (160 tons), owned by Lewes Owen, William Lancaster, William Angell and John Halseye of London, fishmongers, was chartered to 'George Kennethorpe and others intending a viadge for Virginia' for nine months from 10 March 1606 at £30 a month, Arthur Chambers of London fishmonger, to be master. Delays prevented the ship leaving the Thames until June, and further delays occurred at the Downs, so that it was July before she entered Weymouth (Chambers being accused of misappropriating some of her provisions). She made her way to Irish waters eventually anchoring at 'the Poole of Glamtath' (Clontarf, Dublin Bay). From there she sailed for Kinsale on the south coast of Ireland where she was to pick up her captain, Ralph Bingley. She lost masts and rigging off Pwllheli and limped to Waterford for repairs. Bingley joined her there but fell out with Chambers, though, since her men refused to sail without her master, this was glossed over. She was at Kinsale at the end of the year [after her charter had expired] and from there 'went to sea one viadge & returned to Baltimore' (elsewhere referring to 'one viadge to the quost of Spaine'). Her owners began proceedings for her recovery, Bamford admitting that 'the said Arthur Chambers both [before] the expiration of the nine menethes & after did well knowe that the viadge intended for Virginia could not be performed Fo[rasmuch] that there was not victualle & other provision for the viadge [which] could not be provided'.

22   5 April 1608. Sir Ralph Bingley to the earl of Salisbury[1]

I knowe that my doinges at sea have bein lykwyse made verie odious to your lordship good my lord geive me leave to set them downe unto you fullie, and trulie, for a more honorable Iudge I cannot fynde.

First when throughe a most terrible storme I had beine tossd for vj weekes together vppon the coast of Spaine, all my lower Tyce of bere, and vj Tonne of water was leakt out, almost vij score men aboarde mee, & not above three buttes of drinke lefte in the whole ship, with a badd winde for England, In this distress I met with a smale barke that had in her some litle quantitie of Syder & water, which I tooke

[1] P.R.O., State Papers, Ire., James I, SP 63/223, 64, extract (*NAW*, III, 402). Bingley was first charged with piracy on the criminal side of the High Court of Admiralty (*Oyer et Terminer*) on 25 June and 7 July 1607, but by influence (and a gift to the earl of Nottingham), these charges were dropped on August 7 (HCA 1/5, 150; HCA 1/62, 29). He was supported by Sir Arthur Chichester, lord deputy of Ireland, who glossed over his actions (letters of 16 July and 6 August to Salisbury, *Cal. S.P. Ire.*, *1606–8*, pp. 224–5). He was not involved in the civil proceedings against Chambers in the Instance and Prize Division of the H.C.A., but he was challenged for damages in a case brought by French merchants in 1608 (HCA 24/72, 95; HCA 14/39, 149), and again supported by Chichester (*Cal. S.P. Ire.*, *1606–8*, p. 473). Finally he wrote this totally insincere 'vindication' to Salisbury who appears to have accepted it. The episode did not hamper his subsequent career in Ireland.

and gave the owners my bill for. of this if anie on complayne I knowe
he had neither Comission nor Cawse to doe it. Another time I was
forced for Savinge of my selfe & Companie when wee weare readie
to sinke in the seas/to possess a Frenche ship that I met with by chaunce,
close aboarde the shoare of Spaine, wheare wee weare seekinge out a
harbour after a great storme to save our lyves in, to them of this ship
because the men desyrd to be set on shoare. I gave directions where
they sholde fynde me out, and receave back boethe ship & such goodes
(which was onlie wheate) that was in hir, which I after performed as
the honorable Deputie can certefie your lordship which I doe here most
earnestlie protest on my fayethe and credit was all & everie jott of harme
that in all my voyadg I did at sea. Which if anie man can amplefie
with a larger relacion (most honorable lord) I am well content to lose
my lyffe.

When I intended first my voyadge to sea my thoughtes did soare
to highe to stoope at those base & forbidden baytes that Pyrates oft
are wont to byte at, And at my beinge at Sea, when that men did see
how my buisines was bruisde, & my voyadge broken, woulde I then
have changd my mynde, as my fortunes did change, I lackt no offers
that weare daylie presented mee by men of that qualletie whoe with
their shippes & them selves proffered mee their service, with whome
if ever I acted or plotted anie thinge save that tooke on of them in
Baltemore by order & warrant from Sir Harry Brunnkern the Lord
President[1] then let no man spare to speake, nor Iustice prolonge to
punishe....[2]

[*Endorsed*:] 5° Aprilis 1608. Sir Ralph Bingley to my Lord in his
iustification.

---

[1] Sir Henry Brounker, lord president of Munster.

[2] He is implying throughout, though avoiding to state, that the *Triall* was on her
way to Virginia early in 1607, when shortage of victuals and water prevented him from
proceeding with the voyage.

This evasive and lying letter tails off into incoherence.

CHAPTER VIII

THE NORTH VIRGINIA VOYAGES
UNDER THE 1606 VIRGINIA COMPANY
CHARTER: GENERAL ACCOUNTS

The charter of the Virginia Company of 10 April 1606 (preceded by the Chancery Warrant of 5 April) was the culmination of a series of events, of which the previous voyages to North Virginia formed one part.[1] The tradition of the Roanoke colonies, the revival of voyages to the southern region by Sir Walter Ralegh from perhaps 1599 onwards, the possible reconnaissance of Chesapeake Bay in 1603 (bringing rumours of Lost Colonists surviving nearby) and perhaps again in 1605 by Captain Newport, together with a sheaf of economic incentives, turned most of the Londoners to the southern colony, and so its organisation was centred there. The western adventurers, on the strength of the ventures of Gosnold, Pring and, above all, Waymouth focused their attention on North Virginia. Of the 'two severall Colonies and Companies' one was of Londoners and courtiers and concerned with land between 34° and 41° N lat. 'and the other consisting of sondrie Knightes Gentlemen merchauntes and other Adventurers of our Citties of Bristoll and Exeter and of our towne of Plymouthe and of other places which doe ioyne themselues vnto that Colonie' whose plantations and colonies were to lie between 38° and 45° N lat., the overlap to be provided for later. As usual in such charters the persons named as the petitioners were not necessarily the leading men in each enterprise, though they were persons intimately concerned with the project. In the case of the 'Second Colonie', as the North Virginia enterprise was to be known officially, they were 'Thomas Hannam [Hanham] and Raleighe Gilberde [Gilbert], William Parker and George Popham'. Each colony was to have a council of thirteen persons, and there was to be an official seal for the colony, in this case 'Sigillum Regis Magne Britanie Francie & Hibernie' on one side and 'pro Consilio secunde Colonie Virginie' on the other. (No record of its use has yet been found.) Over and above the two

---

[1] Edited versions of all the documents on the foundation of the dual Virginia company will be found in Philip L. Barbour, *The Jamestown voyages under the first charter, 1606–1609*, 2 vols. Hakluyt Society, 1969; the texts are in *NAW*, v, 183–232. An incomplete copy of the charter of 10 April 1606 and of the instructions of 20 November 1606 are among the Plymouth records, the latter being printed on pp. 390–6. Subsequent chapters will provide texts and annotations in detail: it should be noted however that the fragments which we have on the important Hanham and Pring voyage of 1606 are almost all contained in the general accounts which follow, pp. 342–3, 348.

company organisations and their colonies was to be established a royal council. Some of its members were officials who had no special concern with either company; others were, or were to be, prominently associated with one or other company. For the 'Second Colonie' the former were 'Sir Francis Popham K*night*, Sir Ferdinando Gorges K*night* Thomas James of the Citty [of] Bristol Merch*aunt* and Iames Bagge of Plymouth in ye County of Deuonshire merch*aunt*'. The royal council had the duty to appoint the councils in the colonies and to define, according to rules established by them on 20 November 1606, their duties and responsibilities. Moreover, for the first five years, the adventurers of the second colony were 'to elect and choose out of themselues one or more Companies [= Committees or Councils], each Company consisting of three persons att y^e least', who were to be resident at or near Plymouth, who were 'to take charge of the trade, and accompt of all such goods, wares, merchandizes, and other things, which shall be sent from thence, to y^e Company of y^e same Colony or Plantation in Virginia, and likewise of all such wares, goods and merchandizes, and other things, which shall be sent from thence, to y^e Company of y^e said Colony or Plantation, vnto y^t place within our realme of England [= Plymouth], and of all things concerning y^e mannaging of y^e affaires and profits concerning y^e aduenturors of that Company, which shall so passe out, or come into the place or port.' The Virginia Charter is cited from the Patent Roll (though a somewhat damaged copy remains at Plymouth), but the 'Articles' of 20 November 1606 are represented by a summary in Plymouth also. On 9 March 1607 additional members were added to the royal council, a group for each of the 'Colonies': 'Sir Edw*ard* Hurgerford [Hungerford] K*night*, Sir Iohn Mallet K*night*, Sir Iohn Gilbert K*night*, Sir Thomas Feake (Freake) K*night*, Sir Richard Haukins [Hawkins] K*night*, Sir Barthollomew Mitchell K*night*, Edw*ard* Seynior [Seymour] Esq*uire*, Bernard Greenville [Grenville] Esq*uire*, Edw*ard* Rogers Esquire, and Mathew Sutcliffe Doctor of Diuinity [Dean of Exeter] named to Vs, by and on behalfe of the said second Colony, Shall...bee Our Councill.' This is almost all we know about the organisation of what is generally called the Plymouth Company. The effective officer was in the case of each of the companies the treasurer, and in the case of the Plymouth Company, this was Sir Francis Popham. But so long as his father, Sir John Popham, lived (until June 1607) he remained the driving force. We might assume that the persons named in the charter and the two groups named in the documents constituting the Royal Council for Virginia would be, or were likely to be, members of the Company (Committee or Council) at Plymouth, but few have been identified so far as having had much to do with the North Virginia ventures. Of those who did, Sir Ferdinando Gorges was by far the most prominent. He had been teaching and been taught by three of the Indians whom he had had since Waymouth's return, and it is probable that the other two Indians were also put under his care when the Plymouth Company was formed. He took an active part in the preparations of the initial voyages, followed their progress, communicated with Lord Salisbury about them, and arranged for relief to be sent when necessary, though he did maintain in a legal case that he did so only as a member of the royal council and implied he was not a member of the local council. Sir Francis Popham does not, indeed, seem to have given full-time attention to the Plymouth Company. He resided for a time with Gorges in 1607, but he does not appear to have been present in 1608 when his presence was needed, though his father's death and the consequent diversion of his activities to the Popham seat at Wellington and properties elsewhere no doubt distracted him from the Virginia venture. We have indeed a mention of 'Commissioners' but much of the business may have been carried on at intermittent meetings of Popham with Gorges, Seymour and Sutcliffe, who are the only persons, previously named, who have been found to be active in the affairs of the Company in Plymouth, though they are likely also to have had a member of the Corporation of Plymouth present. Consequently, except for the impetus given initially by Sir John Popham (who supplied the ship the *Gifte of God* and perhaps other vessels), and the continuing support of Sir Ferdinando Gorges, the Company did not have much continuing direction. Thomas Hanham indeed appears briefly in 1606 but then retires, so far as we can see, from further activity in the venture (his journal alone passing to Richard Hakluyt).

The enthusiasm of Sir John Popham ensured the Plymouth Company was first off the mark in August 1606, but the faulty course taken by Captain Henry Challons in the *Richard* and his capture by the Spaniards in November lost them some advantage. The successful reconnaissance of Captain Thomas Hanham and the experienced Martin Pring in the months from September or early October 1606, onwards, and their return towards the end of the year, renewed Plymouth's advantage (since the London Company was not ready until December with its first expedition). The initial thrust appears to have been fur-trading, fishing and searching for metals in that order, but it would appear that Hanham and Pring brought information of French activity on the coast (from the Port Royal base) and so the 1607 preparations had to be at least partly military, a reason perhaps for the choice of the elderly George Popham (a grantee of the 1606 charter), an experienced soldier, as the first governor, and the decision to fortify strongly on the River Kennebec, chosen by Hanham and Pring as the best location for the first settlement, probably after some consultation with the Indians who knew the country. Agricultural objectives were marginal, though the assembly of naval stores (masts being a first consideration) and the building of ships (the *Virginia* pinnace) was to prove promising, while the collection of plants and roots of medicinal value or of possible use for textiles, and the search for minerals, precious or otherwise, were sufficient to provide some incentives, apart from the fur trade from which much was hoped (even if the English knew little or nothing of how to conduct it), and the possibility of exporting some of the Kennebec fish (sturgeon and salmon) which was so plentiful, as well as developing a sea fishery even if seasonal visiting fishing vessels, independent of the settlement, were likely to appear to exploit Monhegan and other islands.

The outline of the first stage in the colony is well known. Starting in reasonable time, if not early, the *Gifte of God* and the *Mary and John* left Plymouth on 31 May, making a landfall in modern Nova Scotia on 31 July, but choosing a site for settlement just behind Sabino Head on the Kennebec River only on 18 August. Between then and 8 October a fortified settlement was built and a limited amount of exploration done. The *Mary and John* was at this point sent home with letters, specimens of 'salsaparilla' (smilax) and milkweed (the down of which was considered to be a sort of cotton), and very few skins (since the season was wrong and the English failed to adapt to Indian methods of trading). The ship may also have brought back a few settlers (since the physician Dr Turner had come back to acquire supplies for his profession). She arrived at Plymouth on 1 December. If timber and furs sounded promising, the absence of any immediate tangible return was a major disappointment. Nothing further was heard until February. After the *Gifte of God* was unloaded it was intended that she too should return. But Indian rumours that there were prospects of French attacks (unjustified so far as is known) led to her retention as a guard-ship. By December, winter had set in severely: men were suffering hardships in their flimsy dwellings; the ship was buffeted with ice coming downstream and finally holed. This forced the president and council to take stock of their situation. There was too little food and too many men. What could be spared was given to the *Gifte of God* (an estimated six-week ration), some 30 or more settlers were put on board bringing her complement to about 50. She was carrying also 33 masts of white pine and a few staves of timber. Her Captain, John Elliott, and master, John Havercombe, were given permission to sell what they needed if stores were running short when they came to the Azores. They did so, disposing of the masts, three staves, a cable and leaving a cannon as pledge. They reached Topsham at the beginning of February and Plymouth by 7 February. The return was another disappointment; the settlers are likely to have given a very poor account of their situation; there were no proceeds. (Sir Francis Popham and his mother even took an action against the master of the ship for selling the masts and staves but the judge of the High Court of Admiralty threw it out.)

It seems likely that many of the subscribers of 1606 failed to pay their second instalments on their shares, but Sir Ferdinando Gorges and a few others used all their influence to raise money for supplies. In the meantime, the President, George Popham had died in February and command had devolved on Raleigh Gilbert (of whose irresponsible conduct Gorges had earlier received reports, true or false). A fire destroyed part of their storehouse and some of their dwellings so that conditions must have been very uncomfortable if not desperate. We have little knowledge of how they fared in the spring but the indications are that the Indians, during and after the hunting season, were able to supply them with some meat, and that trading for furs was begun on a satisfactory basis, though perhaps not on a large scale. When the thaw came some further exploration up the Kennebec river proved possible.

By 20 March Gorges had managed to despatch two small supply ships from Topsham. We have no indication when they arrived but it was probably some time in May. They do not appear to have found the remaining settlers, now reduced apparently to some 45 in number, in too poor shape, though we are unable to discover whether they were able to bring back any substantial quantity of furs received in trade. Further reinforcements, a 200-ton ship, the *Gifte of God* under Captain Robert Davies, was to be got to sea before the end of May but did not leave until July. Again her arrival date is unknown but it is likely to have been some time in September or early October. Once more conditions appear· to have been tolerable but somewhat static. When, however, it became clear that Raleigh Gilbert was determined to return home (his brother's death having left him head of the family and his brother's heir) the settlers refused to stay under another president. It might appear that the supply of furs had again dried up and few other prospects were in view – we cannot tell if the first two supply vessels made up a cargo of fish on their way home but they may well have done so. Fort St George was thereupon evacuated, and the survivors were back in England about November. The fact that nothing survives to tell us of their last days or the date of their return indicates the sense of failure the abandonment of the colony created. Early in 1609 the London company invited the subscribers to the Plymouth Company to switch to the Jamestown venture and some did so (with no more profit). Sir Ferdinando, with a small band of enthusiasts, continued to send exploring and trading expeditions to the New England coasts (1611, possibly 1612, and 1614), and Sir Francis Popham sent out cod-fishing vessels which used Monhegan as a base. Until John Smith took up New England as an interest in 1614 nothing substantial was attempted in exploration, while the first settlement had to await another half-dozen years.

The English were right, as Champlain had been, to concentrate on the fur-trading and fishing zone of New England. Southern New England was eventually to offer better prospects, indeed very fine ones in the end, but not while it was thickly occupied by sedentary Indian farmers. Lack of experience and persistence, as well as the drawing off of the furs of the interior Indians to the St Lawrence River marts, led the fur trade to languish (even if we may suspect that Gorges received some return on his money from it). The military character of the 1607 colony; its too great size for a trading venture; the slow realisation that agricultural production, even for subsistence, was likely to be minimal; the drainage of support from the west of England, all made its failure as a settlement inevitable. It could only have been sustained by mineral discoveries, or by official government support if French intervention took place. The English gained something from the Indians brought over in 1605. They did not deal with them very effectively in 1607, though they learned a good deal from them: they seem to have been more successful in employing them as intermediaries in 1608. The Eastern Abenaki they encountered showed a considerable degree of independence and were in no way subservient; they do not appear to have been greatly interested in absorbing European culture though they passed on much (most of which has been lost) about their own. Culture contact was indecisive, if to some extent mutually advantageous at this stage. The chief result of the 1607–8 colony was an extension of the exploration of New England, by penetration of the Kennebec River valley by a second European nation, and the enabling of the explorations by the English between 1602 and 1608 and of the French 1604–9 to be synthesized on the English map sent to Spain (the Velasco map) early in 1611 which we must reckon as the cumulation of nearly a decade's venturing.

23   1622. Retrospect by the Council of New England on the events of 1606–1608[1]

When this designe was first attempted, some of the present company[2] were therein chiefly interessed;[3] who being carefull to haue the same accomplished, did send to the discouery of those Northerne parts a braue Gentleman, Captaine Henry Challons, with two of the Natiues of that Territory, the one called Maneday, the other Assecomet.[4] But his misfortunes did expose him to the power of certaine Strangers, enemies to his proceedings, so that by them, his company were seized, the ships and goods confiscated, and that Voyage wholly ouerthrowne.

   This losse, & vnfortunate beginning, did much abate the rising

[1] The president and councell of New-England. *A briefe relation of the discouery and plantation of New England: and of sundry accidents therein occuring, from the yeere of our Lorde M.DC.VI. to this present M.DC.XXII* (1622), sig. B1 *v*. It may well have been composed by Sir Ferdinando Gorges.

[2] The council of New England had been constituted on 3 November 1620, and contained no less than 40 members. (C. M. Andrews, *Colonial period of American history*, I (1934), 322–3.) The pamphlet was intended to encourage projectors to apply to them for patents for land by giving some historical perspective on earlier activities (especially by Gorges whose creature the Council largely was) as well as providing a prospectus for current grantees.

[3] In the surviving 'Records of the Council of New England' (incomplete but representative), American Antiquarian Society, *Proceedings* (1867), 1–5, it is clear that only Gorges, Matthew Sutcliffe, dean of Exeter, and Sir Edward Seymour, of the old Plymouth group, took any active part.

[4] This is the first mention in print of which Indians were sent with Challons, namely Maneddo (whose subsequent fate is unknown) and 'Saffacomoit, a servant', as described by Rosier. Gorges later indicated that the latter, his 'Assacumet', had been by some means recovered from his Spanish captivity (Baxter, *Gorges*, II, 22). The place appointed as their destination was designated as 'Pama Quidda in Mayasho' (Pemaquid in Mawooshen) (p. 356).

courage of the first Aduenturers; but immediately vpon his departure, it pleased the Lord chiefe Iustice, Sir Iohn Popham knight, to send out another ship, wherein Captain Thomas Haman went Commander, & Martine Prinne of Bristow Master, with all necessarie supplies, for the seconding of Captaine Challons and his people; who arriuing at the place appointed, and not finding that Captaine there, after they had made some discouery, and found the Coasts, Hauens, and Harbors answerable to our desires, they returned. Vpon whose relation[1] the Lord Chiefe Iustice, and wee all waxed so confident of the businesse, that the yeare following euerie man of any worth, formerly interessed in it, was willing to ioyne in the charge for the sending ouer a competent number of people to lay the ground of a hopefull plantation.

Here vpon Captaine Popham, Captaine Rawley Gilbert, and others were sent away with two Ships, and an hundred Landmen,[2] Ordnance, and other prouisions necessarie for their sustentation and defence; vntill other supply might bee sent. In the mean while, before they could returne, it pleased God to take from vs this worthy member, the Lord Chiefe Iustice, whose sudden death did so astonish the hearts of the most part of the Aduenturers, as some grew cold, and some did wholly abandon the businesse. Yet Sir Francis Popham his sonne, certaine of his priuate friends, and other of vs, omitted not the nexte yeare (holding on our first resolution) to ioyne in sending forth a new supply, which was accordingly performed.[3]

But the Ships arriuing there, did not only bring vncomfortable newes of the death of the Lord Chiefe Iustice, together with the death of Sir Iohn Gilbert, the elder brother vnto Captaine Rawley Gilbert, who at that time was President of that Councell: But found that the old Captaine Popham was also dead; who was the onely man (indeed) that died there that Winter, wherein they indured the greater extremities; for that, in the depth thereof, their lodgings and stores were burnt,[4] and they thereby wondrously distressed.

[1] This usefully, if not specifically, supplements what little we have elsewhere on the Hanham–Pring voyage. It does not state specifically that they recommended a settlement on the Kennebec rather than the St George River, but this was almost certainly the case.

[2] The figure of 100 settlers given here would seem to be authoritative (cp. p. 353).

[3] We have no details of the dissensions at Plymouth consequent on Popham's death but the account of what follows is, it would appear, a fair one, namely that Sir Francis Popham continued to act as treasurer, though the main responsibility for the relief expeditions fell on Gorges' shoulders (even if he is not mentioned by name).

[4] The information that the store (though not necessarily all their stores) and some of their houses were destroyed is only given here. The precise extent of the loss is not particularised elsewhere. This disaster must have occurred after the departure of the *Gifte of God* in December 1607.

This calamitie and euill newes, together with the resolution that Captaine Gilbert was forced to take for his owne returne, (in that hee was to succeed his brother, in the inheritance of his lands in England) made the whole company to resolue vpon nothing, but their returne with the Ships; and for that present to leaue the Countrey againe, hauing in the time of their abode there (notwithstanding the coldnesse of the season, and the small helpe they had) built a prettie Barke of their owne, which serued them to good purpose, as easing them in their returning.[1]

The arriuall of these people heere in England, was a wonderfull discouragement to all the first vndertakers, in so much as there was no more speech of settling any other plantation in those parts for a long time after; only Sir Francis Popham hauing the Ships and prouision, which remained of the company, and supplying what was necessary for his purpose, sent diuers times to the coasts for trade and fishing; of whose losse or gaines himselfe is best able to giue account.

24 Extracts from Sir Ferdinando Gorges, *A briefe narration* (1658), on the New England voyages, 1605–1608

Sir Ferdinando Gorges wrote an account of his long-standing concern with North America only late in life, between 1640 and 1647, but his recollections of the early voyages are of value, even if he is sometimes inaccurate and does not give specific information on matters on which he had been well informed. His *A briefe relation* (1658) was published by his grandson, Ferdinando Gorges, as an appendix to his *America painted to the life* (1659). The earlier date attached to Sir Ferdinando's tract suggests it was originally intended to have been published first, but that his grandson then decided to append it to a rather lightweight, but wider-ranging work of his own. Gorges gives the impression that throughout he was the moving spirit in the 'North Virginia' ventures, 1606–8, whereas it is clear from the cases Popham *v.* Havercombe in the High Court of Admiralty in 1608 and in the series of chancery cases between himself and Abraham Jennings, 1608–15 (*NAW*, III, 442–64) that his involvement in the preparation of the Sagadahoc venture of 1607 was not very extensive, though he took on himself the task of reporting to Lord Salisbury such news as came from there, and implied that he was the expedition's chief representative at Plymouth, who in fact was Sir Francis Popham. He was, however, largely responsible for the relief measures of 1608. As he lived in Plymouth and the

[1] The account of the last period of the settlement adds nothing to what was available to Strachey in 1612 (pp. 414–15).

Pophams at Wellington and London, he was very much 'the man on the spot' and so could take more credit than perhaps he merited. At the same time, whatever his misrepresentations, he did pursue his interest in the area long past the period with which we are concerned and his perspective on the earlier period is of some appreciable value.

CHAPTER II.[1]

The reasons and meanes of renewing the undertakings of
Plantations in America.

This great Monarch Gloriously ascending his Throne, being borne to greatnesse above his Ancestors, to whom all submitted as to another *Salomon*, for wisedome and justice, as well as for that he brought with him another Crown, whereby those Kingdomes that had so long contended for rights and liberties, perhaps oft times pretended rather to satisfie their present purposes, then that justice required it; But such is the frailty of humane nature as not to be content with what we possesse, but strives by all meanes to enthrall the weaker that is necessitated to prevent the worst, though by such meanes sometimes to their greater ruine; With this Union there was also a generall peace concluded between the State, and the King of *Spaine*, the then onely enemy of our Nation and Religion, whereby our Men of war by Sea and Land were left destitute of all hope of imployment under their owne Prince; And therefore there was liberty given to them (for preventing other evils) to be entertained as Mercenaries under what Prince or State they pleased; A liberty granted upon shew of reason, yet of a dangerous consequence, when our friends and Allyes that had long travelled with us in one and the fame quarrell, should now finde our swords sharpned as well against, as for them; Howsoever reason of State approved thereof, the World forbore not to censure it as their affections led them, others grew jealous what might be the issue, especially when it was found that by such liberty the sword was put into their hands, the Law had prohibited them the use; Some there were not liking to be servants to forreigne States, thought it better became them to put in practice the reviving resolution of those free Spirits, that rather chose to spend

---

[1] Sir Ferdinando Gorges, *A briefe narration of the original undertakings of the advancement of plantations into the parts of America. Especially showing the beginning, progress and continuance of that of New-England* (1658). Extracts. Pp. 2–9.

339

themselves in seeking a new World, then servilely to be hired but as Slaughterers in the quarrels of Strangers;[1] This resolution being stronger then their meanes to put it into execution, they were forced to let it rest as a dreame, till God should give the meanes to stir up the inclination of such a power able to bring it to life; And so it pleased our great God that there hapned to come into the harbour of *Plymouth* (where I then commanded) one Captain *Waymouth* that had been imployed by the Lord *Arundell* of *Warder* for the discovery of the North-west passage.[2]

But falling short of his Course, hapned into a River on the Coast of *America*, called *Pemmaquid*, from whence he brought five of the Natives, three of whose names were *Manida*, *Skettwarroes*, and *Tasquantum*, whom I seized upon;[3] they were all of one Nation, but of severall parts, and severall Families; This accident must be acknowledged the meanes under God of putting on foote, and giving life to all our Plantations, as by the ensuing discourse will manifestly appeare.

CHAPTER III.

Of the use I made of the Natives.

After I had those people sometimes in my Custody, I observed in them an inclination to follow the example of the better sort; And in all their carriages manifest shewes of great civility farre from the rudenesse of our common people; And the longer I conversed with them, the better hope they gave me of those parts where they did inhabit, as proper

[1] Sir Ferdinando remained resolutely anti-Spanish and resented particularly the formation of an English regiment to fight on the side of the Archdukes and Philip III after the peace (and of which Lord Arundell was the first commander) when Tristram Winslade's scheme for Catholic ex-soldiers broke down. He may not have resented so much the employment of English regiments on the side of the United Provinces. His emphasis on the effects of the ending of war on the willingness (or even anxiety) of former soldiers to take their chance in North America is of interest. The Sagadahoc and Jamestown colonists of 1607 were both predominantly composed of men who had recently been discharged from one army or another.

[2] Gorges is confused. Waymouth had gone to search for the Northwest Passage in 1602: his voyage in 1605 had nothing to do with it. The 'river of Pemmaquid' which follows is not the St George River, but the area around Pemaquid Point with which direct contact was only made in 1606. The names of the men taken by Waymouth are discussed above. It does not emerge elsewhere that they were members of several bands and not that of Pemaquid only.

[3] The 'seizure' of the three Indians is inexplicable, since what authority could Gorges as commander of Plymouth Fort have to take men brought by Waymouth to England? Either he enticed them by bribes or else he bought them from Waymouth (who kept quiet about the transaction).

for our uses, especially when I found what goodly Rivers, stately Islands, and safe harbours those parts abounded with, being the speciall marks I levelled at as the onely want our Nation met with in all their Navigations along that Coast, and having kept them full three yeares. I made them able to set me downe what great Rivers ran up into the Land, what Men of note were seated on them, what power they were of, how allyed, what enemies they had, and the like of which in his proper place.[1]

CHAPTER IV.

Captain Henry Challoung sent to make his residence in the Countrey till supplyes came.

Those credible informations the Natives had given me of the condition and state of their Countrey, made me send away[2] a Ship furnished with Men and all necessaries, provisions convenient for the service intended under the command of Captain *Henry Challoung*, a gentleman of a good Family, industrious, and of fair condition, to whom I gave such directions, and instructions for his better direction as I knew proper for his use, and my satisfaction, being grounded upon the information I had of the Natives, sending two of them with him to aver the same, Binding both the Captain his Master, and company strictly to follow it; Or to expect the miscarriage of the Voyage to be laid unto their Charge, Commanding them by all meanes to keep the northerly gage, as high as Cape Britton, till they had discovered the Maine, and then to beate it up to the Southward, as the Coast tended, till they found by the Natives they were neer the place they were assigned unto; Though this were a direction contrary to the opinion of our best Sea-men of these times; yet I knew many reasons perswading me thereunto, as well as for that I understood the Natives themselves to be exact Pilots for that Coast, having been accustomed to frequent the same, both as Fishermen and in passing along the shoare to seek their enemies, that

---

[1] This would appear to make Gorges the inspiration of the document 'The description of the country of Mawooshen' (pp. 470–6 below), and it may be true, but he would need someone with linguistic knowledge, such as Rosier possessed, to work out the complexities of the Eastern Abenaki territory in English. He is wrong about the 'three years' and 'Tasquantum' was not one of those he obtained in 1605. Both those named 'Manida' and 'Skettwarros' left England in 1606 or 1607. Tasquantum did not come until 1614.

[2] Gorges takes sole credit for the inception of the voyage of Henry Challons in the *Richard*, but the expedition was fitted out by the Plymouth Company, primarily under the supervision of Francis Popham.

341

dwelt to the Northward of them; But it is not in the wit of Man to prevent the providence of the most High.

For this Captain being some 100 leagues of the Island of *Canara*, fell sick of a Feaver, and the windes being Westerly, his company shaped their course for the *Indies*, and coming to *St. John De Porteriko*, the Captain himselfe went a shoare for the recovery of his health, whiles the Company took in water, and such other provision as they had present use of, expending some time there, hunting after such things as best pleased themselves; That ended, they set their course to fall with their owne height they were directed unto; By which meanes they met the *Spanish* Fleet that came from *Havana*, by whom they were taken and carried into *Spaine*, where their Ship and goods were confiscate, themselves made Prisoners, the voyage overthrowne, and both my Natives lost; Thus[1] the gaine of their breach of Order, which afterwards observed, brought all our Shippes to their desired Ports; The affliction of the Captain and his Company put the Lord Chief Justice *Popham* to charge, and my selfe to trouble in procuring their liberties, which was not suddainly obtained.

CHAPTER V.

The Lord Chief Justice dispatching Captaine Prin *from* Bristoll
for the supply of Captaine Challounge.

Shortly upon my sending away of Captaine *Challounge*, it pleased the Lord Chiefe Justice[2] according to his promise to dispatch Captain *Prin* from *Bristoll*, with hope to have found Captaine *Challounge*, where by his instructions he was assigned, who observing the same, happily arrived there, but not hearing by any meanes what became of him, after he had made a perfect discovery of all those Rivers and Harbours he was informed of by his instructions, (the season of the yeare requiring his return), brings with him the most exact discovery of that Coast that ever came to my hands since, and indeed he was the best able to performe it of any I met withall to this present,[3] which with

---

[1] Misprinted 'this'?

[2] Gorges here gives credit to Sir John Popham for the rapid follow-up of the Challons expedition. He does not mention that Thomas Hanham (for whom see p. 76, his father was Popham's daughter's husband) commanded the vessel and was accompanied by Martin Pring as master. The information that the expedition started from Bristol does not appear elsewhere; by this time, however, the City of Bristol had begun to subscribe to the Plymouth Company (pp. 381–3).

[3] These tantalizing references indicate how valuable the Hanham journal would have proved had it survived.

his relation of the Country, wrought such an impression in the Lord Chiefe Justice, and us all that were his associates, that (notwithstanding our first disaster) we set up our resolutions to follow it with effect, and that upon better grounds, for as yet, our authority was but in motion.

CHAPTER VI.

Of his Lordships care in procuring his MAJESTIES *Authority for setling two* COLONIES.[1]

In this Interim his Lordship failed not to interest many of the Lords and others to be Petitioners to his MAJESTY for his Royall Authority, for setling two Plantations upon the coasts of *America*, by the names of the *First* and *Second* Colonie; the first to be undertaken by certaine Noble Men, Knights, Gentlemen, and Merchants in and about the City of *London*; the second by certaine Knights, Gentlemen, and Merchants in the western parts: This being obtained, theirs of *London* made a very hopefull entrance into their designe, sending away under the command of Sir *Thomas Gates*, Sir *George Summers*, and many other Gentlemen of quality, a very great and hopefull Plantation to repossesse the parts of *Virginia*, Sir *Thomas Gates* hapily arrived in the Bay of *Jessipiock*, in which navigation Sir *George Summers* unhapily cast away his Ship upon the Islands of *Bermathaes*, since called the *Summer Islands*, in memory of him that deserved the honour for the great paines, care, and industry he used out of the carkasse of his wracked Ship, to build a New Barque sufficient for the transportation of himselfe, distressed company, and provision to finde out Sir *Thomas Gates* who timely arrived to the wonder of the rest of his consorts.[2]

CHAPTER VII.

The dispatch of the first Plantation, for the second Colonie sent from Plymouth.

By the same Authority all things fully agreed upon between both the Colonies the Lord cheife justice his friends and associates of the West Country, sent from Plymouth Captain Popham as president for that imployment with Captain Rawley Gilbert, and divers other Gentlemen

---

[1] The retrospect on the Virginia Company is simply wrong. The charter was granted before the Challons and Hanham–Pring voyages, which were both the product of the Plymouth Company ('the Second Colony' as he calls it).
[2] The Gates expedition was of course the fourth not the first to 'South Virginia'.

of note in three saile of ships with 100. land-men, for the seizing such a place as they were directed unto by the counsell of that Colonie, who departed from the coast of England the one and thirtieth day of May, Anno 1607.[1] and arrived at their Rendezvouz the 8th of August[2] following; as soone as the President had taken notice of the place, and given order for landing the provisions, he dispatcht away Captain Gilbert with Skitwarres his guide[3] for the through discovery of the rivers and habitations of the Natives, by whom he was brought to severall of them where he found civill entertainment, and kind respects far from brutish or Savage natures, so as they suddainely became familiar friends, especially by the meanes of Dehamda, and Skitwarres, who had been in England, Dehamda being sent by the Lord cheife justice with Captain Prin[4] and Skitwarres by me in company, so as the President was earnestly intreated by Sassenow,[5] Aberemet,[6] and others the principall Sagamores (as they call their great Lords) to go to the Bashabas, who it seemes was their King, and held a State agreeable, expecting that all strangers should have their addresse to him, not he to them.

To whom the president would have gone after severall invitations, but was hindred by crosse winds and foul weather, so as he was forced to return back, without making good what he had promised, much to the greife of those Sagamores, that were to attend him.[7] The Bashabes notwithstanding hearing of his misfortune, sent his own son

---

[1] The Davies Journal placed the departure from the Lizard on 1 June, but departure (from Plymouth) on 31 May is almost certainly correct (cp. p. 417).

[2] The journal (pp. 425–6) makes the reuniting of the *Mary and John* and the *Gifte of God* take place at Georges Harbor on 7 August. (It is clear Gorges is using some documents for his brief account of the 1607–8 venture which are not identical with the others which have survived.)

[3] The use of Skidwarres (the Journal's name) for this purpose is not elsewhere indicated.

[4] Nahanada, as the Journal calls him, was sagamore of the Pemaquid band of Indians of the Eastern Abenaki group: he had gone out with Hanham and Pring and had stayed.

[5] Sabanoa appears in the Journal as sagamore of a band inhabiting a district some way up the Kennebec River. He claimed to be lord of the river and had been involved in fighting with the Pemaquid band though he afterwards made friends with them (p. 409 below).

[6] Abermot does not appear in the Journal but in the Mawooshen document (p. 471), but was probably among those who visited the colonists on either 5 September or 4 October, more probably the latter (pp. 311, 477).

[7] This attempt to make contact with Bashabes took place during the week 8–15 September, and its failure was significant. Bashabes had been used to Europeans and had traded with the French: had the colonists made friends with him, the outcome of the venture might have been different.

to visit him, and to beat a trade with him for furrs.[1] How it succeded, I could not understand, for that the ships were to be dispatched away for England,[2] the Winter being already come; for it was the 15. day of December before they set saile to return, who brought with them the successe of what had past in that imployment,[3] which so soon as it came to the Lord cheife justice hands, he gave out order to the Councell for sending them back with supplies necessary.

CHAPTER VIII.

The sending supplies to the Colonie, and the unhappie death of the Lord cheife justice before their departure.

The supplies being furnished and all things ready onely attending for a faire wind, which hapned not before the news of the chiefe justice death was posted to them to be transported to the discomfort of the poor Planters, but the ships arriving there in good time, was a great refreshing to those that had had their store-house and most of their provisions burnt the Winter before.[4]

Besides that they were strangely perplexed with the great and unseasonable cold they suffered with that extremity, as the like hath not been heard of since, and it seemes, was universall, it being the same yeare, that our Thames were so lockt up that they built their boates upon it, and sould provisions of severall sorts to those that delighted in the Novelties of the times, but the miseries they had past, were nothing to that they suffered by the disasterous news they received of the death of the Lord chief justice, that suddainely followed the death of their President, but the latter was not so strange, in that he was well stricken in years before he went, and had long been an infirme man.[5]

---

[1] The visit of 4 October was headed, according to the Journal (p. 413) by Bashabes' brother, not his son. We do not have any other mention of the beginnings of a fur trade at this time. Bashabes was not likely to have any great store of pelts for sale until late spring or early summer.

[2] Gorges admits he is relying on information brought by the *Mary and John* which set out on 8 October and arrived on 1 December 1607 and did not have any detailed account of the economic results of the whole period of the colony's existence.

[3] This (or 16 December) was the date of the departure of the second ship, the *Gifte of God*, from Fort St George, which arrived on 6 or 7 February 1608, and would have had full information on fur-trading if any had taken place in the previous October.

[4] There is much vagueness about what happened in 1608 which is not clarified here, Sir John Popham having died in June 1607 (cp. pp. 354, 378), not after the return of the *Mary and John*.

[5] We may well wonder why George Popham was selected as governor if he was in such poor health in 1607. See his letter of 30 May (p. 446).

Howsoever heartned by hopes, willing he was to dye in acting something that might be serviceable to God, and honourable to his Country, but that of the death of the cheife justice was such a carrasive to all, as struck them with despaire of future remedy, and it was the more augmented, when they heard of the [death of] Sir John Gilbert, Elder brother of Ralph[1] Gilbert that was then their President, a man worthy to be beloved of them all for his industry, and care for their well being; The President was to return to settle the state his Brother had left him, upon which all resolved to quite the place, and with one consent to away, by which means all our former hopes were frozen to death, though Sir Francis Popham could not so give it over, but continued to send thither severall years after in hope of better fortunes, but found it fruitlesse, and was necessitated at last to sit down with the losse he had already undergone.[2]

CHAPTER IX.

My resolution not to abandon, the prosecution of the business, in my opinion so well grounded.[3]

Although I were interested in all those misfortunes, and found it wholly given over by the body of the adventurers, aswell for that they had lost the principall support of the designe, as also that the Country itself was branded by the returne of the Plantation, as being over cold, and in respect of that not habitable by our Nation.

Besides, they understood it to be a taske too great for perticular persons to undertake, though the Country it selfe, the Rivers, Haven, Harbours, upon that coast might in time prove profitable to us.

These last acknowledgements bound me confidently to prosecute my first resolution, not doubting but God would effect that which Man despaired of, as for those reasons, the causes of others discouragements, the first onely was given to me, in that I had lost so Noble a Freind,

---

[1] For 'Raleigh'.

[2] Gorges sums up the causes of the break-up as (1) climate, (2) knowledge that their chief backer, Sir John Popham, had died, (3) the decision of their second Governor, Raleigh Gilbert, to return for family reasons. All these are valid: it may well be that the conclusive reason was that trade was not profitable, though we are told china root (smilax) and furs had been obtained in some quantity. But would the men not insist on leaving before enduring another winter?

[3] Sir Ferdinando's peroration is given to indicate how he saw in retrospect the earliest New England voyages and how he regarded them as inspiring him to continue, as he did until 1643 at least, to pursue a series of New England ventures, none very successful, many of them rather costly.

and my Nation so worthy a Subject. As for the coldnesse of the Clyme, I had too much experience in the World to be frighted with such a blast, as knowing many great Kingdomes and large Territories more northerly seated, and by many degrees colder than the Clyme from whence they cam, yet plentifully inhabited, and divers of them stored with no better commodities from Trade and Commerce than those parts afforded, if like Industry, Art, and Labour be used, for the last I had no reason greatly to despaire of meanes when God should be pleased by our ordinary frequenting that Country, to make it appeare, it would yeild both profit and content, to as many as aimed thereat, these being truly (for the most part) the motives that all men labour, howsoever otherwise adjoyned with faire colours and goodly shadows.

25 North Virginia Voyages, 1606–1608, from Samuel Purchas, *Pilgrimage*, in Second (1614) and Subsequent Editions.[1]

After this followed the plantation by the present Aduenturers, for the foundation of a New Britan Common-wealth: and the East and[f] West parts of England ioyned in one purpose of a two-fold Plantation in the North and the South parts of Virginia. Of the North part our Method requires first mention. Mawooshen was many yeers together visited by our men, extending between 43. and 45. degrees, 40. leagues in bredth, and 50. in length.[2] They found therein nine Riuers, Quibiquesson, Pemaquid, Ramassoc, Apanawapaske, Apaumensek,[3] Aponeg, Sagadahoc, Ashamahaga, Shawokotoc. Sagadahoc is in 43. degrees, it is a mile and halfe at the mouth, holding the same bredith a dayes iourney, and then makes a sound three dayes[g] iourney broad, in which are sixe Ilands: it hath two branches, the one from the Northeast 24. dayes

f. Their Patents Prescribe that they plant not within 100 miles of each other: & containe from 30. deg. to 45.

g. The Sauages reckon thus by dayes iourney.

---

[1] The first edition of Samuel Purchas, *Pilgrimage* (1613) did not contain the American material. It was obtained for the second edition in 1614 from Richard Hakluyt and was used in a highly compressed form (pp. 755–7). There were a few changes in the 1617 edition (pp. 938–9), but none in the final edition, 1626 (p. 829), which is used here. This appeared as what was in effect a fifth volume to his four-volume *Pilgrimes* of 1625. Unfortunately he did not develop his brief summaries of most of the documents cited in the *Pilgrimage* and they are lost (cp. p. 352).

[2] The Mawooshen document (pp. 470–6 below) covers the whole of the Eastern Abenaki territory which owed a degree of allegiance to a high chief, Bashabes, residing on the Penobscot. Purchas obtained the document from Hakluyt, but it was probably compiled in the first place for Sir Ferdinando Gorges (p. 341 above).

[3] The 1614 edition has 'Apaumensek'. There are some slight variations in spelling in the Mawooshen document itself, p. 473. The other details on the Kennebec River are discussed there.

iourney, the other North-West 30. dayes iourney. At the heads are two Lakes the Westermost 8. dayes iourney long and foure wide, the Eastermost halfe so large. This is Bashabaes his dominion. The Tarentines[h] country is in 44. de*grees* two thirds parts where the Sauages tell of a Rock of Allum, neere the riuer of Sasnowa.[2] Captain[i] Thomas Hanham sayled to the Riuer of Sagadahoc 1606.[3] He relateth of their beasts, doggs like wolues, of colours blacke, white, red, grisled:[4] red Deere, and a beast bigger, called the Mus,[5] &c. of their fowles fishes, trees:[6] of some Oare proued to be siluer.[7] Bashabes hath many vnder-Captaines, called Sagamos:[8] their houses built with withs, and couered ouer with Mats, sixe or seuen paces long.[9] He expresseth also

h.
Christopher
Fortescue.[1]
i. Tho.
Hanham.
M. Chalenge
made a viage
hitherward
the same
yeere, but was
taken by the
Spaniards.

[1] Nothing is known of Christopher Fortescue as Purchas did not print or retain his narrative. His expedition was probably made from Fort St George in 1608 and was a visit to the Micmac ('Terantines') territory on the Bay of Fundy. Sasinou was the Micmac name which Champlain collected for Little Manan Island near the mouth of the Bay (*Works*, I, 282).

[2] It is possible here that Purchas is confusing two similar but distinct names. There was an alleged rock of alum on the Sasanoa River, the modern Back River, linking the Kennebec River with Hockomock Bay and the Sheepscot River. Champlain had been brought uncomfortably along it (ibid. p. 315).

[3] Thomas Hanham and Martin Pring followed the Challons expedition in late 1606 to give help in establishing an advance camp or initial settlement. Gorges pays tribute to its success in exploration and it is clear the establishment of the Sagadahoc colony owed much to its reports. Purchas did not attribute the journal (which he discarded) to Hakluyt's collections so he may have had it direct from Hanham or from Gorges.

[4] Hanham is the only early writer to discuss the colours of dogs in this area. N. Denys, *Description and natural history of Acadia* (1908) has something on the Micmac attachment to their dogs and use in hunting. Driver and Massey, 'Comparative studies of North American Indians', *Trans. Amer. Phil. Soc.* (1957), no. 2, on maps 6 and 21 show them being used for food on ceremonial occasions, and their employment in fish-poisoning operations as well as hunting. G. M. Allen, 'Dogs of the American aborigines', *Bulletin of the Museum of Comparative Zoölogy, Harvard University*, LXIII (1920), 431–517, remains the standard monograph. E. M. Butler and W. S. Hadlock, 'Dogs of the northeastern woodland Indians', *Bulletin of the Massachusetts Archaeological Society*, X (1949), 17–35, survey the surviving materials.

[5] Wapiti or Elk, *Cervus canadensis* L., which is very similar to the European Red Deer, *C. elaphus*. Moose, *Alces americana* Jardine. The Sieur de Monts brought a female moose ('elan') to France in 1605 for Henry IV, and it remained alive in captivity for some time. See R. Le Blant and R. Baudry, *Nouveaux documents sur Champlain et son époque*, I (1967), 102. This is the earliest use of the Abenaki-derived word in English.

[6] Hanham continued, and possibly improved on, the collection of materials on the natural resources of New England, most recently demonstrated by James Rosier.

[7] No locations of silver or lead–silver ores in the area can be indicated.

[8] For the dominance of Bashabes see p. 106. See Snow (in *Handbook*, p. 140) for 'sagamores'.

[9] This is the earliest description of the Abenaki long house, with the framework of bent saplings, covered with mats. A length (at four feet to the pace) of 24 to 28 feet seems credible.

the names of their twelue Moones or moneths: as Ianuary Mussekeshos, February Gignokiakeshos, &c.[1]

Anno 1607. was settled a Plantation in the River Sagadahoc,[2] the ships called the *Gift*, and the *Mary and Iohn*[k] being sent thither by that famous English Iusticer Sir Iohn Popham and others. They found this coast of Virginia full of Ilands, but safe. They chose the place of their Plantation at the mouth of Sagadahoc, in a Westerly Peninsula: there heard a Sermon, read their Patent and Lawes, and built a Fort. They sailed vp to discouer the Riuer and Countrey, and encountered with an Iland where there was a great fall of water, ouer which they haled their Boat with a Rope, and came to another fall, shallow, swift, and vnpassable. They found the Countrey stored with Grapes white and red, good Hops, Onions, Garlike, Okes, Walnuts, the soil good. The head of the Riuer is in forty fiue and odde minutes.[4] Cape Sinieamis in 43. deg*rees* 30. min*utes* a good place to fortifie.[5] Their Fort bare name of Saint George. Forty fiue remained there. Captaine[6] George Popham being President, Raleigh Gilbert Admirall. The people seemed affected with our mens deuotions, and would say, King Iames is a good King, his

k. James Dauies[3]

l. Io. Eliot, G. Pop. Let. to S. I. Gilbert and E.S.[7]

---

[1] The two month names are not in Rosier's vocabulary. It might appear that Hanham compiled his own Abenaki vocabulary, or that he may have had Rosier's (pp. 310–11) and supplemented it.

Dr Philip Barbour writes on these words:'"Massekeshos", January, can be compared with Abn. *mekᵂasigᵂe*, "Janvier, lorsqu'il fait grand froid" (probably the lunar month 19 December 1606–17 January 1607 according to the then English calendar (–*keshos* [Abn. *kizws*] being "moon, month"). "Gignokiakeshos", February, seems to correspond to Abn. *names kizws*, "Fevrier, qu'on prend du poisson", namely the lunar month 18 January–15 February 1607.'Their year would therefore appear to have comprised twelve lunar months.

[2] The 1614 version is the earliest published account, brief as it is, of the Sagadahoc colony.

[3] Purchas evidently had a journal which he attributed to James Davies, and it has been generally identified with that in the Lambeth MS and also used by Strachey. Strachey, however, attributes it to 'Captain R. Davies' and incidental indications virtually establish it as that of Robert Davis or Davies (pp. 80–1, 401). The following few sentences are compatible with it being the surviving journal but they do not constitute proof. Purchas in any case is quite capable of confusing the two Davieses.

[4] Cp. p. 412.

[5] 43° 15′ N. This is 'Sinio-amis' in 1614. Cape Semeamis is discussed on pp. 407–8, 433.

[6] This is the authority for suggesting that the *Gifte* removed in December 1607 more than half of the original number of settlers, though a few may have gone with the *Mary and John* in October, since the total complement of the *Gifte* was only about 50. Cp. pp. 464–5.

[7] The authorities cited, the journal of Captain John Elliott, who commanded the *Gifte* on her return voyage (p. 462) and the letters of George Popham to Sir John Gilbert and to Edward Seymour, if it is he, do not survive. They presumably were dated on or about 13 December 1607 (cp. p. 452).

God a good God, and Tanto naught. So they call an euill spirit which haunts them euery Moone, and makes them worship him for feare. Hee commanded them not to dwell neere, or come among the English, threatning to kill some and inflict sicknesse on others, beginning with two of their Sagamos children, saying he had power, and would doe the like to the English the next Moone, to wit, in December.[1]

m.
Ral. Gilbert.
n. These seem
to be the
deformed
Armouchiqois
made in the
telling more
dreadfull.

The people[m] told our men of Canibals,[n] neere Sagadahoc, with teeth three inches long, but they saw them not.[2] In the Riuer of Tamescot[3] they found Oysters nine inches in length:[4] and were told that on the other side they were twice as great. On the 18. of Ianuary they had in seuen houres space, thunder, lightning, raine, frost, snow,[5] all in aboundance, the last continuing. On February 5. the President died.[6] The Sauages remoue their dwellings in Winter neerest the Deere.[7] They haue a kinde of shooes a yard long, fourteene inches broad, made like a Racket, with strong twine or sinewes of a Deere; in the midst is a hole wherein they put their foot, buckling it fast.[8] When a Sagamo dyeth, they blacke themselues, and at the same time yerely renue their

[1] This is the earliest material we have on the animistic beliefs of the Eastern Abenaki, but they did not differ appreciably from those of the other hunting tribes. The religious cults were maintained by the shaman of each band who was also often the chief (Brasser, in *Handbook*, p. 84). Tanto was evidently a Moon spirit, and the prophecy was evidently the result of contacts made in November 1607. The threat of the shaman (from which band we do not know) indicates continuing suspicion, evidently intermittently between August and October 1607, in the Abenaki contacts with the English, though this gradually appears to have broken down. We cannot say whether or not the sagamore's children died from poison (from the shaman), from disease contracted from the English or from normal causes. The second would not be unlikely as contagion could easily spread, for example, with fatal measles. The propaganda in favour of King James seems to suggest an elementary indoctrination programme as the colonists developed some knowledge of the language. Presumably the ethnographic material was in Raleigh Gilbert's lost journal. Cp. p. 352.

[2] These are Abenaki myths about their enemies Micmac or Malicite, the authority being, apparently, the Journal of Captain Raleigh Gilbert.

[3] The Tamescot was the Daramiscotta river, which joins the Kennebec from the west. Eckstorm, *Indian place-names of the Maine coast* (1941), p. 108; Huden, *Indian place-names of New England* (1962), p. 246.

[4] This sounds exaggerated. Oysters, *Crassostrea virginica* Gmelin do not now exceed 6 inches or the Northern Quahog, *Mercenaria mercenaria* L. 5 inches. Abbott, *Marine shells*, pp. 150, 162.

[5] The major storm may have coincided with damage by fire to their storehouse (pp. 337, 345).

[6] Our authority for the date of Popham's death.

[7] The hunting area for each family band appears to have been confined to a particular drainage basin of a tributary stream or a defined part of a major valley. Moose, caribou and bear were hunted; beaver, muskrat, otter and other small animals were trapped. See Snow (in *Handbook*, pp. 137, 139).

[8] The description of the snowshoe is valuable. Movement on snowshoes and by toboggan was essential during the hunting season (ibid.).

mourning with great howling: as they did for Kashurakeny[1] who died the yeare before. They report that the Canibals haue a Sea behinde them.[2] They found a Bath about two miles about, so hote that they could not drinke it.[3] Master Patteson was slaine by the Sauages of Nanhoc, a Riuer of the Tarentines,[4] Their short Commons[o] caused fear of mutiny. One of the Sauages, called Aminquin, for a straw hat and knife giuen him, stript himselfe of his cloathinge of Beuers skinnes, worth in England 50. shillings, or three pound to present them to the President, leauing only a flap to cover his priuities. He would also have come with them for England.[5] In winter they are poore[p] and weake,[6] and do not then company with their wiues, but in summer when they are fat and lusty.[7] But your eyes wearied with this Northerne view, which in that Winter communicated with vs in the extremitie of cold,[8] looke now greater hopes in the Southerne Plantation, as the right arme of his Virginian body, with greater costs and numbers furnished from hence.

o. Edward Hartley.

p. Other notes *apud* Hakluyt.

[1] The account of an annual mourning festival for their dead sagamores is not elsewhere recorded for the Eastern Abenaki. Kaskhurakeny may possibly have preceded Nahanada as sagamore of the Pemaquid band, his place being taken in 1606 by the latter on his return from England.

[2] This would be the Gulf of St Lawrence at the northern limit of the Micmac area (or possibly Lake Ontario?). [3] No such hot spring or lake is known.

[4] Neither Patteson (Patterson?) nor the Nanhoc River in Micmac territory is known. If Edward Harlow (not Hartley) kept a journal for 1606–7 it is not otherwise referred to, but it may be that Purchas is using a record of his from a later voyage (cp. pp. 476–80).

[5] Amenquin (as the name is there spelt) is recorded in Strachey as visiting Fort St George on 4 October 1607 and staying on when his companions left on 6 October (p. 413). His action in presenting Popham with his beaver-skin cloak demonstrates that he had previously traded with the French and that they had already expressed their preference for coat beaver (i.e. beaver already worn by the Indians, so losing the long outer hairs and leaving the close fur only which was used for felting). This left him with a sufficient covering, his breechclout. His gift did, however, clearly express his appreciation of what the English had given him. His desire to come to England is not otherwise mentioned. The information that a single cloak was worth £2 10s–£3 is of value (almost the only piece of economic information we have for this colony).

[6] From Cartier's time onward the debilitation of the hunting Indians after the hunting season was over and the meat consumed is a commonplace of French accounts of the St Lawrence Indians: it is the only early evidence that we have of this for the Eastern Abenaki.

[7] We have only one other piece of evidence on the copulatory practices of the coastal peoples (p. 279). If correct it was an astute observation, gleaned (possibly by Raleigh Gilbert) from intimate conversation with Indians (possibly the English-speaking ones from Pemaquid).

[8] Writing in 1614 Purchas could see no hope of developing settlement in North Virginia. Only with the publication of John Smith's *Description* in 1616 did any wide interest revive, though activity on the New England coast was not altogether lacking in the interim.

26 Purchas' omissions on North Virginia, 1625[1]

Reader, I had by me the Voyage of Captaine Thomas Hanham (written by himselfe) vnto Sagadahoc:[2] also the written Iournals of Master Raleigh Gilbert which stayed and fortified there in that vnseasonable Winter (fit to freeze the heart of a Plantation)[3] of Iames Davies,[4] Iohn Eliot,[5] &c. but our voluminousnesse makes me afraid of offending nicer and queasier stomackes: for which cause I haue omitted them, euen after I had with great labour fitted them to the Presse:[6] as I haue also done a written large Tractate of Mawaushen,[7] and the Voyage of Master Edward Harlie (one of the first Planters with Cap*tain* Popham)[8] and Nicholas Hobson[9] to those parts 1611. with diuers Letters from Cap*tain* Popham and others.[10] You must obserue, that it was in those times called by the name of Virginia, and the Northerne Plantation or Colonie.

[1] Samuel Purchas, *Pilgrimes*, IV (1625), 1837 (XIX (1906), 296). This is in some ways for us one of the saddest passages Purchas wrote, since the materials he did not print have proved irreplaceable, except for the Davies Journal in the Lambeth MS and as used by Strachey.

[2] The Hanham Journal has defied all attempts at discovery. Dene House at Wimborne was burnt in the early eighteenth century, and if a copy of the journal remained there it was lost then.

[3] Gilbert's journal would have been specially valuable as a picture of the colony from the inside and more especially as filling in the narrative from October 1607 to the departure of the colony late in 1608.

[4] James Davies is also cited elsewhere by Purchas (pp. 80–1).

[5] John Elliott's deposition in Popham *v*. Havercombe (*NAW*, III, pp. 452–4) is the only evidence we have from him.

[6] Purchas must have been pressed for space if he was going to complete his coverage in his over–large fourth volume. That he had prepared texts for the press shows he wished to print them: space was probably the over-riding consideration, but he strongly implies that parts of the journals at least would have made unpleasant reading, perhaps because they described the hardships of the winter 1607–8 in grim detail, though also because they revealed too much about divisions in the colony (even if he had already given George Percy's journal on the first Jamestown expedition which also in part made grim reading).

[7] Does this mean that he had a larger treatise on Mawooshen than the one he did after all print, or does it mean that he changed his mind and managed to include it in spite of this statement? (Cp. p. 30).

[8] Very little is known of Edward Harlow's voyage (p. 476) of 1611. 1612 is sometimes given for the date but Purchas should be authoritative on this. He implies that Nicholas Hobson accompanied him but this is not certain. Smith, *The description of New England* (1616), p. 46, gives some details.

[9] It may be that he is referring to Hobson's voyage in June 1614 for which Harlow appears to have compiled the advice given on pp. 476–80.

[10] Letters referred to above, p. 349.

27   John Smith on North Virginia.[1]

[1] Now this part of America hath formerly beene called *Norumbega*, *Virginia*, *Nuskoncus*,[2] *Penaquida*,[3] *Cannada*,[4] and such other names as those that ranged the Coast pleased. But because it was so mountainous, rocky and full of Iles, few haue aduentured much to trouble it, but as is formerly related; notwithstanding, that honorable Patron of vertue, Sir Iohn Popham, Lord chiefe Iustice of England, in the yeere 1606. procured meanes and men to possesse it, and sent Captaine George Popham for President, Captaine Rawley Gilbert for Admirall, Captaine Edward Harlow master of the Ordnance, Captaine Robert Dauis Sargeant-Maior, Captaine Elis Best Marshall, Master [Robert] Seaman, Secretary, Captaine Iames Dauis to be Captaine of the Fort, Master Gome [Gawyn] Carew chiefe Searcher: all those were of the Councell,[5] who with some hundred more[6] were to staye in the Country: they set saile from Plimoth the last of May,[7] and fell with Monahigan[8] the eleuenth of August. At Sagadahock 9. or 10. leagues southward, they planted themselues at the mouth of a faire nauigable Riuer, but the coast all thereabouts most extreme stony and rocky: that extreme frozen Winter was so cold they could not range nor search the Country,[9] and their prouision so small, they were glad to send all but 45. of their companye backe againe:[10] their noble President Captaine Popham died,[11] and not long after arriued two ships well prouided of all

Sir Francis Popham Treasurer.

---

[1] John Smith, *The generall historie of Virginia* (1624), pp. 203–4.

[2] Nusconcus for Muscongus Sound (J. C. Huden, *Indian place names of New England* (1962), 128, 153).

[3] Pemaquid, and variations.

[4] See p. 404 for the use of 'Canada' for this area, but this was a measure of the prevailing ignorance of northeastern North American geography.

[5] Smith is our main authority for the personnel of the ruling group in the colony, even for the description of Sir Francis Popham as treasurer (the organisation at Plymouth has never been satisfactorily spelled out). The council in action appears in Popham *v.* Havercombe. Popham as president, Gilbert, Gawyn Cary (modifying Smith), Robert Seaman (adding a Christian name), James Davies, Edward Harley, and one other, John Elliott, being present at a council meeting early in December 1607 (*NAW*, III, 444–54).

[6] Smith is not certain of the round figure of 100. Cp. pp. 337, 344.

[7] The Journal begins one day later, off the Lizard.   [8] Monhegan I.

[9] The impediments placed on the movement of the colonists by the severe winter (which also arrived early) is a point well made.

[10] If Smith is right it might seem that all these were carried on the *Gifte of God*, but some may well have come with the *Mary and John* (as we saw the physician Master Turner did, p. 334). If Elliott and Havercombe had so many supernumeraries on board it would help to explain why so much had to be spent on food in the Azores, but they speak of 50 in all which suggests about 30–35 colonists (p. 464).

[11] On 5 February, according to Purchas, p. 350.

necessaries to supply them, and some small time after another, by whom vnderstanding of the death of the Lorde chiefe Iustice, and also of Sir Iohn Gilbert: whose lands there the President Rawley Gilbert was to possesse according to the aduenturers directions, finding nothing but extreme extremities, they all returned for England in the yeere 1608.[1] and thus this Plantation was begunne and ended in one yeere, and the Country esteemed as a cold, barren, mountainous, rocky Desart.[2]

[1] This general description does not add anything to what we know from other sources.

[2] Smith's comment is significant. His own emphasis in *The description of New England* (1616) was on the comparatively greater fertility of the land to the south, from Casco Bay to the Upper Cape. However, Maine offered possibilities as an outpost against French intrusion (met by direct aggression later on by Samual Argall for the Virginia Company), as a fur-trading post (later posts were to be established, e.g. by the Plymouth Colony on the Kennebec), and as a supply base for fishing vessels. The lands to the south were undoubtedly much more suitable for colonisation with an agricultural base.

We may add what Smith considered to be advantages which might be enjoyed by his colony planned in 1615. 'The main assistance next God, I had to this small number, was my acquaintance among the Saluages; especially, with *Dohannida* one of their greatest Lords; who had liued long in *England*. By the means of this proud Saluage, I did not doubt but quickly to haue gotte that credit with the rest of his friends, and alliants, to haue had as many of them, as desired in design I intended, and that trade also they had, by such a kind of exchange of their Countrie commodities; which both with ease & securitie in their seasons may be vsed. With him and diuerse others, I had concluded to inhabit and defend them against the Terentynes; with a better power then the *French* did them; whose tyranny did inforce them to imbrace my offer, with no small deuotion' (pp. 45–6). This stresses a line of continuity from 1605 to 1615.

THE FIRST EXPEDITION TO NORTH VIRGINIA UNDER THE 1606 CHARTER: THE FATE OF THE *RICHARD*, HENRY CHALLONS CAPTAIN

The abortive expedition of Henry Challons in the *Richard*, 1606, which was captured by the Santo Domingo fleet in the Florida Channel, was the earliest to get to sea after the Virginia Company was chartered. It was unwise enough to take the longer southern route by Madeira, the Canaries, Santa Lucia (or possibly Marie Galante), Dominica, southern Puerto Rico and then through the Florida Channel. By 10 November 1606 *Richard* was in the Florida Channel and suddenly found herself surrounded by a fleet of Spanish merchantmen coming from Santo Domingo. She expected to be allowed to pass and her crew showed their English flag and produced credentials. When the Spaniards boarded they treated the English as enemies (the Santo Domingo merchants had lost many ships to English privateers, some of whom were still operating in the Caribbean), wounding several of them, dividing the prisoners between several vessels, and making for Seville. The fleet was scattered in mid-ocean and one vessel, on which were Daniel Tucker, the cape merchant, and three others made port at Bordeaux, and they were freed by French officials. In turn they had the Spanish ship arrested and tried (unsuccessfully) to use her release to get the *Richard* back from Spain (Tucker was finally non-suited on 20 February 1609). Members of the crew brought in the first ship to reach Spain were kindly treated by the duke of Medina Sidonia at San Lúcar, but were later taken prisoner to Seville, as were the others as they arrived. The *Casa de la Contratación*, to begin with, treated the matter as if the *Richard* was the prize of Captain Francisco Mison commanding the ship which made the capture. Challons, St John, and the two Stonemans were released on securities, the remainder were imprisoned. Tucker came to England and made a statement on 4 February 1607 which Gorges sent on to Cecil.

Salisbury was very conscious of the political implications of the case and was anxious to avoid associating himself with the Virginia venture. He was right, since already on 21 May 1607 the Council of the Indies (A. G. Simancas, Estado 843, under date, item 4), decided to use the treatment of English prisoners taken in the Indies for political pressure. The result was a long tug-of-war in which many of the *Richard*'s men were sent to the galleys (along with other English prisoners) to put pressure on James I to withdraw from

North America. Finally, and unexpectedly, in November 1608 the Spaniards gave way and released the surviving eighteen men from the galleys. The political story is told in D. B. Quinn, 'James I and the beginnings of empire in America', *Journal of Imperial and Commonwealth History*, II (1974), 135–52. Later, the pilot John Stoneman gave a full account of the voyage and of his experiences in Spain. A fuller selection from the extensive documentation of this case is given in *NAW*, III, 403–19.

---

28   16 February 1607. Deposition of Nicholas Hind, master of the *Richard* in the High Court of Admiralty[1]

16 February 1606[–7] Nicholas Hind of Cockenton, Devon, seaman and late master of the ship called the *Richard* of the port of Plymuthe, aged 44 years or thereabouts, being sworn, and examined deposes as follows:

Q. 1. Whether the *Richard* left Plymouth in the months of June, July or August 1606 and who set her out?

A. 'To the first article he sayth that he doth nowe know that the said shipp the Richard did in the moneth of Auguste last past & in the xij[th] day thereof as he remembreth did sett sayle from the porte of Plymouth & was sett out on that voyadg by Sir Ferdinando Gorge[2] [   ] Waddon[3] merchant of Plymouth captaine Morgan & captaine Thomas Love[4] of Plymouth merchantes together & others & was bound for the coast of Virginia called Pama Quidda in Mayaushon[5] in trade of marchandizes by sufficient authority from the kinges Maiesty of England & the Lordes

---

[1] The materials in the case of Henry Challons and the capture of his ship the *Richard* by the Spaniards in the Florida Channel are complex. In the High Court of Admiralty depositions were taken from members of the crew as they escaped from France or Spain: most of them were taken in Latin (or put into Latin) in case they were needed for legal proceedings in France or Spain. In this case a personal answer in English was made by Nicholas Hind, master of the *Richard*, to draft interrogatories, three days before the interrogatories were put into formal shape and the deposition he had already made put into Latin. The formal documents in this case are in P.R.O., HCA 14/38, 118 (with the deposition in Latin), and dated 19 February 1606/7; while the personal answer (in English) is in HCA 13/8, under date. In what follows the substance of the Latin interrogatory is given before the reply in English. They are given separately in *NAW*, III, 410–12.

[2] It is interesting that all mention of the Pophams as originators of the voyage is omitted (though Sir John is at the head of the list in Stoneman's narrative (Purchas, *Pilgrimes*, IV (1625), 1833)), since Sir John's participation might involve the king's government in legal cases which might follow on the continent.

[3] This may be the clerk's attempt at William Parker.

[4] For Love see p. 385. This is the only occasion he appears as 'captain'.

[5] This is the earliest appearance of either of these names, Pemaquid and Mawooshen, for Pemaquid Point and the Eastern Abenaki homeland generally, respectively.

of his Ma*iestes* privy counsell, which he knoweth to be true being m*aste*r of the s*ai*d shipp the s*ai*d voyadge.'

Q. 2. Whither was the *Richard* bound? And did she carry in her two persons of that land of America or Virginia?

A. To the second article he says and deposes 'that the s*ai*d shipp the Richard was bound for Pama Quidda in Mayushon in Virginia aforesaid[1] & and that there were two men borne in that Cuntry of Virginia[2] on boord the s*ai*d shipp the Richard at her going from Plymouth & xxviij Englishemen & none els of this ex*amin*ate*s* knowledg being m*aste*r thereof the s*ai*d voyadg'.

Q. 3. Whether the *Richard* followed her course towards America or Virginia without any violence offered towards any?

A. To the third he affirms 'that the s*ai*d shipp the Richard & there company thereof did w*i*th as much speed as they could (as wind & weather would suffer them) sayle towards the fores*ai*d port of their discharge whither they had directions to goe being Mayoushen & to no other port & being on their s*ai*d voyadg were driuen by force of wether & stormes to an Island called Andozia[3] being an Island which doth border on the West Indies, where they remayned three dayes & did theire take in some wood & water & so departed to sea againe towardes Mayowshen aforesaid & sayled along by S*ain*t Iohn de Porterrico where there was a certein Friar which was amongst the Salvages & this ex*amin*ate & company sett him on shore at Porterico & saued his life from the Saluages[4] & w*i*th all the speed, & with the wind & weather they might they made for the port of Mayaushen afores*ai*d which he knoweth to be true being m*aste*r of the s*ai*d shipp as aforesaid'.

Q. 4. In what circumstances did the *Richard* encounter the Spanish fleet?

A. To the fourth he affirms 'that the company of the said shipp the Richard being on their course as afores*ai*d did vppon the high seas & about xxv degrees & a halfe[5] meete with a fleet of Spanish shippes comming for Santo Domingo & bound for Spaine being all m*e*rchantes

---

[1] No mention is made of their being engaged in reconnaissance for a colonial settlement.

[2] The two Pemaquid Indians were Rosier's Maneddo and Sassacomoit (who are Mannido and Assacomoit in Purchas, *Pilgrimes*, IV (1625), 1833). For the latter's survival (though badly wounded) and return see Baxter, II, 22: Maneddo's fate is unknown.

[3] 'Andozia' is the clerk's version of Santa Lucia: the rescue of the friar took place at Dominica.

[4] He was put ashore on the east or south coast of Puerto Rico, cp. pp. 365–7.

[5] John Stoneman (p. 367, below) gives 27° 30′ or somewhat more, both being definitely inside the waters of coastal Spanish Florida. This took place on 10 November (20 November N.S.).

shipps[1] & the company of the said shipp the Richard as soone as they descried the said Spanishe fleet did sett out theyr colors being an englishe flagge to the intent that the said Spaniardes shall see from whence they came, & notwithstanding the said flagg sett out the said Spaniardes in the said fleete did shoot at the said shipp the Richard & the said company of the Richard seeing the Spaniardes did offer them violence did offer them selues voluntaryly to show what they were and whence they did beare vpp to the Admirall of the Fleete which he knoweth to be true as aforesaid'.

Q. 5. In what circumstances did the Spanish fleet take the *Richard*?

A. To the fifth he affirms it to be true 'that notwithstanding the voluntary submission & bearing vppe to the Admirall of the said Fleete, yet the shipps still shott of att the said shipp the Richard & Shot here throwghe & throughe & laid her violently on board & toke the posession thereof & after they came on boord the Richard they did beset the company with their naked rapiers & thrust one of the two Indiens which were on boord the Richard at least six inches into the body & throughe & throughe the Arme[2] & cutt one Robert Cooke an Englisheman in the head with an rapier & abused & beate euery man in the shipp & took from them all that euer they had & made them go barefoote & almost naked & kept this examinate & the capten in one of their shipps with Cassatha being the pithe of the tree & water & ferkin beefe once a week whiche was full of maggottes & they would creepe vppon the spitt for the space of ix weekes & had water but once a day & then they went two to a pint, And so he hard the rest of the Company being in other of the Spanishe shippes were vsed which he knoweth to be true giuing his resons of his knowledg as aforesaid'.

Q. 6. What did the commander of the Spanish fleet do when he was shown that the *Richard* was going with the king's leave to Mayowshen in Virginia?

A. To the sixth he affirms it to be true 'that before the said Spaniardes came on boord the master & company of the Richard did certyfy & declare to them that they were englishmen bound for the partes of

---

[1] The fleet into which Challons blundered was not the *flota*, which had sailed earlier under guard, but the Santo Domingo merchant vessels which had missed the main fleet. The flagship was evidently well armed, however. Her commander is described by Neville Davis, writing to Salisbury, on 24 August 1607 (14 August O.S.?) from Seville as 'one francisco Mison who was the cheif that touck them, and had their shippe vnder his charge and kept with Spaniards' (Cecil papers, CP 193/144; *Cal. Cecil MSS*, XIX, 216–17).

[2] The Indian was Sassacomoit and he did recover from his wound, eventually getting back to England. Mannedo may have died in Spain.

Virginea to a place called Mayowshen & had nothing on boord of them but what they brought from England neither had they touched anywhere since theyr cominge from England[1] & wished them to come on boord quietly and after theyr comynge on boord wished them to search their shipp without any resistance at all & tould them they were bound for Mayoushen aforesaid & theyr commodytyes were fitt for no other place but that & that they were bound for no place els but that, which he knoweth to be true as aforesaid'.

Q. 7. What did the commander of the Spanish fleet do with regard to the master, sailors, goods and merchandise of the *Richard* when she was taken?

A. To the seventh he affirms 'that the captens & company of the said Spanishe Fleete notwithstanding the premisses did presently vppon the company of them on board the said shipp the Richard did dispossesse the captaine & company thereof & greatly abused them as aforesaid & putt some into one ship & some into another, & master Henry Challens being capten of the Richard & this examinate were put into one shipp & they arived at Saint Lucar in Spaine, and most of the rest of the company of the Englishemen are in prison in Sivill in Spaine with the capten saving some which were left in the Richard, & what is become of them on the shipp & goodes he knoweth not'.

Q. 8. In which ships was Henry Challeng taken and in which the two natives of America or Virginia?

A. To the eighth he affirms as above 'that master Challen & this examinate & one of the two Indians were putt into one shipp & carried for Spayne, where both master Challenge & those two Indians & some xx[ty] more of theyr company remayned prisoners'.

Q. 9. Whether those of the Richard intimated to the Spaniards that the king of England was in amity with the king of Spain, and whether they showed their pass from the king and council, and whether they voluntarily submitted themselves to the Spaniards?

A. To the ninth and last he says 'that the capten & company of the Richard did voluntarily subiect themselues to the said Fleet for that theyr was peace & league betwixte England & Spayne at that tyme they mistrusted nothing especially no mercy to be offered to them by any Spaniardes showing theyr passe from the King of England his counseile

---

[1] They had watered at Madeira, 31 August–3 September 1606 and were well treated there (p. 360, below). Precisely what sort of pass they had is unknown. It was probably a specific pass from the royal council for Virginia established under the Virginia Company charter, apparently citing part of the charter of 10 April 1606.

& for that they had bine kindly vsed before at Madares vppon the sight of that passe   And he sayth that if they had mistrusted they would haue offered them any violence they might haue escaped them being that they were of farr better sayle then they were'.

[*Signed*:] Nicholas Hyns[1]

29   4 February 1607. The relation of Daniel Tucker[2]

The Relasion of Daniell Tucker merchant beinge Implyed by diuers Adventerars of Plimmothe to goe as Facttor of a shipe bownd for Floredae wrytten by him selfe the 4th of February 1606.

The wind beinge faer we departed from Plimmothe the 12th of Auguste, which winde contenued tell we came within 80 Leages of the westward Ilandes, and then the wind westerd with a grete storme, where by we waer put for the Iland of Maderes, where we wattered with the Governers Licence one the 4th of Septtember and there staed tell the 8th daye/

And from thens we stude owr Corse for the coste of Floredae, but after we had saled some 100 Leges we waer be Calmed 14 daes together, and by Reson of the exstrem hete owr freshe water scanted vppon vs so as we waer forsed to the outter moste Ilandes of the weste Inges.[3]

And about the Laste of october we a Rived at a niland Called

---

[1] Hind's (or 'Hyns' as he signs himself) deposition was supported by depositions by two of the leading members of the Plymouth Company. Matthew Sutcliffe, dean of Exeter, and John Barlee, merchant of Plymouth (13 Feb.), as well as the Reverend Henry Wallis of Plymouth (14 Feb.), were mobilized to give evidence about the setting out and objectives of the *Richard* (recorded in HCA 13/8, between 13 and 14 Feb.), as well as Edward Lithaby an escaped member of the crew (13 Feb.). They give a number of names of members of the *Richard*'s company, Henry Challons, captain, Nicholas Hine of Cockington, master, John Stoneman, of Plymouth (who had been with Waymouth), pilot, Daniel Tucker, cape merchant, John Walrond, steward, William Stone, carpenter, Nathaniel Humfrie, boatswain (murdered in prison in Spain), Robert Cooke, of London (died in Spain), James Stoneman, brother of John, Master St John (a gentleman), Pierce Gliddon, Daniel Tooke, George Barton, with the Indians, here called 'Hossa-Commowet and Monita', plus some 13 others. The *Richard* was a small vessel of 55 tons.

[2] Hatfield House, CP 115/89; *Cal Cecil MSS*, XIX, 36–37; Baxter, *Gorges*, III, 139–31; *NAW*, III, 409–10. Tucker as factor would have acted as cape merchant of the expedition (cp. p. 280). His literacy was limited but his brief deposition after his return to England is an essential counterpart to that of John Stoneman.

[3] Tucker makes clearer than Stoneman (p. 365) that the decision to sail as far south as the Canaries was fatal to the original intention to sail directly across the Atlantic from Madeira and led to the vessel being hopelessly becalmed in the doldrums until she worked her way southwards to the southeast trades. Stoneman, being pilot, passes over this, as he evidently does not wish to take responsibility for the mistakes in navigation, even though these may have been due primarily to the captain's orders.

Margethanta,[1] wher we wattered and Refresshed owr selues with suche
Frutes as the Iland did afford, and staed ther 4 daes, from thens we
wente by a Niland called Domeneca, wher a Spanishe Frier Came a
bord owr shipe, in a small Cannoe with 5 Ingens[2] which brought Frutes
with them. The saed Frier desired vs for Godes Caes to geue him
passage for some part of Cristendom, whos shipe had bene Caste a waye
some 13 monthes befoer and all his Company drownned and slaned
by the Engians, only hee saved a Liue.

Whiche saed Frier[3] we tooke into owr shipe, and some 4 daes after
we sete him a shoer at the Estward of Portarecca, and ther delevered
him vnto two Spanniardes which waer herdes men of Cattell, wher
we staed two daes, and goinge from thens owr shipe Came a grownd,
but with out anye harme we got Cleer, and so stude owr Corse to
Floredae.

And beinge at see in the hithe of 26 degres & some 60 Leges from
the shoer we met with a Flete of a 11 shipes (all Spanniardes) merchant
men, on the 10th of November in the morninge we waer in the
middeste of the saed Flete, we standinge owr Corse, one of the
windward shipes shot at us, wher vppone we wente to the Admerall,
and Comminge vnder his Lee, the Admerall shot at vs two shot, and
came a borde of owr shipe in most veyholent manner,[4] and disposeste
vs of owr shipe and goodes, and sent vs a bowrde of his one shipe,
and the nexte day parted vs some 4 & 5 in a shipe and put Spanniardes
a borde of owr shipe and stud for Sevell in Spane But by Resen the
Admerall had a grete Lecke the Reste of the shipes Lefte him onlye
with owr shipe and soe parted from the Admerall, and 6 daes after we
Loste all owr Flete in a grete storme with moer winde then we Cowlde
well stere afoer, and by Resen of exstreme fowle wether and hauinge
a bad Pilote who Cowld not tacke his Iuste hithe we[5] Continued
at see two monthes in grete meserie & exstremetie, and soe not

---

[1] Stoneman is clear that the island on which they first landed was St Lucia and not
Marie Galante. He is almost certainly correct.

[2] 'Ingens' and 'Engians' are original to Tucker for Indians, but probably show how
west countrymen pronounced the word at the time. They were Caribs on whom Stoneman
gives a little more detail.

[3] Friar Blasius (the Latinized form of Blas?) has not yet been identified.

[4] The summary description of the capture should be compared with that of Hind
and Stoneman (pp. 358, 368).

[5] Stoneman had to help pilot the ship on which he was placed into the Guadalquivir
(p. 369). The fact that the vessel in which Tucker was imprisoned was carried so far off
course as to put into Bordeaux shows that Spanish navigation throughout this group of
merchant vessels was very poor.

knowinge where we waer, we ariued at the Reuer of Burdes the second of Januarye/

And the Master and the Reste of the Spanniardes knoinge theme selues to bee in Burdes, thaye Commanded my selfe with the three other of my Companye, to bee put into the shipes howld and there thaye kepte us Fiue daes and Fiue nites, in that manner, tell the Iuge of the Admerralte Came a borde of the shipe Riddinge aganste the Towne of Burdex and Exsamened my selfe, And the Iuge vnder-standinge the truthe of owr Caues Carried me and the three other a shoer to Burdex.

And when I was at Lebertie I wente to one of the Cheffeste Counseller and sertefied him of owr veyage & howe the Spanniardes had used vs and in what manner they had tacken vs. I desired his Cownsell what Course was beste to tacke a ganste the Spanniardes, who aduised me to see a Procter, and macke a petesion to the Parlemente and to the Admerall to have the Master of the Spanishe ship & the rest of my Company exsammened, which I did, and shoed the Copie of all owr exsammenasions to my Cownseller, who aduised me to macke a Letter of a Turnie to my Procter and to some other whome I thought good, and thaye to folloe the Caues a ganste the Spaniardes in my Absence, and my selfe to Repaer for England with all spede, and to Returne with serteficate to Conferme owr exsammenasion to bee truthe.[1]

Where vppone I made a Letter of a Turnye to my Procter and to a nother my solester which hathe order to areste the saed Spanishe shipe and goodes, tell furder profe Comethe out of England.

This beinge Finneshed I departed from Burdex and at my departtuer my Cownseller and my Procter saed ther was no dowt but the worthe of the shipe and gudes with all dammages wold bee Recouered of them/[2]

By me / Daniell Tucker

[Endorsed:] 4 Feb 1606/1607 The Relation of Daniell Tucker going to Terra Florida.

[1] Tucker's success in getting the Spanish ship impounded after he had obtained his and his companions' release, and his subsequent legal activity in attempting to use this as an instrument for the release of the *Richard* and her men at Seville, shows his business acumen and some knowledge of French legal procedures. That he was non-suited in the end is no criticism of his vigorous efforts. It may well be that records of his activities are traceable in French archives.

[2] Once he had set legal procedures going Tucker's best tactic was to return to England to get documentation on the *Richard* through the High Court of Admiralty. This led to

a series of depositions being taken there, a number of them in Latin, so that they could be forwarded under the seal of the Admiralty as evidence of the peaceful intent of the *Richard* and the consequent criminality of the Spaniards whose ship was retained at Bordeaux. Since the case was a far from straightforward one and involved matters of international jurisdiction it is not surprising that the French courts rejected the English case and released the Spanish vessel.

The documentation of the case included a series of documents intended to assist the prosecution in the French courts of Daniel Tucker's claim as factor, on behalf of those who set out the *Richard*, that the Spanish vessel, the *amiral* of the squadron, from which he had escaped at Bordeaux, should continue to be held there and should be awarded to him and his backers in lieu of the *Richard*, held by the Spaniards, or exchanged for her. This was unlikely to succeed but it meant that the ship was held at Bordeaux for more than a year until the court decided on her release, so that the Spaniards suffered some loss through retaining and eventually sinking the *Richard*. The documents issued in support of the case by the High Court of Admiralty consisted of an exemplification, dated 19 February 1607, by the Lord High Admiral (draft in HCA, 14/138, 18) of the data which had been produced in the Admiralty court by the plaintiffs in the case, including the deposition of Nicholas Hind which was the primary statement on what had happened. This was supported by three depositions (HCA 13/38, ff. 189v–190v), taken on 13 February 1607, purporting to show that the voyage was a peaceful one. The first was by Edward Lithaby of Salternowne by Launceston, who testified to the departure of the *Richard* in August 1606, in virtue of a commission under the Great Seal, and to her being set out by the chief justice, Sir John Popham, Sir Ferdinando Gorges (clear evidence of his involvement at this early stage), William Parker gentleman, William Morgan gentleman, and a certain Waddon and others, natives of England. He outlined the voyage, stressing her call at Madeira, but glossing over her penetration of the Caribbean, and explained how she was taken by the Spaniards in spite of assurances given that she was on her way to Virginia. He stated that certain of the Englishmen, Daniel Tucker ('Tooker'), Pierce Elisson, and George Barby, were on board the Spanish admiral when she was driven into Bordeaux, while the *Richard* was taken to Spain. The next was by Matthew Sutcliffe, doctor of laws, of Efford, near Plymouth, aged 53 years (but not described as Dean of Exeter), who explained that the *Richard* was a merchantman of Plymouth and not a ship of war. She was fitted out to go to a place called Mayoushon, which was no great distance from the River of Canada, was supplied with goods for that purpose, and carried with her two Virginians and 28 Englishmen. She had been taken by the subjects of the king of Spain, though he knew no details, but he considered her factors deserved restitution for their losses. John Barlee of Plymouth, gentleman ('armiger') confirmed that the *Richard* was a merchantman of the port of Plymouth and not a ship of war. He reaffirmed what had already been said about her destination and her complement, and added that she was worth £400 and that the Spaniards should be distrained for her retention. These documents, all in Latin, for the benefit of the French courts, presumably all made their appearance there in due course. Their value is largely in making more specific the character of the ship, her complement and, especially, the backing she received in the preparation of her voyage.

30 [December 1607]. Narrative of John Stoneman, pilot of the *Richard*, after his return to England[1]

The Voyage of Master Henry Challons intended for the North Plantation of Virginia, 1606. taken by the way, and ill vsed by Spaniards: written by Iohn Stoneman Pilot.

On Tuesday the twelfth of August, 1606. Master Henry Challons Gentleman set forth from Plimouth, in our small Ship of the burthen of fiftie fiue Tunnes or thereabout, called the Richard of Plimouth. Wherein went twentie nine Englishmen, and two of the fiue Sauages (whose names were Mannido and Assacomoit) which were brought into England the yeere before out of the North parts of Virginia, from our goodly Riuer by him thrice discouered,[2] called ___³ in the Latitude of 43. de[g]rees, 20. minutes were imployed for a farther discouery of these Coasts: And if any good occasion were offered, to leaue as many men as wee could spare in the Country.[4] Being victualled for eleuen or twelue moneths, at the charges of the Honourable Sir Iohn Popham Knight, Lord chiefe Iustice of England, Sir Fardinando Gorges Knight, Captaine of the Fort of Plimouth, together with diuers other worshipfull Knights, Gentlemen and Merchants of the West Countrye: Iohn Stoneman of Plimouth being Pilot, who had beene in the foresaid parts of Virginia the yeere before, with George Waymouth:[5] The Masters name was Nicholas Hine of Cockington, neere Dartmouth;[6]

Madera.   The last day of August wee fell with the Ile of Madera, where we watered and refreshed our selues, and stayed three dayes, being very

---

[1] Purchas, *Pilgrimes*, IV (1625), 1833–7, XIX (1906), 284–96; *NAW*, III, 404–8. This Purchas obtained from Hakluyt's papers.

[2] Cp. pp. 309–10 for their names and subsequent histories.

[3] Rosier recorded no name for the St. George River which he had explored in 1605, but perhaps the missing name was the Eastern Abenaki name for their region, Mawooshen, as this appears in the depositions made in the High Court of Admiralty by members of the *Richard*'s complement.

[4] The intention to establish a small settlement was clear, but out of a total of 29 not more than about 15 could be left. This would compare with what Gosnold intended in 1602. Here, presumably, they could depend, they thought, on the protection of the Pemaquid Indians. The intention to settle a small party also helps to explain why Hanham and Pring were sent so promptly to reinforce and supply them, though they were unable to do so (cp. pp. 76, 337). To attempt to found a settlement as late as October was surely risky, but little was known as yet of the climate in winter.

[5] Stoneman may or may not have acted as pilot on Waymouth's voyage but at least he was aware of the direct route to North Virginia, which the *Richard* did not follow.

[6] For his deposition see above, pp. 356–60.

kindly vsed by the Inhabitants. The third day of September wee departed from thence, passing betweene Gomora and Palma, two of the Canary Iles,[1] and from thence were driuen by contrary winds, to take a more Southerly course then we intended,[2] and so spent more then sixe weeks before wee could recouer any of the Ant-Iles.[3] The first that wee could recouer, was the Ile of Saint Lucia,[4] in the Latitude of 14. degrees, 20. minutes, where we refreshed our selues with Wood and Water. And saw certaine of the Sauages there, about fortie or fiftie, came vnto vs at our Ship in one of their Cannoas, bringing vnto vs Tobacco, Potatos, Plantins, and Cassaui Bread, the which Sauages had slaine more then fortie of our Nation, the yeere before, 1605. as after wee vnderstood by Philip Glasco, and Miles Pett, being two of Captaine Nicholas Saint Iohns company, which was there treacherously slaine among the rest.[5]

Saint Lucia.

Fortie English slaine by Sauages, 1605.

Hauing stayed heare three dayes, about the two and twentieth of October we departed thence to the Northward. And in passing by the Ile of Dominica,[6] wee chanced to see a white Flag put forth on the shoare, whereat maruelling, wee supposed that some Christians had sustained shipwrack their. And forthwith a Cannoa came off from the shoare towards vs, which when they came neere, being very little wind, we layed our Ship by the lee and stayed for them a little, and when they were come within a little distance of the Ship, wee perceiued in the Cannoa a Friar, who cried aloud in the Latine tongue, saying, I beseech, as you are Christians, for Christ his sake to shew some mercy and compassion on mee, I am a Preacher of the Word of God, a Friar of the Order of Franciscus in Siuill, by name Friar Blasius. And that hee had beene there sixteene moneths a Slaue vnto those Sauages; and

Dominica.

Friar Blascus his request.

[1] The decision to attempt to sail from Madeira southwards to the Canaries was fatal to any prospect of a direct voyage. Stoneman does not explain why a course was not kept for the Azores as in the previous year.

[2] Sailing from the Canaries the *Richard* would now be in the grip of the SE trades: in attempting to escape northwestwards she was becalmed in the doldrums and after 14 days turned back into the trades to be carried to the Caribbean, or so Tucker (p. 360 above) said.

[3] In spite of all protestations to the contrary Challons, or at least his pilot, may have aspired to do some plundering in the Caribbean if opportunity offered, since English pirates as well as traders were still active in the area.

[4] St Lucia, Windward Is, 14° N, 61° W.

[5] John Nicol's story of the attack on 67 deserters from Sir Oliph Leigh's ship, *Oliph Blossom*, on her way to reinforce Charles Leigh's colony on the Wiapoco is in *Pilgrimes*, IV (1625), 1255–60, XVI (1906), 324–7. They landed on St Lucia to plunder Spanish wrecks and were themselves overwhelmed by a large force of Caribs who killed most of them; a few survivors, after many adventures, reached England in February 1607.

[6] 15° 30′ N, 61° 30′ W.

that other two Friars which were of his company they had murthered and throwne into the Sea. We demanded of him then, how he got so much fauour to preserue his life, his Brethren being murthered: Hee answered, because hee did shew the Sauages how to fit them Sayles for their Cannoas, and so to ease them of much labour often in rowing, which greatly pleased the Sauages as appeared, for wee saw them to vse sayles in their Cannoas, which hath not beene seene before.

Then we demanded of him where they had this Linnen Cloth to make those Sayles: hee answered, That about two yeeres before that, three Gallions comming to the West Indies were cast away on the Ille of Gwadalopa,[1] where abundance of Linnen Cloth and other Merchandise was cast on shoare. We demanded farther, what was the cause of his being in this place, and how he came thither: he answered, That the King of Spaine did euery yeere, send out of euery great Monastery certaine Friars into the remote parts of the Indies, both to seeke to conuert the Sauages, as also to seeke out what benefits or commodities might be had in those parts, and also of what force the Sauages were of, and what number of them were in the seuen Ant-Iles, viz. Saint Vincent Granado, Saint Lucia, Mattalina, Dominica, Gwadalopa, Aisey.[2] The which the said Friar Blaseus said he had diligently noted and obserued, and did hope to make perfect relation of such great benefits and riches as was to be drawne from thence, as he doubted not but would bee greatly accepted of this King, if hee might liue to returne to declare it: For, said hee, I haue seene in one Riuer discending from the Mountaines in the Ile of Dominica, the Sand to glitter like Gold or find Copper, whereupon I tooke some of it, and chewed it betweene my teeth, and found it perfect Mettall, the Sauages noting me, began to haue some ieolousie of me, so as I durst not take any farther notice of it, neither would they suffer him forward to come neere to that place. And farther hee said, That if the great plentie of diuers Fruits and Roots fit for mans sustenance were perfectly knowne, together with the Sugar-canes that they haue in those Iles, and the fertilitie of the soyle he thought it would be very shortly inhabited; and as for the number of Sauages there, as neere as we could vnderstand, was scarce one thousand of all sorts of men, women, and children in all the said seuen Iles.

Now, being moued with pittie at the lamentable complaint, and

Three gallions lost at Guadalupa.

Causes of yeerly sending of Friars out of Spaine.

old in ominica.

---

[1] Guadeloupe, 16° 10′ N, 61° 30′ W.

[2] St Vincent, Grenada, St Lucia, Martinique, Dominica, Guadeloupe, and (?) Antigua in the Lesser Antilles.

humble suit of this distressed Friar, wee tooke him into our Ship, and sent away the Sauages much discontented. And from thence wee sayled to the Ile of Saint Iohn De-port-rico, where on the nine and twentieth of October, wee arriued on the Southside,[1] and forthwith sent the Friar on shoare, and deliuered him to two Heardsmen, which most thankfully receiued him, and of their courtesie brought vs a fat Cow, and proferred vs more with Hogs, Calues, or any thing else that they could procure vs in recompence of the good deed done to the Friar.

They land the Friar on Port Rico.

Wee departed from thence, and sayled out betweene the Iles of Saint Iohn De-portrico, and Hispaniola standing away to the Northward.[2] And leauing the great shoalds called Abrioio, on our Larboord side,[3] being in the Latitude of 21. and 22. degrees, from thence Westward, our course North North-west, and North-west and by North, vntill wee were in the Latitude of 27. degrees or better,[4] and about one hundred and eightie leagues from Saint Iohn de Port Rico.

In this place hauing had a very great storme of Wind and Raine continuing fiftie six houres and more before on the tenth day of Nouember, about ten of the clocke in the morning, suddenly we found our selues in the middest of a Fleet of eight Sayle of ships[5] in a very thicke fogge of mist and raine, so as we could not see them before they were very neere, and within shot of them, wherein three of them were on the wind-ward of vs, on a third and fourth more to lee-ward: those at the wind-ward came rome vnto vs, and shot at vs, requiring vs to speake with their Admirall.[6] When we saw that by no meanes we could auoid them, but they would speake with vs, we put abroad our Colours, and went toward the Admirall, before wee came vnto him, he likewise strooke downe our Sayle, and came vnder his lee, demanding his pleasure: the other ship which first shot vs, all our Sayles being downe, and shot our mayne Sayle in pieces lying on the Decke. And forthwith the Admirall came on boord of vs, with two and

They by vnhappy hap fall amongst Spanish ships.

They are borded, taken and abused.

[1] The coast runs just south of the parallel of 18° N.

[2] They entered the Mona Passage opening at 18° N, 68° W.

[3] Not identified, but presumably at the southern approaches to the Grand Bahama Bank where there are many dangerous shoals.

[4] At 27° N or somewhat more they would be well clear of the Bahamas and nearly out of the Florida Straits.

[5] Though Tucker says 11 (p. 361), 8 seems to be correct. They were the Santo Domingo merchantmen which had evidently arrived at Havana too late to join the *flota* which had sailed without them. Being without a guardship they were peculiarly sensitive to the possibility of an attack by pirates and their reaction was easily understandable.

[6] Francisco de Mison was captain of the *capitana*, the name of which has not been found.

twentie men in their ships Boate with Rapiers, Swords, and halfe-pikes. We being all in peace stood readie to entertayne them in peace. But assoone as they were entred on boord of vs, they did most cruelly beate vs all, and wounded two of our Company in the heads with their Swords, not sparing our Captayne nor any. Also they wounded Assacomoit, one of the Sauages aforesaid, most cruelly in seuerall places in the bodie, and thrust quite through the arme, the poore creature creeping vnder a Cabbin for feare of their rigour:[1] and as they thrust at him, wounding him, he cried still. King Iames, King Iames, King Iames his ship, King Iames his ship. Thus hauing beaten vs all downe vnder the Deckes, presently they beat vs vp againe, and thrust vs ouer-boord into their Boate, and so sent vs on boord of the Admirall ship. Neither would they suffer any of vs to speake a word, to shew the cause of our passing the Seas in these parts. Neyther regarded they any thing, our Commission which the Captayne held forth vnto them in his hand: vntill that the Admirall with the Company of foure other of the ships, had rifled, spoyled, and deliuered all the Merchandize and goods of the ship among them: which beeing done, they also diuided vs beeing thirtie persons in all into the said fiue ships, by seuen, six, fiue, and foure to a ship.[2]

King Iames his name little respected by Spaniards.

Three of the former eight Sayle made Sayle away, and neuer came neere vs, neither were partakers of our spoyle. Then they also repayred our Maine Sayle which was torne with the shot aforesaid, and put their men into her. And after because they could not make her to sayle well, they tooke two of our men, and put into her to helpe them, the other fiue ships and our ship kept company two or three dayes together.[3] After this they separated themselves either from other, not through any tempest or storme, but through wilfull negligence or simple Ignorance, by shaping contrary courses the one from the other. So as not two of them kept company together. My selfe and sixe more of our company in the Vice-Admirall (of the burthen of one hundred and eightie tunnes; called the Peter of Siuill, the Captaynes name was Andreas Barbear) beeing alone, and hauing lost the company of the Fleet, continued our course vntill the middle of December: at which time being about

---

[1] Sassacomoit survived and eventually made his way to England from Spain (p. 336).

[2] Though the prize crew placed on the *Richard* was evidently from the *capitana* and she was regarded as Mison's prize, the distribution of the captives among the other ships was a wise precaution. Later two were taken from the flagship and put on board to help in sailing her.

[3] According to Tucker (p. 361), the *capitana* was leaking and made slow progress, the other ships outsailing her.

twentie leagues off from the Ile of Santa Maria, one of the Iles of the Azores[1] the Vice-Admiral and the whole company disliking the great Ignorance of the Pilot, because he had told them ten dayes before that he was very neere the Ilands, and had waited all this time, and could find any of them, entreated me very earnestly to shew my skill. And the Pilot himselfe brought mee his Instruments, and besought mee most earnestly to assist him, and to appease the company. Whereunto by there much importunitie I yeelded. And by Gods assistance on Christmasse Eeue, after our English account, I brought them safe to the Barre of Saint Lucas, being the first ship of the whole Fleet that arriued there.[2]

One of the ships of this Fleet, by the great Ignorance of the Spanish Masters, Pilots, and Mariners was driuen beyond all the Coast of Spaine, into Burdeaux in Gascoyne, In which shippe the Officers of the Admiraltie of France, finding foure of our Englishmen prisoners vnder the Deckes in hold; to wit, Master Daniell Tucker, who was our Cape Merchant, Pierce Gliddon and two others, did very friendly set them at libertie; and the said Daniel Tucker presently arrested the Spanish ship and goods beeing of great value, which of long time remayneth vnder arrest.[3] *French courtesie.*

The good Duke of Medina[4] hearing of the arriuall of certaine English prisoners taken here, the Coast of the West Indies, sent command to the Captaynes of the Spanish ships, to bring foure of the chiefest to be brought before him. Whereupon my selfe, Master Thomas Saint Iohn, Iohn Walrond our Steward, and William Stone our Carpenter were brought before him. The ship wherein Master Challons was, was not yet come.

Master Dauid Neuill an Englishman dwelling in Saint Lucas, was appointed our Interpretor. And then the Duke required me vpon my oath to yeeld a true and faithfull answere, according to the whole state and manner of our Voyage and proceedings, which I did, according to the former Relation afore written, wherevpon his Excellencie replyed vnto the Spanish Captaynes which had brought vs, saying, if

[1] Santa Maria, 37° N, 25° W. The absence of an efficient pilot was also the reason for the miscarrying of the ship on which Tucker was (p. 361).

[2] A voyage from 10 November to 24 December from the Florida Straits to San Lúcar was a good one for the *San Pedro* to make.

[3] See Tucker's version, p. 362.

[4] Pérez de Gúzman, duke of Medina Sidonia, had lived for the most part since the Armada's failure on his virtually autonomous estate of San Lúcar de Barrameda at the mouth of the Guadalquivir. His kindness to the English and his willingness to believe their story throws an interesting sidelight on his personality.

this bee true which this Englishman affirmeth, you haue greatly wronged these men. And so commanded them to prouide meate, drinke, and fit lodging for vs, and to bring vs againe the next day before him. They sent vs neuerthelesse to Siuill, where wee were brought to a Dutchmans house, called Signior Petro, where we were reasonably lodged, and entertayned that night.

The next morning being New yeeres day we were brought before the President of Siuill, at the Contractation, who hearing of our comming, and not vouchsafing to speake with vs, sent foure Officers to vs, and cast vs into Prison.[1] Where for the space of fiue dayes wee had publike allowance, but such as poore men which were there Prisoners, also did of their mercie bestow on vs. At length after many humble Sutes, and earnest Petitions exhibited to the President, we had a Riall of Plate allowed to each man a day, which is sixe pence English, which by reason of the dearth of all sorts of victuall in those parts, will not goe so far as three pence in England.

Their imprisonment.

And so at seuerall times, within one moneth after eleuen more of our Company were committed to Prison, as they came home, whereof our Captaine was one. Notwithstanding that the good Duke of Medina had discharged both him and all those of his Company, which came into Spaine with him, and willed him to goe home to the Court of England, or to the Court of Spaine where he thought to haue best reliefe for his poore imprisoned Company. Wherevpon Nicholas Hine our Master, and two more of our men wisely foreseeing what was like to bee the Issue, made haste away out of the Citie, and so got passage and escaped into England.

Before the comming of our Captaine to Siuill, my selfe and eleuen more of my Company were examined before the President of the Contractation: who finding no iust cause of offence in vs, did often earnestly examine me of the manner and situation of the Countrie of Virginia, together with the Commodities and benefit thereof.[2] And

---

[1] Once the matter had come to the attention of the Casa de la Contratación, the capture of the *Richard* soon ceased to be a simple matter of prize-taking by the Santo Domingo vessels, and was taken over as an example of English piracy in the Spanish zone in America, in which the Spaniards attempted to insist that any infringement of the waters off Spanish America (in this case off Florida) was punishable by death. The very fact that the *Richard*'s men alleged that they were going to found a colony farther north made their case more serious from one aspect, especially in view of the action against the *Castor and Pollux* (p. 215) in 1605, well to the north of where the *Richard* was taken.

[2] In the initial stages some compassion was shown and an easy attitude taken with the captives from whom was squeezed all the information they had about North America. As Stoneman had been with Waymouth, this was considerable. His deposition, if found

after the comming of our Captaine, they likewise examined him to the same purpose. We answered both to one purpose, according to our Commission in writing,[1] which the Spaniards at our taking at Sea, had preserued and deliuered vp vnto the hands of the President. Within few dayes after, they gaue our Captaine and Master Thomas Saint Iohn, libertie of mayne Prison, vpon the securitie of two English Merchants, which were Master William Rapier, and Master John Peckeford, whereof the later is dwelling and maried in Siuill.[2] The rest of the Company being one and twentie in Prison, continued still in miserable estate. And about two moneths after, Robert Cooke of London one of our Company fell sick of a Fluxe, whereof he languished three moneths and more, and by no meanes that wee could make, could get him forth to bee cured, although wee spent more then sixtie Rials in Supplicaues and Sutes to get him out. At length being dead, they caused his bodie to bee drawne vp and downe the Prison by the heeles, naked, in most contemptible manner, crying, Behold the Lutheran, as fiue others of our Company beeing then in Prison beheld: and so laid him vnder the Conduit, and powred water into his dead bodie. This done, they cut off his Eares, Nose and Members, as the Spaniards themselues confessed vnto vs, and so conueyed his bodie wee could neuer learne whether, although we proffered them money to haue his dead corps to burie it.

Hard hearted Spaniard.

Cruell immanitie.

Shortly after Nathaniel Humfrie our Boatswaine was stabbed into the belly with a Knife by a Spaniard, what was a slaue in the Prison, and fourteene dayes after dyed, who beeing dead I went vnto the Keeper of the Prison, desiring to buy his dead bodie to burie it, and so for twenty Rials I bought his bodie, and buried it in the field. Then we besought the President for Iustice on this slaue which had slaine our Boatswaine: he demanded what we would haue of the slave. And we requested, that as he had slaine an honest and worthy man of ours causelesse that hee might die for it according to the Law. The President answered no,

---

at Seville, could throw further light on the 1605 voyage and also on Challons' objectives. The escape of Nicholas Hine (see deposition, pp. 356–60) and others may have made things worse for the rest.

[1] Probably a copy of the Virginia Company charter with some explanatory material from the royal council for Virginia, explaining their purpose and function in North Virginia. In the later long negotiations with English officials the fact that they had such documentation is never mentioned.

[2] The release of the captain, Henry Challons and Thomas St John, probably described as Master because he was a gentleman, and not defining him as the ship's master, on sureties was probably on account of their social status. This applied to Stoneman after he had found sureties three months later.

but if we would haue him condemned for two or three yeares more
to the Gallies he should. For said hee, The King of Spaine will not giue
the life of the worst Slaue that he hath, for the best Subiect the King
of England hath, and so sent vs away with this answere. Whereupon
being out of all hope of Iustice with the President, we repaired vnto
the Regent being an Ecclesiasticall man, one of the chiefest Iudges of
the Citie, desiring likewise Iustice on the Murtherer aforesaid: who in
kind tearmes promised vs Iustice, and so willed us to retaine counsell
and Atturnies to prosecute our Sute; which wee did accordingly, and
so after two monethes Sute, and the cost of more then two hundred
Rials on Lawyers, Scribes and other Officers at length we had him
hanged by the fauour of the Regent, which otherwise we had neuer
obtained.[1]

And now I may not omit to shew how I got the libertie to haue
the scope of the Citie for my Race to come, and go. Hauing beene three
monethes in close Prison with our poore company as aforesaid. At length
I got the fauour of two Englishmen inhabiting in Siuill named
Constantine Collins, and Henry Roberts who did ingage themselues
for me. The Spaniards were very desirous to have me to serue their
State, and proffered me great wages, which I refused to doe, affirming,
that this imployment which I had in hand, was not yet ended vntill
which time I would not determine any.

Then the Alcadie maior of the Contractation House and diuers others
Merchants perswaded me to make them some descriptions and Maps
of the Coast and parts of Virginia, which I also refused to doe.[2] They
being discontent with me, sent mee againe to Prison, where I continued
two and twentie dayes, and then I making meanes vnto my good
friends borrowed money, and so gaue diuers bribes vnto the keepers
of the Prison, whereupon they gaue mee libertie to goe abroad againe

---

[1] The story of the treatment of the seamen and settlers in prison would certainly excite
sympathy in England when he put this account on paper, since anti-Spanish feeling in ports
like Plymouth was just as strong as anti-English feelings were in Spain, even though English
merchants could now reside and trade with Spain (though not without constant struggles
with Spanish officialdom). The successful appeal to the governor of Seville to intervene
to punish the officials of the prison of the Casa de La Contratación and the hanging of the
murderer shows that the civil authorities recognised that until they were convicted English
prisoners had some civil rights.

[2] Stoneman's story of how the authorities of the Casa wished to engage him as a
pilot, tried to persuade him to make maps of the location of the English explorations in
north Virginia, and finally turned against him for this and for his participation in
Waymouth's voyage sounds credible. It also reflects the hardening of official Spanish
opinion on the case, as they gradually increased the pressure on King James to abandon
the Virginia enterprise.

Spanish
Presidents
respect to the
English.
Honest
Spaniards.

into the Citie at my pleasure. And wayting euery day for some order from the Court of Spaine of our discharge, there came none but delayes and prolonging of our troubles and miseries. So as we began almost to despaire of libertie.

At length an honest Dutch Merchant dwelling in Siuill, named Hanse Eloyse, sent vnto mee to speake with me, which when I came vnto him, signified vnto me what he had learned of one of the Iudges of the Contractation: who told him as he reported vnto me, that the Spaniards had a great hate vnto me aboue all others, because they vnderstood that I had beene a former Discouerer in Virginia, at the bringing into England of those Sauages; and that they thought it was by my instigation to perswade our State to inhabit those parts. And because they had receiued so small knowledge of those parts by my confession: and that they could not perswade mee to serue that State, neither would make them any note draught, or descriptions of the Countrie. They resolued to bring to the Racke and torment me, whereby to draw some further knowledge by confession from me, before any discharge might come for vs. The which this honest Merchant considering, and the Innocencie of our case, gaue me to vnderstand. And wished mee rather to flie and preserue my selfe, then to stand to their mercie on the Racke, I hearing this the next morning, being the three and twentieth of October, suddenly fled from Siuill, and with me Master Thomas Saint Iohn aforesaid, and one other of our Company named Iames Stoneman my Brother, whom through great cost and charges bestowed on the Keepers of the Prison a little before I had got forth to bee cured of a Callenture. Thus wee fled from Siuill, leauing Master Henry Challons our Captaine at libertie vpon sureties, and sixteene more of our Company in close Prison.

From thence on the fiue and twentieth of October, wee came to a Mount in the Cundado, where finding no passage by any shipping into England, France or Flanders.[1] Wee trauelled through Algaruie, to the Port of Setunall, and finding no passage there, wee trauelled to Lisbone in Portugall. Where wee arriued the one and thirtieth of October, and there found ships readie bound to goe to England, but the wind was contrary for fourteene dayes.

At the time of our abode at Lisbone, wee vnderstood that three

---

[1] Their route was probably eastwards (though 'a Mount in the Cundado' is not explained) to the port of Huelva, which would likely be where they did not find shipping. Thereafter they passed through the Algarve to Setúbal and Lisbon where they found a ship, the *Margaret* of Bideford, since security was less strict there than at Seville or Cadiz.

Carrickes were come from the East Indies: whereof one was arriued safely at Lisbone tenne dayes before our comming thither. Another was driuen to leeward, and put in Veego, as wee heard. The third Carracke beeing at the Ile of Tercera, was so leake that they could not bring her home into Portugall, but vnloaded her into three of the King of Spaines great Armadoes, to bring the goods more safely to Lisbone. Which Ships at their comming before the mouth of the River of Lisbone in the night within three dayes after my comming thither, were all cast away on certaine shoaldes there called Oscachopos, or as wee commonly call them the Catchops, where of nine hundred men, as the Portugalls reported, but only thirtie seuen were saued, and of the goods very little at all: because the said ships being cast away on the ebbe. The goods were driuen off into the Sea, the dead bodies of many that were drowned, I my selfe saw cast on the shore with the sundry wrackes of the parts of the Ships Masts and Yards, with other wracke of Caske, Chists, and such like in great abundance.

Three ships cast away.

The fourteenth day of Nouember the winde being faire, wee tooke passage from Lisbone in a small Barke belonging to Bidiford, called the Marget, and on the foure and twentieth of the same we were landed at Saint Iues in Cornwall, and from thence I hasted to Plimmouth, where I shewed vnto Sir Ferdinando Gorges and diuers others the Aduenturers, the whole Discourse of our vnhappie Voyage together with the miseries that wee had, and did indure vnder the Spaniards hands. And then hasted with all the speed I could toward the Court of England, where I was assured to my great comfort; that they either were alreadie, or very shortly should bee deliuered.[1]

Before my departure from Siuill, I should haue remembred, that about Whitsontide last there were brought into the Prison of the Contractation there, two young men brought out of the West Indies,

[1] Gorges had for many months been aware of the capture and had been in communication with Challons, while he had also seen Tucker's deposition. Proceedings in the High Court of Admiralty had been begun in February 1607, and Gorges had been instrumental in having depositions sent to Challons who was still hoping to recover the *Richard* or damages for her capture by a civil action, after having proved in the courts that his objective was an innocent one, though the Spaniards were playing a cat-and-mouse game with him. On 13 March Gorges had urged him not to press a claim for damages of more than £5,000. He said 'that the Iourney hath bene now small charge vnto vs that first sent to the Coast and had for our returne but the fiue salvadges [implying he had helped to sponsor Waymouth's voyage] whereof two of the principall you had with you and since within two monthes after your departure [October 1606] we sent out another shippe to come to your supplie and now againe we haue made a nue preparacion of diuers all which through your misfortune is likely to be frustrate and our time Chardge lost'. (P.R.O., CO 5/15; Baxter, *Gorges*, III, 144–5.)

in one of the Kings Gallions, which were of Captaine Iohn Legats company of Plimmouth, which departed out of England, about the latter end of Iuly 1606. bound for the River of Amazons, as hee told me before his going forth, where hee had beene two yeeres before. And comming on the Coast of Brasill as those young men (the name of one of them is William Adams borne in Plumpton neere Plimmouth) reported vnto mee whether falling to the leeward of the Riuer of Amazons, or deceiued by his Master they knew not. And not being able to recouer the said Riuer, were constrayned to refresh in the West Indies, in which time there fell a great disorder betweene the said Captaine Legat and his company, so as one of his company, in a broyle within themselues aboard there ship, slue the said Captaine Legat, whether in his owne priuate quarrell or with the consent of the rest of the Company, they could not tell mee. But this is the more to bee suspected for that he alwayes in former Voyages dealt very straitly with his company. After his death his company coming to the Ile of Pinos, on the Southside of Cuba, to refresh themselues, being eighteene persons were circumuented by the trecherie of the Spaniards, and were there betrayed, and taken Prisoners: and within foure dayes after, of eighteene persons, fourteene were hanged the other foure being youths were saued to serue the Spaniards, whereof, two of them, refusing to serue longer in there ships, were put into the Prison at Siuill, the other two remayne still as slaues to the Spaniards.

This I had the rather noted to the end that it may be the better considered what numbers of ships and men haue gone out of England, since the conclusion of peace betweene England and Spaine, in the way of honest Trade and Traffique, and how many of them haue miserably miscarried. Hauing beene slaine, drowned, hanged or pittifully captiued, and thrust out of their ships and all their goods.[1]

Captain Iohn Legat of Plimmouth.

Mutine. *Captain* Legat slaine by his mutinous crew, which knew not when they had done to bring home their ship, and so stumbled on Spanish Iusticers. I haue heard him much commended for a proper and expert Seaman.

---

[1] The news is again not directly relevant to the Challons affair but helped to stoke the fires in England over Spanish cruelties to Englishmen caught in the Caribbean, as his concluding passage shows.

CHAPTER X

THE PRELIMINARIES TO THE 1607 VOYAGE

The very end of 1605 or the opening of 1606 saw the sudden entry into the Virginia project of the Lord Chief Justice, Sir John Popham. His vigorous support for the project of a major colonial enterprise overrode the plans set out in the Rosier pamphlet (p. 252) earlier in the autumn of 1605, though they did not entirely swallow up the Waymouth–Zouche project (pp. 314–17, 319–20). Sir Walter Cope was closely associated with the earl of Salisbury and was, almost certainly, a principal instrument in getting the London merchants to co-operate in a Virginia venture (p. 378). The participation of Popham gave the enterprise standing and no doubt helped greatly to get the venture going, but it also injected a West Country element into it. Popham's connections extended through Somerset (his main seat being at Wellington) and so brought in Sir Edward Seymour and probably his influential relatives and friends. George Popham was customer of Bridgwater. His contacts with Bristol were consolidated through Thomas Hanham of Wimborne, Dorset (married to his daughter Penelope) (their son, recorder of Bristol, led the second 1606 expedition). Through his legal activities he had contacts with the southwest in Exeter and Plymouth in particular. In Exeter his influence was exerted through the dean, Matthew Sutcliffe, rather than the corporation. In Plymouth he is likely to have known the leading merchants who made up the corporation, but his most important contacts were the privateering captain, William Parker, now a merchant, and Sir Ferdinando Gorges, commander of the fort.

The westerners were to have exclusive rights to explore, trade with and settle north Virginia, the area to which Gosnold, Pring and Waymouth had gone. The support of the western towns was not gained without friction. The Common Council of Bristol first of all refused to participate unless they were assured that it was to be a national not a local enterprise but, when so assured, agreed to put up a useful if not exceptionally large sum of money (pp. 381–3). Exeter City Chamber refused to have anything to do with the project and may have persisted in this attitude, though individual Exeter merchants may later have subscribed. The charter of 10 April 1606, when it created the London and Plymouth divisions of the Virginia Company, under a royal council (see pp. 331–2), did not please the Plymouth Town Council, even though Hanham, George Popham and Parker were named in it, since the supervisory royal council did not appear to represent sufficiently West Country as against

London interests (pp. 384–7). They enlisted the support of Sir Ferdinando Gorges, Fort Major of Plymouth (and a man with interests in the Bristol area — his family lived at Wraxall), and a member of the royal council, who wrote strongly to Salisbury on their behalf (pp. 388–90). It is clear too that the Plymouth Council expected to dominate the enterprise and were jealous of Bristol. However, they were mollified, and the orders set down by the royal council on 20 November 1606, of which a version survives in the City Archives (pp. 390–6), gave a clear lead as to the degree of autonomy which the north Virginia enterprise would enjoy. The early frictions, however, did not make for harmonious working later or for adequate subscriptions. Sir Francis Popham, Sir John's son, also made Plymouth his headquarters as treasurer, and this must have had a poor effect on the Bristol men.

In the series of actions in the Court of Chancery between 1608 and 1615 (printed in *NAW*, III, 454–65, but not excerpted here) some light is thrown on the preparations for the 1607 voyage. Abraham Jennings made it appear that Sir Francis Popham stayed with Sir Ferdinando Gorges at the Fort while he, as treasurer, was preparing the expedition and that Gorges bought 'Iron pottes boxes Chafyng disshes lockes & and divers other wares' for £36 19s 11d from the warehouse of Abraham Jennings, a Plymouth merchant, who became a subscriber, to help equip the settlers. Gorges, Jennings said, had also received sums of £20 each from Matthew Sutcliffe, dean of Exeter, and Sir Edward Seymour, and 'dyvers other somes of mony' as subscriptions towards the voyage. The cases hinged on the circumstances under which Jennings did or did not pay Sir Francis Popham the sum paid out for the goods and a further sum which he alleged Gorges owed him, making up £100 in all. Gorges denied buying anything towards the voyage, but said he had advised Popham about purchases only since he was 'a Counsellour chosen and allowed by his Majestie in that behalfe and no otherwise' (he was saying he was not one of the commissioners in charge of the Company but only a member of the royal council for Virginia). He did admit owing Jennings money for other purposes and claimed to have repaid it. The rights and wrongs of the matter were argued in detail by both parties and no decision was finally recorded, but the fact that the sums involved were so small suggests the preparations in 1607 were made on a shoestring and so were inadequate for their purposes. The documents also help to indicate why the Company broke down in 1609, since quarrels had broken out amongst the subscribers.

31 [December 1605 or January 1606]. Sir Walter Cope to the earl of Salisbury[1]

Sir

my Lorde cheffe Iustyce, foreseeynge In thexperyence of hys place The Infynite numbers of Cashiered Captaines & Soldyers, or pore artezan that would, & cannot worke, & of Idell vagrantes that maye & will not worke, whose Encrease threateneth the state,[2] ys affectionately bent to the plantation of Virginia, in the which he hathe allredye taken greate paynes,[3] & meaneth to disburse 500li. per annum for fyve yeares[4]   If the action prosper[5] / he desyreth for hys better expedicion two Lynes from your Lordship in particular[6] / or from the Lordes in generall / by vertue wherof he maye cawle the vndertakers gentleman marchantes &c vnto him / & by ther advyse to sett downe the best manner of proiect, which beyng agreed vpon, shalbe spedely Retourned to your Lordshipps,[7] because the best Season for the Iorney approcheth; & after Receave such further dyrection as to your wysedomes maye be thought fytt.

Your honours most humbly
Walter Cope[8]

[1] Hatfield House, CP 191/120 (*Calendar of Cecil MSS*, xviii, 84).

[2] This is the most famous justification of plantation in North America as a social panacea. On its results see N. Canny, 'The permissive frontier', K. R. Andrews, N. P. Canny and P. E. H. Hair, ed., *The westward enterprise* (Liverpool, 1978), pp. 17–44.

[3] This might seem to suggest Sir John Popham's interest in and possible financial support for a previous transatlantic enterprise or enterprises. If so investment in the Waymouth voyage would seem the least implausible.

[4] This was a very substantial investment and one on a scale which his son Sir Francis Popham did not contemplate after his father's death. If he supplied £500 for the Plymouth enterprises of 1606 this was enough to give him a major stake in those small ventures. He lived long enough to provide another £500 in 1607, which would have materially assisted in the equipment of the *Gifte of God* and the *Mary and John* (though he may have done even more for them). The question of whether he left any money for the continuance of the enterprise has not been answered. He probably did not, as his will, probated on 17 June 1608, had been made as far back as 21 September 1604, before his involvement in the Plymouth venture. (P.R.O. PROB 11/58, ff. 18v–20v.)

[5] Though Rosier claimed (p. 252), when his pamphlet on Waymouth's voyage was published (before 31 Dec. 1605 or before 24 Mar. 1606?) that the king and some privy councillors approved the continuance of the north Virginia project, he may have been speaking in hope rather than in knowledge, but if he wrote after contact with Sir John Popham and especially after this approach to Salisbury he would indeed be correct.

[6] Popham would be satisfied with a note from Salisbury himself to read to the assembly of intending subscribers and settlers he intended to convene, but he clearly would have preferred an official letter from the privy council. This he does not appear to have obtained, but the registers for this year are not extant.

[7] Popham envisaged, after the meeting, a report to the privy council, seeking advice and, most probably, official backing for the project.

[8] Sir Walter Cope (d. 1614) had been gentleman usher to Lord Burghley and was

[Addressed:] to the Right honorable the Earle of Salisbury hys Ma*iestes* Princypall Secretary at the Court.

[Endorsed:] 1605 Sir Walter Cope to my Lorde.

32   27 March 1606. Exeter City Chamber refuses to participate in the voyage[1]

xxvij die Martij An*no* Ja*cobi* Quarto[2]

And they[3] agree where my Lord Cheefe Justice hathe by his Le*ttr*es moc*i*oned to the Cittie to haue an Adventure from them to Terr*a* Virginia to be borne. That a answer shalbe made therunto that the m*er*chantes of this Cittie haue bene Charged in form*er* tymes with such Adventures very muche to ther Losse & hinderans   That they are not mynded to adventure to the seme   And that M*aster* Recorder M*aster* Periam M*aster* Howell & M*aster* Dorchester shall in ther descrecon.[4]

---

rising rapidly in the political firmament under his son. He had long been interested in overseas ventures and was an eminent collector of 'curiosities', especially those relating to America. He frequently exhibited his museum to visiting foreign dignitaries (*Thomas Platter's travels in England, 1599,* ed. Clare Williams (1937), pp. 171–3; B.L., Cotton MS Julius C III, ff. 101, 108). For his interest in Indians brought to England in 1603 see Quinn, *England and the discovery of America,* pp. 422, 429, 431, 483. He became a member of the royal council for Virginia on 3 March 1607 (*NAW,* v, 199). For Waymouth's association with him see p. 61 above.

[1] Devon Record Office. Exeter, Exeter City Records, Chamber Act Book, 1601–11, p. 208; *NAW,* III, 427–8.

[2] The date indicates that well before the Virginia charter was issued Popham was sending out circular letters inviting participation in the north Virginia venture.

[3] The Chamber was the ruling body of the city. Exeter city merchants, through their Merchant Adventurers Guild, had lost money in supporting the North-west Passage ventures of John Davis, 1585–8, but there does not seem to be any surviving record of the City Chamber itself having been involved in these ventures.

[4] The following can be identified: William Martin, the younger, recorder; John Periam, the younger, mayor, 1598–9; John Howell, mayor, 1599–1600; Richard Dorchester, sheriff, 1596–7, mayor, 1607–8. Henry Hall (not present) was mayor when this decision was made. (R. Izaake, *Memorials of the City of Exeter,* pp. 53, 141–3; W. T. MacCaffrey, *Exeter 1540–1640* (1958), pp. 255, 262–3 (Martin); 63, 109, 172, 197, 214, 223, 239, 253, 260, 262 (Periam); 255 (Howell); 239 (Dorchester). Martin at his death in 1609 left gross personal estate of £6,381, while John Periam was also a rich man (W. G. Hoskins, 'The Elizabethan merchants of Exeter', in S. T. Bindoff [*et al.*], ed., *Elizabethan government and society* (1961), pp. 169–70, 172, 176, 185 (Periam); 173 (Martin)). The persons named were evidently to draw up a suitably diplomatic reply embodying the decision.

33 12 March 1606. Bristol Common Council reserves its decision to participate in the voyage[1]

xij die Martij 1605[–6] Anno *Regni Regis* Jacobi 3.

[Ciu]itas ⎫
[Bri]stoll ⎭ *Presens*

Thomas James Mayor absens[2]
Williamus Hickes alder*mannus*
Franciscus Knight alder*mannus*
Williamus Perphey alder*mannus*
Johannes Welbe alder*mannus*
Williamus Ellis alder*mannus*
  Deputy Maior
Johannes Hopkins alder*mannus*
Williamus Vawer alder*mannus*

Radulphus Hurte alder*mannus*
Johannes Whitsone alder*mannus*
Christoferus Kedgwine
  alder*mannus*
Johannes Rowbero ⎫
Johannes Guy ⎭ *vicecomites*
Johannes Barker
Ricardus Smithe
Mathewe Havelande
Thomas Pyther
Johannes Butcher
Robertus Aldworthe
Johannes Eglesfielde

This daye my Lord Chiefe Justice his *lettre* to *Master* mayors deputye and the aldermen touchinge the plantacon in Virginia was redde to the Com*mon* then presente, Who were all of opynyon not to adventure any thinge in that action vnles yt shall please the kinges ma*iestie* to vndertake the same and to Giue in that chardge[3] And then they will be contributary and adventure in some reasonable proportion, to w*hich* effecte It is agreed that an answer shalbe fourth*with* made to my Lorde Chieffe Justices let*tre*, as shalbe thought fitte by the advise of *Master* John Rowberowe *Master* John Guy[4] nowe sheryfes and *Master* Barker and *Master* Kytchen Cou*n*cyllers appoynted for drawinge the sayd answere /

---

[1] Council House, Bristol, Bristol City Archives, Council Book, II.

[2] Thomas James was M.P. for Bristol, 1604–11. He had earlier been active in English plans to exploit the Gulf of St Lawrence between 1591 and 1597 (Quinn, *England and the discovery of America*, pp. 318–25). A succinct biographical note will be found in P. McGrath, ed., *Merchants and merchandise in seventeenth century Bristol* (Bristol Rec. Soc. XIV, 1955), p. 139. The other members of the Common Council who offered later to play an active part in the enterprise are discussed below, p. 383.

[3] Popham's request for their support was met with scepticism. The demand that the King should participate before they would agree to become involved arose from the lack of success of earlier colonising ventures (Bristol had had a hand in those of Sir Humphrey Gilbert and Christopher Carleill, 1583–4).

[4] The involvement of John Guy in the committee to draw up a reply may indicate that he was already becoming interested in colonial projects.

Ricardus George
Williamus Cary
Abell Kythen
Johannes Harrison
Johannes Boulton
Thomas Hopkins
William Hopkins
Johannes Aldworthe
Thomas Farmer
Williamus Barnes
Georges Richardes
Williamus Cole
Georgius Harrington
Georgius White
Thomas Parker
Johannes Robertes
Robertus Rogers
Hugo Murcet
Thomas Aldworthe
Thomas Moore
Williamus Younge
Hugo Pears
Artherus Needes

34   1 April 1606. Bristol Common Council opens subscriptions for the north Virginia venture[1]

primo die Aprilis Anno Regni Regis Jacobi quarto 1606.[2]

Thomas James mayor[3] absens ad parliament /   xx[tie] markes yeerelye
for fyve yer[es]

[1] Council House, Bristol, Bristol City Archives, Council Book, II.

[2] Since 12 March there had evidently come a reply to the earlier negative response. This was clearly the information that a major charter for the Virginia enterprises was about to be granted by the crown, that Richard Hakluyt was one of the petitioners (he had long been a prebendary of Bristol Cathedral and had been associated with American ventures in 1583, in the 1590s and in 1603 (see p. 214)), that word had been received from Thomas James that it was wise for them to be associated with the venture and, particularly, that the West Country interests were to be concerned with North Virginia, to which Pring's expedition had been profitably made in 1603 (pp. 214–30).

[3] Thomas James' letters (referred to later), and his offer to head the list with £13 6s 8d a year for 5 years, produced 13 other offers of subscriptions amounting (with that of the mayor) to £101 14s 8d a year (or £553 13s 4d for five years), a respectable but not a notable

Willie*l*mus Hickes alder*mann*us   x^{li} for fyve yeres
Franciscus Knighte alder*mann*us   o
Willie*l*mus Perphey alder*mann*us   o
Jo*hann*es Webbe alder*mann*us   o
Willie*l*mus Ellis alder*mann*us deputatus maioris /   iij^{li} for fyve yeres.
Jo*hann*es Hopkins Alder*mann*us   xij^{li} x^{s} for fyve yeres.
Willie*l*mus Dawer alder*mann*us
Rad*ulph*us Hurte alder*mann*us   o
Jo*hann*es Whitsone alder*mann*us   o
*Christ*oferus Kedgwine aldermannus   o
Jo*hann*es Rowbero ⎱
Jo*hann*es Guy ⎰ *vicecomites*   o
                                                xx^{tie} marks yeerelye
Jo*hann*es Barker   o
Rich*ard*us Smithe   o
Matheus Ḥaveland   o
Thomas Pitcher   o
Jo*hann*es Butcher   o
Rob*er*tus Aldworthe   xij^{li} x^{s} yeerelye
Jo*hann*es Eglesfielde
Ric*ard*us George   o
Willie*l*mus Cary   o
Abell Kychen   o
Jo*hann*es Harrison
Jo*hann*es Boulton   xl^{s} yeerelye
Thomas Hopkins   iij^{li} yeerelye
William Hopkins
Jo*hann*es Fowens   v^{li} yeerelye
Jo*hann*es Aldworthe   vj^{li} xiij^{s} iiij^{d} yeerelye
Thomas Farmer
Willie*l*mus Barnes
Georgius Richard*es*
Willie*l*mus Cole   v^{li} yeerelye
Georgius Harrington   o
Georgius White
Thomas Parker

---

sum for such a wealthy corporation. It is significant that there were 17 noes and 13 without a figure and probably undecided, less than one-third being committed. This indicates something considerably less than wholehearted support. Whether this money went to the North Virginia venture over the years 1606, 1607 and 1608 is not certain, but the last 2 years' contributions, if collected, would have gone (with the issue of the 1609 charter) to the London venture.

Joha*nn*es Robertes
Robe*rt*us Rogers   iij^{li} yeerelye
Hugo Murcet
Thomas Aldworthe
Thomas Moore   o
Willie*l*mus Younge
Hugo Pears
Arthuerus Needes   iij^{li} yeerelye[1]

An yeerelye Contribution for fyve yeeres for the plantac*i*on and Inhabitinge of Virginia

M*aste*r Thomas Hopkins and M*aste*r Thomas Aldworth m*e*rchauntes[2] are appoynted to Confe*rr*e and deale with the Inhabitant*es* of bristoll and to Certifye M*aste*r deputye and the aldermen his bretherne what every man will adventure towardes this action of Virginia / thus aunswer may be therevpon made to M*aste*r Mayors le*tt*res with as convenient speede as may bee /.

---

[1] Of the 13 members of the Common Council who contributed Thomas James who, with John Guy, offered the largest subscription, has already been mentioned (p. 381). Of the other twelve all will be found referred to except John Hopkins, Robert Rogers and Arthur Needes, in *Bristol Wills*, ed. E. A. Fry (British Record Soc. XVII, 1897). William Hickes, William Ellis, John Guy, John Hopkins, Robert Aldworth and John Aldworth, John Bolton, John Fowans (Fowens, Fawnes), William Cole, Robert Rogers and Arthur Needes were associated with either or both the organisation of the Spanish Company in March 1605 and the revival and reorganisation of the Society of Merchant Adventurers of Bristol in December 1605 (*Records relating to the Society of Merchant Adventurers of Bristol*, ed. P. McGrath (Bristol Rec. Soc. XVII, 1952), pp. 2–5). John Hopkins, fishmonger, had sailed his own ship in the Cadiz attack in 1596 (Latimer, *Annals of Bristol*, II, 25). John Guy was to establish the first English colony in Newfoundland in 1610 (Cell, *English activity in Newfoundland*, passim), and until 1631 to play a very active part in Bristol history (see biographical note in McGrath, ed., *Merchants and merchandise*, p. 143). The Aldworth family, along with John Whitson (see p. 219), was to play a vital part in the development of Bristol trade (see especially McGrath, *Merchant Adventurers*, passim). Together they made up the most active and innovative group in Bristol mercantile affairs during this period.

[2] Hopkins and Thomas Aldworth (the latter's family being very deeply involved in overseas ventures) were to canvass further subscriptions from Bristolians outside the Common Council. We have no record of their success or failure. But they were probably able to give Thomas James in London some idea of the total measure of support to be expected from Bristol not long after the charter was sealed on 10 April.

35   10 May 1606. Walter Mathewe, for Plymouth Corporation, to the earl of Salisbury[1]

Righte Honorable:

our humble dutyes remembred. It hath pleased our very good Lorde, the Lord Chiefe Iustice of Englande out of an Honorable disposicion to recomende vnto vs an enterprice for establishmente of a Plantacion in the partes of America; wherevnto we weare drawen to assent (vppon hope to obtayne suche free and reasonable Condicions as had in former tymes ben graunted, by her late Maiestye of famous memorye, to certeine particular Gentlemen): But sithence, it appeares, that it hath ben thoughte more Convenyent (for respectes beste knowne to your Lordshipp) to assigne vs to be dyrected (vnder his Maiestye) by a Councell of dyuers, some very worthie and worshipfulle persons, others of the same rancke and quallityie our selues are, the greatest parte, strangers to vs & our proceedinges, which neuerthelesse, being donne with your Lordshipps preuetye, we doubte not of anie inconuenyence or discomoditye which maie growe thereby; And therefore doe whollye referre ourselues to your Honorable Care ouer vs[.] And for our further desires to your Lordshipp we leaue to be more largely related by Captain Loüe the bearer hereof whome we haue purposely sent vpp to that ende, and (amongeste the reste, to become an humble sutour to your Lordshipp, that it woulde please you to Voushsafe vs your favorable protection and helpe, as one in whome, we in this behalf, as in all other thinges (nexte vnto his Maiestye) doe desire to make our cheefe dependencye, and to be assisted by yourself with suche other Honorable & worthie persons as in your wisdome shalbe thought fitt, amongeste whome we Cannot but remember the Lord Cheefe Iustice with our humble thankes for his good affection towardes vs in this behalf.[2] And for that we haue had many testimonyes & apparances of your Lordshipps loue & fauour towardes vs herein, we are bold at this

---

[1]   Hatfield House, CP 116/39; *Cal. Cecil MSS*, XVIII, 133; printed in Baxter, *Gorges*, III, 133–3.

[2]   The letter is very much a threat of withdrawal from the enterprise by Plymouth if the royal council for Virginia, established under the charter of 10 April 1606, is not reconstituted to contain persons who are familiar to them and who understand their problems. It is curious that this representation should have been made, as Thomas Hanham (of Wimborne and Bristol), William Parker (of Plymouth) and George Popham (of Bridgwater, but closely representing Sir John Popham) were all named in the charter of 10 April 1606 to represent the western interests, and the personnel of the royal council had not yet been published. They were indeed not formally constituted until 20 November 1606 (*NAW*, v, 200–5), though it is clear from this and from the letter which follows that the proposed composition was already known. He probably received assurances from

present to beseeche the Contynewance thereof, and haue promised with ourselues not to proceede further without yt, whollye relyinge vppon your favour & wisdome, to be disposed of, both in bodye and goodes, so farre further, as you shalbe pleased to Comaund. And in the meane tyme we will contynewallye praie for all Honour and happines to you and yours, humbly crauinge pardon for our ouerboldnes in beinge thus trowblesome to your good Lordshipp: to whome we doe reste in all dutifull seruice./

    Your Lordshipps moste humblie to Comaund/
        Waltere Mathewe[1]
      deputie maior and his bretherin
From Plymouth this 10th. of Maye 1606.

[Addressed:] To the Right honorable my verie good Lord the Earle of Salisbury.

[Endorsed:] 10 May 1606. Maiour of Plymmouth to my Lord.

36   11 June 1606. Plymouth Corporation to Sir John Popham[2]

Right Honorable our humble dueties remembred We haue receaved two letters from your Lordshipp the one being dated the 21 of Maye the

---

Salisbury that the royal council would not interfere in the detailed preparations and running of the north Virginia settlement and also that when fully constituted it would contain adequate representation of Plymouth interests. It would not have been practicable, in view of his duties, for Sir John Popham to be a member and, indeed, in the list of 20 November, officials of the second rank were joined to gentry and merchant representatives. It may well be that no formal organisation of the Plymouth Company ever took place, and that it remained primarily an informal joint-stock enterprise in the hands of the Popham family. See Preston, *Gorges*, pp. 140–5.

    Captain Thomas Love had earlier been associated with Waymouth (p. 316). During the year 1606–7 we have the entry in the Plymouth City Records, Receivers' Accounts (West Devon Record Office), 'Item paid for the hire of a horse for Thomas Love to ride to Exon [Exeter] about yᵉ Virginia voyage'. He may have been sent to try to wean the City from its earlier refusal to contribute. Dr Matthew Sutcliffe, Dean of Exeter, remained a loyal supporter of the venture.

[1] Walter Mathewe had been mayor 1604–5. The mayor in 1606 was the influential merchant, formerly deeply involved in privateering, James Bagge. (Worth, *History of Plymouth*, 2nd ed. (1890), 214.) The government of Plymouth was in the hands of the mayor with twelve aldermen and twenty-four common councilmen (ibid. p. 184). James Bagge was appointed to the royal council for Virginia along with Sir Francis Popham and Sir Ferdinando Gorges some time after 10 April 1606, so as to give the western interests some representation on it (*NAW*, v, 199). This was either not yet known to them or was regarded by them as insufficient.

[2] West Devon Record Office, Plymouth. Plymouth City Records, W 360/18; *NAW*, III, no. 495.

other the 29 of the same[1] in boath there seemeth to be some Contrarietie that gaue occasion of some distraction for in the firste itt pleased Your Lordship to resolue that all thinges should be performed from this place according whervnto we haue made our resolution giving order for the performance thereof as by our former letters in answer of Your Lordships itt doth appeare   But this devision hath disioynted itt much for nowe we neither do knowe What the particulars are that shalbe necessarie to be provided out of Severne nor can they tell what may be convenientlie had here[2] and before theise thinges cann be resolued on the tyme wilbe spent And the Confusion withall wilbe infinite Wherefore itt may please your Lordship to hold your firste deter-mynacion that We may builde altogeather vppon a Certentie with one mynde and one order so shall we be sure neither to staye one for the other att places vnsaufe nor one to surchardge or confounde the other by vnnecessarie provisions neither be subiect to the vnconstencie of Wyndes and Weather which may be good for vs here when itt is evill for theym there And to the end we may be the better vnderstood in this behalf we haue appoynted this gentleman master Challange more particularlie to giue your Lordship our reasons herein[3] Withall we haue made an estimate of the whole voyage the which we haue likewise sent to Your Lordship to thend you may perceaue what we conceaue is necessarie for the present out of the particuler vnderstanding We haue of the place. Whereof more att large your Lordship shall receaue farther advertisement from Sir Fardinando Gorge hereafter[4] And whereas there

---

[1] In the absence of the act books of the town council it is not possible to follow the involvement of Plymouth in the north Virginia venture. The initial invitation is likely to have been made about the beginning of March (cp. the approach to Bristol, pp. 380–1), and the co-operation of the town fully assured before the issue of the Virginia Company charter on 10 April. It would appear that the town was fully committed to assist in the venture by May when Popham wrote on the 21st and 28th, but in the first letter he committed himself (the Plymouth council believed) to the full fitting out of the vessels at Plymouth, while in the second he laid down that some of the victualling should be done from the Severn, i.e. in association with Bristol, which was now committed to the venture, but whose links with Plymouth remain undefined.

[2] The argument is that the ships should stay at one port and be totally equipped there, and this should be Plymouth, though this did not exclude part of the materials coming by sea or road from Bristol to Plymouth.

[3] Richard Challons, who had recently escaped from Seville, having broken his bond there (see pp. 355–6). He was a good envoy as Popham had already much to do with him before and since his unfortunate voyage.

[4] Sir Ferdinando Gorges, as a member of the royal council for Virginia constituted shortly after the issue of the Company charter (NAW, v, 199), was clearly regarded, already, as a major spokesman for the Plymouth interests.

are diverse gentlemen of Somersett[1] willing to aduenture some necessarie provisions If we may but knowe what itt is wee shall easilie take order by whatt meanes it may convenientlie be brought hither[2] And as for any quicke Cattell the[y] will with great ease com by lande.[3] Farther we are to craue of Your Lordship that in case we shall not be able voluntarilie to git men willing to goe fitt for the service that you wilbe pleased to be a meanes we may obteyne some letters from the Lordes to Certaine Iustices for ther assistance in that behalf[4]

Thus much vnder you Lordships favor we are bold to recomend to your wisdome and withall to remember yo[u] that the firste establishing of an vniforme order in all thinges wilbe occasion to the Contynewan[c]e hereof the better besides there wilbe taken awaye all occasion of envie or disgrise howe sorie we are that this occasion of protraction is falne out[5] is needeles here to write notwithstanding we cannot but infinitelie acknowledg our selues bound vnto your Lordship for the Contynewance of your Honores favour to wardes vs humblie beseeching you to thinke vs worthie to hold them and to register vs among those you have most power of   Even so with acknowledgement of our dueties we humblie take our leave

Plymouth this xjth of   Your Lordships most humblie
Iune 1606 //   to be comaunded /[6]

[*Endorsed*:] A lettre from the Town ye 11 of Iune 1606 to ye Lord Chief Iustice of England.

[*Later hand*:]   I. A: No. 32
    :11:th Iune 1606

---

[1] The Seymour family, which had extensive interests in Somerset, was already involved (pp. 349, 377), but we do not know who was associated with them.

[2] Popham, having his seat at Wellington, Somerset, was, they considered, best able to arrange about victualling from the country.

[3] They anticipated that part of the Somerset contribution might be live cattle which could come by road.

[4] Clearly, recruiting men to go was not being easy and what they are asking here is that Popham should obtain powers of impressment to make up numbers if necessary. We do not know if this had to be resorted to, but at least J.P.s could be (and probably were) asked to assist by consigning some able-bodied unemployed and perhaps minor criminals to the enterprise. There is no evidence that minor criminals were transported to the colony.

[5] The council is concerned at the lack of any overall plan of organisation (it seems itself to have been acting as the interim executive for the enterprise) and desires to have this rectified and existing delays and confusions cleared up.

[6] The mayor who would have signed it was still James Bagge (see p. 332 above).

A Letter from the Town to the Lord Chief Justice of England relative to the fitting out some expedition at this Port.

37 10 May 1606. Sir Ferdinando Gorges to the earl of Salisbury[1]

Right Honorable:

My humble dutie remembred: Thorough the mocion att firste of some particular persons, and well afected of these partes in this Idle tyme to bring to passe somethinge worthie his Maiesties gratious acceptance. It hath pleased my Lord Iustice out of an honorable disposition to aduance theire proceedinges and (as yt seemed) to be a meanes for the obteyninge of his highnes free leaue and good liking as by his letters Pattentes yt doth att lardg appere to seuerall parties graunted. But some thinges there are whereunto they finde themselues tied which hath exceedinglie cooled the heate of theire afections that att firste did make profer of theire aduentures. As namelie they are vpon all occasions to expecte their directions. for their gouerment from certayne whome his maiestie hath elected to of his councell for those afaires in and about the Cittie, and although many of them exceeding worthie, yet diuers Citizens both of London, Bristow, and Exon. [Exeter] well knowen to haue no manner of vnderstanding what belongeth thereunto more then ordinarie.[2] Besides for them heere to be tyed vpon all occasions to Poste yt to London, is a matter soe tedeous and chargeable as they are wholie distasted with the imagination thereof,[3] and as I perceaue they haue written to his Lordship they vtterlie refuse to proceede any farther, vnles they may be soe happie, as to obteyne your Lordships honorable favour to ioyne with his Lordship for the deliuering of them from soe heauie a yoake as they ymagine this in tyme wilbe vnto them.[4] And indeed when yt was once bruted that

---

[1] Hatfield House, CP 116/40; *Cal. Cecil MSS*, XVIII, 133–4; Baxter, *Gorges*, III, 123–6.

[2] Gorges is more specific and forthright about the Plymouth revolt against the royal council than Mathewe had been (Love was no doubt given the details to present to Salisbury). It appears certain that some announcement of the personnel of the royal council had been made by the end of April, but in what form we do not know.

[3] The jealousy of London by the outports is balanced by the outposts' jealousy of one another, Exeter refusing to be associated with Plymouth, Bristol refusing at first and then coming in under some pressure from one of her M.P.s (pp. 381–2).

[4] The allegation that the day-to-day business of Plymouth in regard to the colonising expedition and the colony would be the concern of the royal council and that frequent visits to London would be needed on matters of detail rests on a misunderstanding, possibly deliberate, of the role of the council as envisaged in the charter, but perhaps defined in whatever document we have lost listing the initial membership.

soe many Cittizens and Tradesmen weare made councellours to his
highnes for the disposing of theire afaires that one theire priueate chardg
vndertooke the enterprize, all the gentlemen that before weare willing
to be lardge aduenturers presentlie withdrew themsealues and by noe
meanes will haue to do therein.[1] But now the pore Townesmen of
Plymouth relyeing themselues vpon your protection hoping by your
honors meanes to find releefe or otherwise the[y] doe dispayer of any
future good hereof to ensew vnto them. And vndoubtedlie (yf my
judgment doe not much deceaue me) yt wilbe a matter of that momente
and the consequence both vnto his maiestie and our whole nation as
yt weare greate pittie yt should be suffered to fall to the grounde.
Neyther can theare be any thinge more honorable then free Condicions
to be graunted to such as willinglie doe hazard themsealues and their
estates without farther chardge to his highnes, to sease him of soe lardge
Territories as they promyse to doe. And for ought I perceaue theire
desier (more then is graunted alreadie) is principally that they may be
assigned to your Lordship and my Lorde Cheife Iustice with such other
honorable and worthie persons as you shall thinke fitt to take vnto you
for your more easie execution of his highnes pleasuer as occasion from
tyme to tyme shall require, and that there may be certeyne Comyssiones
authorized and by you chosen out of these partes that may at all tymes
be presente redelie to receaue and execute those directions to the ease
of all heere without their farther trouble or chardge, and that they may
be exempted from hauing to doo with those Citizens and townesmen
nomynated in his Maiesties graunte, whome they see are like heereafter
to preuayle agaynste them in that they haue alreadie gotten the
gouerment ouer them, soe as they can looke for noe manner of libertie
more then shall stand with theire likinge, or sorte to the profitt of their
seuerall Corporacions, and therefore they are become humble suters to
your good Lordship for obteyninge theire release in that behaulfe.[2] And

---

[1] Gorges maintains that the larger potential subscribers have already withdrawn,
which was quick going unless they had signed on before the charter was granted on 10
April (which is quite possible since the Plymouth project in so far as it derived from the
Waymouth venture could well have been in the making early in the year).

[2] The request for a council headed by Salisbury, Sir John Popham and a collection
of Plymouth men was disingenuous, since there was to be a single royal council to oversee
all the colonies, but it seems clear that it was not defined what the local organisation of
the London and Plymouth companies was to be like. We know each was to have a treasurer,
but precisely what kind of local council representing the subscribers was in mind is not
clear, nor has it been wholly clarified since the evidence is not adequate. At the same time
some local organisation was worked out which quelled some of the fears of the Plymouth
men in giving the Plymouth Company adequate latitude within general principles worked

that being graunted yt is doubtles that many worthie and braue spirites will easilie be drawen to Ingage themselues in this Designe, and the rather yf they finde they may walke vnder the shelter and by the direction of soe honorable a person as your sealfe, which I proteste I speake not to flatter, as I doubte not but the sequell will manyfestlie mencion, and weare my meanes answerable I would say more then now I can, but as yt is I will for euer acknowledge yt your Lordship and sealfe to be disposed during liefe as,

    Your Lordships in all seruices most humblie to be commaunded
                                Fardinando Gorges

From the forte bie Plymouth the 10th of maie 1606.

[*Addressed*:] To the righte Honorable my verie good Lord the Earle of Salisburie.

[*Endorsed*:] 10 May 1606. Sir Ferdinando Gorges to my Lord.

38   [20 November 1606]. 'A note of the orders sett downe for the gouernment of y^e Colonie in Virginia'[1]

After that the kinges Maiestie by his privie Seale hath established his Councell for Virginia betweene the degrees of 34 and 45 of the lyne northward in America   It is this [= thus] sett downe   And the said Councell of Virginia shall nominate and appoint the first seuerall

---

out by the royal council for the organising of the Company so as to allow for adequate local initiative. Gorges, Sir Francis Popham and Bagge were on the royal council from the beginning but we do not know the date on which it was constituted, though possibly only after these letters were written (or before information on its composition had been conveyed to them). An attempt was made to balance Court, London and Western interests though it could be argued that the westerners were under-represented. On 20 Novembe 1606 additional members specifically to represent the interests of each division were appointed. Sir Edward Hungerford, Sir John Mallet, Sir John Gilbert, Sir Thomas Freake Sir Richard Hawkins, Sir Bartholomew Mitchell, Edward Seymour, Bernard Grenville Edward Rogers, and the Very Rev. Matthew Sutcliffe were to represent the westerner (*NAW*, v, 200). Presumably they were all subscribers and were intended to involve both the landed and urban interests in the west more fully in the venture. We know from othe sources only of the involvement of Seymour and Sutcliffe as subscribers, but the other are likely also to be contributors, Sir John Gilbert for one.

[1] West Devon Record Office, Plymouth, Plymouth City Records, W 360/89, ff. 1–5 This is a summary version of the 'Articles, Instructions and orders' set down by the roya council for Virginia for the operation of the two colonies in America. It accompanies damaged copy of the letters patent of 10 April 1606 (W 360/57). There is no authoritativ copy of this document, but working texts of it are given in Barbour, *Jamestown voyages* I, 34–44, *NAW*, v, 200–5.

Councellours of those seuerall Councells which are to be appointed for those two seuerall Colonies which now are to make their plantacion in Virginia & America betwene the degrees before mencioned according to our said lettres Pattentes in that behalfe made   And that each of the same Councells of the said seuerall Colonies shall by the Maior parte of them Chose one of the same Councell not being the Minister of godes worde to be President of the same Councell and to contynue that Office by the space of one whole yere vnles he shall in the meane tyme die or be removed from that Office   And we doe further establish and ordaine that it shalbe laufull for the Maior parte of either the said Councells vpon anie iust Cause either of absence or otherwise to remove their President or anie other of that Councell being either President or anie of that Councell, And that vpon the death or removall of him the same President or Councellors   It shall be laufull for the more parte of that Councell to elect another in the place of the partie so dieing or remoued so allwaies as they shall not be aboue thirteene of either the said Councells, And we doe establish & ordaine that the President shall not contynue in his Office of Presidentships aboue the space of one yere, And doe speciallie ordayne Charge and require the said President and Councells and the Ministers of the said seuerall Colonies respectiuelie within their seuerall lymittes and precynctes That they with all diligence care and respect do prouide that true word & seruice of god and Christian faith be preached planted and vsed not onlie within euerie of the said seuerall Colonies and plantatcions but also as much as they maie amongest the sauage people which be or shall adioyne vnto them or border vpon them according to the doctryne rightes and relygion, nowe professed and established within our Realme of England, And that they shall not suffer anie person or persons to withdrawe anie of the subiectes or people inhabiting or which shall inhabite within anie of the said seuerall Colonies and plantacions from the same or from their due allegeance vnto vs our

Plymouth would have been the natural repository for documents connected with the north Virginia venture. There were 'Commissioners', a ruling council for the western venture, but we have no record of their meeting or of their organisation, except that Sir Francis Popham was treasurer, and did, initially, most of the work, though it later fell mainly to Sir Ferdinando Gorges. At the same time it is clear that the Plymouth Council regarded itself, and was regarded by the council of the London division, as the body ultimately responsible for the western venture after the deaths of Sir John Popham and Sir John Gilbert (see p. 335).

George Popham was appointed president before the colonising expedition sailed in 1607 and it is probable that the composition of the colony council (p. 353) was also known before 31 May 1607.

heires and Successors as their Imediate soueraigne vnder god, And if they shall finde within anie of the said Colonies and Plantacions anie person or persons so seeking to withdrawe anie of the subiectes or people of those landes or places they shall withall diligence cause him or them [in] manner so offending to be apprehended arrested and imprisoned vntill hee shall be fullie and thoroughlie reforme himselfe or otherwise where the Cause so require that he be with all convenient speed sent into oure Realme of Englande there to receaue Condigne punishment for his and their said offence and offences   And moreouer we do hereby ordaine & establish for vs our heires and Successors that all landes Tenantes and heredytamentes to be haide [= had] and enioyed by anie of our subiectes within anie the precinctes aforesaid shalbe had inherited and enioyed according as in the like estates they be had and enioyed by the lawes within this Realme of England, And that the offences of mutynie Conspiracies and seditions which maie be dangerous to the state there, Murther, Manslaughter, incest, Rape and adulterie comitted in the partes within the precinctes of anie the degrees aboue mencyoned and no other offence shalbe punished by death, And that without benefitt of Clergye excepte in the Case of manslaughter in which Clergie shalbe allowed   And that the said seuerall Presidentes and Councells and the greater number of them within anie of their seuerall lymittes and presynctes shall in full power & authoritie heare and determyne all and euerie the offences aforesaid within the precynctes of their seuerall Colonies in manner and forme following   That is to saie by twelue honest and indifferent persons sworen vpon the Evangelistes to be returned by such ministers and officers as anie of the said presidentes and Counsells or the moste parte of them respectiuelie shall assigne, And we doe in like manner establish and ordaine if anie of either of the said Colonies shall offend anie the offences before mencioned within anie parte betweene the degrees aforesaid out of the precinct of his or their Colonies, That then euerie such offender shalbe tried and punished as aforesaid within his or their proper Colonie And the twelue persons so returned and sworen shall according to their evidence to be geauen vnto them vpon oath and according to the truth in their conscience either convict or acquite euerie of the saide persons so to be accused and tried by them   And that all and euerie person and persons which shall voluntarielie confesse anie of the said offences to be comitted by him he shall vpon such his confession thereof be convicted of the same as if he had ben found guiltie thereof by the verdict of anie such twelue Iurors as aforesaid; And that euerie person and persons which shalbe accused of anie of the said offences and which shall stand mute or refuse to make direct answeare therevnto the said persons so standing mute or so refusing to make direct answeare shalbe and be held convicted of the said offence as if he had confessed guiltie by the verdicte of anie such twelue Iurors as aforesaid   And that euerie person and persons so conuicted either by verdict of his own confessions or by standing mute or refusing directlie to answeare as aforesaid of anie the offences before menciioned

The said Presidentes and Councell or the greater number of them within their seuerall preceintes and lymittes where such conuiccion shalbe hadd & made as aforesaid shall haue full power and authoritie by theis presentes to geue iudgment of death vpon euerie such offender, without benefitt of Clergie except onlie in the Case of Manslaughter, And that no person so adiudged attainted and condempned shalbe repriued from thexecucion of the said Iudgment without the Consent of the said President and Councell, or the moste parte of them by whome such Iudgement shalbe geuen, And that no person shall receaue anie pardon or be absolutlie discharged of anie the said offences for which he shalbe condempned to death as aforesaid except in the Case of Manslaughter, but by the pardon of vs our heires and Successors vnder our great seale of England, And that euerie of the said Presidentes and Councells within their seuerall lymittes and precinctes or the Maior parte of them shall haue full power and authoritie by these presentes to heare and determyne all and euerie other trespasses offences and misdemeanours whatsoeuer other then those before mencioned vpon accusation of anie person and proofe first made by sufficient witnes vpon oath. And that in all the said Cases the said President and Councell and the greater number of them shall haue full power and authoritie by these presentes respectiuelie as aforesaide to punish the offender or offenders therin either by Corporall punishment and imprisonment or else by fyne and awarding damages or their satisfaccion to the partie grieued as to the said President and Councell or the more parte of them respectiuelie shalbe thought fitt and Conuenient   And that also the said President & Councell shall haue power and authoritie by vertue of these presentes to punish all manner of accesse [= excess] through drunkennes or otherwise   And all idle loytring and vagrant persons which shalbe found within their seuerall lymittes and precinctes according to their best discretions and with such punishment as they or the most parte of them shall thinke fitt and conuenient   Also our will and pleasure is that in euerie the iudiciall proceedinges abouesaid the same shalbe summarie & verballie without wrighting vntill it come to the iudgment or sentence, And yett neuertheles our will and pleasure is that euerie Iudgment and sentence thereafter to be geuen in anie the Causes aforesaid or in anie other by the said seuerall presidentes and Councells or the greater number of them, within their seuerall lymittes and precinctes shalbe registred into a book to be kept for that purpose together with the Cause for which the said Iudgment or sentence was geuen, And that the said Iudgment and sentence so registred and wrytten shalbe subscribed with the thandes or names of the said President and Councell or such of them as gaue the same sentence or iudgment, Also our will and pleasure is and we doe hereby establish and ordeyne that the said seuerall Colonies and plantacions and euerie person and persons of the same seuerallie & respectiuelie shall within euerie of their seuerall precinctes for the space of fyue yeres next after their first landing vpon the said Coast of Virginia or America trade together in anie [= one] Intier stocke and bring not onlie all the fruites of their labours there but alsoe all such other goodes and Comodities which shalbe brought out of England or anie other place into the same into seuerall Maggesens or storehouses for that purpose to be made and erected for the said seuerall Colonies there, And our will and pleasure is and we doe in like manner establish and ordaine that in euerie of the said seuerall Colonies and plantations there shalbe chosen and elected yerely by the President and Councell or euerie of the said seuerall Colonies and plantacions or the more parte of them one person of the same Colonie and plantacion to be Tresurer or Cape merchant of the same Colonie & plantacion to take the Charge and managing of all such goodes wares and Comodities which shalbe brough[t] into or taken out of the said seuerall Maggesens or Storehouses   The same Tresurer or Cape merchant to contynue in his office by the space of one said yere next after his said election vnles he shall happen to die within the said [yere] or voluntarielie geue over the same or be remoued for anie iust or reasonable cause, And that therevpon the said President and Counsell or the moste parte of them shall haue power and authoritie to elect him againe or anie other in his roome or steede to contynue in the said Office as aforesaid   And that alsoe there shalbe two persons of good discretion within euerie of the said seuerall Colonies and plantacions elected and chosen yerelie during the said terme of fyue yeres by the President and Councell of the said Colonie or the moste parte of them respectiuelie within their seuerall lymittes and precinctes The one to be to keepe one booke in which he shall register and enter all such goodes wares and merchandizes as shalbe receaued into the said seuerall Maggesens & Storehouses within his seuerall lymittes and precinctes and the other to be to keepe a like booke wherein he shall register all goodes wares and merchandizes which shall issue or be taken out of the said seuerall Maggasens and storehouses which clarkes shall contynue in their said places but at the will of the said President and Councell of that Colonie whereof he is or of the moste part of them And that euerie person of euerie of the said Colonies and Plantacions shalbe furnished withe all necessaries out of those seuerall Maggesens or storehouses which shall belong vnto the said Colonie and plantacion of which the partie is for and during the said terme and tyme of fyue yeres by the appointment direccion and order of the President and Councell thereof or of the said Cape Marchaunt and two Clarkes or of the moste of them within the said seuerall lymittes and precinctes of the said Colonies and plantacions   Then here folowes a direction to those that be of the seuerall Colonies for setting their trade in England concerning what shalbe sent out or brought in, Also our will and pleasure [is] that no person or persons shalbe admitted into anie of the said Colonies and Plantacions there to abide and remayne but such as shall take a Corporall Oath such as is lymitted in his Sessions of Parliament nowe holden for their due obedience vnto vs our heires and Successors that the said President and Councell of each of the said Colonies and the more parte of them respectiuelie shall and laufullie maie from tyme to tyme constitute make and ordaine such constitucions ordynaunces and officers [orders?] for the better order gouernement and peace of the people of their seuerall Colonies so as allwaies the same Ordynaunces or Constitucions shall stand and contynue in full force vntill the same shalbe otherwise altered or made voyde by vs our heires and Successors, or our or their Councell of Virginia   So allwaies the same alteracions be such as maie stand with or be in substance Consonant vnto the Common lawes of England or the equitie thereof

Furthermore our will and pleasure is and we doe hereby determyne and ordaine that euerie person and persons being our subiectes of euerie the said Colonies and plantacions shall from tyme to tyme well entreate the Saluages in those partes and vse all good meanes to drawe the Saluages and heathen people of the said seuerall places and of the territories and Countries adioining to the true service of knowledge of god   And that all iust kinde and charitable Courses shalbe holden with all such of them as shall conforme themselues to anie good and sociable trafique and dealing with the Subiectes of vs, our heires and

Successors which shalbe planted there whereby they maie be the sooner drawen to the true knowledge of god and to the obedience of vs our heires or Successors vnder such severe paynes and penalties as shalbe inflicted by the same seuerall Presidentes and Councells or the moste parte of them within their seuerall lymittes and precinctes on such as shall offend therein or do the Contrarie, And that as the said Terrytories and Countrie of Virginia and America within the degrees aforesaid shall from tyme to tyme increase in plantacion by our Subiectes, We our heires and Successors will ordaine and geue such other and further instruccions, Lawes Constitucions and ordynaunces for the better rule order and gouernment of such as shall so make plantacion there as to vs our heires and Successors shall from tyme to tyme be thought fitt and conuenient which allwaies shalbe such as maie stand with or be in substance Consonant with the Common lawes of England or the equitie thereof: And lastlie we doe ordaine and establishe for vs our heires and Successors that such Oath shalbe taken by each of our Councellors here for Virginia concerning their place and office of Councell as by the Priuie Councell of vs our heires and Sucessors of this Realme of England shalbe in that behalfe lymitted and appointed. And that each Councellor of the said seuerall Colonies shall take such Oath for the execucion of their place and Office of Councellor as by the Councell of vs our heires and Successors here of virginia shall in that behalfe be lymitted and appointed. And that aswell Articles & instruccions herein mencioned and conteyned as also all such as by vertue hereof shall hereafter be made and ordayned shall as need shall require by the aduise of our Councell here of Virginia be transcripted ouer vnto the said seuerall Councells of the said seuerall Colonies vnder the Seale to be ordayned for the said Councell hereof of Virginia/ In witnes whereof &c /

[*Endorsed*:] A note of the orders sett downe for the gouernment of the Colonie in Virginia

[*Other irrelevant hand*:] Newfoundland

CHAPTER XI

THE DAVIES JOURNAL OF THE 1607 NORTH VIRGINIA VOYAGE

39 The narrative of the North Virginia voyage and colony, 1607–1608. William Strachey, 'The historie of trauaile into Virginia Britania'

The earliest account of the outward voyage in 1607 and of the establishment of the colony on the Kennebec River was put together by William Strachey between 1610 and 1612. He used the journal kept on the outward voyage of the *Mary and John* and during the early period of the colony by Captain Robert Davis (or Davies) (pp. 398–414). The copy of the Journal from an original in Sir Ferdinando Gorges' papers after his death in 1647 is given below (pp. 416–41), but Strachey's has a certain priority. It was included in the three surviving copies of Strachey's uncompleted book, 'The historie of Travaile into Virginia Britannia', in B.L., Sloane MS 1622, edited as *The historie of travaile into Virginia Britannia* by R. H. Major (Hakluyt Society, 1849), where it occupies pp. 162–80; 'The Historie of travell into Virginia Britania', edited as *The historie of travell into Virginia Britania* by L. B. Wright and V. Freund (Hakluyt Society, 1953) from the Princeton MS, where it appears on pp. 158–73, and 'The Historie of Travaile into Virginia Britannia', in Bodleian Library, MS Ashmole 1758, folios 65–73, which is here published for the first time. The first of these was presented to Sir Francis Bacon as late as 1618, the second to Henry, ninth earl of Northumberland, while he was still a prisoner in the Tower, but probably in or about 1612, and the third to Sir Allen Apsley, purveyor to the navy, at an unknown date. Strachey may have received the manuscript from the officials of the Virginia company of London during 1610 or 1611, but he clearly (pp. 81–2) completed it in 1612, when it might appear that all three copies were written out in the same hand, but were only afterwards distributed to possible patrons, none of whom responded to the receipt of their manuscript by financing its publication. The first copy omits a few passages, but has a number of profiles of the New England coast which are the first of their kind (and which are added here). The other two are textually much closer but they do not include the profiles, though blank spaces are left for them at or near the appropriate places, some lack of care in the final preparation having led to their omission. They are closely related to those in the MS of the Journal, though there is one additional item in Strachey. The Journal is turned by Strachey into a smoothly flowing narrative, omitting much navigational detail but sticking fairly closely to the text as we have it for particulars of the exploration of the Kennebec River and relations with the Eastern Abenaki Indians. The final leaf was absent in the Journal as we have it and is represented in Strachey. A puzzling feature is that details here and there (pp. 399, 401–2, 406) are clearly authentic and are not in the Journal. It would seem that the version which he had was not identical with that possessed by Sir Ferdinando Gorges. No clear explanation of why Robert Davis (or Davies) should have prepared two varying versions of his journal is forthcoming. Annotation has concentrated on variations between Strachey and the Journal as given in the next chapter.

[f. 65] At what tyme the Adventurers of the first Colony Anno 1606. had prepared all things fitt with a fleet of 3. saile for Cap*tain* Christopher Newport to transport a Colony of 100. to begynne the plantac*i*on within the Chesapeak Bay, the foresaid S*ir* John Popham likewise prepared a tall shipp well furnished belonging to bristoll, and the River of Severne, with many Planters, w*h*ich sett out from Plynmouth about Maie [blank], Cap*tain* Haines Mas*ter* to settle a plantation in the River of Sachadehoc, w*h*ich, making his Course[1] for the Islandes of Flores [f. 65 v] and Corvez, one morning about the Island of Gratiosa, the Spanish Fleet com*m*ing from Mexico, had sight of yt, gaue yt chase, and soone tooke yt, and vnderstanding by exam*i*nac*i*on whither she was outward bound, and for what purpose, they tooke the Captaine whose name was Martin Prin[2] out of her, togither with the master and most of the Passengers, dispersing them into divers shippes of their owne, & so held their Course, carrying ours along with them for Spaine, howbeit, one of the Fleete wherein 3. or 4. of the English were togither, by the Steridge of the English, who tooke their turnes at the helme and not being observed, altered their Course, or whether

[1] Strachey is very vague about the beginnings of the North Virginia enterprise. The *Richard*, Henry Challons captain, Nicholas Hinds (or Hynd) of Cockington (not 'Haines') master, left Plymouth on 12 August 1606, while Christopher Newport did not leave the Thames until 20 December 1606. We do not know they had decided to go to 'Sachadehoc': their objective was Pemaquid in Mawooshen (p. 356 above). The choice of the Kennebec was made only after the return of Hanham and Pring late in the year, after they had failed to find the *Richard* at the Georges Is. or Pemaquid.

[2] The captain, of course, was not Pring but Challons. Strachey did not clearly understand there were two expeditions from Plymouth to North Virginia in 1606, so he confuses the leaders' names. The capture of the *Richard* in the Florida Channel on 10 November 1606 is told on pp. 367–8. Where he got the idea that the capture took place off Graciosa, while the ship was making for Flores and Corvo, we cannot say: it was in any case not the Mexico but the Santo Domingo squadron which took the *Richard*.

by Contrary windes Compelled, true yt is vponn observacion, the spanish Pilot not knowing where he was vnlooked for fell vpon the coast of Fraunce, within the River of Burdeux where they would haue concealed the English, and stowed them therefore vnder hatches, had they not happely bene perceaved by some of the French, which came abourd, who obteyned them of the Spaniard and carryed them ashore, at what tyme one of them Daniell Tucker[1] Gentleman made Complaint vnto the officers of the place of this wrong offred vnto themm, and in his Maiestes name caused this shippe to be stayed & arrested vntill the Court in Paris might determine of the same: but the Spaniard had too golden an Advocate, a West Indian Purse coming newlie from thence, and therefore after some little attendaunce, easely freed himself from the Incombrance and made for Spaine with mallice enough to entreat the other Captived English, whome they had dispersed & made slaues in their Gallions./

Howbeit, the aforesaid late Lord Chief Iustice would not for all this hard handsell, and Spanish mischief giue over his determynacion for planting of a Colony within the aforesaid so goodly a Country vponn the River of Sachadehoc, but against the next yeare prepared a greater nomber for Planters and better provisions, which in two shippes he sent thither, a fly-boat, called the guift of God. wherein a kinsmann of his, George Popham commaunded, and a good shippe called the Mary and John of Londonn, wherein Raleigh Gilbert comaunded which with 120. persons for Planters[2] brake grownd from Plynmouth in June <u>1607</u>.[3] which the 25.th fell with Gratiosa, and the 28.th tooke in wood and water at Flores & Coruez. [f. 66] from whence they alwaies kept their Course to the westward as much as wynd and weather would permitt, in which Course to the west, and west-nor-west as the wynd would giue leaue they rann twoo hundred leagues from Flores, and in the Latitude of 42. degrees they found the Compasse to be varyed one whole point.[4]

---

[1] He has picked up something of Daniel Tucker's story about the fate of the men whose Spanish captor was driven into Bordeaux, and of the action (ultimately unsuccessful) to hold the vessel as pledge for the return of the *Richard* and her men. Daniel Tucker's narrative of his experiences is given above: the final result of the action was much later, cp. pp. 360–3.

[2] Strachey's figure of 120 intending planters is not confirmed elsewhere, and is almost certainly too high: 100 or thereabouts seems more nearly correct (pp. 337, 344).

[3] He is gradually picking up the material from the Davies Journal: we know the ships left Plymouth on 31 May, but the Journal begins with them leaving the Lizard on 1 June.

[4] Apart from the misspelling of Corvo (the work of his amanuensis?), the account summarizes the Journal except that there is no mention that at 200 leagues west of Flores a variation of one point (11¼ degrees) was noted (cp. p. 419). This indicates either that he had a second journal (which seems unlikely) or that he had a slightly fuller MS of the Davies Journal.

From thence they stood still to the west-ward, vntill the 27. of July being the*nn* in the Latitude of 43. and $\frac{2}{3}$. where they threwe out the dipsing lead,[1] and had grownd but xx^{ty} fathome & 22. fathome vpo*nn* a Banck, and here they fisht some 3. howres and tooke nere 200. o Cod, very great Fish, and where they might haue lade*nn* their shippe in little tyme./

From hence they stood in for the Maine, the wind being at so-west and as they ra*nn* in for the land, they alwaies sounded from this banck and having ru*nn* some 12. leagues from the banck nor-west they sounded and had 60 fathome ouze ground black the wynd now growing scant, they were constrayned to stand for the so-ward, and made south so-west waie and sounded againe the next daie, being the 28. of Julye, and had 30. fathome, smale stones and white shells fishing ground./[2]

29. they made a west waie vntill noone and then sounded had 160 fathome black oze.

30. about [blank][3] of the Clock in the morning, they had sight o the land, and yt bore of them norwest, they sounded being 10. league from the shoare, and had 100. fathomes black oze they made towarde the shoare, but Could not recover yt before the night tooke the*mn* for w*h*ich they were constreyned to beare off a little from the land and lie a hull all that night where they found aboundaunce of Fish very large and great and the water deepe, hard abourd the shoare 18. o 20. fathome/

31. standing in for the shoare in the afternoone, they came to an ancre vnder an Island, for all this Coast is full of Islandes but very sounc and good for shipping to passe by the*mm*, and the water deepe harc abourd the*mm*, they had not bene at an ancre 2 howres when there came a spanishe shallop[4] to them from the Shoare, in her eight Salvadg men*n*, and a little Salvadge boy, who at the first rowed about the*mn* and would not come abourd, notwithstanding they proffered then bread,[5] knives, beades, and other smale triffles, but having gazed a whil vpo*nn* the Shippe they made shew to depa*r*te, howbeit whe*nn* [f. 66v they were a little from them, they returned againe, and bouldly Cam

---

[1] The dipsing lead is not mentioned in the Davies Journal. It was a line with lea sinkers for sounding depths.

[2] The soundings for the 28th are not in the Journal (cp. p. 419). The narrative conflate events of 27–30 July.

[3] The gap is in all the MSS of Strachey: in the Journal (p. 420) it is given as ' 10 '.

[4] 'a biskey shallop' in Journal, Ibid.

[5] 'biskett' in Journal, Ibid.

vp into the shippe and 3. of them staied all night abourd, the rest departed, and went to the Shoare, shewing by signes that they would returne the next daie

The first of August, the same Salvages returned with 3. womenn with them in another Biskey Shalloppe, bringing with themm manie[1] Bever skinnes to exchaung for knives & beades the sagamo of that place[2] they told them, was called Messamot seated vponn a River not far of which they called Emanuett the Salvages departing, they hoisted out their boate, and the Pilot Captain R. Dauies[3] with 12. others, rowed into the Bay wherein their ship road, and landed on a gallant Island, where they fownd Gooseberries, Strawberries, Raspices, Hurts, and all the Island full of hugh high Trees of divers sortes, after they had delighted themselues there a while, they returned abourd againe, and observed the place to stand in 44. degrees & $\frac{1}{3}$.[4]

2. about midnight the Moone shyning bright,[5] & the wynd being faire, at nor-east they departed from this place, setting their Course so-west for so the Coast lieth

3. yearly in the morning, they were faire by the Shoare a league from yt and saw manie Islandes of great biggnes, & many great Sowndes going betwixt themm but made proufe of none of themm, but found great store of fish all alongst the Coast.

4. They were thwart of the Cape or head-land which standes in 43. degrees, the ship being in 42. degrees 50. minutes,[6] betwixt the place they were now at, and the said Cape or head-land yt is all full of Islandes and deepe soundes for any shipping to goe in by themm, and where is exceeding good fishing for Cod great and smale. bigger then what comes from the Banke of the new fownd land, this Cape is low land, shewing white like sand, but yt is all white Rockes, and a strong tyde goeth there, they rann within half a league of the Cape and from thence the land fell away and falls in from this head-land nor-west, and by nore, & nore-west, They kept their Course from this head-land west, and west, and by south 7. leagues from this head-land, and came to three Islandes, where they found a ledge of Rockes to the so-ward which made them hale of from them, and the wynd being at nor-east,

---

[1] 'Som feow' in Journal, p. 421.

[2] 'the sagamo of that place' for 'the Cheef Commaunder' in Journal, Ibid.

[3] 'the Pilott, Captain R[obert] Dauies' This helps to establish that the Journal was written by Robert Davies (or Davis) rather than James Davies (see above, pp. 80–1).

[4] The latitude, 44° 10′, is not given in Journal, p. 422.

[5] 'the moone shining bright' not in Journal, Ibid.

[6] 'and cam very near vnto ytt' [no figure for lat. given] in Journal, p. 423.

they passed the*m*m keeping their Coast still west and by south, and west so-west vntill 12. of the Clock at night, and made from this head-land in all 30. leagues.[1]

[f. 67] 5. they made a west nor-west waie from 4. of the Clock in the morning, vntill 3. of the Clock in the after-noone, & made 15. leagues, and then they sawe the land againe, for from the Cape before named, they saw no more land, but those 3 Island*es* vntill now in w*h*ich tyme they ra*n*n 45. leagues, and the land bore of them, whe*n*n they saw yt first norwest & by north and yt shewed yt self in this forme[2] 9 leagues or more from yt, There be three high mountaynes that lye in on the land, the land called Segohquet,[3] nere about the River of Penobscot

Fig. 17.

they stood towardes this high land, vntill 12. of the Clock noone the next daie and they found the shippe to be by observac*i*on in $43\frac{1}{2}$

6. from 12 of the Clock noone, they kept their Course due west, and came neere vnto the 3. Island*es*, lying low & flat by the water, shewing white to the water, as if yt were sand, but yt is white rock, making shewe afarre off almost like Dover Cliffs there lieth so-west from the eastermost of the 3. Island*es*, A white rocky Island, and those other 3. Island*es* lye one of the other east and west, so they stood their Course west fast by them and as they stood to the westward, the high-Land before spoke*n*n made shew of this forme herevnder, bearing of them then Nore norwest west[4]

---

[1] The Journal does not give the distance (30 leagues) made good, p. 423.

[2] The profiles are reproduced from the B.L. MS: those in the Journal are broadly similar in design but all three are in line, and not two above and one below as in Strachey, cp. p. 424. The Bodleian MS merely leaves a gap below where the B.L. version is inserted.

[3] 'the lande called Segohquet' not in Journal, Ibid. The name is normally applied to the St George River (Eckstorm, *Indian place-names*, pp. 84–5; Huden, *Indian place-names*, p. 225), but it could well have been applied by the Pemaquid band to the land on either side of the river and refer to a territory there. It appears as Segocket in Smith, *Description* (1616), pp. 8, 24.

[4] A gap is left which is filled from the B.L. MS. The two profiles in the Journal are broadly similar in form, but here that on the left is relatively larger and reached the sea

Fig. 18 [i].

From hence they kept still their course west & by nore towardes 3 other Islandes, which they saw lying from those Islandes 8 legues, and about 10 of the Clock at night, having sent in their boat before night to make yt, they bore in for one of themm, the which they afterwardes named St Georges Island,[1] they sounded all along as they came in and found very deepe water hard abourd yt 40. fathome, so here they ancored for y^t night, within this Island in 12. fathome: in the morning they were envyroned every waie with Islandes, they told vpward of 30 Islandes, from abourd their shippe very good sayling out betweene them

[f. 67v] 7. they weyed anchor, thereby to ride in more saffetye howsoever the wynd should happenn to blow, howbeit before they put fromm the Island they found a Crosse sett vp, one of the same which Captain George Waymann[2] in his discovery for all after occasions, left vponn this Island, having sayled to the westward they brought the high Land before spoken of to be north and thenn it shewed thus[3]

Fig. 18 [ii].

About midnight Captain Gilbert caused his Shippes boat to be mand with 14. persons, and the Indiann called Skidwares (brought into

---

in a gentle curve and not a steep cliff. Further, here on both islands vegetation is crudely indicated (as tree cover?) whereas in the Journal the surface is smooth. Presumably this version is closer to the original.

[1] 'which they afterwardes named St Georges Island' is probably Strachey's mistake. In the Journal it is 'this Illand we Call St Georges Illand' but this was because they knew it to have been so called by Waymouth in 1605 (though it was also known to Rosier as Santa Cruz Island).

[2] The Journal assigns the cross to 'Captain George Wayman' for Waymouth, under 6 August, p. 425.

[3] The last sentence is not in the Journal nor is the profile which is taken from the B.L. MS, a gap being left in the Bodleian MS. These are the hills on the mainland (Camden Mts) indicated above, p. 260. Once again vegetation is suggested, very slightly for the larger mountain on the left, more positively for the smaller one on the right.

403

England by Captain Waymann)[1] and rowed to the westward from their shippe, to the River of Pemaquid, which they found to be 4 legues distant from their shippe where she road, the Indian brought them to the Salvadges howses, where they found 100. menn womenn and Childrenn and their Chief Comaunder or sagamo amongst them named Nahanada, who had bene brought likewise into England by Captayne Wayman[2] and returned thither by Captain Hanam setting forth for those partes and somme parte of Canada the yeare before, at their first Coming the Indians betooke themm to their Armes, their bowes and arrowes, but after Nahanada had talked with Skidwares and perceaved that they were English menn, he caused them to lay asyde their bowes & arrowes, and he himself came vnto and ymbraced them and made them much welcomme, and enterteyned them with much Chierfulnes, as did they likewise him, and after 2. howers interchaungeably thus spent, they returned abourd againe.

9. Sonday, the Chief of both the Shippes with the greatest part of all the Company, landed on the Island, where the Crosse stood, the which they called St Georges Island, and heard a Sermon delivered vnto themm by master Seymour their Preacher and so returned abourd againe

10. Captain Popham, manned his Shallop, and Captaine Gilbert his Shipboat with 50. persons in both and departed for the Riuer of Pemaquid, carrying with them Skidwares and being arryved in the mouth of the River, there came forth Nahanada with all his Company of Indians with their bowes and arrowes in their handes, they being before his dwelling howse would not [f. 68] willingly haue all our people come on shore, being fearefull of themm, to giue them satisfacion the Captaynes, with some 8. or 10 of the Chiefest landed, but after a little parlie togither they suffred them all to come a shore, vsing them in all kynd sort after their manner, nevertheles after one howre, they all suddenly with drew themselues into the woodes, nor was Skidwares desirous to returne with them any more abourd, our people loth to proffer any violence vnto him by drawing him by force,

---

[1] The information that Skidwarres had been brought to England by 'Captain Wayman' is not included in the Journal, p. 425.

[2] The initial absence of the Indians, stressed in the Journal, is not included: 'or sagamo' (for sagamore) is not in the Journal nor is the information that Nahanada had been captured by Waymouth and brought back by 'Captain Hanam, setting forth for those parts and some part of Canada the year before', Ibid. The reference to Hanham setting out for some part of Canada is somewhat puzzling (but 'Canada' is used elsewhere for New England, p. 353).

suffred him to stay behind, promising to returne vnto them the daie following, but he did not, after his departure they imbarked themselues and rowed to the further side of the river, and there remayned on the shoare for that night.

11. they returned to their shippes towardes the Evening, where they still road vnder St Georges Island.

12 they weyed anchors and set saile to goe for the River of Sachadehoc, they had little wynd and kept their Course west

13. they were south of the Island of Sutquin a league from yt, and yt riseth in this forme here vnder but they did not take yt to be Sutquin[1]

Sutquin, being sowth of it. The high mountains being north from you rise thus.

Fig. 19.

so the weather being very faire, they sought the island further to the west-ward, but at length fynding y^t they had overshott yt, they bore vp helme but were soon becalm'd by which meanes they were constreyned to remaine at Sea, when about midnight there arrose a mightie storme vpon them which putt them in great daunger by reason they were so neere the shore and could not gett off the wynd all the while at south and yt blew very stiff so as they were compelled to turne yt to & againe hard abourd the Lee shore, many Rockes & Islandes vnder their Lee hard by themm, but (god be thancked) they escaped vntill yt was daie, the storme still contynuing vntill noone the next daie.

14 so soone as the daie gaue light, they perceaved that they were hard abourd the shore in the Bay, that they were in the daie before, which made them looke out for some place to thrust in the Ship to saue their lives, for towing the long boat, yt laye suncke at the sterne

[1] There are considerable variations in the profiles in B.L. MS and that in the Journal, and there is a gap in the Bodleian MS only at the end of the entry for the 13th. There is little difference with regard to that on the left, the view of Seguin I. from the south, except that here vegetation is indicated. The other presents not another view of Seguin I. but a more elaborate version of high ground on the mainland, with the inscription 'The high mountains being north from you rise thus'. There is little, if anything, above the 200 ft contour to be seen from this point, and it might seem this is transposed from a view northward from the Georges Islands.

2 howers & more[1] yet would they not cut her off lyving in hope to
saue her so bearing vp helme they stood in right with the shore, whenn
anonn they perceaved twoo little [f. 68 v.] Islandes, to which they made,
and there they found (god be thancked) good anchoring, where they
road vntill the storme broke, which was the next daie after,[2] here they
freed their boat, and had her ashore to repaire her, being much torne
and spoyled: these Islandes are twoo legues to the west-ward of
Sachadehoc[3] vponn one of themm they went on shore, and found
4. Salvadges and one womann.   the Island all rocky and full of pine-trees

15. the storme ended, and the wynd came faire for them to goe for
Sachadehoc, the River whither they were bound too, and enioyned to
make their plantation in, so they weyed Anchor and sett sayle and came
to the eastward, and found the Island of Sutquin, and anchored vnder
yt, for the wynd was off the shore, by which they could not get in
to Sachadehoc yet Captain Popham with the Flie-boat[4] got in

16. in the morning Captain Popham sent his Shallop[5] to helpe in
the Mary & John, which weyed anchor, and being calme was soone
towed in and anchored by the Guifts syde.

17 Captain Popham in his Pynnace with 30. persons, & Captain
Gilbert in his long boat, with 18. persons more, went early in the
morning fromm their shippe into the River of Sachadehoc, to view the
River, and to search where they might fynd a fitt place for their
plantationn,   they sailed vp into the River nere 14 legues[6] and found
yt to be a very gallant River very deepe and of a good breadth, and
full of Fish leaping aboue the water and seldome lesse water then 3.
fathome, when they found least, wherevponn they proceeded no
further, but in their returne homewardes they observed manie goodly
Islandes therein and manie braunches of other smale Rivers falling
into yt

18 they all went on shore, and there made Choise of a place for their
plantationn at the mouth or entry of the River on the west syde (for
the River bendeth yt self towardes the nor-east and nor-east and by
east)[7] being almost an Island of a good bignes, being in a province called

---

[1] 'two howers and more' is additional to the Journal, p. 430.

[2] The sequence differs from the Journal, according to which shelter was found under
the two small islands on the 13th, not the 14th, Ibid.

[3] Here 'Sachadehoc' is usual; in Journal 'Sagadehock' is normal, Ibid.

[4] The description of the *Gifte of God* as 'the flie-boat' is not in Journal.

[5] 'pynnace' here and 'shallop' in Journal, p. 431.

[6] It is argued that 4 or 5 leagues (not this nor the Journal's '14' nor the '40' of the
B.L. MS) is correct. Ibid.

[7] The bracketed material is not in the Journal, Ibid.

by the Indians Sabino[1] so called of a Sagamo or Chief Commaunder vnder the graund Bashaba, as they were a shore 3 Canoas full of Indians came to themm, but would not come neere, but rowed awaie vp the River

19 they all went to the Shoare, where they had made Choise for their plantationn, and there they had a sermonn delivered vnto them by their preacher, and after the Sermonn the Presidentes Commission was read, with the lawes to be observed and kept[2] George Popham gentleman was nomynated President [f. 69] Captain Raleigh Gilbert, James Dauies, Richard Seymour Preacher Captain Richard Dauies, Captain Harlow,[3] the same who brought awaie the salvadg at this tyme shewed in Londonn from the River of Canada,[4] were all sworne Assistentes and so they returned abourd againe

20. all went to shoare againe, and there beganne to entrench and make a Fort, and to build a storehowse,[5] so contynuing the 21. 22. 23. 24. 25. 26. 27.

28. whilst most of the handes laboured hard about the Fort, and the Carpenters about the building of a small pinnace,[6] the President overseeing and applying every one to his worke Captain Gilbert departed in the shallop vponn a discovery to the westward and sayled all the daie, by manie gallant Islandes, the wynd at night coming contrary, they came to anchor that night vnder a head-Land, by the Indians called Semiamis, the land exceeding good and firtile, as appeared by the trees growing there onn being goodly and great, most oake and walnut with spacious passadges betweene, and no rubbish[7] vnder, and a place most fitt to fortefie on being by nature fortefyed on twoo sydes, with a spring of water vnder yt

[1] The material which indicates the site as being in an Indian district called Sabino, and under a sagamore who in turn was under 'the graund bassaba [Bashabes]' is not in the Journal, p. 431.

[2] See above, p. 353.

[3] The additions to the Journal naming the president and council are useful. George Popham as president, Captain Raleigh Gilbert, James Davies, Richard Seymour, preacher, Captain Richard [for Robert] Davies, Captain [Edward] Harlow. Strachey got these from another source. For a fuller and more precise list see John Smith's version, Ibid.

[4] 'Captain Harlow, the same who brought away the salvadg at this tyme shewed in London, from the River of Canada' (the St Lawrence) but from southern New England, having been captured in 1611 and exhibited in London in 1612 when Strachey was there (cp. p. 82). The item is useful as showing that Strachey completed this part of his narrative in 1612. In the B.L. MS and the Princeton MS (Wright and Freund, p. 167) the plural 'saluadges' is used.

[5] The storehouse does not appear in the Journal at this stage, p. 432.

[6] The Journal puts the beginning of work on the pinnace as 21 August, Ibid.

[7] 'no rubbish' for 'no thickett', Journal, p. 437.

29. they departed from this headland Semeamis lying in the height of $43\frac{1}{2}$ degrees, and rowed alongest the shore to the west ward for that the wynd was against them, and which blew so hard that they reached no further then an Island 2 legues off, where whilst they anchored twoo Canoas passed by them but would not come nere them.

30. they returned homeward, before the wynd sailing by manie goodly and gallant Islandes, for betwixt the said head-Land Semeamis and the River of Sachadehoc is a very great bay, in the which there lyeth so manie Islandes, and so thicke & neere togither, that cann hardly be discerned the nomber, yet may any Shippe passe betwixt the greatest parte of them, having seldome lesse water then 8. or 10. fathome about them,[1] these Islandes are all overgrowne, with woodes, as oake, walnut, pine, Spruse-trees, hasel nutes sarsaperilla, and hurtes in aboundaunce only they found no Saxafras at all in the Country, and this night they arryved at the fort againe

September. 31. and 1. of September 2. 3. & 4 nothing was done but only for the furtheraunce and building of the Fort and Storehouse to receaue ashoare their Victualls / [f. 69 v]

5. about noone there came into the entraunce of y^c River of Sachadehoc, and so vnto the Fort, as our people were at their worke 9 canoas with 40. saluadges in them, men women and children, and amongest them was Nahanada, and Skidwares, they came vp into the fort, and the President gaue them meat and drinck and vsed them exceeding kyndly, two or three howres they remayned there,[2] and then they parted, Skidwares and another Saluadge staying still with whome at night Captain Gilbert, James Dauies, and Ellis Best[3] went over to the furthest syde of the River, whether all the rest had withdrawne themselues, and there remayned with themm all the night, and early in the morning, the Salvadges departed in their Canoas for the River of Pemaquid, promising Captain Gilbert to accompany him in their Canoas to the River of Penobscot, where the Bashaba dwells.[4]

6. & 7. the busines of the Fort only attended.

8. Captain Gilbert with 22. others departed in the shallop for the River of Penobscot taking with him divers sortes of Marchandizes to trade with the Bashaba, but by reason the wynd held Easterly being contrary yt was 3. daies before he got vnto the River of Pemaquid[5]

---

[1] 'never Lesse Watter then 8 fetham', Journal, p. 436.

[2] 'Two or three howers they remayned there' not in Journal, p. 438.

[3] 'James Dauies, and Ellis Best': 'James Davis and Captain Ellis best', Journal, Ibid.

[4] 'bassaba'; 'bashabe', Journal, p. 439.

[5] 'yt was 3 daies before he got ynto the river of Pemaquid'; 'Ytt was the xjth daye beffor he Could gett to the ryver of Pemaquid', Journal, Ibid.

11. early in the morning they came into the Riuer of Pemaquid there to call Nahanada and Skidwares, to goe along with them, but being arryved there, they found that they were all gonne from thence vnto the Riuer of Penobscot[1] before, wherefore they sett saile for that River, and all that daie, as likewyse the 12. and 13. they sayled and searched to the east-ward, yet by no meanes could fynd the River, for which they returned their victualls spent, and the wynd larg and good, and in 2 daies arryved againe at the fort having had a sight the 15th in the morning of a blasing starre in the noreast of them

The 16. 17. 18.19. 20. 21. 22. all laboured about the Fort, and building vp of the Storehowse.

23. Captain Gilbert accompanied with 19. others departed in his Shallop[2] to goe for the head of the River of Sachadehoc, they sayled all this daie, and the 24th the like vntill 6. of the Clock in the Afternoone, whenn they landed on the Rivers syde, where they fownd a Championn Land, and very firtile, where remayned all that night [f. 70]

25. in the morning they departed from thence, and sayled vp the River and came to a flatt low Island, where is a great Cataract or Downefall of water,[3] which runneth by both sides of this Island very shold & swift   In this Island they found great store of grapes both red and white, good hoppes, as also Chiballs and garlick,   they haled their boat with a strong roape through this downefall perforce, and went neere a legue further vp, and here they lay all night, and in the first of the night there called certayne Saluages on the further syde of the River vnto them in broken English, they answered them againe, and parled long with themm, when towardes morning they departed

26. in the morning there came a Canoa vnto them, and in her a Sagamo and 4. Saluages[4] some of those which spoke to them the night before,   the Sagamo called his name Sebenoa[5] and told vs how he was Lord of the River of Sachadehoc,[6]   they entertayned him freindly and

---

[1] 'gonne from thence vnto the River of Penobscot'; 'gone from thence', Journal, p. 436.   [2] Adds 'in his shallop'.
[3] 'a great Cataract or Downefall of water'; 'a great down Fall of watter', Journal, p. 440.
[4] 'in her a Sagamo and 4 Saluages'; 'in her fower saluages', Journal, p. 441.
[5] 'Sebenoa'; 'Sabenoa', Journal, Ibid.
[6] At this point the Journal ends. Strachey appears to have had the clear impression that the Journal he was using was written by Captain R. Davies (p. 401). It recorded events only up to the eve of the departure of the Mary and John from Fort St George on October 8, the date of the plan which was also brought with the ship (pp. 441–3; Fig. 25). According to Gorges, it was the Captain, Robert Davis or Davies, who gave him a full report of what had occurred in the course of the outward voyage and in the establishment of the colony

tooke him into their boat and presented him with some triffling thinges, which he accepted   howbeit he desired somme one of our menn to be put into his Canoa as a Pawne for his saffety,[1] wherevpon Captayne Gilbert sent in a mann of his, when presently the Canoa rowed awaie from themm, with all the speed they Could make vp the River,   they followed with the shallop, having great Care that the Sagamo should not leape over bourd   the canoa quickly rowed from them and landed, and the men made to their howses, being neere a league in on the land from the River syde, and carryed our mann with them,[2]   the shallop making good waie, at length came vnto another downefall, which was so shallow and so swift, that by noe meanes they could passe any further,[3] for which Captain Gilbert with 9 others landed and tooke their fare the savage Sagamo with them and went in search after those other Saluadges, whose howses the Sagamo told Captain Gilbert were not farr off[4]   and after a good tedious March they came (indeed) at length vnto those Saluadges howses, where they found neere 50 able menn very strong and tall, such as their like before they had not seene,[5] all new paynted & armed with their bowes and arrowes,   howbeit after

---

(p. 451). Purchas indicated in his *Pilgrimage* (1614) that he depended on a journal by James Davies, but he may well have been mistaken in the authorship (pp. 349, 352). James Davies is referred to in the third person in the Journal while the author always refers to himself in the first person. Each had, according to Smith (p. 353), a position in the colony's hierarchy. James Davies, as captain of the fort, could not well leave in October. Is his Ric. for Rob., the sergeant major? As such he would be second in command of the military element in the colony, Popham being the commander. Once the fort was fully established Richard (Robert) Davies could be spared. He was evidently a close associate of Raleigh Gilbert throughout the outward voyage and in the colony. He was also a skilled pilot, and either acted as pilot on the outward voyage, or checked the reckonings of the master during the voyage. The assumption that James Davies must have been the author is not supported by Strachey.

[1] This assumes some degree of communication. Could Sabenoa speak a little English? Did some of the English by this time know a little Algonquian? Or was it all done by signs? Most probably he had one of the Pemaquid band with him to translate.

[2] It is clear from what follows below that the canoe with the English hostage was beached, portaged, and that the party passed some 3 miles into the interior.

[3] Thayer (pp. 77–8) followed by Burrage (p. 414) identify the island, now gone, as Cushnoc Island, five miles above which were Bacon's Rips, at modern Augusta, near where they went ashore.

[4] We here have Gilbert obeying Sabenoa's directions. Thayer (p. 77) considered they were heading up Seven Mile Brook, but no clear indication can be given.

[5] We can probably identify Sabenoa with the Sabenaw (Sabnoa) of the Mawooshen document (p. 473 below), or even the Samowessa of Harlow (p. 477), but this is not certain. There his band is located on the Andrascoggin River, the western branch of the Kennebec River basin complex. He appears to have exercised some local superiority over the bands of the central Kennebec, but recognising Bashabes' superiority. His 50 warriors would imply a village of some 200 people.

that the Sagamo had talked with them, they delivered back againe the mann and vsed all the rest very freindly, as did ours the like by them, who shewed themm their Commodities of beades, kniues and some Copper of which they seemed very fonnd,[1] and by way [f. 70v] of trade made shew that they would come downe to yᵉ boat, and there bring such thinges as they had to eschaung them for ours,[2] so Captain Gilbert departed from them, & within half an howre after he had gottenn to his boate, there came 3. Canoas downe vnto them, and in them some 16. Saluages, and brought with them some Tobacco & Certayne smale skynns, which were of no value, which Captain Gilbert perceauing, and that they had nothing ells wherewith to trade, he caused all his menn to come abourd[3] and as he would haue put from the shore, the saluadges perceiuing so much subtilly devised how they might put out the fire in the Shallop, by which meanes they sawe they should be free from the daunger of our mens pieces, and to performe the same, one of the Saluadges came into the Shallop and taking the fire brand which one of our Company held in his hand, thereby to light the Matches, as if he would light a pipe of Tobacco, as soone as he had gottenn yt into his hand, he presently threw it into the water & leapt out of the Shallop,[4] Captain Gilbert seeing that, suddenly Commaunded his menn to betake them to their muskettes, and the Targettiers to from the head of the boat, and bade one of the menn before with his targett on his arme to steppe on the shoare for more fier, the Salvadges resisted him & would not suffer him to take any,[5] and some others holding fast the boat rope that the Shallop could not

---

[1] Their special interest in copper might suggest they were not part of the trading chain which brought copper along the coast from the Bay of Fundy to southern new England (p. 109 above).

[2] Gilbert would probably have been wise to give them some of the objects he showed them as an earnest of this good intentions.

[3] Gilbert's refusal to accept what the Indians brought was unwise. They were not accustomed to matching exchanges precisely and regarded the refusal to accept their offerings as proof of bad faith. Gilbert is here applying European concepts of exchange which were foreign to the Indians, namely exchange at rates of equal value. Had he accepted and paid for what was offered, he would have given evidence of his good intentions and laid the foundations for future trade, whether or not it was true that at this time the Indians had no further trade objects.

[4] This episode shows how dependent a small party was on maintaining fire for the matchlocks, and the ingenuity of the Indian who perceived the connection between the match and the percussion of the guns was considerable.

[5] It is not clear whether Gilbert was totally dependent on matches for fire, but striking fire from flint and steel and lighting a fresh match from it would take time and concentration. It was easier to attempt to secure fire from the Indians' own fire in their village.

put off, Captain Gilbert caused the Musquettiers to present their pieces, the which the Saluadges seeing presently lett goe the boat rope,[1] & betooke them to their Bowes & arrowes, & ran into the bushes nocking their arrowes, but did not shoot neither did ours at themm, so the Shallop departed from themm to the further side of the River, where one of their Canoas came vnto them and would have excused the fault of the others   Captain Gilbert made shew as if he were still freindes and entertayned them kindly[2] and so left them, returning to the place where he had lodged the night before, and there came to an anchor for that night,   The head of this River[3] standeth in 45. degrees & od minutes   vponn the contynent they found aboundaunce of Spruse Trees,[4] such as are able to maast the greatest shippe his Maiestie hath, and many other Trees, oake Walnut Pineapple,[5] fish aboundaunce, great store of grapes hoppes and Chiballs,[6] also they found Certaine Codes in which they [f. 71] supposed the Cotton wooll to growe,[7] and also vponn the banckes manie shells of Pearle. /[8]

27. here they sett vp a Crosse,[9] and then returned homeward in the waie seeking the by ryver of some note called Sasanoa,[10]   this daye

[1] How serious the attempt to hold up the shallop was, is hard to say; in the event both sides showed restraint in not coming to blows, but at least the episode was a test of the Englishmen's determination. Perhaps the gesture was made primarily to reprimand them for the bad manners (in Indian eyes) with which they had spurned the tobacco and skins.

[2] The peace gesture and its acceptance would seem to support the suggestions just made.

[3] It is difficult to know what he means by 'the head of the river'. Thayer (p. 81) is inclined to think that Gilbert considered the rapids he encountered marked the end of boat navigation, which they did not. It may be that some indications of the river rising in a lake some 70 to 80 miles farther on could be had from the Mawooshen description (p. 475). While Augusta is at 44° 15′ N, the Moosehead Lake headwaters lie between 45° 28′ and 45° 55′: any approach so far inland would appear to be out of the question.

[4] Probably White Spruce, *Picea glauca* (Moench) Voss, the prevailing species.

[5] For oaks p. 304. White Walnut, *Juglans cinerea* L. is near the limit of the natural range (Hyland and Steinmetz, *Woody plants*, p. 12): Shagbark Hickory, *Carya ovata* (Mill) K. Kohn has a somewhat more northerly range. Pineapple is simply pine (see p. 408).

[6] On grapes, hops and chiballs (wild onions) see pp. 409, 440.

[7] The 'codds' were the seed pods of the milkweed, whose cotton-wool-like seeds had apparently by this time dispersed. *Asclepias syriaca* L. is the most commonly found species in this area. From the time of the Roanoke voyages onwards it was regarded as a possible textile source (see Quinn, *Roanoke voyages*, index of subjects).

[8] These are most probably shells of the Freshwater Mussel, *Unio complanatus* L., the source of mother-of-pearl.

[9] No clear idea of where the cross was erected can be gained from the narrative.

[10] Thayer considered, and probably correctly, that they were looking for the Sasanoa River much too far north (pp. 81–2). The river, later found (p. 474), opens opposite the site of Bath and links the Kennebec proper with Sheepscot Bay. The fog and rain of late September are still characteristic of the river valley.

and the next they sought yt, when the weather turned fowle and full of fogg and rayne, they made all hast to the Fort before which the 29. they arrived.

30 and 1. & 2. of October all busy about the Fort   October.

3. there came a Canoa vnto some of the people of the Fort as they were Fishing on the sand in which was Skidwares,[1] who bade them tell their President, that Nahanada, with the Basshabaes brother[2] and others were on the further syde of the river, and the next daie would come & visit him

4. there came 2. Canoas to the fort, in which were Nahanada and his wife[3] and Skidwares, and the Basshabaes brother and one other called Amenquin a Sagamo,[4] all whome the President feasted, and entertayned with all Kindnes both that daie and the next, which being Sondaie the President carryed them with him to the place of publique praiers, which they were at both morning and evening, attending yt with great reverence & sylence.

6. the Salvadges departed all except Amenquin the Segamo, who would needes stay amongest our people a longer tyme,[5]   vponn the departure of the others, the President gaue vnto euery one of them Copper beades, or kniues, which contented them not a little, as also deliuered a President [= Present] vnto the Basshabaes brother, to be presented vnto the Bashaba and another for his wife, giving him to vnderstand, that he would come vnto his Court in the River of Penobscot, and see him very shortly, bringing many such like of his Country Comodities with him.[6]

You maie please to vnderstand how whilst this busines was thus followed here soone after their first arrival [f. 71 v] that had dispatcht

[1] This visit of Skidwarres was an important attempt to establish closer relations and avoid future misunderstandings. The Pemaquid community was now confident that it could, with the authority of Bashabes' brother behind it, deal on equal terms with the English settlers.

[2] We are not told the name of Bashabes' brother. He may have been Asticon who succeeded him in 1615 (Snow, in *Handbook*, p. 141).

[3] The bringing of his wife showed that Nahanada was now confident he would not again be abducted and could safely introduce the two leading men he had with him to Captain Popham.

[4] Amenquin, we are told, offered his own beaver-pelt garment to Popham (p. 351). We do not know where his community was situated.

[5] Amenquin's curiosity and desire to stay represent a wish to make some independent contact with the English, possibly in expectation of exchanging furs with them after the winter hunting season. Did he offer to go to England?

[6] Popham's promise to visit Bashabes on the Penobscot River was never kept, but we cannot be sure that after his death an English party did not visit Bashabes in the late spring or summer of 1608.

awaie Captain Robert Dauies in the Mary and John to advertize both of their safe arrivall and forwardnes of their plantationn within this River of Sachadehoc with Lettres to the Lord Chief Iustice, importuning a supplie for the most necessariose wantes to the subsisting of a Colony to be sent vnto them betymes the next yeare[1]

After Captain Dauies departure they fully finished the Fort, trencht and fortefyed yt with 12. pieces of ordinaunce and built 50. howses therein, besyde a Church and a Storehowse,[2] and the Carpenters framed a pretty Pynnace of about some 30. tonne, which they called the Virginia,[3] the chief Shipwright being one Digby of London.[4]

Many discoveryes likewise had bene made both to the Mayne and vnto the neighbour Rivers, and the Frontier Nations fully discovered by the diligence of Captain Gilbert had not the winter proved so extreeme vnseasonable & Frostie,[5] for yt being in the yeare 1607. whenn the extraordinary Frost was felt in most parte of Europe, yt was here likewise as vehement, by which no boat could stirre vpon any busines, howbeit as tyme & occasion gaue leaue, there was nothing omitted which could ad vnto the benefitt or knowledge of the Planters. For which whenn Captain Dauies arrived there in the yeare following[6]

---

[1] The *Mary and John* was unloaded as soon as a storehouse (perhaps an additional section) was completed. She was laden with specimens of timber, and other plant specimens as indications of the products of the country. These included 'sarsaparilla', smilax (p. 449). Sassafras, also looked for, does not grow as far north as the Kennebec, but some may have been found during the expedition southwards to Casco Bay (cp. Hyland and Steinmetz, *Woody plants*, p. 19). Strachey is clearly unable to link the journal which he was using with the captain of the *Mary and John*. She left, in fact, on 8 October, immediately after the journal ends, and arrived, with Robert Davies as captain, at Plymouth on 1 December.

[2] Strachey's brief characterisation of the fort is unlikely to have relied on written evidence, but on the sight of a plan of the fort. There may have been several, but the *Mary and John* brought one, completed only on 8 October.

[3] The pinnace *Virginia*, 30 tons, was probably employed on coastal trading voyages in 1608 on which we have no information so far. She returned to England late in 1608 and subsequently served the London Virginia Company well on voyages to and from Jamestown.   [4] Nothing is known of the shipwright, Digby.

[5] The final long paragraph is Strachey's own addition from materials not now extant. What we know of the colony between October and December 1607 derives from the case Popham v. Havercombe (pp. 459–65), which shows something of the effects of the early hard winter.

[6] Nothing is said of the two small vessels sent out in early summer of 1608 by Sir Ferdinando Gorges and the remaining members of the Company at Plymouth. It was they who discovered that George Popham was dead and Raleigh Gilbert (of whom disquieting stories had reached Gorges in February (pp. 449–50)) was acting as president. It was probably during the time these vessels were present that active trading took place up-stream (we hear of the Sasanoa River being traversed, p. 474), and along the coast. After the winter hunting, and allowing some time for preparing furs, the trading season would start in late April (possibly) but certainly in May. How far afield furs were obtained cannot be ascertained, but it is possible that direct contacts were in fact made with Bashabes. The

sett out from Topsam, the port towne of exciter with a shippe laden full of victualls, armes, Instrumentes and Tooles &c albeit he found Master George Popham the President and some others dead yet he found all thinges in good forwardnes and manie kindes of Furrs obteyned from the Indians by waie of Trade, good store of Salsaparilla gathered, and the new Pynnace all fynished, but by reasonn that Captain Gilbert receaved Lettres that his brother was newlie dead[1] and a faire portion of land fallenn vnto his share, which required his repaire home, and no mynes discovered, nor hope thereof, being the mayne intended benefit expected to vphold the Charge of this plantacion,[2] and the feare that all other winters would proue like this first, the Companie by no meanes would staie any longer in the Country especially Captain Gilbert being to leaue them,[3] and Master Popham as aforesaid dead wherefore they all embarqued in that this new arrived shippe and in the new Pynnace ye Virginia [f. 72] and sett saile for England,[4] and this was the end of that northerenn Colony vponn the Riuer of Sachadehoc./[5]

---

mention, farther down that sarsaparilla had been obtained in quantity indicates considerable concentration on smilax roots (p. 449.)

The vessel which Captain Robert Davies commanded in 1608 was probably the *Gifte of God*, which left Topsham after 9 July and reached the Kennebec some time in late August or early September. Gorges knew the settlers had been reduced in number to no more than 45, but the supplies mentioned here were evidently for this number and apparently did not include anything for reinforcements for the settlement. If this was so it may well have contributed to the unwillingness of the settlers to face another winter.

[1] Sir John Gilbert of Greenway died on 9 July 1608, so the vessel set out later than this. His Will, P.R.O., PROB 11/98, ff. 309v–10r, bequeathed a number of leases to 'my brother Rawleighe'. Probate was granted on 15 November 1608. Raleigh Gilbert's determination to return to take up his inheritance was natural, but it indicates also that he did not foresee any great advantage to be gained by continuing the settlement.

[2] We are not told whether the colonists included a mineral expert, but Gorges was clearly disappointed that no mines had been reported by February. Later an alleged deposit of alum was claimed to have been found (p. 448), but this was not worked (if indeed it was alum). The presence of minerals alone could make up for what were evidently poor agricultural prospects (what did they grow in their garden in 1608?). The fur trade, and a fishery, it was clear, could be carried on (unless there was severe French competition which evidently did not appear in 1608) by seasonal voyages. The military aspect of the colony, which was strong in 1607, was apparently considered a luxury in 1608. Fishing too could best be continued on a summer seasonal basis.

[3] Here primary responsibility for the decision to abandon the colony was placed on Gilbert's shoulders.

[4] We do not know when they left, but suspect that it was in late September and may assume that all were back in England by November. Purchas had Gilbert's journal, as well as others, but did not print it (p. 352), and so almost all record of the 1608 season is now lost.

[5] The assimilation of many participants in the North Virginia venture into the London Company is discussed in Preston, *Gorges*, pp. 149–50. The appeal to the Plymouth merchants to join the Company appears on pp. 466–8.

40 [Robert Davies] 'The Relation of a Voyage unto New-England'. The Journal of Robert Davis (or Davies) of the voyage to North Virginia in 1607 and of the founding of Fort St George on the Kennebec River, 1 June–26 September 1607

This celebrated account of the 1607 New England voyage and of the first steps to establish the first English colony on the Kennebec River was evidently written by Robert Davis, as pilot of the *Mary and John* (184 tons), serving under Raleigh Gilbert on the voyage outwards, and commanding the ship on her return to England between 6 October and 1 December. A copy of the original, containing missing material between 26 September and 6 October, was in William Strachey's possession at some time between 1609 and 1612 (pp. 397–415 above). The transcript here printed from Lambeth MS 806 no. 14, ff. 1–12 is evidently a faithful attempt to reproduce the original, with all its warts of punctuation and spelling, by an otherwise unknown William Griffith, working from what was almost certainly the original, found among the papers of Sir Ferdinando Gorges shortly after his death in 1647. It was admirably edited by Henry O. Thayer, *The Sagadahoc colony, comprising The relation of a voyage into New England* (The Gorges Society, 1892). This was reprinted in slightly modified form in H. S. Burrage, ed., *Early English and French voyages chiefly from Hakluyt, 1534–1608* (1906), pp. 399–419, and in *NAW*, III, 429–37, all the editions adding the additional matter lacking from the Lambeth MS and representing, apparently, a single leaf at the end which was absent from the copy when it was made by William Griffith.

[f. 1]   In the nam of god Amen

The Relation of a Voyage, unto New-England. Began from the *Lizard*, yᵉ first of June 1607. By Cap*tai*n Popham in yᵉ ship yᵉ Gift, & Cap*tai*n Gilbert in yᵉ Mary and John:

Written by   & found amongst yᵉ Papers of yᵉ truly Wor*shi*pfull S*i*r Ferdinando Gorges, Kn*ight* by me William Griffith.[1]

---

[1] Lambeth Palace Library, MS 806, item 14, foliated at the top left-hand corner of the recto 1–12, endorsed on f.12v. 'The Relation of a Voyage to Virginia' to which 'New England' had been added in a later (but still early) hand. An excellent edition, with very few misreadings, was published by The Gorges Society, Portland, Maine, vol. IV (1892), *The Sagadahoc colony, comprising The Relation of a Voyage into New England; (Lambeth Ms.)* with an introduction and notes by Henry O. Thayer. Henry S. Burrage based his edition

[f. 2] Departed from the Lyzard the firste Daye of Iune Anno Domini. 1607.[1] beinge Mundaye about 6 of the Cloke in the afternoon and ytt bore of me then Northeste and by north eyght leages of.

from thence Directed our Course for the Illandes of flowers & Corve in the which we wear 24 dayes attainynge of ytt all which time we still kept the Sea and never Saw but on Saill beinge a ship of Salcom bound for the new Foundland whearin was on Tosser of Dartmoth Master in her.[2]

The 25th daye of Iune we fell with the Illand of Garseasa [overwritten Gersea] on of the Illandes of the Assores & ytt bore of vs then South & by est ten Leages of, our Master & his mattes makinge ytt to be flowers but my Selffe withstood them & reprooved them in thear errour as afterward ytt appeared manyfestly and then stood Roome[3] for flowers.

The 26th of Iune we had Seight of flowers & Corv[o] & the 27th in the mornynge early we wear hard abord flowers & stod in for to fynd a good rod for to anker[4] Whearby to take in wood and watter the 28th we Descryed to Sailles, standinge in for flowers whearby we presently wayed anker & stood towardes the rod of Sainta Cruse beinge

---

in *Early English and French voyages chiefly from Hakluyt, 1534–1609* (New York, 1906), pp. 399–415 on this, including the conclusion from Strachey (1849) and adding a few notes of his own. The MS is republished with the permission of the Librarian. The earlier ascription to James Davies has been abandoned. William Griffith is untraced, but it may not prove irrelevant that Gorges was associated with George Griffith, merchant of London, and Mary Griffith, possibly his wife, in 1629 (Preston, *Gorges*, p. 279).

[1] Smith says (p. 353 above) that the *Gifte of God* and the *Mary and John* left Plymouth Harbour, on 31 May. This ship was the *Mary and John*, with Raleigh Gilbert captain. The rapid departure from the Lizard (lat. 49° 5′ N, long. 5° 13′ W) indicated that both ships were favoured by easterly winds. Marsden, 'English ships of the reign of James I', p. 325, gives the tonnage of the *Mary and John* as 184.

[2] Twenty-four days out to Flores (lat. 39° 13′ N, long. 31° 8′ W) and Corvo (lat. 39° 35′, long. 31° 8′) indicates that progress after a good initial start was slow. The sighting of the Salcombe Newfoundlander (Tosser of Dartmouth, not identified, master), indicates that the ships, which so far had been keeping company, were so far taking the orthodox route of the Newfoundland fishing vessels, first to the Azores and then northwesterly to about 50° N. From the Azores, however, they were to keep a more southerly course than the normal fishing vessels.

[3] Come about before the wind.

[4] The copyist first wrote Garseasa (Graciosa, 39° 13′ N, 38° 3′ W) and then wrote over it (or someone else did) 'Gersea'. The mention of Flores and Corvo above indicates not that they had been attained but that the course was set towards them: in that case Graciosa would have been encountered first (as indeed is clear from the Strachey version, p. 399 above). Davies' reproving of the master for his false identification of the island helps to show that his position was that of pilot.

near three Leages from the place. Whear we wattered.[1] thear Captain
Popham ankered to take in wood and watter but yt was So Calme that
we Could nott recouer or gett vnto hem beffor the daye cam on. /[2]

The 29th of Iune beinge Mundaye early in the morn[ing] those to
Sailles we had Seen the nyght beffore Wear neare vnto vs & beinge
Calme they Sent thear botes beinge full of men towardes vs. And after
the orders of the Sea they hailled vs demandynge vs of whense we wear
/ the which we told them: & found them to be Flemens & the States
shipes.[3] on of our Company named John Goyett of Plymoth knew
the Captain of on of the shipes for that he had ben att Sea with hem.[4]
havinge aquainted Captain Gilbert of this & beinge all frindes he
desyered the Captain of the Dutch[man] to Com near & take a Can
of bear the which hee thankfully excepted we still keepinge our Selves
in a redynesse both of our small shott & greatt; the Dutch Captain
beinge Com to our ships syde Captain Gilbert Desyered hem to com
abord hem & entertand hem in the beste Sort he Could.[5] this don they
to requytt his kind entertainment desyrd hem that he wold go abord
with them & vppon their earnest intreaty he went with them takinge
three or 4 gentellmen with hem. but when they had hem abord of them
they thear kept hem perfforse Charginge him that he was a pyratt &
still threatnynge hemselffe & his gentellmen with hem to throw them
all overbord & to take our ship from vs. in this Sort they kept them
from ten of the Clok mornynge vntill eyght of the Clok nyght vssinge
Som of his gentlemen in most vile maner as Settinge Som of them
in the bi[l]bowes & buffetinge of others & other most vyle & shamefull
abusses but in the [f. 3] end havinge Seene our Comission the which
was proffered vnto them att the firste but they reffussed to See yt and
the greatest Cause doutinge of the Inglyshe men, beinge of thear owne
Company who had promist Captain Gilbert that yf they proffered to
perfform that which they still threatned hem. that then they all woold
Rysse with hem. & ether end thear Lyves in his Deffence or Suppresse
the shipe. the which the Dutch perseavinge presently Sett them att

---

[1] The best anchorage at Flores is south of the town of Santa Cruz das Flores.

[2] The two ships were not able to make contact thereafter, until off the coast of Maine.

[3] Piracy was still rampant and the Dutch were still at war with Spain, so that any
strange ships were potential robbers. Though the ships were those of the United Provinces
their sailors could still be called Flemings (later reserved for inhabitants of the Spanish
Netherlands) as well as Dutch.

[4] John Goyett, evidently one of the Plymouth seamen on the expedition, could well
have served with a Dutch ship in a privateering voyage in the Caribbean.

[5] The invitation of the Dutchmen on board the *Mary and John* was a normal courtesy
of the sea, provided adequate precautions were taken.

Lyberty & Sent them abord vnto vs aggain to our no small Ioye.[1]
Captain Popham all this tyme beinge in the Wind of vs never woold
Com roome vnto vs notwithstandinge we makinge all the Seignes that
possybell we myght by strykinge our topsaill & hoissinge ytt aggain
three tymes & makinge towards hem all that ever we possybell Could.[2]
so hear we Lost Company of hem beinge the 29th daye of Iune about
8 of the Clok att nyght beinge 6 Leages from flowers West norwest
wee standinge our Course for Vyrgenia the 30th wee Laye in Seight
of the Illand.

The firste Daye of Iully beinge Wensdaye wee departed from the
Illand of flowers beinge ten Leages South weste from ytt.[3]

From hence we allwayes kept our Course to the Westward as much
as wind & weather woold permytt vntill the 27th daye of Iully duringe
which time wee often times Sounded but Could never fynd ground.
this 27th early in the mornynge we Sounded & had ground but 18
fetham beinge then in the Lattitud of 43 degrees & $\frac{2}{3}$[4] hear w[ee] fysht
three howers & tooke near to hundred of Codes very great & large
fyshe bigger & larger fyshe then that which coms from the bancke of
the new Foundland. hear wee myght have Lodden our shipe in Lesse
time then a moneth.[5]

from hence the Wynd beinge att South west wee sett owr Saills &
stood by the wind west norwest towards the Land allwayes Soundinge
for our better knowledg as we ran towardes the main Land from this
bancke.

from this bancke we kept our Course west norwest 36 Leages which
ys from the 27th of Iuly vntill the 30th of Iuly in which tyme we ran

[1] The ill-treatment of the English visitors may well have been merely because the
Dutch (rugged privateers as they were and probably drunk) wanted some rough sport with
the gentlemen of the expedition. Whether there was real danger of major violence it is
hard to say, but the steadiness of the English eventually brought the Dutch to their senses.

[2] Since such wind as there was was contrary, Popham in the *Gifte* would not have
been able to reach the *Mary and John*, except perhaps by his ship's boat. Evidently his
lookout, in any case, did not interpret the signals made to him correctly. They may have
simply signified to him that the *Mary and John* had at last caught up, or they may not have
been seen at all. Davies' sense of grievance is evident.

[3] At 8 p.m. on the 29th Flores stood 18 miles WNW, and apparently on the morning
of 1 July they were 30 miles SW of the island, not an auspicious start.

[4] Thayer (p. 40) points out that with Davies' figure of 18 fathoms (and Strachey's
of 22) they could only have been in the close vicinity of Sable Island (on which they were
fortunate not to ground). The Canadian Chart 4490 gives a line of depths within this range
at 43° 50', so that 43° 40' was an exceptionally accurate observation, if this was indeed the
location.

[5] Seamen on board would be familiar with average cod sizes from Newfoundland
fishing voyages.

36 Leages as ys beffor sayed & then we Saw the Land about 10 of the Clok in the mornynge bearinge norweste from vs about 10 Leages & then we Sounded & had a hundred fethams blacke oze. hear as we Cam in towardes the Land from this banck we still found deepe watter the deepest within the bancke ys 160 fethams & in 100 fetham you shall See the Land yf ytt be Clear weather after you passe the bancke the ground ys still black oze vntill you Com near the shore[1] this daye wee stood in for the Land but Could nott recover ytt beffor the night tooke vs so we stood a Lyttell from ytt & thear strok a hull vntill the next daye beinge the Laste of Iuly hear Lyeinge at hull[2] we tooke greatt stor of Cod fyshes the bigeste & Largest that I ever Saw or anny man in our ship. / This Daye beinge the Last of Iuly about 3 of the Clok in the after noon we recouered the shore & Cam to an anker vnder an Illand for all this Cost ys full of Illandes & broken Land but very Sound & good for shipinge to go by them the watter deepe / 18 & 20 fetham hard abord them.

[f. 4] This Illand standeth in the Lattitud[3] of 44 degrees & $\frac{1}{2}$[4] & hear we had nott ben att an anker past to howers beffore we espyed a biskey shallop Cominge towardes vs havinge in her eyght Sallvages & a Lyttell salvage boye / they cam near vnto vs & spoke vnto vs in thear Language.[5] & we makinge Seignes to them that they should Com abord of vs showinge vnto them knyues glasses beades & throwinge into thear bott Som biskett[6] but for all this they wold nott Com abord of vs but makinge show to go from vs we Suffered them. So when they wear a Lyttell from vs and Seeinge we proffered them no wronge of thear

[1] The direction can scarcely have been much more than one point north of west. As the limit of the 100-fathom line land was more than 30 miles away. Thayer's choice of their landfall, La Hève Island and the high land of Apostogeon behind (p. 41), would appear to be correct, their latitude approaching it being about 44° 10′ N.

[2] A-hull, sails being furled and rudder lashed to prevent, as far as possible, drifting in the night. It was still too deep for them to anchor.

[3] 'this Illand standeth in the' is written twice.

[4] If this is La Have (La Hève) Island (there are other small islands around it in Green Bay, including Ironbound I.), the latitude determination was some 20′ too high, but this was well within the current range of error. The bay and its islands were described and illustrated by Champlain in 1604, Works, I (1922), pl. LXIV.

[5] This is again a Basque shallop being sailed by a Micmac crew (cp. pp. 117, 145). Many of the French sailors knew some Micmac words and the Indians might well expect this English ship to have someone on board who could reply to them in their own language, while it is clear that they, themselves, could speak some French.

[6] The offerings of knives, beads and looking glasses would be attractive (though ships' biscuits may have seemed more like weapons than gifts): however, since the shallop may recently have been stolen their reluctance to put themselves into the power of the Europeans is natural.

owne accord retorned & Cam abord of vs & three of them stayed all that nyght with vs the rest departed in the shallope to the shore makinge Seignes vnto vs that they wold retorn vnto vs aggain the next daye.[1]

The next daye the Sam Salvages with three Salvage wemen[2] beinge the fryst daye of Auguste retorned vnto vs bringinge with them Som feow skinnes of bever in an other biskey shallop[3] & propheringe thear skinnes to trook with vs but they demanded ouer muche for them & we Seemed to make Lyght of them[4]   So then the other three which had stayed with vs all nyght went into the shallop & So they departed. ytt Seemeth that the french hath trad with them for they vse many French wordes   the Cheeff Commander of these partes ys called Messamott & the ryver or harbor ys called emannett.[5] we take these peopell to be the tarentyns[6] & these peopell as we have Learned sence do make warrs with Sasanoa the Cheeffe Comander to the westward whea[r] we have planted & this Somer they kild his Sonne.[7] So the

[1] Their return so soon indicated that they had decided the newcomers were not likely to take the shallop from them. The staying on board of three men was a clear sign that they were prepared to trade.

[2] The appearance of the party with some women shows a further advance in their trust of the English.

[3] The use of a second Basque shallop indicates how well they had supplied themselves with stolen transport.

[4] The Micmac were experienced traders, but would have expected their first offering to be accepted at the price they offered; if this was done they were more likely to bargain over subsequent consignments. The English did not understand this, and their rejection of the skins made the Micmac lose interest in developing commercial dealings with them. Their departure indicated that they considered the episode at an end.

[5] Norman, Breton and, above all, French Basque vessels (with occasional Spanish Basques) fished and traded on this coast, so they could have picked up either French or Basque words. Messamouet, as the French called the chief of La Have, had been in France, was well equipped with French goods of all sorts, and acted as a guide to the French in the Bay of Fundy, playing an important part in the politics of the region. (Champlain, *Works*, I, 278, 393–6 (especially 395n.); Lescarbot, *History*, II, 323.) The English were much at sea with such a Europeanized Indian and did not know how to deal with him at his sophisticated level (he was liable to make long harangues when he felt inclined). A Micmac name sounding like 'Emannett' for La Have has not been found in the early narratives.

[6] Frank T. Siebert, Jr, 'The Tarrantines', *Studies in Linguistics*, XXIII (1973), 72–6, considers the name to be 'a jargon term for the Micmacs, used by fishermen and voyagers on the North Atlantic coast during the late sixteenth and early seventeenth centuries'. He suggests it is in origin Basque *tarantari*, 'babbler, chatterer', the name being given by the French Basques who could not understand their language.

[7] Sasanoa will be found (p. 433) as the sagamore who claimed to control the central part of the Kennebec River to which the expedition was bound, so that information he could give was of considerable value, though it may not have been sufficiently exploited. The sentence referring forward to events of August may have originally been added in the margin of the journal.

Salvages departed from vs & cam no mor vnto us. // After they wear departed from vs we hoyssed out our bot [and went to the shore] whearin my Selffe was with 12. others & rowed to the shore & landed on this Illand that we rod vnder the which we found to be a gallant Illand full of heigh & myghty trees of Sundry Sortes. hear we allso found aboundance of gusberyes strawberyes rasberyes & whortes So we retorned & Cam abord.[1]

Sondaye beinge the second of Auguste after dyner our bott went to the shore again to fill freshe watter whear[2] after they had filled thear watter thear Cam fower Salvages vnto them havinge thear bowes & arowes in thear handes makinge show vnto them to have them Com to the shore but our Saillers havinge filled thear watter wold nott go to the shore vnto them but retorned & cam abord beinge about 5 of the Clok in the afternoon[3] So the bott went presently from the ship vnto a point of an Illand & thear att Lo watter in on hower kild near .50. great Lopsters you shall See them Whear they ly in shold Watter nott past a yeard deep & with a great hooke mad faste to a staffe you shall hitch them vp. Thear ar greatt store of them you may near Lad a ship with them. & they are of greatt bignesse I have nott Seen the lyke in Ingland.[4] So the bott retorned abord & wee toke our bott in & about myd nyght the wynd Cam faier att northest we Sett Saill & departed from thence keepinge our Course Southwest for So the Cost Lyeth.[5]

[f. 5] Mundaye beinge the third of Auguste in the morninge we wear faier by the shore & So Sailled alongste the Coste We Saw many Illandes all alonge the Cost & great Soundes goinge betwyxt them. but

---

[1] 'Whorts' is the southwestern English form of whortleberry (hurtleberry) applied to the indigenous bilberry, but in America extended to all species of *Vaccinium* including blueberry. Gooseberries, strawberries, raspberries, and several *Vaccinia* would have been found on either of the more likely islands, La Have or Ironbound. (See p. 420 above.)

[2] Fresh water was a prime necessity after an ocean oyage.

[3] This was legitimate caution not cowardice: the Micmac had in the past killed many Europeans on this coast. At that time, however, they were co-operating closely with the French.

[4] This is the earliest English advertisement for the Nova Scotia lobster.

[5] The arrival of the *Mary and John* coincided almost with the French abandonment of Port Royal (which the English might have occupied as it was left undamaged, had they maintained close and friendly relations with the Micmac and arrived a little later). One boat had left there by 20/30 July; two more followed on that day; in the fourth Poutrincourt and Champlain set out on 1/11 August and a few days later in Green Bay Champlain drew his sketch of the bay and islands (*Works*, I, 456–60, pl. LXIV; Lescarbot *Nova Francia* (1928), p. 136). Marcel Trudel, *Histoire de la Nouvelle-France*, II (1966), 73–6 notes the curious fact of the English arrival immediately following the French departure

We could make prooffe of non for want of a penyshe [pinnace].[1] hear we found fyshe still all allonge the Cost as we Sailled.

Tusdaye beinge the 4th of Auguste in the morninge 5 of the Clok we wear theawart of a Cape or head Land Lying in the Latitud of 43 degrees and cam very near vnto ytt. ytt ys very Low Land showinge Whytt Lyke sand but ytt ys Whytt Rockes and very stronge tides goeth hear from the place we stopt att beinge in 44 degrees & ½ Vntill this Cape or head Land ytt ys all broken Land & full of Illandes & Large Soundes betwixt them & hear we found fyshe aboundance so large & great as I never Saw the lyke Codes beffor nether any man in our shipe

After we paste this Cape or head Land the Land falleth awaye and Lyeth in norwest & by north into a greatt deep baye.[2] We kept our course from this head Land West and Weste and by South 7 Leages and cam to thre Illandes[3] whear cominge near vnto them we found on the Southest Syd of them a great Leadge of Rocks Lyeinge near a Leage into the Sea[4] the which we perseavinge tackt our ship & the wynd beinge Large att northest Cleared our Selves of them kepinge still our Course to the westward west & by South & west Southwest vntill mydnyght. then after we hald in more northerly.[5]

Wensdaye beinge the 5th of Auguste from after mydnyght we hald in West norwest vntill 3 of the Clok afternoon of the Sam and then we Saw the Land aggain bearinge from vs northweste & by north and ytt Risseth in this forme hear vnder.[6] ten or 12 Leages from you they ar three heigh mountains that Lye in vpon the mayn Land near vnto

[1] The *Gifte of God* was carrying their pinnace in sections, but the observation here indicates how essential a small vessel was for inshore exploration. At this time the *Mary and John* was running down the coast (sounding no doubt from time to time) towards Cape Sable, that is to approximately 43° 30′ (Strachey is more specific, p. 401 above).

[2] The gradual opening of the wide entrance to the Bay of Fundy.

[3] Apparently Seal I. and Mud I., with a number of smaller islets nearby.

[4] Thayer (pp. 47–8) thinks this ledge comprised Blonde Rock (uncovered at low water) and the shoals adjacent to it, over which there is a heavy rip as the tide flows into the Bay of Fundy.

[5] Varying their course, with the aid of a favouring wind, brought them into open water well south of the entrance to the Bay of Fundy and quite rapidly towards the wide opening of Penobscot Bay.

[6] The sight of the three mountains is marked by rough profiles placed below. They appear also in the B.L. MS of Strachey (Major, p. 167), see p. 402 above, but with only the first two in line and the third below. This makes some alteration of Thayer's identifications (p. 49) within the Matinicus group necessary. Wooden Ball I. would appear on the starboard side, Matinicus I. to port and Ragged I. below it, presuming they were sighted, some little way SE of Matinicus Rock. These are highly likely but not certain identifications. Lat. 43° 50′ N, long. 68° 50′ W gives a medial position for the group: the *Mary and John* would be at approximately 43° 44′ N, 68° 45′ W when the profiles were made.

the ryver of Penobskott in which ryver the Bashabe makes his abod the Cheeffe Comander of those partes & streatcheth vnto the ryver of Sagadehock vnder his Command[1] You shall see theise heigh mountaines when you shall not perseave the main Land vnder ytt   they ar of shutch an exceedinge heygtes: And note that from the Cape or head Land beffor spoken of vntill these heigh mountaines we never Saw any Land except those three Illandes also beffor mensyoned.[2] We stood in Right with these mountaines vntill the next daye.

Fig. 20.

Thursdaye beinge the 6th of Auguste we stood in with this heigh Land vntill 12 of the Cloke noon[3] & then I found the shipe to be in 43 degrees & $\frac{1}{2}$ by my observacion[4] from thence we Sett our Course and stood awaye dew weste & Saw three other Illandes Lyenge together beinge Lo & flatt by the watter showinge whytt as yff ytt wear Sand but ytt ys whytt Rockes makinge show a far of allmoste Lyke vnto Dover Cleeves.[5] & these three Illandes Lye dew est & west on of the other   So we Cam faier by them and as we Cam to the Westward

[1] Knowledge of the Penobscot Bay and River, and of Bashabes was gained after the settlement was established.

[2] Perhaps Ingraham Hill (280 ft) in the foreground, and Mt Battux (620 ft) and Dodge Mt (660 ft) in the rear. It is debatable whether the higher peaks of the Camden range, which lie well inland (Pleasant Mt 1,064 ft, Ragged Mt 1,300 ft and Bald Mt 1,272 ft) would be seen clearly unless in exceptional circumstances.

[3] 'Standing right in with' is too vague a phrase to be of much value in determining their position. They may have sailed as far as Two Bush Channel (north of Metinic I., which is not mentioned) as this would give them an easy westward course to the Georges Is.

[4] The position suggested would place them at about 43° 55', so they may have been farther south, but not below 43° 50' so that the observation was 20' out, a very usual margin of error. Robert Davies is giving an indication of his position on board by mentioning that the observations were made by himself.

[5] There are problems (Thayer sets them out fully, pp. 50–1) in making anything except the more southerly of the Georges Is. from the three islands seen to the west. (Cp. p. 402 above.) There were no chalk limestone cliffs like those at Dover, but bare sandy shores, gleaming in the sunshine, could look white. The journal (even when amplified slightly in Strachey's version, p. 403) is scarcely precise enough to be dogmatic about the course of the *Mary and John*. If she was sailing along the parallel of 43° 50' she would indeed see Metinic I., Metinic Green I. and Hog I. first, before continuing westward to bring the Georges Islands into view.

the heygh Land beffor spoken of Shewed ytt selffe in this form as followith.

Fig. 21.

[f. 6] From hence we kept still our Course West & Weste by north towardes three other Illandes that we Sawe Lyenge from these Illandes beffor spoken of[1] 8 Leages and about ten of the Clok att nyght we recovered them & havinge Sent in our bott beffore nyght to vew ytt for that ytt was Calme & to Sound ytt & See whatt good ankoringe was vnder ytt[2] we bor in with on of them the which as we Cam in by we still Sounded & founde very deep watter 40 fetham hard abord of yt. So we stood in into a Coue In ytt & had 12 fetham watter & thear we ankored vntill the mornynge. and when the daye appeared we Saw we weare environed Round about with Illandes you myght have told neare thirty Illandes round about vs from abord our shipe.[3] this Illand we Call St Georges Illand for that we hear found a Crosse Sett vp the which we Suppose was Sett vp by George Wayman[4]

Frydaye beinge the 7th of Auguste we wayed our Ankor whearby to bringe our shipe in mor better Safty how Soever the wynd should happen to blow[5] and about ten of the Clok in the mornynge as we wear standinge of a Lyttell from the Illand we descried a saill standinge in towardes this Illand & we presently mad towardes her & found ytt

---

[1] This time there is no doubt that the Georges Is. were seen.

[2] Sending a boat ahead to sound so late in the evening suggests there was a very bright sky. She presumably rowed in just to the north of Little Burnt I. into Pentecost Harbor (Georges Harbor) where indeed 42 feet is on the chart (U.S., 1203).

[3] She was now lying approximately where the *Archangell* was in 1605 (pp. 510–12), but the thirty islands said to be seen from the crow's nest is an exaggeration. Though the journal does not admit it, the presence of one or two men who had been with Waymouth is very likely. The run into the harbour could however have been aided instead by possession of Waymouth's lost chart (p. 299).

[4] The location of the cross on Allen I. overlooking Pentecost Harbor is marked by the monument erected in 1905 on the advice of Henry R. Burrage. A position a little to the east might have been more appropriate. The ship at least had the 1605 pamphlet and knew the name given by Waymouth. Why his name was given as Wayman (and elsewhere Waiman) is not known (cp. pp. 58–62). The additional profile given by Strachey (Major, p. 168) is not clearly identifiable.

[5] She was anchored first in the channel between Little Burnt I. and Allen I. and was now brought up into the harbour defined by Allen I., Benner I. and Davis I.

to be the Gyft our Consort[1] So beinge all Ioyeffull of our happy meetinge we both stood in again for the Illand we ryd vnder beffor & theare anckored both together.[2]

This night followinge about mydnyght[3] Captain Gilbert caussed his ships bott to be manned & took to hemsellfe 13 other my Selffe beinge on. beinge 14 persons in all & tooke the Indyan skidwarres with vs the weather beinge faier & the wynd Calme we rowed to the Weste in amongste many gallant Illandes and found the ryver of Pemaquyd to be but 4 Leages weste from the Illand we Call St georges whear our shipp remained still att anckor. hear we landed in a Lyttell Cove[4] by skydwarres Direction & marched over a necke of the Land near three milles[5] So the Indyan skidwarres brought vs to the Salvages housses whear they did inhabitt although much against his will for that he told vs that they wear all remoued & gon from the place they wear wont to inhabitt. but we answered hem again that we wold nott retorn backe vntill shutch time as we had spoken with Som of them.[6] at Length he brought vs whear they did inhabytt whear we found near a hundreth of them men wemen and Children. and the Cheeffe Comander of them ys nahanada.[7] att our fryste Seight of them vppon a howlinge or Cry that they mad they all presently Isued forth towardes vs with thear bowes & arrows & we presently mad a stand & Suffered them to Com near vnto vs then our Indyan skidwarres spoke vnto them in thear

[1] The *Mary and John* moved out before anchoring due east to meet the newcomer. Popham and Havercombe in the *Gifte of God* had also evidently sufficient knowledge of *Archangell*'s 1605 position to make directly for it.

[2] After greetings and information on their respective course had been exchanged both vessels entered and anchored in Pentecost Harbor.

[3] This was midnight on 7 August: again the night must have been exceptionally clear. The boat's crew of 12, with Gilbert, Davies and Skidwarres, making 15, was numerous enough to resist a surprise attack.

[4] New Harbor, on Pemaquid Neck, was about 8 miles directly from Pentecost Harbor, across Muscongus Bay. Skidwarres must have remembered how to pilot them so as to avoid frequent rocks and shoals.

[5] The village of the Pemaquid band lay across the Neck from New Harbor near the mouth of Pemaquid River on John Bay. There was probably a trail (and canoe carry) from New Harbor to Pemaquid ('Pemaquidda' of 1606).

[6] Skidwarres (who may have been left signs to guide him) was not to forget his capture by Waymouth in 1605, and retained some suspicions of the English. On the other hand he would know that the village might well be partly or wholly unoccupied during the fishing. In spite of what appear to have been friendly relations established by Hanham and Pring in 1606, the band could not be certain who the strangers were, so they adopted a course by which they could ambush the intruders if it should seem necessary. Skidwarres evidently gave some indication that he did know where they had gone.

[7] Nahanada (Tahánedo, etc.) (cp. p. 309), had been returned as sagamore to the Pemaquid band by Hanham and Pring the previous year. He was to continue to maintain a somewhat ambivalent attitude towards the English for some time.

Language showinge them what we wear[1] which when nahanada thear
Comander perseaved what we wear he Caussed them all to laye assyd
thear bowes and arrowes and Cam vnto vs and imbrassed vs & we did
the Lyke to them aggain.[2] So we remained with them near to howers
& wear in thear housses.[3] Then we tooke our Leave of them & retorned
with our Indyan skidwarres with vs[4] towardes our shipp the 8th Daye
of August being Satterdaye in the afternoon.

[f. 7] Sondaye beinge the 9th of Auguste in the morninge the most part
of our holl Company of both our shipes Landed on this Illand the which
we call St Georges Illand whear the Crosse standeth and thear we heard
a Sermon Delyvred vnto us by our preacher gyvinge god thankes for
our happy metinge & Saffe aryvall into the Contry & So retorned abord
aggain[5]

Mundaye beinge the xth of Auguste early in the morninge Captain
Popham in his shallope[6] with thirty others & Captain Gilbert in his
ships bott with twenty others acompaned Departed from thear shipes
& Sailled towardes the ryver of Pemaquyd & Caryed with vs the Indyan
skidwarres and Cam to the ryver ryght beffore thear housses[7] whear
they no Sooner espyed vs but presently nahanada with all his Indians

[1] Skidwarres was evidently unsure what his reception would be or else he would
have gone forward as soon as the Indians came within view.

[2] The Indian war cry followed by cautious manoeuvring of both sides was replaced
dramatically by recognition, the dropping of the Indians' arms, and warm greetings once
Skidwarres spoke in Abenaki. But would Nahahada not have immediately recognised
English as spoken by Gilbert and his men? The event may indeed have been only a
traditional gesture of response to visitors from outside.

[3] This is our first record of an English visit to a New England Indian village, but
it is probable that Hanham and Pring had been there. Snow (*Handbook* pp. 139–40), says
'Houses were either hemispherical with circular floor plan, or pyramidal, in which case
the floor plan could be square. Houses were shingled with sheets of bark. There was a center
post and slab of rock to protect it from the adjacent fire. There were normally two doors,
each covered by a deerskin. One was usually left open to provide an adequate draft
exiting through a smokehole at the apex of the house.'

[4] Skidwarres made no difficulty about returning with them on this occasion. We may
assume that the remainder of the company of both ships were relaxing during Gilbert's
absence.

[5] The assembly both of crews and planters on Sunday morning on Allen I. and the
service held by the clergyman, Richard Seymour, who was to remain with the colonists,
was primarily to set thes tone of orthodoxy in religion, in obedience to the law of England,
as well as, genuinely, to give thanks to God for the safe crossing.

[6] We lack information on whether the shallop was carried intact on the *Gifte* or was
brought in sections and was reconstituted between their arrival and the 10th. Earlier
indications (pp. 146–7) were that sectional shallops were easier to handle, but the *Gifte*, a
fly-boat, may have had a large enough deck to accommodate her complete.

[7] This time the boats (the ship's boat as well as the shallop probably carrying a sail)
sailed round Pemaquid Point into Johns Bay, some 13 or 14 miles, and anchored at or near
the mouth of the Pemaquid River.

with thear bowes and arrows in thear hands Cam forth vppon the Sandes[1]
So we Caussed skidwarres to speak vnto hem & we our Selves spok
vnto hem in Inglyshe givinge hem to vnderstand our Cominge tended
to no yvell towardes hem Selffe nor anny of his peopell. he told vs
again he wold nott thatt all our peopell should land. So[2] beccause we
woold in no Sort offend them.   hearvppon Som ten or twelffe of the
Cheeffe gentlemen Landed & had Som parle together & then afterward
they wear well Contented that all should Land   So all landed we
vssinge them with all the kindnesse that possibell we Could. never-
thelesse after an hower or to they all Soddainly withdrew them Selves
from vs into the woodes & Lefte vs[3]   We perseavinge this presently
imbarked our Selves all except skidwarres who was nott Desyerous to
retorn with vs. We Seeinge this woold in no Sort proffer any Violence
vnto hem by drawing hem perfforce Suffered hem to remain and staye
behinde vs.[4] he promyssinge to retorn vnto vs the next Daye followinge
but he heald nott his promysse   So we imbarked our Selves and went
vnto the other Syd of the ryver & thear remained vppon the shore the
nyght followinge.[5]

Tuesdaye beinge the xj[th] of Auguste we retorned and Cam to our
shipp whear they still remained att ankor vnder the Illand we call S[t]
georges

Wensdaye being the xij[th] of Auguste we wayed our anckors and Sett
our sailles to go for the ryver of Sagadehock.[6] we kept our Course from

[1] The alarm was clearly an automatic response to the approach of strangers but the
number of Englishmen (52) might appear to constitute a new threat.

[2] It is clear that by this time Nahanada was willing to admit that he understood
English.

[3] Nahanada's anxiety that only a few Englishmen should land indicates his continued
caution, but he was gradually reassured by Skidwarres so as to allow the whole party, apart
from those needed to keep the boats, to land. No doubt presents were given as well as
reassurance of benevolent intentions, but the intimations that the English intended to stay
permanently nearby on the Kennebec re-aroused suspicions and led to the retreat of the
band into the woods.

[4] Skidwarres was naturally attracted by the opportunity to remain with his own
community after two years' absence. Had he been forced to stay, then hostilities might
well have begun and the trading prospects, at least, of the settlement impaired. His failure
to return the next day aligned him with Nahanada in his caution, but later he took the
opportunity to represent his community alongside the sagamore in dealings with Fort St
George (p. 408).

[5] Their anchorage and campsite would have been at the mouth of Johns River on
the west side of Johns Bay, probably on Rutherford I.

[6] The leisurely progress of the expedition showed they had little conception of how
short a season they had left to found their settlement. At the same time it is clear they had
a chart (from the Hanham and Pring voyage) which indicated the location of the Kennebec
River on which they expected to settle.

thence dew Weste vntill 12 of the Clok mydnyght of the Sam   then
we stroke our sailles and layed a hull vntill the mornynge Doutinge
for to over shoot ytt

Thursdaye in the mornynge breacke of the daye beinge the xiij[th] of
Auguste the Illand of Sutquin bore north of vs nott past halff a leage
from vs[1] and ytt rysseth in this form hear vnder followinge the which
Illand Lyeth ryght beffore the mouth of the ryver of Sagadehocke South
from ytt near 2 Leages but we did nott make ytt to be Sutquin so we
Sett our sailles & stood to the westward for to Seeke ytt 2 Leages farther
& nott fyndinge the ryver of Sagadehocke we knew that we had
overshott the place[2]   then we wold have retorned but Could nott &
the nyght in hand the gifte Sent in her shallop & mad ytt & went into
the ryver this nyght but we wear Constrained to remain att Sea all
this nyght and about mydnight thear arosse a great storme & tempest
vppon vs the which putt vs in [f. 8] great daunger and hassard of
Castinge awaye of our ship & our Lyves by reasons we wear so near
the shore   the wynd blew very hard att South right in vppon the shore
so that by no means we Could nott gett of hear we sought all means
& did what possybell was to be don for that our Lyves depended on
ytt / Hear we plyed ytt with our ship of & on all the nyght often times
espyeinge many soonken rockes & breatches hard by vs enforsynge vs
to put our ship about & stand from them bearing saill when ytt was
mor fytter to have taken ytt in but that ytt stood vppon our Lyves
to do ytt & our bott Soonk att our stern yett woold we nott Cutt her
from vs in hope of the appearinge of the daye   thus we Contynued
vntill the daye Cam   then we perseaved our Selves to be hard abord
the Lee shore & no waye to escape ytt but by Seekinge the shore[3] then
we espyed 2 Lyttell Illandes Lyeing vnder our lee   So we bore vp the
healme & steered in our shipe in betwyxt them whear the Lord be

---

[1] If they sailed due west for the mouth of the Kennebec R. they must, initially,
have gone at least as far south as Monhegan I. (Seguin is about 5′ S of the latter.) At
midnight their (approximate) position would be 43° 45′ and they had sailed some 25 to
30 miles.

[2] These profiles of Seguin (fair approximations to actuality) are correctly placed by
Strachey, p. 405.

Robert Davies as pilot had not been fully briefed. Clearly, the chart was on the
Gifte of God, whose pilot (or master) was able to identify Seguin at the first attempt, possibly
because he had been with Hanham and Pring.

[3] Davies' description of the perils of a southerly gale is a striking one and it is clear
that only excellent seamanship (his?) kept the Mary and John from being broken up on
a lee shore. Many rocks are marked on the chart westward from Seguin Ledges (to the
north of the island).

praised for ytt we found good and sauffe ankkoringe & thear anckored
the storme still Contynuinge vntill the next daye followynge.[1]

<table>
<tr><td>this forme
beinge South
from ytt</td><td>beinge est & west
from the Illand
of Sutqin
ytt maketh in this
form /</td></tr>
</table>

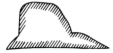

Fig. 22.

Frydaye beinge the xiiij[th] of August that we anckored vnder these
Illandes thear we repaired our bott being very much torren &
spoilled then after we landed on this Illand & found 4. salvages &
an old woman this Illand ys full of pyne trees & ocke and abondance
of whortes of fower Sortes of them.[2]

Satterdaye beinge the 15th of Auguste the storme ended and the wind
Cam faier for vs to go for Sagadehock so we wayed our anckors &
Sett Saill & stood to the estward & Cam to the Illand of Sutqin
which was 2 Leages from those Illandes we rod att anker beffor, & hear
we anckored vnder the Illand of Sutqin in the ester syde of ytt for
that the wynd was of the shore that wee Could not gett into the ryver
of Sagadehock[3] & hear Captain Pophams shipes bott Cam abord of vs
& gave us xx freshe Codes that they had taken beinge Sent out a
fyshinge[4]

Sondaye beinge the 16th of Auguste Captain Popham Sent his

---

[1] These are most likely to have been Seal I. and islets near it. They lie north of Small
Point (then an island) which provides a little protection, particularly if the wind had gone
round towards the southwest. Thayer (pp. 62–3) and Burrage (p. 409), both of whom knew
the coast, came to this conclusion also.

[2] On Seal and Small Point Islands pine and oak were everywhere, but to distinguish
four species among the varieties of *Vaccinium* was something of a botanical feat, though
blueberries and cranberries, the two main groups, could easily be differentiated. Hyland
and Steinmetz, *Woody Plants of maine* (1944), pp. 50–2, distinguish 19 Maine species of the
genus.

[3] Once the wind had died down, the course to Popham Point and the entrance to
the Kennebec would have become clear enough, but sightings and soundings could indicate
shoals and rocks on the way.

[4] The pilot was perhaps excessively cautious but the rounding of Seguin I. and an
approach from the east may well have been dictated by prevailing winds: it might seem
that by the time she anchored off the east side of Seguin I. the wind had gone round to
the northerly quarter. Popham's actions after entering the river (led by his shallop and

shallop vnto vs for to healp vs in   So we wayed our anckors & beinge Calme we towed in our ship & Cam into the Ryver of Sagadehocke and anckored by the gyftes Syd about xj of the Cloke the Sam daye[1]

Mundaye beinge the 17th Auguste Captain Popham in his shallop with 30 others & Captain Gilbert in his shipes bott accompaned with 18 other persons Departed early in the morninge from thear shipes & sailled vp the ryver of Sagadehock for to vew the Ryver & allso to See whear they myght fynd the most Convenyent place for thear plantation my Selffe beinge with Captain Gilbert. So we Sailled vp into this ryver near 14 Leages and found ytt to be a most gallant ryver very brod and of a good depth[2] we never had Lesse Watter then 3 fetham when we had Least & aboundance of greatt fyshe in ytt Leaping aboue the Watter on eatch Syd of vs as we Sailled.[3] [f. 9] So the nyght aprochinge after a whill we had refreshed our Selves vppon the shore about 9 of the Cloke we sett backward to retorn & Cam abourd our shipes the next day followinge about 2 of the Cloke in the afternoon We fynd this ryver to be very pleasant with many goodly Illandes in ytt & to be both Large & deepe Watter havinge many branches in ytt that which we tooke bendeth ytt Selffe towards the northest.

Tuesdaye beinge the 18th after our retorn we all went to the shore & thear mad Choise of a place for our plantation which ys at the very mouth or entry of the Ryver of Sagadehocke on the West Syd of the Ryver beinge almoste an Illand of a good bygnesse[4] whylst we wear

---

possibly with a chart) are not known to us. He evidently had already reconnoitred some possible sites for the settlement, and was able to afford the luxury of sending his ship's boat out to fish for cod and, no doubt, to try to sight his consort. Once contact had been made it was only a question of time before the *Mary and John* could enter the river.

[1] It is worth noting that it was only on the 11th day after their reunion at Georges Is. that the two ships were ready to set to work to establish the settlement. At least a week could have been saved had they been as efficient as Waymouth.

[2] The expedition upstream is more likely to have been one of something over 4 leagues rather than 14 (and Strachey's 40 a mistake for the smaller number, p. 406 above), as some 15 nautical miles would bring them far enough into Merrymeeting Bay to observe the northeast trend of the river. The impression which the river makes is a powerful one and there is no exaggeration in Davies' account.

[3] Thayer, p. 65, and Burrage, p. 410, have no doubt the fish were Sturgeon, *Acipenser oxyrynchus* Mitchill, whose habits in the Kennebec were well known to both of them.

[4] Atkins Bay is the first inlet on the west side of the Kennebec R., separated from a sea-beach (Popham Beach) by the high bluff, Sabino Head. They evidently rejected Hunniwells Point, the point at its entry, as being too exposed and too narrow, and chose the second land-projection into the bay as the site for the fort. This has suffered much in the course of time from wind erosion and human interference, so that the problem of aligning their chosen site in detail with what now survives is a difficult one (cp. pp. 515–19).

vppon the shore thear Cam in three Cannoos by vs but they wold nott Com near vs but rowed vp the Ryver & so past awaye

Wensday beinge the 19th Auguste we all went to the shore whear we mad Choise for our plantation and thear we had a Sermon delyvred vnto vs by our precher and after the Sermon our pattent was red with the orders & Lawes thearin prescrybed & then we retorned abord our shipes again[1]

Thursdaye beinge the 20th of Auguste all our Companyes Landed & thear began to fortefye our presedent Captain Popham Sett the fryst spytt of ground vnto ytt[2] and after hem all the rest followed & Labored hard in the trenches about ytt

Frydaye the 21th of Auguste all handes Labored hard about the fort Som in the trentch Som for fagettes[3] and our ship Carpenters about the buildinge of a small penis or shallop.[4]

The site offered a high lookout point to the main channel of the river and was sheltered from the south and east, though exposed to northerlies coming down the river, while providing a modest expanse of low ground to the west. Atkins Bay now provides anchorage for small vessels at high tide but dries out in part at low water: ships would have to stand off Hunniwells Point in the exposed river channel. It was well concealed from European enemies at sea, and was defensible from attack from the river, but it could be put in jeopardy in the rear if any enemy was able to erect a battery on Sabino Head itself (though dense forest gave cover even there). There was timber in abundance, rock sand and muddy clay, sufficient to enable the quick erection of primary entrenchments. Clearly military considerations – a possible French attack – dominated the early stages of the settlement at St George's Fort. The two ships anchored offshore in the river and the shallop and ship's boat ferried the men ashore. They may have done a little clearance of the site and some preliminary staking of the bounds of the settlement, but went back to the ships without more being done.

[1] A further shore expedition saw the formal steps being taken, the ground was marked out, a dedication ceremony held with a sermon by the Rev. Richard Seymour, appropriate parts of the charter of 10 April 1606 and the instructions of 20 November (pp. 390–6 above) were read, and the president and council formally nominated and presented with the oaths of office. Strachey gives some detail (p. 407). Since George Popham was designated governor before they left England, the names and offices of the council would already be known.

[2] The turning of the first spit marked the formal establishment of the settlement. The entrenchment no doubt followed lines that had been marked out during the previous two days. The digging of trenches along the north and west sides would have been straightforward (except for the segregation of rocks from sand and soil): on the east side the rocky elevation involved more complex engineering work, while to the south the close tree cover would delay entrenchment until enough timber had been felled and uprooted.

[3] Faggots were short lengths of wood, probably cut mainly from the trees on the south, which (laid laterally) were used to consolidate the steep sloping banks thrown up from the trenches to create an outer embankment for the fort. They can be seen on John Hunt's plan (pp. 441–3; fig. 25). For the bulwarks stone as well as wood was probably employed as suitable pieces were unearthed or gathered.

[4] The immediate beginning of the building of the shallop (or pinnace) indicated both the need for smaller vessels for reconnaissance purposes and also the desirability of

Satterdaye the 22th Auguste Captain Popham early in the morninge departed in his shallop to go for the ryver of Pashipskoke.[1] thear they had parle with the Salvages again who delyvred vnto them that they had ben att war with Sasanoa & had slain his Soone in fyght skidwares and Dehanada wear in this fyght[2]

Sondaye the 23th our presedent Captain Popham retorned vnto vs from the ryver of Pashipscoke

The 24th all Labored about the fort

Tuesdaye the 25th Captain Gilbert imbarked hem Selffe with 15 other with hem to go to the Westward vppon Som Discouery but the Wynd was Contrary & forsed hem backe again the Sam daye

The 26th & 27th all Labored hard about the fort

Frydaye the 28th Captain Gilbert with 14 others my Selffe beinge on Imbarked hem to go to the westward again[3] So the wynd Servinge we Sailled by many gallant Illandes & towardes nyght the winde Cam Contrary against vs So that we wear Constrained to remain that nyght vnder the head Land called Semeamis[4] whear we found the Land to be most fertill the trees growinge thear Doth exceed for goodnesse & Length being the most part of them ocke & wallnutt

---

experimenting as soon as possible with the suitability of the local timber for shipbuilding, so that this could be reported to the promoters.

[1] Their initial reconnaissance having taken them as far as Merrymeeting Bay, they were now attempting to make the first exploration of the western branch of the Kennebec R., the modern Androscoggin R. This appears in the 'Description of Mawooshen' (pp. 473-4).

[2] There is evidence of warfare amongst the Eastern Abenaki groups. Sabanoa was to inform Gilbert later that the Kennebec R. proper, the lower channel before Merrymeeting Bay, was his domain. It is likely that his principal settlement or settlements were on the Sasanoa R. (Back R.). The Pemaquid group, including Nahanada and Skidwarres, were now allied to Sasanoa's people though they had formerly fought with him. Sasanoa, though subject to Bashabes, was evidently building up a heritage from other bands along or near the Kennebec.

[3] Gilbert was evidently given the use of Popham's shallop which would have been employed upstream. His objective was probably to attempt to follow the coast westwards beyond Cape Small to the corn-growing area (of which he would have heard by this time) in the lower part of Casco Bay. Robert Davies was with him as pilot and it is likely that the crew came from the Mary and John. The initial setback indicated that winds blowing southwards from the river constituted a continuing hazard for small vessels.

[4] After passing Cape Small the shallop would keep within sight, but barely within sight, of the islands which occupy much of Casco Bay. After a sail of some 20 nautical miles in a generally southwesterly direction, the mainland from Portland Head to Cape Elizabeth would come into view. The headland 'Semeamis' was thought by Eckstorm (Indian place names, p. 166) to be Cape Elizabeth, but she is not supported by Huden (Indian place names, p. 397). Burrage (1906), p. 412, preferred Richmond I. Deep water and shelter could have been found northeast of Richmond I. and south of the southernmost part of Cape Elizabeth (now known as High Head).

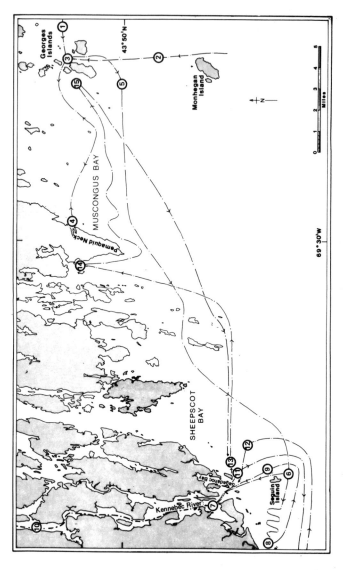

Fig. 23. August–October 1607. Courses of *Mary and John*, *Gifte of God*, and pinnace.
Figs. 24 (i) and (ii) show courses immediately to W.

Fig. 23. Key to general map

1 6 August 1607. *Mary and John* arrives in roadstead in Georges Is, between Allen, Benner, and Burnt Islands, and enters Georges Harbor, north of Allen I. (but see Appendix pp. 510–13).

2 7 August. Suggested route of *Gifte of God* towards Georges Is.

3 7 August. Union of ships at roadstead, though *Gifte* may not have entered the Harbor.

4 a. 7–8 August. First boat trip (ship's boat of *Mary and John*) to Pemaquid Neck (they crossed the Neck to the Eastern Abenaki settlement on its western side).

   b. 10–11 August. Second boat trip (*Gift*'s shallop and *Mary and John*'s boat) around Pemaquid Point to the Indian settlement. (Not illustrated.)

5 12–13 August. *Gifte of God, Mary and John*, and shallop sail from Georges Is. to attempt entry to Kennebec R.

6 13 August. Successful entry of shallop and *Gifte of God* into Kennebec (Sagadahoc) R.

7 Initial anchorage to the north of Sabino Head. 18 August. Choice made of site for Fort St. George at Atkins Point. See Fig. 24 (ii).

8 13–14 August. *Mary and John* carried westwards past Seguin I. in storm: anchored under some small islands.

9 15–16 August. Successful return of *Mary and John*, entry into Kennebec River, and junction with *Gifte of God*.

10 17 August. Shallop and boat explore lower reaches of Kennebec R.

11 28 August. Voyage of *Mary and John* W. and S.W. from Kennebec R. See Fig. 24 (i).

12 30 August. Return voyage through Casco Bay to re-enter Kennebec R.

13 8 September. *Mary and John* sets out for Penobscot R.

14 11 September. Visits Pemaquid Neck and finds Indian settlement deserted.

15 11–13 September. Makes slow headway against contrary winds and is forced to turn back before reaching Georges Is.: returns to Kennebec R.

Fig. 24 (i). 28–30 August 1607. Westward exploration of the Maine coast. Continued from fig. 23.

1. 28 August. Voyage of *Mary and John* W and SW from Kennebec River.
2. 28–29 August. Sights high headland (Semeamis) at Cape Elizabeth.
3. 29 August. Anchors off Richmond I.
4. 30 August. Return voyage through Casco Bay to re-enter Kennebec River.

Fig. 24 (ii). August–September 1607. Exploration of the Kennebec River.

1. 17–18 August. Point of departure and return in first reconnaissance.
2. Approximate limit of first reconnaissance.
3. 22–23 August. Second reconnaissance to the Androscoggin River.
4. 23–29 September. Third reconnaissance in search of the head of the river (see p. 412, n. 3).

rowinge a greatt space assoonder on from the other as our parkes in Ingland and no thickett growinge vnder them   hear wee also found a gallant place to fortefye whom nattuer ytt Selffe hath already framed without the hand of man with a runynge stream of watter hard adioyninge vnder the foott of ytt[1]

[f. 10] Satterdaye the 29th Auguste early in the mornynge we departed from thence & rowed to the westward for that the wind was againste vs but the wynd blew so hard that forsed vs to remain vnder an Illand 2 Leages from the place we remayned the night beffore   whilst we remayned vnder this Illand thear passed to Cannoos by vs but they wold nott Com neare vs   After mydnyght we put from this Illand in hope to have gotten the place we dessyered but the wind arose and blew so hard at Southwest Contrary for vs that forsed vs to retorn.[2]

Sondaye beinge the 30[th] Auguste retornynge beffore the wynd we Sailled by many goo[d]ly Illandes for betwixt this head Land called Semeamis & the ryver of Sagadehock ys a great baye in the which Lyeth So many Illandes & so thicke & neare together that you Cannott well desern to Nomber them   yet may you go in betwixt them in a good ship for you shall have never Lesse Watter the[n] 8 Fethams These Illandes ar all overgrowen with woodes very thicke as ockes wallnut pyne trees & many other thinges growinge as Sarsaperilla hassell nutes & whortes in aboundance.[3] So this day we retorned to our fort att Sagadehock.

Munday beinge the Last of Auguste nothinge hapened but all

---

[1] This could indeed have been on the north shore of Richmond I. A successful fishing and trading plantation was operated here for Richard Trelawney from 1632 onward and tends to bear out Davies' choice of it as a fertile and defensible site (*The Trelawney papers*, ed. J. P. Baxter (Portland, Me., 1884)). Davies may be of the opinion that a faulty choice was made in placing Fort St George on the Kennebec. White Walnut, *Juglans cinerea* L. is not mentioned amongst the more northerly trees: it needs rich moist soil. The openness of the woods suggests that the Indians had cleared the underbrush for hunting.

[2] If the Richmond I. identification is sound, this could be Wood I., off the mouth of the Saco River. The Indians would be those of the Saco R., whose chief Champlain (*Works*, I, 323, 395–9, 457–8, III, 373), named as Onemechin, and who were linked by language and agriculture with the Indians of southern New England, notably the Massachusetts (see Salwen in *Handbook*, p. 160).

[3] The shallop evidently came closer to the maze of islands in Casco Bay than she had on her southward run. Cushing, Peaks, Long, Jewell, Bailey and Ragged Is. are among the more prominent she is likely to have sighted. He is right about deep water, but there were many hidden dangers. Clearly some landings were made, but the descriptions are not indicative of where. Oaks, pines, hazelnuts and whortleberries (see pp. 304–5, 308) were universal. This is his earliest mention of Sarsaparilla, the Green-brier, *Smilax rotundifolia* L., thought to be a kind of China Root and its roots of value in medicine (see p. 449).

labored for the buildinge of the fort & for the storhouse to reseave our vyttuall.[1]

Tuesday the first of September thear Cam a Canooa vnto vs in the which was 2 greatt kettelles of brasse   Som of our Company did parle with them but they did rest very doutfull of vs and wold nott Suffer mor then on att a tyme to Com near vnto them   So he departed[2]

The Second daye third & 4th nothinge hapened worth the wryttinge but that eatch man did his beste endevour for the building of the fort

Satterdaye beinge the 5th of September thear Cam into the entraunce of the ryver of Sagadehocke nine Cannooas in the which was Dehanada & skidwarres with many others in the wholl near fortye persons men women & Children   they Cam & parled with vs & we aggain vssed them in all frindly maner We Could & gave them vyttailles for to eatt   So skidwarres & on more of them stayed with vs vntill nyght the rest of them withdrew them in thear Canooas to the farther syd of the ryver. but when nyght Cam for that skidwares woold needes go to the rest of his Company[3]   Captain Gilbert accompaned with James Davis & Captain Ellis best[4] took them into our bott & Caryed them to thear Company on the farther syd the ryver & thear remained amongst them all the nyght. & early in the mornynge the Sallvages

[1] The outer entrenchments would now have been complete and the men (living under canvas and aboard ship) would have begun construction of utility buildings and, perhaps, dwellings. The intermittent reference by Davies to work at the Fort when he was present indicates that he, like all the rest of the seamen, had to work on the construction when he was available. The storehouse under construction on 31 August was evidently the 'old storehouse' later referred to and is likely to have been near the wharf: the storehouse shown on the plan (p. 443) appears to have been the larger one built later. Unloading of perishable cargo from the *Mary and John* was possible only when safe storage was ready.

[2] The brass kettles were greatly prized by the coastal Indians for preparing food or for cutting up for ornaments. Many were stolen and some traded by the French farther north, and the canoe is not unlikely to have been a Micmac one, trading along the coast, but deciding that the English settlers were unlikely to be friendly (cp. pp. 109, 420–1).

[3] Towards the end of the fishing and gathering season the Pemaquid band made the decision that a large proportion of them should go to see what the English were doing at Fort St George. Nahanada and Skidwarres were now willing to resume contact and the visit was to convince Popham and Gilbert that they could act as intermediaries with Bashabes, whose political and economic control of the region was a vital element in the success or otherwise of English commercial activity. The discussion was almost certainly about the fur trade and the part the Pemaquid band could play in promoting it in their own interest. They gave evidence of their goodwill by their leaders remaining some time in the English fort, but of their intention to remain autonomous by insisting in camping across the river. Their short-term mission was to arrange a meeting between the English and Bashabes.

[4] James Davis (or Davies) is here referred to impersonally: one small indication that the author of the journal was not he: for Captain Ellis Best see pp. 353, 408.

Departed in thear Cannooas for the ryver of Pemaquid promyssinge Captain Gilbert to accompany hem in thear Cannooas to the ryver of Penobskott whear the bashabe remayneth

The 6th nothinge happened the 7th our ship the Mary & John began to discharge her vyttualles[1]

Tuesday beinge the 8th September Captain Gilbert acompaned with xxij others my Selffe beinge on of them Departed from the fort to go for the ryver of Penobskott takinge with hem divers Sortes of Merchandise for to trade with the [f. 11] Bashabe who ys the Cheeffe Comander of those partes[2] but the wind was Contrary againste hem so that he could nott Com to Dehanada & skidwares at the time apointed for ytt was the xj[th] daye beffor he Could gett to the ryver of Pemaquid whear they do make thear abbode[3]

Frydaye beinge the xj[th] in the mornynge early we Cam into the ryver of Pemaquyd thear to Call nahanada & skidwarres as we had promyste them but beinge thear aryved we found no Lyvinge Creatuer they all wear gon from thence[4] the which we perseavinge presently departed towardes the ryver of Penobskott Saillinge all this daye & the xij[th] & xiij[th] the Lyke yett by no means Could we fynd ytt So our vitall beinge spent we hasted to retorn So the wynd Cam faier for vs and we Sailled all the 14th & 15th dayes in retornynge the Wind blowinge very hard att north[5] & this mornynge the 15th daye we perseaved a blassing star in the northest of vs[6]

---

[1] The date of 7 September then marks a stage in the completion of a storehouse, though it may not have been the only one (cp. p. 407).

[2] Once again Gilbert is apparently using the shallop, along with Robert Davies, and 21 others, to make his way to the Penobscot seat of Bashabes, some 100 miles distant, to which the Pemaquid leaders had undertaken to pilot him. The object was clearly to trade. Bashabes had had close earlier trading connections with Champlain. His domination of the Eastern Abenaki is here acknowledged. Moose hides, rather than beaver, were what he most likely would have to offer.

[3] However difficult it may have been for Gilbert to get his vessel to Pemaquid it is strange he did not try to send a messenger by boat, as the distance was not great. His failure to do so might suggest a certain contempt for the Indians, who must await his arrival.

[4] The arrival of the English over two days late broke the arrangements between them and the Pemaquid band. Nahaneda and Skidwarres had probably gone off on the 9th to inform Bashabes that the English had not appeared. Their absence was proof of their independence rather than of their unreliability. The movement of the remainder of the band is less explicable.

[5] Davies was unlucky, as before, in finding the entrance to the river: it may show up some of his weaknesses as a pilot. But wind conditions in September can be very severe.

[6] This can scarcely have been the comet which Thomas Harriot observed on 22 September (J. W. Shirley, ed., *Thomas Harriot, Renaissance Scientist* (1974), p. 11), unless Davies' dating is wrong by a week, even if Harriot is using N.S. dating. If it was not the same Davies is more likely to have meant a shooting star.

The 16th 17th 18th 19th 20th 21th 22th nothinge hapened but all Labored hard about the fort & the store house for to land our wyttailles[1]

The 23th beinge Wensdaye Capt*ain* Gilbert acompaned wit*h* 19 others my Selffe on of them dep*ar*ted from the fort to go for the head of the ryver of Sagadehock   We Sailled all this daye   So did we the Lyke the 24th vntill the evenynge then we Landed thear to remain that nyght. hear we found a gallant Champion Land & exceedinge fertill So hear we remayned all nyght[2]

[f. 11 v.] The 25th beinge frydaye early in the mornynge we Dep*ar*ted from hence & sailled vp the ryver about eyght Leag*es* farther vntill we Cam vnto an Illand beinge Lo Land & flatt   att this Illand ys a great Down Fall of watter / the w*h*ich run*n*eth by both Sydes of this Illand very swyfte & shallow[3]   in this Illand we found greatt store of grapes exceedinge good and sweett of to Sortes both red butt the on of them ys a mervellous deepe red.[4] By both the syd*es* of this ryver the grapes grow in aboundance & allso very good Hoppes[5] & also Chebolles and garleck.[6] and for the goodnesse of the Land ytt doth so far abound [in goodnesse] that I Cannott allmost expresse the Sam   hear we all went ashore & with a stronge Rope made fast to our bott & on man in her to gyde her against the Swyfte stream we pluckt her vp throwe ytt p*er*force   after we had past this Down Fall we all went into our bott again & rowed near a Leag*e* farther vp into the ryver & nyght beinge att hand we hear stayed all nyght,[7] & in the fryst of the night about ten of the Cloke thear Cam on the farther syd of the ryver sartain

---

[1] Either unloading was painfully slow or else it was necessary to accommodate some of the cargo in a second storehouse which had then to be built.

[2] The exploring expedition was much the same as on previous occasions and again, apparently, in the shallop. They proceeded up river, allowing for exploration of entering tributaries, some 50 miles. The stop for the night would have been well north of their previous limit in Merrymeeting Bay.

[3] Thayer, pp. 73–4, makes a convincing case for this being Cushnoc Island, just below modern Augusta (42 miles from Fort St George), swamped in the nineteenth century by the damming of the river. It lay near the eastern bank, with a swift current on either side.

[4] Fox-grape, *Vitis labrusca* Michx. (not sweet by our taste) and Forest Grape, *V. riparia* Michx. (with the intermediate species *V. novae-angliae* Fern.) would be found. All would be ripe.

[5] *Humulus lupulus* L., the American Hop, being that found also in England, and recognizable especially by men from the southeast.

[6] 'Chibolls' are onions and the plants probably *Allium canadense* L., though other species are possible, as the mention of garlic would suggest (the distinction may have been merely the size of the bulbs, or possibly the smell).

[7] After getting past the rapids they would have had a straight course ahead. They would seem to have camped just north of present-day Augusta.

Salvages Callinge vnto vs in broken inglyshe   we answered them aggain   So for this time they departed[1]

The 26th beinge Satterdaye thear Cam a Canooa vnto vs & in hear fower salvages those that had spoken vnto vs in the nyght beffore his name that Came vnto vs ys Sabenoa   he makes himsellfe vnto vs to be Lord of the ryver of Sagadehocke./[2]

41   8 October 1607. John Hunt's plan of St George's Fort[3]

The Draught of s[t] Georges fort Erected by Captayne George Popham Esquier one the entry of the famous Riuer of Sagadahock in Virginia taken out by Iohn Hunt the viij[th] day of october in the yeare of our lorde · 1607.

[1] Almost certainly members of the Pemaquid band who were trading or hunting along with the leading Sagamore of Androscoggin, Sabanoa. They had perhaps been following the shallop upstream but keeping out of sight. As already suggested, Sabanoa appeared to have asserted some pre-eminence along the lower reaches of the Penobscot and Androscoggin Rivers, but still subordinate to Bashabes.

[2] The ending of William Griffiths' transcript here is possibly due to his having a faulty MS, but more probably a leaf has been lost. Strachey's version (above pp. 397–417) continues it. The endorsement leaf shows that the MS was originally folded down the middle, the endorsement being written on the left-hand side. 'The Relation of the whole Voyage to Virginia' is followed in another hand by 'New England'.

[3] The detailed drawing, or picture plan, of the fort as completed by 8 October 1607 by John Hunt (sent by Pedro de Zúñiga to Philip III, and in Archivo General de Simancas, Estado Inglatierra 2586, f. 147) gives some basis for discussion of this fort (fig. 25, also pp. 514–19). Some writers have considered that more than 15 structures could not have been constructed between 20 August and 8 October, and that 50 is a mistake for 15. There are grounds for challenging this. Eighteen separate structures can be distinguished, containing 22 chimneys, plus the church, storehouse, munition store and one other which have no chimneys which would provide 26 buildings. But a house in the almost contemporary plantation of Ulster was a unit of 16 square feet in plan, and rising 1½ storeys (one room and an attic), with a chimney. A composite containing more than one of these units was called by the number of units ('his dwelling of two houses', etc.). Allowing for such units, which can usually be distinguished on the plan, we can count up to 54 or 55 units in all, some being very small, little more than sheds attached to dwellings. This approach makes the '50 howses' credible. It cannot be regarded as fully established. However pole frames, if not more than about 16 feet wide, with cross-pieces and a pitched roof, roughly thatched, could be put up very rapidly. The filling-in of the walls with matting, lath and plaster (here clay rather than plaster), and the gradual covering of them inside with timber sheathing, could take very much longer than the simple erection, and the plan does not mean that any buildings were wholly finished for winter comfort by 8 October. Chimneys would be of wood plastered inside with clay (and so very vulnerable to fire). The details given by Hunt (of whom we know nothing in other connections) – the president's house, the chapel, the admiral's house, the munition house (magazine), the storehouse (it may have been rebuilt as we hear of the old storehouse, probably near the wharf (p. 403)), the munition master's house, the vice-admiral's house, the buttery general (refectory), the provost's (provost marshal's) house, the sergeant major's house, the corporal's house, the

· A · a demy Culueringe   · 10 · the Sargent Maiors howse
· B · Sakers   · 11 · the Corporals howse
· C · Min*n*yons   · 12 · the kitchin generall
· D · fawcons   · 13 · the Smithes howse
· 1 · the Presedente howse   · 14 · the Coupers howse
· 2 · the Chapell   · 15 · the Bake house
· 3 · the Admirals howse   · 16 · the Court of goarde
· 4 · the Munition howse   · 17 · the lake
· 5 · the Store howse   · 18 · the Land gate
· 6 · the Munition M^r howse   · 19 · the water gate
· 7 · the Vice Admirals howse   · 20 · the posterne gate
· 8 · the Buttery general.   · M · the Market place
· 9 · the Prouostes howse   the rest are priuat lodgins

kitchen general (a separate building on account of danger from fire, but surprisingly far from the buttery general), the smith's house, the cooper's house, the bakehouse (again separate for reasons of fire danger but again far from both kitchen and buttery), the court of guard (the guard house), are all convincing and most can be attached to named individuals. The small sheds attached to some of these buildings, e.g. those of the smith and cooper, were clearly workshops to enable them to carry on their trades.

The fortifications consisted of a trench, except where 'Clyffe' is marked, and made a ditch round the whole settlement; inside was a revetment of sand, clay or rock, kept in place by horizontal lines of timber faggots, and making a sloping rampart. Substantial bastions were constructed on which to place the heavier cannon and large enough in several cases to contain small buildings as well, and with embrasures between bastions on two sides to give complete covering fire towards the water, eight large cannon being shown mounted. There were three gates: a land gate, a water gate and a postern gate, the first two with towers, all of which may well have been much more primitive in appearance and construction than is indicated. The nature of the site precluded following the traditional star fort pattern, but many of its features were incorporated. The small headland to the north of the site was revetted with stone to make a small pier, off which the newly built pinnace *Virginia* is shown lying (she would not have been complete). A path is laid down from the water gate to the water. A fenced garden area is laid out to the west. The basic layout was of a rough rectangle, modified by the nature of the ground. The N–S side was roughly 229·6 ft with an extension to the south for a further 100 ft (and some 50 ft wide) for a bastion covering the river approach. The E–W side by the water was some 340·7 ft long; the inner side N–S was about 196·2 ft and the E–W inner side (including the southern bastion's width) some 211·1 ft. The total area enclosed was about 45,000 sq. ft. 5,000 sq. yds). This considerable area has now been much eroded and has yielded almost nothing in the way of artefacts. The site has recently been considered by Andrew Wahll in the light of such cartographical evidence as exists. The results of archaeological activity in 1963 and 1964 and of some cartographic research are given on pp. 515–19 below.

442

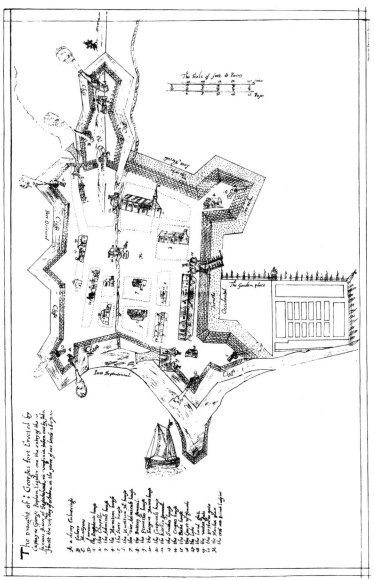

Fig. 25. 8 October 1607. John Hunt's Picture-plan of Fort St. George, Kennebec River.

CHAPTER XII

INCIDENTAL DOCUMENTS ON THE
1607–1608 VOYAGES

Though we are reasonably fully informed about the voyage and the early stages of the progress of the venture at Fort St George on the Kennebec River, we are very poorly informed about what happened after 8 October 1607 until the final evacuation in the autumn of 1608, Purchas having discarded the essential documents (p. 352). We start with George Popham's final acceptance of the presidency on the day that he started from Plymouth in command of the *Gifte of God* (for which we have no surviving journal). We are, thereafter, largely dependent on Sir Ferdinando Gorges' letters to Lord Salisbury from 1 December 1607 onwards. They are full of his own concerns and may scarcely be regarded as wholly objective but they do record the arrival of the *Mary and John* at Plymouth on 1 December 1607, give some details about the sample cargo she carried (not very satisfactory for the subscribers), and retail gossip about divisions in the settlement between the president and his 'admiral' and second-in-command, Raleigh Gilbert (p. 450), but they are only adjuncts to the Robert Davies diary and to the plan of the fort brought back by the ship.

The second vessel, the *Gifte of God*, retained as guardship against a possible French attack, was forced by ice floes in the river to leave on 13 December 1607. She carried letters to Sir John Popham and to Edward Seymour but they are lost (p. 349), and all we have is the pompous and grossly misleading Latin letter sent by George Popham to James I, which might suggest that the president was in his dotage (pp. 452–5). We are not told that she was carrying back a substantial number of the colonists, whom Popham could not feed (45 only out of 100 being left). She was instructed, if she had not enough food to bring her home, to visit the Azores and dispose of her cargo there (since apparently no one had any money in Fort St George). She sold off masts and spars and pledged a cannon, but reported on her arrival at Plymouth on 7 February 1608 that all the survivors were well but suffering from cold and shortages of food and clothing. Gorges (pp. 455–6) had much to say of the 'idle proceedinges' of the colonists in not sending home viable cargoes, but little on the internal situation in detail.

Sir John Popham having died, his widow and his heir, Sir Francis, took an action against the ship's master John Havercome, for disposing of the ship's cargo on the way home, which the High Court of Admiralty eventually threw out (summaries on pp. 459–65; full report *NAW*, III, 442–547). The Pophams seem to have taken the action to assert a claim to all goods brought from the colony, Captain John Elliott's journal, which Purchas also threw away, would have given us much more detail, but we learn a little about the internal working of the colony between October and December 1606 and of the effects of an early and hard winter on it. On 20 March 1608 Gorges, who had now taken over executive authority from Sir Francis Popham, reported that he had got two ships sent from Topsham with supplies and hoped to send another in May. Thereafter darkness surrounds the colony. Purchas had a journal of Christopher Fortescue apparently covering at least part of this period, but he disposed of it also. We gather that after George Popham's death in February, Raleigh Gilbert, as president, kept the colony viable. Either before or after the arrival of the ships, he was able to get further exploration going and was also able to engage substantially in the fur trade with the Abenaki after they had furs and skins ready for sale in late spring and early summer. We do not know whether or not he made his postponed visit to Bashabes on the Penobscot. This should have been the situation if the ships had arrived at the end of May or early in June as they should have done if Gorges had told the truth on 20 March. We may probably assume that they left for home not long after with a cargo of some value but all reference to their arrival (in August?) is lacking.

The third vessel was the *Mary and John* once more. She did not leave until after 9 July and she would have been in the colony by late August or early September. It may well be that she did not bring enough stores to instil any confidence in the remaining settlers (who may or may not have been reinforced by the supply ships). She did bring news that Sir John Gilbert, who before his death on 9 July may well have contributed to the rescue operations, had left his property to Raleigh Gilbert, his younger brother. He now felt obliged to return and so the colonists, we learn (pp. 414–15), insisted on going too and dismantled the fort, not expecting to return. We can take it that the venture ended with their arrival in the West Country about November 1608. But even such a slight sketch of the later stages is based on hints and supposition rather than documents. Of the journals which Purchas disposed of so rashly, that of Raleigh Gilbert would have been the most informative on the final phase of the enterprise, of which we know almost nothing.

We may well consider the letter of the royal council for Virginia to the mayor and aldermen of Plymouth on 17 February 1609, assuming that the North Virginia venture had failed, and inviting their association henceforth in a renewed Virginia Company concerned with the Jamestown colony only, to mark the formal end of the North Virginia enterprise as planned in 1606. The persistence of both Sir Francis Popham and Sir Ferdinando Gorges in continuing the venture may indicate that the proposal found no further corporate support in Plymouth, and we may doubt whether there were further meetings of the Commissioners who supposedly formed the governing council of the Western venture.

42   31 May 1607. Captain George Popham to the earl of Salisbury, accepting the presidency of the North Virginia colony[1]

My Lord:

Remembringe my self on all humble dutifulnes vnto my right honorable good lord, doe by theis make bold to aduertize, that I directed my late lettres vnto your Lordshipp concerninge a commaunde I had from my Lord Cheife Iustice of England, to appointe my self vnto the discouerye and populacion of the western Colony in Virginia.[2] I wishe my desire mighte goe accompanyed with any of the leaste acceptable seruice therein, yet durste I promise by due endeuours to giue my beste addicion vnto the same. Sente alsoe a lettre in that of myne enclosed, concerninge the passage of our merchantes aboute theire occassions in Spaine & Portugall,[3] whereof I thoughte fytt to acquaint your honor.

[He recommends the bearer, Rowland Jones, collector at Bridgwater,[4] for preferment in Somerset.]

From Plymouth this Laste of Maye. 1607:[5]

Your honors moste humble to Commaund /
George Popham

[Addressed:] To the righte honorable my verie good lord the Earle of Salisburye principall Secretary to his moste excellente Maiesty and of his highnes moste Honorable Priuye Counsaile.[6]

---

[1] Hatfield House, CP 121/65; *Cal. Cecil MSS*, XIX (1965), 141–2; printed in Baxter, *Gorges*, III, 144–5; *NAW*, III, 426. George Popham was born in the early 1550s. He was a first cousin of Sir John Popham, being the son of Edward Popham of Huntworth, Somerset, brother of Sir John's father. He was active at sea in the privateering war in 1594 (Ralegh, *The discouerie of Guiana* (1596), pp. 102–12), and commanded a pinnace under Sir Robert Dudley in the Caribbean in 1594–5 (*The voyage of Robert Dudley, 1594–5*, ed. G. F. Warner (1899), pp. 43, 71, 75–6). See Brown, *Genesis*, II, 968–9.

[2] Though Gorges regarded him as too old and infirm to be in command, George Popham evidently regarded the command from his uncle as something he could not resist. He would in any event, according to the instructions, not have to serve for more than a year. See p. 391.

[3] Bridgwater had some trade with the Iberian peninsula where English merchants were still in some difficulties.

[4] Popham was customer of Bridgwater and he might appear to be commending Jones for promotion from collector to acting customer during his absence.

[5] Popham made his will the same day. He leaves part of his estate to his nephew, Edwarde Popham, who was to go with him on the voyage, with £5 to his servant Thomas Oxnam, and the remainder to Lettice Maior, who was to be his sole executrix. P.R.O., PROB 11/112, ff. 413r–414r. See Thayer, pp. 249–50. Probate was granted on 8 December 1608.

[6] His earlier letter is not now extant. It may be significant that he left his confirmation

43   1 December 1607. Sir Ferdinando Gorges to the earl of Salisbury, reporting the return of a vessel from North Virginia.[1]

Right Honor*abell*. This present day, heere is ariued on of our shipps out of the Partes of Virginia,[2] with greate newes of a fertill Contry, gallant Riuers, stately Harbors, and a people tractable, (so discreete Courses bee taken with them,) but no returne, to satisfy the expectation of the Aduenturers, the which may bee an occasion, to blemish the reputac*i*on of the designe, although in reason it could not bee otherwayes,[3] both bycause of the shortnes of theyr aboad there (which was but two monethes), as also, theyr want of meanes to follow theyr directions, theyr number being so small, and theyr busines so great, beside in very truthe, the defect and wante of vnderstandinge of som of those imployed, to performe what they weare directed vnto, from whense, there did not only proceede confusion, but thorough pride and arrogansay, faction, and priuat resolution, as more at large your Lor*dshipp* shall perceaue, by my next, with the particulars therof, in the meane time,[4] I haue sente this inclosed, humbly beseeching, it may bee deliuered to Sir Fransis Popham, whome I doubt not, but will at large accquaynte your Lor*dshi*pp what he receaueth, although I beleeue

---

of his acceptance of the presidency and the making of his will until the day of sailing. It might appear that his appointment was made late in the preparations for the voyage and possibly as the result of another declining the post.

[1]   Hatfield House, CP 123/77, *Cal. Cecil MSS*, XIX (1965), 353-4, printed Baxter, *Gorges*, III, 154-6, *NAW*, III, 437-8. Extracts.

[2]   Sir John Popham having died on 10 June 1607, Sir Ferdinando Gorges had now taken over the business side of the project at Plymouth, though Sir Frances Popham and his mother, Sir John's heirs, still continued to regard the proceeds as their private property (see p. 459 below). The *Mary and John*, Robert Davies captain, had left the Kennebec River on October 8 (arriving December 1).

[3]   Gorges attempts to mitigate the unfavourable things he has to say by expressing his confidence in the location of the colony and his belief in its ultimate potential, though he does not regard the specimens of commodities brought back as being of any value to the investors.

[4]   He distributes blame between smallness of numbers, shortness of time, inability to follow their instructions and also their own divisions (pp. 449-50). He does not pay tribute to the achievement of the colonists in constructing a substantial defensive settlement (which preoccupied them to the partial exclusion of the search for profitable commodities). But it can be argued that their initial dealings with the Eastern Abenaki Indians were also unskilled and not calculated to produce even the small amount of furs and tobacco available in the autumn (cp. pp. 333-5).

hee will not heare of all, that hath paste.[1] For my owne opinion, I am confident, there will bee diuers reasons to perswade a constant resolution, to persue this place, as firste the bouldnes of the Coaste, the easines of the nauigation, the fertility of the soyle, and the seuerall sortes of Commodityes, that they ar ashured, the contry do yealde, as namely fish in the season, in great plenty, all the Coste alonge mastidge for shipps, goodly Oakes, and Ceaders, with infinit other sortes of trees, Rasom [= resin?], hempe, grapes very fayre and excellent good, wherof they haue already made wine, much like to the Claret wine that comes out of France, rich Furrs if they can keepe the Frenchmen from the trade, as for mettals, they can say nothinge, but they ar confidente there is in the Contry, if they had meanes to seeke for it, neither could they go so high, as the Allom mines ar, which the Sauages doth ashure them there is great plenty of.[2] Thus mouch I humbly desire may satisfy your Lordshipp at this present, vntill I bee better able to furnish your Lordshipp with the rest that they can say...

> Your Lordshipps humbly to bee Commaunded/
> Fard: Gorges.

[1] No report from Popham to Salisbury has survived, but other letters had also come, among them the letters from Captain George Popham to Sir John Popham and Edward Seymour (referred to above by Purchas but now lost, p. 349).

[2] After his initial pessimism he is tempted to bring as many goods as he can to Salisbury's attention. The boldness of the coast can be admitted; the easiness of the navigation can be qualified by the rugged nature of the Maine shore and the dangers imposed both by its many islands and its incalculable weather. The fish, cod and sturgeon alike, were good recommendations if not very relevant to the short-term objectives of the company. Masts from the white pine were certainly an asset and timber from oak attractive (though it did not prove economical to bring it to England). So far as cedar is concerned the reports (and probable specimens) are more likely to be from the Northern White-cedar, *Thuja occidentalis* L., rather than the Eastern Red-cedar, *Juniperus virginiana* L., earlier brought from southern Massachusetts by Gosnold (pp. 160, 207). The 'rasom' has not been met with, but it may well be resin. The 'hempe' has not been identified since hemp was not native. Clearly it was a fibrous plant, many of which were in use by the Indians. Neither the Northern Fox Grape, *Vitis labrusca* L., or the New England Grape, *V. novae angliae* Fernald have won in modern time much esteem for winemaking but both can and have been used. They would be reasonably abundant in this area (Hyland and Steinmetz, *Woody plants*, p. 42).

Raleigh Gilbert had passed up several chances of obtaining at least a few furs and skins so none may have been brought. French competition was certainly a genuine threat since French experience in fur-trading was so much more effective and long-standing.

Descriptions by the Indians of rock which answered the description of rock alum (the compacted chrystalline form of double sulphate of aluminium and potassium) had evidently reached the settlers. Later these rumours were focused on a rock on the Sasanoa River but, in fact, alum-bearing rock was found later in the lower Kennebec basin (Baxter, Gorges, III, 356; Thayer, p. 82). On the importance of alum for cloth manufacture (also tanning): see Quinn, *Roanoke voyages*, I, 327-8.

I should haue remembred your Lordshipp that the Contry doth yealde Sanceparelia in a great aboundance, and a certayne silke that doth grow in small Codds, a sample wherof I will send this night or to morrow.[1]

Plymouth this 1 of December late at night 1607.

[Addressed:] To the Right Honorabell my very good Lord the Earle of Salisbury theise.

[Endorsed:] one December 1607. Sir Fardinando Gorges to my Lord.

44   3 December 1607. Sir Ferdinando Gorges to the earl of Salisbury, with further news from the Kennebec colony[2]

Right Honorabell:

It seems to bee moste certayne, that ther is no enterprise, (how well so euer intended,) but hath his particular impedimentes meeting with many oppositions, and infinite Crosses, as in this small attempt, (begun by my Lord Cheefe Iustice out of a noble zeale to his prince and Contry, (amongst many others,[)] it is experiensed for firste as hee was honorable himselfe, so hee thought all others weare, beleeuing what they toulde him, and trustinge to what, they promised, by which meanes, his Lordshipp was not a litle deceaued of what hee expected,[3] for neither were his prouisions answerable to his Charge bestowed,[4] nor the persons imployed such as they ought; in as much as the wantes of the on was cause of inabilety to performe what was hoped; & the Childish factions, ignorant timerous, and ambitiouse persons, (for of that nature I founde the commposition to bee) hath bread an vnstable resolution,

[1] Sarsaparilla was equated with the supposedly medicinal China root and it in turn with species of *Smilax*. Here it is Common Green-brier, *Smilax rotundifolia* L. (Hyland and Steinmetz, *Woody plants*, p. 4; Gleason and Cronquist, *Manual*, p. 214). The 'Codds' are the seed-pods of the Milkweed, *Asclepias* family, of which a number of species grow in Maine, *A. syriaca* L. being the most prominent. The down was thought to make a silky cloth.

[2] Hatfield House, CP 123/81, *Cal. Cecil MSS*, xix (1965), 356–7, printed in Baxter, *Gorges*, iii, 158–60, *NAW*, iii, 438–9.

[3] It is difficult to decide on the basis of this letter how much is gossip, retailed by the returned members of the *Mary and John*, how much Gorges' own attempt to establish himself (rather than George Popham or Raleigh Gilbert on the spot, and Sir Francis Popham at home) as the chief inspiration of the continuing enterprise.

[4] The inadequate victualling of the settlers is undoubted (p. 455). Gorges suggests that Sir John Popham was deceived in his agents. As these included both Gorges and Francis Popham (pp. 332–3 and *NAW*, iii, 442–54), there is an element of ingenuousness in his disposition of the blame.

and a generall confusion, in all theyr affayres.[1] For firste the President himselfe is an honest man, but ould, and of an vnwildy body, and timerously fearfull to offende, or contest with others that will or do oppose him, but otherwayes a discreete carefull man.[2] Captayne Gilberte is described to mee from thense to bee desirous of supremasy, and rule, a loose life, prompte to sensuality, litle zeale in Religion, humerouse, head-stronge, and of small iudgment and experiense, other wayes valiant inough,[3] but hee houldes that the kinge could not giue away that, by Pattent, to others, which his Father had an Act of Parliament for, and that hee will not bee put out of it in haste. With many such like idle speeches, which (allthough hee bee powrlesse to performe oughte) weare not vnfit to bee taken notice of bycause it weare good in my opinion that all such occasion were taken way, as may hinder the publique proceedinge, and let the cause of sedicion bee plucked vp by the Roote, before it do more harme;[4] besides hee hath sent (as I am farther informed) into England for diuers of his freindes, to com to him, for the strenghning of his party on all occasions (as hee termes it) with much more that I haue receaued notis of to this effect;[5] which I thought it my duety to aduertise your Lordshipp in time, that some course may bee taken, to preuent mischiffe. Which must bee don by immediate authority from thense, taking no farther notise

[1] Robert Davies, most probably, and others on the *Mary and John* carried to Gorges a picture of a sharply divided community. In isolation, without clearly defined objectives, a small settlement such as this did split into contesting groups which could seriously damage its effectiveness; this was only too well demonstrated at Jamestown at precisely the same time. (See the evidence on this for the first Jamestown colony running through P. L. Barbour, *The Jamestown voyages*, 2 vols., 1969.)

[2] The picture of the president, George Popham, is a balanced one, and may well be correct. It remained in Gorges' mind and he was to repeat it in later life, basically unchanged, p. 345.

[3] The picture of Raleigh Gilbert, who as admiral of the colony was second in command until George Popham's death, is not confirmed (or denied) from other sources, but it may well be biased since Gorges may have wished to avoid giving Gilbert and his brother Sir John Gilbert, who had a considerable following in the Dartmouth area, too much influence in the affairs of the venture. Gilbert was to succeed George Popham as president in two months from the date of this letter.

[4] Sir Humphrey Gilbert's patent of 1578 was for six years only, and in effect expired at his death at sea in 1583, while it was replaced by the patent to his half-brother, Walter Ralegh, in February 1584 (which in turn became void in 1603). There was no such 'Act of Parliament'. The story that Raleigh Gilbert was attempting to revive his father's supposed rights may well be a canard. (See Quinn, *Gilbert*, I, 188–94, and p. 334 above.)

[5] That Raleigh Gilbert should have sent letters to his brother and to his friends (by the *Mary and John*), inviting them to join him, is very probable, but does not necessarily carry the implication which Gorges gives it (namely the intention to overthrow the North Virginia enterprise under the charter of 1606), but rather underlines the Gorges–Gilbert rivalry suggested above.

heerof, then your wisdom shall thinke good, but the better to manifest, and to bringe all to light, without callinge the authors in Quaestion, your Lordshipp mey bee pleased to sende downe present commaunde, to intercept all letters whatsoeuer, and to whomesoeuer, and to cause them to bee sent vp, (for I know in whose possession these letters ar yet, and I thinke I shall finde the meanes to keepe them from being deliuered in haste[)],[1] As for the reste of the Persons imployed, they ar either fit for theyr Places or tolerable, But the Preacher is moste to bee commended,[2] both for his Paynes in his place, and his honest indeuors; as also is Captayne Robert Daues,[3] and likewise Master Turner theyr Phisition,[4] who is com ouer, to sollicite theyr supplyes, and to informe the state of euery Particular. I haue sayde in my laste to your Lordshipp what I thinke how necessary it is, this busines should bee thoroughly followed, but if I should tell your Honor how much I am affected vnto it in my owne nature, it may bee that my commendations therof, would bee of the lesse credit, but I desire in my soule, that it would please God, his Maiesty would take it into his owne handes, vnto whome (of right) the conquest of kingdoms doth appertayne, and then should I thinke my selfe moste happy to receaue such imployment in it, as his highnes should thinke mee fit for, and I woulde not doubte, but with a very litle charges, to bringe to passe infinite thinges. I will say no more of it, as this present, only I make no quaestion but that your Lordshipp will finde it to bee of greater moment, then it can easily bee beleeued to bee;[5] I haue sent vnto your Lordshipp the Iournalls

---

[1] The proposal to put the Gilbert correspondence under surveillance and to impound it sounds malicious, and there is no evidence that Salisbury took any notice of it. Gorges goes on to consider what he knows or has heard of other members of the colony.

[2] The Reverend Richard Seymour.

[3] Captain Robert Davies is said by Strachey to have been pilot of the *Mary and John* on the outward voyages and is implied to have been the author of the journal he used (cp. p. 401). He was, John Smith says, designated to be sergeant-major in the colony, effectively second in command on the military side (p. 352). The sergeant-major's house is shown on John Hunt's plan (pp. 441–3), but he was mainly employed as Gilbert's right-hand man in exploration.

[4] Master Turner, the physician of the colony, perhaps a member of the well-known medical family, William (d. 1568), his son Peter (d. 1614), the latter, however, too grand by this time to go discovering. George (d. 1610), not a relation, was too involved in Cambridge politics. His return to plead for additional medical supplies is a little specious since he would be absent from the colony during the winter period when his services would be most in need. His intention to report on the colony and act, in effect as its Thomas Harriot, is more credible. Turner's report, if ever put on paper, would be a most valuable document. No mention of it has been found.

[5] Gorges pleads in rather confused rhetoric his own desire to be placed in a position of more responsibility for the colony.

that were taken by on of the Shippes, as I receaued it from theyr going out, vntill theyr returne, by which the nauigation will appeare to bee as easy as to Newfound lande, but much more hopefull.[1] Euen so commending your Lordshipp to Gods holy protection I will euer rest during life

Your Lordshipps humbly to bee commaunded/

Fard: Gorges.

Plymouth, 3 of December.

[Addressed:] To the Right Honorabell my very good Lord the Earle of Salisbury.

[Endorsed:] 3. December 1607. Sir Fardinando Gorges to my Lord.

45   13 December 1607. Captain George Popham to King James I, from Fort St George[2]

GEORGE POPHAM, President of the Second Virginia Colony, does humble obeisance at the feet of his most illustrious Sovereign.[3] If your Divine Majesty's indulgence may be pleased to accept a few words from a most diligent and devoted, howbeit unworthy, servant, I consider that they will far from detract from your Highness's fame, since they seem to be conducive to the glory of God, to the scale of your Eminence and to the advantage of the British people.

The idea that James should take direct responsibility for the colony might fit in with Gorges' own ambitions as the would-be royal governor, but it would appeal neither to James nor to Salisbury, who at that time were fighting off, rather feebly, the Spanish demand that the whole Virginia enterprise be abandoned. In effect disengagement was very much in the air. (See Quinn, 'James I and the beginnings of empire in America', *Journal of Imperial and Commonwealth History*, II, (1974), 135–52.)

[1] He may well include the journal which Strachey used of which there is the incomplete copy in Lambeth Palace Library, derived from Gorges' papers after his death, which we have attributed to Robert Davies. If the original went to Salisbury this could have been the route by which Strachey obtained his copy, possibly by way of the Virginia Company, with which Salisbury was closely linked. This could explain discrepancies from the ex-Gorges copy at Lambeth.

[2] P.R.O., CO 1/1, 16. This was printed in Latin and with an English translation in Edward Ballard, ed., *Popham memorial volume* (Portland, Me., 1860), pp. 220–6, and this translation has subsequently been followed. Baxter, *Gorges*, III, facing 164, contented himself with a facsimile of the Latin. The translation has been wholly revised by Dr Neil M. Cheshire.

[3] This was sent with the *Gifte of God*. Gorges may have seen it before it was sent on to the King or also other similar letters since he expressed some contempt at Popham's sentiments, p. 455.

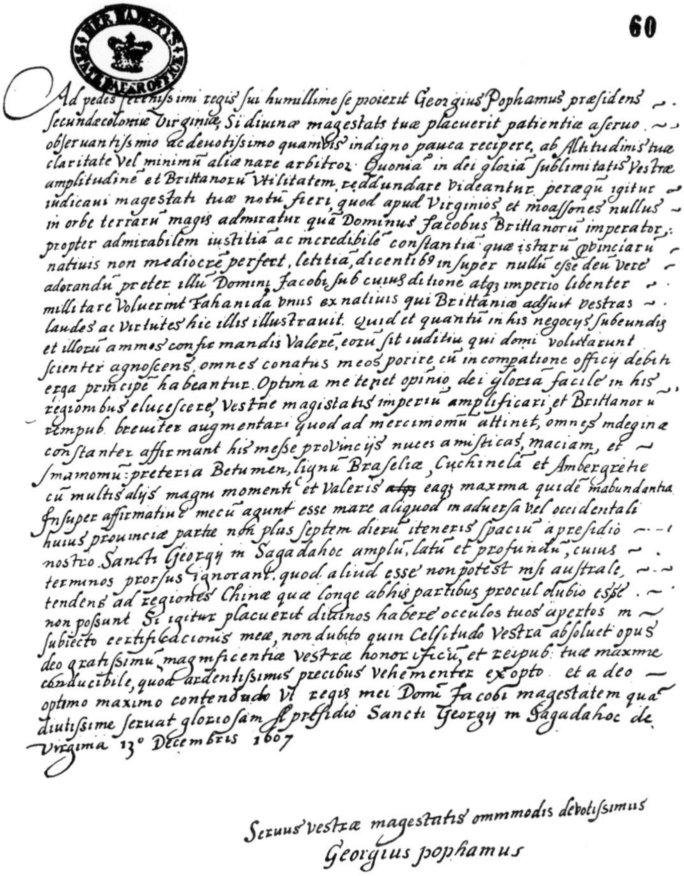

[Manuscript letter in Latin in secretary hand, beginning:] Ad pedes serenissimi regis sui humillime se proiecit Georgius Pophamus præsidens secundæcoloniæ Virginiæ. Si diuinæ magestati tuæ placuerit patientia aseruo obseruantissimo ac deuotissimo quamuis indigno pauca recipere, ab Altitudinis tuæ claritate vel minimu aliæ nare arbitror. Quonia in dei gloria sublimitatis Vestræ amplitudine et Brittanoru Vtilitatem, redundare videantur, peræqu igitur iudicaui magestati tuæ notu fieri, quod apud Virginios et moassones nullus in orbe terraru magis admiratur quam Dominus Jacobus Brittanoru imperator, propter admirabilem iustitia ac incredibile constantia quæ istaru prouinciaru natiuis non mediocre perfert, letitia, dicenti si in super nulli esse deu vere adorandu preter illu Domini Jacobi sub cuius ditione atqu imperio libenter militare voluerint Tahanida vnus ex natiuis qui Brittaniæ adsuit vestras laudes ac virtutes hic illis illustrauit. Quid et quantu in his negocys subeundis et illoru ammes confer mandis Valere, eoru sit iudiciu qui domi voluerunt scienter agnoscens, omnes conatus meos ponere cu in comparatione officy debiti erga principe habeantur. Optima me tenet opinio, dei gloria facile in his regionibus elucescere, Vestræ magestatis imperiu amplificari, et Brittanoru rempub breuiter augmentari. Quod ad mercimonii attinet, omneis mdeginæ constanter affirmant his mense prouincys nuces a musticas, maciam, et amamomu preterea Betumen, lignu Braseliæ, Cuchinela et Ambergrete cu multis alys magni momenti et Valeris atqu eaqu maxima quide inabundantia. Insuper affirmatiue mecu agunt esse mare aliquod in aduersa vel occidentali huius prouinciæ parte non plus septem dieru iteneris spaciu a presidio nostro Sancti Georgy in Sagadahoc amplu, latu et profundu, cuius terminos prorsus ignorant. Quod aliud esse non potest nisi australe, tendens ad regiones Chinæ quæ longe abhis partibus procul dubio esse non possunt. Si igitur placuerit dictinos habere occulos tuos apertos in subiecto certificationis meæ, non dubito quin Celsitudo Vestra absoluet opus deo gratissimu, magnificentiæ Vestræ honorificu, et reipub tuæ maxime conducibile, quod ardentissimis precibus Vehementer exopto. et a deo optimo maximo contendu vt regis mei Domini Jacobi magestatem qua diutissime seruat gloriosam. E presidio Sancti Georgy in Sagadahoc de Virginia 13° Decembris 1607.

Seruus vestræ magestatis ommodis deuotissimus
Georgius pophamus

Fig. 26. 13 December 1607. Captain George Popham to King James I.

I have therefore deemed it perfectly proper to inform your Majesty that nobody in the world is more admired by the people of Virginia and Moasso [Mawooshen][1] than the Lord King James, Emperor of the Britons, because of his wonderful sense of justice and his scarcely credible constancy which bring great happiness to the natives of your provinces. For they say moreover that no God is truly worthy of worship except the Lord King James's, and that they would willingly

---

[1] 'apud Virginios et moassones' = among the Virginians and the Mawooshonians! The Eastern Abenaki territory being known as Mawooshen.

give military service under his authority and command.[1] Tahinda,[2] one of the natives who has been to Britain, has broadcast your praise and your fine qualities to them here.

What good I might do, and how much, in undertaking this enterprise and in consolidating their feelings, is for those to judge who have given it informed consideration at home; for I recognise that all personal endeavours are as nothing when compared with my obligations towards the King. I am firmly convinced that the glory of God is beginning to shine out freely in this region, that your Majesty's empire is being enlarged and that the common welfare of the British (settlers) has been increased in a short time. As regards commercial resources, all the native inhabitants repeatedly assert that there are nutmegs, mace and cinnamon in these parts;[3] furthermore there is bitumen, Brazil wood, cochineal and ambergris,[4] along with many other important and valuable things, and all very plentiful at that.

Moreover they impress upon me that, in the opposite or western part of this province no more than seven days journey from our Fort St. George at Sagadahoc, there is some Sea which is extensive, wide and deep; but they have no idea how far it extends. This can be none other than the Southern Ocean, stretching towards the land of China which doubtless cannot be far away from this region.[5]

Therefore, if it may please you to take divine notice of the subject

---

[1] How far Christian opinions had been exposed to Nahanada and Skidwarres in England is not known or precisely how much missionary work was attempted, at what level, by the Rev. Richard Seymour and others. Their presence and that of others at an Anglican service (pp. 407, 427) gives little evidence to support Popham's claim, but it is all we have.   [2] Tahanida, Nahanada etc. see p. 309.

[3] 'nuces a misticas. maciam, et sinamomum': it is difficult to get nutmegs from the first spice as Latin but the Spanish for nutmeg-tree was *miristica*. None of these products could, of course, be found in North America.

[4] 'Betumen, lignum Braseliae, Cuchinelam et Ambergetiae': pitch could be made from tar products of conifers: it is just possible that the Indian mention of red dyes, from vegetable sources, which they used themselves (cp. p. 268), suggested brazil wood and cochineal: ambergris could certainly have been within the bounds of possibility, but whether any had been found on shore (as sometimes happened) is wholly unknown. This whole passage had best be taken as wishful thinking of a very injudicious sort, though the Indians who had been in England and learned the names of desirable trade objects may have been only too willing to delude the settlers.

[5] The sea within 7 days' journey can only have been Moosehead Lake, in which the Kennebec river takes its rise. Otherwise vague tales of the Great Lakes may have been passed on. They could have been known to the Eastern Abenaki through the ramifications of the fur trade. This is precisely the sort of wish-fulfillment that should not have been expressed at this time. It was bound to raise false hopes. Gorges clearly felt so from other letters he had seen (pp. 455–7).

of my testimony, I have no doubt that Your Highness will accomplish a task which is most acceptable to God, which brings honor to Your Majesty and which is of great advantage to your kingdom; and this with fervent entreaties I earnestly implore you to do. I pray also to God, the Good and the Great, that he will long preserve the glorious Majesty of my Sovereign Lord James.

At Fort St. George, Sagadahoc, Virginia; 13th December, 1607. Your Majesty's devoted servant in all things,

George Popham

46   7 February 1608. Sir Ferdinando Gorges to the earl of Salisbury, reporting the return of the *Gifte of God*[1]

Right Honorable:

Our second shipp is returned out of the partes of Virginia,[2] but with advertisement of nothinge more, then wee receaued at the first, only the extremity of the winter, hath ben great, and hath sorely pinched our People, notwithstanding (thankes bee vnto God) they haue had theyr healthes exceedingly well, although theyr Cloathes were but thinne and theyr Dyets poore, for they haue not had on sicke from the time they came thither, to the instant of theyr comminge away.[3] Yᶜ President, and his People, feedes vs still with hopes of wonders that wilbee had from thence in time, but I feare mee, ther must go other manner of spiritts, to settle those busines, before it wilbe brought to passe,[4] for I finde the continuance of theyr idle proceedinges, to haue mutch preiudicialld the publique good, deuidinge themselves into factions, each disgracing the other, euen to the Sauages, the on

---

[1] Hatfield House, CP 120/66; *Cal. Cecil MSS*, xx (1968), 55-7; printed in Baxter, *Gorges*, III, 161-4; *NAW*, III, 440-1.

[2] The *Gifte of God*, John Elliott (said to be a member of the council of the colony but not on Smith's list), captain, John Havercombe, master, reached Helford, apparently, on 28 February, moved on to Topsham where she presumably was when Gorges wrote. For her problems on the voyage the proceedings in Popham *v*. Havercombe, in the High Court of Admiralty give detailed, if sometimes conflicting, information (*NAW*, III, 442-54).

[3] She left on 16 December 1607 (having apparently on board not only a cargo of masts but a number of the settlers), spent nine days at the Azores, selling her masts and pledging a gun for food supplies. Gorges stresses that, by report of the returned men, in spite of inadequate food and clothing, the remaining colonists were well when they left. He stresses the extremity of the weather but does not go into any detail.

[4] Captain Popham's letters and other reports (which Gorges has evidently seen) remained optimistic, but Gorges is sceptical, as Popham's surviving letter would make anyone who had spoken to John Elliott, the captain, or other member of the company.

emulatinge the others reputation amongst those brutish people;[1] whose conuersation, & familiarity they haue most frequented, which is on of the cheefest reasons, wee haue to hope in time, to gayne that which presently cannot bee had, they shew themselues exceeding subtill and conninge, concealing from vs the places, wheare they haue the commodityes wee seeke for, and if they finde any, that hath promised to bringe vs to it, those that came out of England instantly carry them away, and will not suffer them to com neere vs any more.[2]

These often returnes without any commodity, hath much discouraged our aduenturers, in espetiall in these partyes, although in common reason, it bee not to bee looked for, that from a sauage wildernes, any great matters of moment can presently bee gotten, for it is arte, and industry, that produceth those thinges, euen from the farthest places of the worlde,[3] and therfor I am afrayde, wee shall have much a doo, to go forwardes as wee ought, wherfor it weare to bee wished, that som furtherance might bee had (if it weare possible) from the cheefe springe of our happines, I meane his Maiesty who at the laste, must reape the benefit of all our trauell, as of right it belonges vnto him; besides if it please your Lordshipp to looke into it with those eyes, with the which you pearce the greatest, and most obscure coniectures, you will finde it most necessary, it should bee so, both for many publique, and priuate reasons as first the certaynty of the commodityes, that may bee had from so fertill a soyle, as that is, when it shalbee peopeled, as well for buildinge of shippinge, hauinge althinges risinge in the place, wherwith to do it, as also may other hopes therof to insew, as the increase of the Kinges Nauy, the breedinge of marriners, the imployment of his People, fillinge the world with expectation, and satisfyinge his subiects with hopes who now ar sicke in despayre, and in time will growe desperate through necessity, also hee shall sease that to himselfe, & to his posterity,[4] thewhich hee shall no sooner quite,

[1] Gorges is saying in effect that the right men to run an effective colony are not present, but that other 'manner of spirits' (i.e. men chosen by himself) must go out to make a success of it.

[2] It is difficult to make sense of his references to the colony's dealings with the Indians. It is made to appear that one group in the colony was too friendly with them and obtained commodities from them, while others found them hostile, and that they were encouraged by the party friendly to them to conceal their commodities from the rest. There may well have been a strain of hostility to the settlers, some attempt to exploit them and even some close fraternisation (pp. 105–8).

[3] Gorges' plea for continuing colonisation is vague and general, but his point that the application of art and industry is necessary before profits can be made is an elementary and sensible one.

[4] Salisbury is urged to look at the long-term national benefits of persistence, but is

but his nighbors will enter into, and therby make themselues greate, as hee might haue don, for at this instant, the French ar in hande with the natiues, to practise vpon vs, promisinge them, if they will put vs out of the Contry, and not trade with none of oures, they will com vnto them, and give them succors, agaynst theyr Enèmyes, and as our People heares, they have ben this yeare with fowre shippes to the Southwardes of them, som 50 Leagues[1] and the truthe is, this place is so stored with excellent harbors, and so boulde a coaste, as it is able to inuite any actiuely minded to indeuor the possessinge therof, if it weare only to keepe it out of the handes of others. I could say much more in this, but I am loathe to bee over troblesom to your Lordshipp and therefor I will thus conclude vnder your Lordshipps Fauor, that I wish his highnes would bee pleased, to aduenter but on of his middle sorte of shippes, with a small pinnace, and withall to giue his letters, and commission, to countenance and authoresy, the worthy enterpriser, and I durste my selfe, to vndertake, to procure them to bee victualled by the Aduenturers, of these partes, for the discouery of the whole coaste alonge, from the firste to the Seconde Colony, espetially to spende the most parte of the time in the searche of those places allready possessed, and for myne owne parte, I should bee proude, if I might bee thought worthy to bee the man, commaunded to the accomplishment heerof, by his Highnes, and should thinke it a season well spente, wherin I should haue so many hopes, to serue my Contry, wherof the least would bee in this sleepy season, the inablinge of my owne iudgment, and experience, in these maren causes, therby, the better heerafter on all occasion, to discharge my duty to my Souerayne.[2] Al which I humbly recommend to your Honors wisdom, to bee so handled as you shall vouchsafe to thinke good, for the reputation of him, whome you haue tyed to you, by many obligations, and euen

---

not given any very specific reasons why he should do so, except, perhaps, that Gorges' interests might be better served if he did.

[1] That fear of the French influenced the colony in their concentration on fortification and in keeping the *Gifte of God* as a guardship until ice threatened her safety is clear, but evidence of 4 French ships trading some 150 miles to the south, in southern New England, in 1607 is not yet borne out from other sources. It can only have rested on Indian rumours.

[2] His request for one of the king's ships and a pinnace to explore the whole New England coast and the intervening territory down to the South Viriginia colony is unlikely even to have been passed on to James. He fears that parts of the coast may have been occupied by other nations. This was not so, but failure to make such a reconnaissance did lead to the rediscovery of the Hudson in 1609 and the subsequent entry of the Dutch.

Gorges' offer was never accepted, and he never in fact made an expedition to North America in spite of his continued preoccupation with it until his death in 1647.

so I will humbly commend your Lordshipp to Gods holy protection, restinge euer

Your Lordshipps humbly to bee commaunded

Fard: Gorges.

Plymouth this 7 of February.

[Addressed:] To the Right Honorabell my very good Lord the Earle of Salisbury/

[Endorsed:] 7 February 1607. Sir Ferdinando Gorges to my Lord.

47   20 March 1608. Sir Ferdinando Gorges to the earl of Salisbury reporting the despatch of additional ships to the colony[1]

As concerninge our Plantation, we haue found the meanes to encowrage our selues a newe,[2] and haue sent two shippes from Tapsome[3] for the supplies of those that be there, with victualles & other necessaryes, hauinge sett downe the meanes how we shalbe able, by Maye next, to send one more of 200 tunnes.[4] We frame vnto our selues many reasons of infinite good, that is likely to befall our countrye, if our meanes fayle vs not to accomplish it. But we hope, before Summer be past, to giue such satisfaction to the wordle [world] here of, as none that ar louers of their Nation, but will (for one cause, or other) be willinge to wish it well at the least, what crosses soeuer we haue receaued heretofore. Yet I am verely perswaded, that yᵉ end will make amendes for all;   For it is sure, it is a very excellent countrye both in respecte of the clyme, as also the multitude of goodlye Riuers &

---

[1] Hatfield House, CP 120/130; *Cal. Cecil MSS*, xx (1968), 109–10; printed in Baxter, *Gorges*, III, 165; *NAW*, III, 441–2. Extract.

[2] The raising of additional funds cannot have been easy, but clearly Gorges was the leading figure in the equipping of two further vessels to go to the colony. His relations at this time with Sir Francis Popham do not seem to have been good since he and his mother were carrying on an action to recover the value of the masts, etc., disposed of by the *Mary and John* at the Azores (*NAW*, III, 442–54 and pp. 459–65).

[3] We do not know when the vessels left Topsham, what were their names, whether they carried additional settlers, or when they arrived at the Kennebec (though they did so safely, but later, we suspect, than was intended). The blackout in our information largely arises from Purchas's failure to preserve Raleigh Gilbert's and other journals of the colony (p. 352).

[4] The *Mary and John* was the vessel eventually sent. She did not sail until after the death of Sir John Gilbert on 9 July 1608, so that she can scarcely have arrived until very late August or early September, unless she had a very fortunate crossing. Her removal of the colonists is briefly noted, p. 415.

harboures it doth abound with all; besides the seuerall commodityes that a fertile soyle will yeelde; when arte, and industrye shalbe vsed for the ease of Nature, the which seemes to shewe her selfe exceedinge bountifull in that place.[1] But, here of to trowble your Lordshipp: noe more at this present.

I humbly commend your Honor to Godes holye protection, & rest during lyfe.

Your Lordshippes in all seruice to be commaunded /

Fard: Gorges.

Plymouth March 20. 1607

[Addressed:] To the right honorabell my very good Lord the Earle of Salisbury these /

[Endorsed:] 20 Martii 1607. Sir Far: Gorges to my Lord.

48   12 May–23 June 1608. Sir Francis Popham and Lady Anne Popham *v.* John Havercombe[2]

I. 7 June 1608. Personal answer of John Havercombe, master of the *Gifte of God*.[3] He says that he was appointed by the council of the colony in Virginia to sail first to the Azores and furnish himself and his company with victuals by the sale of masts, spars and other things. On reaching the Azores he had left only 2 hogsheads of beef, 2 hogsheads of bread, and meal for 2 days unspent.

'He beleveth that according to the commaundemente & direction of George Popham president & others of the Counsell articulate he this

---

[1] Gorges' optimism was artificial at this point, but genuine, as he demonstrated by his continued concern with Maine for most of the remainder of his life. (The best general study of this remains R. A. Preston, *Gorges of Plymouth Fort* (Toronto, 1953); see also R. E. Moody, ed., *The letters of Thomas Gorges* (Portland, Me, 1978)).

[2] Documents in the case are given in outline only. The principal parts of the depositions, except for Havercombe's personal answer, are given in C. F. Banks, 'New documents relating to the Popham expedition, 1607', American Antiquarian Society, *Proceedings*, XXXIX (1929), 307–33; and in extenso in *NAW*, III, 442–54. The charges against Havercombe seem not to bear the weight of the proceedings brought against him, as the judge ultimately decided. They show that the Pophams regarded all the proceeds of goods from the colony as being their return for their investment, and they resented the disposal of £33 worth of cargo at the Azores to buy food to bring the ship's company home. It should be remembered that she carried not only her crew (of perhaps 20) but also perhaps 30 or more colonists being sent back (thus she had some 50–55 persons on board). Captain Elliott, for the Pophams, certainly did not press any effective case against Havercombe.

[3] P.R.O., HCA 13/104, ff. 210v–24v; *NAW*, III, 444–5, in full, though with a mistaken reference to HCA 13/91.

respondent for that the said Governor Counsell & cuntrey could not sufficiently victuall and furnish this respondent with necessaries fitt to cary the said shipp articulate and company home into England did sayle with his said shipp vnto the places articulate, there to releve him self and companye, & there stayd to make provition of victualls for the space of nyne dayes & not above as he belevethe And he further beleveth that xxxiij mastes[1] & thre spars & one cable specified in the scedule articulate were with this respondentes privitye and consente sould, and one sacre was pawned by the said Captaine Elliot at the places articulate for the some of thirtie one pound fourtene shillinges sixpence & no more as he beleveth.' 33 masts were sold for £7 10s; 3 spars for 4s 6d; cable for £80; one sacre pawned for £10.

II. 8 June 1608. John Havercombe's further reply to the allegations of Sir Francis and Lady Popham.[2]

'Item that presently vppon the arrival of the said shipp the Guift of God in the North partes of Virginia aforesaid the said John Havercombe master of the said shipp the Guift of God did Comitte himself his shippe and Companie and her ladeinge vnto the Comaund and governmente of the said President and others of the Counsaile aforesaid and did serve him and others of the Counsaile boath with their boat and men and did all such service and labor as the said President and Counsaile did direct and appoint them.'

'Item that shortly after the premises vizt. about the ninth of October the Mary and John (wherewith the said Havercome and Guift of God was consorted) did departe from the said Havercombe out of the harbor of Sakadahoc in the Northe partes of Verginia before such tyme as the said Havercombe had discharged the said Guift either of her victualls or salte and presently after the unladeing of the salt and victuall aforesaid the said governor and others of the Counesaile aforesaid did determine to send the said Havercombe and his said shipp presently for England but by reason of some spech of the people of that Countrie that gave intelligence to the Governor and others of the Counsaile that the French would come and besiege them the said governor and

---

[1] Thirty-three masts, if they were long ones, made up a substantial lading for a ship not adapted to carry them: at the same time their monetary value (after duty had been paid on them) at the Azores was small. How much more they would have made in England cannot be ascertained. Havercombe was entitled to put on record his own personal answer as well as to answer the questions devised by his opponents in the case.

[2] P.R.O., HCA 24/73, 449; *NAW*, III, 445–6, in full. This is Havercombe's formal reply on the second round of the proceedings. It makes a straightforward story, even though we do not have the interrogatories on which it was based.

Counsaile Commaunded the said Havercombe and Companie to stay thither in the said Countrie and not to departe.' By reason of the commandment of the president and council they were 'to stay in the harbor of Sakadahoc aforesaid...for the space of...at least two monethes together'.

'Item that dureing the aboad of the said Havercombe and Companie with the Guifte of God aforesaid in the harbor aforesaid there happened much fowle weather and Ice in the said Countrie the extremitie whereof did much indanger and hurt the said shipp the Guifte of God whereuppon the President and others perceaving it did give directions vnto the said Havercombe to ballast the said shipp and delivered vnto the said Havercome such store of victuall as they could well spare.'

'Item that the said President and Counsaile had not sufficient provision of victualls and other things to furnishe the said shippe to send for England when the said shipp the Mary and John were gone for England but were forced by reson therof as alsoe for that the said shipp would have bine vtterly spoiled by the ice and fowlnes of weather aforesaid to send the said ship for England.'

'Item that the said President and Counsaile did appoint one Captain [John] Elliott Captain of the said shippe the Guifte of God in her return towardes England and did give commaundment and directions unto him and to the said Havercombe and Company to depart with their said shipp the Guift of God towards England with such smal provision of victualls as they could spare and appointed him the said Havercombe and Eliot to dispose of and sell 30 mastes, a peece of ordinance and any other thing of goods they had aboard the said shipp at the Island of the Asseraes [Azores] and appointed them to stay and victuall themselves and Company there and fitt the said shipp the Guift of God with such necessaries as she wanted.' On their arrival there they had 2 hogsheads of beer, 2 hogsheads of bread and two days' provision of meat left.

'Item that befor such tyme as the said Havecombe did put into the Assores with his said ship the Guifte of God he and his Company were for wante of drinke forced to drink water and endured such penury and want that divers of the said Company died for lack of food and others for want thereof (yf they had not bine spedely relieved) would have likewise perished.'

III. 10 June 1608. Examination of Lancelot Booker, cooper.[1]

He says 'that on the vth of Iuly last this examinate being in a shipp of London called the Penelope belonginge to Master Richard Hall homeward bound from the West Indies mett with the articulate shipp called the Gifte of God about thre score leages from the Island of Flowers bound for Virginia, whereof the articulate John Havercom was master and George Popham Captain. And they wantinge a Cooper havinge lost their consorte intreated this examinate to leave the Penelope & to goe with them for Virginea, & made wages with him for xxxiiij[s] the monethes. And so this examinate went for Cooper with the said Havercom and knowethe that the said shipp arrived in savety in the North partes of Virginea. And that the said Havercom was master of the said shipp all the viadge, & as Master behaved himself very painfully & carfully vntill the ships returne into England.'

He served with Havercombe under the governor and council. The *Mary and John* was sent back in October. The savages reported the French would come and besiege them. The *Gifte of God* was commanded 'to stay longer in the harbor of Sakadahoc & to keep watch & warde both a shipp bord & a shore so longe as they continued there which was by the space of viij or ix weekes as he remembreth'. During this time 'there hapened much fowle weather & great floes of Ise wherewith the said shipp was much endangered and hurte for as he sayethe the force of the Ise one night struck in a pece of a planck of the said shipp of a foote & a halfe longe so as if the same had [not] byn presently spied and repayred the shypp had byn in greate danger of sinkinge'.[2] The president and council ordered the ship to return to England, giving such provisions as they could spare.

Captain Elliott was appointed captain of the *Gifte of God* and he and Havercom were given 'directions in writinge' to sail to the Azores, dispose of masts etc. for necessities they might require, 'and this he knoweth to be true for he was present in the house of Captaine Gilbert, when as the said directions were given in writinge by the said President

[1] P.R.O., HCA 13/39, under date; *NAW*, III, 447–8, in full. The acquisition of a cooper from an English ship met near the Azores is a curious example of hiring practices at sea. He is likely to have remained on the ship and so may not have occupied the cooper's house inside Fort St George (pp. 422–3).

[2] The detail which he gives of the staving of a plank indicates clearly the peril presented by floating ice on the Kennebec. How real the threats of French attacks were we cannot say, as there does not appear to be any evidence so far of French activity in 1607 after the Sieur de Monts abandoned Port Royal in July 1607, but Popham is unlikely to have been aware of the French decision to leave Acadia.

and Counsell to the said Captaine Elliott & John Havercom & this examinate then reade the same and saw that the said President gave the Captaine a letter in Spanish & Lattin which he willed him to deliver to the officers of the Island at his arrival there'. At the Azores 33 masts and a cable were sold, and a gun pawned for provisions. They were reduced to such penury that they were inforced to drink water so that 1 died before they came to the Islands and 2 more after.

They left on December 16 '& arrived at Opsam [Topsham] about the last of February last'.

The commission and directions 'was don in the house of Captaine Gilbert in the towne newe builte there called St George. And there were present George Popham president, Rawleigh Gilbert, Gawyn Cary, Robert Seaman, James Davies, Edward Harley [Harlow], John Elliott of the counsell, master [Christopher] Foscue, John Havercom, this examinate & who else he remembreth not'.

IV. 10 June 1608. Examination of John Deaman, seaman.[1]

He was hired by Sir John Popham and was quartermaster on the *Gifte of God* and sailed to Virginia, 'and that the articulate George Popham wente in the said ship from Plimouth to Virginia to be president of the Counsel there, and at his arrival at Virginia he was admitted & allowed for President & so held & accompted there'.

On a report 'that the Frenche men would come & make spoile of them' the president and council stayed the *Gifte of God* to keep watch and ward for three months. 'For as he sayth the extreemity of the Ise was such that yt bruck a planck of the said shipp as she rode in the harbor to the indaungering of the said shipp if yt had not byn espied and amended of this examinates knowledge.' The president and council gave order in writing to Captain Elliott and John Havercom to put in to the Islands 'to refreshe them selves of victualls with the sale of such things as were in the shipp'. He was present and heard the directions read. By the time they reached the Islands there was not a hogshead of beer and about a hundred weight of bread left. Masts and spars and a cable were sold and a gun pawned, and 'two of the company of the said shipp by reason of the wante of victualles to bring them home were starved & died at sea & a thirde died also a little before the ships arrival in England'.

[1] P.R.O., HCA 13/39, under date; *NAW*, III, 448-50, in full.

V. 10 June 1608. Examination of Timothy Savage, sailor.[1]

He was appointed by Sir John Popham and served as one of the quartermasters on the *Gifte of God*. He confirms what Deaman has said.

He arrived back at Helford about February 8. They might have come sooner if they had not wanted victuals. He received 1 month's wages, 23s, from Sir John Popham, and £3 more from Sir Francis Popham. At Topsham on March 10 Sir Francis promised to pay the rest of their wages but has not paid him or any of the rest.

VI. 10 June 1608. Examination of John Fletcher, seaman.[2]

He virtually repeats what Deaman and Savage have said.

VII. 23 June 1608. Examination of Captain John Elliott on behalf of Sir Francis Popham and Lady Popham.[3]

He is from Newland Fee, Essex, gentleman, aged 24. Sir John Popham was accounted to be the owner of 'the Guifte of God & of her tackle apparrel & furniture'. He went out in her to Virginia. 'And the cable & sacre & a roule of canvas mentioned in the sedula ar*ticu*late were in the said ship.' John Havercomb was appointed master by Sir John Popham. The ship stayed at Virginia from 14 August to 16 December following, '& then the President & Counsell there gave directions to the said Havercom to sayle directly for England with the said shipp & fifty men & boyes and a proportion of victualls for six weekes according to the said number of men by haverdepois waighte was allowed to the said Havercom to bringe the said shipp & company for England   And this examinate being appointed to returne home in the said shipp told the said President that the said shipp was coming from England ten weekes & od dayes, & he feared the said proportion of victualls would be little to bringe them for England, & he answered that they had the sea, the Banks for fisheing & the Islandes to frende if they were scanted of victualls, & appointed him to sell anything in the shipp rather then they should be in want in their returne'.

He said 'that the said Havercomb havinge his directions to come for England came from Virginea, and kepte his directe course towardes England, vntil the 'company were come on the heighte of the Islandes or thereaboutes and then there was a generall mutiny in the shipp amongst the company that they wanted victualls & should be starved if they had not supply   Wherewith this ex*amina*te beinge appointed

---

[1] P.R.O., HCA 13/39, under date; *NAW*, III, 450–2, in full.
[2] P.R.O., HCA 13/39, under date; *NAW*, III, 452, in full.
[3] P.R.O., HCA 13/39, under date; *NAW*, III, 452–4, in full.

Captaine of the shipp, was acquainted therewith and tould the Master & company that they were appointed to goe directly for England, & that if they should goe for the Islandes & make any stay there, they should greatly wrong the company left in Virginea for that theire want of victualls there required all haste that could be made for England to send them supply, and the company of the shipp answered that their wante being at sea was more desperate, & that they should perishe if they were not releeved. Whereuppon this ex*aminate* consented they should goe for the Islandes of Treserues [the clerks' version of 'the Azores'] & sayled thither accordingly & stayed there viij dayes, & in that tyme theye sould by the consente of this ex*aminate*, the said Havercom & the officers of the shipp one cable one sacre xxx spars that this ex*aminate* knewe one roule of canvas & some ropes belonging to the said sacre & nothinge else to his knowledge, & xxxij^li. sterling made thereof as he remembreth & bestowed all in victualls togeather also with thre pound of this ex*aminate*s money for the vse of the said shipp & company.' He knows nothing further, 'Savinge he thinketh that they might have come for England with the victualls that they brought out of Virginea if the Master & company had byn spareing & would have dealt honestly with the said victualls, & the rather for that they had thre barrels of breade & a busshel of pease in the shipp as he hath heard, more then this ex*aminate* had knowledge of & [swore] themselves with drinkinge of whole cans of beere not to confesse yt as he hath byn told by Peter Grislinge of Plymouth Masters mate & Iohn Diamand one of the quarter masters.' He said 'that the sailors in the said shipp vnder hand as he beleeveth consumed and spilte more victuals then were necessary to bee so in excesse, and by reason thereof the rest were in wante and a mutiny grew amongst them when they perceved they were come vnto the height of the Islandes & therevppon they putt into the Islandes with this respondents consent to make supply of victualls'. He says 'there was no salte water droncke in the viadge to his knowledge neyther doth he knowe what victualls were lefte when they arrived at the Islandes. And sayth that one for wante of victualls & partly by his owne beastlines in not cleneing him selfe of lise & vermyn, & two others died afterwards in the like maner.' And 'he thynketh that many more mighte have died if they had not byn releeved at the Islandes for that they had wastefully spent there victualls before'.[1]

---

[1] Formal proceedings in court 12 May–23 June 1608, Book of Acts, 1608–10, fols. 56, 59v, 63, 67v, 79; *NAW*, III, 443–4, add little to what has been included. Havercombe had been imprisoned at the suit of the Pophams but was released by the judge, Sir Thomas

49   17 February 1609. The Royal Council for Virginia to Plymouth Corporation[1]

After our hartie Comendacions.[2] Having vnderstood of your generall good disposition towardes your advancing of an intended plantacion in Virginia begun by divers gentlemen and Marchauntes of the Westerne partes which since for want of good supplies and secondes here, and that the place which was possessed there by you: annswered not those Comodities which meight keepe lief in your good beggyninges, it hath not so well succeeded as soe worthy intentions and labours did meritt But by the Coldenes of the Clymate and other Connaturall necessities your Colonie was enforced to retorne:/: We haue thought fitt (nothing doubting that this one ill successe hath quenched your affections for soe hopefull and godlye an action) to acquaynt you briefely with the Progresse of our Colonie the fitnes of the place for habitation and the Comodities that through gods blessing our industries haue discouered vnto vs. Which though perhapps you haue heard at large Yet vppon lesse assurednes and Creaditt, then this our informacion: We having sente 3: yeres past and foun[d] [a] safe and navigable Riuer, beginn to builde and plante 50 myles from the m[outh] [th]ereof, haue since yerelie supplyed and sent 100 men from whome we haue ass[uraun]ce of a most frutefull countrey for the

---

Crompton, on assurances that he would appear when he was required. The Pophams wished to have witnesses examined in Devon and a commission was accordingly issued to Sir Amias Bamfield, Sir William Pole, Sir Bartholomew Michell, Matthew Suckliffe [Sutcliffe], dean of Exeter, and — Ward, gent. who were assigned to meet Havercombe's representatives in the parish church of Aslam [Topsham?], between Thursday and Saturday, after Trinity Sunday [26–28 May], but no records of these proceedings have been found. On 8 June the following took oaths to give evidence [on behalf of Havercombe]: Timothy Savage, Michael Fernal [deposition not entered], Lancelot Buckar [Booker] and John Fletcher. On 23 June 1608 sentence was pronounced in favour of John Havercombe (the formal sentence is in P.R.O., HCA 24/73, no. 443, and is printed in Susan M. Kingsbury, ed. *Records of the Virginia Company*, III (1935), 10–12).

[1] West Devon Record Office, Plymouth, Plymouth City Records, W 359/54. The letter is imperfect and gaps have been filled conjecturally but plausibly.

[2] During the period from late 1608 until the issue of the second charter to the Virginia Company of London on 23 May 1609, the initiative in organising the dual ventures sanctioned in the 1606 charter lay with the royal council for Virginia created in the first charter. The poor success of the North Virginia ventures of 1606–8 led the council to plan to bring the latter to an end, and to enlist the support of the west country in the major venture planned for Jamestown in 1609. This letter, and the others mentioned in it which have not survived, stressed the advantages of South Virginia over North Virginia and proceeded to assume that the co-operation of the Plymouth venturers would be forthcoming. The Spanish ambassador, Zúñiga, reported on 15 January 1609 that the colony sent by the chief justice had returned in sad plight (Brown, *Genesis*, I, 197–8).

maytenaunce of mans lief and aboundant in rich commodities safe from any danger of the Saluages or other ruyn that maye threaten vs, yf we ioyne freelie togeather and with one Common and patient purse mayneteyne and perfecte our foundations: The staple and certayne Comodities we haue are Sope Asshes, Pytch, Tarre, dyes of soundry sortes and rich values, Tymber for all vses, Fyshing for Sturgeon and divers other sortes, which is in that Baye more aboundant then in any parte of the world knowen to vs, making of Glasse and Iron, and noe vnprobable hope of Richer mynes, the assurednes of these besides many other good and publicque endes haue made vs resolue to send in the month of March a lardge supplye of 800 men vnder the goverment of the Lord De la Warr accompan[ied] with divers knyhtes and gentlemen of extraordinarye rancke and sufficiene[ie. And] because the greate Chardge in furnishing such a nomber [of men can be (?)] hardly drawne from our single adventures we haue tho[ught good to ask (?)] your Corporacion of Plymouth to ioyne your indeavors w[ith our own (?)] which if you please to do, We will vppon your Lettres incert you[r]se[lues into] our Patent and admytt and receive so many of you as shall adventure 25 [li][1] i[n] [this] Corporacion Of which to all priviledges and liberties he shalbe as free, as if he hadd begun with vs at the first difficultie. And whereas we haue intreated the Right ho[nourable] the Earle of Pembrooke[2] to adress his lettres to his officers in the Staneries, for providing vs 100 mynerall and laboring men We do desire that such adventures as shalbe consented to amonge you mayebe disbursed by some officer, chosen among yourselues for the providing a Shipp marryners and victualls for 6 monethes for such a nomber, and to be readie by the last of March,[3] About which tyme we purpose with our fleete to put in at your Haven, or where els you shall appoynt vs to take them in our Companye. / It wilbe to lardge to discourse more perticularities of this business by lettre or to promote with many reasons so good and forward inclinations as we hope and receive yours to be, And therefore desiring onelie your speedie annswere of this, and that you will please to conferr with Sir

---

[1] This did not involve any financial concession.

[2] William Herbert, third earl of Pembroke (1580–1630), lord warden of the stannaries since 1604. The Cornish tin mines were often regarded as a source of skilled labourers and craftsmen and Herbert was here expected to impress them for the Virginia voyage.

[3] The specific request for a ship to be equipped as their part of the 1609 venture shows considerable confidence in the co-operation of Plymouth Corporation and its associates.

Ferdinando Gorge[1] and Master doctor Sutcliffe Dean of Exon[2] to whome we haue written to assist you and vs herein[.] We bid you hartelle farewell, London the 17th of february 1608

your verie louing freindes

W. Waad   Tho Smythe

Edwyn Sandys   Tho. Roe   William Romany[3]

To the right Worshipfull our
verie loving freindes the
Mayour and Aldermen of
the towne of Plymouth /

[Endorsed] A lettre from ye councell of Virginia to the Corporation of Plymouth ye xvijth of Februarie 1608
And an Annswere to ye same from ye Corporation[4]

[1] Though he had himself been a member of the royal council since 1606, Gorges' reply is not extant, but it is likely to have been a decided negative as he was determined by this time to keep the northern venture alive on his own account. Yet he had become a member of the Virginia Company by 1619 (Brown, *Genesis*, II, 902). Sir Francis Popham also continued to send ships to fish and explore so that the North Virginia venture was not formally abandoned.

[2] Matthew Sutcliffe, dean of Exeter, a major supporter of the Plymouth venture, was also a member of the royal council for Virginia, 1606–9. He subscribed to the Virginia Company (Brown, *Genesis*, II, 1028–9).

[3] Sir William Waad (1546–1623), lieutenant of the Tower of London; Sir Thomas Smith (or Smythe) ((1558?–1625), M.P., governor of the East India Company, 1600 and 1603; Sir Edwin Sandys (1561–1629), M.P.; Sir Thomas Roe (1581?–1644); Sir William Romney (d. 1611), governor of the East India Company, 1606.

[4] The reply is not extant but it almost certainly refused a corporate association with the London Virginia Company, though leaving it open to individual members to subscribe.

CHAPTER XIII

EVIDENCE ON NEW ENGLAND FROM INDIAN SOURCES, 1605–1614 THE DESCRIPTION OF THE COUNTRY OF MAWOOSHEN, *CIRCA* 1606

The name Mawooshen was clearly derived from the Indians brought back by Waymouth in 1605, as they learned English. It was the objective of Challons in 1606 and continued to be used as the Eastern Abenaki name for the region comprised within the Plymouth division's effective area over the next three years or more. Bashabes, the Abenaki chief located on the Penobscot, considered himself, or was considered, to be the high chief of this whole area (the evidence on the range of his effectiveness is impressive but limited in detail). In terms of space the distance Southwest to Northeast along the coast might be thought to correspond very roughly with that from Casco Bay to Mount Desert Island, while the inland area Southeast to Northwest would include not only the hunting territories of the Eastern but also parts of those of the Western Abenaki. There may have been some overlap, or else the inland extension indicated is exaggerated by the Eastern Abenaki informants.

Purchas' head-note in 1625 is not to be taken too literally. The contributions of Dean. R. Snow on the Eastern Abenaki (and his paper 'The ethnohistoric baseline of the Eastern Abenaki' in *Ethnohistory*, XXIII (1976), 291–306) and of Gordon M. Day on the Western Abenaki, in *Handbook of the North American Indians*, ed. Bruce G. Trigger (Washington, D.C., 1978), pp. 137–59, have done much to clarify the pattern of Indian life in all this area. Much preliminary work on this document was done during his lifetime, but not published, by Wendell S. Hadlock.

50 Eastern Abenaki captives describe their country of Mawooshen[1]

The description of the Countrey of Mawooshen,[2] discouered by the English, in the yeere 1602. 3. 5. 6. 7. 8. and 9[3]

This description of Mawooshen I had amongst Master Hakluyts papers.

Mawooshen is a Countrey lying to the North and by East of Virginia, betweene the degrees of 43. and 45. It is fortie leagues broad, and fiftie in length, lying in breadth East and West, and in length North and South.[4] It is bordered on the East side with a Countrey, the people

[1] This document was compiled under the direction of Sir Ferdinando Gorges from what the three Indians, Nahanada (Tahanedo), Manido (Maneddo), and Saffacomoit (misprint for Sassacomoit, and also Assacomoit) aided probably by Amoret and Skicowaros (Skidwarres), see pp. 309–10. A version of it came into the hands of Richard Hakluyt before 1613 and was available to Purchas in 1614 (when he published his short summary of it, pp. 347–8 above). It was probably ready by the time the colonists left England at the end of May 1607 (see p. 399), and it was certainly known to the author of a summary description of New England, Edward Harlow, by 1614. It is a remarkable document, the first to be furnished as a geographical summary of their Eastern Abenaki territory, Mawooshen, by any Indians who were brought to England. It may be compared with the material on the Coastal Algonquian area in modern North Carolina assimilated into Barlowe's narrative about the end of 1584 (Quinn, *Roanoke voyages*, I (1955), 110–13). It was printed in Purchas (*Pilgrimes*, IV (1625), 1873–4, XIX (1906), 400–5; *NAW*, III, 421–4), even though he had already stated that he had 'a Tractate' of the country of Mawooshen, which raises the supposition that he might have had a longer version also in his possession and chose only to print the shorter (p. 352).

[2] The document covers the Eastern Abenaki territory from Mount Desert Island to the Saco River. Fannie Hardy Eckstorm's *Indian place-names of the Penobscot valley and Maine coast* (1941), paid frequent, but usually puzzled, attention to it, but provided one or two important clues to identifications. More ambitious was W. D. Spencer's attempt in *Pioneers on Maine rivers* (Portland, Me., 1930), p. 258, to provide a complete key: though this was not successful as a whole it provided several identifications which have been sustained. Dean A. Snow, in *Handbook*, pp. 137–8, used it for its definition of the Eastern Abenaki homeland about 1600 and for its clues to the distribution of population. In 'The ethnohistoric baseline of the Eastern Abenaki,' in *Ethnohistory*, XXIII (1976), 291–306, he has given a full treatment of the Mawooshen document from the aspects of topography, social leadership, and population. Wendell S. Hadlock was interested in the document for a long time and gave me the benefit of his extensive Maine studies before his death, as have Gordon M. Day and Bernard G. Hoffman.

[3] Purchas's generalization in the heading is not accurate since it was not available to expeditions in 1602, 1603 or 1605. We cannot tell whether it was ready by the time of the expeditions of 1606; it was certainly at the disposal of the Sagadahoc colonists in 1607–8; only Purchas (since all knowledge of an expedition in this year appears to have died with him) could tell what value it was in 1609. It continued to be of value down to 1614, at least, though it was probably not made available to John Smith for his voyages of 1614 and 1615.

[4] The length fits well enough into the area mapped by Snow, *Handbook*, p. 138. A penetration into the interior of 120–130 miles is probably about right, though in places to the south the Western Abenaki territory extends to something less than 50 miles from

whereof they call Tarrantines:[1] on the West with Epistoman,[2] on the
North with a great Wood called Senaglecounc, and on the South with
the mayne Ocean Sea, and many Ilands.

In Mawooshen it seemeth there are nine Riuers,[3] whereof the first to
the East is called Quibiquesson;[4] on which there is one Towne, wherein
dwell two Sagamos or Lords, the one called Asticon [= Asticou], the
other Abermot. In this Towne are fiftie houses, and 150. men. The
name of which Towne is Precante; this Riuer runneth farre vp into
the Mayne, at the head thereof there is a Lake of a great length and
breadth; it is at the fall into the Sea tenne fathoms deepe, and halfe
a mile ouer.

The next is Pemaquid,[5] a goodly Riuer and very commodious all
things considered; it is ten fathoms water at the entrance, and fortie
miles vp there are two fathoms and a halfe at low water; it is halfe a mile
broad, and runneth into the Land North many daies iourney: where
is a great Lake of 18. leagues long and foure broad. In this Lake are
seuen great Ilands: toward the farthest end there falleth in a Riuer,
which they call Acaconstomed, where they passe with their Boates
thirtie daies iourney vp, and from thence they goe ouer Land twentie
daies iourney more, and then come to another Riuer, where they haue
a trade with Anadabis or Anadabijon, with whom the Frenchmen haue
had commerce for a long time. Neere to the North of this Riuer of
Pemaquid are three Townes: the first is Vpsegon,[6] where Bashabes their

Sidenotes: Climate and quantitie. Tarantines are said to be the same with the Souriquois. 1. Quibequesson Riuer. Asticon Sagamo. A great Lake. 2. Pemaquid riuer A great Lake. Anadabis. Three townes Bashabes.

---

the coast (Day, in *Handbook*, p. 148). With such an indented coast as that of Maine, 'inland'
is too vague to define with any approach to accuracy, but the approach to the actual area
is remarkably close.   [1] Micmac.

[2] Epistoman not identified (Eckstorm, pp. 121–2, discusses it), nor is the wood (but
see Huden, p. 226).

[3] We might well say at least 9 rivers since the document in fact defines 11, and there
are also omissions of major streams in the coastal areas covered. What is important is the
emphasis the Indians placed on them.

[4] Quibiquesson (most probably transcribed or printed wrongly and more correctly
Quibiquessou; it is Quibesquissue in the 1614 document) is identified by Snow as the Union
River, to the east of Mount Desert I. Precante, with its two sagamores, Asticon (for Asticou)
and Abermot, illustrates Snow's view that each village community had two sagamores,
a senior and a junior perhaps (Snow, 'Ethnohistoric baseline', on which the following notes
are also heavily dependent).

[5] Pemaquid here presents a problem and is almost certainly a corruption. Challons was
bound for 'Pam Quidda in Maoashen' in 1606 (pp. 356–7), and the river of Pemaquid
in 1607 (p. 404). This was evidently one of the waterways beside Pemaquid Point. This
river is the Penobscot, and the corruption is revealed in the 1614 document which gives
it in its right place in the series as 'Panawabsack' (p. 477; see the synonymy in Snow,
Handbook, p. 147), agöet being an elision or a dialectal version.

[6] Upsegon is on the site of modern Bangor: for Bashabes see p. 476. Caiocame and
Shasheokinge were (it is suggested by Snow) facing each other across the Penobscot (Indian

chiefe Lord doth dwell. And in this Towne are sixtie houses, and 250.
Caiocame. men, it is three daies iourney within the Land. The second is Caiocame;
the third Shasheokeing. These two last Townes are opposite one to the
other, the Riuer diuiding them both, and they are two daies iourney
from the Towne of Bashabes. In Caiocame dwelleth Maiesquis, and
in Shasheokeing Bowant, two Sagamos, subiects to Bashabes. Vpon
both sides of this Riuer vp to the very Lake, for a good distance the
ground is plaine, without Trees or Bushes, but full of long Grasse, like
vnto a pleasant meadow, which the Inhabitants doe burne once a yeere
to haue fresh feed for their Deere. Beyond this Meadow are great
Woods, whereof more shall bee spoken hereafter. The Riuer of
Pemaquid is foure dayes iourney from the mouth of Quibiquesson.

Ramassoc. The third Riuer is called Ramassoc,[1] and is distant from the mouth
of Pemaquid foure daies iourney; it is twentie fathoms at the entrance,
and hath a mile ouer; it runneth into the Land three daies iourney, and
within less then a daies iourney of the dwelling of Bashabes: vpon this
Panobscot a Riuer there is a Towne named Panobscot, the Lord whereof is called
Towne. Sibatahood; who hath in his Town fiftie houses, and eightie men.

4. The fourth Riuer Apanawapeske,[2] lying West and by South of
Apanawa- Ramassoc, at the entrance whereof there is twentie fathoms water, and
peske. it is a mile broad: it runneth vp into the Countrey fiue daies iourney;
and within three daies of the mouth are two Townes, the one called
Meecombe, where dwelleth Aramasoga, who hath in his Towne fiftie
houses, and eightie men. The other is Chebegnadose, whose Lord is
Skanke, and hath thirtie houses and ninetie men. The mouth of
Apanawapeske is distant from Ramassoc three daies iourney.

To the South-west foure daies iourney,[3] there is another excellent

---

Island and Old Town being modern equivalents). Asticou succeeded Bashabes in 1614 or
1615 (Snow in *Handbook*, p. 141). Abermot is mentioned above p. 344.

[1] Ramassoc appears as the Orland R. entering Penobscot Bay on the east (Eckstorm,
pp. 188–9), though the town of Panobscot is ambiguous, its location, and its sagamore not
being otherwise known.

[2] Apanawapeske is a river entering Penobscot Bay rather farther towards its mouth
and fits the Bagaduce R. The villages of Meecombe and Chebegandose, with their
sagamores, have not been located. (Again see Eckstorm, pp. 199–200.)

[3] It should be clear that a day's journey varied according to the terrain and method
of transport: by open water it was a full day's canoe ride, but with rapids and carries it
could be much shorter, while through rough country, with frequent carries, it could be
very short indeed. These problems of lengths of journeys were not rapidly understood by
the English. J. W. Thornton, 'Ancient Pemaquid', Maine Historical Society, *Collections*,
II (1857), 155–7, thought it could be as short as four miles. Wendell Hadlock considered
15 to 20 as a fair estimate of what a canoe could do under reasonable conditions.

Riuer; in the entrance whereof is twentie fathoms water, and it is a quarter of a mile broad, it runneth into the Land two daies iourney[1], and then there is a great fall, at the head whereof there is a Lake of a daies iourney long and as much in breadth. On the side of this Lake there is a Strait, and at the end of that Strait there is another Lake of foure daies iourney long, and two daies iourney broad; wherin there are two Ilands, one at the one end, and another at the other end. I should haue told you that both these Lakes, as also the rest formerly spoken of, doe infinitely abound with fresh water fish of all sorts, as also with diuers sorts of Creatures, as Otters, Beeues, sweete Rats, and such like.[2]

5. Apanmensek.

A Lake.

Another Lake.

All the Lakes full of Fish, Beeues, and sweet Rats.

The sixt Riuer is called Apponick,[3] on which there are three Townes; the first is called Appisham, where dwelleth Abochigishic: The second is Mesaqueegamic, where dwelleth Amniquin, in which there is seuentie houses and eightie men; the third is Matammiscowte, in which are eightie houses and ninetie men, and there dwelleth Narracommique.

6. Aponeg [sic].

To the Westward of this there is another Riuer called Aponeg:[4] it hath at the entrance ten fathoms water, and is a mile broad: it runneth vp into a great Sound of fresh water. Vpon the East side of this Riuer there are two Townes, the one called Nebamocago, the other called Asshawe. In the first dwelleth Mentaurmet, and hath in his Towne 160. housholds, and some 300. men. In the second dwelleth Hamerhaw, and hath in his Towne eightie housholds and seuentie men. On the West side there is another Towne called Neredoshan, where are 120. housholds, and 100. men. There is a Sagamo or Lord called Sabenaw.

7. Aponeg.

Three daies iourney from Aponeg to the Westward, there is a goodly Riuer called Sagadahoc:[5] the entrance whereof is a mile and an halfe

8. Sagadahoc.

[1] Apanmensek (Apassimensek), clearly a river to the west of the Penobscot and one of the rivers (St George or Medemak) entering Muscongus Bay. It is almost certainly the St George R. linked with Rosier's comparable (and possibly connected) exaggerations in his narrative (pp. 295–6).

[2] Otter, *Lutra canadensis* L.; Beaver, *Castor canadensis* L.; Muskrat, *Ondatra zibethica* L. Presumably the principal skins obtained by the colonists during the summer trading of 1608.

[3] Apponick (Aponog), with its villages Appisham, Mesaqueegamic and Matammiscowte, is the Damariscotta R., the third village being closely linked with this name (Eckstorm, p. 107).

[4] Lying between the Damariscotta R. and the Kennebec R., Aponeg is the Sheepscot R. (The seventh river in the 1614 document, though intervening ones differ, is Aponeg, p. 477.)

[5] There is much detail on the topography of the Sagadahoc R. (Kennebec R., below the junction with Androscoggin R. and Eastern R.) and the complex of interlocking streams from these points northward. As far as exploration went in 1607 and as far as it continued in 1608 (though we do not have details of this), the indications would be of very great value to the settlers at Fort St George.

Here C.
Popham built
S. Georges
Fort, and
planted.

Great Sound.

ouer, holding that breadth a daies iourney, and then it maketh a great
Sound of three daies iourney broad:[1] in which Sound are six Ilands,
foure greate and full of Woods, and two lesse without Woods: The
greater are called Sowaghcoc, Neguiwo, Neiwoc. And in the verie
entrance of this Riuer there is another small Iland:[2] from the West of
which Iland to the Maine, there is a Sand that maketh as it were a bar,
so that that way is not passable for shipping: but to the Eastward there
is two fathoms water. This Sound diuideth it selfe into two branches
or armes,[3] the one running North-east twentie foure daies iourney, the
other North-west thirtie daies iourney into the Maine: At the heads
whereof there are two Lakes, the Westermost being eight daies iourney
long, and foure daies iourney broad; and the Eastermost foure daies
iourney long, and two daies broad. The Riuer of Aponeg runneth vp
into this Sound, and so maketh as it were a great Iland between
Sagadahoc and it. From the Iland vpward the water is fresh, abounding
in Salmons, and other fresh-water fish.[4] Some thirteene or fourteene
daies iourney from the entrance in the North-east branch, there is a
little arme of a Riuer that runneth East some daies iourney, which hath
at the entrance foure fathoms water. Vpon this arme there is one ouer
fall, which standeth halfe a daies iourney aboue this branch: vpon this
arme there are foure Townes: The first is called Kenebeke, which hath
eightie houses, and one hundred men. The Lord whereof is Apomhamen.
The second is Ketangheanycke, and the Sagamos name is Octoworthe,
who hath in his Towne ninetie housholds, and three hundred and thirtie
men. This Towne is foure dayes iourney from Kenebeke, and eight
dayes iourney from [   ][5] To the Northward is the third Towne, which
they call Naragooc; where there are fiftie housholds, and one hundred
and fiftie men. The chiefe Sagamo of that place is Cocockohamas. And
on the small branch that runneth East standeth the fourth Towne,
named by Massakiga; where there are but eight housholds, and fortie
men. Vpon the Northwest branch of this Sound[6] stand two Townes

Two Lakes.

A great Iland.

Kenebeke.

[1] The sound is the broad reach above Bath to Merrymeeting Bay, the Androscoggin
trending northeastwards from it, the main stream (Kennebec not Sagadahoc) above it.

[2] Returns to entrance to Sagadahoc R., stresses Seguin I., with a sand bar to W. and
a channel to the E., as experienced by the *Mary and John* in August 1607 (pp. 429–30).

[3] Reverts to linking of rivers – then the Sheepscot links with the 'Sound' by way
of the Sasanoa (or Back) R. The great island is Arrowsic I.

[4] Fish seen in quantity in 1607 were probably sturgeon (p. 467): salmon were
probably available to the colonists in 1608.   [5] Gap in narrative as printed.

[6] The detailed sequence up the Androscoggin cannot be followed from this
information, but Snow (*Handbook*, p. 138) says 'Arosaguntacosk' identifies the inhabitants
of the Androscoggin drainage.

more: The first is called Amereangan, and is distant from Kenebeke six dayes iourney. In this place are ninetie housholdes, and two hundred and sixtie men, with two Sagamoes; the one called Sasuoa, the other Scawas. Seuen daies iourney hence there is another Sagamo, whose name is Octoworokin, and his Townes name Namercante, wherein are fortie housholds, and one hundred and twentie men. A dayes iourney aboue Namercante there is a downefall, where they cannot passe with their Cannoes, but are inforced to carrie them by Land for the space of a quarter of a mile, and then they put them into the Riuer againe: And twelue dayes iourney aboue this Downfall there is another, where they carrie their Boates as at the first; and sixe dayes iourney more to the North[1] is the head of this Riuer, where is the Lake that is of eight dayes iourney long, and foure dayes broad before mentioned.[2] In this Lake there is one Iland; and three dayes iourney from this Lake there is a Towne which is called Buccawganecants, wherein are threescore housholds, and foure hundred men: And the Sagamo thereof is called Baccatusshe. This man and his people are subiects to the Bashabez of Mawooshen, and in his Countrey is the farthest limit of his Dominion, where he hath any that doe him homage.

To the Westward of Sagadahoc, foure dayes iourney there is another Riuer called Ashamahaga,[3] which hath at the entrance sixe fathoms water, and is halfe a quarter of a mile broad: it runneth into the Land two dayes iourney: and on the East side there is one Towne called Agnagebcoc, wherein are seuentie houses, and two hundred and fortie men, with two Sagamos, the one called Maurmet, the other Casherokenit.

9. Ashamahaga.

Seuen dayes iourney to the South-west of Ashamahaga[4] there is another Riuer, that is six fathoms to the entrance: This Riuer is named Shawakotoc, and is halfe a myle broad; it runneth into the Land fiftie

10. Shawakotoc.

---

[1] The long relatively straight course of the Kennebec northward from Merrymeeting Bay was relatively easy travelling, apart from the penetration of tributaries and occasional rapids.

[2] The lake is the many-branched Moosehead Lake, nearly 150 miles from the sea. This is stated to be the limit of Bashabes's influence, and fits in with the 40 leagues penetration: 'where he hath any that doe him homage' indicates strong attachment: Snow (*Handbook*, pp. 137, 140) considers it reflects personal dominance rather than military or institutional power.

[3] Ashomahaga is taken by Snow (in *Handbook*, p. 137) to be the Presumpscot R., flowing into Casco Bay: it is ignored on the 1614 document (pp. 477–8).

[4] Shawanatoc, elsewhere Shawokotoc (Sawaquatock in 1614 document, and see Eckstorm, pp. 172–3) is the Saco R. Only the upper reaches of the river belonged to the Eastern Abenaki group: other inhabitants were 'Souriquois' enemies (see map in *Handbook*, p. 138).

dayes iourney, but foure dayes from the entrance it is so narrow, that the Trees growing on each side doe so crosse with their boughes and bodies on the other, as it permitteth not any meanes to passe with Boates that way: for which cause the Inhabitants that on any occasion are to trauell to the head, are forced to goe by Land, taking their way vpon the West side. At the end of this Riuer there is a Lake of foure dayes iourney long, and two dayes broad, wherein are two Ilands. To the North-West foure daies iourney from this Lake, at the head of this Riuer Shawakatoc there is a small Prouince, which they call Crokemago, wherein is one Towne. This is the Westermost[1] Riuer of the Dominions of Basshabez, and Quibiquisson the Westermost.

A Lake foure dayes iourney long & 2. broad.

51 [1614] A document, apparently by Edward Harlow, using the 'Description' and other sources as a guide for Nicholas Hobson's voyage of 1614[2]

[1] This should of course read 'eastermost'. Snow's summary (*Handbook*, pp. 137–8), is that there were 21 known villages with 23 sagamores (including one village with no sagamore mentioned) and a total of 1,238 houses (averaging 59 houses to the village, which seems high), and with 2,930 adult males. He takes the latter to represent some thirty per cent of the population which would therefore indicate a population of more than 10,000 for the years 1605–7. If these appear high, they omit the toll of war from 1607 onward and the early incidence of European-carried disease. On the other hand, the concepts of the Indians from whom the information derived about number may well have not been very precise. There are, so far, no wholly reliable means of checking such statistics, but that they exist at all is notable. Further considerations of populations of hunting-fishing people of this and comparable areas will have to take into account sophisticated demographic factors. The general tendency during the 1970s was to expand substantially the size of Indian populations at the contact stage. Francis Jennings, *Invasion of America* (1975) tends to give weight to these assumptions, and they are borne out by local estimates throughout *Handbook*, xv. In a forthcoming publication Dean Snow will discuss the need to revise pre-epidemic figures for New England as a whole very radically upward.

[2] B.L., Egerton MS 2395, ff. 412–13 v (between nos. 33 and 34). This was amongst a number of earlier items on New England collected for the use of the Board of Plantations 1681–5, in connection with its dealings with Massachusetts. There is no indication of its source: it may have misreadings in detail. It was printed by David I. Bushnell, Jr, 'New England names', *American Anthropologist*, XIII (1911), 235–7, but has not been used by historians of New England. It was brought to my attention by Dr Ives Goddard.

The author was clearly a person who had had access to the description of Mawooshen (pp. 470–6); he had been a member of the Sagadahoc colony of 1607–8; he had made a voyage to New England earlier which had brought him to Nantucket Sound; he was writing in support of a leader of an expedition to New England to whom instructions had already been issued; his recommendations preceded Captain John Smith's voyage in 1614. The only person of whom we know who could have met these conditions was Captain Edward Harlow. He had been a member of the 1607–8 colony and had left some written record of it (now lost, p. 352); he had gone on an expedition to New England in 1611 during which he had reached Martha's Vineyard (and brought back several Indians). Sir Ferdinando Gorges sent out to New England ahead of John Smith in June 1614 a vessel [f. 412r] The Names of the Rivers and the names of ye cheif Sagamores y^t inhabit vpon Them from the River Quibequissue to the River of Wenesquawan.

First there is Quibesquissue upon the East syde whereof dwelleth Abermite and upon the West syde Astighoo.[1]

The next is Panawabsack[2] described to bee a great River.

The next is Pemaquid or Sagakett[3] and there dwelleth the Bashabe.

Then there is Panawapaske or Nepammocagan where dwelleth Sebathahood.[4]

The next is Panawapaske or Nepammocagan where dwelleth Aramasoge.[5]

Then there is Apumcossock where did Dwell Abecogissick Amenqum & Nedicomoma.[6]

Then you have Aponegeg[7] and there did dwell Menteroermitt Hamerhow & Esabany.

The next is Sagadahock and that Divides it self into two great Branches the one Running to thee northwest, the other to the North East   To the West did Dwell Agamaquos Amorcogant & Samowessa two brothers. But I have forgotten the Rivers name to ye Northwest

---

to explore and trade under the command of Captain Nicholas Hobson, which was a failure. The document here reprinted should therefore take its place as subsidiary information given to Captain Hobson by Captain Harlow in the early part of 1614. A number of suppositions are made in this reconstruction and it must depend on circumstantial evidence rather than direct information, but it appears to fit the case.

[1] The river is the Union R. and the sagamores are identical with the Abermot and Asticou of the 'Description' (p. 471).

[2] As is explained above, the name Panawabsack is a correction of the corrupt 'Pemaquid' of the 'Description' (Ibid.). It is clear that the writer had not been to the Penobscot.

[3] This differs from the 'Description'. 'Segoquet' is clearly a name for the St George River (Eckstorm, pp. 84–5). Pemaquid is not the name, but the modern Pemaquid Point or the two Indian harbours, New Harbor on the east and Pemaquid Harbor on the west (cp. Eckstorm, pp. 102–3). It is probable, going back to Waymouth, that Muscongus Bay, of which Pemaquid Point forms the southern boundary, was known by the name (cp. p. 473).

[4] The Ramassoc of the 'Description' where a sagamore Sibatahood is named (p. 472). As this is the Orland R., running into Penobscot Bay, the author is not following a strictly N–S sequence, having perhaps misunderstood the 'Description'.

[5] The Apanawapeske of the 'Description', of which Nepammocagan is an additional name (not otherwise found), and is the Bagaduce R., again entering Penobscot Bay and again confusing the N–S sequence. Aramasoga is a sagamore in the 'Description'.

[6] For Apanmensek, the Damariscotta, where the sagamores were Abochigishic, Aniquin, and Narracommique. Amenquin appears above, pp. 311, 351, 413, 473.

[7] The Aponeg of the 'Description', the Sheepscot, where the sagamores are Mentaurmet, Hamerhaw, and Sabenaw, whom Esabeny replaces.

dwelt Apunhamon, Sassanow, Sawes and Ochowomakin   To the north East did dwell Ochoworth & Ocockhamys   And at ye River head above the Lake, Baccasossom.[1]

[f. 412 v] Then there is Sawaquatock and there did Dwell Agemohock.[2]

Then you have another Riuer called Wedopekeg[3] where dwelleth one Ageewhahasnon.

Next unto this a great Broad Riuer or bay vpon ye west Side whereof, there was one Squamiock that was ye cheif Sagamore, the Rivers name is Merimack as I take it.[4]

These Rivers you are to take particular Notice of with their Sagamores, as farr forth as possible shall be able & so to cause them to be Artificially set Downe in your Card as you find them with their true distances one from ye other,[5] as also the Island of Teponege.[6]

For these I make Account bee all of them to ye Eas(t)wards of Cape Code with many others. /[7]

[1] Even if what is said of the Kennebec basin is somewhat vague, it indicates that the writer has been a member of the 1607–8 colony and, though he is using the 'Description', is not as clear as he might be about the complexities of the river system. Dean Snow, in a personal communication (7 April 1980), considers that the river the author cannot recall is neither the Kennebec (which I had been inclined to think) nor the Androscoggin, but another river (unidentified) to the west, upon which Agamaquos, Amorcogant and Samowessa lived. He considers than 'to ye Nortwest dwelt Apumhamon' looks like the beginning of a new thought, not a continuation of the previous fragment. He goes on to say that the rivers to the northwest and the northeast appear to be the Androscoggin and the Kennebec respectively, the sagamores listed being distributed just as in the 'Description', exept only that Apumhamon (Apombamen) is placed on the Androscoggin instead of the Kennebec. The 'Description', he says, puts Bacctusske on the Androscoggin, while the Egerton MS leaves Baccatusshe, on the lake, unclearly located. This would, in turn, put Sassanow and Sawes on the northwest river (Androscoggin) with Apumhamon and Ochwomakin.

[2] This is clearly the Shawakotoc of the 'Description', the Saco River, though no sagamore was named, indicating additional information.

[3] The 'Description' is now left behind and we are in the area of the Eastern Abenaki's enemy whom Champlain called the Almouchiquois. The river should be taken, provisionally, as the Piscataqua.

[4] The Merrimack R. is unmistakable. The instructions do not penetrate southward into the main Massachusetts–Cape Cod area.

[5] Here the document reveals its didactic intentions. The recipient is to carry his search northward along the coastline already described and beyond, that is to the Maine shore northward from Mount Desert I.

[6] Teponege is possibly Monhegan but, if so, the name was a mistake. By 1614 this was the main focus of the summer cod-fishing vessels sent out by Sir Francis Popham and others, so that a detailed map of it would be of value in assessing its full potential for drying fish on shore and providing summer (and possibly winter) quarters for fishermen.

[7] The main intructions to the recipient (which have not survived but most probably derived from Gorges) were evidently to round 'Cape Cod' (effectively Monomoy Point), and chart (as well as trade with) the area into which Gosnold had first penetrated and where Harlow had followed.

To the West of Cape code (as in your Instructions is said) you shall meet with Severall Islands as namely Natcea,[1] Ioucanoke Akeucanack[2] and Capawick[3] which is the Largest of them all & which hath vpon the northsyde thereof towards the Mayne, 3 Rivers ye Eastemost is Sasquiaca. /

The next is Quatanque the last is Weiwyout.[4]

At the Eastward end there is another Riuer but evill coming to it, by reason of thee Slates & Sands and that is called Whackwhigh[5] (and the Sogum) for here they are not called Sagamores as before,[6] This name was Wavenot who Commands all that part, of the Island[7] as doth Tadoshwme, the middle part who doth Command thee west part I have forgotten but hee hath been enemye to both ye other two if I be not mistaken. /[8]

These Islands use your best Diligence to make a perfect discovery, of, as also ye land to the North of them [(| according to your [f. 413 r] Instructions) for there is great hope they will afford matter of good Consequence[9] but you will find thee people very false & Malitious in

---

[1] The novelty of this information makes interpretation very much a matter of guesswork. Natcea would appear to be Nantucket (the Nohono seen by Harlow in 1611). Bushnell finds 'Natocke' on a 1671 map of Novi Belgii, which may be indicative of its earlier sixteenth-century name (cp. Smith, *Works*, p. 197).

[2] Ioucanoke and Akeucanack offer guesses as to which of the four possible islands these are, Capoag (almost certainly known as that and so it can probably be eliminated, see pp. 500–2). Chappaquiddick I. is likely to be one of them. We do not know if Muskeget I. and Tuckernuck I. had anything like their modern form: it seems not improbable they formed a single island and that this is the other. Unless some indications can be found from early land deeds this is as far as the question can be taken.

[3] Capawick is not, if the explanations above are correct (Fig. 3, p. 119), a problem, being Martha's Vineyard. See W. F. Gookin, *Capawack*.

[4] The three rivers on the north shore of Martha's Vineyard offer some problems – Vineyard Haven is probably Sasquiaca; an outlet from Lake Tashmoo (if there was one) or Lamberts Cove could be Quatanque; while Menemsha (then open, see p. 126) would be Weiwyout. There does not appear to be any confirmation of these names.

[5] Whackwigh must clearly be Edgartown Harbor if it is to the east, but the difficulties of the approaches appear exaggerated.

[6] 'Sogum' is sachem. While among the Eastern Abenaki the chiefs are sagamores, to the south they become sachems (*Handbook*, pp. 140, 166–7).

[7] Wavenot must have been sachem of the East Chop and Edgartown areas. Tadoshwme would apparently control West Chop and the parts to the south and west.

[8] Harlow's memory of his 1611 visit was failing. Clearly the sachem of the Gay Head Indian group was intended. (This passage strongly reinforces the view that Harlow is the author.)

[9] There is no clear evidence that Harlow visited Upper Cape Cod in 1611. According to Smith (*Works*, II, 697, 699) he was well received by the people of 'Agawom', but whether this was the 'Agawam' northwest of Cape Ann, the later Ipswich, is uncertain as the name was frequent in New England. The tenor of his instructions was that Hobson should indeed make contact there. His description of them as hostile to strangers bears out Champlain's experience at Stage Harbor with the Nausets (*Works*, I, 420–3).

which respect you must be more cautious how you deal with Them, they are plentifull in Corne & Tobacco but have not many Scinns. if you cannot otherwayse Deale with them, first making Tryall of all Fayr Courses, then do your best to Seize their Corne & provision for that will inforce them to commerce & supply their want and necessityes espetially when they see they cannot offend you but that you are still offensive unto them.[1]

In coming along y[e] Coast I could wish you to endeavour to take with you (for to bee your Guide or interpreter) Mentoermit who is the onely Traveller in all these parts / That I have heard of & hath y[e] opinion of a very honest man & one that doth understand many of their Languages;[2] [sic]

I Could Speak of other places more Westerly but that I leaue to your Industry to find out at your best leisure.[3]

[f. 413 v] [Endorsed:] The Names of the Rivers in New England

[1] Harlow's familiarity with this area seems more definite here. Certainly there were many cornfields and tobacco patches and, as Champlain earlier discovered, few skins. The device of seizing their corn and forcing them to trade shows how Harlow himself is likely to have behaved in 1611.

[2] This was probably the Kennebec sagamore, Météournite, encountered by Father Biard early in November 1611. He was certainly an experienced talker (whether traveller or not) assuring Biard of his hostility to the English and feeding him very dubious tales of their behaviour, while at the same time offering him skins to sell (alleging they grew maize, which is possible but far from certain, but did not have any to spare). L. Campeau, *La première mission d'Acadie*, I (1967), 243–6, 678. His double-dealing is more evident than his honesty.

[3] Harlow's voyage of 1611 is so poorly documented that we have no definite evidence of his sailing to the west of Martha's Vineyard, though he may have done so. But he could have acquired information on Buzzards Bay and the mainland to the west from the Indian brought back with him in 1611.

JAMES ROSIER'S LIST OF INDIAN (EASTERN ABENAKI) WORDS, RECORDED IN SAMUEL PURCHAS, *PILGRIMES* (1625): A PRELIMINARY ANALYSIS BY PHILIP L. BARBOUR

I

The objective of this review is to list, and to attempt to throw light upon, nearly a hundred Indian words taken down by James Rosier during his brief association with George Waymouth in 1605. The region explored by Waymouth was the northeast coast of New England, where the Indians encountered spoke what is now called Eastern Abenaki. This language differs from the languages spoken in the Maritime provinces of Canada and extreme eastern Maine (Maliseet-Passamaquoddy and Micmac) roughly as French differs from Italian or Spanish, and it differs to a similar degree from the languages then spoken to the west and south of Maine, including Massachusett and Narragansett. All of these languages, in addition to several more, are collectively known as the Eastern Algonquian languages.

Curiously, Rosier did not include his list of Indian words in his book *A true relation* (*1605*), though he claimed there to have collected between four and five hundred. We cannot tell how many words were in the manuscript Hakluyt obtained and passed to Purchas or how many of these Purchas eliminated when he published his extracts from the manuscript in his *Pilgrimes* in 1625. Nor can we tell how accurately he reproduced Rosier's original manuscript. Thus, between the likelihood of original mishearing and of copyists' errors of transcription, we have the possibility that Purchas pruned the list in such fashion that the wrong English definition might accompany an Indian term, or that Rosier did not quite understand what his Indian interlocutor meant. It is one thing to point at an animal or a tree and indicate that what is wanted is the name of it. It is much more difficult to get the term for a relative, a season of the year, or such a natural phenomenon as rain. Yet the analysis of his Indian words given below shows that Rosier was remarkably accurate, especially in view of the short period of time at his disposal on land, on the sea voyage home with the five captives and in the few months within which he could speak to some of them in England.

Taking these and other matters into consideration, as will appear below, the writer has chosen the least intricate method of linguistic analysis for this study: the identification of words and their conformable meanings through comparative linguistics. Granted the uncertainty of the phonetic value of Rosier's transcriptions, and our own lack of complete certainty about the specific language or languages of the Indians who were interviewed though they were almost certainly Eastern Abenaki, relevant Algonquian-English vocabularies have been investigated for words of potentially similar sound with the same or similar meaning in English. That the bulk of Rosier's words were Abenaki (variously spelled) was obvious from the outset. Fortunately, the *Dictionary of the Abnaki Language* begun by Father Sebastien Rasles (variously spelled) in 1691 soon provided clues to most of them. James Hammond Trumbull's admirable *Natick Dictionary* (1903), which contains cognates in several related languages, provided *inter alia* almost contemporary words in the language now called Massachusett into which the Reverend John Eliot translated the Bible beginning in 1646. Two words were very recently tracked down through living Indian languages (Micmac and Maliseet-Passamaquoddy) thanks to the courtesy of friends: Professor Vincent O. Erickson, University of New Brunswick, and Peter Paul, of the Woodstock (Maliseet) Reserve. The linguistic connections are clear, and with the supplementary help of a little 'informed guessing', it may be said that Rosier's vocabulary has been confirmed, along broad lines. The groundwork has been laid for specialists in Algonquian dialectology.

Parenthetically, it should be noted that this method of analysis through related words, or cognates, is at variance with that of James A. Geary in the Carolina Algonquian word-list in Quinn's *Roanoke voyages* (II, 873–1000) and in his analysis of William Strachey's vocabulary in the Wright/Freund edition of Strachey's *Historie of travell* ((1953), pp. 208–14), where reference is made to Proto-Algonquian (PA) forms. Proto-Algonquian is the hypothetically reconstructed ancestral language of more than two dozen varieties of speech used at one time or another across a large part of Canada and the United States from the Rocky Mountains to the Maritime Provinces and south through

New England into North Carolina. Territorially, it is comparable to the sweep of the Indo-European languages from Portugal to Sweden and Russia and south into India. Just as Proto-Indo-European is a matter of concern primarily to professional linguists, so proto-Algonquian (or the more recent development of Proto-Eastern-Algonquian (PEA)) can be confusing to lay-readers. In this study, consequently, in place of attempting to specify the hypothetical PA or PEA forms, self-evidently cognate words or terms are cited from various kindred languages wherever possible. For example, Rosier's *ibider*, meaning 'teeth', is compared with Abenaki *wipit*, 'his tooth' (plus *-er*, plural), and with Strachey's *neputts* '[my] tooth', to which Geary added PA 'nīpitc'. The hypothetical form has been omitted here, but in order to make these comparisons clearer, further examples or illustrations from other, more remote, languages have also been introduced here and there.

Although little of this is of grave importance to any but linguistic specialists, one detail should be mentioned. Rasles consistently used a ligature of the Greek letters *omicron* and *upsilon* to transcribe an Abenaki sound that must have been very close to the vowel in the English word 'pool' or in French 'tout'. This ligature was formed by superimposing the *upsilon* on the *omicron*, to form a character resembling the numeral '8' with the top open (often printed in linguistic studies today as a plain '8'). Rasles also used this ligature, however, where the Abenaki sound was clearly that of an English 'w', as in the word *wipit*, already mentioned, and has added diacritical marks on occasion, as in *maskŵé*, 'écorce de bouleau à cabaner.' In order, therefore, to avoid the typographical clumsiness of a Greek ligature or an Arabic numeral in roman type, the writer has used 'w' throughout, adding such accents, etc., as are found in Rasles: *mashquere*, 'bark of a tree,' is compared with *maskŵé*, as above, and *moose* is shown in its Abenaki form, *mŵs*, with *mŵsŵk* as the plural. This fits in reasonably well with Natick (Massachusett) *mœs*, an English ligature often used in Rosier's day.

II. BIBLIOGRAPHY, AND ABBREVIATIONS

Abn. The Eastern Abenaki language, and *A dictionary of the Abnaki language in North America*, by Father Sebastian Rasles, published with introduction and notes by John Pickering, American Academy of Arts and Sciences, New Series, Vol. I (Cambridge, Massachusetts, 1833).
Alg. Algonquian.
app. apparently.
cf. compare.

Cree   The Cree language, and *A dictionary of the Cree language*, edited by Ven. R. Faries (Toronto, 1938).

Del.   The Delaware or Lenape (Renape) language.

Douglas-Lithgow   R. A. Douglas-Lithgow, *Dictionary of American Indian place and proper names in New England* (Salem, Mass., 1909).

Eckstorm   *Indian place names of the Penobscot Valley and the Maine Coast*, by Fannie Hardy Eckstorm. University of Maine Studies, 2nd ser., No. 55 (repr. Orono, Me., 1960).

etc.   In addition to its usual meaning, *etc.* here stands for "plus similar forms, words, or spellings".

Geary   The Reverend James A. Geary, author of monographs on Carolina and Powhatan Algonquian languages in Quinn, *Roanoke voyages*, and in WS.

JS   Captain John Smith, *Works*, ed. by Edward Arber (Birmingham, 1884). (The present writer's new, annotated edition is in the press.)

Mathews   *A dictionary of Americanisms*, ed. by Mitford M. Mathews (Chicago, 1951).

Mic.   The Micmac language, and the *Dictionary of the language of the Micmac Indians*, by Rev. Silas Tertius Rand (Halifax, Nova Scotia, 1888).

Narr.   *A key to the [Narragansett] language of America*, by Roger Williams (1643; most recent and most useful ed. is in John J. Teunissen and Evelyn J. Hinz, eds., *Roger Williams, A key into the language of America* (Detroit, 1973)).

Nat.   *Natick dictionary*, by James Hammond Trumbull. Smithsonian Institution, Bureau of American Ethnology, *Bulletin* 25 (Washington, DC, 1903).

OED   *The Oxford English dictionary* (Oxford, 1933).

Pen.   The Penobscot language or people.

Peq.   The Pequot language or people.

pl.   Grammatical plural.

Prince   John Dyneley Prince, "The Penobscot language of Maine," *American Anthropologist*, new ser., 12 (1910).

Purchas   Samuel Purchas, *Hakluytus posthumus or Purchas his pilgrimes* (1625; repr. Glasgow, 1905–1907).

Quinn   *The Roanoke voyages 1584–1590*, ed. by David Beers Quinn (1955).

Rand   Silas T. Rand, *Dictionary of the language of the Micmac Indians*. Halifax, N.S., 1888.

Rasles   See Abn.

rel.   Linguistically related. [In the comparisons, vowel length is indicated by ˘ for short vowels, and ‾ or ˆ for long vowels. Rough breathing represents the glottal 'catch' preceding German 'ach!'.

Trumbull   Refers to the *Natick Dictionary* (Nat.) when another language than Natick is mentioned.

Walam Olum   *Walam Olum, or Red Score*, translated with notes, etc., by various authors, published by the Indiana Historical Society (Indianapolis, 1954).

Williams   See Narr.

Wood   William Wood, *New Englands prospect* (1634).

WS   William Strachey, *The historie of travell into Virginia Britania* (c. 1612), edited by Louis B. Wright and Virginia Freund (1953).

III. ANALYSIS

I. *Nature*

Bemoquiducke 'the mainland'; not in Rasles; identical with the place-name Pemaquid. The meaning of this is 'long point' or 'that runs into the water' [44]. The termination *-ucke* is merely the locative case ending.

Cheemuck 'sand'. Apparently the word is a contraction–distortion of something like *-amki-hemuk* [*Wassamkihemuk*, 'white sand place'], meaning 'sandy spot'. Cf. Abn. *nega'kw*, 'sable' [525, abbreviated to *a'kŵ*]. and Eckstorm, p. 14, Cree *yakow* and WS. *racawh* [200], 'sand'.

Kashterush [*Cash-*] 'a weed'; not in Rasles; Nat. *mosketuash* (pl.), 'hay, pasture' [64–65]; JS. *attasskuss*, 'leaves, weeds, or grass' [44]; WS. *attasqwus*, 'weeds' [205, copied from JS?]. App. derived from a radical meaning 'it is green.'

Kesus 'sun or moon'; Abn. *kizŵs*, 'le soleil' [529], 'la lune' [477]; Nat. *kēsuk*, 'the sky' [35]; JS. *keskowghes* [for *keshowghes*], 'suns' [45]; WS. *keshowse*, 'the sun' [202].

Machoucke [for *Wachouke*?] 'mountain'; app. not in Rasles, though this is a common Alg. word as is seen by: Nat. *wadchu*, 'mountain' [179]; Cree *wuche*, 'a hill' [519].

Nabscurr 'a stone'; Abn. *pnapeskŵ* plural *-kŵr*, 'pierre' [506].

Puckchawsen 'wind'; cf. Abn. *péderañmpsen*, 'le vent vient' [541], and Nat. *pœtau*, 'he blows' [132]. There is probably miscopying in this word, with 'ck' for 'd' or 'ct', and poss. 'w' for 'm'.

Shamogoon 'water'
Shomogon 'rainbow' } These must be studied together
Soogoran 'rain'

Rosier was obviously confused: *Sœgoran* 'rain', represents Abn. *sŵgherañn*, 'il pleut, pluie', [508] which is cognate with Natick *sokanon*, 'rain' [312]; *shomogon*, 'rainbow', then, is Abn. *ŵsañmerañn*, 'il a trop plu' [508], derived from the same root. *Shamogoon*, 'water', is not Abnaki, but Micmac and Passamaquoddy *samaguan*, '[salt?] water' [Prince, 197], and related to the word for 'sea', which follows.

Shoubbe 'sea'; Abn. *sŵbékŵ*, 'la mer, eau salée [485], cognate with Micmac *samaguan*; cf. Del. *šewánpi*, 'salt water, ocean' [Walam Olum, 109].

Squida 'fire'; Abn. *skŵtâi*, 'feu' [455]; Narr. *sqútta*, 'fire' [Trumbull 155]; Cree *iskatāo*, 'fire' [76].

Toboogg 'wave of the sea' [misprinted as 'wane of the sea']; Abn. *tegŵ*, *tegïwak* (pl.), 'vague' [540], 'flot' [456]; Nat. *tukkœg*, 'waves' [166]. [The 'b' is prob. a misprint for a 'k']; the form in -*œg* is obviously pl., -*ak* in Abn., -*og* in Nat.]

II. *Animals*

Coribo 'fallow-deer' [*Rangifer arcticus*]; this is clearly the word which has become caribou, though it is not found in Rasles. It came into English in 1609. See M. Lescarbot, *Nova Francia*, ed. H. P. Biggar (1928), p. 118 (see Quinn, *Hakluyt handbook*, II, 554–5, from the first edition of Marc Lescarbot's *Histoire de la Nouvelle France* (1609), and in 1610 it appears in the *Jesuit relations and other documents*, ed. by Reuben Gold Thwaites (Cleveland, 1890–1901), I, 82. Cf. Narr. *kuttíomp*, 'a great buck' [Trumbull 243]; and Pen. *magalibo*, 'caribou' [Prince, 195].

Madoso 'hog' [*Erethizon dorsatum*]; Abn. *mañdawessŵ*, 'porc-épic' [383]; Pen. *madaweso*, 'porcupine' [Prince, 194].

Moosurr 'red-deer' [*Alces americana*]; Abn. *mŵs*, [pl. *mŵsŵk*], 'original [moose]' [383]; Nat. *mŵs*, 'fallow-deer' [297]; the name seems to mean 'he trims (the bark from trees while feeding)' [Trumbull, 66].

Narsim 'a beast' [*Lynx rufus*]; Abn. *mañrsem*, 'loup-cervier [lynx]' [382]; cf. Nat. *puppinashim*, 'a beast' [136].

Nymemano 'otter' [*Lutra canadensis*]; Abn. *nañbékikŵ*, 'loutre, *sic dicitur* de la marte' [383]; cf. Nat. *nehnēkikom*, 'he tears or rends (it)' [82], and Cree *nekit*, 'otter' [357].

Paneah 'beaver' [*Castor canadensis*]; Abn. *hépana,kessŵ*, 'marte' [383, beaver ('castor') is *tema kwé*]; Nat. *openock, wappenaugh*, 'marten' [294]; cf. WS. *pohkeuwh*, 'an otter or rather a beaver' [196, perhaps for *ponkeuwh*?].

Pisho 'a beast' [Wild Cat, Lynx]; not in Rasles [*pesŵ*, 'fourmi', seems out of the question (383-]; cf. Saginaw dialect of Ojibwa *pee shoe*, 'the lynx' [Trumbull, 136]. [It is possible that this is confused with *pushuck*, q.v.]

Pocamka 'pole-cat' [*Mephitis mephitis*]; almost certainly a misprint for *secamka* [as -*po* for -*te*, under *Birds and Insects*, chussuah, below], as in Abn. *ségñkŵ*, 'bête puante' [383]; cf. Cree *sikak*, 'skunk' [456] and Peq. *squnck* [Josselyn, quoted in Trumbull, 323], which may have given us the word 'skunk' [Mathews, *Dictionary*, s.v.].

Pushuck 'cat' [Wild Cat, Lynx]; Abn. *peswis* (pl. *peswisak*), 'chat' [409, with (erroneous) explanation that the word was borrowed from English 'pussy']; the reference is probably to the wildcat [lynx], Cree *pisew*, Narr. *pussoúgh* [Trumbull 136]. The root-idea is prob. to be found in Cree *pussoo*, 'he scents (as an animal scents a human being)' [442].

Remoose 'dog'; Abn. *aremŵs*, 'chien' [413]; a 'classic' example for illustrating consonantal changes between the various Algonkian languages: Nat. *anùm*, Nipmuck *alùm*, Narr. *ayím* [all in Trumbull, 246–247], and WS. *attomois* [175] or *attemous* [181]. The matter is explained by Professor Geary in Quinn, *Roanoke voyages*, 878.

Rogsoo 'bear' (*Ursus americanus*); Abn. *awéssŵs* (pl. -*ak*), 'ours' [383], the throaty 'w' being mistaken for an 'r'. [Cf. Mohegan *mquch*, 'bear', in Trumbull, 345]. Compare Penobscot *awēsos*, 'bear' [Prince, 190]. Rosier's *rogsoo* for Abn. *awéssŵs* helps clear up the 'mystery' in Strachey's *amonsoquath*, [175] and *momonsacqweo*, id. [176]; if 'm' is a misreading or misprint for 'w', *awonsoquath* would bear a striking resemblance to a nasalized *awĕssŵak* [or *awĕssûak*], pl. of 'bear'.

Romcaneek 'tortoise'; prob. Abn. *amikenakŵ*, 'écaille de la tortue' [536]; cf. Cree *mi'kina'k*, and Ojibwa *mik e nok* [Trumbull, 337], 'turtle'. As in *rogsoo*, the initial throaty sound was more 'aw' than 'rog-' [here 'rom-'] and the Abn. '-i-' elided.

Sanuke 'rat' [*Ondatra zibethica?*]; The Abn. word recorded by Rosier was not the rat but may have been muskrat or another animal. We therefore have Abn. *mesánikŵ*, [il a] un beau poil' [383], applied to the invader-rat. Compare JS. *mussaneekes* [128, 441, untranslated] and WS. *moussomko*, *mussane* [193] and *mussanek* [202], 'a squirrel (or beast so called)', the elements of which seem to be 'big' and 'squirrel' (or chipmunk).

Tasquus 'a beast' [*Sylvilagus floridanus*]; Abn. *mattegwéssŵ*, 'lièvre' [382]; Narr. *waûtuckques*, 'the coney' [Williams, 128 – 'there is some Deitie in it']; Nat. *môhtukquás-og*, 'conies' [62].

III. *Fish*

Anego 'plaice [flounder]'; not in Rasles; the only comparable word seems to be Mic. *anagwāách*, 'flounder' [113], although Nat. has *anneganuhtuk*, 'a fish spear' [10], in which -*uhtuk* represents 'stick, spear' [325].

Biskeiore 'codfish'; not in Rasles; no readily recognizable cognate in

Nat., Mic., Peq., etc., or in JS. or WS. Since Eckstorm mentions the influence of the Basques on Micmac trade vocabulary [xviii], it is remotely possible that the fish most sought after [codfish] acquired the name of the seekers [Basques] who were called *Biscayans* in English, or *Vizcaínos* in Spanish. [Hypothetical.]

Hesucke 'cockle'; Abn. *és* (pl. *éssak*), 'coquille' [418]; Cree *ās*, 'mussel' [249].

Manedo 'a fish with horns'; this seems to be a misunderstanding. *Manit* or *manitto*, etc., is a common word for 'god, spirit'. Williams reports that the Narragansetts "cry out *Manittóo*...'it is a god' at the apprehension of any excellence in men, women, birds," etc. [Trumbull, 49]. This appears to be what happened with Rosier – the 'fish with horns' causing the exclamation.

Muscopeiuck 'porpoise'; Abn. *meskŵamegŵ* (pl. *-ak*), 'saumon' [510], with 'p' for 'm'; Narr. *mishcùp* (pl. *-paŭog*), 'bream', corrupted to *scuppaug* and the popular (but loosely used) American 'porgy', a name applied to a variety of fishes.

Powdawe 'a whale'; Abn. *pŵdébé*, 'baleine, grand poisson' [391]; Nat. *pŵtâop*, 'whale' [343]; cf. WS. *potawaugh*, 'a porpoise' [197]. The root is illustrated by Nat. *pŵtau*, 'he blows'; cf. *puckchawsen*, 'wind'.

Shagatocke 'a rock-fish'; Abn. *sañgŵategŵé*, 'petits [poissons]' [510].

Shoggah ' lobster'; Abn. *tsañghé* (pl. *-gak*), 'écrevisse' [383]. The common word for lobster seems to have been some form of Narr. *ashaŭnt*, Peq. *muschúndaug*, or WS. *ahshaham* [191].

Shoorocke 'mussel'; Abn. *sarahaghé*, 'écaille de poisson' [510]. The derivation is obscure.

Tattaucke 'cunner-fish [golden wrasse?]'; not in Rasles; cf. WS. *tatamaho*, 'gar-fish' [185]. This is the fish known as *tautauog* in Narr., and thought by Williams to mean 'sheep's-head'. It is commonly called *tautog* in New England, and blackfish elsewhere. (Mathews, *Dict.*, v. *tautog*.]

Wussorasha 'crab'; not in Rasles. A difficult word, for which no cognate appears to have been recorded in the seventeenth century. We may hazard a guess that what Rosier heard was merely a cognate of Nat. *ussowessu* meaning, more or less, 'its name is...', and that he mistook the word for the name of the fish.

IV. Birds and insects

Chussuah 'a [gnat, or] garnepo fly'; Abn. *tsé'swé* (pl. *-ak*), 'mouche' [383]; WS. *mowchesoh*, 'a fly' [184]; cf. Del. *utscheuwes* [Prince, 44].

Garnepo appears to be a misprint for 'ganatte', a spelling of gnat found as late as 1562 [OED, s.v. 'gnat']. In MSS of the period, 'e' was often mistaken for 'o', and vice versa, while in Rosier's MS 's', 't', 'm' and possibly 'k' have all been printed at least once as 'p' – though it is possible that 'p' for 'm' was due to mishearing.

Cagagoose [for *Kagagoose*] – 'crow'; Abn. *mkazes*, 'corbeau' [418]; Nat. *konkont*, 'crow, raven', and other onomatopoetic names in other New England languages [Trumbull, 40]. Cf. WS. *coiahqwus*, 'gull' [187]. Rosier's form is undoubtedly influenced by the English word 'goose'.

V. *Trees, flowers and vegetables*

Asheemena 'currant tree'; Abn. *asebañmskŵéminar* (pl.), 'groseilles' [460]. Cf. *ushcomono*, 'peas'. It is impossible to be certain just what word Rosier heard; if the 'sh' is an error for 'sk', the word was probably a compound of some form of *aske* or *uske*, 'green', 'raw' [found in many Alg. languagues], plus *-min*, a radical meaning berry or fruit, etc.; if the 'sh' represents a palatal 's', the first element could be *hassun* or *ussinne*, etc., meaning 'stone, little stone', etc. The same applies to *ushcomono*, q.v.

Askabesse 'oak'; Abn. *anaskamesi*, 'chêne qui porte des glands' [386]. Cf. Carolina Alg. *ascopo*, 'sweet bay' [Quinn, *Roanoke*, 885].

Epsegan 'plum-tree'
 Epsegononino 'cherry-tree' } These must be studied together.

Epsegan appears to be Abn. *espakŵse* (pl. *-sar*), 'ils ressemblent aux sa'tar, "fruits frais"' [460].

The longer word, *espegononino*, 'cherry-tree', may be a mistake for the same word, or it may be derived from (or related to) Abn. *pañbeséganimin* (pl. *-ar*), 'fruits bons' [460], which is of little help.

Kiskeemy 'raspberry'; Abn. *kepeskimin*, 'framboises' [460]; cf. WS. *muskeskimmins* 'strawberries' [192].

Mashquere 'bark of a tree'; Abn. *maskŵé* (pl. *-kŵar*), 'écorce de bouleau à cabaner' [439].

Mebeere 'a leaf'; Abn. *mibi* (pl. *-ar*), 'feuille' [455].

Minusheck 'wild-rose'; not in Rasles, but cf. Abn. *asekkŵhessŵ*, 'rose' [524] which seems to contain the second element. It is possible that the first element is the common radical *min*, 'berry, fruit, etc.' and that the word meant 'berry-like rose'. [Hypothetical.] Cf. Professor Geary, on *minsal*, 'small beads' [Quinn, *Roanoke*, 891–892].

Pasquar 'birch'; Abn. *maskwémŵsi*, bouleau' [386]; Cree *wuskwi*, 'birch (tree), birch-bark' [522]. Cf. *mashquere*, 'birch-bark'. The 'p' seems to be a mishearing for 'm', and *pasquar* may be the same word as *mashquere*.

Pishoa 'strawberry'; possibly Abn. *meskikŵiminse*, 'fraises', but highly conjectural; 'p' may be a mishearing of 'm' and 'sh' an error for 'sk'; *-minse* is evidently for *-min*, 'berry' (probably a diminutive), but we must add assumed distortion from slovenly speech, or even miscopyings or printing. Rosier's abbreviation of some words seems to have been arbitrary.

Poco 'pitch and tallow'; Abn. *pekŵ*, 'goume, gomme [vegetable gum]' [462]; Mic. *üpkoo*, 'pitch'; WS. *pickewh*, 'gum (that issueth out of a certain tree called the Virginian maple)' [186]; Cree *pikew*, 'gum, pitch, tar, rosin' [422]. Waymouth's 'pitch and tar' for 'rosin' reflects the current interest in finding supplies of those commodities for ships.

Seteock 'a fir-tree'; Abn. *sediak*, app. a synonym for *pŵpŵkanikŵ*, 'sapin' [386]; cf. Cree *setakwun*, spruce brush' [454].

Shewanor 'gooseberry'; this is app. the same word as *asheemena*, 'currant tree', with 'w' for 'm' (a common exchange): Abn. *asebañmskŵéminar*, 'groseilles' [460]. There may have been confusion with *shoanor*, 'bow', however, especially since that word itself was confused (see below).

Tomoch 'tobacco'; Abn. *ŵdámañ*, 'pétun', and *ŵdamañgan*, 'calumet' [505 and 402], prob. the latter; Narr. *wuttamâuog*, 'tobacco', *wuttámmagon*, 'pipe', and Peq. *wuttummunc*, 'a pipe' [Trumbull 210]; modern Mohegan-Pequot *tummoung* [pronounced *tümüñg*], 'a pipe' [Prince 41].

Ushcomono 'peas'; Abn. *aŵennŵtsŵiminar*, 'pois à manger' [509], but see *asheemena*. Cf. Cree *uskeminu*, 'swampberries, etc.,' [491]. The meaning may have been 'greenberries.'

VI. *Mankind and the human body*

Breeche 'a hand and a finger'; Abn. *meretsi*, 'main' [487]; cf. WS. *meteingeies*, 'fingers' [183], *meihtinge*, 'hand' [187] and *metinge*, 'hand' [192].

Ibider 'teeth'; Abn. *wipit*, '[son] dent' [419]; WS. *neputts*, (for *nipits*), 'the [my] tooth' [212]. [Parts of the body had to have a personal-possessor prefix, which could have been 'ne- for 'I', ke-for 'thou', we- for the third person, or me- for an indefinite person. *Ibider* may stand for *wibider*, 'his or her teeth' etc.]

Canoah [for *kanoah*] 'the cheek'; Abn. *manüé*, 'joue', *nanüé*, 'ma joue' [419]; Rosier prob. heard *kanüé*, 'thy cheek'.

Codd 'a leg'; Abn. *nekañt, kekañt*, etc., '[*dicitur genericé*] depuis le pié inclusive jusqu'au dessus de la hanche' [419]; Rosier's spelling hints that Abn. kanwé, 'thy cheek' was pronounced *ka-noo-ay*, not *kan-way*; hence 'w̄' was vocalic. Rosier dropped the prefix entirely here.

Cushe 'a nail of the hand'; Abn. *mekas* (pl. *-ak*), 'onge' [495]; WS. *mekonse*, 'nails' [192]; prefix again dropped.

Meris or *Messer* 'hair'; Abn. *nepiésŵmar* (pl.), 'mes cheveux' [412]; WS. *merersc* or *mexersc*, 'the hair of the head' [187]; indefinite possessor.

Metoan 'a lip'; Abn. *nedŵn*, 'ma bouche, mes lèvres' [419]; WS *mettone*, 'mouth' [192]; indefinite possessor.

Momon 'eyelid'; Abn. *mañmañn*[ak], 'sourcil[s]' [419]; not in Strachey.

Musseete 'a foot'; Abn. *nesit*, 'mon pié' [419]; WS. *messeate*, 'foot' [192]; indefinite possessor.

Nicowur 'a beard'; Abn. *mi'tŵar*, 'barbe', *nŵitŵi*, 'j'ai de la barbe' [392];

Pagâgocun 'blood'; Abn. *ba'akkañn*, 'sang' [526]; WS. *neh paangunnu*, 'bluid [blood]' [177].

Peech-ten 'a nose'; Abn. *ki'tan*, 'nez' [419], with 'p' for 'k'; cf. Cree *miskiwun*, 'nose' [328], corresponding to WS. *meskew* [192].

Queh 'the chin', Abn. *nkŵi*, 'mon menton', *wkwi*, third person [419]; app. not in Strachey; cf. Cree *mikwakun*, 'the face', *mikwaskonāo*, 'the chin' [325].

Sagamo 'a chief lord'; app. not in Rasles; this word appears in English as sagamore or sachem, and is said to be derived from a root which appears in Nat. as *sohkau*, 'he has mastery' [Trumbull 151]; Narr. *sâchim* 'a king', Del. *sakímau*, 'he is a chief' [Trumbull, 316]. Cf. JS. 'The *Massachusets* call...their Kings Sachemes...The Pennobscots...their Kings, Sagamos.' [939] and p. 93 above.

Scottooquah 'forehead'; Abn. *meskátegŵe*, 'front' [419]; WS. *muskan*, 'forehead' [192]; prefix dropped.

Sheesuck 'an eye'; Abn. *tsísekŵ*, 'oeil' [419]; cf. WS. *muskiendguk* [-*d*(*g*)*ues*], 'eye, eyes' [182], and *muskins*, 'the eyes' [192].

Tawwucke [misprinted as *Fawwucke*] 'an ear'; Abn. *mtawakŵ*, 'oreille' [419]; WS. *meihtawk*, 'ear' [182], *metawke*, 'ears' [192]; prefix dropped.

Usto 'son' ⎱ Take together.
Wado 'father' ⎰

Rosier's informant would probably not have thought of either word in terms of 'father' or 'son', as expressed in an Indo-European language. He would most likely have used an Alg. term meaning a specific individual (*my* father, *my* or *your* son), or a genuine expression such as 'the one who has a son', or 'he who is a father'. No immediately corresponding word in the modern Eastern Abenaki language has yet been traced; possibly probably due to an error in transcription by Rosier, Purchas or the Printer.

VII. *Artifacts*

Edagawancke 'sword'; app. Abn. *maghi‛kaïn*, 'je le bats, je le lapide', [Trumbull 161], with 'w' for 'm', related to 'tomahawk' (q.v. under ('tomaheegon').

Cogosho [for *Kogosho*] 'black paint'; not in Rasles, although the word seems to be connected with *cagagoose*, 'crow' (v. sup.) – cf. Abn. *mkazéŵighen* and rel. *nemikazéŵséŵé*, 'mon habit est noire' [492]. It is curious that this word is troublesome, while *red paint* is quite clear.

Makeecon 'a fish-hook'; Abn. *mkíkan*, 'hameçon' [465]. and *maghi kaïn*, id. [382]; WS. *mowhkohan*, 'a fish-hook' [192].

Paune 'bread'; Abn. *abaïn*, 'pain' [496]; JS. *ponap*, 'bread' [63], WS. *appoans*, etc., 'bread' [178, and elsewhere with other spellings]; a fairly common Alg. word, based on a radical meaning 'to bake', which has come into English as (corn-) pone [see OED, s.v.].

Quiden 'a ship or boat'; Abn. *agwíden*, 'canot' [403]; WS. *aquointan*, 'a canoe or small boat' [178], and *aquintayne*, 'ship, boat or canoe' [175]; Pen. *agwed'n*, 'canoe' [Prince 189].

Quodogon 'knife'; not in Rasles. A difficult word, since (European) knives did not exist in America. Vincent O. Erickson, with the concurrence of Peter Paul, suggests that *Quodogon* is likely how Rosier heard *mikudakon*, the contemporary Maliseet-Passamaquoddy for knife (personal communication, 6 December 1978).

Shoanor 'a bow' }
Tobood 'an arrow' } These must be studied together.

Rosier seems again to have confused related objects. *Tobood* is fairly obviously Abn. *taïbi*, which means 'bow' [386], and has cognates in Mic. *abe*, 'bow', *nootäbeech*, 'a small bow' [41–42] and in JS. *attawp*, 'bow' [44], and WS. *auhtab*, 'bow' [177]. *Shoanor* is a little less clear, but seems derived from some such word as Abn. *arŵssar*, 'arrows', perhaps in compound form (e.g. *kaïkskarŵs*, 'flèche où il y a des plumes') [386]. Rosier's form *shoanor* seems to have been influenced by the completely unrelated *shewanor*, 'gooseberry'. (There are several examples of such haphazard influences in these words.)

Speesone 'white bone whereof they have chains, girdles, bracelets'; not in Rasles. Peter Paul saw it as the Malisseet-Passamaquoddy word for belt: Vincent O. Erickson suggested the Micmac word for belt (from Rand), pointing that neither Rosier nor Peter Paul noted the R-sound, possibly a dialectal difference.

Tenoganuke 'a shirt or coat'; Abn. *aïtûréhaïwé*, 'chemise' [412]; Mic. *chenŭmōgwŏn*, 'shirt' [233]; cf. Nat. *wuttunkum, wuttunkhumunát*, 'to cover with' [213] and the Narr. word for Englishman *Waútacon-ûaog*, 'coat-men' [Trumbull, 183].

Tomaheegon 'an axe or hatchet'; Abn. *temahígan*, 'hache' [465]; JS. *tomahacks*, 'axes' [44], WS. *tamohake* [203], *tamahaac* [187], 'hatchet'; the source of English tomahawk. The Abn. form shows the instrumental ending *-hikan, -higan*, partly cut off by JS. WS. and modern English.

Woroman 'red paint'; Abn. *ŵrámaïn*, 'peinture' [502], *ŵrámaïn* 'peinture vermillion [541], obviously the same word; Narr. *wunnàm*, 'their red painting, which they most delight in' [Trumbull, 200]; cf. Del. *coláman* [ooláman?], 'Indian paint, red paint' [Walam Olum, 105].

Wuttohoganor 'an oar'; Abn. *ŵ'tahagan*, 'aviron' [390]; Mic. *ootagun*, 'oar' [189]; Nat. *wuttuhhunk*, 'a paddle' [213].

493

APPENDIX II

DISPUTED POINTS OF THE VOYAGES OF
1602–1608

Since evidence on many matters of detail is so tenuous in the documents it is not surprising that there is controversy about many of the points on where exactly the explorers went and what they saw. Some of this is very much a matter of personal idiosyncrasy and the desire to set up the place where one lives as somewhere of importance; sometimes it is a matter of genuine difficulty which cannot finally be resolved, but in other cases a stand has got to be considered in the light of what evidence there is, if it does seem on reflection and study to point one way rather than another. Some problems have been resolved satisfactorily in the notes but other voices deserve to be heard also on some of them and on a few others not treated there in detail. No comprehensive coverage is attempted here but it seemed best to give critics of the views expressed above some leeway and put forward additional evidence rather than extend the introduction further or make the notes still more unwieldy. We follow through chronologically.

Gosnold's Sailings from 3 p.m. on the 14th to 9 a.m. on the 15th of May
(24–25 May by the Gregorian calendar)

John C. Bower Jr, who is experienced in sailing these waters, expressed to me both in 1970 and 1978 his doubts about the capacity of the *Concord* to sail from Cape Elizabeth or Cape Neddick to the southern part of Cape Cod Bay near modern Barnstable between 3 p.m. on the 24th and 9 a.m. on the 15th, but thought she might make it from Cape Ann. An important factor is the age of the moon. Mr Bower kindly supplied me with the following note.

'The age of the moon on 15 May 1602, Julian, according to Philip Harvey's formula, published in *British Astronomical Association Journal*, LI (July 1941), 209. Here follows Harvey's method of finding the moon's age, which must be entered with the Gregorian date, that is to say ten days later than the Julian, or 25 May 1602.

1 Divide given year by 19; find remainder
2 Multiply remainder by 11
3 To remainder add $\frac{1}{3} + \frac{1}{4}$ of century, excluding fractions

4   Add constant 8
5   Sum of items 2, 3, 4
6   Subtract number of century
7   Add month (March = 1)
8   Add day of month
9   Sum of items 6, 7, 8
10   Subtract multiples of 30. Remainder is age of the moon in days after new, $\pm$ one day.

Applied to 25 May 1602, the sequence follows

$$
\begin{array}{lll}
1 & 1602 \div 19 & = 6 \\
2 & 6 \times 11 & = 66 \\
3 & +\frac{1}{3} \times 17 & = 5 \\
  & +\frac{1}{4} \times 17 & = 4 \\
4 & +8 & = 8 \\
5 & 66+5+4 & = 83 \\
6 & -17 & = 66 \\
7 & \text{March}+2 & = 3 \\
8 & 25 & = 25 \\
9 & 66+3+25 & = 94 \\
10 & -(3 \times 30) & = 90 \\
 & & = 4 \text{ days}
\end{array}
$$

Antedating Harvey is, of course, the William Bourne sequence, which appears in *The regiment for the sea*, published first in 1571. The modern edition for citation here is Hakluyt Society, Series 2, cxxi, 60–2, edited by E. G. R. Taylor, where a determined reader might dig out the sequence from Master Bourne's interesting prose for himself. Lacking that ambition, he may now follow the sequence as applied to our Julian date, 15 May 1602:

$$
\begin{array}{llll}
1 & \text{Given year}+1 & = & 1603 \\
2 & 1603 + 19. \text{ Remainder Prime} & & 7 \\
3 & \text{Prime} \times 11 & = & 77 \\
4 & 77+30. \text{ Remainder Epact} & & 17 \\
5 & \text{March} = 1, +2, \text{ for May} = & & 3 \\
6 & +\text{day of month} & & 15 \\
7 & \text{Sum of items } 4, 5, 6 & = & 35 \\
8 & \text{Subtract multiples of } 30 & = & 30 \\
9 & \text{Age of the moon} & = & 5 \text{ days}
\end{array}
$$

From this the following deductions appear likely: the distances from Cape Elizabeth being about 120 nautical miles, from Cape Neddick nearly 100, from Cape Ann about 65.

With a four–five day old moon there would be little light for nearly 8 out of the 18 hours available. Suppose *Concord* made six knots for six hours in daylight, she would still have covered 36 miles and from dawn to 9 a.m. another 24. This leaves 60, 40 and 5 nautical miles respectively to be covered in darkness in eight hours, giving her speeds of 7·5, 5, and 0·625 knots. The maximum figure seems too high, the intermediate possible and the third too low. But suppose she made 8 knots while it was light, this would leave her only to do 40, 20, or less than nothing in darkness, with 5, 2·5, and nil knots according to the distance.'

Sailors were accustomed to sailing by star-light and if the North Star was visible it appears to us that she could come from Cape Elizabeth in this time, even if we scale her sailing speed in daylight to 7 knots, making under 6, under 3, or nil for the three distances. Consequently we can still keep Cape Elizabeth in the running, though Cape Neddick cannot be excluded, and it seems unnecessary to bring her as far south as Cape Ann. The 'fresh gale' which drove her southwards makes it possible to consider a high average rate of sailing (as much as 8 knots), but luck as well as good seamanship must be taken into account. However John Bower did attempt to estimate the *Concord*'s sailing speed on her way across the Atlantic, and on 12 September 1970 wrote: 'The sailing speed of *Concord* is best determined by her passage from Falmouth to the North American coast. She left Falmouth on March 26 and passed St Mary's in the Azores on April 14: 19 days and 1200 miles. From there to Lat. 43 on the American Coast is 30 days and 1800 miles. Thus *Concord* made good 3000 miles in 39 days; 76·92 mi./day, or 3·2 knots over the ground upon the rhumb lines.' This is very helpful, but as we have no log we cannot say how the weather and winds were and whether a record of distance made good each day was kept. Conditions offshore on the New England coast, with the wind behind her most of the way (though she might have had to claw her way from off Barnstable around Cape Cod), were very different and we could, perhaps, expect something like double her ocean sailing speed. On the evidence dogmatism does not seem advisable.

Gosnold's Vantage Point on the Upper Cape

Warner Gookin was the first to pick up the significance of Brereton's statement that Gosnold had climbed up to a high point above the southern end of the Bay (Cape Cod Bay) where he found himself at

9 a.m. on the morning of May 15. He suggested that the lookout point was Shoot Flying Hill (200 ft), which is still a tree-covered refuge between the up and down lanes of Route 6. This is one of the highest points on the ridge which forms the spine of the Upper Cape and a lookout from one of the tall trees of the climax forest would have provided an excellent place to see what lay to the southward. The shore party had, according to Brereton, a long hot march but finally saw 'this headland to be part of the maine, and sundrie Islands lying almost round about it' (pp. 146–7). At the start the ship was riding in some 90 feet of water off Barnstable Harbor. Before her to the south was a sandy spit (Sandy Neck) (this part of the shoreline does not change so rapidly as that outside the protection of the Cape but some silting takes place), from which the profile of a low range of hills could be seen. A boat, the half-shallop, was put out to row into land. It would have rounded Beach Point, entered Barnstable Harbor and, most probably, entered the creek on which the modern town of Barnstable stands. From the Creek there was a gentle slope up to the ridge, the highest point to the south being now 138 ft above sea level. Sending a man aloft up the high trees from time to time, they could accumulate a picture of what lay to the south. They may indeed, if they spent five hours on the operation, have reached Shoot Flying Hill where the best observation was possible, but that involved twelve miles in all, there and back, with some marshes to begin with, then virgin forest, and, if the Indians had not cleared it for hunting, thick undergrowth. Experienced walkers are a little sceptical about whether they got as far as Shoot Flying Hill and back in the time, but other points less far distant would have produced an adequate picture of the coast to the south.

What did they see? Visibility varied greatly on the three occasions when looking southward from Shoot Flying Hill was attempted by the editors (though from the ground not the tops of trees). Nantucket was never seen and it seems unlikely that it ever can be. What a clear day will show is sun-flashes from beaches on Muskeget or Tuckernuck Islands lying between Chappaquiddick and Nantucket. Capoag, even, might well be too distant, so Brereton's 'islands' remain something of a mystery. What would be seen clearly is the shore of the Upper Cape, trending steadily southwestwards, though it would not be evident that it eventually breaks off just past Woods Hole and becomes a chain of islands. To the south the main bulk of Martha's Vineyard would stand out, since East and West Chop would be seen, and the adjoining land to the west, which also might have been seen to trend somewhat to the southwest, may have been visible also. Gosnold would get the impression that what he was seeing was a broad channel into the mainland to the southwest. If he was looking, as he was, for Verrazzano's 'Refugio', then this was a sufficiently strong hint that it lay beyond the channel and justified his rounding of the great peninsula of the Cape in order to see it. Gookin appreciated this but he thought more could be deduced from the viewpoint than is, in fact, the case.

The sail round Cape Cod to Nantucket Sound

Warner Gookin spent some years struggling with this problem and eventually brought the *Concord* (sketch-map as frontispiece to Gookin and Barbour, *Gosnold* (1963) and following) from the evening of May 15 to the evening of May 16 all the way south to round Nantucket Island (and incidentally through Nantucket Shoals) to lie off Muskeget Channel to the southeast of Martha's Vineyard. He refused to accept that Gosnold could do what Champlain was to prove possible, namely to enter Nantucket Sound by a channel south of Monomoy Point. This involved some 120 nautical miles at the very least but with the moon only one day older and with a very much more circuitous course. Rounding Cape Cod might have been done before dark. But with the water shoaling off the entrance to Nantucket Sound, and especially with a course to be picked all the way across the very dangerous Nantucket Shoals, which would involve constant soundings, sailing south and west of Nantucket was a different matter. Neither Mr Bower, nor any other experienced sailor we have consulted, regard this as feasible, and if it was attempted then the *Concord* was one of the most fortunate vessels on record. Gookin's difficulty was that Archer said they had to go twelve leagues south of Cape Cod. He was obsessed with the Velasco Map (pp. 520–5 below) which put Cape Cod in the position of Monomoy Point at the southern extension of the Lower Cape, whereas it is clear Gosnold meant by Cape Cod what we mean, the northern promontary, and this would be a reasonable landsman's estimate of the distance from Cape Cod to an entry into Nantucket Sound south of Monomoy Point. My view is that we must discard Gookin's carefully worked-out hypothesis and have the *Concord* make a slow, carefully-sounded entry to Nantucket Sound during the 16th, possibly following the same route as Champlain was to do, even though Mr Bower says that he and his sailing friends would not now care to attempt it, though it can be done.

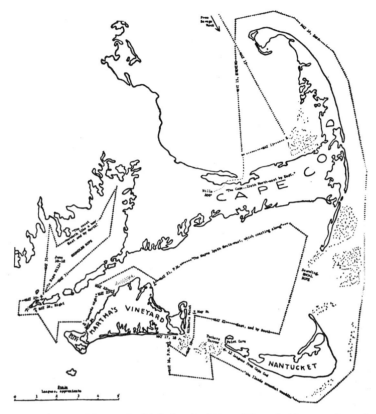

Fig. 27. C. 1950. Warner Gookin's sketch of Gosnold's probable route through the islands.

The text along the marked route reads: in Buzzards Bay, 'The coast bendeth like a bow East and by North'; off Martha's Vineyard 'towards night'; in Nantucket Sound, 'The Mayne lyeth South-east, which coasting along'; and in Cape Cod Bay 'The Cape...lieth North-east by East'.

Gosnold, when he rounded Cape Cod, would not need to sail very far off the southward trending shore of the Lower Cape since sounding would find him deep water not more than two miles off shore, but he would need to be careful as he got to the stretch between Nauset Harbor and Chatham, as Champlain showed that an island, long gone, stood in the way (Webbs Island nine miles southast of Chatham) and that shoals extended some way out to sea. Champlain gives conflicting

499

testimony on the coastal topography of the southeast tip of the Cape where shorelines have changed with bewildering rapidity. His sketch of Stage Harbor after he had rounded what we call Monomoy Point into Nantucket Sound shows a long barrier beach, curving close inshore to the east around the southeast part of the Cape. On the other hand his narrative states that this was a long point, presumably extending southward, standing out to sea for three leagues, S by SE from the mainland, more or less like Monomoy Point in the 1970ties (*Works*, I, pl. LXXVIII, pp. 407–8). *The English Pilot. The fourth book* (London, 1689, facsimile, Amsterdam, 1967) in its final plate shows Monomoy as an island, trending NE–SW to the south of which is a channel into Nantucket Sound showing 6 and 7 fathoms of water, more than the modern Pollock Rip Channel in this place, or the Great Round Shoal Channel farther south, nearer Nantucket Island. There seems little doubt that Gosnold did enter Nantucket Sound in this manner.

Capoag

The argument that Cape Poge was an island in the seventeenth and early eighteenth century is irrefutable; the probability that it is Gosnold's first Martha's Vineyard is very high indeed. In the Registry of Deeds, Court House, Edgartown, there are deeds which establish this clearly. On 16 June 1668 Pahkepunnasto, sachem of Chappaquiddick, ceded to Thomas Mayhew certain rights on the island of Natack (an alternative name for Capoag) (Deeds, I, 388): on 31 March 1726 Micijah Mayhew, in turn, leased 'the Island of Natick alias Capoag near unto the island of Chappaquiddick' (Deeds, IV, 158–9), and again on 7 February 1729 he leased part of 'the Isle of Capoag...[which] lieth a little to the East or Northard of the Isle of Chapaquidet' (Deeds, IV, 395). The junction of Capoag with Chappaquiddick came during a storm between 1729 and 1742 (though David M. Ludlum, *Early American hurricanes* (Boston, 1963), records nothing of this sort between 1727 and 1743). However, on 28 October 1742, Benjamin Pease (aged about 66 years) testified 'that forty years ago & upward They were well knowing that there was a Constant Course of Water Running through between the Island of Chappaquiddick and Natick *alias* Capoag' until 'about Twenty yeare Agoe when it was Stopped up with Sand which was Occasioned by a grate Storm', until which the two 'were and have been known esteemed and improued as towe Distinct and Seperate Islands' (Deeds, VI, 401, confirmed by VI, 520, 4 March

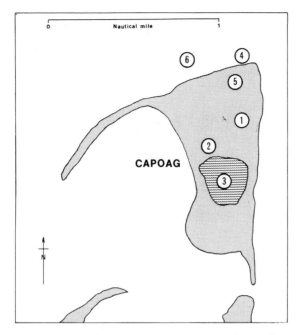

Fig. 28. Reconstruction of Capoag I., 1602. (Now the northern part of Chappaquiddick I.)

(1) 'we saw a disinhabited island...we bore with it, named it Marthaes Vineyard...the Iland is fiue miles, and hath 41. degrees and one quarter of latitude' (Archer). 'foure English miles in compasse' (Brereton). (2) 'Beeches and Cedars' (Brereton). 'we went ashore, and found it full of wood...' (Archer). (3) 'a greate standing lake of fresh water, neere the sea side, and English mile in compasse' (Brereton). (4) 'on the north side of this Island we found many huge bones and ribbes of whales' (Brereton). (5) 'Heere we had...Birds which there at that time vpon the Cliffes being sandy with some Rockie stones, did breed...' (Archer). (6) 'heere we rode in eight fathome neere the shoare...' (Archer).

1743). Some of these instances were cited by C. E. Banks, *History of Martha's Vineyard*, I, 21, 35, II, 206.

The precise size of the island as it would have been before the junction with Chappaquiddick is not easy to calculate. The large freshwater pond, marked by the projection of Little Neck, is still a semicircular bay inside the greater Cape Poge Pond. Great Neck, the long barrier beach which, with North Neck, almost encloses Cape Poge Pond, may then have been shorter, but it almost certainly already existed. The promontary of Cape Poge, as by then it had come to be known, in the profile drawing of 1776 (Fig. 3) *The Atlantic Neptune*, III (1781), has had its tree-cover removed, and has been subject to continuous erosion. As early as 15 November 1797 J. Thaxter wrote to Jeremy Belknap 'it is certain that the shoals shift & that Cape Poge in the memory of man has washed into the sea, some say 30 or 40 Rods' (Belknap Papers, 61 C, in Massachusetts Historical Society). Today, the glacial clay and sand, embedded with large rocks, as Archer saw them, still make a substantial cape. From the disused lighthouse, which erosion has approached but had not in 1978 reached, the impression of a separate island is strongly present. In the lee of the Cape tall trees, now mainly Scotch pine and recent Cedar, grow, as Francis Jennings and one of us found in August 1978. Wilcomb Washburn filmed a few ancient, moss-covered cedars there in 1963, and found white pine, blueberry, and grapes growing. Gale Huntington and Dorothy R. Scoville of the Dukes County Historical Society in 1964 confirmed the survival of old cedars, large beeches, wild strawberries, raspberries and gooseberries, so that evidence from the 1960ties fitted, within reason, the criteria of the 1602 narratives at almost every point. There may well have been deer on the island then.

It is necessary to add this detailed material to the notes since Warner Gookin, in his version of the voyage, brought the *Concord*, once she was through the Muskeget Channel on the south coast, on a tour of the north coast of Nantucket, north to Upper Cape, and westwards to discover East Chop on Martha's Vineyard as Gosnold's first Martha's Vineyard. East Chop has a pond near its base but was never an island within recent historic times. So much of his careful work was thus wasted, or perhaps not wholly so, since he was the first to weigh up each word in the narratives and to attempt identifications on a systematic basis even if he was not correct in his final conclusions.

The route to the Elizabeth Islands

The discovery of Martha's Vineyard I (Capoag) and the translation of the name to Martha's Vineyard II (the main island) is not particularized in the accounts, but once the *Concord* had a clear view down Vineyard Sound (her previous route may well have suggested its nature already), Gosnold could be certain that it was a passage between two groups of islands since he saw Capoag, the main part of Martha's Vineyard, and Gay Head as three islands to the south and the continuation of the

Upper Cape as another chain of islands to the north and, at the southwestern end of the channel, open sea once again: there was no entrance to 'Refugio' this way. Nonamesset, Naushon, Pasque, Nashawena and Cuttyhunk Islands made up the chain as it is now. Even if the islands were somewhat differently divided then, the sequence remained the same. Once he left his anchorage on the northwest of Martha's Vineyard (Lambert's Cove?) Gosnold would find the Sound widening and would keep closer to the islands as he moved west of them, finding at the very end the Sow and Pigs Reef, which was sufficiently prominent then to find itself on the Velasco Map of 1610 (Fig. 34, p. 521 below). The ultimate island appeared to be a place to stay and he named it 'Elizabeths Ile', celebrating his Queen and, Gookin suggested, his sister Elizabeth also (Gookin and Barbour, p. 143). The group remains the Elizabeth Islands to this day. The great sound which stretched before the *Concord* after she came to anchor in deep water on the western side of the modern island of Cuttyhunk was Buzzards Bay, stretching as far as could be seen to the N.E. with a mainland shore to be glimpsed on the northern side. This ought to be the 'Refugio' at last! At least the final island would provide a base for further searching.

What was 'Elizabeths Ile' in 1602?

It has been suggested that if the island which Gosnold picked for a base was sixteen miles in circuit it could not be Cuttyhunk as we have it today. Harold C. Wilson and William C. Carr, in 'Gosnold's Elizabeth's Isle: Cuttyhunk or Naushon?' *American Neptune*, XXXIII (1973), 131–45, make a case for regarding the chosen island as not Cuttyhunk but the third island in the present chain, Naushon, which is by far the largest (and incidentally retains some climax forest, almost the last on the east coast). *The English Pilot. Fourth book* (1689), last plate, does name Naushon 'Elizabeth'. They find a pond and make the terrain sound attractive: certainly it has been cared for as Cuttyhunk and Nashawena have not, but the case simply will not work. To make it so the documents have to be twisted and turned in a way that is just not possible. We are thus thrown back on the suggestion made in the notes that 'Elisabeths Ile' was what are now the two islands of Cuttyhunk and Nashawena. A long sand-spit almost joins them, and the Canapitsit Channel which divides them is only 12 to 14 feet deep. But it was there already in the late eighteenth century, since it shows up on *The Atlantic Neptune*, III. It seems a reasonable hypothesis that the channel was cut by a pre-1776 hurricane. Proof, unless an earlier map turns up or legal documents are found, is impossible and it has been accepted with some doubts about Archer's accuracy in recording the size of 'Elizabeths Ile'. Amelia Forbes Emerson (of Naushon), in her *Early history of Naushon Island* (Boston, privately printed, 1935), p. 46, gave it as her opinion that in 1602 Cuttyhunk and Nashawena were one and were divided by a storm. She gives instances, from her personal knowledge of this kind of thing happening elsewhere in the islands and, moreover, states that Canapitsit Channel was dredged to give it its modern depth only about 1930.

The Fort on Elisabeths Ile

That the fort and storehouse were built on an island in a pond on an island, that a flat-bottomed punt was constructed to carry materials from the main island to the inner island, that it was fit, Archer considered, to hold twenty men for a year, when Gosnold decided to abandon it, can be established. In 1902, to mark the third centenary of Gosnold's visit, a Committee from New Bedford, headed by the Honorable Charles S. Randall, celebrated the anniversary and raised money to erect a stone tower in 1903 which effectively obliterated all remains of the 1602 structures. We have to go back to the eighteenth and nineteenth centuries to see what can be found. In the Belknap Papers in the Massachusetts Historical Society a brief journal was entered on Thomas's *Almanack* for 1797 by Jeremy Belknap, who had a little earlier committed himself to the view that the Gosnold fort had been on Naushon but had been induced to reconsider this and visit Cuttyhunk Island where he convinced himself he had found on the island in the island pond there the site of Gosnold's building. It reads:

12 [June 1797]. I went in ye stage to New Bedford.
19 [June]. Saild from New Bedford to Cuttihunk Island & returned – 20 [June] – I there found the Island in ye Pond where Capt Gosnold built his fort & house 1602. The cellar remains.
21 [June]. Returned to Boston.

As a result, in the second volume of his *American biography* (Boston, 1798), II, 114–16, he expanded on this discovery:

In this island, at the west end, on the north side, is a pond of fresh water, three quarters of a mile in length, and of unequal breadth; but if measured in all its sinuosities, would amount to two miles in circuit. In the middle of its breadth, near the west end, is a rocky islet, containing near an acre of ground.

To this spot I went, on the 20th day of June 1797, in company with several gentlemen, whose curiosity and obliging kindness induced them to accompany me. [In the margin: Noah Webster, Esq. of New-York, Captain Tallman, Mr. John Spooner, Mr. Allen, a pilot, of New Bedford.]
The protecting hand of Nature has reserved this favourite spot to herself. Its fertility and its production are exactly the same as in Gosnold's time, excepting the wood, of which there is none. Every species of what he calls 'Rubbish', with strawberies, pease, tansy, and other fruits and herbs, appear in rich abundance, unmolested by any animals but aquatic birds. We had the supreme satisfaction to find the cellar of Gosnold's store-house; the stones of which were evidently taken from the neighbouring beach; the rocks of the islet being less moveable, and lying in ledges.

The whole island of Cuttyhunk has been for many years stripped of its wood; but I was informed by Mr Greenhill, an old resident farmer, that the trees which formerly grew on it, were such as are described in Gosnold's Journal. The soil is a very fine garden mould, from the bottom of the vallies to the top of the hills, and affords rich pasture [suggesting sheep farming had already begun].

The length of the island is rather more than two miles, and its breadth about one mile. The beach between the pond and the sea is twenty-seven yards wide. It is so high and firm a barrier, that the sea never flows into the pond, but when agitated by a violent gale from the north-west. The pond is deep in the middle. It has no visible outlet. Its fish are perch, eels and turtles, and it is frequented by aquatic birds, both wild and domestic.

The breach which let the sea into the pond and made it salt, and open to the north, has not been firmly dated. Belknap is invaluable but by no means the last word. Mr John C. Bower, Jr., with his usual caution, writes:

It seems to me that I would be wary of the cellar hole business. We must surmise that fishermen of many nationalities in many times before and after 1602 dug 'cellar holes' wherein they cool-stored their flaked [sun-dried on flakes] fish until they were ready to carry a cargo back to Europe. No other refrigeration, protection from the elements, animals and marauding natives were at hand. An ample shallow hole was dug, lined with available stone, and covered with rough hewn planks, sod, and branches.

He does not think that Belknap's 'cellar' alone carries conviction. Mrs Clifford riposted, in the correspondence I have seen, that she could not imagine a fisherman building a 'cellar-hole' fifteen feet square. Without subscribing to any firm view, the editors suggest that

Belknap's 'cellar' was merely a slight depression, marking foundations of a building. The size would be appropriate for a storehouse or fort.

In 1971 Charlotte B. Clifford completed a paper 'Gosnold's Fort on Cuttyhunk' (the present location of the original is not known) in which she traced all the pre-1902 references she could find to the 'remains' on Cuttyhunk. She did not publish it, and later attempts to get in touch with her failed. However, she cited a paper by Francis C. Gray, 'Visit to the Elizabeth Islands', *North American Review*, V (1817), 313–24, which is worth extracting:

In the western end of the pond is a high islet, surrounded by a rocky margin and covered with very rich soil, in which were growing the wild gooseberry, the grape, the elder, mallows, primrose, eglantine, yarrow, sumach, wild parsnip, volvulus, thoroughwort, and red clover. The stump of a red cedar stood near the shore, and we brought home a piece of it as a remembrancer of our expedition.

On the northern bank of the islet, about ten yards from the water, we found a small excavation overgrown with bushes and grass, on the one side of which were three large stones in a row at the distance of three feet from each other, having under them stones of the same size lying in the same direction. Between these were smaller stones, which appeared from their form and smoothness to have been taken from the beach. In another slight excavation twenty yards south of the former near the center and highest part of the islet, were similar stones, but very few in number, and not disposed in any apparent order. On digging in other parts of the islet, we found none of the same kind. We conjectured that the first excavation was all that remained of Gosnold's cellar [influence of Belknap only?], and the latter a part of the trench dug for the purpose of forming the fort.

A few years later a party visited the spot and on the highest point of the islet James Howland II found 'what they concluded to be three sides of the cellar of Gosnold's house, which he estimated to have been about fifteen feet square.' This was cited by Mrs Clifford from Daniel Ricketson, *History of New Bedford* (New Bedford, 1858), which has not been seen.

The 'fifteen feet square' gives us one credible set of measurements, namely the sixteen feet by sixteen feet which made up a 'house' plan when plantations were being made shortly after this time in Ulster and which was the size of a pole-and-frame building which was practical, quickly, to erect (though occasionally with a stone base and even an excavation below it, stone-lined). My own view is that perhaps two 'houses' of this sort could have been constructed for the fort and the storehouse, or that two plus two might be a safer guess. To provide adequate accommodation for twenty men and give them a storehouse as well would require something like four 'houses', with a half-storey upstairs. This type of dwelling could, as is argued for the 1607 colony Fort St George (p. 441), be very rapidly constructed in outline, roofed, and the walls left to be finished later on, as winter came in.

The scene shifts to 1868. Commodore S. O. Blake U.S.N. and William A. Goodwin, a civil engineer in the U.S., naval service, visited Cuttyhunk on naval business and were sufficiently interested to visit the island in the pond and to make a sketch of what they regarded as the remains of the Gosnold Fort. Afterwards, Commodore Blake wrote to Samuel Foster Haven, Director of the American Antiquarian Society at Worcester, Mass. (the letter being in the Society's files and the enclosed plan in the Graphic Arts Department of the same Institution, as Miss Kathleen A. Major, Assistant in the Manuscripts Department informed me when she located the letter):

Boston 2$^{d.}$ Sept 1868

Dear Sir,

I send you at length the sketches of Gosnold's Is^{d}.

They are, as you will see, but very slight, & for the reason that there is very little to sketch.

What we regarded as the remains of a wall seems very interesting.

M^{r}, Goodwin, the engineer who accompanied me, had no doubt of its being artificiall, & as I told you I rely more upon his judgement than my own. – You will observe that it is upon that portion of the shore which is within arrow flight of the opposite shore, – which seems to strengthen his opinion.

We had no doubt either in regard to the excavation.

The growth upon the Island is still very much as described by the historians.

This little contribution is hardly worth your notice but you will at any rate receive it as an evidence of my interest in such matters & in the hope that my next one may be of more value. I remain

very truly y^{rs}

S. F. Haven Esq.   S. O. Blake

This evidence is more specific in some respects and less so in others. William Goodwin, being a civil engineer, ought to have been able to distinguish an artificial embankment from a natural one. He ought also, especially with S. O. Blake's endorsement, to have been able to identify an uncompleted wall. Since we do not know of any later habitation on the island (the cellar-digger, if he was not Gosnold, apart) it would seem that we have on his sketch the outline of the outer works. Where he falls down is in only marking 'Site of Blockhouse' without any indication of what could be seen on the ground. He does, however, give us some idea of what the plan for the Fort and Storehouse may have been.

A final note on Nashawena-Cuttyhunk before the 1902–1903 depredations comes from A. Hollack, 'A reconnaissance of the Elizabeth Islands', New York Academy of Sciences, *Annals*, XIII (1901), 387–418. He found on Nashawena 'some quite extensive clumps of stunted trees, which are mostly massed in the depressions and on the sheltered slopes of the northeastern portion'. The vegetation was more abundant than on Pasque Island and similar to that of Naushon I. 'except for the greater relative abundance of oaks as compared with beeches'. On Cuttyhunk he noted that while there were no living trees left there was plenty of evidence of previous afforestation: 'near the western end, on the south shore is a depression once occupied by a swamp, one edge of which is exposed by the breaking away of the bluff. In the bottom of this depression may be seen numerous large stumps and logs, buried in a peat-like mass of fine vegetable debris, and subsequent examination showed these to be oak and beech.'

Where did Waymouth make his landfall in 1605?

Burrage in 1887 said Sankatty Head, the highest point of S.E. Nantucket, and almost all subsequent writers have followed him but the soundings he gives will not allow it. Before stating a point of view we might suggest that Waymouth may have been playing a double game. Arundell almost certainly wanted to go back to the Old Verrazzano 'Refugio' at his estimated 41° 40'; Waymouth, with fishing interests backing him, preferred to go farther north where Gosnold and Pring alike had found evidence of good fishing to be had. Therefore when he found land at about this latitude or a little farther north, instead of turning south and then west, he continued to the northward, thus showing that fishing interests came first with him. The possible identification of Georges Bank as he moved towards the North American coast (it is on the Velasco Map but in the wrong place) may have influenced him to follow it northward; his identification of Monhegan I. as a fine fishing base was enough to satisfy his Plymouth backers. His subsequent explorations from Allen Island gave him a single possible location for Arundell's colony. He deliberately did not explore the Maine coast to avoid complications with either of his backers. He had something for each, even if Rosier had to exaggerate

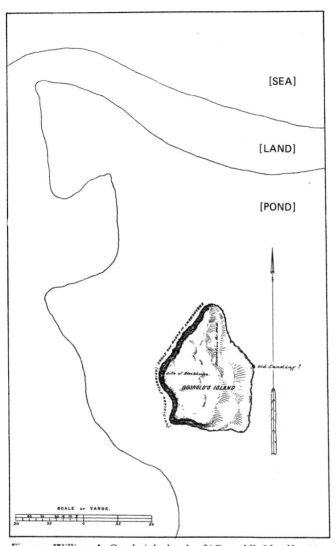

Fig. 29. William A. Goodwin's sketch of 'Gosnold's Island', 1863.
The inscriptions on the island read (left to right): 'Embankment of earth and
stone (evidently artificial)'; 'Site of Blockhouse'; 'Excavation for wall'; 'Old
Landing?'.

the size and fertility of the St George River in order to sell it to Arundell, or his possible successors.

The 100-fathom line comes reasonably close to land only at 41° 50′ offshore from Nauset Harbor: the rapid shoaling to 5 fathoms must therefore have taken place north of this off the Lower Cape, and the land seen was most probably the Lower Cape Cod Highlands in the vicinity of 42°. It will be noted that from there he kept on a northerly course.

Waymouth's Anchorage and Expeditions

Enough has been said (p. 219) about the preference for Provincetown over Plymouth for Pring's landing in 1603. Waymouth however still attracts devotees of the Sheepscot and the Kennebec Rivers because the Rosier account does not fit the distances required for the St George River entrance. The other circumstances, however, cannot be made to fit any route except Monhegan I., the Georges Is and St George River. The first clear exposition of this in words and on a map was by George Prince whose *Rosier's narrative of the Waymouth voyage to the coast of Maine*, with remarks by George Prince (Bath, Me, Eastern Times Press) forms a landmark. His map is impeccable except that he makes the St George River above Thomaston appear too wide and the river below, by contrast a little too narrow. He was followed and developed by Henry S. Burrage in his *Rosier's Relation of Waymouth's voyage to the coast of Maine in 1605* (The Gorges Society, Portland, Me, 1887), and his other editions and publications down to 1923. Burrage put flesh and detail on to Captain Prince's 'remarks' and map and, basically, his interpretation stands.

Waymouth's anchorages and locations in the Georges Islands

Rear-Admiral William F. Royall has questioned the assumption, to which we are inclined to adhere, that Waymouth anchored and moored the *Archangell* in Georges Harbor (also known as Pentecost Harbor), just north of Allen Island, and that most of his activities in the Georges Islands were concentrated on Allen Island, where there is still a fresh spring. He prefers Burnt Island as his landing place. He writes 'I believe that she stood in through the "harbour mouth" between Dry Ledges and Burnt Island. That Cam, the mate, sounded and found an anchorage north of the Dry Ledges which were "in the middest of the harbour" and formed a breakwater to protect the harbor. There the

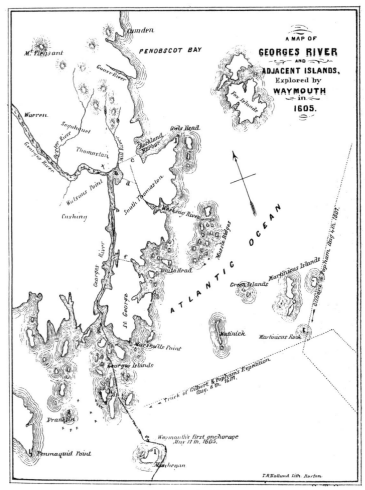

Fig. 30. Waymouth's route as sketched by George Prince in 1860.

ship was moored. The landing place on Burnt Island was in clear sight from the ship on her way in and from her berth.' There is some problem about terminology here. Admiral Royall takes 'harbour' to mean the roadstead between Allen I. and Burnt I. We take it to mean the much smaller part of the sheltered area almost surrounded on three sides by Allen, Benner and Davis Is. As a naval officer, he distinguishes mooring from riding at anchor, swinging free to wind or swell in a

511

roadstead, and mooring which involves fixing her in one position in a harbour with more than one fastening, whether by anchors or by cables to fixed objects (trees in this sort of set-up) on the shore. To us it appears that *Archangell* moored in the harbour north of Allen Island precisely because she was not intended to swing freely but to be as close in, in a confined space, as was possible if Allen I. was to be the expedition's base. If she stayed in the roadstead, where Admiral Royall would have her, there was no need for her to moor. And we are convinced that when Waymouth was setting out on his expeditions to the mainland he took her out into the roadstead until he was about to set out and brought her back to anchor there when he returned before taking her into the enclosed harbour to be moored. Admiral Royall considers she was moored in the roadstead, instead of anchoring only, because Waymouth 'wanted to cover his landing with her guns. He had some expectation of encountering hostile natives when he landed and afterwards when he marched about the islands under arms'. This seems to us unjustified by anything in the text. The march round Allen Island was to give his men some military exercise in the sort of rough terrain they might encounter on the mainland and to 'show the flag', an annexation ceremony. Benner I. seemed to me, when Admiral and Mrs Royall took us to see it in 1970, a very inhospitable place compared with Allen I., but of course the vegetation cover has greatly changed and it is hard to be dogmatic. His views are certainly worth taking into account but they are far from being established. Fig. 31, opposite.

We give his suggested locations. No. 1 is where Waymouth sent Cam forward to find a roadstead or harbour. No. 2 is the roadstead where Admiral Royall says he moored and we consider he used as an occasional anchorage when arriving or departing. No. 3 is the present site of a substantial spring and pond of fresh water. No. 4 is W. F. Royall's choice of the place where Waymouth landed, completed his pinnace, and used as his land-base. We have placed No. 5 at the place where Burrage thought the *Archangell* was moored, and which we accept, and we would put his landing-place on the north shore of Allen Island, just below the bluff on which (under Burrage's influence) the memorial cross was placed in 1905.

We conclude this section, however, by allowing W. F. Royall his considered opinion:

As to the island where the wells were dug, the pinnace assembled and the cross erected, it would appear to be Burnt Island because of the little island adjoining. The cove where the abandoned Coast Guard Station stands is the

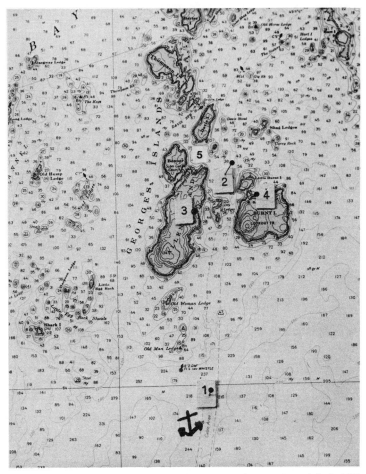

Fig. 31. Waymouth in the Georges Islands, according to Rear Admiral W. F. Royall's placings on the modern chart.

first landing place to be seen and would be passed close aboard by a vessel entering from the southward. Also the sandy beaches in the cove and on Little Burnt offer some of the few spots in the vicinity where a seine might be drawn. I would expect Waymouth to anchor within sight of his activities ashore in the event of attack.

The argument will probably continue. It is a small but, perhaps, significant issue.

Whaling

Correspondence with Philip F. Purrington of the Old Dartmouth Society's Whaling Museum at New Bedford, in 1975, about Indian whaling indicates considerable scepticism on his part about the capability of New England Indians to take large whales. We wondered outselves about the possibility that the Eastern Abenaki Indians were romancing about the whale hunts and feasts that Rosier describes. We have finally come to the conclusion that they are authentic and that the birch-bark canoe together with the multi-barbed harpoons, which are so plentifully found in Eastern Abenaki sites, and which are fairly formidable weapons, would enable whaling to take place. Mr Purrington, however, gives us a lesson on the Black Right Whale, *Balaena glacialis* L., which is up to sixty feet in length. This, he says, summers in the latitude of Iceland. Whales of this species then come to southern New England between 1 November and late January, and at times find difficulty in getting clear of Cape Cod, and sometimes are stranded there on their way south to winter quarters between Bermuda and South Carolina. From 1 March to early May they were on their way north, again sometimes having difficulty in getting past Long Island and Cape Cod where they were stranded. If they were stranded they could be and were exploited by the Indians for food and oil. He does not think they were close enough inshore to be found in the Gulf of Maine accessible to fleets of birch-bark canoes.

He states very firmly that 'the best works at my disposal indicate no artifacts of New England useful for the capture of whales nor any skeletal whale parts. Nor was the Indian dug-out or canoe a practical vessel for whale hunting.' We are entirely prepared to accept his views on the Southern New England Indians who were primarily agriculturalists and gatherers, but not, necessarily, about the Eastern Abenaki of Maine. They were hunters, whose fishing range extended as far out as Monhegan and the evidence for whose whaling activities appears to be good. Whaling by the Eastern Abenaki was acceptable to Wendell S. Hadlock who had a very long acquaintance with their canoes and their artifacts. It is accepted by Dean S. Snow in *Handbook of the North American Indians*, xv, and must, we think, now be taken as established. What is not established is that it was the Right Whale they caught and here Mr Purrington's views carry much weight. Precisely what cetacean – Killer Whale, Porpoise or whatever – must be left in some doubt for the present.

St George's Fort on the Kennebec River

The documents seem clear enough that George Popham entered the Kennebec River and chose the site for his fort round the first point on the left-hand side as he advanced upstream. Many other sites, nearby and farther away, have been suggested by local enthusiasts. But the site itself, especially when looked at in the light of John Hunt's plan, over the past eighty years has not seemed very adequate. It seems too small, too rocky, not in the least suitable for agriculture, though good enough for defensive purposes. Its choice, out of sight of possible French coasting vessels, its safety against attack except from the somewhat precipitous and wooded Sabino Head, seemed to be in its favour. The U.S. government built Fort Popham nearby before the Civil War and sited military installations (Fort Baldwin) twice in the twentieth century on Sabino Head, pushing construction vehicles through the western part of the site. Until their records have been examined, no details of the changes they made can be estimated. Two events of recent years are worth recording which bear on the site's feasibility as the 1607 fort. The first is that the National Park Service carried out excavations at the site between 1962 and 1964 (in that of 1964 our younger son, Roderick E. N. Quinn, took part) and the full, unpublished report is deposited in the Maine State Library, Archives Division, at Augusta, to which I am indebted for a copy.

'Fort St. George, Popham Colony', historical research by George Carey; archaeological report by Gardner Lane; project supervisor Wendell S. Hadlock (1966), pp. 68, contains most of what is known. On the historical side George Carey is able to call to his support an early record which is not widely known, that of Samuel Maverick, 'A description of New England', *New England Historical and Genealogical Register*, xxxix (1885), 34–5, which records his visit to the Sagadahoc site about 1624 when, he says, 'I found Rootes and Garden hearbs and some old Walles there, when I first went over which showed it to be the place where they had been.' Carey is sceptical, as I have suggested he need not necessarily have been (pp. 441–3 above), the fort plan representing what was actually built or in process of being completed on 8 October 1607, and yet he fits the plan neatly (too neatly in my opinion) to the present topography of the site. Their concluding assumptions (or their conclusions?) are:

1. The Hunt map is an authentic document which, though accurate

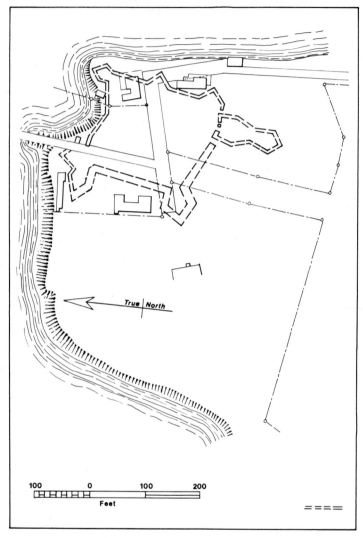

Fig. 32. Sketch of conjectural location of the 1607 fort on the ground 1966.

geographically, depicted the colonists' aspirations for a fort, not the fort itself.

2. The Popham colony was indeed established for a short time on Sabino Head and not in any of the other locations suggested by oral traditions.

3. Subsequent agricultural pursuits on Sabino Head, the activities of Fort Baldwin through two World Wars, and the process of natural erosion have obliterated any hope of locating a trace of the fort itself.

With this there is little to quarrel. But excavation is hampered by the existence of a number of houses on and near the point, by the cutting of a road through the lower part of the site, and the clearing away to bare rock (by erosion or excavation) of the upper or southern part of the site. Wendell Hadlock also recognised the erosion which took place from winds sweeping down the Kennebec itself and the removal of loose materials from the foreshore and its crumbling and removal into Atkins Bay over the longer period since the fort was in existence.

The archaeological effort was directed primarily, as Gardner Lane observes (with some elisions from his discussion) to unearth evidence of the

north-east wall of the fort...to discover a stream which was believed to have run through the site, and to excavate part of the southwest bastion. There was also an attempt to find the garden (or what appeared to be a garden) on the Hunt plan, at the western edge of the fort site. The stream was indeed located as it appears in the Hunt map, though it returned nothing in the way of artifacts, nor did any trace of the southwest bastion remain. This, and the excavation of a well, produced evidence of extensive nineteenth century agricultural activity. Indian and late European artifacts were recovered in some quantity. Of early modern European artifacts there were very few: the three more important ones, which may be reasonably dated to the time of the colony (or within a generation or so of it) are:

1. Lead bale seal used to seal bales of cloth. Similar to those excavated at Jamestown. Double X's probably mean 20 yards, while the other mark is the merchant's insignia.

2. Earthenware, in particular pan sherds of pinkish earthenware. Probably made in North Devon, England. Similar in body color and glaze to sherds of same origin found at Jamestown. Could be early 17th Century...Other western England wares were excavated.

3. 'Seal Head' of an English latten spoon – late 16th or early 17th Century: but could be as late as 1650.

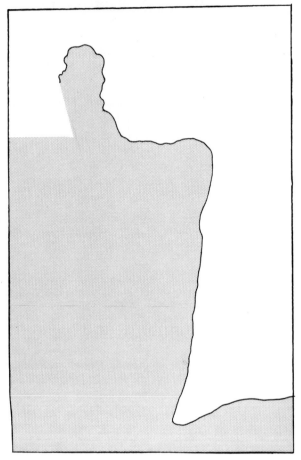

Fig. 33. Sketch of Hunniwell's Point, Kennebec River, by J. J. Lee, 1857.

The report concludes, however, that the actual fort cannot now be found, owing to subsequent human intervention.

A second development has been the examination of the topography at the time of the construction of Fort Popham. Andrew J. Wahll, of the cartographic Division of the National Geographic Society, has located a draft map of 'Hunniwell's Point', surveyed by J. J. Lee, for the U.S. Corps of Engineers (Fortifications File, National Archives,

Washington, D.C.) in 1857. A section of this shows a very much rounded shoulder to the point and a much larger land projection out into Atkins Bay than Thayer, using an 1891 map, was able to point to and this, in turn, enables the Hunt plan to be fitted much more plausibly to the then shorelines. Wahll concludes that the coastline appears to have changed less between 1607 and 1857 than between 1857 and 1891 or subsequently, and is inclined to attribute this to the removal of material for the construction of Fort Popham, which at that time was taking place a few hundred yards to the east. When his work is complete we will have a much more credible means of placing the Hunt plan on what was, probably, the then site and the adjacent shoreline. The removal of material from the shore may also have been accompanied by the excavation and scouring of the mainland, and consequently a major cause of the loss of 1607–8 artifacts, though some may still be found offshore.

MAPS OF NEW ENGLAND OF THE 1606–1610 PERIOD

THE SO-CALLED 'VELASCO MAP'

The origin of the Velasco Map, enclosed in a letter of Alonzo de Velasco to Philip III from London (Archivo General, Simancas, Estado 2588/25 (M.P. y D.I. 1)) on 22 March 1611, and named for its sender, has remained a mystery. It was clearly compiled by an Englishman who had an exceptionally up-to-date knowledge of the activities of the English, French and Dutch from Virginia, the Hudson Valley, New England, Acadia and the St Lawrence Valley. His sources for New England are not known. The map of Penobscot Bay and of the Penobscot River contains far more knowledge than the English ever accumulated during this period and the nomenclature is clearly French but it is far from being identical with the Champlain map of 1607, his printed map of 1612 (which deals with the coast southwestward from Acadia rather cursorily) or the map of 1616 (known only from the John Carter Brown Library copy), so another map of Champlain or even Lescarbot must be suggested as a source. The lower course of the Kennebec River is given by the name the English called it, 'R. Sagadahock', in 1606 perhaps or certainly 1607, but that for the upper course is near Champlain's, namely 'Cinebague' for 'R. de quinibeguy' of his 1616 map. Far to the south of the group of French names for islands in Penobscot Bay lies 'St Georges Banck', a shoal accompanied by four unnamed islands. It may be suggested that this derives from the lost Waymouth map of 1605 to which Rosier refers (p. 299), and that it has been moved very far to the east. What appears to be St George River is given a name 'Tahanock' which is not on any other map and it appears more like the Sheepscot River than the St George River, if it were not for the small islands off its mouth and one standing well to the south and named 'I. St George'. This we would expect to be Monhegan, discovered by Waymouth, but he also called the islands nearer the mainland, Allen Island and the rest, now known as the Georges Islands, by that name. 'C. Porpos', 'Ile Lobster' and

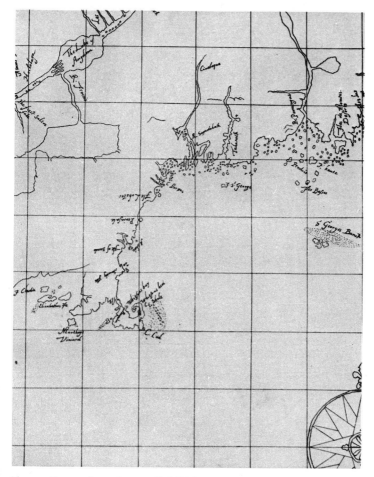

Fig. 34. Extract from the so-called 'Velasco Map', 1610, showing the area explored by the English 1602–1608.

'Peninsale' are not on any other map. Cape Porpoise appears to be Cape Elizabeth, Lobster I. Richmond I., and 'Peninsale' Cape Neddick, though the name might appear to be taken from the French. We then have on the Massachusetts coast, not very helpfully, 'A shole', 'Isle of Sands' and 'Sandy Isle', the last apparently for Cape Ann. These could have come from any voyage between Gosnold and Hanham. There is a strong suspicion that the river names in Maine come from a lost map compiled on the Hanham–Pring voyage, but they could well have emerged from the 1607–8 colony, the *Mary and John* sailing southwest to Richmond Island (p. 437) and a number of expeditions having gone up the Kennebec, those we know of in 1607 and others merely hinted at in 1608 (pp. 335–6, 409–12, 440–1). For Cape Cod Bay however the map clearly depends on Pring, with 'Whitsons Bay' for Cape Cod Bay, and 'Whitsons head' for Cape Cod, the map helping by its shape to suggest the winding-like-a-snail effect which indicates Provincetown Bay as his landing place. Outside the Lower Cape we have 'C: Shole' and a very large shoal marked all the way down to Monomoy Point, which has Gosnolds 1602 name for it, 'C. Cod'. It might seem that the shoals are in reality those south of Monomoy Point, since the waters off the Lower Cape shelve rather rapidly and, though there are shoals before Monomoy Point is reached, the really dangerous shoals are those guarding the entrance to Nantucket Sound. We are inclined to attribute this feature to a misreading of a map brought home by Gosnold. The length and the deep indentations of the Upper Cape, with a long shoal extending southwest at one point, strongly suggest Archer's narrative, which has given so much difficulty. There is no Nantucket as we would expect and 'Martheys Viniard' lies at the opening of a passage to the west, only a small shoal being indicated on its western side and no division into a larger and smaller island made (which is what we would expect once the name had been transferred from Capoag to Capawack, Martha's Vineyard as we know it (pp. 500–2)). The Elizabeth Islands are set at some distance to the north of their actual position and are well inside Buzzards Bay. The long shoal correctly appears extending from 'Elizabethes Ile', and the island itself is on a scale strongly suggestive of the then union of Cuttyhunk and Nashawena (Fig. 3, p. 119) while Naushon I. appears in its correct relative position. Rocks, two small islands, one Penikeet, and the other perhaps 'Haps Hill' (Fig. 6, p. 131) are on the unnamed and uncompleted Buzzards Bay, while to the west 'I Claudia', Verrazzano's old name for Block Island, appears with no hint of an opening into Narragansett Bay in between. Clearly then the compiler had a number of maps, possibly mere sketches and also narratives, before him and he made the best of them, giving us a remarkable if not wholly complete or entirely correct depiction of the New England coast. It fits in by and large with the narratives, though less well with Waymouth's than with the Brereton–Archer and Pring accounts, but it leaves open the question of who made what between 1606 and 1608, but with a strengthened supposition that Hanham and Pring were responsible for some of it since the 1607 colony was directed so firmly to the Kennebec River and not the St George River as Waymouth and Rosier had urged. How the French material on the east and north came in is a complete mystery, as is the knowledge shown of Hudson's discovery of the river bearing his name to the west. The Virginia materials clearly came, in some way, from John Smith. Henry Hudson, himself, moving about between Dutch and English, and noting some French materials on the way, could have had something to do with it before he set out on his last disastrous voyage, but there is so far not the slightest evidence that he did. Velasco's supplier was probably the same person who supplied the plan of Fort St George to his predecessor, Pedro de Zúñiga, but no hint of his identity has been found, though he must have been closely associated with the Virginia Company and also with the members of the pre-1606 ventures.

NOMENCLATURE FOR NORTHEASTERN NORTH AMERICA: NORTH TO SOUTH

Isles des Sauvages (not on Champlain 1607)
Iles de Montes Deserts (1607 Champlain, Mont Desert)
R. Pemetogat (Pentigoet, do.)
I. Haute (Isle haute, do.)
Penduis (Isles Perdier, do.)
Isles Basses (not on Champlain, 1607)
S Georges Banck (1605, Waymouth?)
Tahanock (1606, Hanham?)
Cinebague (1606, Hanham?)
R. Sagadahock (1606 Hanham?)
I. St George (1605 Waymouth)
C. Porpos (1606 Hanham?)
Isle Lobster (1606 Hanham?)
Peninsale (1606 Hanham?)
A shole (not specific)
Sandy Isle (not specific)
Whitsons bay (1603, Pring)
Whitsons hed (1603, Pring)
C. Shole (not specific)
C. Cod (1602, Gosnold)

Penquin (1602, Gosnold)
Martheys Viniard (1602, Gosnold)
Elizabethes Ile (1602, Gosnold)
I. Claudia (1524, Verrazzano)

Sources

(1) Gosnold
(2) Pring
(3) Waymouth
(4) Hanham (or 1607–8 colonists)
(5) Champlain, 1607
(6) An otherwise unknown French (or other) version of a Champlain map. R. de Pemetegit; R. de quinibequy, and R. de Chouacoit are on Champlain's map of 1616 (published by the John Carter Brown Library, with an introduction by Lawrence C. Wroth, in 1956, and reprinted in Champlain, *Works* (Toronto, 1970), portfolio, after Pl. LXXXII).
(7) A map retaining older Verrazzanian features (e.g. 'I. Claudia,' in C. Wytfliet (1597), *NAW*, V, Map no. 131).

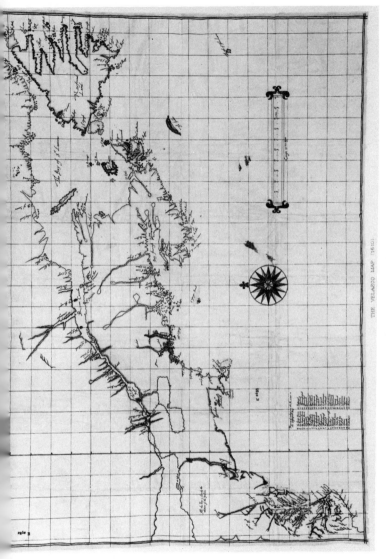

Fig. 35. The so-called 'Velasco Map', 1610.

'THE VIRGINIA CHART'

'The Virginia Chart' owes it name to a former owner, I. N. Phelps Stokes, from whose collections it came into the New York Public Library. It is of much less interest and importance than the Velasco map, but is the only other one of the period between 1600 and 1616 covering the area with which we are concerned (and much besides). It gives the impression of being a routine professional job by one of the commercial cartographers of the Thames School who were emerging at that time. It has material from many sources but for eastern North America it uses it perfunctorily: its Virginia is a mere outline, but showing a slight acquaintance with the maps being made of it by Smith and others in 1608 and later. It does show a large river which could well be the Hudson but it could possibly even be the traditional Rio de Gamas, the Penobscot, wildly out of place. If it is the Hudson we should date the map 1610, if not then 1608 would be more likely. What it does show is the Upper and Lower Cape, with 'Cape Cod' intermediately between Cape Cod and Monomoy Point. It also has something on Gosnold's discoveries on and to the south and southwest of the Upper Cape, a somewhat larger island for Martha's Vineyard and two small islands, mere pinpoints, for the Elizabeth Islands, but with no names. It therefore made use of maps or sketches brought back by Gosnold and possibly Pring, the former being possibly the same, though used perfunctorily, as that used for the Velasco Map. For the Maine coast it has only a number of undifferentiated inlets with offshore islands, and on one of the smaller rivers the name 'Sagdo Hok', again showing a nodding acquaintance with sketches brought back from the Maine coast, 1606–8, but not employing them to any effective purpose. French names are given for a few places in Acadia and farther north, while Canada appears as the name of the land dividing the Maine Rivers from those flowing into the St Lawrence, the name 'Nova Francia' being confined to the land north and northwest of the St Lawrence River.

The maps which survive can only be a relatively minor supplement to the narratives, though the Velasco Map has a few major features. John Smith's map of New England in 1616 did not venture south and west beyond Monomoy Point (which he leaves in some suspense), but for the coast to the north he gave much more information of a reliable character, though on the printed map he had covered the older names with new English ones chosen by Prince Charles, though most of the Indian names often survive in his text. With him, however, we come an important stage nearer towards seeing New England as such and as a whole.

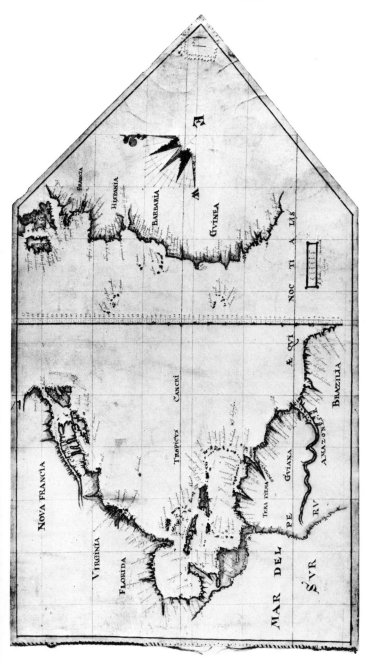

Fig. 36. The so-called 'Virginia Chart', c. 1610.

BIBLIOGRAPHY

Manuscript Sources

1. Public Record Office

CO 1/1,15. 13 Mar. 1607. Sir F. Gorges to H. Challons.
CO 1/1,16. 13 Dec. 1607. G. Popham to James I.
SP 14/28,34. 18 Aug. 1607. D. Carleton to J. Chamberlain.
SP 63/223,64. 5 Apr. 1608. Sir R. Bingley to E. of Salisbury.
C2, James I, G 1/26. Chancery cases between A. Jennings and Sir F. Gorges, 1608–15.
HCA 1/46. 13 Nov. 1605. Deposition of W. Parker.
HCA 1/46. 29 Apr. 1607. Deposition of R. Bulkeley.
HCA 3/27. 12 May–23 June. Popham *contra* Havercombe, proceedings.
HCA 13/38. 13–14 Feb. Depositions of M. Sutcliffe, J. Barlee, W. Wallis, E. Litheby.
HCA 13/38. 16 Feb. Deposition of Nicholas Hind.
HCA 13/38. 3 Sept. Deposition of R. Bamford.
HCA 13/39. 10 June 1608. Depositions of L. Booker, J. Deaman, T. Savage, J. Fletcher.
HCA 13/39. 23 June. Deposition of J. Elliott.
HCA 13/91. 7 June 1608. Personal answer of J. Havercombe.
HCA 14/38,6. 26 May 1606. Passport for Sir R. Bingley and A. Chambers.
HCA 14/38,65. 3 Nov. 1606. Commission for arrest of *Triall*.
HCA 14/38,19. 19 Feb. 1607. Exemplification by E. of Nottingham in case of *Richard*.
HCA 14/39,196. 3 Jan. 1607. Circular letter by R. Roche.
HCA 24/67, between 4 and 5. 19 Sept. 1599. Inventory of *Diamond*.
HCA 24/72,97. 3 Sept. 1607. Interrogatories for R. Bamford.
HCA 24/73,449. 1608. Allegation by John Havercombe.
HCA 24/73,443. 23 June 1608. Sentence in Popham *contra* Havercombe.

2. British Library, Reference Division

Egerton MS 2395, ff. 412–13 v. [E. Harlow]. 'The names of the Rivers.'
Additional MS 15208, ff. 510–11. 9 May 1600. Nottingham to Caesar.
Additional MS 19889. George Waymouth, 'The Jewell of Artes'.
Sloane MS 1622. William Strachey, 'The historie of trauaile into Virginia Britannia'.
Sloane MS 1447. Pamphlets by R. Hakluyt, the elder, 1578, and D. Ingram, 1583.
Harley MS 6792, f. 126. 7 June 1607. Sir F. Bacon's report to the House of Commons.

3. Lambeth Palace Library

MS 806, no. 14, ff. 1–12. [Robert Davies], 'A Voyage into New-England.'

4. Bodleian Library

Ashmole MS 1758. William Strachey, 'The historie of trauaile into Virginia Britania.'

5. West Devon Record Office, Plymouth

Plymouth City Records.

MS W360/18. 11 June 1606. Corporation of Plymouth to Sir J. Popham.

MS W360/89. [20 Nov. 1606]. Orders for the colony of Virginia.

MS W359/54. 17 Feb. 1609. Council for Virginia to Corporation of Plymouth.

6. Devon Record Office, Exeter

Exeter City Records, Chamber Act Book, 1601–11, p. 208. Proceedings on Virginia.

7. Bristol Records Department

Bristol City Records, Common Council Book II, 12 Mar., 1 Apr. Proceedings on Virginia.

8. Ipswich Public Library

Transcripts of parish registers. Register of Sproughton, Suffolk, 1540–1771.

9. Lancashire County Record Office, Preston

Documents by Queen Elizabeth for Waymouth to take on his 1602 voyage to Asia.

10. Stonyhurst College, Lancashire

MS Anglia III, no. 53. 8/18 March 1605. Robert Persons S.J. to Tristram Winslade.

11. Marquess of Salisbury, Hatfield House.

Cecil Papers

CP 94/160. 21 Aug. 1602. Sir Walter Ralegh to Sir Robert Cecil.

CP 115/89. 4 Feb. 1607. Relation of Daniel Tucker.

CP 116/39. 10 May 1606. William Mathewe to the earl of Salisbury.

CP 116/40. 10 May 1606. Sir Ferdinando Gorges to the earl of Salisbury.

CP 120/66. 7 Feb. 1608. Gorges to Salisbury.

CP 120/130. 20 March 1608. Gorges to Salisbury.

CP 121/65. 31 May 1607. Capt. George Popham to the earl of Salisbury.

CP 123/77. 1 Dec. 1607. Gorges to Salisbury.

CP 191/120. [Dec. 1605 or Jan. 1606]. Sir Walter Cope to the earl of Salisbury.

CP 192/96. William Udall to the earl of Salisbury.

12. Washington, D.C. U.S. National Archives.

Corps of Engineers, Fortifications File.

13. Washington, D.C. Library of Congress, Geography and Map Division.

Samuel de Champlain. MS map of Northeastern North America, 1607.

14. Washington, D.C. Smithsonian Institution, Department of Anthropology.

Report, Call no. 1118, 11 July 1973, by Martha Goodway and R. M. Organ, 'Copper beads from the Titicut site' (Conservation Laboratory, U.S. National Museum).

15. Augusta, Maine. State Library, Archives Division.

George Carey and Gardner Lane 'Fort St. George, Popham Colony', Typescript, 1966.

16. Cambridge, Massachusetts. Harvard University Library.

George Prince's 'Waymouth' (1860), with anonymous MS notes for a new edition of Rosier's *True relation* (1605).

17. Boston. Massachusetts Historical Society

Jeremy Belknap Papers. Copy of Thomas's *Almanack* for 1797, with Belknap's diary of his visit to the Elizabeth Islands.

Jeremy Belknap Papers, 61C. 15 Nov. 1797. J. Thaxter to J. Belknap.

18. Worcester, Mass. American Antiquarian Society

Department of Manuscripts. Letter from Commander S. O. Blake, U.S.N., to Samuel Foster Haven, 2 Sept. 1868.

Department of Graphic Arts. William A. Goodwin, Plan of Gosnold's Fort on Elizabeth Island, 1868 (formerly enclosed in the preceding item).

19. Edgartown, Martha's Vineyard, Mass. Court House

Deeds, volumes I, II & VI.

20. Edgartown, Dukes County Historical Society

Warner F. Gookin Papers.

21. New York, Public Library

'Virginia Chart', *c.* 1610 (I. N. P. Stokes Collection).

22. Charlotteville, Va. University of Virginia, Alderman Library

Rich Papers (Tracy McGregor Collection) (1) 30 October 1605. Agreement between George Waymouth and Sir John Zouche. (2) 1611. Commission by Sir James Bond to George Waymouth to have a ship built for him. [Formerly deposited by the duke of Manchester in the P.R.O.]

23. Simancas. Archivo General

Estado 843, no. 4. 21 May 1606. Decision of Consejo de Indias on Virginia.

Estado Inglatierra 2586, f. 147. 8 Oct. 1607. John Hunt's plan of St. George's Fort on the Kennebec R.

Estado Inglatierra 2588/25 (M.P. y I. 1). [22 March 1611] 'Velasco' Map of Eastern North America [1610].

PRINTED WORKS

Abbott, R. Tucker. *American seashells*. N.Y. 1954.

Adney, E. T. and Chappelle, H. L. 'The bark canoes and skin boats of North America', Smithsonian Institution, National Museum, *Bulletin* 230 (1964), 1–242.

Aiton, Arthur. 'The impact of the flora and fauna of the New World upon the Old World during the sixteenth century,' *Biologia*, II (1950–5), 121–6. (Chronica Botanica, 12, nos. 4–6.)

Allen, Glover M. 'Whales on the coast of New England,' Boston Society for Natural History, *Memoirs*, VIII, pt. 2 (1916).

'Domesticated dogs of the American aborigines', Museum of Comparative Zoology, *Bulletin*, LXIII (Cambridge, Mass., 1920), 431–517.

'List of the *Aves*', *Fauna of New England*, pt. 3 (1904). Boston Society of Natural History, *Occasional Papers* 7.

'List of the *Mammalia*', *Fauna of New England*, pt. 11 (1909).

Andrews, Charles M. *The colonial period of American history* (4 vols. 1934–8), I (New Haven, 1934).

Andrews, Kenneth R. *Elizabethan privateering*. Cambridge, 1964.
  English privateering voyages to the West Indies 1589–95. Cambridge, 1959.
  Hakluyt Soc. 2nd ser. 111.
  'English voyages to the Caribbean, 1596 to 1604: an annotated list', *William and Mary Quarterly*, XXX (1974), 250–2.
  The Spanish Caribbean, 1530–1630. London and New Haven, 1978.
Andrews, K. R., Canny, N. P. and Hair, P. E. H., ed. *The western enterprise*. Liverpool, 1978; Detroit, 1979.
Anstruther, Godfrey, O. P. *The seminary priests, 1603–1659*. 1977.
Arber, Edward, ed. *A transcript of the registers of the Company of Stationers of London 1554–1640 A.D.* 5 vols. Birmingham. 1875–94.
Archer, Gabriel. 'The relation of Captaine Gosnols Voyage to the North part of Virginia, begunne the sixe and twentieth of March, Anno 42. Elizabethae Reginae 1602', Samuel Purchas, *Hakluytus posthumus, or Purchas his Pilgrimes*, IV, (1625), 1647–51.
  Bartholomeus Gosnols reys van Engeland na het norder gedeelte van Virginien. anno 1602. Leiden, Pieter van der Aa. 1706.
  'The relation of Captain Gosnold's voyage', Massachusetts Historical Society *Collections*, 3rd ser. VIII (1843), 72–81.
  The relation of Captaine Gosnols voyage to the north part of Virginia. Boston, 1902. Old South Leaflets, General Series, V, no. 120.
  'The relation of Captaine Gosnold's Voyage', in H. S. Burrage, *English and French voyages 1534–1608*. N.Y. 1906. Pp. 330–9.
  'The relation of Captain Gosnols voyage to the north part of Virginia', in Charles H. Levermore, *Forerunners and competitors of the Pilgrims and Puritans*, I (Brooklyn, N.Y. 1912), 43–54.
Bailey, Liberty H. 'Genus Rubus', *Gentes Herberum. Occasional papers on the kinds of plants*, V, fasc. 1–7 (Ithaca, N.Y., 1941, 1943, 1944).
  Manual of cultivated plants. N.Y. 1924.
Baker, William A. *Colonial vessels*. Barre, Mass. 1962.
  'Notes on a shallop', *American Neptune*, XVII (1957), 105–6.
  'Gosnold's *Concord* and her Shallop', *American Neptune*, XXXIV (1947), 231–42.
  Sloops and shallops. Barre, Mass. 1966.
Ballard, Edward, ed. *Popham memorial volume*. Portland, Me, 1860.
Banks, Charles E. 'Capowack. Is it the correct Indian name for Martha's Vineyard?', *New England Historical and Genealogical Register*, LII (1898), 176–80.
  'Martin's or Martha's Vineyard? What is the proper nomenclature?', *New England Historical and Genealogical Register*, XLVIII (1894), 201–4, 468–9.
  The history of Martha's Vineyard. 3 vols. Boston, 1911. Repr. Edgartown, Mass., 1966.
  'New documents relating to the Popham expedition, 1607', American Antiquarian Society, *Proceedings*, XXXIX (1929), 307–33.
Barbour, Philip L., ed. *The Jamestown voyages under the first charter*. 2 vols. Hakluyt Soc. 2nd ser. 136–7. 1969.
Baxter, James Phinney, ed. *The life and letters of Sir Ferdinando Gorges*. 3 vols. Boston, 1890. Prince Society Publications 18–20. Repr. N.Y. 1967.

ed. *The Trelawney papers*. Portland, Me, 1884. Maine Historical Society, Documentary History of Maine, III.

Beck, Horace Palmer. *The American Indian as a sea fighter*. Mystic, Conn., 1959.

Belknap, Jeremy. *American biography*. 2 vols. Boston, 1794–8.

Bigelow, Henry B., 'Physical oceanography of the Gulf of Maine', U.S. Board of Fisheries, *Bulletin* 40, pt. 2 (1928).

Bigelow, Henry B. and Schroder, William C. *Fishes of the Gulf of Maine*. U.S. Board of Fisheries, *Bulletin* 74 (1953).

Biggar, Henry P., ed. Samuel de Champlain, *Works*. 6 vols. and portfolio. Toronto, 1922–36. Champlain Society Pubns. new. ser. 1–6, and portfolio. Repr. Toronto, 1971. 7 vols.

Bliss, William R. *Colonial times in Buzzard's Bay*. New ed. Boston, 1900.

Blomefield, Francis. *An essay towards a topographical history of the County of Norfolk*. 2nd ed. 11 vols. 1805–10.

Bolton, Charles K. *The real founders of New England, 1602–1628*. Boston, 1929. *Terra Nova: the northeast coast of America before 1602*. Boston, 1935.

Bourne, William. *A regiment for the sea*. Thomas Hacket, 1574. STC 3422. Further editions [1576?], 1577, 1580, 1584, 1587, 1594. STC 3423–6. Newly corrected by Thomas Hood, 1596. STC 3427.

A regiment of the sea, ed. Eva G. R. Taylor. Hakluyt Society, 2nd ser. no. 121. 1963.

Bovill, E. W. *The golden trade*. 2nd ed. 1965.

Bradford, William. *History of Plymouth Plantation*, ed. Charles W. Bradford. Boston, 1912.

Of Plymouth Plantation, ed. Samuel E. Morison, N.Y. 1952.

Braun, Emma Lucy. *Deciduous forests of eastern North America*. Philadelphia, 1950.

Breder, Charles M. *Field-book of the marine fishes of the Atlantic coast*. N.Y., 1929. New ed. 1948.

Brereton, John. *A briefe and true relation of the discouerie of the north part of Virginia*. Imp. George Bishop, 1602. STC 3610.

A briefe and true relation... *With diuers instructions of speciall moment newly added in this second impression*. Imp. G. Bishop, 1602. STC 3611.

A briefe and true relation. First edition. Facsimile reprint. Supplement to *The Bibliographer*, 1 (N.Y. 1902).

A briefe and true relation. First edition. Facsimile with introduction by L. S. Livingston. N.Y. 1903.

A briefe and true relation [reprint of 2nd ed.]. Massachusetts Historical Society, *Collections*, 3rd ser. VIII (1843), 83–123.

A briefe and true relation. [Brereton narrative only], in G. P. Winship, *Sailors' narratives* (1905), pp. 31–50.

A briefe and true relation. [Brereton narrative only], in H. S. Burrage, *English and French voyages* (1906), pp. 325–40.

A briefe and true relation. [Brereton narrative only], in C. H. Levermore, *Forerunners and Competitors of the Pilgrims and Puritans*, 1 (1912), 31–41.

'A briefe and true relation' [Brereton narrative only], ed. H. F. Howe, *Massachusetts Archaeological Bulletin*, 1 (no. 4, 1940).

'A briefe and true relation' [Brereton narrative only], in Quinn, *New American World*, III (1979), 347–52.

Bridenbaugh, Carl. *Vexed and troubled Englishmen*. N.Y. 1968; rev. ed. 1971.

Britton, Nathaniel L. and Brown, Addison. *An illustrated flora of the northern United States, Canada and the British possessions.* 3 vols. 3rd edition. N.Y. 1936.

Britton, Nathaniel L., Brown, Addison and Gleason, Henry A. *The new Britton and Brown illustrated flora of the northeast United States and adjacent Canada.* N.Y. 1952.

Brown, Alexander. *The genesis of the United States.* 2 vols. N.Y. 1890; London, 1891; repr. N.Y. 1965.

Burrage, Henry S., ed. *Early English and French Voyages, 1534–1608.* N.Y. 1906; repr. 1969.

Gorges and the grant of the province of Maine, 1622. A tercentenary memorial. Printed for the state of Maine, 1923.

ed. *Rosier's Relation of Waymouth's voyage to the coast of Maine in 1605.* Portland, Me, 1887. Gorges Society Publications.

The beginnings of colonial Maine. Portland, Me, 1914.

Burton, R. J. 'Zouche of Codnor', Derbyshire Archaeological and Natural History Society, *Journal*, XXXI (1909), 35–8.

Bushnell, David I., Jr. 'New England names', *American Anthropologist*, XIII (1911), 235–8.

Butler, Eva and Hadlock, Wendell S. *A preliminary survey of the Musungan–Allagash waterways.* Robert Abbe Museum. 1962.

'Uses of birchbark in the northeast', Robert Abbe Museum, *Bulletin*, VII (1957).

'Some uses of birch bark in northern New England', Massachusetts Archaeological Society, *Bulletin*, XVIII (1957), 72–5.

'Dogs of the northeastern woodland Indians', Massachusetts Archaeological Society, *Bulletin*, X (1949), 17–36.

Byers, Douglas S. and Johnson, Frederick. 'Two sites on Martha's Vineyard', Robert S. Peabody Foundation, *Papers* (Andover, Mass. 1940).

Campeau, Lucien, S.J. *La première mission d'Acadie (1602–1616).* Monumenta Novae Franciae, 1. Rome, Monumenta Hist. Soc. Iesu; Montreal, Presses de l'Université Laval. 1967.

Canny, Nicholas P. *The Elizabethan conquest of Ireland; a pattern established.* Dublin, 1976.

Carew, Richard. *The suruey of Cornwall.* S. S[tafford] for J. Jaggard, 1602. STC 4615.

Carr, Archie F. *Handbook of turtles.* Ithaca, N.Y. 1952.

Caton, John D. *The antelope and deer of America.* 2nd ed. Boston, 1881.

Caulfield, Richard, ed. *The council book of Kinsale.* Guildford, Surrey, 1879.

Cell, Gillian T. *English activity in Newfoundland, 1577–1660.* Toronto, 1969.

Chamberlain, Barbara B. *These fragile outposts; a geological look at Cape Cod, Martha's Vineyard, and Nantucket.* Garden City, N.Y. (for American Museum of Natural History), 1964.

Champlain, Samuel de. *Les voyages.* Paris, Jean Borjon, 1613.

Works, ed. H. P. Biggar. Toronto, 1922–36. Champlain Society, new ser. I–VI, plus portfolio; repr. 7 vols. Toronto, 1971.

Chapin, Henry and Smith, F. G. W. *The ocean river.* N.Y. 1952.

Chapin, Howard M. *Sachems of the Narragansetts.* Providence, 1931. Rhode Island Historical Society.

Cheyney, Edward P. *History of England from the defeat of the Armada to the death of Queen Elizabeth.* 2 vols. 1914–33.

Chiapelli, Fredi, ed. *First images of America.* 2 vols. Berkeley and Los Angeles, 1976; repr. 1979.

Chute, Newton E. *Geology of the coastline between Point Gammon and Monomoy Point, Cape Cod, Massachusetts.* Boston, 1939.

Clapham, Arthur, Tutin, T. G. and Warburg, E. F. *Flora of the British Isles.* 2nd ed. Cambridge, 1962.

Cokayne, George E. *The complete peerage.* Ed. Vicary Gibbs. 13 vols. 1910–59.

Collinson, Patrick. *Archbishop Grindal, 1519–1583.* 1980.

Conant, Roger. *A field guide to reptiles and amphibians.* Boston, 1975.

Coon, Nelson, 'Sassafras', *Dukes County Intelligencer,* xv (Edgartown, Mass. 1974), 119–29.

Cooper, C. H. and T. *Athenae Cantabrigienses.* 2 vols. Cambridge, 1858–1913.

Copinger, Walter A. *County of Suffolk.* 5 vols. 1904–5. Index. By N. B. Copinger. Manchester, 1907.

Council of New England. 'Records of the Council of New England', American Antiquarian Society, *Proceedings, 1865–7* (1867), 53–181. (Proceedings for 24 April 1867.)

A briefe relation of the discouery and plantation of New-England: and of sundry accidents therein occurring, from the yeere of our Lorde M.DC.VI to this present M.DC.XXII. J. Haviland, sold by W. Bladen, 1622. STC 18483.

Crapo, William W. 'Remarks by William W. Crapo on Gosnold's voyage' Massachusetts Historical Society, *Proceedings,* 2nd ser. xvi (1903), 247–9.

Crosby, Everett U. *Nantucket in print.* Nantucket, Mass. 1946.

Cumming, W. P., Skelton, R. A. and Quinn, D. B. *The discovery of America.* 1971.

[Davies, Robert?]. 'The Relation of a voyage, unto New England. Began from the Lizard, the first of June 1607.' In B. F. De Costa, 'The Sagadahoc colony', Massachusetts Historical Society, *Collections,* 1st ser. xviii (1880), 82–117.

'The relation...' Henry O. Thayer, ed. *The Sagadahoc colony.* Gorges Society Pubns. 4. Portland Me, 1892.

'The relation...' In C. P. Winship, *Sailors' voyages* (1905), 153–77.

'The relation...' In H. S. Burrage, *Early English and French voyages* (1906), pp. 395–419.

'The relation...' In C. H. Levermore, *Forerunners and competitors of the Pilgrims,* i (1912), 352–381.

'The relation...' In Quinn, *New American world,* iii (1979), 429–37.

Davis, William M. *Geographical essays.* Ed. Douglas W. Johnson, 1909; repr. 1954.

Day, Gordon M. 'Western Abenaki', in *Handbook of the American Indian,* xv (1978), 148–59.

'English–Indian contacts in New England', *Ethnohistory,* ix (1962), 24–40.

'The Indian as an ecological factor in the northeastern forest', *Ecology,* xxxiv (1953), 329–46.

Deane, C. and Woods, L., ed., Richard Hakluyt, *A discourse on western planting.* Cambridge Mass. 1877.

De Costa, Benjamin Franklin. *Ancient Norumbega.* Albany, 1890.

'Gosnold and Pring', *New England Historical and Genealogical Register*, XXXII (1878), 79–80.

Cabo de Baxos, or the place of Cape Cod in the old cartology. N.Y. 1881.

'The Prings of Awliscombe, Devonshire, England', *New England Historical and Geneological Register*, XLI (1887), 86–8.

'The Sagadahoc colony', Massachusetts Historical Society, *Collections*, VIII (1880), 82–117.

Denys, Nicolas. *Description and natural history of the coast of North America (Acadia)*. Ed. W. F. Ganong. Toronto, 1908. Champlain Society 2.

Dexter, Lincoln A. *The Gosnold discoveries...1602*. Brookfield, Mass., 1982.

Diamond, Sigmund, 'Norumbega: New England's Xanadu', *American Neptune*, XI (1951), 95–107.

Ditmars, Raymond L. *A field book of American snakes*. N.Y. 1939; repr. 1948.

Dodge, Ernest S. and Hadlock, Wendell S. *A canoe from the Penobscot River*. Salem, Mass. 1951.

Driver, Harold E. and Massey, William C., *Comparative studies of North American Indians*. American Philosophical Society, *Transactions*, XLVII, pt. 2 (Philadelphia, 1957).

Eames, Aled. *Ships and seamen of Anglesey*. Llangefni, 1973.

Eckstorm, Fannie H., 'The handicrafts of the modern Indians of Maine', Abbe Museum, *Bulletin*, 3 (1932).

'The Indians of Maine,' in Louis C. Hatch, ed., *Maine; a history*, I (N.Y. 1919), 43–64.

Indian place-names of the Penobscot valley and the Maine coast. Orono, Me, 1941. University of Maine, *Bulletin* 44.

Old John Neptune. Portland, Me, 1945.

Eden, Richard. *The decades of the newe world or West India*. I. Iug in aed G. Powell, 1555. STC 645–8.

Edwards, Edward. *The life of Sir Walter Ralegh with his letters*. 2 vols. 1860.

Elvin, Joseph B. *The fishes of Martha's Vineyard*. Edgartown, Mass. Dukes County Historical Society.

Emerson, Amelia F. *Early history of Naushon Island*. Privately printed, 1935.

Felter, Harvey W. *The genesis of the American materia medica*. Cincinnati, Ohio, 1927. Lloyd Library of Botany, *Bulletin* 26.

Fernald, M. L., 'The Portland catalogue of Maine plants', Portland Society of Natural History, *Proceedings*, II, pt. 2 (1892), 41–72, pt. 3 (1895), 73–96, pt. 4 (1897), 123–37.

Fernald, Merritt Lyndon, ed. *Gray's manual of botany*. 8th ed. N.Y. 1950.

Fernald, M. L. and Kinsey, Alfred Charles. *Edible plants of North America*. N.Y. 1943.

Fernald, M. L., Kinsey, A. C. and Rollins, Reed C. *Edible plants of North America*. 2nd ed. N.Y. 1958.

Fernández de Oviedo y Valdes, Gonzalo. *De la natural hystoria de las Indias*. Toledo, 1526.

Fidalgo de Elvas. *Relaçam verdadeira dos trabalhos q̃ hõ gouernador dõ Fernãdo d'Souto*. Evora, Andree de Burgos, 1557.

Virginia richly valued, translated by Richard Hakluyt. F. Kyngston for M. Lownes. 1609. STC 22938.

True relation of the hardships suffered by Governor Fernando de Soto, edited and translated by James A. Robertson. 2 vols. De Land, Fla., 1932–3. Florida State Historical Society.

'True relation of the hardships suffered by Governor Fernando do Soto', in D. B. Quinn, ed., *New American World*, II (1979), 97–158.

Flannery, Regina. *An analysis of coastal Algonquian culture.* Washington, D.C., 1939. Catholic University of America, Anthropological Series 7.

Fobes, Charles B. *Climatic divisions of Maine.* Orono, Me, 1946.

Foley, Henry, S.J. *English records of the society of Jesus.* 1875.

Forbush, Edward H. and May, John Richard. *Natural history of the birds of eastern and central North America.* N.Y. 1939; repr. 1955.

Foster, Joseph. *Alumni Oxonienses.* 4 vols. Oxford, 1891–2.

Fotherby, Martin, Bp: *Atheomastix clearing foure truthes against atheists.* N. Okes, 1622. STC 11205.

Fry, E. A. *Bristol wills.* 1897. British Record Society 17.

Galvão, Antonio. *Tradado…dos diuersos & desuayrados caminhos, por onde nos tempos passados a pimento i especaria viejo de India as nossas.* Lisbon, Ioam da Barreira, 1563.

The discoueries of the world, vnto the yeere 1555, translated by Richard Hakluyt. George Bishop, 1601. STC 11543.

Gatchet, Albert S., 'The Timucua language', American Philosophical Society, *Proceedings*, XVI (1876–7), 626–42, XVII (1877–8), 499–504, XVIII (1878–80), 465–502.

G.E.C. *see* Cokayne, G. E.

Gerard, John. *The herball.* E. Bollifant for B. and J. Norton, 1597. STC 11750.

Catalogus arborum, fruticum ac plantarum tam indigenarum quam exoticarum in horto J.G.…nescantium. ex officio R. Robinson, 1596. STC 11748. Another ed. A. Hatfield, imp. J. Norton, 1599. STC 11749.

A catalogue of the plants cultivated in the garden of John Gerard in the years, 1596 to 1599. Ed. B. D. Jackson. 1876.

Gleason, Henry A. *The new Britton and Brown illustrated flora.* 1952. See Britton, Nathaniel L.

Gleason, Henry A. and Cronquist, Arthur. *Manual of vascular plants of northeastern United States and adjacent Canada.* Princeton, 1963.

Godfrey, W. Earl. *Birds of Canada.* Ottawa, 1966.

Goodale, George L. 'New England plants seen by the earliest colonists,' Colonial Society of Massachusetts, *Publications*, III (1896), 180–94.

Goodspeed, Thomas H. *The genus Nicotiana.* Waltham, Mass., 1954. Chronica Botanica 16.

Gookin, Warner F. 'The first leaders at Jamestown', *Virginia Magazine of History and Biography*, LVIII (1950), 181–93.

Capawack. Edgartown, Mass. Dukes County Historical Society. 1947.

'Who was Bartholomew Gosnold?', *William and Mary Quarterly*, 3rd ser. VI (1949), 410–15.

'Notes on the Gosnold family', *Virginia Magazine of History and Biography*, LVII (1949), 312–14.

A voyage of discovery to the southern parts of Norumbega. Edgartown, Mass. 1950.

'Family connections of Bartholomew Gosnold', *New England Historical and Genealogical Register*, CIV (1950), 27–36.

'The ancestry of Bartholomew Gosnold', *New England Historical and Genealogical Register*, CV (1951), 5–22.

Gookin, Warner F. and Barbour, Philip L. *Bartholomew Gosnold*. Hamden, Conn. 1963.

Gorges, Sir Ferdinando. *A briefe narration of the original undertakings of the advancement of plantations into the parts of America. Especially showing the beginning, progress and continueance of that of New-England.* Nathaniel Brook. 1658.

See Baxter, J. P.; Council of New England. *A briefe relation.* 1622.

Gorges, Ferdinando, the younger. *America painted to the life.* Nathaniel Brook. 1659.

Gosnold, Bartholomew: see Brereton, John; Archer, Gabriel; Burrage, H. S.; Levermore, C. H.; Winship, G. P.

'Master Bartholomew Gosnolds letter to his father, touching his first voyage to Virginia.' In Purchas, Samuel, *Pilgrimes*, IV (1625), 1646.

'Documents relating to Bartholomew Gosnold's voyage to America, A.D. 1602', Massachusetts Historical Society, *Collections*, 3rd ser. VIII (Boston, 1883), 70–2.

'Master Bartholomew Gosnold's letter to his father.' C. H. Levermore, *Forerunners and competitors of the Pilgrims*, I (1912), 55–6.

'Letter of Bartholomew Gosnold.' Quinn, *New American world*, III (1979), 357–8.

Grant, W. L. See Lescarbot, Marc.

Gray, Asa. *Gray's manual of botany.* See Fernald, M. L.

Gray, Francis C. 'Visit to the Elizabeth Islands', *North American Review*, V (1817), 313–24.

Grieve, Maud. *A modern herbal.* N.Y. 1959; repr. 1971.

Gunther, Robert G. T. *Astrolabes of the world.* Oxford, 1932; repr. 1976.

Hadlock, Wendell S., 'Bone implements from shell heaps around Frenchman's Bay, Maine', *American Antiquity*, VIII (1943), 341–53.

'Warfare among the northeastern woodland Indians', *American Anthropologist*, new ser. XLIX (1947), 204–21. See Butler, Eva.

Hakluyt, Richard, the younger. *Diuers voyages touching the discouerie of America.* Thomas Woodcocke, 1582. STC 12624.

The principall nauigations, voiages and discoueries of the English nation. George Bishop and Ralph Newberie. 1589. [See Quinn, D. B. and Skelton, R. A.] STC 12625.

The principal nauigations, voiages, traffiques and discoueries of the English nation. 3 volumes. George Bishop, Ralph Newberie and Robert Barker. 1598–1600. [For states and issues see Quinn, *Hakluyt handbook*, II, 498–509.] STC 12626–12626a.

'Discourse of Western Planting' ('A particuler discourse'), 1584. See Deane, C.; Taylor, E. G. R.; Quinn, D. B.

A notable historie. 1587. See Laudonnière, René de.

The discoueries of the world. 1601. See Galvão, Antonio.

Virginia richly valued. 1609. See Fidalgo de Elvas.

Hale, Edward E., 'Gosnold at Cuttyhunk', American Antiquarian Society, *Proceedings*, new ser. xv (1902), 98–102.

Hall, Albert F., 'The vegetation of the Penobscot Bay region, Maine', Portland Society of Natural History, *Proceedings*, iii (1923), 339–438.

Hall, E. Raymond and Kelson, Keith R. *The mammals of North America*. 2 vols. N.Y. 1959.

Hallet, L. F., 'Cultural traits of the southern New England Indians', Massachusetts Historical Society, *Bulletin*, xv (1954), 59–64.

Harriot, Thomas. *A briefe and true report of the new found land of Virginia*. 1588. STC 12785.

Haskell, Louisa T. *The story of Cuttyhunk*. New Bedford, Mass. 1953.

Hatch, Louis C., ed. *Maine: a history*. 4 vols. N.Y. 1919.

Hewson, John, 'Micmac placenames in Newfoundland', *Regional Language Studies: Newfoundland* 8 (St John's Newfoundland, 1978), p. 15.

Higginson, Francis. *New Englands plantation*. T. & R. Cotes for M. Sparke. 1630.

Hine, T. A. *The Gosnold monument on Cuttyhunk. A description of the exercises held at the dedication in August 1903*. N.Y. 1903.

Hoskins, William, 'The Elizabethan merchants of Exeter', in Bindoff, S. T. *et al.*, *Elizabethan government and society*. 1961.

Hough, Franklin B., ed. *Papers relating to the island of Nantucket..., Martha's Vineyard, and other islands adjacent, known as Dukes county*. Albany. 1856.

Howe, Henry F. *Early explorers of Plymouth Harbor, 1525–1619*. Plymouth, Mass. 1953.

Prologue to New England. N.Y. 1943.

'The sources of New England history prior to 1620', Massachusetts Archaeological Society, *Bulletin*, iii (1942), 19–24.

Howells, W. W. 'Physical types of the Northeast.' See Johnson, Frederick.

Huden, John C. *Indian place names of New England*. N.Y. 1960. Museum of the American Indian, Heye Foundation, *Contributions* 18.

Hughes, Thomas, S.J. *History of the Society of Jesus in North America*. 3 vols. in 4. London and N.Y. 1907–17. Text, vol. i (1907). Documents, vol. i (1908).

Hulton, Paul H. *The work of Jacques Le Moyne de Morgues*. 2 vols. 1977.

Hulton, Paul and Quinn, D. B. *The American drawings of John White*. 2 vols. London and Chapel Hill. 1964.

Hussey, Christopher. *Parham Park*. 1950.

Hyland, Fay and Steinmetz, Ferdinand H. *The woody plants of Maine*. Orono, Me. 1944. University of Maine Studies, 2nd ser. no. 59.

Izaake, Richard. *Antiquities of the City of Exeter*. 1677.

Jackson, B. D. *A catalogue of the plants cultivated in the garden of John Gerard in the years, 1596–1599*. 1876.

James, Sidney V., ed. *Three visitors to early Plymouth*. Plymouth, Mass. 1963.

Jameson, J. F. 'Notes and queries', *Virginia Magazine of History and Biography*, xix (1911), 195–6.

Jenney, Charles Francis. *The fortunate island of Monhegan*. Worcester, Mass. 1922.

Jennings, Francis. *The invasion of America*. Chapel Hill. 1975.

Johnson, Douglas W. *The New England–Acadian shoreline*. N.Y. 1925.

Johnson, Frederick, ed. *Man in northeastern North America*. Andover, Mass. 1946. Robert S. Peabody Foundation for Archaeology, *Papers* 3.

Jordan, David S. and Evermann, Barton W. *A checklist of the fishes of North and Middle America*. Washington, D.C. 1896. U.S. Bureau of Fisheries, *Report of the Commissioner for 1897.*

A checklist... Revised by H. W. Clark. Washington, D.C. 1930. U.S. Board of Fisheries, *Report, 1928*, app. 10.

Josselyn, John. *New Englands rarities discovered.* G. Widdowes. 1672. Facs. by Massachusetts Historical Society. 1972.

A relation of two voyages to New-England. G. Widdowes. 1674.

'New-Englands rarities discovered', ed. E. Tuckerman. American Antiquarian Society. *Transactions and Collections*, IV (1860), 105–238.

An account of two voyages to New-England, ed. William Veazie. Boston. 1866.

Keith, Allan R. *The mammals of Martha's Vineyard.* Edgartown, Mass. 1969. Dukes County Historical Society.

Kelly, Wilfred, S.J., ed. *Liber ruber venerabilis collegii anglorum de urbe.* 1940. Catholic Record Society Publications, XXXVII.

Kendall, William C. *An annotated catalogue of the fishes of Maine.* Portland, Me. Portland Society of Natural History, *Proceedings*, III, pt. 1.

'List of the *Pisces.*' *Fauna of New England*, pt. 8. Boston. 1908. Boston Society of Natural History, *Occasional Papers* 7.

Kenny, Anthony, S.J., ed. *The responsa scholarum of the English College, Rome.* 1962. Catholic Record Society Publications, LIV.

Kerry, C., 'Codnor Castle and its ancient owners', Derbyshire Archaeological and Natural History Society, *Journal*, XIV (1892).

Kingsbury, Susan M., ed. *Records of the Virginia Company of London.* 4 vols. Washington, D.C. 1906–35.

Kinietz, V., 'Notes on the roached headdress of animal hair among the North American Indians', Michigan Academy of Sciences, Arts and Letters, *Papers*, XXVI (1940), 463–7.

Kittredge, Henry C. *Cape Cod: its people and their history.* Boston and N.Y. 1936.

Latimer, John. *Sixteenth century Bristol.* Bristol and London. 1908.

Laudonnière, René de. *L'histoire notable de la Floride.* Paris, Guillaume Auuray. 1586.

A notable historie containing foure voyages made by certayne French captaynes vnto Florida, translated by Richard Hakluyt. Thomas Dawson, 1587. STC 15316.

Lea, J. Henry, 'Genealogical gleanings among the English archives [Gosnold family]', *New England Genealogical and Historical Society Register*, LVI (1902), 402–7; LVII (1903), 93–100; LVIII (1904), 311–14, 396–400; LIX (1905), 101–3.

Le Blant, René and Baudry, Robert, ed. *Nouveaux documents sur Champlain et son époque*, I. Ottawa. 1967. Public Archives of Canada Publications 15.

Lescarbot, Marc. *Histoire de la Nouuelle France.* Paris. Iean Milot. 1609.

Noua Francia, translated by Pierre Erondelle. [Eliot's Court Press] imp. George Bishop. 1609. STC 15491.

Nova Francia, ed. H. P. Biggar. 1928.

Works, ed. Grant. W. L. and Biggar, H. P. 3 vols. Toronto. 1907–14. Champlain Society Publications, 1, 7, 11.

Levermore, Charles H. *Forerunners and competitors of the Pilgrims and Puritans.* 2 vols. Brooklyn, N.Y. 1912.

Lorimer, Joyce. 'The English contraband tobacco trade in Trinidad and Guiana,

1590–1617', in Andrews, K. R., Canny, N. P. and Hair, P. E. H., *The westward enterprise* (1976), pp. 124–50.

Ludlum, David M. *Early American hurricanes*. Boston. 1963.

Lussagnet, Suzanne, ed. *Les français en l'Amérique pendent la deuxième moitié du xvie siècle*, part ii. Paris. 1958.

Lyte, Henry, ed. and trans. Rembert Dodoens. *A new herball*. N. Newton. 1586. STC 6985.

McCaffrey, Wallace T. *Exeter, 1540–1640*. Cambridge, Mass. 1958.

McGrath, Patrick, ed. *Records relating to the Society of Merchant Adventurers of Bristol*. Bristol. 1952. Bristol Record Society Publications, XVII.

ed. *Merchants and merchandise in seventeenth century Bristol*. Bristol. 1955. Bristol Record Society Publications, XIV.

John Whitson and the merchant community of Bristol. Bristol. 1970. Bristol Historical Association Pamphlet Series.

Mackeever, Frank C. *Native and naturalized plants of Nantucket*. Amhurst, Mass. 1968.

Maine Historical Society. *Tercentenary of Martin Pring's first voyage to the coast of Maine, 1603–1903*. Portland, Me. [1903].

Tercentenary of the landing of the Popham colony, August 29, 1907. [1907].

Manning, Charles and Moore, Merrill, 'Sassafras and syphilis', *New England Quarterly*, IX (1936), 473–5.

Marsden, R. G., 'English ships in the reign of James I', Royal Historical Society, *Transactions*, n.s. XIX (1905), 309–42.

Martin, Calvin. *Keepers of the game*. Berkeley, 1980.

Mason, John. *A briefe discourse of the New-found-land*. Edinburgh. A. Hart. 1625. STC 17616.

Mathews, Ferdinand S. *Field book of American wild flowers*. Revised by Norman Taylor. N.Y. 1955.

Maverick, Samuel, 'A briefe description of New England' in Massachusetts Historical Society, *Proceedings*, 2nd ser. I (1884–5), 231–49.

A briefe description of New England [1660], ed. John W. Dean. Boston. 1885.

Mayhew, Elizabeth R., ed. *Martha's Vineyard: a short history and guide*. Edgartown, Mass. 1956. Dukes County Historical Society.

Mayhew, Experience. *Indian converts, or some account of a considerable number of the Christianized Indians of Martha's Vineyard*. Boston. 1727.

Observations on the Indian language. Ed. John S. H. Fogg. Boston. 1884.

Monardes, Nicolás. *Primera y segunda y tercera partes de la historia natural...de nuestras Indias*. Seville. Alonso Escriuano. 1574.

Ioyfull newes out of the newe founde worlde, translated by John Frampton. [J. Kingston for] W. Norton. 1577; W. Norton. 1580. E. Allde, by thassigne of B. Norton. 1595. STC 18005a–18007.

Joyfull newes out of the newe founde worlde. Ed. Stephen Gaselee. 2 vols. 1925.

Mood, Fulmer, 'Bartholomew Gosnold': 'John Brierton', *Dictionary of American Biography*.

'Richard Hakluyt and John Brierton', *New England Historical and Geneological Society Register*, LXXXIII (1929), 505–7.

'Martha Gosnold and Martha's Vineyard', *New England Historical and Genealogical Society Register*, LXXXIII (1929), 373–4.

'Why the "Vineyard?"' *New England Quarterly*, VI (1933), 131–6.

Moody, Robert E., ed. *The letters of Thomas Gorges, 1640–1643*. Portland, Me. 1978. Maine Historical Society.

Moore, C. B. 'Sheet copper in the mounds not necessarily of European origin', *American Anthropologist*, V (1903), 27–49.

Morton, Thomas. *New English Canaan*. Amsterdam, J. F. Stam. 1637. STC 18202.

    The New England Canaan, ed. Charles F. Adams, Jr. Boston. 1883. Prince Society Publications 14; repr. N.Y. 1967.

Mourt's relation or Journall of the plantation at Plymouth. Ed. Henry B. Dexter. Boston. 1865. See Winslow, Edward.

Murdoch, George P. and O'Leary, T. J. *Ethnographic Bibliography of America*. 4th ed. 5 vols. New Haven. 1975.

Old Dartmouth Historical Sketches. A. R. Wall, 'Gosnold and his colony at Cuttyhunk'; E. Watson, 'The Modern settlement at Cuttyhunk'; W. Ricketson, 'The Gosnold memorial shaft and something of the geology of Cuttyhunk'; 'The Gosnold memorial at Cuttyhunk, September 1, 1603'. Old Dartmouth Historical Society, New Bedford, Mass. [1903].

Parks, George B. *Richard Hakluyt and the English voyagers*. N.Y. 1928; repr. 1961.

Pett, Phineas, *Autobiography*, ed., W. G. Perrin. Navy Records Society, 1904.

Pope, Clifford H. *Turtles of the United States and Canada*. N.Y. 1939.

Preston, Richard A. *Gorges of Plymouth Fort*. Toronto. 1953.

Prince, George, 'The Voyage of Capt. Geo. Waymouth to the coast of Maine in 1605', Maine Historical Society, *Collections*, VI (1859), 291–306.

    'In Waymouth's tracks,' in *Historical articles relating to Captain Waymouth's voyage*. Rockland, Me., 1897, pp. 55–7.

Pring, James H. *Captain Martin Pring, the last of the Elizabethan seamen*. 1888.

Pring, Martin, 'A voyage set out from the citie of Bristol...for the discouerie of the north part of Virginia', Samuel Purchas, *Pilgrimes, IV* (1625), 1647–57.

    'A voyage...' H. S. Burrage, *English and French voyages* (1906), pp. 341–52.

    'A voyage...' G. P. Winship, *Sailor's narratives* (1905), pp. 50–63.

    'A voyage...' C. B. Levermore, *Forerunners and competitors of the Pilgrims and Puritans*, I (1912), 61–8.

    'A voyage...' D. B. Quinn, *New American world*, III (1979), 359–62.

Purchas, Samuel. *Hakluytus Posthumus or Purchas his pilgrimes*. 4 vols. W. Stansby for H. Fetherstone, 1625. STC 20509.

    Hakluytus posthumus, or Purchas his pilgrimes. 20 vols. Glasgow. 1905–7.

    Purchas his pilgrimage. 2nd edition. W. Stansby for H. Fetherstone, 1614. STC 20506.

    Purchas his pilgrimage. 3rd edition. W. Stansby for H. Fetherstone, 1617. STC 20507.

    Purchas his pilgrimage. 4th edition. W. Stansby for H. Fetherstone, 1626. STC 20508.

Quinn, David B., ed. *The voyages and colonising enterprises of Sir Humphrey Gilbert*. 2 vols. Hakluyt Soc., 2nd ser. nos. 83–4. 1940.

    ed. *The Roanoke voyages, 1584–90*. 2 vols. Hakluyt Soc., 2nd ser. nos. 104–5. 1955.

'The voyage of Étienne Bellenger to the Maritimes in 1584; a new document', *Canadian Historical Review*, XLIII (1962), 328–43.

ed. (with Paul H. Hulton). *The American drawings of John White*. 2 vols. London and Chapel Hill. 1964.

ed. (with R. A. Skelton). *Richard Hakluyt, The principall navigations (1589)*. 2 vols. Hakluyt Soc., extra ser. 39. 1965.

Richard Hakluyt, editor: with facsimiles of Divers voyages (1582), and A journal of several voyages into New France (1580). 2 vols. Amsterdam. 1967.

(with Warner F. Gookin). 'Martin Pring at Provincetown in 1603,' *New England Quarterly*, XL (1967), 79–91.

'The voyage of *Triall*, 1606–7: an abortive Virginia venture', *American Neptune*, XXXI (1971), 85–103.

England and the discovery of America, 1481–1620. N.Y. 1974.

ed. *The Hakluyt handbook*. 2 vols. Hakluyt Soc., 2nd ser., nos. 144–5. 1974.

'Thomas Harriot and the New World', in John W. Shirley, ed. *Thomas Harriot, Renaissance Scientist*. Oxford. 1974.

'James I and the beginnings of empire in America', *Journal of Imperial and Commonwealth History*, II (1974), 135–52.

'An Anglo-French "voyage of discovery" to North America in 1604–5, and its sequel', in *Miscellanea offerts à Charles Verlinden*, II, 513–34. Ghent. 1975.

'Renaissance influences in English colonization', *Transactions of the Royal Historical Society*, 5th ser. XXV (1976), 73–93.

North America from earliest discovery to first settlements. N.Y. 1977.

ed. (with Alison M. Quinn and Susan Hillier). *New American world*. 5 vols. N.Y. 1979.

Sources for the ethnography of North America to 1611. Ottawa, Museum of Man, Mercury Ser. no. 76, 1981.

Rainey, F. G. 'A compilation of historical data contributing to the ethnography of the Connecticut and southern New England Indians,' Connecticut Archaeological Society, *Bulletin* 3 (1936)), 1–89; repr. 1956.

Ralegh, Sir Walter. *The discouerie of...Guiana*. R. Robinson. 1596. STC 20634–6.

Rasles, S. 'A dictionary of the Abnaki language', American Academy of Arts and Sciences, *Memoirs*, new ser. I (1833), 375–574.

Rathbun, Mary J. 'List of the *Crustacea*', *Fauna of New England*, pt. 5. Boston, 1905. Boston Society of Natural History, Occasional Papers 7.

Rich, Louise D. *The coast of Maine, an informal history*. N.Y. 1956; 2nd ed. 1962.

Ricketson, Daniel. *History of New Bedford*. New Bedford, Mass. 1858.

Robbins, Chandler S. *et al*. *Birds of North America*. N.Y. 1966.

Robbins, Maurice. 'Indians of the Old Colony', Massachusetts Archaeological Society, *Bulletin*, XVII (1956), 59–73.

'Some Indian Burials from southeast Massachusetts', Massachusetts Archaeological Society, *Bulletin*, XXI (1959), 26.

'The Titicut site', Massachusetts Archaeological Society, *Bulletin*, XXVIII (1966), 33–6.

Robbins, W. *Botany of crop plants*. 3rd ed. N.Y. 1931.

Rogers, S. L. 'The aboriginal bow and arrow of North America and East Asia', *American Anthropologist*, new ser. XLII (1940), 255–69.

Rosier, James. *A true relation of the most prosperous voyage made in this present yeere*

1605, by Captaine George Waymouth. [Eliot's Court Press] imp. George Bishop. 1605. STC 21322.

A true relation... Massachusetts Historical Society, *Collections*, 1st ser., VIII (1843), 125–57.

Rosier's narrative of Waymouth's voyage, ed. George Prince. Bath, Me. 1860.

Rosier's relation of Waymouth's voyage to the coast of Maine, 1605, ed. Henry S. Burrage. Portland, Me. 1887. Gorges Society Publications 3.

The grant of the Province of Maine, 1622 (1923), pp. 39–75.

'An account of a Voyage to Virginia', in John Harris, *Navigantium atque itinerantium bibliotheca*, I (1705), 817–18.

A true relation, ed. Charles Whittingham. 1877.

'A true relation', in G. P. Winship, *Sailors' voyages* (1905), pp. 99–151.

'A true relation', in H. S. Burrage, *English and French voyages* (1906), pp. 353–95.

'A true relation', in C. H. Levermore, *Forerunners and competitors of the Pilgrims and Puritans*, I (1912), 313–51.

'A true relation', in D. B. Quinn, *New American world*, III (1979), 365–80.

'Extracts of a Virginian voyage made in 1605 by Captain George Waymouth', in S. Purchas, *Pilgrimes*, IV (1625), 1659–67, XVIII (1906), 335–60.

'Extracts of a Virginian voyage made in 1605 by Captain George Waymouth', in D. B. Quinn, *New American world*, III (1979), 380–91.

Rowse, Alfred L. *Shakespeare's Southampton.* 1965.

Rye, Walter, ed. *The visitacion of Norffolk...1563* [etc.]. Harleian Society Publications, 32. 1891.

Salwen, Bert. 'Indians of southern New England and Long Island: early period', *Handbook of North American Indians*, XV. *The Northeast*, ed. Bruce Trigger (1978), 160–76.

Sanford, Samuel N. F. *New England herbs.* Boston. 1937. Boston Museum of Natural History.

Sargent, Charles S. *Manual of the trees of North America.* 2nd ed. N.Y. 1922.

Schneider, Jürgen, ed. *Wirtschaftskräfte und Wirschaftswege. Festschrift für Hermann Kellenbenz.* 4 vols. Nürnberg. 1978.

Schroeder, P. L. and Ruhl, K. C. 'Metallurgical characteristics of North American copper work', *American Antiquity*, XXXIII (1968), 162–9.

Schurz, William L. *The Manila galleon.* N.Y. 1939; repr. 1959.

Sewell, R. K. 'Popham's town of Fort St. George', Maine Historical Society, *Collections.* 1st ser. VII (1876), 291–322.

Shaler, N. S. *Report on the geology of Martha's Vineyard.* Washington, D.C. 1888. United States Geological Survey.

Shea, John Gilmary. *The Catholic church in colonial days, 1521–1763.* N.Y. 1886.

Shirley, John W., ed. *Thomas Harriot, renaissance scientist.* Oxford. 1975.

Siebart, Frank I., Jr. 'The identity of the Tarrantines, with an etymology', *Studies in Linguistics*, XXIII (1973), 69–76.

Slijper, Everhard J. *Whales.* Translated by A. J. Pomerans. N.Y. 1962.

Sluiter, Engel. 'Dutch-Spanish rivalry in the Caribbean, 1594–1609', *Hispanic American Historical Review*, XXVIII (1948), 165–96.

Smith, John. *A description of New England.* H. Lownes for R. Clerke. 1616. STC 22788.

A map of Virginia, with a description of the countrey. Oxford. I. Barnes, 1612. STC 22791.

The generall history of Virginia. I D[awson] and I. H[aviland] for M. Sparkes, 1624. STC 22790.

Works, ed. E. Arber. Birmingham, 1884; London, 1895; ed. E. Arber and A. G. Bradley. 2 vols. Edinburgh, 1910. Repr. N.Y. 1967.

Smith, Marion Jacques. *A history of Maine*. Portland, Me. 1949.

Smith, Nicholas N. 'Wabanaki uses of greases and oils', Massachusetts Archaeological Society, *Bulletin*, XXI (1960), 19–21.

'Smoking habits of the Wabenaki', Massachusetts Archaeological Society, *Bulletin*, XVIII (1957), 76–7.

'Wabanaki dances', Massachusetts Archaeological Society, *Bulletin*, XVI (1955), 29–37.

Snow, Dean S. 'Eastern Abenaki', *Handbook of North American Indians*, XV. *The Northeast*, ed. Bruce Trigger (1978), 137–47.

'The ethnohistoric baseline of the Eastern Abenaki', *Ethnohistory*, XXIII (1976), 291–306.

Speck, Frank G., 'The functions of wampum among the eastern Algonkians', American Anthropological Association, *Memoirs*, VI (1919), 3–71.

Penobscot man. Philadelphia. 1940; repr. N.Y. 1970.

Speck, F. G. and Dexter, R. W. 'Utilization of marine life by the Wampanoag Indians of Massachusetts', Washington Academy of Sciences, *Journal*, XXXVIII (1948), 257–65.

Spedding, James. *The letters and life of Sir Francis Bacon*. 7 vols. 1861–74. IV (1868), 553–4.

Spencer, W. D. *Pioneers on Maine rivers*. Portland, Me. 1930.

Squires, William A. *The birds of New Brunswick*. St John, N.B. 1952. The New Brunswick Museum, Monographic Series 4.

Stafford, Joseph. *The Canadian oyster*. Ottawa. 1913.

Stock, J. F., ed. *Proceedings and debates of the British parliaments respecting North America*, I (Washington, D.C. 1924).

Stommel, Henry. *The gulf stream*. Berkeley. 1958; 2nd ed. 1965.

Stout, A. B., 'Vegetable food of the American Indian', New York Botanic Garden, *Journal*, XV (1914), 50–60.

Strachey, William. *The historie of travaile into Virginia Britannia*, ed. R. H. Major. 1849. Hakluyt Society, 1st ser. no. 6.

The historie of travell into Virginia Britania, ed. Louis B. Wright and Virginia Freund. 1953. Hakluyt Society, 2nd ser. no. 103.

Sturtevant, William C., general editor. *Handbook of North American Indians*. 20 vols. Washington, D.C. 1977– [in progress].

Strype, John. *The history of the life and acts of the Most Reverend Father in God, Edmund Grindal*. 1710.

The history of the life and acts of Edmund Grindal. Oxford. 1821. (*Works*. 27 vols. in 24. Oxford, 1820–40, XIX.)

Sverdrup, Harald U., Johnson, Martin W. and Fleming, Richard H. *The oceans*. N.Y. 1942; repr. 1946.

Taylor, Eva G. R., ed. *The original writings and correspondence of the two Richard Hakluyts*. 2 vols. 1935. Hakluyt Society, 2nd ser., nos. 76, 77.

Taylor, E. G. R. and Richey, Michael. *The mathematical seaman*. 1962.

Thayer, Henry C., ed. *The Sagadahoc colony*. Portland, Me. 1892. Gorges Society Publications 4.

Thoreau, Henry David. *Cape Cod*. Boston. 1865.

The Maine Woods. Boston. 1864.

Thornton, J. W., 'Ancient Pemaquid', Maine Historical Society, *Collections*, II (1857), 155–7.

Trigger, Bruce, ed., *The northeast*. Washington, D.C. 1978. *Handbook of North American Indians*. XV.

Trudel, Marcel. *Histoire de la Nouvelle-France*. 3 vols. Montreal. 1963–79.

Trumbull, James Hammond. *Natick dictionary*. Washington, D.C. 1903. Smithsonian Institution, Bureau of American Ethnology, *Bulletin* 25.

Venn, John and Venn, John A. *Alumni Cantabrigienses*. 4 vols. Cambridge. 1922–7.

Wallis, Wilson D. and Wallis, Ruth S. *The Micmacs of Eastern Canada*. Minneapolis. 1955.

Warner, G. F., ed. *The voyage of Sir Robert Dudley to the West Indies, 1594–1595*. 1899. Hakluyt Society, 2nd ser., 3.

Waymouth Tercentenary. An account of the celebration of the landing of George Waymouth. [n.p. 1905]

Whitford, A. C. 'Textile fabrics used in eastern aboriginal North America,' American Museum of Natural History, *Anthropological Papers*, XXXVIII (1938), 1–22.

Whiting, Henry L. 'Report of changes in the shore-line and beaches of Martha's Vineyard, as derived from comparison of recent with former surveys', U.S. & C.G. Survey, *Report for 1886* (1887), app. 9, 263–6.

Whitson, John. *A pious meditation...with additional memoirs*, ed. John Eden. Bristol. 1829.

Willan, Thomas S. *The early history of the Russia Company, 1555–1603*. Manchester. 1956.

Williams, Clare, ed. *Thomas Platter's travels in England, 1599*. 1937.

Williams, Penry. *The council of Wales and the Marches under Elizabeth I*. Oxford. 1958.

Williams, Roger. *A key into the language of America*. Gregorie Dexter. 1643.

A key into the language of America, edited by John J. Teunisen and Evelyn J. Hinz. Detroit. 1973.

Willoughby, Charles C. *The antiquities of the New England Indians*. Cambridge, Mass. 1935.

'Houses and gardens of the New England Indians', *American Anthropologist*, new ser. VIII (1906), 115–32.

Willson, David H., ed. *The parliamentary diary of Robert Bowyer*. Minneapolis and London. 1931.

Wilson, H. C. and Carr, W. C., 'Gosnold's Elizabeth's Isle; Cuttyhunk or Naushon?', *The American Neptune*, XXXIII (1973), 131–45.

Winship, George P., ed. *Sailors' narratives of voyages along the New England coast 1524–1624*. Boston. 1905.

Winslow, Edward. *Good newes from New England*. I. Dawson [at Eliot's Court Press] for William Bladen and Iohn Bellamie. 1624. STC 25855.

[Winslow, Edward]. *A relation or iournall of the begining and proceedings of the*

English plantation setled at Plimouth in New England. [I. Dawson, for] Iohn Bellamie. 1622. [Also known as *Mourt's Relation.*] STC 20074.

Winsor, Justin, ed. *The memorial history of Boston*, I (1880). 4 vols. Boston. 1880–1.

Wood, William. *New Englands prospect.* Thomas Cotes for Iohn Bellamie. 1634. STC 25957.

 New Englands prospect, ed. C[harles] D[eane?]. Boston. 1865. Prince Society Publications 1; repr. N.Y. 1967.

Woodworth, Jay B. and Wigglesworth, Edward. *Geography and geology of the regions including Cape Cod, the Elizabeth Islands, Nantucket, Martha's Vineyard, No Mans Land and Block Island.* Cambridge, Mass. 1934. Museum of Comparative Zoology at Harvard College, *Memoirs*, LII.

Worth, Richard N., ed. *Calendar of Plymouth municipal records.* Plymouth. 1893. *History of Plymouth.* Plymouth. 1871; 2nd ed. 1873, 1890.

Wright, Albert H. and Wright, Ann A. *Handbook of snakes of the United States and Canada.* Ithaca, N.Y. 1957.

Wright, Edward. *The description and vse of the sphaere.* [E. Allde] for J. Tap. 1613. STC 26021.

Wroth, Lawrence C. *The voyages of Giovanni da Verrazzano.* New Haven. 1970.

Yanovsky, Elias. *Food plants of the North American Indians.* Washington, D.C. 1936. U.S. Department of Agriculture, Miscellaneous Publication 237.

INDEX

A reference number followed by 'n' only indicates the carry-over of a footnote from the previous page.

Micmac Indians (*cont.*)
enemies to Abenaki, 350n2; fire-making,
156n5; language, 158n6, 481, 482, 488;
paddles, 232n1; porpoise oil used by,
280n7; traders, 9, 89, 110, 145n7,
268n2, 273n4, 275n1, 438n2; whalers,
304n
Milford Haven, Wales, 216
Milkweed, 334, 449n2; *Asclepias syriaca*,
412n7
Mill Creek, Barnstable, 146n5
Mill River, St George R., 293n5
Minas Basin, B. of Fundy, copper at, 109
minerals, 165n70, 191; as incentives to
colonisation, 3–4, 170, 171, 415
mines, 156, 157, 467; copper, 170, 184;
gold, 184; silver, 170, 184
Mint, 19
Mishaum Point, Mass., 129(fig.), 152n9,
153n4
Mison, Francisco, captain of Spanish ship,
355, 358n1, 367n6
missions, 168n1, 246–7
Mississippi River, 292n3
Mitchell, Sir Bartholomew, 466n; member
Virginia Co. royal council, 332, 390
momonsacqweo, bear, 487
Monardes, Nicolás, *Joyful news* (1574), 197,
198, 225n1
Monhegan I., 116(fig.), 285n1, 434(fig.),
478n6, 511(fig.); on maps, 253n2
flora, 25, 259–60, 266n6, 304n6; fishery,
4, 64, 73, 263n3, 287n1, 301n1,
334, 335, 508; Indian hearth site,
262n3; Sagadahoc colonists at, 353,
429n1; Waymouth at, 259–60, 261n1,
298n2, 510
Monomoy Point (Point Care), 119(fig.),
120n6, 121n1, 122n5, 147n7, 148n1,
229n6, 478n7, 498, 500, 522, 526
Monts, Pierre du Gua de, 252n5, 266n3,
348n5, 462n2
Monument Hill, Mass., 219n4
moon, calculating age of, 494–5
Moore, Thomas, Bristol councillor, 381,
383
Moose, 26, 155n3, 170n5, 348, 350n7; hides,
439n2; Abenaki name, 27, 310, 486;
Alces americana, 348n5; *A. alces americana*, 306n7, 307n, 486
Moosehead Lake, 412n3, 454n5, 475n2
Morgan, William, 70, 316, 356, 363
Morison, Samuel E., 177n2

Morocco, 180
Morton, Thomas, 14; *New English Canaan*
(1637), 15, 22, 27
Mosquito I., Pemaquid, 283n
mother of pearl, 266
Mountain Lion, 23; *see* Puma
Mount Desert I., 469, 470n2, 478n5,
521(fig.), 523
Mountnessing, Kent, 34n1
mourning ceremony, 106, 350–1
Muasacoromoneete, Abenaki Indian, 311
Mud I., B. of Fundy, 423n3
muffs, 158n4
Mulberry, 21, 193, 195, 199
Mullet, 24, 200; Common, *Mugil cephalus*,
226
Murcet, Hugo, Bristol councillor, 381, 383
Murre, 17; Atlantic, *Uria aalge aalge*, 115
Muscongus Bay, Maine, 94n3, 217n4,
353n2, 426n4, 434(fig.), 473n1, 477n3
Muscovy (Russia), Company, 59, 180, 183
Muskeget Channel, Martha's Vineyard,
121n, 146n5, 498, 502
Musket I., 479n2, 497
Muskhogean language, 195n6
Muskrat, 155n3, 170n7, 350n7; Abenaki
name, 27, 310, 487; *Ondatra zibethica*,
473, 487
Mussel, 18, 24, 132, 152, 161, 200; Abenaki
name, 27, 310, 488; Blue, *Mytilis
edulis*, 165n62, 226, 266, 307; Fresh-
water, *Unio complanatus*, 412n8;
Hooked, *Brachicontes recurvus*, 165n6;
Northern Horse, *Modiclus modiclus*,
165n62, 226
mustard, 134, 154

Nagle, Richard, merchant of Cork, 322,
323, 327
Nahanada (Bdahanedo; Dehamda;
Tahánedo), Abenaki sagamore, 106,
282n3, 357n1, 354n2; captured by
Waymouth, 284n6, 309, 311; at
Pemaquid, 6, 76, 404, 409, 427–8, 433,
439; at Plymouth, 105, 470n1; rela-
tions with English, 9, 107, 344, 454;
visits to Fort St George, 408, 413, 438–9
nails, 216
Namercante, Abenaki village, 475
Nanhoc River, 351
Nantucket Bank, 257n4, 258n1
Nantucket I., 21, 121n, 146n5, 479n1, 497,
498, 499(fig.), 502, 522